D O N N A   K O O L E R ' S

encyclopedia
of
needlework

A L E I S U R E A R T S P U B L I C A T I O N

DONNA KOOLER'S

encyclopedia
of
needlework

A LEISURE ARTS PUBLICATION

10 9 8 7 6 5 4 3

Library of Congress Cataloging-in-Publication Data
    Kooler, Donna
    Donna Kooler's Encyclopedia of Needlework
    "A Leisure Arts Publication"

I S B N :   1 - 5 7 4 8 6 - 1 8 4 - 0

contributors

produced by

KOOLER
DESIGN
STUDIO inc.

published by

LEISURE ARTS

If you have questions or comments
please contact:

LEISURE ARTS CUSTOMER SERVICE
P.O. BOX 55595
LITTLE ROCK, AR 72215-9633
www.leisurearts.com

KOOLER DESIGN STUDIO, INC.
399 TAYLOR BLVD. SUITE 104
PLEASANT HILL, CA 94523
kds@koolerdesign.com

PRINTED IN THE U.S.A. BY
R.R. DONNELLEY & SONS, CO.
WILLARD, OHIO

editor & creative director
DONNA KOOLER

editorial director
DEANNA HALL WEST

writer
KIT SCHLICH

book design & production
NANCY WONG SPINDLER

illustrations
JO LYNN TAYLOR

needlework design
LINDA ABEL, BARBARA BAATZ,
MARY POLITYKA BUSH, DIANE CLEMENTS,
LINDA GILLUM, RAE IVERSON, SANDY ORTON,
NANCY ROSSI, DEANNA HALL WEST

stitch gallery samples
SARA ANGLE

line drawings
SANDY ORTON

support
SHELLEY CARDA, JOAN CRAVENS, JENNIFER DRAKE,
ANITA FORFANG, LINDA GILLUM, LAURIE GRANT,
VIRGINIA HANLEY-RIVETT, MARSHA HINKSON,
ARLIS JOHNSON, CHAR RANDOLPH, GIANA SHAW,
PRISCILLA TIMM, JOYCE TOBENKIN

photography
DIANNE WOODS, BERKELEY, CA

photo styling
DONNA KOOLER

color separations
PREPRESS ASSEMBLY, SAN FRANCISCO, CA
CAMERA GRAPHICS, LAFAYETTE, CA
JO LYNN TAYLOR, SAN ANSELMO, CA

digital prepress
PREPRESS ASSEMBLY, SAN FRANCISCO, CA

framing
FRAME CITY, PLEASANT HILL, CA

We dedicate this book to all the anonymous stitchers of yesteryear—
the medieval master who wrought threads of gold
upon hallowed vestments and altar cloths,
the grand dame who hung her drafty hall with tapestries,
the schoolgirl who persevered at her sampler,
the housewife who filled her parlor with cushions,
the lady's maid who monogrammed her mistress' linens,
and all the mothers, grandmothers, sisters, cousins, and aunts
who took the time to pass along not only the techniques of stitching
but the appreciation for the value of handwork as well,
leaving for us a legacy that we will not allow to vanish.

∞∞∞

We wish to thank Anne Van Wagner Childs,
Vice President and Editor-in-Chief of Leisure Arts Publications,
and Sandra Graham Case,
Executive Director of Leisure Arts Publications.
Without their support, encouragement,
and faith in our ability,
it would be difficult to imagine that this book
could have been created.

contents

needlepoint

embroidery

counted thread

for your information

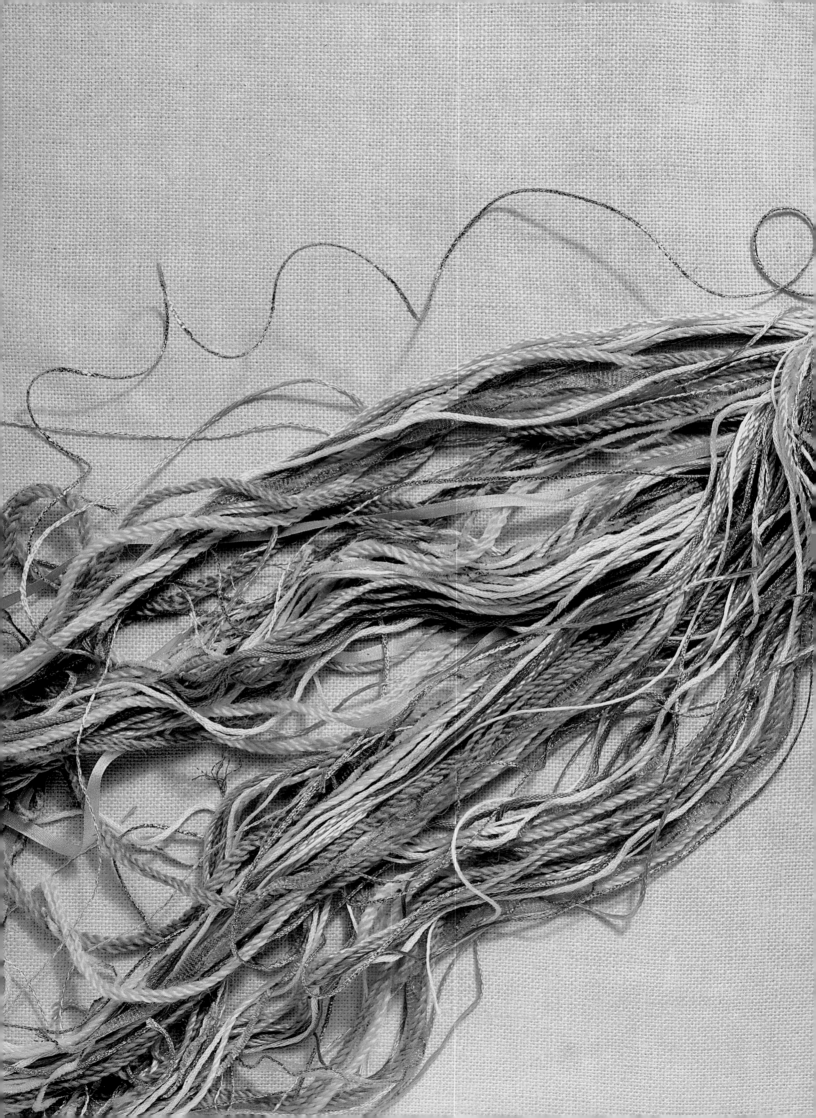

NEEDLEWORK is as old an art form as painting and sculpture, but unlike them is humble in nature and often cloaked in anonymity. Except on samplers, the names of the accomplished stitchers of the past have not survived, but their work has. Nevertheless, the practice and enjoyment of needlework provides us with a human connection to centuries past.

Because needlework came to be considered a feminine art, women desired to master it, for proficiency signified their status. Finesse at stitching was the sign of an educated woman. Our value is no longer measured by the perfection of our stitches, yet needlework is more popular than ever. Besides the obvious link to the past, why do modern women and men enjoy stitching?

Needlework captures the beauty of the physical world. Pictorial designs reflect the love that stitchers have for the natural world and the desire to recreate it and bring it into their immediate lives. The earliest fragments of embroidery show us that plants and flowers are universally beloved, and offer endless design possibilities.

Needlework expresses the beauty of pure form and substance. Abstract and geometric designs, pleasing in their own right, show off the beauty of fibers—nubby wools, glistening silks, soft and subtle cottons, bold metallics—as well as offer an opportunity to play with limitless combinations of stitches.

Needlework records and celebrates significant human events. From documenting history as the fabled Bayeux Tapestry does to marking personal experiences such as births and weddings, needlework offers the opportunity to document human affairs in an enduring and aesthetically pleasing form. Throughout the history of most cultures of the world, needlework has embellished ceremonial apparel and items of sacred observance such as altar cloths.

Needlework offers a creative outlet. A stitcher may duplicate a beautiful work of the past, or borrow the same elements and recombine them, casting them in a new light for a fresh and personal statement. It satisfies our yearning for authenticity in a pre-fabricated world.

To accompany you on your quest for greater understanding and knowledge of our needlework heritage, this book organizes needlework into three great families—needlepoint, embroidery, and counted thread. Although their origins are similar, each has an individual story as well as fascinating subcategories; some you'll know, others will be new.

Each chapter shows you how to select the right materials and tools for your chosen stitching project. The three Stitch Galleries are the heart of the book, combining diagrams, stitching directions, and suggested uses for over 400 stitches. Fifteen original projects from expert designers give you a taste of the delights that needlework has to offer. A source list and bibliography will help you find what you need and to explore further.

A stitching adventure awaits you!

needlepoint

 NEEDLEPOINT, also known as canvas work or tapestry, is defined as counted stitches worked on an even, openly woven canvas, which is usually (but not always) completely covered by the stitcher's work. Technically it may be classified as a counted thread technique, but differs from the other counted thread work in that the stitches usually fill the canvas completely, creating an additional textile layer. Each individual stitch actually wraps around the threads of the canvas to produce a remarkably strong finished piece of needlework.

Needlepoint does a beautiful job of blending old and new expressions. You may choose to reproduce a 17th-century seat cover, or you may create something strictly contemporary to show off a new synthetic fiber. Needlepoint is naturally well suited for items which will receive a lot of wear and need durability, so it's a natural choice for furnishings such as cushions, chair seats and backs, wall hangings, church kneelers, and such.

The building blocks of needlepoint are the stitches themselves, which are grouped in the Stitch Gallery into four families: diagonal, straight, crossed, and composite. One needlepoint design may be worked in repetitions of a single stitch, another may be composed of a variety of stitches. As you read, you'll acquaint yourself with stitches—such as the tent stitch and its variations—that needlepointers used centuries ago, as well as newer configurations such as the Rhodes stitch family, developed by Mary Rhodes, a 20th-century needleworker.

Traditionally wool has been the most popular needlepoint thread, but you can find old pieces stitched with silk, cotton, or linen. Now exciting synthetic threads join the time-honored natural fibers to raise needlepoint to a sophisticated art form, worthy of pictorial or geometric masterpieces fit for framing.

Cushion Cover Fragment; England, 1599, wool on linen. Courtesy of Fine Arts Museums of San Francisco, Gift of Mr. A. Middleton Beckett, 6141.

THE ORIGINS OF NEEDLEPOINT

Needlepoint, surface embroidery, and counted thread work share a common ancestry. Because natural plant fibers disintegrate with time, it is our misfortune that examples of very early needlework are lost to us. We must rely on the written accounts of what people wore, what textiles they used in their homes, and how they stitched upon fabric. We know that stitched decoration on fabric coincided with the development of linen textiles in the Middle East—Egypt, Syria, Persia, and Byzantium—in pre-Christian times. Trade and conquest brought textile and decorative influences from as far away as India and other Asian civilizations.

Early Christian Europe adopted needlework traditions from Byzantine and Coptic (Egyptian Christian) influences. Medieval documents shed some light on the subject of needlework, although it's often impossible to determine whether the needlework in question was what we now call needlepoint, or whether it was other forms of counted thread work or embroidery. An example of this dilemma is contained in an English description from the year 679, the first mention of needlework recorded in the English language—"a fine and magnificent embroidery in gold and precious stones" given to St. Cuthbert by St. Etheldreda, the Abbess of Ely. Is it counted thread work or surface embroidery?

It's clear that the finest needlework of the Middle Ages served ecclesiastical needs, primarily church vestments and altar cloths, often stitched with silk and metal threads. Actual vestments (a stole and maniple) from the tomb of St. Cuthbert at Durham, England, have survived from the 10th Century. Needlework had developed into a fine art by this time, and designs show a strong link to those used in the great medieval illuminated manuscripts. In England, for example, professional embroiderers were organized into a guild known as the "Gild of Broderers" which established rules for the training of apprentices and ensured the maintenance of standards of excellence for both technique and materials.

At the heart of historic needlepoint is the tent stitch, in which a decorative thread diagonally crosses one thread intersection of a ground fabric. The tent stitch appears in several forms: as the half cross, the continental, and the basketweave stitch, all of which appear in needlework over the centuries throughout the known world. The earliest pieces of conclusive evidence concerning needlepoint's direct ancestry are altar cloths from 13th-century Germany and Switzerland, bearing geometric patterns created by stitchers counting the threads of the linen ground fabric.

The term "tapestry" confuses many who study accounts of historic needlework. Originally it referred to large textile pieces with pictures and scenes which were woven on looms, and denoted both the process and the finished product, usually great wall hangings brought to the highest degree of excellence during the Middle Ages. Attempts to mimic the look of woven tapestries through hand-stitching were successful, for the tent stitch created a fair facsimile of the loom work.

As the medieval world waned and the Renaissance dawned, the uses for needlework shifted from ecclesiastic to royal. Emerging dynasties both major and minor required the display of heraldic symbols on items of practicality that could also be beautified, such as wall hangings, bed curtains, and horse trappings. A privileged class of ladies could devote themselves solely to stitching for their household, or perhaps a royal family could afford to pay a retinue of expert artists and stitchers who contributed to a great house's furnishings. This outpouring of needlework reached a zenith in the 15th and 16th Centuries, and many items from this era survived in their ancestral halls; others became today's museum exhibits.

Mary Queen of Scots and Elizabeth, Countess of Shrewsbury (Mary's stitching companion during her period of house arrest), left a vast needlework legacy, much of which has survived. Elizabeth's home, Hardwick Hall in Devonshire, England, is a treasure house of furnishings from the late 1500s, and includes bed valances, wall and window hangings, "table rugs," cushions, book bindings, "cupboard carpets," and more, many executed in tent stitch. Of particular interest are Mary's "emblem" motifs, small pictorial designs stitched separately then appliquéd upon velvet wall hangings and bed curtains. These emblems often held a double meaning for the Scottish queen whose life was defined by political intrigue.

Needlepoint as we now know it came into its own during the 16th and 17th Centuries. In 1500s Turkish rugs became a rage; because they were very expensive they were often copied in wool thread on canvas. On a far finer scale, a purse now in the Victoria and Albert Museum (London) shows needlepoint from exactly the same time period: tiny tent stitches on fine linen with approximately 1,250 stitches to the square inch.

The invention of the steel needle and its availability made needlework possible and practical for many people; previously needles were precious, being composed first of bone, bronze, and iron, then later of ivory, silver, and gold. The Moors first brought steel needles to Europe; records indicate they were manufactured in Nuremberg as early as 1370. Steel needles made in Spain were exported to England in great quantities by the end of the 16th Century.

The invention of the printing press encouraged the publishing of images from the graphic arts, which offered many design sources for stitchers. Inspiration came from the woodcut illustrations printed in religious and scientific books, especially herbals (such as *The Herball of General Historie of Plantes*, 1636) and bestiaries (such as *The Historie of Foure Footed Beastes and Serpents*, 1607) with beautifully detailed botanical and zoological illustrations. Publishing also served needlework directly in such forms as lace pattern books with designs printed on a grid that could be used by the needle-pointer as well. Some early English books were directed to the needleworker, with such titles as *New and Singular Patternes and Workes of Linnen* (1591) and *A Schole-house for the Needle* (1624).

Furniture was upholstered for the first time in the 17th Century; previously, the only sources of comfort were loose cushions. Needlepointed canvas was sturdier and more durable than woven fabrics, and the first coarse but evenly woven canvas was developed for use as a foundation for upholstery at this time. The Florentine stitch and a style known as bargello achieved popularity (see related story on page 14). Purely decorative items such as wall panels and framed pictures became popular.

A wonderfully detailed and illustrated guide to the origin, early history, and development of needlepoint is Mary Rhodes' *The Batsford Book of Canvas Work*, published in 1983.

The next three sections explain more about distinct branches of needlepoint that developed since the turn of the 16th Century which we still practice today: *gros point* and *petit point*, bargello, and decorative needlepoint.

GROS POINT & PETIT POINT

Needlepoint offers many pleasures to those who practice it, from the satisfaction of working with the hands to the sheer joy of creation. But one of its greatest charms is one the needle-pointer shares with other fine artists—the creation of pictures and images. We humans never tire of reproducing the world around us through any and all means possible. All the better to do it using beautiful threads on canvas, in a style that is generally known as flat needlepoint.

This was the goal of the 18th-century European lady of affluence who desired decorative furnishings for her home. By the early 1700s she was able to purchase painted canvases, sold at the same shops that sold the woolen threads to fill these canvases. These designs required the services of artists who painted directly onto canvas in colors representing the threads the stitcher should use. The prices of the painted canvases and colored wools were, not surprisingly, high.

A favorite intended use of painted canvas at this time was to cushion fitted chair seats and backs. Some surviving specimens were stitched by professionals, but most were finished by amateurs who nonetheless did splendid work. In the account books of the great English furniture designer Thomas Chippendale is mention of high-quality wooden chairs which were waiting for the seats to be covered with the purchaser's own needlework. Flowers—singly, in bouquets and arrangements, and as borders—were the most favored subjects, but scenes were also popular. Stitchers also blessed with good artistic judgment may very well have drawn their own designs, using printed pictures as guides.

To render the fine details required for pictorial subjects, designs incorporated stitches made over single thread intersections of the canvas (for central motifs, especially faces) surrounded by stitches made over two threads, which were larger and coarser but suitable for filling and backgrounds. The finely-stitched areas became known as *petit point* (French for "small point") which were executed primarily in the tent stitch and its variations. By today's definition, true *petit point* is stitched on canvas finer than 18 mesh, and up to 24, 30, 40, 56 per inch. The larger, less-detailed areas came to be called *gros point*

Needlepoint rug; Greek Islands, c. 1960, tent stitch. From the collection of Lillian Daniels Dunn.

13

(French for "large point") worked in larger tent stitches as well as cross stitches. This style of stitching remains popular, as thousands of painted and printed canvases are eagerly purchased every year. Penelope canvas, with its double mesh, is ideally suited for a mixture of *gros* and *petit point*.

Needlepoint in wool went briefly out of fashion at the turn of the 18th Century as silk embroidery and tambour work became the rage. By the time woolwork appeared again—early and middle 19th Century, the era we call Victorian—a new class of woman embraced it in a different form, a style known as Berlin woolwork. The Industrial Revolution created an ever-widening middle class which enjoyed material prosperity as never before. Millions of women in Europe and America could now afford the mass-manufactured materials for needlepoint, and had the leisure time to pursue it. More than ever, stitching was a sign of gentility and upward mobility, and Berlin woolwork blossomed into a craze. It's easy to picture the overstuffed Victorian parlor packed to the rafters with decorative stitchery for rugs, cushions, album covers, window valances, fire screens…

Bargello's graduated shades of color and stepped stitches create an illusion of depth.

Berlin woolwork required the stitcher to read a charted grid and count the canvas threads as she stitched, filling the canvas with primarily tent and cross stitches. These charts were the brainstorm of an engraver in Berlin, Germany, whose innovation inspired stitchers in Europe and America to pick up their tapestry needles, canvas, and charts.

Originally Berlin woolwork charts were individually hand-painted over a printed grid by a cottage industry of women and young girls, but advances in color printing eventually streamlined chart production. One of the gifts we have from this era is the survival of some of the original charts, from which we may now stitch. The designs reflect the favorite themes of the Victorian Era—flowers of all kinds, domestic and wild animals, stylized natural forms such as leaves and vines, reproductions of famous paintings (Leonardo Da Vinci's "Last Supper," for example), and portrayals of historical personages, biblical figures, and beloved characters from literature.

The materials used to stitch these designs were not always of the highest quality. Chemical dyes gave the wool harsh colors that faded with time and looked ugly. The commonness of Berlin work eventually signaled its decline, as well as changes in taste typified by the Arts and Crafts movement.

Today, Berlin woolwork designs have been rediscovered by needlepointers and cross-stitchers alike. The actual Berlin work charts have been dusted off and reprinted, and needlepoint designers copy the characteristic style for original designs with a vintage flair. Moreover, contemporary needlepointers enjoy the resurgence of high-quality materials—wools in particular—that ensure their work will withstand many decades of display and wear to become tomorrow's treasures.

BARGELLO

What's in a name? If the name is "Bargello" you're in for a journey down many roads with fascinating destinations. Bargello is an ancient palace, a decorative style, a stitch.

The palace is in Florence, the jewel of Tuscany, birthplace of the Italian Renaissance. Built in 1255, the Palazzo del Podestà is one of the city's oldest public buildings with its imposing tower and (later) Gothic enhancements, originally serving as the town hall, then the ministry of justice. In 1574, under the rule of the Medici family, it became the residence of the chief of police—the *bargello*—and the city's prison.

Now the former Palazzo del Podestà houses something far more illustrious than felons—immortal works of art by Michelangelo, Donatello, della Robbia, and Cellini, among many others. The palace was converted to a museum in 1859 by the provisional government of Tuscany and dedicated primarily to statuary and so-called "minor arts" including jewelry, items of ivory and amber, and rare fabrics. Of interest to us are eleven 17th-century armchairs, upholstered in a particularly striking style of needlepoint now known as… bargello!

"Bargello" is only one of the many names for the stitch that provides the foundation of bargello style. "Florentine" refers to the city where the famous chairs reside. "Hungary" and "Hungarian Point" hearken to the legendary birthplace of the stitch. "Irish" hints at an altogether different country's tradition; did the stitch originate in more than one locale, or did it emigrate without a trace? We don't know. The name "Flame" is perfectly descriptive.

Where did this style and stitch originate? What scant information we have about bargello's development is that it achieved its early prominence during the 14th Century, possibly in the kingdom of Hungary. A number of intriguing legends exist, all involving Hungarian women—Saint Elizabeth of Hungary who worked with the poor, a Princess named Jadwiga, and an unnamed princess who married into the Medici family—all who were reputed to have popularized this style of stitching. An alternate tale tells of the marriage of a 15th-century Hungarian king to an Italian princess who reputedly brought her country's artistic influences to the Hungarian court along with her trousseau. There is probably some basis for at least one of these legends, for the Italian name for this distinctive style of stitching is *punto ungaro*, or Hungarian Point. It's likely that one or more dynastic unions guaranteed a successful marriage of Italian and Hungarian styles of needlework. Another famous royal, the great 18th-century Hapsburg Queen Maria Teresa, produced fine needlework in bargello style which is preserved in the Hungarian National Museum.

Bargello is characterized by its structured pattern of stepped, elongated, parallel stitches repeated in a sequence, and is rarely pictorial in nature. As the steps rise and fall, they form either sharp peaks and valleys or rounded scallops, depending on the steepness of steps. The ratio of the stitch length to the "jump" affects the steepness of the zigzag or scallop.

The secret of bargello's appeal is that, although it is based on a geometric concept, it appears fluid—sometimes almost wildly so—as it takes on the shapes of zigzags, waves, or even flames (an alternate name for the stitch is Flame) in an infinite number of color combinations and patterns. (Learn more about the Florentine stitch on page 45.) Bargello's beauty derives from the relationship between color, pattern, and texture, which lends itself freely to a personal statement for the stitcher. Intense and highly contrasting colors, especially jewel tones, show off the patterns to perfection. Graduated shades of one color lead to a dramatic illusion of depth. Both of these effects are dramatically illustrated in the Lotus Blossom Kimono design shown on pages 14 and 80.

In addition to up-and-down patterns, bargello also lends itself to four-way orientation. The rosette in the center of the kimono design is a good example of this; notice how the petals radiate from a central point, following the points of the compass. Whichever orientation you favor, begin the bargello pattern in the center of the canvas, and work outward.

This blending of various threads, textures, and stitches typifies decorative needlepoint.

Here's a tip to help you develop a rhythm as you stitch bargello: Stitch UP as you travel down (into the valleys), and stitch DOWN as you travel up (to the peaks). This scheme provides the greatest amount of coverage on the back of the canvas, ensuring that the piece will be durable. In addition to chairs and footstools, beautiful historical examples of bargello adorn bed hangings, fire screens, pillows, and personal items such as pocketbooks, pincushions, and book covers. One of the reasons we can still enjoy viewing antique bargello— whether on a trip to Florence or an American museum—is due to the stitch's excellent longevity. Bargello pieces are meant to last centuries, and very much worth the contemporary needlepointer's efforts.

DECORATIVE NEEDLEPOINT

Something old, something new… venerable old stitches are finding new life in strictly contemporary designs these days. This category of needlepoint has yet to be christened with a definitive descriptive name, but often goes by the titles Decorative Needlepoint or Palette Stitching (as in "a palette of stitches from which to choose"). What it brings the stitcher is unlimited creative ways to explore the beauty and versatility of needlepoint materials and stitches, bringing texture and color to the center stage.

Around the midpoint of the 20th Century, needlework experienced a minor eclipse as other leisure-time pursuits vied for busy people's attention. Many kinds of needlework were associated with fussy, old-fashioned forms of decor, and the

postwar age demanded newer, sleeker expressions. But by the 1960s, a reaction against mass-manufactured goods led those who were artistically-minded to rediscover the value of handwork and the spirit of self-expression.

Women of all ages (and even some exceptional men!) rediscovered needlework, and took advantage of newly available threads, ribbon, beads, and canvas. Decorative needlepoint, with its non-pictorial, free-form melange of colors and stitches, was born. In 1976, Jo Christensen published a landmark book called *The Needlepoint Book*, with over 300 stitches described and diagrammed. It was soon nicknamed "The Needlepointer's Bible," and provided invaluable information and inspiration for experienced and beginning stitchers alike.

In the interest of learning, why not design your own needlepoint sampler in your favorite colors? An easy design plan would be to stitch a sampler of blocks the same proportion as the photos in the Stitch Gallery. But be experimental with the threads. Explore the gamut—woolly and silky, shiny and matte, thick and thin (increase the number of plies to obtain the look you want; this will be great practice)—and before long you'll be ready to plan an entire design, an artistic expression.

The first step in designing your first true needlepoint design is to gain a firm grounding in a variety of stitches. Stroll through the Needlepoint Stitch Gallery (pages 32–73) and study the individual stitch photographs, noting the textures and patterns. Make mental note of the suggested uses. Buy some canvas and try out stitches that interest you, and experiment with new fibers.

Look for design in the world around you. It's amazing how many things in our environment contain patterns that translate into stitchery—patchwork quilts, old tile work, Persian rugs… you'll find many more once you train your eye. Also worthy of your attention are designs by established needlepoint designers. Geometric designs make excellent subjects.

The greatest challenge in this form of needlepoint is to find the delicate balance between unlimited possibilities of stitches, color, and threads, and the judgment required to produce a unified design that makes a strong statement. One possible pitfall is the tendency to do too much—thinking "the sky's the limit"—and create a cluttered design. Mary Polityka Bush's Elizabethan Garden design (on page 84) works because she practiced restraint in her neutral palette while allowing a visually complex pattern of stitches.

Whether or not your first sampler of decorative needlework yields a frame-worthy design is not the point. Falling in love with the process is your goal. Once that happens, you'll find yourself browsing in needlework shops, attending needlework consumer shows, and visiting manufacturer's web sites to view the newest materials for your creative endeavors. ❦

When you embark upon a needlepoint project, begin with a specific design and project in mind first, then select the canvas, next the thread, and last the needle. Each material element you choose depends upon your choice of the previous one.

NEEDLEPOINT CANVAS

Canvas is classified as an open evenweave fabric. The term "mesh" refers to the number of vertical (warp) and horizontal (weft) threads per inch as well as number of thread intersections per inch. The smaller the number the larger the mesh. Canvas for a *gros point* design might be as low as 10 threads per inch, while a diminutive *petit point* design requires a mesh size 18 or greater (finer) and may be as high as 56 threads per inch (or even higher!).

No matter the type and size mesh you choose, one principle remains the same: Always stitch with the warp threads aligned vertically, with the selvage edge (if any) along one of the sides.

When you take into consideration the amount of time you'll spend on a particular project, not to mention the cost of the thread, your best choice of canvas will always be the most well-made (thus more expensive) canvas you can afford. Here's a simple test to determine the quality of a canvas: gently pull apart the cut edge of one of the fibers. Cheaper canvas usually consists of two thin threads held together by chemical sizing. More expensive canvas may consist of as many as six threads twisted together. Because sizing will dissolve when you block the finished canvas, the cheaper canvas will be much weaker in the long run.

WARNING! Never use a product called "waste canvas" (or Blue Line canvas) for needlepoint projects. The glue that holds the threads together is specifically designed to dissolve when wet. It's used by cross-stitchers purely as a guide for stitching over fabrics other than evenweave, and is meant to be removed after stitching.

Most canvases are available in widths of 40" (a few in 54") and are woven of cotton or linen yarns.

Always store canvas flat or rolled; never fold it. If it's rolled, do not set it on end, which will eventually crack the sizing that makes the canvas stiff enough for stitching.

SINGLE THREAD CANVAS

This category of canvas is the most popular with contemporary stitchers. The family of stitches which suits single-thread canvas best is the basic Tent stitch (the Continental and Basketweave stitches) which covers the back with long, slanting stitches, thus adding firmness to the piece. Stitches appear to "blend" together, so shading and curves are easier to effect. It's the best choice for geometric patterns and drawn work. You'll need to use a frame to keep it in shape while you stitch.

MONO This is a plain-weave canvas that comes in white, ecru, or tan (a few more shades are available in some mesh counts). The most popular sizes are 10, 12, 13, 14, 18 mesh (8, 16, 17, 24 are also available). True *petit point* requires a mesh of 18 or finer; silk or polyester gauze comes in even-count sizes: 24, 30, 40, and 56 mesh. Mono canvas is your best choice for pulled-thread work.

CONGRESS CLOTH Available in 24 mesh, this attractive canvas comes in a variety of colors to co-ordinate with your threads. It's a good choice if you intend to leave portions of the canvas unstitched.

LINEN This deluxe canvas (not shown) comes in 13 and 17 mesh, in a cream color. The quality of linen fibers makes this a strong canvas. It's a good choice if you intend to leave portions of the canvas unstitched.

UPPER LEFT: Mono canvas in 10, 13, and 18 mesh.
BELOW: Two colors of Congress Cloth, 24 mesh.

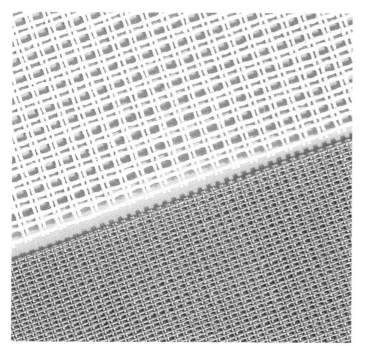

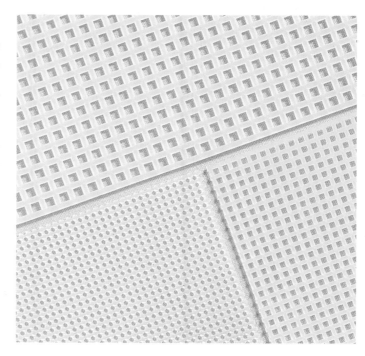

DOUBLE THREAD CANVAS

In double thread canvas, also known as double mesh, close double warps are woven in alternate rows—over one and under one—with pairs of slightly separated weft threads. Because the two paired warp threads are closer to each other than the two paired weft threads are, you can easily determine which axis you should arrange vertically for stitching. Double thread canvas allows you to combine the fine stitches of *petit point* over single mesh and the bolder stitches of *gros point* over double threads within the same design.

PENELOPE (DOUBLE MESH) This strong canvas is a good choice for items that will receive a lot of wear, such as upholstery (chair seats, footstools, etc.) and rugs. The mesh size is expressed as 10/20, 12/24, 18/36; the first number refers to the count for *gros point*, the second for *petit point*. Most needlepoint stitches work well on Penelope. Because it's so firm, you won't need to mount it on a frame if you'll be working with stitches that require uniform tension.

INTERLOCK CANVAS

The mesh threads of interlock canvas appear to be single threads, but the warp is actually composed of a pair of threads that wrap around the weft threads as the canvas is woven. It derives its strength from this feature rather than the thickness of the thread, but it's not as strong as Mono or Penelope canvas. It works well for irregular shapes and does not ravel. Because it does not stretch or drape well, it's not suited for rugs and upholstery. (An exception is Siltek, a polyester interlock canvas which drapes well for garments.) It's unsuitable for drawn-work or cutwork, or for stitches which depend on being worked "on the grain" because the weave is not obvious.

PLASTIC CANVAS AND PERFORATED PLASTIC

Flexible yet rigid, these products are ideal for projects such as handbags, belts, book covers, and boxes. Neither will ravel, and may be cut to size without requiring extra margins for turning. Plastic canvas comes in a translucent white color in 7 and 10 mesh (and a few other colors in 10). Perforated plastic resembles perforated paper (used for cross-stitch) with a grid of small round holes; it's available in 14 mesh and many colors.

UPPER LEFT: Penelope canvas in 5/10 and 10/20 mesh.
UPPER RIGHT: Interlock canvas in 10, 12, and 18 mesh.
ABOVE: Plastic canvas (7 mesh), perforated plastic (14 mesh), plastic canvas (10 mesh).

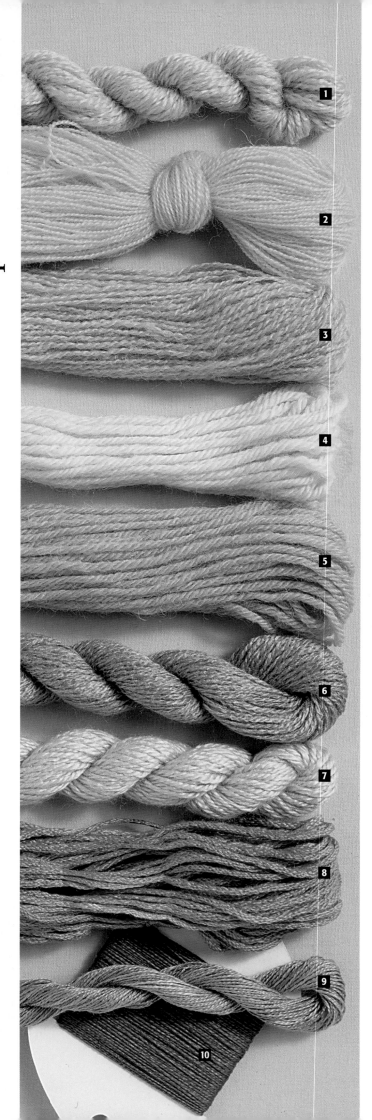

NEEDLEPOINT THREADS

No one single element—except perhaps the design itself—defines a needlepoint project as much as the thread that composes it. Choosing the colors and fibers of threads is one of the most exciting tasks that you will undertake as a stitcher. The look of the piece, as well as the experience of stitching it, will depend on the choices you make.

An important factor to consider is what kind of fiber you like to handle. One of the pleasures of stitching is the tactile experience, and needlepoint in particular offers a wide range of threads—from soft and fuzzy to silky and smooth—to suit your preference.

(Although many needlework fibers, especially needlepoint wool, are often referred to as yarns, this book will refer to them as threads to maintain consistency with other chapters.)

WOOL

Wool is the fiber that first springs to mind when one thinks of needlepoint, and historically it's been a popular choice. Wools range from very fine fibers to heavy rug yarn. Needlepoint requires thread strong enough to withstand repeated pulling through the canvas.

PERSIAN is the most popular and versatile wool thread, and comes in brilliant colors. Three-plied, it's easy to separate and recombine in as many plies as needed: three plies for 10 mesh, two plies for 12-14 mesh, one ply for 18 mesh. Its shorter fibers make it more "woolly" to the touch and less smooth than Tapestry. The name brand Paternayan was originally created to use in restoring Persian rugs.

TAPESTRY is a worsted four-plied wool that does not separate easily and is not intended to. The long, high-quality combed fibers have a round shape that works well in Penelope canvas. It fits only certain mesh sizes—10 to 13—and looks best only when it suitably fits the canvas. Appleton Tapestry Wool and DMC Laine Colbert are well-known brand names.

CREWEL WOOL comes in a single strand of two plies which cannot be untwisted. It's finer than Tapestry and Persian, so you may combine many plies to fill 10 to 24 mesh. You can combine several shades on one needle. Appleton Crewel Wool is a well-known brand name.

MEDICI, a DMC brand name, is very fine and develops a silky sheen with wear. Two or three plies work well on 18 mesh canvas, one ply on 24 mesh.

WARNING! Do not use four-ply knitting worsted wool because it stretches and is too weak for needlepoint.

WOOL/SILK BLENDS

Smoother than wool, more substantial than pure silk, 50% silk/50% wool threads have a lovely hand. Look for Silk and Ivory by Brown Paper Packages; J.L. Walsh and Felicity's Garden also manufacture beautiful wool/silk blends.

FROM TOP: Paternayan's Persian Wool (1), DMC's Medici (2); Appleton's Crewel Wool (3); DMC's Tapestry Wool (4); Appleton's Tapestry Wool (5), Felicity's Garden's wool/silk blend (6), Brown Paper Packages' Silk and Ivory (7), J.L. Walsh's wool/silk blend (8), The Thread Gatherer's Flax 'n Colors (9), Rainbow Gallery's Rainbow Linen (10).

LINEN

This venerable fiber comes in various widths—use size 10/5 on 10 mesh, 20/2 on 13 mesh, 10/2 on 24 mesh. Linen threads are slightly variable in width within one size; this is part of its distinctive character. Take special care to purchase all you need at one time because the dye lots can be irregular. Two excellent linen threads are Rainbow Linen from Rainbow Gallery, and Flax 'n Colors from The Thread Gatherer.

COTTON

Less expensive than wool or silk, cotton is washable and easy to work with but does not wear as well as wool, so it's not a good choice for upholstery.

STRANDED FLOSS (EMBROIDERY FLOSS) is a six-ply cotton with a sheen, available in hundreds of colors. Always separate the plies, then recombine them so the strands can "blossom out" for a fuller look. Use as many as nine plies on 13 mesh, five plies on 18 mesh. The best-known stranded flosses are from DMC and Anchor.

OVERDYED FLOSS is stranded floss dyed for special effects, usually by hand. Colors may be shades within a single color family or several colors that blend gradually from one to another on the same strand. Look for overdyed floss from Needle Necessities, Weeks Dye Works, Sampler Threads from The Gentle Art, and Bravo from Rainbow Gallery.

PEARL COTTON (coton perlé) is twisted, non-separable, and has a lustrous sheen. The three largest sizes work well for needlepoint: Size 3 (closest in size to a single ply of Persian wool) for 12-14 mesh, Size 5 for 18 mesh, Size 8 for 24 mesh. Size 12 can be used for details. Brand names include DMC and Anchor, as well as Overture from Rainbow Gallery. Watercolours from The Caron Collection is a three-ply cotton with a silky sheen in variegated colors (one ply equals one strand of #5 pearl cotton).

SILK

Smoother, stronger, and more expensive than cotton, silk is enjoying renewed popularity. The molecular structure of the silk fiber enables it to reflect light in a distinctive way. Many stitchers find it a pleasure to work with, for it possesses a beautiful "hand" and glides easily through canvas. It requires dry-cleaning and dry-blocking.

Silk threads come in weights similar to cotton threads. Name brands to look for include Soie d'Alger from Au Ver a Soie, Splendor from Rainbow Gallery, Silk 'n Colors from The Thread Gatherer, Silk Mori and Silk Serica from Kreinik Mfg. Co., Impressions by The Caron Collection, and Melange from Cascade Yarns. Needlepoint Inc. makes a eight-ply silk thread.

FROM TOP: Stranded floss from Anchor (1) and DMC (2), The Gentle Arts' overdyed Sampler Threads (3), overdyed floss from Weeks Dye Works (4) and Needle Necessities (5), The Caron Collection's Watercolours (6), DMC's #3 pearl cotton (7), Anchor's #5 pearl cotton (8), Anchor's #12 pearl cotton (9), DMC's #8 pearl cotton (10), Rainbow Gallery's Overture (11), The Caron Collection's Impressions (12), Needlepoint Inc.'s silk (13), Au Ver a Soie's silk Soie d'Alger (14), Cascade House's Melange silk (15), Rainbow Gallery's silk Splendor (16).

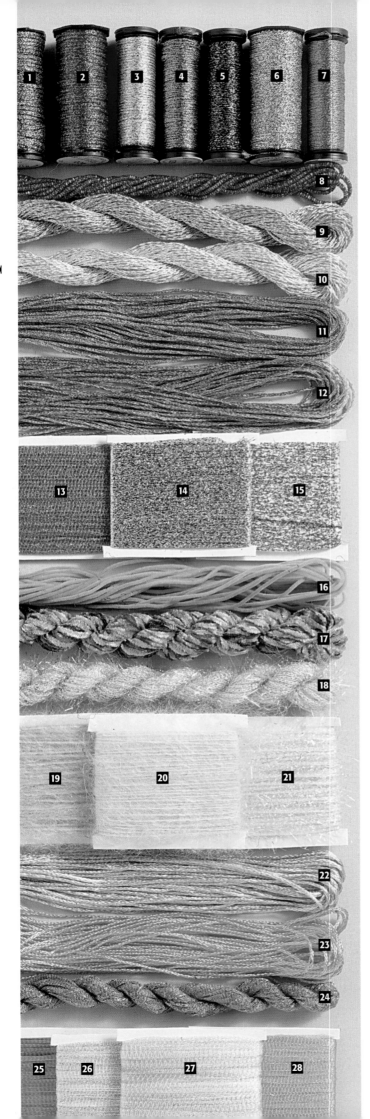

SPECIALTY AND SYNTHETIC FIBERS

This ever-growing category offers many exciting options for the needlepointer. It's not possible to list all the currently available novelty threads, but those mentioned here are some of the more interesting and popular fibers which should enjoy market "staying power."

METALLICS Ribbon from Kreinik Mfg. Co. is a flat metallic ribbon in two widths: 1/16" wide and 1/8" wide. Braid from Kreinik Mfg. Co. is a flat braid with a bright, metallic sparkle, in five weights: #4 Very Fine, #8 Fine, #12 Tapestry, #16 Medium, #32 Heavy. Facets from Kreinik Mfg. Co. is a heavy, three-dimensional thread for couching; it resembles a string of tiny beads. Metallic Pearl Cotton and Metallic Floss from DMC are metallic and viscose blends that resemble their cotton cousins in weight and have relatively "soft hands." Frosty Rays from Rainbow Gallery is a tubular nylon thread with a metallic core. Fyre Werks from Rainbow Gallery is a polyester/nylon blend; colors include hologram gold and silver.

FUZZY SYNTHETICS Nylon Velour from Fleur de Paris has a soft, suede-like appearance. Silk 'n Chenille from The Thread Gatherer is a heavy, napped silk thread for couching and other special effects. Charleston from Needle Necessities, Inc., is a fuzzy, hand-dyed polyamide with a chain center (no core). Santa's Beard & Suit from Rainbow Gallery is a furry, acrylic/wool blend in four colors. Wisper from Rainbow Gallery, a mohair/nylon blend that combines well with other wool threads. Arctic Rays from Rainbow Gallery has a transparent and glistening "wispy fringe."

SHINY SYNTHETICS Marlitt, a four-stranded floss from Anchor, and DMC rayon floss (six-stranded) are rayon threads with a radiant shine. They're a bit slippery and can be difficult to work with because they knot and kink easily. (Moistening the thread as you stitch helps eliminate this.) They're less expensive than silk but have a beautiful silk-like sheen. Rachel and Rachelette from Caron Collections and Flair from Rainbow Gallery are nylon tubular threads with a transparent "watery" look. You can insert other threads into the tubes for special effect, or use these fibers "as they are" over other stitches. Frosty Rays from Rainbow Gallery is tubular nylon thread filled with a narrower, colored thread. Rhapsody from Rainbow Gallery is a nylon, tubular overdyed ribbon. Neon Rays from Rainbow Gallery is a shiny rayon ribbon with great versatility: it spreads out on larger meshes for good coverage, yet compresses to fit on smaller meshes.

FROM TOP: Kreinik's Braid—#32 (1), #16 (2), #12 (3), #8 (4), #4 (5); Kreinik's Ribbon—1/8" (6), 1/16" (7); Kreinik's Facets (8); DMC's metallic pearl cotton (9 & 10); DMC's metallic floss (11 & 12); Rainbow Gallery's Frosty Rays (13), Fyre Werks (14 & 15); Fleur de Paris' Velour Yarn (16); The Thread Gatherer's Silken Chenille (17); Needle Necessities' Charleston (18); Rainbow Gallery's Santa's Beard & Suit (19), Wisper (20), Artic Rays (21); DMC's rayon floss (22); Anchor's Marlitt (23); The Caron's Collection's Rachelette (24); Rainbow Gallery's Flair (25), Frosty Rays (26), Rhapsody (27), Neon Rays (28).

NEEDLEPOINT SCISSORS

Reserve your scissors for needlework only and keep them with your other stitching tools. Have them professionally sharpened when they become dull.

EMBROIDERY SCISSORS Use these for clipping threads and removing mistakes. (Never use a seam ripper for the latter.) Use a scissors sheath or case to protect the points and prevent them from stabbing other items in your stitching bag or basket. If you stitch with metallic and synthetic fibers, consider a second pair of embroidery scissors that are old and duller than your fine ones. (If you only have one good pair, don't cut these fibers using the tips of the scissors; cut closer to the base of the blade.)

SHEARS Use regular dressmaker's shears for cutting your canvas.

TWEEZERS Very useful for picking out threads when you're correcting mistakes.

THIMBLES Definitely a personal preference. In the long run they can prevent callused fingertips.

NEEDLEPOINT NEEDLES

High-quality needles may be more expensive, but are more than worth the investment, for they will make your work a pleasure. Carelessly made needles have small imperfections that can snag on fabric and threads from previous stitching.

The larger the number, the smaller/finer the needle (milliners are exceptions). If needle is too large, it's difficult to pass easily through the canvas and will distort the canvas. If too small, it damages the yarn or thread with each stitch you take.

ABOVE: Needles (from left to right, interspersed with needle threaders)—tapestry, chenille, beading, milliners, and crewel; (at bottom) embroidery scissors, tweezers, thimble, shears.

TAPESTRY The blunt point of this needle prevents splitting the threads of the canvas as you stitch. The large eye makes the job of threading easier. Select the needle according to the mesh size of the canvas. Of course, you must take the thickness of the thread into consideration, too, but this should not be a problem if you've selected the right thread for the mesh.

MESH	NEEDLE
5	Size 13
7	Size 16
10	Size 18
12	Size 20
13 or 14	Size 22
16, 17, 18	Size 24
24	Size 26

CHENILLE These large-eyed needles resemble tapestry needles except for their sharp points, which are useful when securing couched threads.

CREWEL Sharp-pointed, these are shorter-eyed than chenille needles; use them for very fine couching threads.

BEADING These long and narrow needles have very fine eyes which can pass easily through the holes of beads.

MILLINERS These long, sharp-pointed needles have the same diameter along the entire length, which makes it easier to execute Bullion Knots.

NEEDLE THREADERS

These tiny, inexpensive tools are wonderful time-savers and will spare you much aggravation. Tack one to the corner of your canvas so you don't have to search for it every time you need it.

You can make your own threader: Fold a tiny square of stiff paper in half (it should be narrower than the needle's eye), insert the thread end into the fold, and pass the paper through the eye.

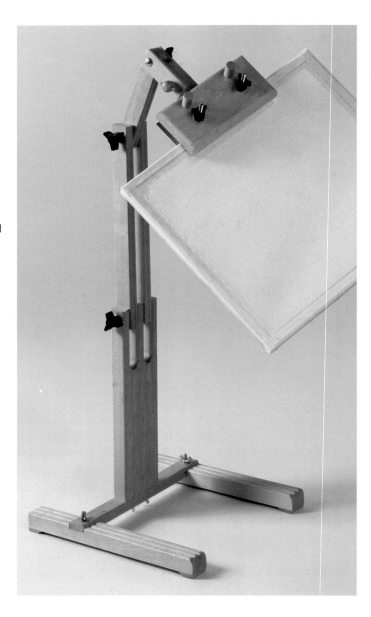

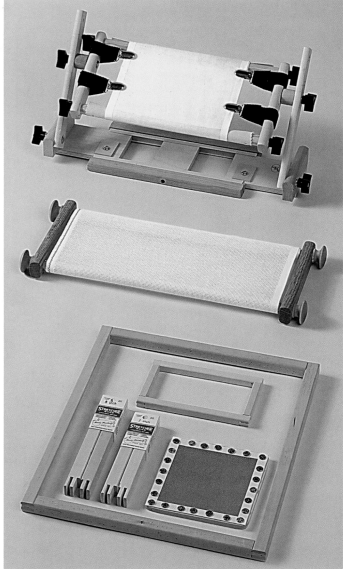

NEEDLEPOINT FRAMES

Using a frame will help you stitch with an even tension and prevents your canvas from becoming misshapen. Experiment with a number of different frame systems to see which one works best for your needs (and your body's needs!).

STRETCHER BARS Easy-to-use and inexpensive, they consist of four ¾"-square wood strips that dovetail at the ends to form an open square or rectangle. They're usually sold in pairs; you need to buy one pair for the width of the canvas, and a second pair for the length. You can tack or staple your canvas directly onto the wood. If you stitch a lot, you'll eventually have an assortment of lengths that will work together to fit many projects. (These bars are specifically intended for needlework; don't confuse them with stretcher bars for painter's canvas.) Sold in pairs or pre-assembled, mini stretcher bars are ideal for projects of 4" to 12" dimensions.

SCROLL FRAMES Scroll frames consist of a pair of round scroll bars that attach to a pair of flat side bars. The scroll bars should be at least as wide as the width of your canvas; they feature a fabric tape or webbing to which you sew the top and bottom edges of your canvas. The ends of the scroll bars screw into the side bars by means of screws or nuts that

you can adjust to achieve your desired tension as you roll the scroll bars in opposite directions. In order to keep the horizontal tension as firm as the vertical, you must lace the side edges of the canvas to the side bars or use frame clips (read below). Scroll frames will crush raised or three-dimensional stitches, so are not recommended for designs with these effects.

TABLE AND FLOOR STANDS Table and floor stands free both your hands for stitching, especially useful when using a laying tool. You can make height and angle adjustments to suit you so stitching is as comfortable as possible. Many come with their own scroll frames, which can be detached for portable stitching, too.

FRAME CLIPS These adjustable clips attach to the sides of scroll frames to ensure that horizontal tension equals vertical tension, and eliminate the fuss of lacing, unlacing, and re-lacing by hand as you move to a new area of your canvas.

ABOVE LEFT: Needlepoint floor stand with a canvas on stretcher bars attached.

ABOVE: Needlepoint frames (from bottom)—stretcher bars packaged and assembled, scroll frame, scroll frame on a table stand with frame clips attached.

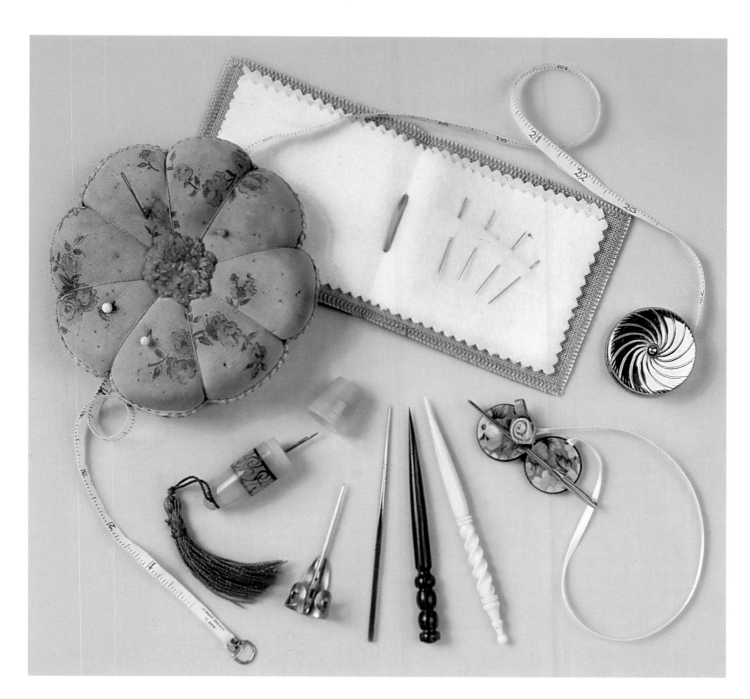

ADDITIONAL EQUIPMENT FOR NEEDLEPOINT

LAYING TOOL When you work with multiple plies on a single needle, you'll need to keep the threads parallel, not twisted, as you stitch. (This is called "laying" the thread.) A variety of laying tools will help you achieve this. The simplest is a large tapestry needle or bodkin. Others specifically designed as laying tools include a stroking tool (also known as a tekobari); one end resembles an awl or stiletto, and the other end is square to prevent it from slipping from your fingers. A trolley needle has a point like a tapestry needle affixed to a metal band that fits on the end of your finger.

PINCUSHIONS Most stitchers find pins useful for such tasks as pinning threads out of the way and marking designated mesh threads on the canvas. Pincushions are also useful for stowing threaded needles if you must change colors often. They come in a variety of sizes and styles both new and antique; select one that fits in your stitching bag or basket. Many stitchers like to make their own personalized models.

Many manufactured pincushions come with an emery, which looks like a very small pincushion filled with a gritty, sand-like material which keeps needles clean and sharp.

NEEDLEBOOK OR NEEDLECASE With "pages" of soft fabric, a needlebook keeps your needles protected (and protects *you* from the needles, too) and organized. Each "open page" is designed to store a particular needle type in a range of sizes. As with pincushions, this is an item you can make yourself to show off your stitching talents.

Many stitchers like to store their needles in needlecases, which may be narrow and cylindrical or large and box-like; some of the latter have magnets to keep needles in place.

THIMBLE Whether or not to stitch with a thimble is a personal preference. Spending time to master using a thimble is well spent if it saves your fingertips, especially if you stitch a lot.

CLOCKWISE FROM UPPER LEFT: Antique pincushion, needlebook, tape measure, magnets, laying tools, trolley needle, needlecase.

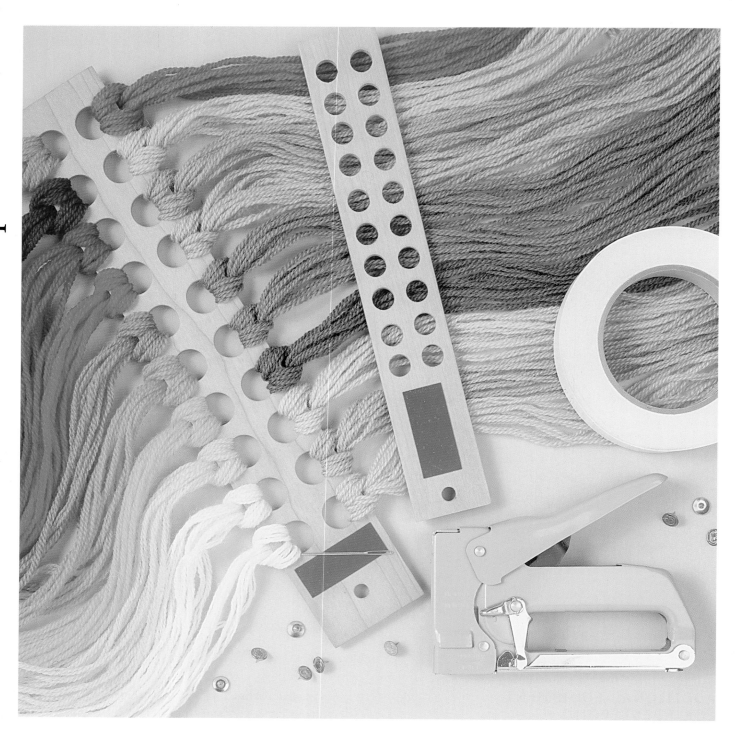

THREAD PALETTE These plastic, wood or paper palettes have a series of holes along the edges to hold individual colors of threads, which you attach using half-hitch knots.

THREAD ORGANIZER There are many products on the market for storing and identifying threads you accumulate. One of the simplest is individual plastic bags held together on a metal binder ring. On the other end are wooden boxes or chests that resemble fine furniture.

MAGNETS A pair of magnets (page 23) that attach to each other from both sides of the canvas are handy to hold needles and small embroidery scissors so they're in easy reach.

RULER AND TAPE MEASURE Clear plastic rulers are invaluable: those calibrated in inches, and those calibrated to particular mesh counts. Both come in a 6" length that fits easily into a stitching bag. For measuring a larger area, a tape measure is useful and takes up little space.

STAPLER AND STAPLES OR THUMBTACKS AND TACK PULLER Choose one of these methods to attach canvas to stretcher bars. Select a lightweight stapler that uses lightweight ¼"-W staples.

DRAFTING TAPE This tape is less sticky than regular masking tape and helps keep your needlework cleaner. Use it for taping the cut edges of your canvas before mounting it in a stitching frame. You can find it at art supply stores. (Masking tape is acceptable if you cannot find drafting tape.)

ABOVE: Wooden thread palettes; drafting tape; tacks and stapler to attach canvas to a frame.

LIGHTING AND MAGNIFICATION Both your eyesight and your needlework deserve optimal lighting. Choose a light that directs a circle (not a spotlight) of light onto your entire stitching surface. Floor lamps and swivel-arm table lamps (such as an architect's light) are good choices. To avoid casting shadows over the work surface, right-handers will benefit from a light directed over the left shoulder, left-handers from the right.

For very fine work on high-mesh count canvas you may want to use a lamp that has a magnifier attached. Other possibilities include magnifiers that hang around the neck or are worn atop the head.

Two table lights (one with magnifier); magnifier designed to be worn on stitcher's head.

NEEDLEPOINT DESIGNS

One of the most important decisions you'll make when choosing a needlepoint project will be whether to use an already-painted canvas or a blank canvas and charted design. Only you can know what will ultimately suit you and bring you the greatest reward for your effort.

PAINTED OR PRINTED CANVAS

Canvases with painted or printed designs allow the stitcher to visualize the finished project, and are excellent for beginners who need to perfect their stitching technique. They're a good choice for those who like to stitch when they're traveling because there are no charts or books to fuss with. The colors are already selected, but you still have the opportunity to select the type of thread (wooly, shiny, metallic) and the stitches.

HAND-PAINTED CANVAS These canvases are painted by a needlework designer, and can be found in two categories: very precise canvas intersection painting in which the individual stitches are prescribed, or the less-precise area painting, which requires you to make more decisions as you stitch. As you might expect, the first is more painstaking for the artist, thus more expensive.

SILK SCREENED CANVAS These canvases are less precise than those that are hand-painted, and less expensive. When selecting one of these designs, look for how well the design elements—especially straight lines—line up with the mesh of the canvas; there should be no overlapping of colors or blank spaces.

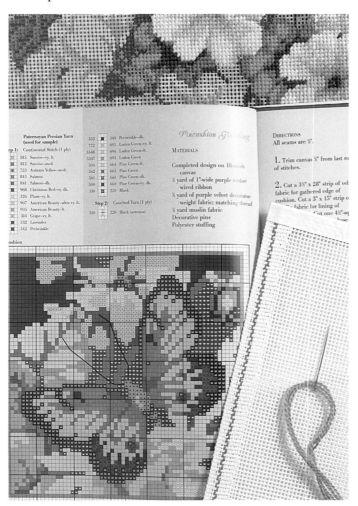

CHARTED DESIGNS

This method relies on counting canvas threads yourself, following a printed chart presented on a grid that indicates the mesh. A chart may be printed in colors that best match the threads or with symbols that represent the various colors, explained in a separate key.

Charted designs offer several advantages over painted canvas: they are less expensive than painted or printed canvas, and afford the stitcher the opportunity to experiment with making design changes. If you're inclined to use various design elements from several sources, your obvious choice would be to begin with a blank canvas.

NEEDLEPOINT KITS

Many manufacturers assemble kits of everything the stitcher needs to complete a design: the design (painted/printed canvas or charted design), threads, embellishments, and instructions. The convenience of kits must be weighed against the fact that you cannot make your own thread choices.

ABOVE: Pre-painted canvases – intersection painting (top) and area painting (bottom).
LEFT: Silk-screened canvas (top) and charted design and blank canvas (bottom).

needlepoint basics

BEFORE YOU STITCH
MOUNTING THE CANVAS ON A FRAME

ALLOW EXTRA CANVAS FOR FINISHING Always allow an extra ½" on all sides for taping (see below); beyond this, let your project be your guide and check instructions for specific amounts. To enable you to block the stitched canvas, allow at least 3" extra to all four sides. You may find it helpful to sew a running-stitch outline of the design perimeter.

ORIENT YOUR CANVAS FOR STITCHING Identify the warp thread and align it vertically (the selvage edge is parallel to the warp). If your canvas does not have a selvage edge, remove a thread in each direction; the warp will show slightly more defined ridges than the weft.

If the size of your canvas permits, make a tracing of the perimeter of the canvas onto paper before mounting it on the frame. Save this paper to guide you when you block the canvas after stitching.

PREVENT THE EDGES OF YOUR CANVAS FROM FRAYING Tape the raw edges using drafting or masking tape. Always cut away these taped edges before framing or otherwise finishing your project. Another solution is to fold purchased hem tape lengthwise and sew to the canvas, using the longest stitch length on your sewing machine.

IF USING STRETCHER BARS First connect the bars at the corners, tapping them together with a hammer or rubber mallet. Check that the corners are perfectly square.

Ideally, the outer edges of your taped canvas should fit the outer edge of the stretcher bars without folding over. Begin stapling or tacking at the midpoint of the top and bottom bars, pulling the canvas as taut as you can. Repeat at the midpoint of the side bars. Work from the midpoints to the corners sequentially on both axes. Place staples or tacks approximately 1" apart. Your canvas should be taut and completely free of wrinkles or ridges.

IF USING A SCROLL FRAME Sew the top and bottom edges of your canvas to the webbing on the scroll bars, using carpet or upholstery thread and firm Backstitches.

To maintain equal tension in the horizontal axis, you'll have to attach the sides of the canvas to the sides of the frame. The easiest solution is to use clips made for this purpose. The alternative is to lace the canvas to the side bars, using upholstery thread, dental floss, or pearl cotton. The disadvantage of this method is that you must unlace—then re-lace—the sides every time you scroll to a different area of the canvas. This may be more of a problem with some designs than others.

ESTIMATING THREAD AMOUNTS

The most accurate method to estimate how much thread you'll need for a given project is to stitch one square inch using
- the intended thread in the correct number of plies
- on the size mesh you plan to use
- in the stitch(es) you plan to use.

From this sample you'll be able to calculate how much thread to buy; you'll also be able to determine if your chosen thread has the coverage you desire. Please note that different colors of the same fiber may vary slightly in thickness depending on how the particular dyes affected them.

As you "stitch your inch" pay close attention to the amount of thread you use. Next calculate (you may have to estimate) how many square inches you'll need for each color of thread. Simply multiply the square inches of the color times the amount you used for your sample. Then add more for starting and stopping threads (especially if the design has frequent color changes) and for correcting mistakes. If you're unsure of your calculations, ask a knowledgeable shop owner for assistance.

PLYING THREADS

Some multiple-ply threads—Persian wool and cotton floss, for example—must be separated before stitching, even if you intend to use the same number of plies in your needle at once. Manufacturing and packaging tend to pack the fibers together, twist, or flatten them. Separating them allows them to fluff out, which results in better coverage on the canvas.

Always test the number of plies you need for a particular canvas. If your thread comes in three plies, but you need to stitch with four plies, cut two equal lengths of three-ply thread, separate them all, and combine four, reserving the remaining two plies for the next "needleful."

Most threads—wool in particular—have nap (direction). Run your fingers first in one direction along the length of the thread, then in the other direction. The smoother direction represents "going with the nap," which is the direction you'll want the thread to enter the canvas, so take note of this as you thread your needle.

MERGING DIFFERENT THREAD DYE LOTS

In an ideal world you'll always buy enough thread at one time to complete your project. Naturally, this will not always be the case! Maybe you'll discover—when you're nearing the midpoint of the design—that you're running out of one or more of the colors, especially if you've had to rip out stitches. If you're lucky, you'll find additional thread at your local shop that was dyed in the same lot with the thread you've already used. If you're not so lucky, the thread you find in the shop may be a slightly different shade than the original, even if the manufacturer labels it with the exact same color name and number. This is simply unavoidable, even by reputable manufacturers, because of the nature of the dyeing process.

How much this affects your project depends on several factors. If the color in question appears in scattered motifs throughout a design that has many colors, the difference in shades may not be noticeable. In this case, just make sure you use only one dye lot within one color block.

If the color in question fills up a large area—as a solidly-filled background, for example—you're faced with the problem of a glaring line of demarcation between the two shades. If you're stitching with one ply of thread, there's no simple solution; you can live with the two shades or you can buy enough of the new shade to re-stitch the entire area. However, if you're stitching with multiple plies, there is a solution if you've reserved some of the original shade and haven't stitched more than half of the area in question. The trick is to introduce increasing amounts of the new shade as you stitch. Instead of an abrupt color change, the stitching will gently blend from one shade to the other. Here's an example of how you would accomplish this when stitching with three plies:

1. Stitch with three plies of the original shade.
2. Stitch with two plies of the original shade and one ply of the new shade.
3. Stitch with one ply of the original shade and two plies of the new shade.
4. Stitch with three plies of the new shade.

TO BEGIN STITCHING
READING A CHART

Charts are arranged so that squares on the grid (negative space) correspond to intersections of the mesh threads. This concept baffles some beginners; the initial tendency is to imagine the lines on the chart represent the mesh threads. (Adding to the confusion is the fact that the mesh threads shown in the diagrams of individual stitches look like a grid.) Allow yourself time for this idea to "click" in your mind; once it does you'll have it for life!

Charted Design   Stitched Design

Many stitchers like to sew lines of running stitches from top to bottom and side to side to divide the canvas into quarters or in a grid of 10 x 10 threads. These lines serve as guidelines as you read a chart. If your chart doesn't indicate the center of each axis, draw the lines yourself with a pencil.

Where on the canvas do you begin stitching? It varies, depending on the design itself: the shape of the design elements, the number of color changes, etc. The obvious choices may be the top of the design, a particularly bold border, or some other dominant area of the design.

When you've completed the first few color blocks of a design, check the number of stitches you've stitched against the chart. The small amount of time you spend checking at this stage may be particularly well-spent if it saves you from ripping out and re-stitching larger areas later on.

STARTING THREADS

In general, use a thread length of approximately 18" long unless specific design instructions specify otherwise; some specialty threads may require a shorter length. Threads longer than 18" may twist or tangle as you stitch, and disrupt your stitching rhythm. Also, the thread closest to the needle will make so many trips in and out of the holes in the mesh that it will become stressed and frayed, and will no longer match the thread at the opposite end.

IN-LINE METHOD Determine the direction in which your first line of stitching will proceed. Hold a 2" tail of thread in place on the back of the canvas as you make the first few stitches, checking to see that the back of the stitches covers the tail.

WASTE KNOT METHOD Make a sturdy knot and insert the needle from the top of the canvas, about four inches from the point you wish to begin stitching. When you're done with that length of thread, clip off the knot, turn the canvas over, then thread the tail into the needle and weave it into the back of the stitches.

IN-LINE WASTE KNOT METHOD Combine both methods for efficiency. Plan the direction you'll be stitching, make a knot and insert it (from the top) along that same path. Clip the knot off just before you reach it; there's no need to hold the thread in place and check for coverage, and no need to rethread and weave later.

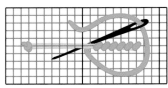

In-line Waste Knot Method

STITCHING TECHNIQUE

TENSION Maintaining consistency of tension within a given stitched area (part or whole of the design, depending on the variety of stitches) is essential for the good appearance of the finished project. Stitching with too tight a tension makes the canvas buckle. Stitching with too loose a tension yields a canvas that looks sloppy, with stitches that tend to snag more easily. Some needlepoint stitches require a looser or tighter than average tension; this will be noted in the individual stitch descriptions in the Stitch Gallery. You may find that longer stitches may require slightly more tension than shorter ones, but be sure to test-check first.

THE STAB STITCH If you use a needlework frame (stretcher bars, scroll frame) you must stitch using the stab method: Insert the needle and thread into the canvas with your dominant hand, then pull the needle through from the back either with your dominant hand or the less dominant hand (this latter is possible only with a floor or table stand that frees you from having to hold the frame).

Some stitchers prefer to use no frame and stitch using the sewing method, in which you insert and pull up the needle in one continuous motion. Because this requires you to bend the canvas as you stitch and affects the tension, this method is not recommended.

USING A LAYING TOOL When you're stitching with multiple plies of thread, the plies may twist or lump together in an unsightly manner. Avoid this by using a laying tool (see page 23) and a floor or table stand to free your less dominant hand. Hold the laying tool in your less dominant hand and stroke the threads with each stitch so they lie flat and parallel.

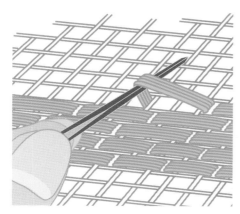

"CLEAN" AND "DIRTY" HOLES This is stitchers' slang for canvas holes that are yet-unstitched (clean) and those that already contain one or more stitched threads (dirty). You'll obtain the best results when you choose to bring your needle up through a clean hole whenever possible. (See the Algerian Eyelet on page 64 for a dramatic example.) If your working thread must share a hole with another stitch, it's preferable that the subsequent stitch be inserted from the top of the canvas, not brought up from the back, which goes against the nap of the previous stitch. However, this isn't always possible if you want the coverage on the back to be consistent.

COMPENSATING STITCHES As you study the stitch diagrams you will notice that some show compensating stitches, which are small "fill-in" stitches not technically part of an individual stitch unit. Their purpose is to fill in small or oddly shaped areas which do not accommodate a perfect stitch unit. Expect to encounter this situation as you stitch. The usual solution is to first place full stitch units, then later fill any open areas with compensating stitches. They should appear to be a complete stitch unit that is partially obscured by surrounding design elements or the edge of the design area.

ENDING THREADS To end a thread, weave it under the stitches horizontally or vertically (never diagonally) on the back of the area you have just stitched. If the stitches are long and loose on the back, double back with a small S-shaped reversed stitch (or two).

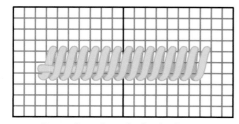

Ending a thread on the back of a canvas

Never weave the tail of a dark-colored thread through the back of an area stitched with light-colored thread. This rule also applies to carrying a dark thread from one color block to the next. No matter what the color, avoid carrying the thread between color blocks more than ½" apart.

WHEN STITCHING IS COMPLETE
BLOCKING THE FINISHED PIECE

If you've stitched your project using a frame, you will have minimized distortion of the canvas. Nevertheless, neglecting to block your finished needlepoint places your entire project in jeopardy, so don't skip this important step.

PREPARE A BLOCKING BOARD You can purchase a ready-made blocking board or make your own. Use insulation boards or fiberboard (you'll find these at a lumberyard or hardware store) and have it cut in a size you can comfortably work with. Cover it with paper; a cut-open grocery bag works fine (tape pieces together if necessary). Using waterproof ink, draw a grid on the paper at least as large as the original outer dimensions of the canvas, with the lines 1" apart. Wet the paper and allow it to dry; this will shrink the paper taut. Draw the exact dimensions of the canvas before you stitched on it.

ATTACHING THE CANVAS If the threads you used are washable, spray the entire canvas with cold water, squeezing out excess water with a towel. If the threads are not washable, lightly press the design on the back and block while still warm. With designs composed of flat stitches, place the design either face down or face up (whichever your preference). Canvases with raised stitches or added embellishments must be placed face up.

For a canvas with margins, use a lightweight staple gun. If there are no margins, use heavyweight, stainless steel T-pins. Begin with several staples/pins at one corner. Proceed to staple/pin an adjacent corner, pulling the canvas as taut as you can so it reaches the corner traced on the paper. Next, pull and staple/pin the opposite corner into place. (You will now have two adjacent sides stapled/pinned in place.) Staple/pin these two sides at the midpoints, and keep stapling/pinning halfway between existing staples/pins until staples/pins are close together. Now pull the fourth corner in place (you may need to remoisten this area and seek the assistance of another person if the canvas is stubborn) and finish stapling/pinning the remaining sides.

Allow the canvas to dry thoroughly. After you remove the staples/pins make sure the blocking produced perfect 90-degree corners. A piece may require additional blocking. 🪡

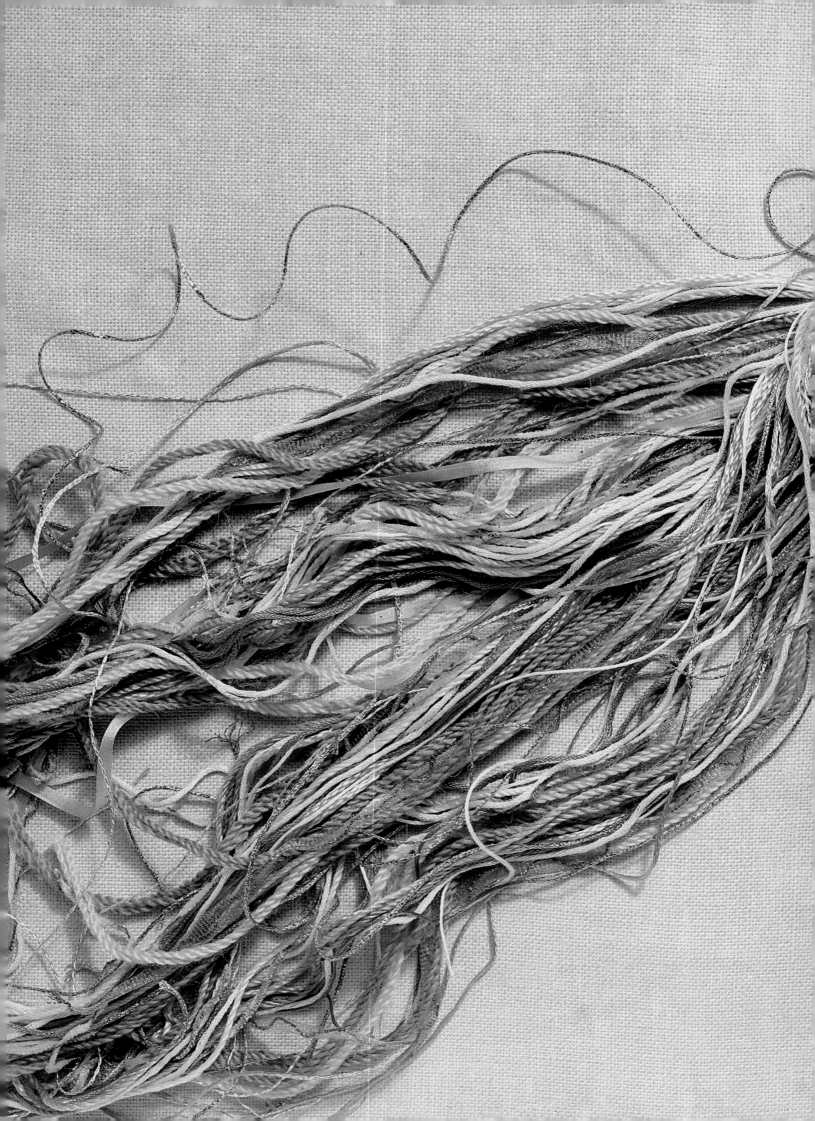

needlepoint
stitch gallery

needlepoint stitches

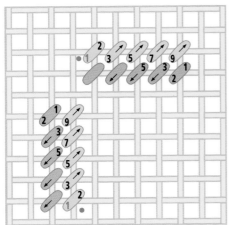

HALF CROSS

DESCRIPTION
One of three stitches classified as "Tent" stitch (a short diagonal stitch over one mesh intersection).

Produces vertical stitches on back (shown in lower half of photo).

Provides poor coverage on back.

Because of poor coverage on back, don't use for upholstery or other items which will receive heavy wear.

HOW TO STITCH
Work from left to right horizontally, then rotate canvas. Work from bottom to top or from top to bottom if stitching vertically.

SUGGESTED USES
Universal

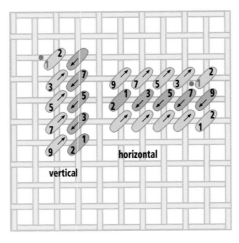

CONTINENTAL
Other Name: Continental Tent

DESCRIPTION
One of three stitches classified as "Tent" stitch (a short diagonal stitch over one mesh intersection).

Produces diagonal stitches on back (shown in lower half of photo).

Provides better coverage on back than Half Cross.

HOW TO STITCH
Work from right to left horizontally, then rotate canvas. Work from top to bottom or the reverse if stitching vertically.

Because succeeding rows come up in already-filled holes, threads don't remain as smooth.

Because it warps the canvas, use a frame and stitch with even tension.

SUGGESTED USES
Universal

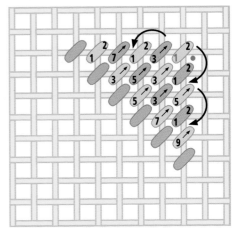

BASKETWEAVE
Other Name: Diagonal Tent

DESCRIPTION
One of three stitches classified as "Tent" stitch (a short diagonal stitch over one mesh intersection).

One of the most popular stitches, good for upholstery.

Produces woven stitches on back (shown in lower half of photo).

Provides good coverage on back.

The stitches are flatter and more consistent than Half Cross or Continental.

Produces negligible distortion of canvas.

HOW TO STITCH
No need to rotate canvas as you stitch.

Descending rows go across vertical warp thread (an aid when skipping around on canvas). As you stitch, remember "vertical, down."

SUGGESTED USES
Universal

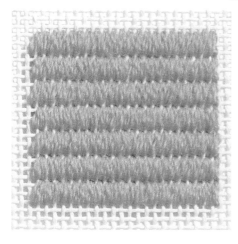

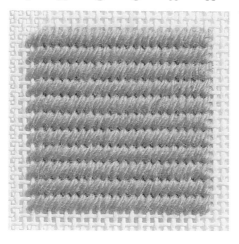

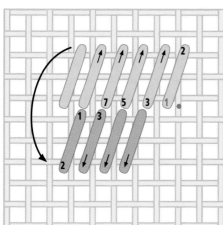

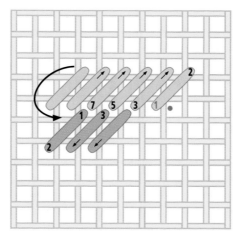

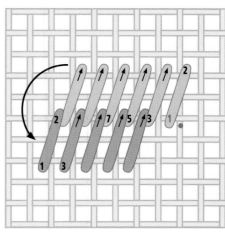

33

SLANTED GOBELIN

Other Names: Gobelin Oblique, Slanting Gobelin

DESCRIPTION

The slant of the stitch may be over one (above) or two (variation at right) threads to the right. (Over one is more common.)

The height of the stitch may vary from two or more threads (usual height is three or four threads).

Requires compensating stitches at beginning and end of each row.

A versatile stitch.

HOW TO STITCH

Work from right to left to give the best coverage on the back.

Take care to keep the slant uniform.

Because it warps the canvas, use a frame and stitch with even tension.

SUGGESTED USES

Background, filling, clapboards on houses

SLANTED GOBELIN VARIATION

DESCRIPTION

Note the difference between this stitch and the one to its left.

This is one of the many possible variations of the Slanted Gobelin.

HOW TO STITCH

Work from right to left to give the best coverage on the back.

Take care to keep the slant uniform.

Because it warps the canvas, use a frame and stitch with even tension.

SUGGESTED USES

Background, filling, clapboards on houses

The red dot in each stitch diagram indicates where to begin stitching.

ENCROACHING SLANTED GOBELIN

Other Names: Interlocking Slanted Gobelin, Encroaching Gobelin Oblique

DESCRIPTION

Each successive row overlaps the previous row by one horizontal (weft) mesh thread.

HOW TO STITCH

Work from right to left or from left to right.

To maintain a uniform slant, be consistent on which side of the previous row you place successive stitches.

Strive for uniform tension.

To achieve a uniform back, rotate canvas 180° and come up in a "dirty" hole (not shown).

SUGGESTED USES

Uniform background, shading, filling

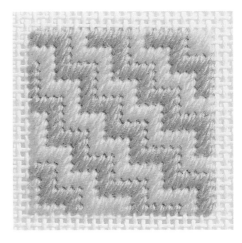

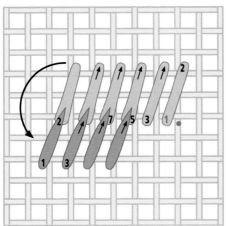

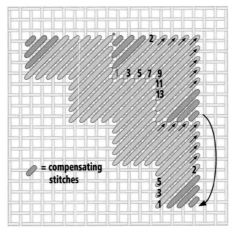

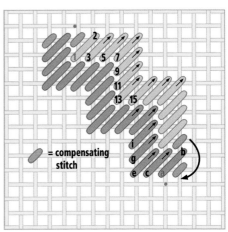

SPLIT SLANTED GOBELIN

BYZANTINE

BYZANTINE VARIATION

DESCRIPTION

Similar to Encroaching Slanted Gobelin (page 33) except each new row splits the threads of the previous row.

Somewhat more tedious to work than other Gobelin variations.

HOW TO STITCH

Split threads exactly in the middle.

SUGGESTED USES

Shading, background, filling

DESCRIPTION

Creates diagonal zigzag stripes.

In diagram, the first three stitches are compensating stitches, then the next five stitches per step establish a pattern to the end of the row.

The stitch length (over two to six vertical mesh threads) and number of stitches per step (2 to 11) may vary, or may be random.

Works up quickly.

Effective in one or more colors.

HOW TO STITCH

When practicable, establish the zigzag pattern by starting at the upper left corner and proceeding toward the lower right corner.

Stitch with a loose tension.

SUGGESTED USES

Stairs, "Southwest" motifs, background, borders

DESCRIPTION

Note the difference between this stitch and the one to its left.

This is one of the many possible variations of the Byzantine.

The smaller stitches and pattern repeat make this more suitable for smaller design areas.

HOW TO STITCH

When practicable, establish the zigzag pattern by starting at the upper left corner and proceeding toward the lower right corner.

Stitch with a loose tension.

SUGGESTED USES

See Byzantine

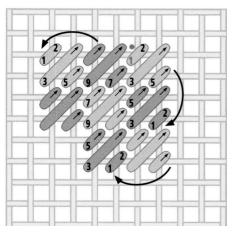
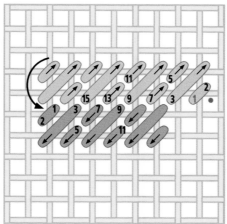
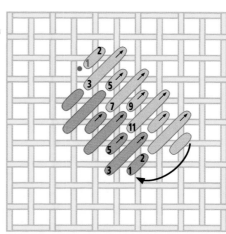

MOSAIC, WORKED DIAGONALLY

Other Name: Diagonal Hungarian

DESCRIPTION

One of the smallest square stitches in needlepoint.

Comprised of three-stitch groups.

Forms diagonal rows.

Two or more colors create a pattern of small diagonal stripes or checkerboard.

Effective in one or more colors.

Works up quickly and easily.

HOW TO STITCH

Because it warps the canvas, use a frame and stitch with even tension.

Start in upper right corner and work in diagonal rows.

SUGGESTED USES

Architectural features (door and window frames), clothing, background, filling; fits well into small areas.

MOSAIC, WORKED HORIZONTALLY

Other Name: Diagonal Hungarian

DESCRIPTION

One of the smallest square stitches in needlepoint.

Forms horizontal rows.

Two or more colors create individual small squares, horizontal stripes, or rows of shading.

Works up quickly and easily.

Effective in one or more colors.

HOW TO STITCH

Work in horizontal rows, from right to left.

To keep the stitch tidy, pull long stitches slightly tighter than the shorter stitches.

SUGGESTED USES

Background, architectural features, clothing, filling

CONDENSED MOSAIC

DESCRIPTION

Creates a look very different from the regular Mosaic stitch.

Note that there's no spacing between the stitch groupings; the last stitch of a previous group is the same as the first stitch of the next group.

Works up quickly and easily.

Effective in one or more colors.

HOW TO STITCH

Work from upper left to lower right.

Set the pattern with the longest diagonal in motif; work compensating stitches later.

SUGGESTED USES

Large and small backgrounds, filling

needlepoint stitches

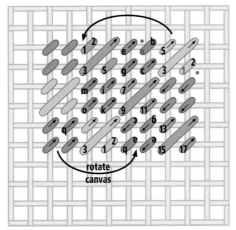

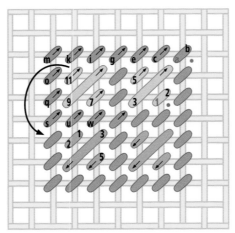

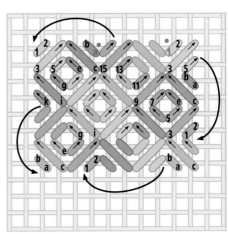

MOSAIC CHECKER

DESCRIPTION
Creates a checkerboard of Mosaic stitches and square of Tent stitches.
Most effective in two colors or two different threads.

HOW TO STITCH
Work the Mosaic stitches, starting in the upper right corner and proceeding diagonally.
Stitch the Tent stitches in Basketweave (page 32) and proceed diagonally to the left.

SUGGESTED USES
Background, clothing, borders, filling

FRAMED MOSAIC

DESCRIPTION
"Framed" refers to a stitch which is surrounded ("framed") by other stitches, usually Tent stitches (shown).
Effective in one or more colors.

HOW TO STITCH
Work the Mosaic stitches first, then the framing stitches.

SUGGESTED USES
Windows, architectural features, background, filling

REVERSED MOSAIC

DESCRIPTION
Suitable for one or more colors; most effective in one color.
Looks attractive with a bead or French Knot added to the central, open area.

HOW TO STITCH
Work Mosaic stitches on the diagonal in opposite directions.

SUGGESTED USES
Small areas, clothing, blankets, background, filling

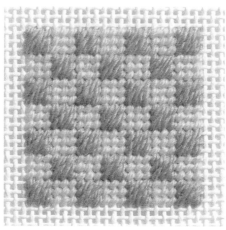
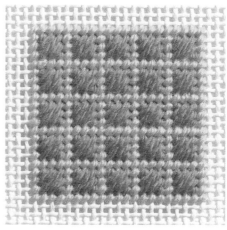

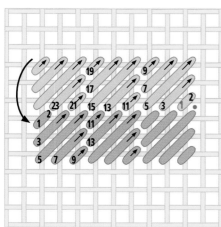
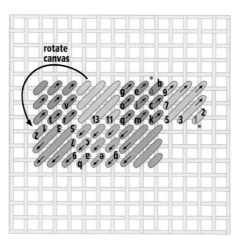
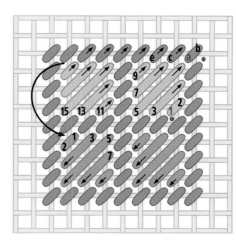

37

SCOTCH
Other Names: Flat, Diagonal Satin

DESCRIPTION
Composed of a five-stitch group.
Slightly larger stitch than Mosaic (page 35).
Works up quickly and easily.
Effective in one or more colors.

HOW TO STITCH
You may also work the stitch so the stitches face the opposite direction.
Work from right to left (as shown), from left to right, or diagonally.

SUGGESTED USES
Background, clothing, architectural features, borders, paths and roads

SCOTCH CHECKER
Other Names: Chequer, Checker

DESCRIPTION
Forms a block-like pattern with alternating blocks of Scotch and Tent stitches.
Creates textured surface.
Provides good coverage on back.
Effective in one or two colors.

HOW TO STITCH
Work from right to left, rotate canvas, continue right to left.
If using two colors, work all Scotch stitches first, then work Basketweave in other color.
Create a checkerboard pattern by using white or black for the Tent stitches and any other color for the Scotch stitches.

SUGGESTED USES
Borders, background, fields, stepping stones, paths

FRAMED SCOTCH
Other Names: Cushion

DESCRIPTION
Comprised of Scotch stitches surrounded ("framed") by Continental stitches.

HOW TO STITCH
Work the "framework" of Continental stitches first, establishing the horizontal rows, then the vertical rows; then fill in empty spaces with Scotch stitches.

SUGGESTED USES
Background, mullioned windows

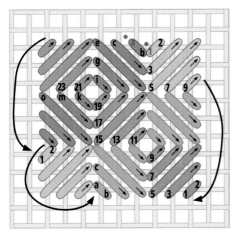
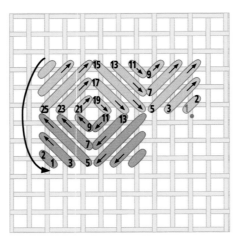
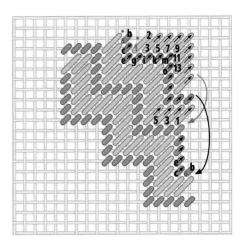

38

REVERSED SCOTCH, WORKED DIAGONALLY

Other Name: Flat

DESCRIPTION

Creates interesting texture.

Effective in one or two colors (checkerboard).

HOW TO STITCH

Work all Scotch stitches oriented in one direction first, then fill in with the others.

SUGGESTED USES

Background, rain on water, tiles, flowers (group of four squares), checkerboard, architectural features

REVERSED SCOTCH, WORKED HORIZONTALLY

DESCRIPTION

Same in appearance as Reversed Scotch, Worked Diagonally.

Creates interesting texture.

Effective on one or more colors.

HOW TO STITCH

Work in horizontal rows.

SUGGESTED USES

Stripes, background

JACQUARD

DESCRIPTION

Comprised of a Byzantine stitch (or regularly stepped Slanted Gobelin) separated by Tent (Half Cross and Continental) stitches.

Usually comprised of five or six long, slanted stitches per step.

Works up quickly.

Effective in one or more colors.

HOW TO STITCH

In general, work the Slanted Gobelin stitches from upper left of each row to lower right, then rotate canvas for subsequent rows.

Work all the Slanted Gobelin stitches first and then fill in with Tent (Half Cross and Continental) stitches, or work row by row.

Because it warps the canvas, use a frame and stitch with loose, even tension.

SUGGESTED USES

Background, sky

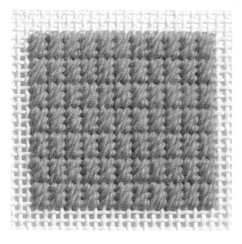
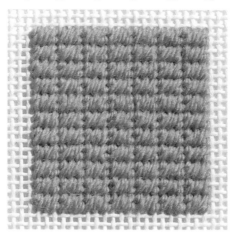

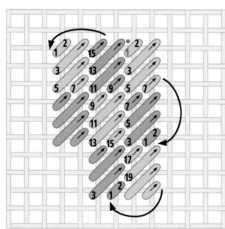
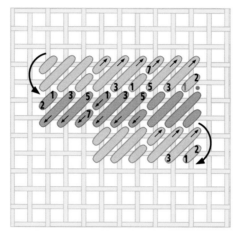
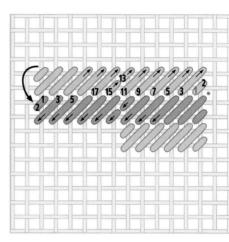

CASHMERE

HORIZONTAL CASHMERE

ELONGATED HORIZONTAL CASHMERE

DESCRIPTION

Resembles Mosaic except it forms rectangles instead of squares.

A versatile stitch.

Effective in one or more colors.

HOW TO STITCH

Work the stitch vertically, horizontally, or diagonally with the stitch pattern still arranged vertically.

You may vary the number of long stitches to form variations (see Elongated Horizontal Cashmere, far right).

Because it warps the canvas, use a frame and stitch with even tension.

SUGGESTED USES

Background, filling

DESCRIPTION

Basically a re-arrangement of the basic Cashmere, worked in horizontal rows.

Creates the appearance of small horizontal rectangles.

Effective in one or more colors.

HOW TO STITCH

Because it warps the canvas, use a frame and stitch with even tension.

SUGGESTED USES

Bricks, houses, walls, pathways, filling

DESCRIPTION

A variation of the Horizontal Cashmere stitch, with the basic "unit" lengthened.

The number of the longer stitches may vary from four to eight.

Effective in one or more colors.

May be stitched vertically to become the Elongated Cashmere stitch.

HOW TO STITCH

You may stagger subsequent rows of the stitch by beginning the new "unit" at a different point horizontally from the previous row; this creates the appearance of brickwork.

Because it warps the canvas, use a frame and stitch with even tension.

SUGGESTED USES

Bricks, elongated thin areas (when vertical), barn siding, wainscoting

needlepoint stitches

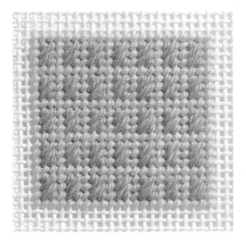

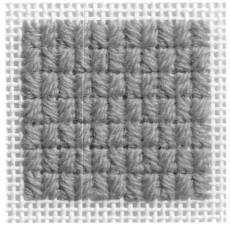

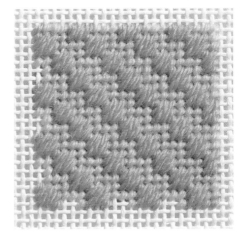

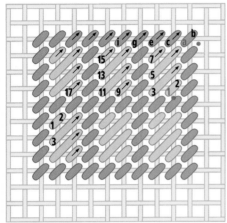

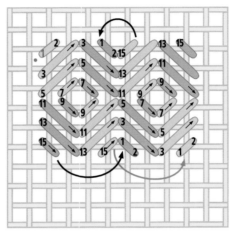

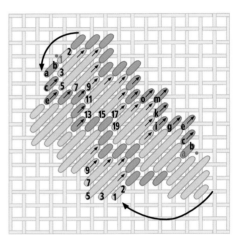

FRAMED CASHMERE

DESCRIPTION

Comprised of basic Cashmere stitches separated by single rows of Continental stitches.

Creates interesting texture.

Effective in one or more colors.

When the Continental stitches are lighter in color than the Cashmere stitches, the effect resembles mortar-and-bricks construction.

HOW TO STITCH

Work Cashmere stitches first, then fill in with Continental stitches.

SUGGESTED USES

Bricks with mortar, buildings, and walls (when oriented horizontally), mullioned windows (when oriented vertically)

REVERSED CASHMERE

DESCRIPTION

Effective in one or more colors.

Looks attractive with a bead or French Knot added to the central, open area.

HOW TO STITCH

Work either diagonally (as shown in diagram) or in horizontal rows.

SUGGESTED USES

Background, clothing, borders, patio bricks, buildings

MOORISH

DESCRIPTION

Comprised of diagonal rows of Condensed Scotch stitches, bordered by Tent (Continental and Half Cross) stitches.

Effective in one or two colors; best with two.

Works up quickly.

HOW TO STITCH

Maintain an even tension.

SUGGESTED USES

Large areas such as background, fields, clothing, rooftops

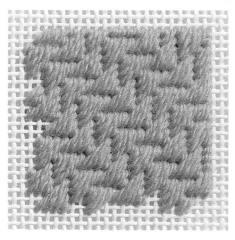
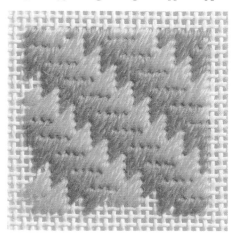
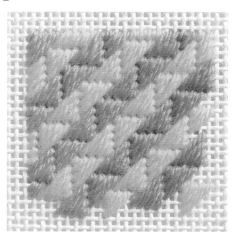

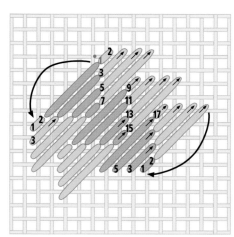
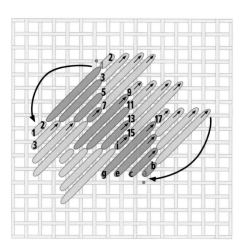
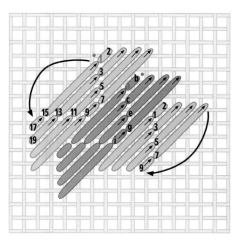

41

MILANESE

DESCRIPTION
An old and venerable stitch.
Creates a "wavy" look.
Effective in one or more colors.
Works up quickly.
The most common pattern is the four-stitch group (shown), but variations include three- and five-stitch groups.

HOW TO STITCH
Work in diagonal rows, from left to right or from right to left.
Maintain an even tension.
Stitch the compensating stitches last.

SUGGESTED USES
Background (good for large areas not broken up with other small motifs), sunset or aurora borealis, sky, "Southwest" motifs

MILANESE VARIATION

DESCRIPTION
Works up quickly.
Effective in two or more colors.

HOW TO STITCH
Work in diagonal rows, changing color for every row.
Work compensating stitches last.
Maintain an even tension.

SUGGESTED USES
Uninterrupted background

MILANESE VARIATION

DESCRIPTION
Effective in two or more colors.
Works up quickly.

HOW TO STITCH
Work in diagonal rows, always starting at the top.
Because it warps the canvas, use a frame and stitch with even tension.

SUGGESTED USES
Rays of sun, background

needlepoint stitches

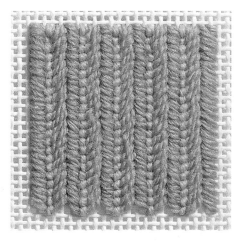

42

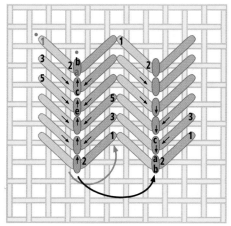
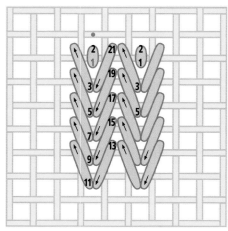
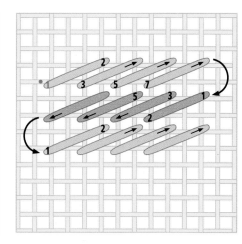

STEM

DESCRIPTION
Not to be confused with the Stem stitch for surface embroidery or counted thread work.

Effective in two colors (this is the advantage over the Fly stitch, page 71).

HOW TO STITCH
Start each left-hand set of diagonal stitches at top.

Work the short stitch as a Backstitch.

SUGGESTED USES
Bands, borders, stripes

KALEM
Other Names: Kelim, Knit, or Knitting

DESCRIPTION
Resembles knitting.

Stitch may cover one to four mesh threads in length.

Effective in one or more colors.

HOW TO STITCH
Work vertically (as shown in diagram) or horizontally.

SUGGESTED USES
Good for stripes, clothing such as sweaters (the smaller the stitch, the smaller the article of clothing), blankets

OBLIQUE SLAV
Other Name: Wide Gobelin

DESCRIPTION
Looks woven, with a smooth, even texture.

Resembles the Slanted Gobelin but with a greater slant.

Commonly stitched two mesh threads high and four mesh threads wide.

Works up quickly.

HOW TO STITCH
Proceed horizontally (as shown in diagram) or diagonally.

Stitch with loose tension.

Use thick threads or increase strands because of the greater distance between the threads (than the Slanted Gobelin stitch).

Fill in empty areas with compensating stitches.

Because it warps the canvas, use a frame.

SUGGESTED USES
Stripes, backgrounds, walls, fences, hills

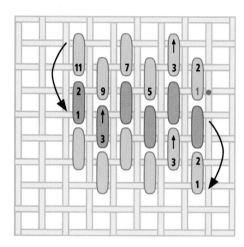
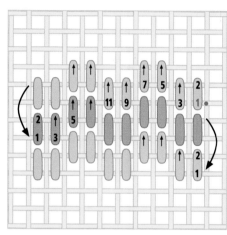
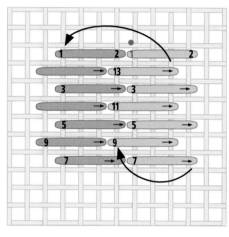

43

BRICK
Other Name: Alternating

DESCRIPTION
Alternates up and down over one mesh (with a two-mesh-tall stitch) or two mesh (with a four-mesh-tall stitch).
Works up quickly.
Blends well with other stitches.

HOW TO STITCH
You may work this stitch over two or four mesh threads, vertically or horizontally.
Work from right to left, then from left to right.
Try overdyed threads for effective shading.

SUGGESTED USES
Tree bark, sky, lakes, meadows or lawns, background, fireplaces, chimneys, petals, clothing

DOUBLE BRICK

DESCRIPTION
Creates a bolder appearance than the basic Brick stitch.
Works up quickly.

HOW TO STITCH
You may work this stitch over two or four mesh threads, vertically or horizontally.
Work from right to left, then from left to right.

SUGGESTED USES
Paths, chimneys, fields, background

HORIZONTAL BRICK

DESCRIPTION
Effective in one or more colors.
Working in pairs of stitches (as in Double Brick) produces the Horizontal Double Brick stitch.

HOW TO STITCH
Work this stitch over two or four (as shown) mesh threads.

SUGGESTED USES
Backgrounds, sky, walls

When using straight needlepoint stitches, you may need to increase the number of strands you use to ensure that the mesh threads do not show through the stitching.

needlepoint stitches

44

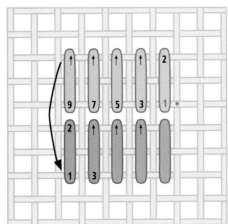
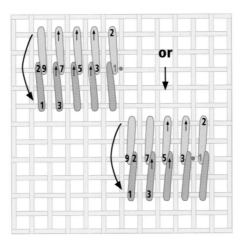
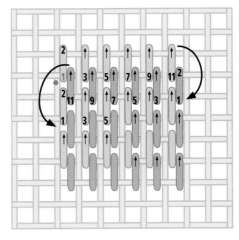

UPRIGHT GOBELIN
Other Names: Gobelin Droit,
Straight Gobelin

DESCRIPTION
Forms distinct rows of upright stitches, resembling woven tapestries.

The stitch length is usually over two to six mesh threads.

Two or more colors create a striped effect.

HOW TO STITCH
Work from the bottom of the stitch to the top.

Work from right to left, then from left to right.

Maintain an even tension.

Keep thread untwisted.

If canvas mesh shows, loosen tension or increase number of strands of thread.

SUGGESTED USES
Background, borders, belts, bands on clothing

ENCROACHING UPRIGHT GOBELIN
Other Names: Interlocking Straight Gobelin, Encroaching Straight Gobelin, Interlocking Gobelin Droit

DESCRIPTION
Comprised of rows of upright stitches which form an even texture.

May cover from two to five mesh threads.

Each successive row overlaps the previous row by one mesh thread.

Stitches appear slightly slanted.

Effective in one or more colors.

HOW TO STITCH
Work from the bottom of the stitch to the top.

Work from right to left, then from left to right.

Be consistent when placing the stitches of a new row to either the left or the right of the stitches of the previous row.

SUGGESTED USES
Uniformly textured background, filling

INTERLOCKING UPRIGHT GOBELIN
Other Names: Interlocking Straight Gobelin

DESCRIPTION
May cover from two to five mesh threads.

Effective in one or more colors.

Good for shading or stripes.

HOW TO STITCH
When stitching successive rows, be consistent as to which side (right or left) of the previous row you place each new stitch.

SUGGESTED USES
Clothing, people, animals, filling

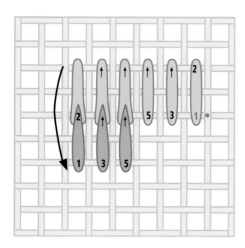

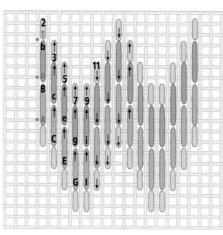

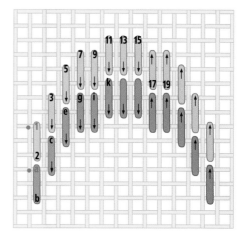

45

SPLIT UPRIGHT GOBELIN
Other Name: Split Gobelin

FLORENTINE
*Other Names: Hungarian Point,
Hungary, Irish, Flame, Bargello,
Punto Ungaro*

DESCRIPTION

First row resembles Upright Gobelin; each successive row covers the same number of mesh threads but overlaps a mesh thread of the previous row by splitting the previously-stitched thread in the middle.

Resembles knitting when worked over two mesh threads.

May cover from two to five mesh threads.

HOW TO STITCH

Always take needle down through previously-stitched thread to make a clean-looking hole.

SUGGESTED USES

Hair, animal fur, background

DESCRIPTION

Historically, there has been considerable difference of opinion and confusion over the distinctions (if any) between Bargello and Florentine.

Comprised of vertical stitches arranged in distinctly repeated pattern of steps (such as zigzags, chevrons, pinnacles, or scallops).

Commonly stitched in five or more color groups with several shapes for each color.

Wears very well; suitable for upholstery, pillows, valances, etc.

Vertical stitches may cover from two to six mesh threads; the longer the stitch, the more likely the finished item will not wear as well.

The steepness of the flame pattern is controlled by how much the successive threads rise or fall in relation to each other.

Not every successive stitch must move up or down (compare diagrams). The number of possible patterns is limitless.

HOW TO STITCH

Maintain an even, consistent tension.

To create the best coverage on the back follow this sequence: for downward steps, stitch from bottom to top of stitch; for upward stitches, stitch from top to bottom.

Make sure the threads completely cover the canvas for a solid effect.

SUGGESTED USES

Background, sky, water, fields, clothing, mountains, sunsets

needlepoint stitches

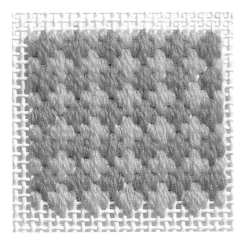

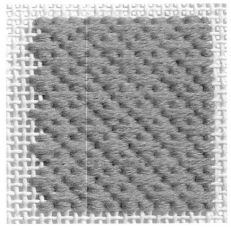

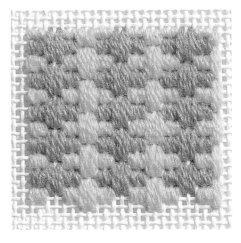

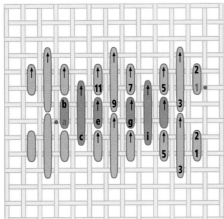

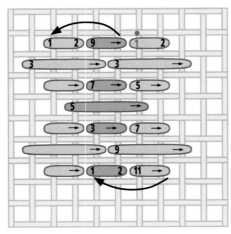

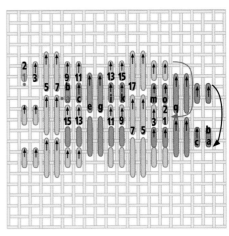

HUNGARIAN
Other Name: Point d'Hongrie

DESCRIPTION
Comprised of three-stitch groups with a space between each grouping.

Each successive row interlocks with the previous row.

Effective in one color (shows off the texture) or more colors (shows off the color pattern).

Versatile; works up quickly.

HOW TO STITCH
Work in horizontal rows, from right to left or from left to right.

Remember to leave a space between each three-stitch group.

SUGGESTED USES
Backgrounds, clothing

HORIZONTAL HUNGARIAN

DESCRIPTION
Similar to Hungarian, except worked in vertical rows to create a horizontal appearance.

Effective in one or more colors.

HOW TO STITCH
Remember to leave a space between each three-stitch group.

SUGGESTED USES
Bodies of water, backgrounds

DOUBLE HUNGARIAN

DESCRIPTION
Effective in one or more colors.

You may align the stitches horizontally (as shown) or vertically.

HOW TO STITCH
Work in rows from from left to right, then from right to left.

SUGGESTED USES
Backgrounds, wavy vertical stripes, clothing, sky, roofs, fields, shrubs, large baskets

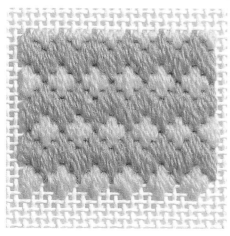
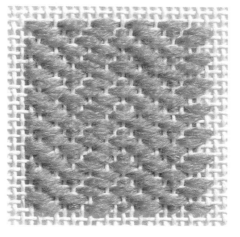

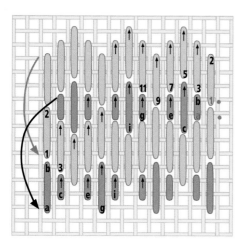
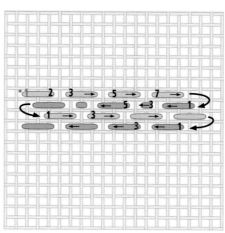
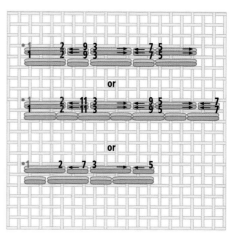

47

HUNGARIAN GROUND
Other Name: Hungarian Grounding

DESCRIPTION
Comprised of alternating rows of Hungarian and Florentine stitches.

You may work it one color, but it's more effective in two colors or two different fibers.

HOW TO STITCH
Work from left to right or from right to left.

In order to always come up in a clean hole, work each row sequentially.

SUGGESTED USES
Background, filling for large areas

DARNING
Other Name: Basting

DESCRIPTION
This basic Running stitch works with the exposed canvas to create patterns.

Numerous patterns are possible.

HOW TO STITCH
Use a loose tension.

Leave a small loop of thread between rows on back of canvas.

SUGGESTED USES
Background, fields, clothing

DOUBLE DARNING

DESCRIPTION
Employs a basic Running stitch.

Most common pattern is "over four, under two" (as diagrammed) but other patterns may be used.

Each row requires four journeys to complete.

Works up slowly.

Uses a lot of thread.

Creates a sturdy back.

HOW TO STITCH
Work horizontally or vertically.

Use a loose tension.

SUGGESTED USES
Backgrounds, small areas, blankets, paths

needlepoint stitches

48

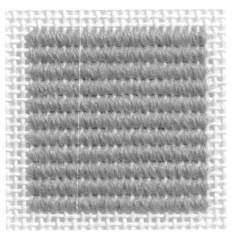

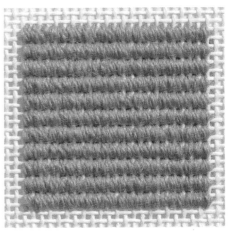

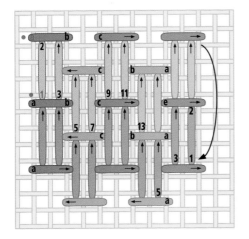

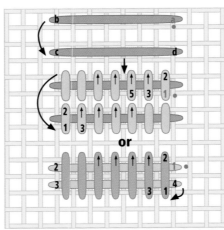

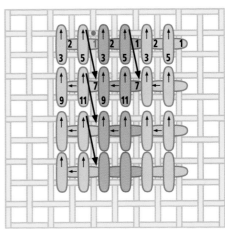

ROMAN II

DESCRIPTION

Comprised of Double Brick stitches with horizontal Running stitches at the top and bottom of each pair.

Effective in one or two colors.

Weaving the horizontal stitches only under the vertical stitches produces an interesting variation known as the *Willow* or *Burden* stitch, with a similar result.

HOW TO STITCH

You may work this stitch horizontally (called *Lazy Roman II*) or vertically (as shown).

SUGGESTED USES

Background, baskets, roofs

RENAISSANCE

DESCRIPTION

Comprised of a long horizontal Straight stitch (Tramé) covered by Upright Gobelin stitches.

Creates subtle texture.

Effective in one or two colors.

Works up more quickly than Renaissance Variation stitch (right).

HOW TO STITCH

Work from left to right, then from right to left.

If the horizontal thread needs to be long, use a Split stitch (see Tramé stitch, page 53).

SUGGESTED USES

Background

RENAISSANCE VARIATION

DESCRIPTION

Comprised of a basic three-stitch unit.

Tight, hard-wearing stitch good for upholstery.

Creates subtle texture.

Works up slowly.

Uses a lot of thread.

HOW TO STITCH

Work each three-stitch unit from left to right, proceeding downward in vertical rows.

Begin successive vertical rows at the top.

SUGGESTED USES

Background

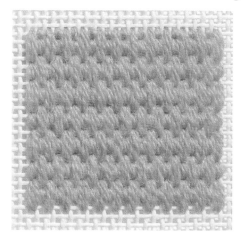

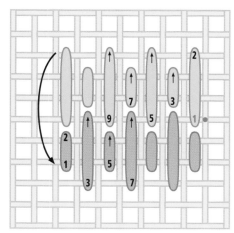
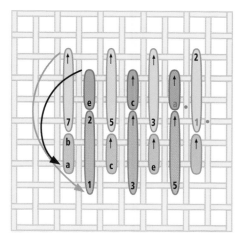
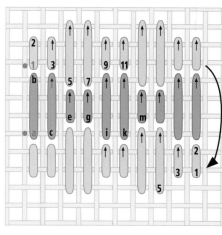

PARISIAN

DESCRIPTION

Comprised of alternating long and short stitches, with successive rows dovetailing.

The stitch patterns may be over four and two threads (as shown), six and two threads, or three and one threads.

Effective in one or two colors; introduce another color for the second row.

Works up quickly.

HOW TO STITCH

Work from right to left or from left to right.

SUGGESTED USES

Background, filling

PARISIAN VARIATION

DESCRIPTION

Comprised of alternating long and short stitches, with successive rows dovetailing.

The stitch patterns may be over four and two threads (as shown), six and two threads, or three and one thread.

Effective in one or two colors; introduce another color for the short stitch of each row.

Works up quickly.

HOW TO STITCH

Work from right to left or from left to right.

SUGGESTED USES

Background, filling, fields

DOUBLE PARISIAN

DESCRIPTION

Comprised of pairs of alternating long and short stitches, with successive rows dovetailing.

The stitch patterns are effective in one or more colors.

HOW TO STITCH

Work in horizontal rows.

SUGGESTED USES

Backgrounds, clothing, hills, buildings, borders, roofs

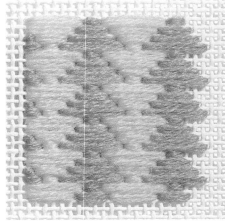

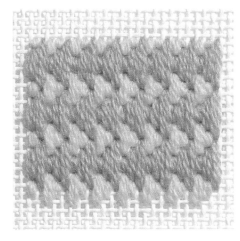

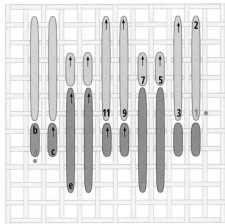

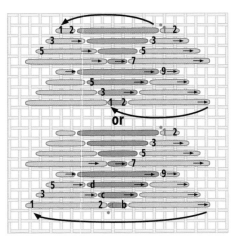

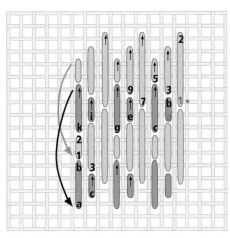

OLD FLORENTINE

HORIZONTAL MILANESE

VERTICAL MILANESE

DESCRIPTION

Comprised of pairs of stitches over six mesh threads alternating with pairs over two mesh threads.

The *Horizontal Old Florentine*—with all short stitches in a darker color—resembles a woven basket.

Effective in one or more colors. Try working all short stitches in one color and the long stitches in another, or alternate colors in each row (as shown).

HOW TO STITCH

Work from right to left or from left to right.

SUGGESTED USES

Borders, paths and roads, chimneys, roofs

DESCRIPTION

Because of the long stitches, it's not suitable for items which will receive a lot of wear.

Effective in one or more colors. The arrowhead pattern is less apparent when stitched in one color.

HOW TO STITCH

Work in vertical rows, from top to bottom, then from bottom to top.

SUGGESTED USES

Background, "Southwest" motifs

DESCRIPTION

Variation of the diagonal Milanese stitch (page 41).

Effective in one or more colors.

HOW TO STITCH

Work in horizontal rows, from right to left or from left to right.

For two-color version, work each row in order.

SUGGESTED USES

Background

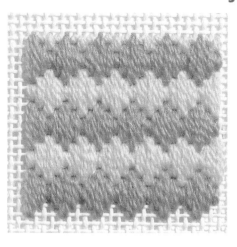

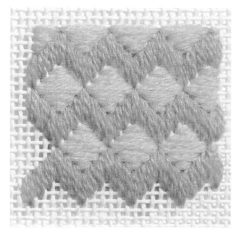

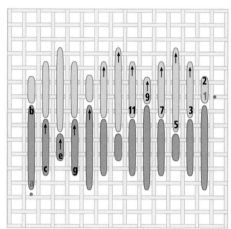
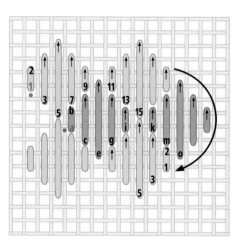
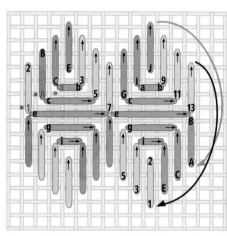

51

PAVILLION
Other Names: Pavillion Diamonds, Hungarian Diamonds

DESCRIPTION
This is a larger version of the Hungarian stitch (page 46): a grouping of five stitches, not three.

Note that there's no spacing between the stitch groupings; the last stitch of a previous group is the same as the first stitch of the next group.

Effective in one or more colors.

HOW TO STITCH
Work from right to left (as shown) or from left to right.

SUGGESTED USES
Background, wallpaper, clothing

PAVILLION DIAMONDS
Other Name: Hungarian Diamond

DESCRIPTION
Note that you must leave a space between each five-stitch grouping so that the diamonds above and below can dovetail into this space.

Works up quickly and easily.

Effective in one or more colors.

HOW TO STITCH
Work in horizontal rows.

SUGGESTED USES
Background, wallpaper, clothing, quilted effects

PAVILLION STEPS

DESCRIPTION
Use three colors to achieve a three-dimensional effect that resembles the Tumbling Blocks quilt pattern.

HOW TO STITCH
Proceed horizontally (note the number sequence).

SUGGESTED USES
Quilts, background

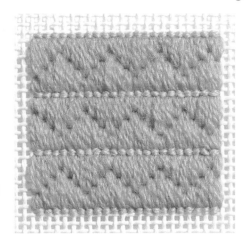

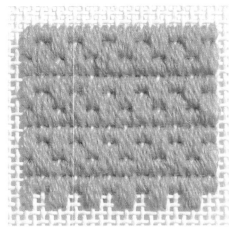

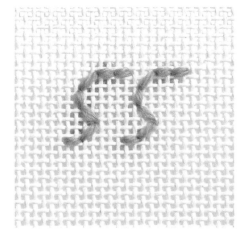

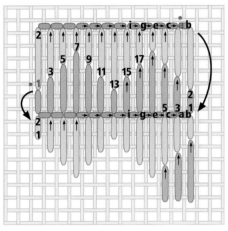

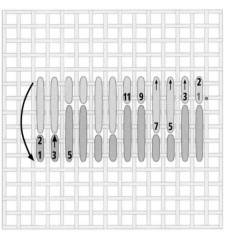

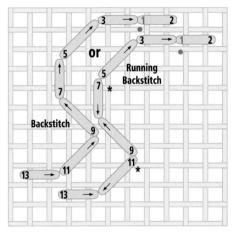

PRINCESS
Other Names: Zigzag, Berlin Border

DESCRIPTION

Backstitches separate opposing rows of vertical stitches.

This stitch has many variations: the pyramids may be larger or smaller, or Straight stitches may separate the opposing pyramids.

Effective in one or more colors; most effective in three.

HOW TO STITCH

Stitch horizontally (as shown) or vertically.

Use a loose tension.

SUGGESTED USES

Borders, edges, stripes, bands

BEATY

DESCRIPTION

Two rows comprise one band.

Effective in one or two colors.

HOW TO STITCH

Work from right to left (as shown) or from left to right.

SUGGESTED USES

Borders, bands, stripes

BACKSTITCH
Other Name: Point de Sable

DESCRIPTION

You may work this stitch over any number of mesh threads and in any direction. (Over one to four threads is most common.)

HOW TO STITCH

Work with a rhythm of "back one stitch, forward two stitches."

Note the stitch sequence for the *Running Backstitch:* this variation avoids carrying the Backstitch thread across an unworked, lightly colored area on the back of the canvas. This is important if you stitch using a dark thread, which might appear as a shadow on the right side of the canvas.

SUGGESTED USES

Use this stitch to cover the exposed canvas between rows of stitches, to hold down long stitches, to outline motifs, and to add accents.

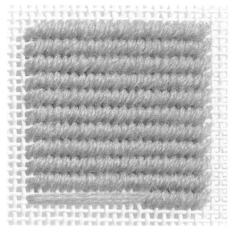

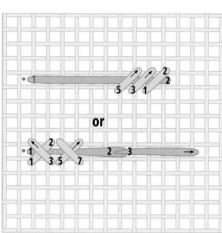

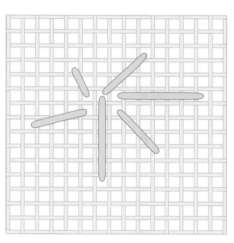

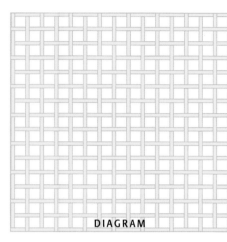

DIAGRAM

53

TRAMÉ

DESCRIPTION

Comprised of horizontal or vertical Straight or Split stitches (the actual Tramé stitch) which serves as padding for added stitches such as Slanted Gobelin (upper diagram) or Cross stitches (lower diagram).

Compare to the Renaissance stitches (page 48).

Effective in one or two colors. (In some cases the Tramé stitch may not show.)

The Tramé layer creates texture.

HOW TO STITCH

If the horizontal Tramé thread needs to be long, use a Split stitch rather than a Straight stitch.

SUGGESTED USES

Borders

STRAIGHT
Other Name: Stroke

DESCRIPTION

Comprised of a single straight stitch in any direction.

HOW TO STITCH

Place this stitch on top of other stitches.

Beware of long stitches snagging.

SUGGESTED USES

Fine details such as cat whiskers, sun rays, rails of a fence, grass, etc.

As you find variations or new stitches not illustrated in this book, add them here and on pages 74–75 to personalize the Needlepoint Stitch Gallery.

STITCH_____
Other Names:_____

DESCRIPTION

_____
_____
_____
_____
_____
_____
_____

HOW TO STITCH

_____
_____
_____
_____
_____
_____
_____
_____
_____
_____
_____
_____

SUGGESTED USES

_____
_____
_____

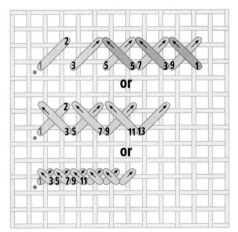

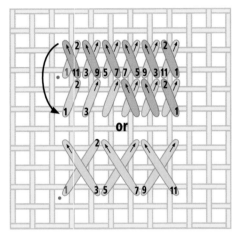

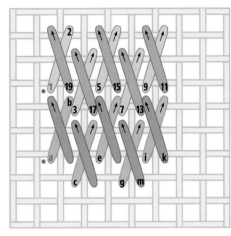

CROSS

Other Name: St. Andrew's Cross,
Cross-stitch, Petite Cross

DESCRIPTION

This basic stitch appears in very old needlepoint pieces.

Works well over one or more thread intersections.

Minimizes distortion of the canvas.

HOW TO STITCH

There are two possible stitching sequences:

1. Complete each cross before stitching the next. This works best on mono canvas and when stitching over only one thread intersection (lowest diagram).

2. Stitch a row of Half Crosses, then complete each cross on the "return journey" (upper diagram). This works best on Penelope canvas.

The top legs of the stitches must always go in the same direction.

SUGGESTED USES

Universal

OBLONG CROSS

DESCRIPTION

Longer than a Cross stitch in one direction (axis), either in width or height.

The ratio of one axis to the other may be 1:2, 1:3, 2:3, 2:4.

HOW TO STITCH

Experiment with different weights of thread; thin threads create a lacy effect.

SUGGESTED USES

Background, clothing, filling

ALTERNATING OBLONG CROSS

DESCRIPTION

Consists of Oblong Cross alternately staggered down one mesh thread.

Produces a staggered stripe effect when stitched in two or more colors.

Effective in one or more colors.

HOW TO STITCH

Work in rows of Half Crosses, crossing the stitches on the return journey, or complete each stitch individually.

SUGGESTED USES

Background, clothing, shrubs and trees, blankets, filling

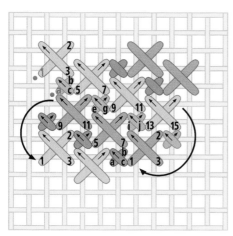

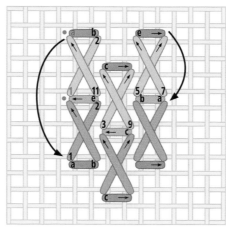

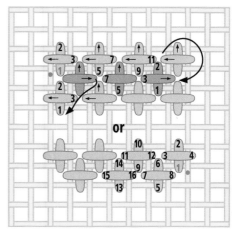

STAGGERED CROSS

DESCRIPTION
Produces a diagonal stripe.
Effective in one or more colors, especially when the smaller stitches are a different color.

HOW TO STITCH
Work in diagonal rows as shown.

SUGGESTED USES
Paths, shrubs, fields, trees, grass, clothing, filling

HOURGLASS CROSS

DESCRIPTION
Most effective when worked in two colors: one for the Oblong Crosses and another for the Straight Stitches.

HOW TO STITCH
Work the Oblong Crosses in rows, crossing the stitches on the return journey.

SUGGESTED USES
Background

UPRIGHT CROSS
Other Names: Straight Cross,
St. George's Cross

DESCRIPTION
Creates a long-wearing, slightly bumpy surface.
Usually each cross is worked in one color, but rows may alternate between two or more colors.
Usually worked over two-by-two mesh threads, but may be larger.

HOW TO STITCH
Work in horizontal rows one at a time.
Make sure that the horizontal stitch is always the top stitch.

SUGGESTED USES
Small areas, background, clothing, tree bark, flower centers, sheep

55

needlepoint stitches

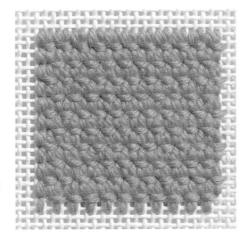

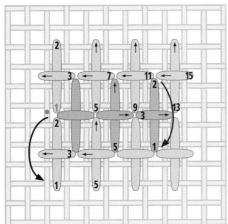

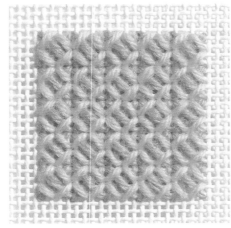

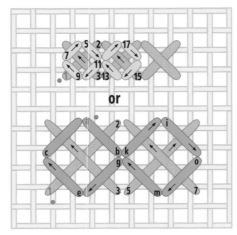

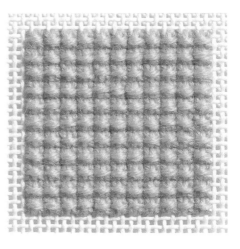

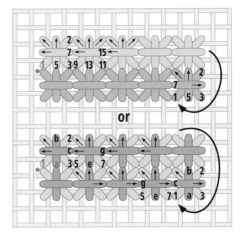

LONG UPRIGHT CROSS

DESCRIPTION
Vertical stitches are always longer than the horizontal stitches.

Creates a woven effect.

Usually each cross is worked in one color, but rows may alternate between two or more colors.

HOW TO STITCH
Work in horizontal rows, alternating from right to left, then from left to right.

SUGGESTED USES
Background

RICE
Other Names: Cross Corners,
William & Mary

DESCRIPTION
Comprised of a basic Cross stitch with each of the four legs tacked down by a short stitch.

Effective in one or two colors.

Works well over two-by-two or four-by-four mesh threads.

HOW TO STITCH
Work underlying basic Cross stitches (page 54) first.

SUGGESTED USES
Borders, background, bands

SMYRNA CROSS
Other Names: Double Cross, Leviathan,
Railway

DESCRIPTION
A combination of a basic Cross stitch (page 54) and an Upright Cross stitch (page 55).

Usual pattern is over two or four threads.

An old stitch, used since the Middle Ages.

Effective in one or two colors.

HOW TO STITCH
Work from left to right, or if worked from right to left, reverse direction of the top stitch.

When working in one color only, complete each cross individually.

When working in two colors, complete first two-leg crosses individually, then work the top upright crosses individually.

SUGGESTED USES
Borders, background, sky, filling, outline; two-color Smyrna Crosses create effective stars

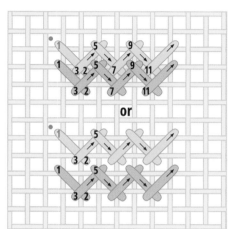
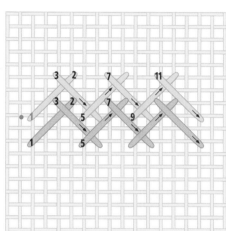
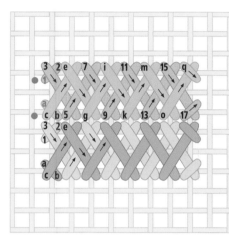

57

HERRINGBONE
Other Names: Witch, Plaited

HERRINGBONE VARIATION

DOUBLE HERRINGBONE
Other Name: Two-Color Herringbone

DESCRIPTION

Creates a zigzag stripe or a woven "tweedy" effect.

Effective in one or more colors.

Offers many variations.

Somewhat time-consuming.

(Stitches in above photo follow the upper diagram.)

HOW TO STITCH

Always work from left to right.

If working with multiple strands, keep strands parallel.

SUGGESTED USES

Borders, background, clothing, trim

DESCRIPTION

Note the difference between this stitch and the one to its left.

This is one of the many possible variations of the Herringbone.

HOW TO STITCH

Always work from left to right.

If working with multiple strands, keep strands parallel.

SUGGESTED USES

Borders, background, clothing, trim

DESCRIPTION

Effective in one or two colors.

Most effective when the first trip (blue threads in diagram) is worked in the darker color.

May be worked over three (as shown), four, five, or six mesh threads.

HOW TO STITCH

Always work from left to right.

SUGGESTED USES

Borders, bands, fields, baskets

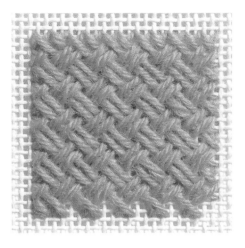

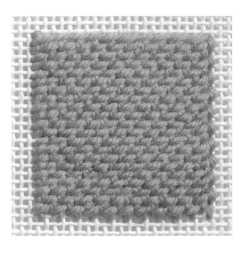

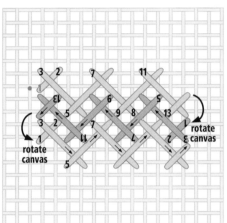

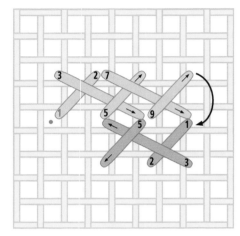

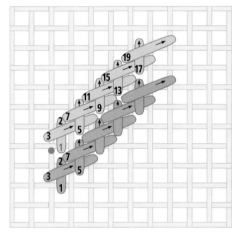

HERRINGBONE GONE WRONG

DESCRIPTION
Produces a rich texture.
Most effective in one color.

HOW TO STITCH
Rotate the canvas at the end of each row.
Work first row from left to right, second row from right to left (left to right if you rotate canvas).

SUGGESTED USES
Background, clothing, baskets

GREEK
Other Name: Double-Back

DESCRIPTION
Resembles a Long-Arm Cross stitch except the long diagonal stitch is in a different direction.
Usually worked over two horizontal threads, but may be worked over more than two.

HOW TO STITCH
Work from left to right, then turn canvas at the end of the row OR end thread at row's end and begin at left side again.

SUGGESTED USES
Small borders, braid, background

DIAGONAL GREEK

DESCRIPTION
Creates diagonal stripes.
Effective in one or more colors.

HOW TO STITCH
Work all rows from left to right.

SUGGESTED USES
Fields, bushes, background

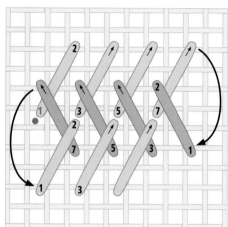

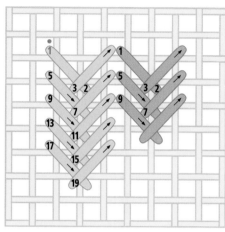

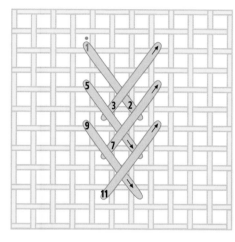

PLAITED GOBELIN
Other Name: Gobelin Plait

DESCRIPTION
Each row overlaps the previous row and slants in the opposite direction.

Works up quickly.

Creates vertical stitches on back.

A variation may be worked over one thread in width and two threads in height.

HOW TO STITCH
Work in horizontal rows, from left to right, then from right to left.

SUGGESTED USES
Background, water, waves, fields, sky, thatched roofs

FERN
Other Name: Canvas Fern

DESCRIPTION
Creates the appearance of a wide braid.

HOW TO STITCH
Work in vertical columns; always begin at the top of the column to keep the braid uniform.

Work vertically or horizontally by turning canvas.

Small Fern stitches work up best on Penelope or interlock canvas.

SUGGESTED USES
Borders, leaves, small trees, bands

FERN VARIATION

DESCRIPTION
Creates the appearance of a wide braid.

HOW TO STITCH
Work in vertical columns; always begin at the top of the column to keep the braid uniform.

Work vertically or horizontally.

SUGGESTED USES
Borders, bands

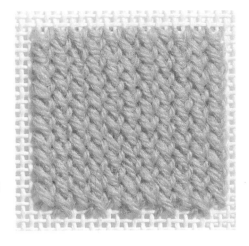

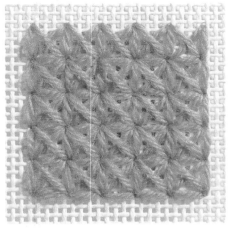

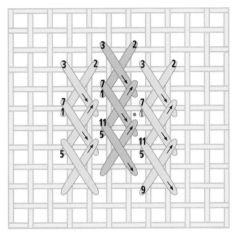

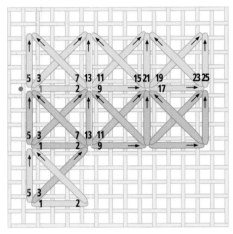

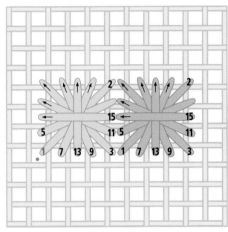

VAN DYKE

DESCRIPTION

Wears well.

Usually worked over two vertical mesh threads and three horizontal mesh threads, but different ratios may be used for different effects.

Creates a braided effect when worked vertically from top to bottom; rotate canvas for a horizontal row.

Alternate effect: Rotate canvas for each new vertical row.

HOW TO STITCH

Begin at right side of canvas, then work vertical rows from top to bottom.

SUGGESTED USES

Vertical stripes, braided or knitted effects, narrow borders

ITALIAN CROSS

Other Name: Two-Sided Italian, Arrowhead Cross

DESCRIPTION

May be worked over two-by-two, three-by-three, or four-by-four mesh threads.

HOW TO STITCH

Work all rows from left to right.

Work in one color. (Two-color variation is a combination of Cross stitches and Backstitches.)

Complete the "framing" of the Cross stitch by adding Backstitches around the outer edges where necessary

An alternate method of stitching is to not stitch the top diagonal stitch until the return journey (diagrammed in the Counted Thread Stitch Gallery, page 198).

SUGGESTED USES

Background, borders, clothing, architectural features, bands

DOUBLE LEVIATHAN

DESCRIPTION

Effective in one or two colors; the top upright cross may be in another color than the underlying stitches.

Usually worked over four-by-four mesh threads, but any even number of mesh threads will work.

May be stitched singly or in groups.

HOW TO STITCH

Work from left to right or from right to left, completing each motif individually.

SUGGESTED USES

Borders, special effects, bands, corners

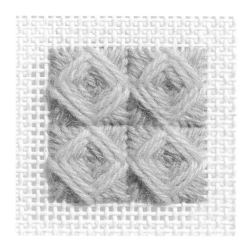

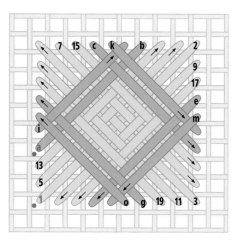
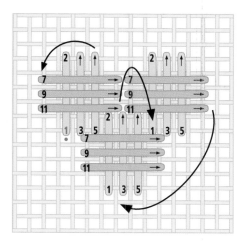
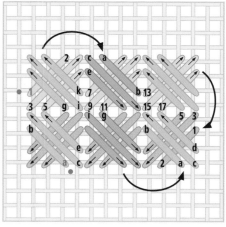

NORWICH
Other Names: Waffle, Southern Cross

DESCRIPTION
Produces a highly textured stitch.
Effective in one or more colors.
Usually worked over nine-by-nine mesh threads but any odd number mesh thread will work: 5, 7, 11, 13, or 15.
Most effective when worked with a smooth thread.

HOW TO STITCH
Always begin with the large Cross stitch.

SUGGESTED USES
Borders, corners, quilt blocks, boxes

BROAD CROSS
Other Name: Barred Square

DESCRIPTION
Produces a bold, raised effect.
Effective in one or two colors.
Covers six-by-six mesh threads.

HOW TO STITCH
Complete each six-stitch cross unit individually.

SUGGESTED USES
Large areas, background, borders, walls, cobblestones, fields

BOUND CROSS
Other Names: Broad Diagonal Cross, Diagonal Broad Cross

DESCRIPTION
Effective in one or two colors.
Create a checkerboard effect by alternating the directions of the crosses.

HOW TO STITCH
Work all the Half Crosses in rows; begin the crosses at the lower left corner and proceed up (as diagrammed), then down the next vertical row, and so on.

SUGGESTED USES
Borders, clothing, cobblestones, paths, bands

61

needlepoint stitches

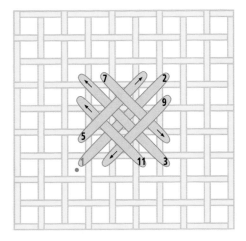
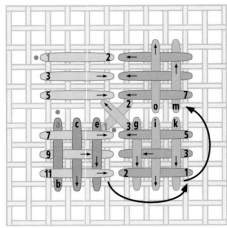
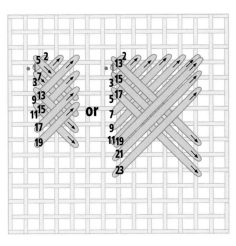

WOVEN CROSS
Other Name: Plaited Cross

WOVEN SQUARE

POINT DE TRESSE
Other Names: Braided, Ribbon

DESCRIPTION
Once you master the sequence, it works up quickly.

Effective in one or two colors.

HOW TO STITCH
First work a Cross stitch over four-by-four mesh threads; then continue with diagonal stitches (in sequence diagrammed); note that the last diagonal stitch (11–12) goes over the 9–10 stitch but under the 5–6 stitch.

SUGGESTED USES
Borders, corners, bands

DESCRIPTION
Effective in one or more colors.

If desired, add a Cross stitch to fill in the empty space between the squares.

HOW TO STITCH
Try rotating canvas when weaving the second set of threads.

SUGGESTED USES
Borders, baskets, blankets and coverlets, paths, bands

DESCRIPTION
Produces a plaited effect.

Easier to stitch than it may first appear.

HOW TO STITCH
Work over three-by-three or six-by-six mesh threads.

As shown, work in pairs (when over three) or trios (when over six) of diagonal stitches.

SUGGESTED USES
Borders, stripes, columns, paths, hair braids, bands

62

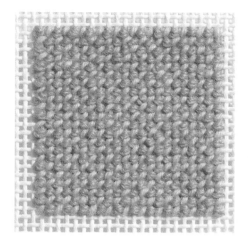

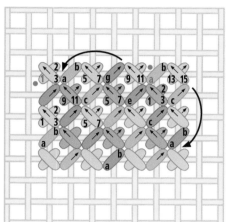

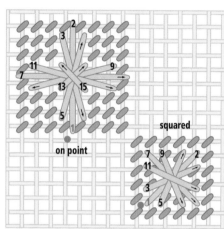

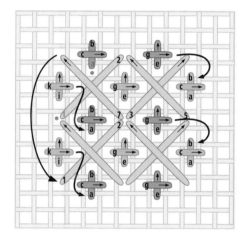

63

DOTTED

DESCRIPTION

Comprised of alternating Cross and
Basketweave stitches.
Produces a small polka-dot pattern.
Most effective in two colors.

HOW TO STITCH

Work the Cross stitches first, completing
each cross individually; work the
first row from left to right, and the
following row from right to left, etc.
Work the small diagonal stitches in the
Basketweave stitch.

SUGGESTED USES

Small areas; clothing, fields

TRIPLE CROSS

DESCRIPTION

Cross may be on point (above) or a
square (below).
Effective in one or two colors.

HOW TO STITCH

On the "on point" variation (above),
stitch a small Cross stitch at center
to help prevent snagging of long
stitches.
On the square variation (below), stitch
Tent stitches first.

SUGGESTED USES

Corners, borders, stars, clothing, bands

DIAMOND CROSS

*Other Names: Large Cross-Straight Cross,
Double Cross, Large St. Andrew with St.
George Fill*

DESCRIPTION

Creates a dramatically decorative effect.
Historically, there is much confusion
over the name(s) of this stitch. Not
to be confused with Smyrna Cross.
Effective in one or two colors.

HOW TO STITCH

Adjust/increase the thread weight so that
no canvas shows.

SUGGESTED USES

Baskets, background, clothing

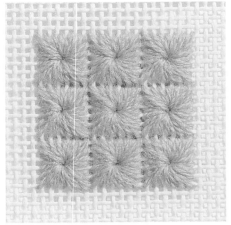

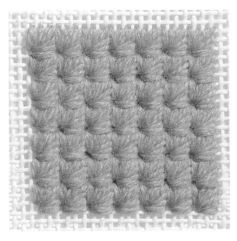

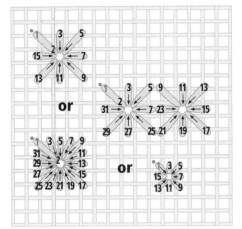

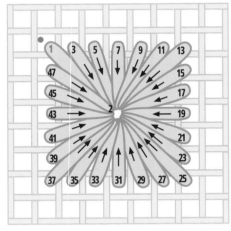

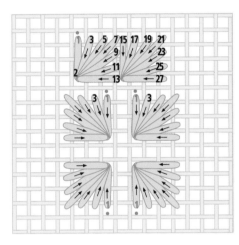

ALGERIAN EYELET, SMALL
Other Names: Square Eyelet, Eye

DESCRIPTION
Usually covers two-by-two or four-by-four mesh threads; anything larger is considered a Large Algerian Eyelet.

HOW TO STITCH
Work in a clockwise pattern and always stitch into the center hole.

To create a pulled Eyelet, pull thread as it emerges along the perimeter.

If you're stitching several Eyelets in a horizontal row, stitch only the top halves of each stitch, then complete each stitch on the return journey.

Take care that the thread on the back does not cover the hole that is created in the center.

SUGGESTED USES
Backgrounds, borders, clothing, bands, corners, alphabets, numbers

ALGERIAN EYELET, LARGE
Other Name: Square Eyelet

DESCRIPTION
Creates a small center hole when stitched with moderate tension; the more tension on the thread, the larger the hole.

May cover six-by-six, eight-by-eight, or ten-by-ten mesh threads.

HOW TO STITCH
Work in a clockwise pattern and always stitch into the center hole.

To create a pulled Eyelet, pull thread as it emerges along the perimeter.

If you're stitching several Eyelets in a horizontal row, stitch only the top halves of each stitch, then complete each stitch on the return journey.

Take care that the thread on the back does not cover the hole that is created in the center.

SUGGESTED USES
Borders, corners, background, eyelet lace, bands, alphabets, numbers

RAY
Other Name: Fan, Square Fan

DESCRIPTION
Equal to one-quarter of an Algerian Eyelet; can face in four different directions.

Works best over three-by-three mesh threads.

Effective in one or more colors.

Can be worked singly or in groupings; particularly effective when alternate rows face in opposite directions.

HOW TO STITCH
Always stitch into the common hole.

Work in horizontal rows.

SUGGESTED USES
Background, corners, borders, flowers, bushes, leaves, bands

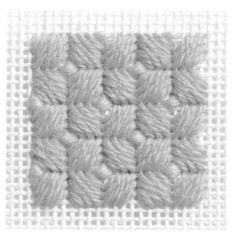

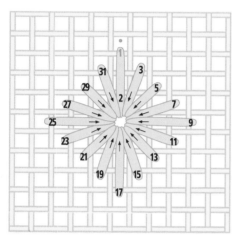
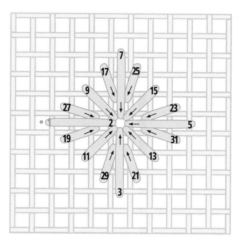
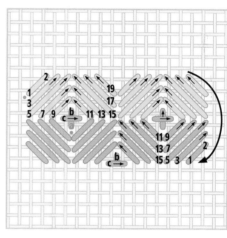

DIAMOND EYELET

Other Names: Star Eyelet, Diamond Star Eyelet

DESCRIPTION

Usually worked over six-by-six or eight-by-eight mesh threads.

Pulling the thread creates a center hole; the more tension on the thread, the larger the hole.

HOW TO STITCH

Always stitch into the common hole.

Because of possible congestion at the center hole, adjust thread thickness to match mesh count.

SUGGESTED USES

Stars, flowers

DIAMOND EYELET VARIATION

DESCRIPTION

This variation prevents congestion of threads at the center hole, so it works well with heavier threads.

HOW TO STITCH

Work in four counterclockwise trips.

SUGGESTED USES

Stars, flowers

BRIGHTON

DESCRIPTION

A variation of the Scotch stitch (page 37); comprised of blocks of five stitches in alternating directions with small Upright Cross stitches between the blocks.

Effective in one or more colors; Upright Cross may be a different color from the diagonal blocks.

French Knots, beads, Cross stitch, or Smyrna Cross stitch may be substituted for the Upright Cross.

HOW TO STITCH

Use one color of cotton or silk floss, or pearl cotton, to accentuate the directions of the stitches by creating light and dark color blocks.

SUGGESTED USES

Background, bands, borders, flowers (single Brighton stitch)

needlepoint stitches

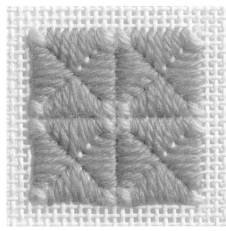

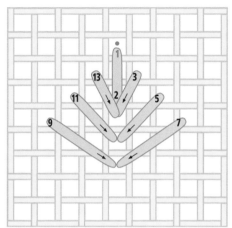
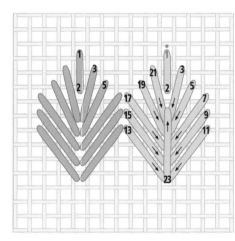
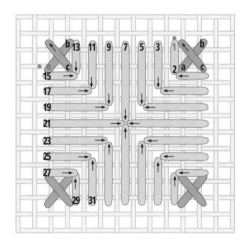

66

LEAF

DESCRIPTION
This stitch has many variations, but they all resemble a leaf.

Most common variation features three diagonal stitches on each side plus one straight stitch at top.

Effective in one or more colors.

HOW TO STITCH
Start at tip and work down left or right side (shown) before completing other side.

Can be stitched on top of Tent stitches for raised effect.

SUGGESTED USES
Leaves, trees, bushes, flower petals, borders

LEAF VARIATION

DESCRIPTION
Most common variation features five diagonal stitches on each side, one straight stitch at top, and one straight stitch for the center vein of the leaf.

Effective in one or more colors.

HOW TO STITCH
Start at tip and work down left or right side (shown) before completing other side.

Can be stitched on top of Tent stitches for raised effect.

SUGGESTED USES
Leaves, trees, bushes, flower petals, borders

TRIANGLE

DESCRIPTION
A large, dramatic stitch which requires a large area to be effective.

Can be worked over 8, 10, 12 or 14 mesh threads (8 or 10 most common).

Effective in one or more colors.

Individual blocks can be separated by Tent or Backstitches.

You may substitute Smyrna Cross, Mosaic, or Tent stitches for corner Cross stitches.

HOW TO STITCH
If the corners are to be in a second color, work the straight stitches first, then the corners.

If the entire stitch is to be in one color, stitch the corner stitches as you come to them.

SUGGESTED USES
Background, corners of borders, walls, paths, buildings

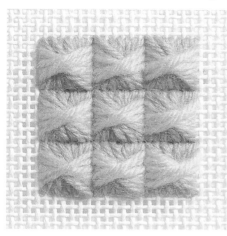

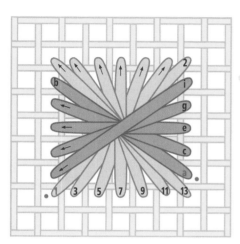
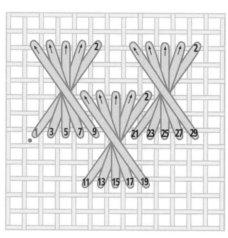
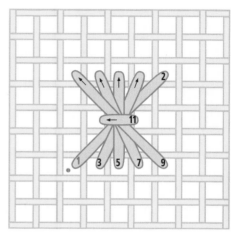

67

RHODES

DESCRIPTION

Named after Mary Rhodes, a British needlework designer.

May be worked to form a square of any number greater than three mesh threads, or a rectangle (eight-by-four, for example).

Does not wear well; the topmost stitches may snag.

Effective in one color or two (shown).

Stitch may be tied (with a short stitch tacking down the topmost spoke at its midpoint) if an even number of mesh threads are covered; tie may be horizontal or vertical.

HOW TO STITCH

Work the stitch counterclockwise.

Work multiples in horizontal or diagonal rows (upper left to lower right).

Use a smooth threads that covers the canvas well; avoid highly twisted threads.

SUGGESTED USES

Corners, borders, architectural features

HALF RHODES

Other Name: Partial Rhodes

DESCRIPTION

Work as a partial Rhodes (at left) with only the first five (or so, depending on how many mesh threads are covered) stitches to form an hourglass shape.

Effective in one color.

May be oriented vertically (shown) or horizontally.

Does not wear well; the topmost stitches may snag.

HOW TO STITCH

Stitch multiples in a diagonal direction.

SUGGESTED USES

Background, filling, baskets, fish scales, bows

HALF RHODES, TIED

Other Name: Partial Rhodes

DESCRIPTION

This partial Rhodes may be tied (shown) or not (see diagram at left).

Effective on one or two colors.

HOW TO STITCH

You may stitch in a single row or interlocked (see photo); over four (diagrammed), six (photo), or more vertical mesh threads.

May be oriented in horizontal direction.

Use a non-fuzzy thread for best definition.

SUGGESTED USES

Bows, fish scales, corn stalks in field. bands

needlepoint stitches

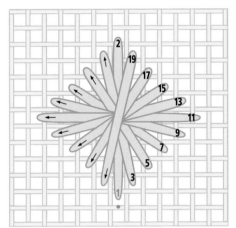

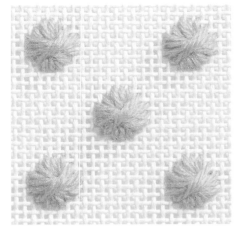

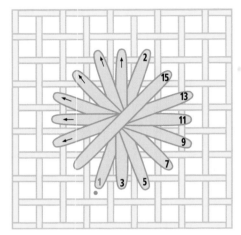

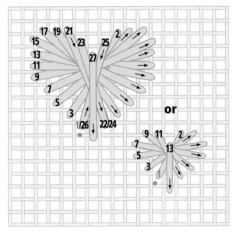

RHODES DIAMOND

DESCRIPTION

Has same characteristics as a basic Rhodes stitch, only the shape is different.

Diamond may cover any number of mesh threads.

Most effective in one color.

HOW TO STITCH

If you want the topmost stitch to be perfectly vertical, begin one stitch to the right (begin at "3" on the diagram; also see page 87).

SUGGESTED USES

Dimensional architectural accents, clothing accents, finials, flowers, windows

RHODES OCTAGON

DESCRIPTION

Octagon may cover any number of mesh threads.

Most effective in one color.

HOW TO STITCH

Work in a counterclockwise pattern.

If you want the topmost stitch to be perfectly vertical, begin one stitch to the right (begin at "5" on the diagram).

SUGGESTED USES

Flowers, dimensional architectural accents, finials, balls, buttons, windows, portholes

RHODES HEART

DESCRIPTION

This is simply a variation of the basic Rhodes stitch but with the needle emerging and inserting at different points to produce a heart shape.

Most effective in one color.

Use this stitch to decoratively fill small heart shapes with texture.

HOW TO STITCH

Work in a clockwise pattern.

Occasionally requires compensating stitches (see 1–26 and 22–24 in diagram) for a large heart.

SUGGESTED USES

Dimensional heart-shaped accents on clothing, fences, houses, jewelry (lockets), butterflies

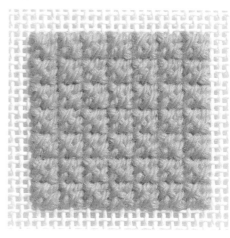

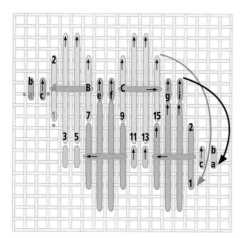

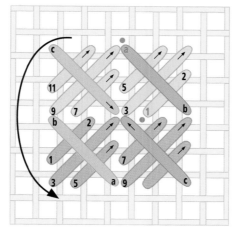

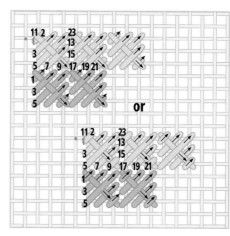

69

WICKER

DESCRIPTION
Effective in one or more colors.
Requires a large area to look effective.

HOW TO STITCH
When stitching in two colors, stitch all vertical stitches in one color, then the tie-down stitch in the second color (stitch is diagrammed in three colors).

SUGGESTED USES
Baskets, furniture, clothing, thatched roofs

CROSSED SCOTCH

DESCRIPTION
Note that the two smallest stitches of the basic Scotch stitch are missing.
Effective in one or two colors.
Works up quickly.

HOW TO STITCH
First work the underlying Scotch stitch in horizontal rows from right to left, then work the single crossing stitch in horizontal rows.

SUGGESTED USES
Background, borders, clothing

WOVEN SCOTCH
Other Names: Scotch, Woven

DESCRIPTION
Produces a "pebbly" appearance.
Effective in one or two colors.

HOW TO STITCH
Work each Scotch stitch first, then weave the long diagonal over and under the previous stitches in either of the two patterns diagrammed.

SUGGESTED USES
Background, borders, clothing, fields, shrubs, beaches

needlepoint stitches

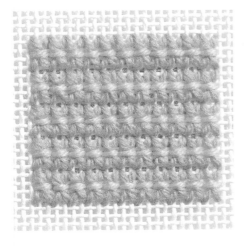

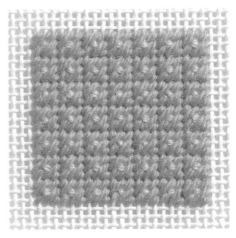

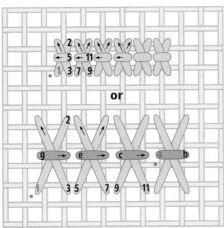

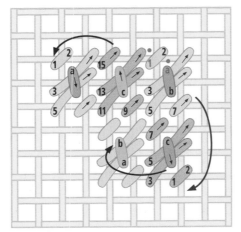

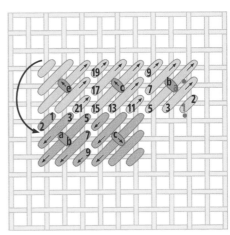

70

TIED OBLONG CROSS
*Other Name: Oblong Cross
with Backstitch*

DESCRIPTION
Comprised of an Oblong Cross tied
down with a Straight stitch or
Backstitch at the midpoint.
Effective in one or two colors.

HOW TO STITCH
You may stitch each unit individually, or
all crosses first, then ties. (Use the
latter when using two colors.)

SUGGESTED USES
Background, bands, borders

TIED CASHMERE

DESCRIPTION
Effective in one or two colors.

HOW TO STITCH
Work Cashmere stitch in diagonal rows.
Work the tie-down stitch in vertical
rows.
Use your thumb to move previous
stitches aside to see where to place
the tie-down.

SUGGESTED USES
Background, borders, clothing, bands

TIED SCOTCH

DESCRIPTION
Produces a polka-dot effect.
Effective in one or two colors.
The tie-down stitch over the longest of
the diagonal stitches reduces the
possibility of snagging.

HOW TO STITCH
Work the Scotch stitch and tie-downs in
horizontal rows.
Use your thumb to move previous
stitches aside to see where to place
the tie-down.

SUGGESTED USES
Background, clothing, bands, borders

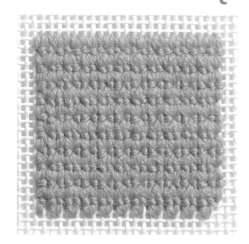

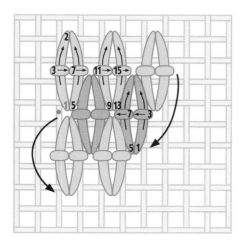

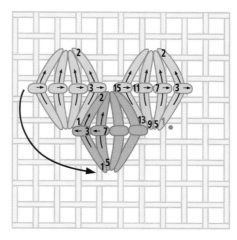

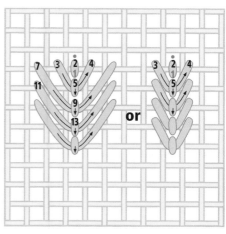

FRENCH
Other Name: Tied Renaissance

DESCRIPTION
Comprised of a pair of upright, tied stitches.

This slightly textured, "tight" stitch is snag-proof and has good coverage on the back.

Effective in one or more colors.

HOW TO STITCH
Work from left to right or from right to left.

Work in horizontal or diagonal rows.

May also be oriented horizontally.

SUGGESTED USES
Small areas, backgrounds

ROCOCO
Other Name: Queen

DESCRIPTION
Comprised of a group of four upright stitches held in place by four short horizontal stitches.

HOW TO STITCH
Usually covers four-by-four mesh threads, but six-by-six and eight-by-eight are possible. Increase the number of legs proportionally: six legs for six-by-six, eight legs for eight-by-eight, etc.

Makes a distinctive, effective pulled stitch; to do so, pull the thread as you begin each short horizontal stitch (small holes will form at the top and bottom of the group of upright stitches).

Use singly or in a grouping.

Work in diagonal or horizontal rows.

SUGGESTED USES
Background, clothing, bows, flowers, insect wings, zigzag band (two rows)

FLY
Other Names: Open Loop, "Y"

DESCRIPTION
Resembles the needlepoint Stem stitch (page 42), but is quicker to stitch.

Usually two or four mesh threads wide and two or three mesh threads deep.

Most effective in one color.

HOW TO STITCH
Stitch vertically or horizontally.

SUGGESTED USES
Stripes, plants, leaves, borders

needlepoint stitches

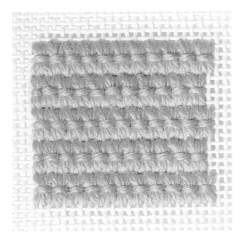

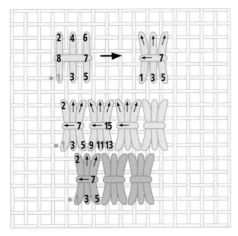

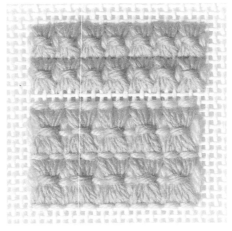

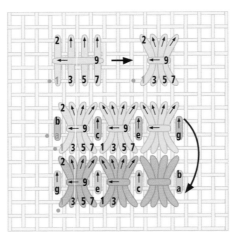

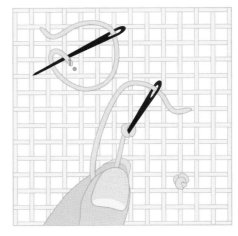

WHEAT
Other Names: Wheat Sheaf, Sheaf, Shell

DESCRIPTION
Comprised of groups of vertical stitches tied down at midpoint.

The number of vertical stitches may vary from three, four, five, or more.

Many variations are possible.

Vertical stitches may vary in height.

HOW TO STITCH
Align or stagger successive rows (latter is shown).

Work from right to left or from left to right (shown), but begin new rows on the same side as the first row.

To prevent puckering the canvas, stitch vertical stitches somewhat loosely so they can bend inward at the tied-down point.

SUGGESTED USES
Background, borders, details in fields and gardens, bands, bows

WHEAT VARIATIONS

DESCRIPTION
Note the difference between these stitches and the one to the left.

Note the addition of Backstitches and Long Upright Cross stitches (top photo); these may be stitched in the same or different colors.

HOW TO STITCH
To prevent puckering the canvas, stitch vertical stitches somewhat loosely so they can bend inward at the tied-down point.

SUGGESTED USES
Borders, bands, bows

As you find new variations for other stitches not illustrated in this book, add them to pages 74 and 75 to personalize the Stitch Gallery.

FRENCH KNOT
Other Names: French Dot, Wound, Knotted, Twisted Knot

DESCRIPTION
Comprised of a raised knot.

HOW TO STITCH
Wrap thread around needle only once or twice.

Keep thread snug around needle while executing stitch.

Insert needle one mesh thread over from the hole from which it first emerged.

Because you must use both hands to complete this stitch, mount your canvas on stretcher bars or a frame to hold the canvas taut.

To create a larger knot, increase the size of the thread, not the number of wraps.

SUGGESTED USES
Flowers, flower centers, flower buds, eye or eye highlights, curly fur or hair, outlines, filling

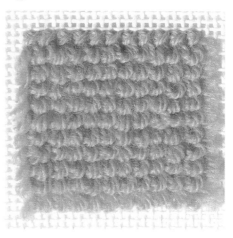

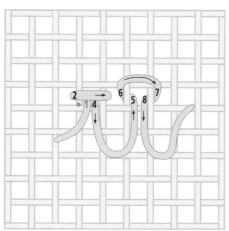
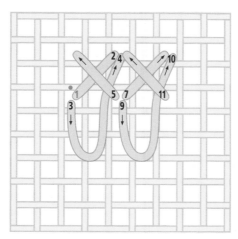
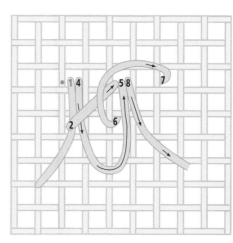

TURKEY WORK

Other Names: Ghiordes Knot, Rya, Turkey Knot, Turkey Tufting, Turkish Knot

DESCRIPTION

Tied-down loops create a fuzzy or raised pile.

The size of the loops determines the depth of the pile.

HOW TO STITCH

You may leave the loops as they are or trim them for a fringed effect.

Work from bottom to top rows to keep loops out of the way.

Work from left to right (as shown) or from right to left.

Hold down the loop with your thumb or a small ruler as you stitch.

Tighten each stitch after Step 4 (as shown).

SUGGESTED USES

Animal fur, flower centers, shag rugs, fringe on rugs, beards, hair

VELVET

DESCRIPTION

Comprised of a loop secured by a Cross stitch.

The length of the loop determines the depth of the pile.

HOW TO STITCH

Work from left to right.

Work from bottom to top row.

SUGGESTED USES

Fringe, beards, animal fur, hair, fur trim on clothing

As you find new variations for other stitches not illustrated in this book, add them to pages 74-75 to personalize the Stitch Gallery.

SURREY

DESCRIPTION

Diagonally tied-down loops create a looped pile.

The length of the loop determines the depth of the pile.

HOW TO STITCH

Work from left to right.

Work from bottom to top row.

Hold down the loop with your thumb as you stitch.

Tighten each stitch after Step 4 (as diagrammed).

If you intend to leave the loops uncut, use a straw or small dowel to keep the length of the loops consistent.

SUGGESTED USES

Fringe, beards, hair, animal fur, fur trim on clothing

F O R Y O U R N O T E S

ATTACH SAMPLE OR PHOTO HERE

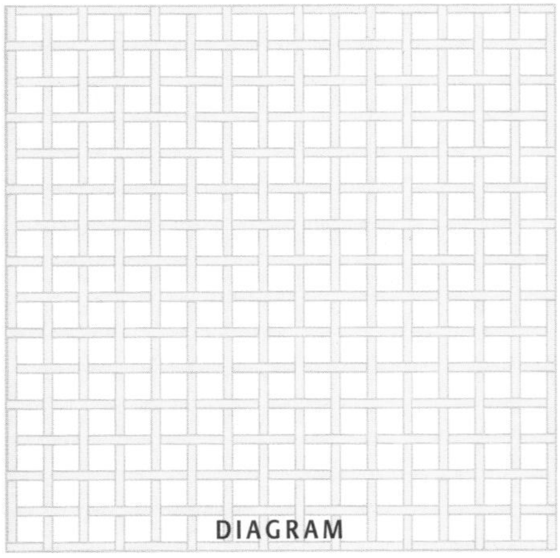

DIAGRAM

STITCH ____________________

Other Names: ____________________

DESCRIPTION

HOW TO STITCH

SUGGESTED USES

ATTACH SAMPLE OR PHOTO HERE

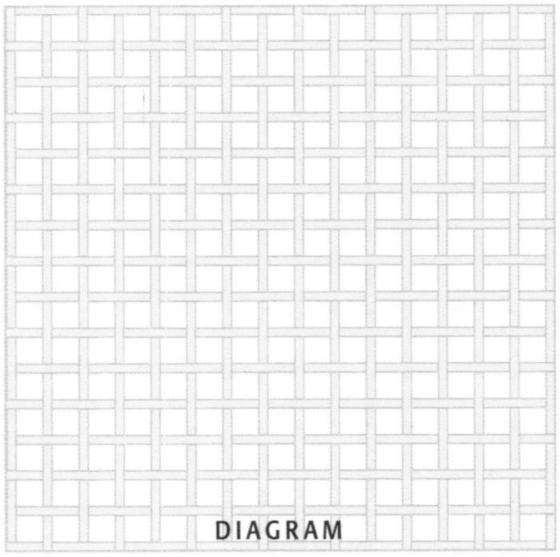

DIAGRAM

STITCH ____________________

Other Names: ____________________

DESCRIPTION

HOW TO STITCH

SUGGESTED USES

ATTACH SAMPLE OR PHOTO HERE

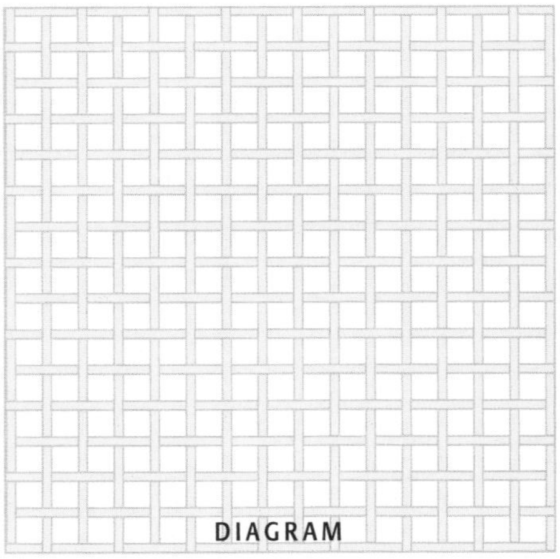

DIAGRAM

STITCH ____________________

Other Names: ____________________

DESCRIPTION

HOW TO STITCH

SUGGESTED USES

ATTACH SAMPLE
OR PHOTO HERE

ATTACH SAMPLE
OR PHOTO HERE

ATTACH SAMPLE
OR PHOTO HERE

DIAGRAM

DIAGRAM

DIAGRAM

75

STITCH_____
*Other Names:*_____

DESCRIPTION
_____
_____
_____
_____
_____
_____

HOW TO STITCH
_____
_____
_____
_____
_____
_____
_____
_____
_____
_____
_____
_____

SUGGESTED USES
_____
_____
_____

STITCH_____
*Other Names:*_____

DESCRIPTION
_____
_____
_____
_____
_____
_____

HOW TO STITCH
_____
_____
_____
_____
_____
_____
_____
_____
_____
_____
_____
_____

SUGGESTED USES
_____
_____
_____

STITCH_____
*Other Names:*_____

DESCRIPTION
_____
_____
_____
_____
_____
_____

HOW TO STITCH
_____
_____
_____
_____
_____
_____
_____
_____
_____
_____
_____
_____

SUGGESTED USES
_____
_____
_____

glorious poppy

This stunning bee's-eye view of a poppy in full bloom relies on bold, vibrant colors for its drama. It's a novice needlepointer's dream project because it's composed of basic stitches from the tent family, and serves as an easy introduction to working with canvas and wool threads.

DESIGN BY BARBARA BAATZ
Finished design size: 11" x 11"
Finished project size: 11½" x 11½" x 2¾"

MATERIALS
17"-sq. mono canvas, 10 mesh
Threads listed in key
Size 18 tapestry needle
Two pairs of 17" stretcher bars (or scroll frame with 18" bars)
½ yd. medium blue, upholstery-weight cotton fabric
2½ yds. of ¼"-W cotton cord
Polyester fiberfill
Blue sewing thread
Drafting or masking tape

INSTRUCTIONS
Read Before You Stitch (page 27) and To Begin Stitching (page 28). Tape the edges of the canvas and mount it on stretcher bars or a frame.

TO STITCH
Each square on the chart represents one thread intersection of canvas. Center and stitch Glorious Poppy design, using Basketweave stitches (or Continental, if that suits a particular color block better) and three strands of thread. Fill the background using a blended needle as specified in the key.

After stitching, block canvas (see page 29) so it measures approximately 11" square.

TO CONSTRUCT
Trim canvas ½" beyond stitching. For pillow back, cut a piece of blue fabric to match. For pillow sides, cut a 45" x 3¾" piece of blue fabric.

With remaining blue fabric, cut and piece two 48" x 2" bias strips. Using a zipper foot, make piping from bias strip and cotton cord. Trim piping seam allowance to ½".

Beginning at bottom of design, baste one length of piping to right side of canvas; leave 2" of piping free on each end. Remove 2" of the stitching on each end of piping and trim cord ends so they just meet. Overlap one end of piping fabric over cord; press under remaining short end, lap it over the other end, and sew in place onto the canvas. Repeat with second length of piping and pillow back.

With right sides facing, sew short ends of pillow side together; press open. Sew side to pillow front and back, clipping at corners and leaving a 4" opening at bottom edge of pillow back. Fill pillow firmly with fiberfill and slip-stitch closed. 🌀

Designer Barbara Baatz of the Kooler Design Studio established her reputation with her elegant angels and realistic floral designs. Her trademark is a dewdrop poised on a flower petal, and this design is no exception.

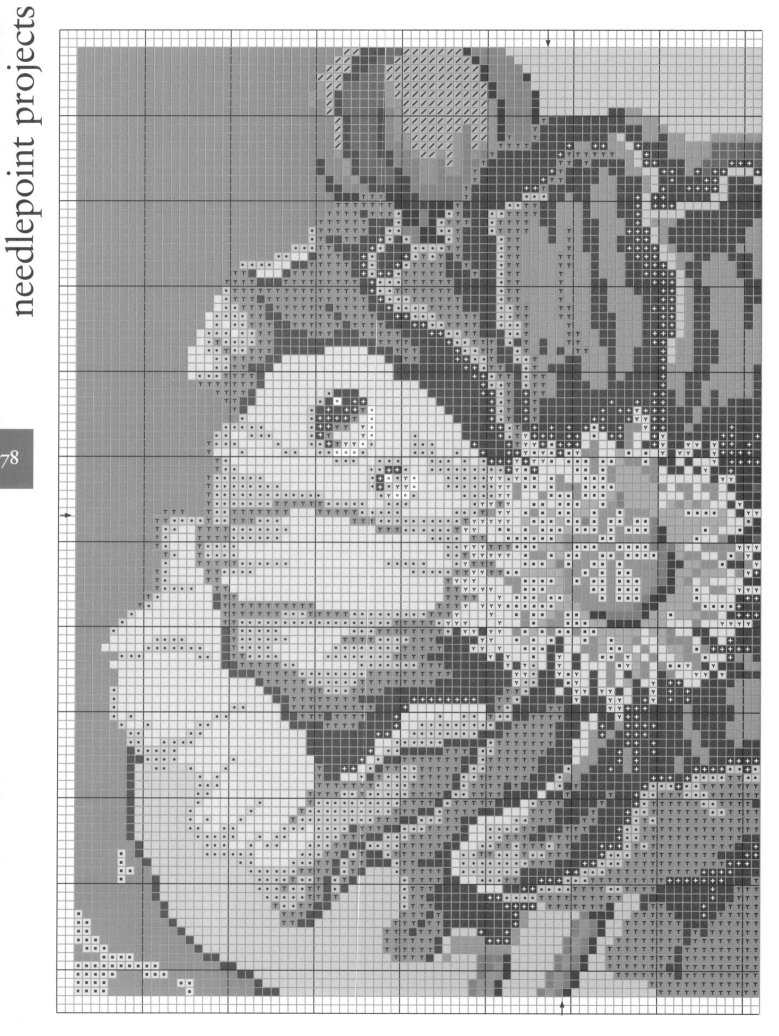

Shaded rows indicate where chart areas overlap.

GLORIOUS POPPY

Paternayan Persian Wool			Basketweave or Continental
001	∘	∘	white
350			plum-med
532			leaf green-dk
602			Nile green
604	╱	╱	Nile green-lt
662			Nile green -med
693			chartreuse
694	▪	▪	hunter green-lt
716	Y	Y	golden yellow-vy lt
811	T	T	tangerine-med
813	∘	∘	tangerine-lt
815			yellow
862			golden brown-lt
900			garnet-dk
961			carnation-lt
963			salmon-vy lt
968	+	+	Christmas red-dk
970			Christmas red-med
			Blended Needle
342/544			342(1x); 544(2x)
343/545			343(1x); 545(2x)

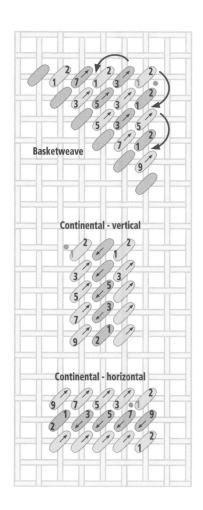

Basketweave

Continental - vertical

Continental - horizontal

lotus blossom kimono

Sumptuous colors and bold graphic design meet in this blending of cultural expressions. From Asia comes the image of the kimono as well as the symbolism of the lotus, beginning at the hem—aqua waves of water, a flight of white birds, the green foliage of the lotus plants, the lotus in bud, then in full bloom. Europe contributes the Florentine stitch, with its creative possibilities and fascinating special effects fully realized.

DESIGN BY BARBARA BAATZ
Finished design size: 11⅞" square
Finished project size: 15" square

MATERIALS
18"-sq. mono canvas, 12 mesh
Threads listed in key
Size 20 tapestry needle
Size 24 crewel needle
Two pairs of 18" stretcher bars (or scroll
    frame with 18" bars)
14½"-sq. gold-tone frame
Black sueded mat with coral bevel and
    11⅞"-sq. opening
Drafting or masking tape
For tassel: 2" x 3" heavy cardboard

INSTRUCTIONS
Read Before You Stitch (page 27) and To Begin Stitching (page 28). Tape the edges of the canvas and mount it on stretcher bars or a frame.

TO STITCH
Each gridline on the chart represents a canvas thread. Center and stitch Lotus Blossom Kimono design, using Florentine stitches, tapestry needle, and three strands of thread. Fill the background using Basketweave stitches, tapestry needle, and three strands of thread. Couch 6 strands of metallic floss with one strand of floss, using the tapestry needle for the laid thread and the crewel needle for the couching stitches.

After stitching, block canvas so it measures approximately 11⅞" square.

FOR EACH TASSEL
Wrap metallic floss around the shorter dimension of the cardboard rectangle 20 times. To make the tassel hanger, thread the crewel needle with two strands of floss (at least 8" long) and slip it under the wrapped floss along one long edge of cardboard. Tie off securely with hanger tails even (do not trim) and remove cardboard. Using a separate length of floss, bind the tassel threads together ¼" below hanger tie and conceal thread ends. Trim loops at bottom of tassel. Thread the hanger tails onto the tapestry needle and attach to design where indicated on chart; secure tails on back of canvas. ✿

Designer Barbara Baatz of the Kooler Design Studio uses her background in oil and acrylic painting to design her needlework. Barbara has received a Charted Designers of America Award, the American School of Needlework Publisher's Award, and the Golden Needle Award.

Shaded rows indicate where chart areas overlap.

LOTUS BLOSSOM KIMONO

Paternayan Persian Wool		Florentine stitch
220		black
260		white
592		aqua - dk
593		aqua - med
594		aqua - lt
595		aqua - vy lt
560		lavendar - dk
343		lavendar - med
553		blue - med
546		blue - lt
610		green - dk
612		green - med
613		green - lt
614		green - vy lt
941		red - dk
943		red - med
944		red - lt
946		red - vy lt
		Basketweave stitch
220		black
DMC Floss		**Couching**
5282		gold - metallic
		Surface attachment
		tassel placement

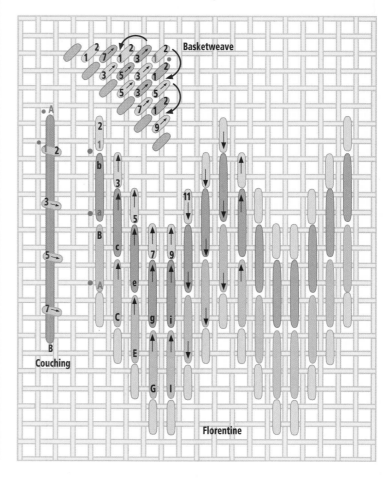

elizabethan garden

The play of light on ivory threads, a glimmer of antique gold, and a restrained palette of neutral colors allow the beauty and rich textures of needlepoint stitches to emerge as the true stars of the show. You can achieve these dazzling effects using five different thread types—and 12 fabulous stitches—as you stitch this lid for an elegant treasure box.

DESIGN BY MARY POLITYKA BUSH
Finished design size: 5" square

MATERIALS
9"-sq. brown mono canvas, 18 mesh
Threads listed in key
Size 22 & 24 tapestry needles
Laying tool of your choice (see page 23)
Two pairs of 9" stretcher bars
8"-square lightweight fabric to match canvas
5½"-square polyester fleece
Black "Betsy Box" with 5"-square design area (Sudberry House)
Drafting or masking tape

INSTRUCTIONS
Read Before You Stitch (page 27) and To Begin Stitching (page 28). Tape the edges of the canvas and mount it on stretcher bars. Locate the center of canvas and enlarge the hole slightly with the laying tool. Designate the side of the canvas inside the "well" of the stretcher bars as the front (right side). Mark one taped edge as "top," and consider it 12 o'clock.

Use the #24 tapestry needle for all stitches except the Rhodes Diamond. Because this design includes areas of unstitched canvas, take care to keep the back of the work as neat as possible.

Work the stitches in the following order, referring to the chart for placement and key for thread type:

RHODES DIAMOND: Use one strand. Note that the last leg of the stitch is vertical. Do not allow the thread to twist as you stitch. Rotate the canvas 90° to begin each new diamond. Take care not to twist the thread or catch the previous stitch as you bring the needle up through a "dirty hole."

CONDENSED MOSAIC: Use four strands.

SLANTED GOBELIN (over two canvas threads): Use four strands.

REVERSED SCOTCH: Use four strands.

BYZANTINE: Use one strand. Stitch with 12:00 at the top.

DOUBLE BRICK: Use one strand. Stitch with 3:00 at the top.

ROMAN II: Use one strand. Stitch with 12:00 at the top. Use #5 pearl cotton for the vertical legs, and #8 for the crossbars.

RHODES HEARTS: Use one strand. Do not allow the thread to twist as you stitch.

NORWICH: Use one strand.

TRIANGULAR RAY VARIATION: Use one strand. Use the laying tool to slightly enlarge the central hole so stitches will lie flat rather than overlapping.

STRAIGHT: Use one strand.

POINT DE TRESSE: Use one strand. Rotate the canvas 90° to begin each new border.

To assemble box, follow manufacturer's instructions. Insert brown fabric and fleece underneath canvas. ✤

Designer Mary Polityka Bush, a professional needlework designer since 1983, has designed needlepoint projects for numerous nationally known magazines, as well as kits for Kreinik Mfg. Co., exploring their extensive line of specialty threads. She teaches for the Embroiderers' Guild of America, the American Needlepoint Guild, and consumer needlework shows.

ELIZABETHAN GARDEN

DMC Color

Double Brick
  #5 Pearl Cotton, ecru (1x)

Roman II
  #8 Pearl Cotton, ecru (1x)

Byzantine
  #8 Pearl Cotton, ecru (1x)

Triangular Ray Variation
  #8 Pearl Cotton, ecru (1x)

Condensed Mosaic
  Cotton Floss, ecru (4x)

Slanted Gobelin Variation
  Cotton Floss, ecru (4x)

DMC Color

Rhodes Diamond
  Rachel, Caron color #B37 (1x)

Rhodes Heart
  1/16" Metallic Ribbon, Kreinik color #102 (1x)

Norwich
  #5 Pearl Cotton, ecru (1x)

Point de Tresse
  #5 Pearl Cotton, ecru (1x)

Reversed Scotch
  Cotton Floss, ecru (4x)

Straight
  #4 Metallic Braid, Kreinik color #102C (1x)

DMC ecru =
Anchor #926

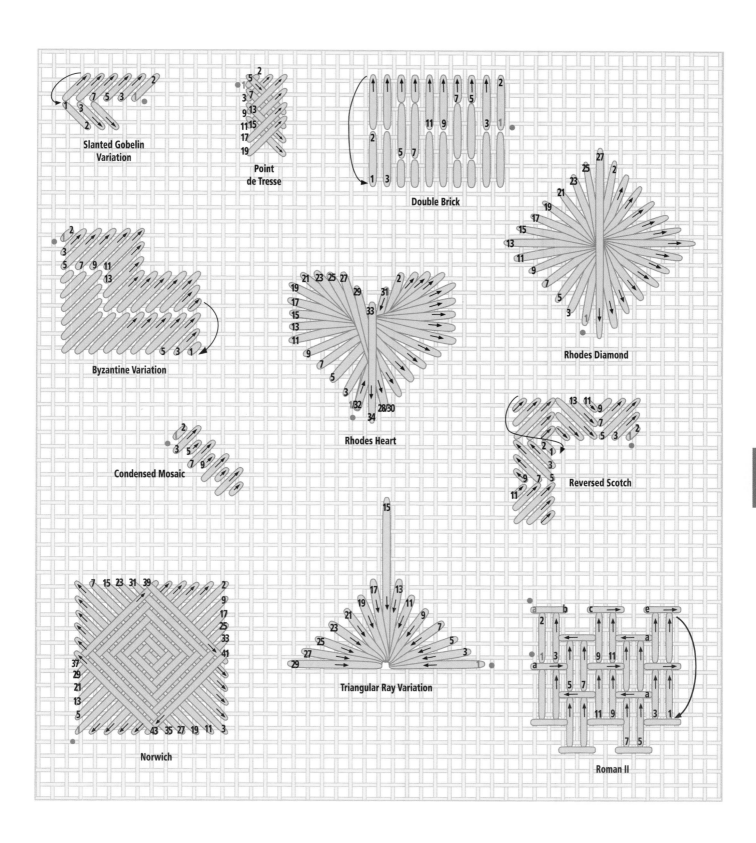

Slanted Gobelin Variation

Point de Tresse

Double Brick

Byzantine Variation

Rhodes Heart

Rhodes Diamond

Condensed Mosaic

Reversed Scotch

Norwich

Triangular Ray Variation

Roman II

embroidery

 The term "EMBROIDERY" means many things to many people, and it's often the source of confusion. To most non-stitchers, it signifies any kind of needlework practiced with needle and thread upon a ground fabric. Because this encompasses needlepoint and counted thread as well as "free embroidery," it's easy to see how misunderstandings arise.

Free embroidery, the subject of this chapter, is also called "surface embroidery," a style of needlework in which stitches are worked independent of the fabric weave. The stitcher may create any shape desired, on any scale desired, using an astonishing variety of fibers on a practically limitless choice of ground fabric. These characteristics makes surface embroidery a natural choice for garment embellishment.

Surface embroidery falls into (but is not limited to) six major categories. Perhaps the most opulent is silk embroidery, born in Asia; its look is adaptable to cotton threads as well. Crewel work using woolen threads hearkens back to Stuart England. Cutwork, in which the ground fabric is cut away for a lacy look, was perfected in 17th-century France. Shadow work, in which sheer fabrics show off the illusion of thread "shadows," originated in India. Silk ribbon embroidery was invented to decorate the gowns of aristocrats in Louis XV's court. During the 19th century, American farm wives practiced candlewicking, a far more modest but charming way to add beauty to simple household goods.

Embroidery stitches in the Stitch Gallery are grouped as flat, looped, chain, knotted, and composite. Combine them to create your favorite pictorial images as well as abstract designs. If you're a beginner, try inexpensive cotton floss until you master a few stitches. Once you gain confidence, why not try silk thread? This fiber deserves your attention as much as you deserve its beauty and luxury.

Memorial Embroidery; Bridgeton, ME, c. 1823; silk embroidery, pencil, and paint on silk. Courtesy of Fine Arts Museums of San Francisco, Gift of W.M. Streehy, DY49410.

THE ORIGINS OF EMBROIDERY

Remains of a Cro-Magnon hunter who lived in Russia 32,000 years ago include a fur garment decorated with rows of beads, the earliest embellished garment yet discovered. Because the desire to dress up utilitarian textiles appears to be universal, embroidery is a worldwide phenomenon.

China was the first culture to elevate embroidery to a high art form. As early as 4500 years ago the Chinese were stitching with silk and precious metals. By 1200 BC, these textiles so beguiled visitors that the known world beat a path to the source (see the related story following). Many embroidery motifs found throughout Europe and Asia can be traced to Chinese designs.

Until fairly recently, embroidery has flourished best when supported by political, religious, or economic power. The intensive labor and great cost of materials ensured that embroidery was reserved for the people of the upper classes as well as for the splendor of important occasions, be they coronations, religious festivals, or simply displays of conspicuous wealth in ancient cultures of Assyria, Persia, Egypt, Greece, Rome, and the Holy Land.

The Near East is the geographic and cultural crossroads of the Old World, and medieval Europe borrowed heavily from its mix of cultural influences. The Crusades brought Europe in contact with the riches of the Near East, such as embroideries from Constantinople. These treasures were carried homeward, and the work copied. This broadening of understanding of the world led to a great flowering of needlework.

As the Hebrews were cast out of their ancestral homeland beginning with the first diaspora (circa 597 BC), they brought their decorative embroidery to the new lands where they settled. Their handwork, which decorated their sanctuaries and ceremonial textiles, included embroidery of numerous styles and materials, noticeably silk embroidery, gold work, and crewel work.

In medieval Europe, needlework served ecclesiastic needs, and common subjects were the human figures of the saints. In England a style called *Opus Anglicanum* (Latin for English work) produced exquisite facial details worked in split stitches of silk thread, as well as gold wire couched down with silk. Often commissioned by popes, these works were stitched by professional embroiderers both male and female, residing in monasteries and convents.

Another style developed concurrently on the Continent, a whitework known as *Opus Teutonicum* (Teutonic work), which featured designs outlined in white linen threads on linen fabric. The lack of color drama led to the development of many new and different stitches—such as chain, buttonhole, encroaching Gobelin, and long-arm cross, and more—for the purpose of introducing varied textures to break up the monotony of white-on-white. Schwalm work is its descendent.

European embroidery never actually declined in popularity but only in fineness, and later forms never surpassed medieval work in complexity and refinement. New woven fabrics such as brocades, damasks, and velvets offered competition to hand-embellished fabrics. But the stitches developed over those centuries remain to this day, to be rediscovered by each new generation of embroiderers.

SILK & COTTON SURFACE EMBROIDERY

A five-thousand year old legend has it that an imperial Chinese princess discovered the secret of the silk fiber. A silkworm cocoon accidentally dropped into a cup of tea, and as she retrieved it, it dissolved to reveal a shimmering filament strong enough to be used for textiles. And so the great silk industry was born.

Just as valued as the silk fiber were the techniques to apply that fiber decoratively to cloth, also perfected by the Chinese. Needles of bronze, ivory, and bone have been found in Chinese archeological sites dated around 3000 BC, which implies that embroidery probably existed at this time.

The crown jewel of Chinese embroidery is the satin stitch, perfectly suited to display silk's beauty. Refinement of technique is necessary, for the perfectly executed satin-stitch motif must appear smooth, flat, and seamless—like satin itself! Exquisite shaded effects are possible thanks to a satin-stitch relative, the long-and-short stitch. It's likely that the backstitch and stem stitch originated in China, and a certainty that the Pekinese stitch did too.

Stitchers around the world have embraced Chinese-inspired designs (referring to them as "Chinoiserie"), which experienced periodic revivals in bursts of activity whenever new exploration or some innovation in transportation brought increased trade with Asia.

One particular American take on silk embroidery were "mourning pictures." Beginning around the time of the death of George Washington in 1799, these personal expressions were stitched on silk fabric (with the faces of the subjects painted) in a technique called needlepainting, achieved by the long-and-short stitch. The designs featured figures languishing by monuments and urns in pretty pastoral settings with weeping willows.

When silk was scarce, embroiderers learned to

Detail of Chinese coat; 20th Century, silk satin embroidery. From the private collection of Donna Kooler.

Chinese coat; 20th Century, silk satin embroidery. From the private collection of Donna Kooler.

91

make do with cotton threads. A world apart from opulent silk work was the simple cotton-on-cotton stitchery popular in America and affordable to all from the late 19th Century onward. You can see the same satin-stitch technique, invented for silk, worked with cotton floss on Flight of Fancy's butterfly (page 150).

Today, cotton embroidery is still practiced as a lively folk art in many areas of the world, from Mexico and Central America where wild colors decorate everyday garments (and attract tourist dollars), to southeast Asia, where the Hmong people of Cambodia embroider stories of recent political conflict on their fabulous quilt-like wall hangings.

GOLD WORK

Gold threads originated in China, and were carried by silk merchants to a fascinated world. By the time of the Roman Empire, most Mediterranean cultures—Italy, Greece, Turkey, Cyprus, Egypt—used gold threads. It is documented that Alexander the Great's tent was "embroidered with gold threads." Numerous biblical passages refer to gold threads. The Hebrews decorated their Torah arks with curtains and valances worked in silk and gold threads, often on velvet ground fabric. In the early Christian era metal threads were used on vestments and altar frontals.

Composed of silver wire covered with a coating of gold, gilt thread comes in many thicknesses and textures—flat, round, crimped, and spiraled. The stitcher usually applies it after all

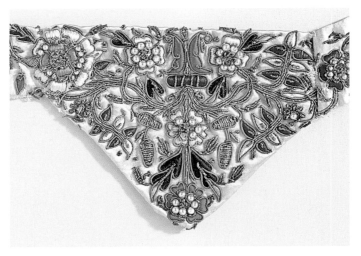

Antique fragment; English, real metal and silk threads, pearls. From the private collection of Deanna Hall West.

other embroidery is complete, because it can snag other threads as they are worked. The metal thread does not pierce the fabric except for the beginning and finishing ends; rather, it is laid and couched with fine silk thread (yellow for gold and gray for silver). In this way, no metal is "wasted" on the wrong side of the fabric. To best show off the light-reflecting qualities of the shiny metal, designs are often worked over padding to create different elevations of the ground cloth so when the gold catches the light, the play of light is dazzling.

Gold work is painstaking, as are most arts that employ precious materials. Even experienced stitchers do not allow themselves to be hurried as they work. Gold threads are sold by the single strand and are, as you might imagine, quite expensive. For beginners, a logical choice would be synthetic substitutes (see page 98); see the example of couched metallic threads in Lotus Blossom Kimono (page 80).

CREWEL EMBROIDERY

The term "crewel" refers to crewel wool threads, and may be applied to any wool stitchery. The great Bayeux Tapestry—famous for its story, figures, and technique—commemorates the Norman Conquest of Britain in the 11th Century, and is the most famous example of crewel work. Its precise date and place of origin are unknown. Stitched in eight shades of wool threads, it is the only major piece of crewel work stitched before the year 1500 to survive. Its long, narrow, horizontal panel is worked in stem stitch and laid stitches of wool on linen ground.

Most historical crewel work now in museums is from the 16th and 17th Centuries, created for household furnishings and costume. During the era known as Jacobean (the reign of the Stuart King James I, "Jacobus Rex," 1603–1625), the English refined crewel work to perfection. Inspired by the illustrations from newly-available printed books, English stitchers favored the Tree of Life, teeming with exotic birds,

Embroidered picture; 17th Century, "work in progress" on silk satin. Courtesy of Colonial Williamsburg Foundation, Williamsburg, VA.

animals, and fanciful flowers and fruits, an ancient theme beloved by the Hebrews and other Near East cultures. The Jacobean Pomegranate (page 144) is designed in this style.

The earliest crewel designs were monochrome outlines worked with stem, backstitch, and chain stitches filled with (first) seed stitches and (later) composite filling stitches called "diaper patterns." Later, when dyes were perfected, designs bloomed with color. By the 18th Century wool embroidery metamorphosed into "needlepainting" with the long-and-short stitch.

A very different style of wool embroidery is *rosesøm*, from the Telemark region of Norway. Stitched on mittens and gloves, socks, purses, and women's folk costumes in brilliant colors of wool thread upon dark backgrounds, the bold floral folk-art motifs dazzle the eye. It was already a well-developed art before the great wave of Norwegian immigrants reached America in the 19th Century.

William Morris, one of the fathers of the Arts and Crafts movement in England in the late 1800s, spearheaded a crewel revival. His daughter Mary kept the traditions of crewel work alive at the Royal School of Needlework, founded in 1872 by one of Queen Victoria's daughters.

SILK RIBBON EMBROIDERY

The emergence of silk ribbon embroidery coincided with the manufacture of silk ribbon, beginning in France around 1750–75, the stylistic era known as Rococo. Used to decorate ladies' gowns, this embroidery was very elaborate and expensive, and was produced by embroidery houses under royal patronage. Because of the way the silk fiber reflects light, and the manner in which narrow ribbons naturally twist and fold, silk ribbons do a splendid job of mimicking petals and leaves, as you can see in the Silk Garden design (page 154).

Ribbon embroidery resurfaced in a series of revivals, although there was very little written about it. Rather, it was passed on by word of mouth from one generation of needleworkers to another. The revival in the 1870s was in part due to the beautiful new variegated ribbon colors available at that time. Fascinated with the language of flowers and their symbolic meanings, Victorian stitchers lavished silk blossoms on crazy quilts, household accessories such as albums and needlebooks, and sumptuous ball gowns that hearkened back to the French gowns of a century earlier. Another revival in the 1920s saw silk ribbon flowers strewn on clothing (including lingerie) from top Parisian couture houses to humble households. We are in the midst of another revival made possible by global communications.

Silk ribbon creates an interesting, raised texture, and works well with many embroidery stitches you'll find in the Embroidery Stitch Gallery (page 109). It also has its own specialized stitches which you'll find in the instructions for the Silk Garden scarf (page 154).

CANDLEWICKING

Simplicity has a special beauty all its own. What could be more basic than plain off-white fabric worked with plain off-white thread? From these unpretentious and inexpensive materials springs the true American folk art of candlewicking, an open-spaced arrangement of knots or "knotting." The technique was perfected on 19th-century Appalachian bedspreads, but no one knows exactly why it's traditionally associated with colonial crafts. It appears to be related to bedspreads from late 17th-century England.

Also called tufting, the earliest candlewicking was stitched on ground fabric of strong linen or cotton fabric in tabby (plain) weave; the thread was a soft, loosely twisted, single-strand cotton called candlewick, always white or off-white (the color of unbleached muslin). The design was outlined in running stitches with a loop of thread between each stitch, shaped over a small stick or gauge. Later the loops might be cut, or not cut and left as loops. Finally, the fabric was washed and would shrink just enough to hold the thread in place. (Modern candlewicking consists of true knots, not loops.)

Candlewicking techniques were passed down from mother to daughter, and each family had a particular pattern. When a girl married, her mother made her a bedspread with the "family pattern" which was now hers to guard and pass down to her daughters. Popular motifs included vines and clusters of grapes, sprays and baskets of flowers, and geometric motifs. Bedspread designs often feature a large central medallion surrounded by intricate borders; the candlewicking borders on Flight of Fancy (page 150) illustrate this.

What was once just a way for farm women to appoint their households became "fashionable" for urban dwellers who visited the mountains for the scenery in the early 1900s. By the 1920s, making these bedspreads became cottage industries in the mountain towns. Many women supported their families by "knotting." A bedspread may take as many as 500 hours of a woman's work, including the hand-tied fringe.

CUTWORK

Imagine fine handwork becoming a political issue between two European powers! When Cardinal Richelieu (1585-1642) of France realized that his countrymen were spending too many francs on Venetian needlelace, he began a program of encouraging his countrymen to make a needlelace to rival the Italian product. He sent lacemakers to Italy to soak up knowledge, then set up French workshops to duplicate it.

For his troubles, he was unofficially honored. The French version of the Venetian needlelace came to be called Richelieu work. Predating the Middle Ages, its ancestry goes back to the

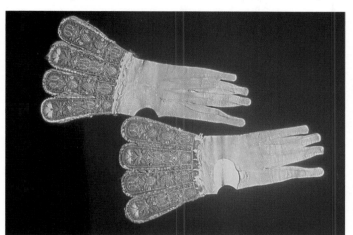

Man's embroidered leather gauntlets; 17th Century. Courtesy of Colonial Williamsburg Foundation, Williamsburg, VA.

Near East, and its direct parentage is the 16th-century Italian *point coupé* that Richelieu had his lacemakers study.

Categorized under the umbrella term "whitework," and sometimes called needlepoint lace (a point of confusion), cutwork features a decorative pattern of small holes incised into the ground fabric and surrounded by buttonhole stitches. The simplest cutwork category is *broderie anglaise*, in which very small holes are made with an awl or stiletto, then finished off by round or oval eyelets.

Renaissance work is more elaborate and decorative than *broderie anglaise*, and looks more like our notion of lace. In this style, the motifs are outlined first with buttonhole stitches, then the surrounding fabric is trimmed away, as if to frame the design. The actual motif is held in place by foundation bars; Rosa Blanca (page 158) shows this effect. Richelieu work, the most elaborate cutwork technique, features decorative picots along these bars. On all varieties of cutwork, the loop edge of the buttonhole stitch faces the cut edge of the fabric. The same stitch also works nicely for the edges of table and bed linens, clothing borders, hems, collars, and cuffs.

Cutwork is still popular in Europe, especially in Italy, where you can buy patterns right off the newsstands.

SHADOW WORK

Originating in India, the home of fine gauzes and lightweight muslins, shadow work was developed to decorate shirts and tunics. It derives its delicate look from the faint whisper of color that shows though sheer white fabric. This effect is created by medium-value colored threads worked densely on the wrong side of the fabric, which, when viewed through the lightweight fabric, become pastel, appearing as "shadows."

The primarily floral designs for shadow work begin as opposing outlines which are filled in with double backstitches. The only stitches visible on the front of the fabric are these delicate backstitched outlines. The back of the fabric, however, is another story; it's filled with criss-crossing herringbone stitches which impart an almost solid appearance.

Fabrics for shadow work projects should be as sheer as possible, such as organdy, batiste, or handkerchief linen. Suitable threads include stranded floss, silk, or floche. Although colors are favored, even white-on-white can be effective, with its subtle contrast between sheer and opaque fabric.

Extra design touches such as stem-stitched vines and French-knot flower centers add realistic details. Ribbons, with their parallel lines and the interesting shapes they make as they twist and turn, make good design additions. Look at the dainty Petite Fleur design (page 162) and judge for yourself. ⚜

94

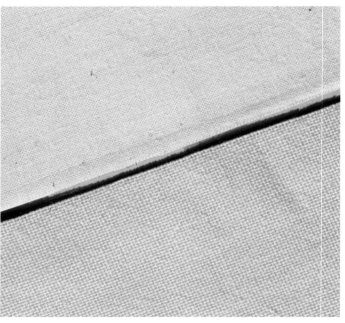

TOP LEFT: Dupioni silk (top) and silk blend (bottom).
UPPER RIGHT: Linen blend (upper left) and Strathaven linen (upper right and bottom).
ABOVE: Cotton muslin (top) and wool (bottom).

EMBROIDERY FABRICS

Unlike needlepoint or counted-thread work, surface embroidery does not require that you stitch on an evenweave fabric. The sharp needles used in embroidery allow you to use any good quality fabric that appeals to you, including fabrics intended for dressmaking and home decorating. Closely-woven fabrics usually yield the best results. However, you can use high-count (32-count and higher) evenweave fabrics such as linen intended for counted thread work. Lower counts are too coarse for many styles of embroidery and make it difficult for you to achieve smooth outlines. A very lightweight fabric may require the additional strengthening of another fabric to back it as you stitch (except for shadow work, in which a single layer of very lightweight fabric is essential). For large projects such as wall hangings, choose a fabric with enough body to hang well and support the weight of the stitchery.

If you intend to wash the fabric after the stitching is complete, be sure to preshrink the fabric first (and the backing fabric, if used). Because the dyes used for silk are usually water-soluble, silk thread must be dry-cleaned; you may stitch silk designs on silk fabric. If you choose to stitch silk thread on linen fabric, take special care to keep the fabric as clean as possible during stitching and wash your hands frequently.

Whatever your choice, check that your intended fabric is clean to begin with, with no heavy crease lines. Buy more fabric than your project requires so you have extra fabric for a "doodle cloth" to try out various stitches and threads.

EMBROIDERY THREADS

The contemporary embroiderer enjoys an array of threads that stitchers of yore would envy. Choosing the colors and fibers of threads is one of the most exciting tasks that you will undertake as a stitcher. The look of the piece, as well as the experience of stitching it, will depend on the choices you make.

One of the pleasures of stitching is the tactile experience, so consider what kind of fiber you like to handle—crewel wool or silky rayon, cotton floss or metallic threads.

Different threads offer varying degrees of difficulty. Depending on the type of thread and the particular stitches you choose, you may need to use a laying tool (pages 23, 102, and 183) to obtain the results you desire.

Many specialty threads listed in the needlepoint chapter (pages 18–20) are too heavy to use for many embroidery stitches, but may be used as couched threads in embroidery.

WOOL AND WOOL BLENDS

Historically, wool is the essential thread for crewel work. These lightweight wool threads are suitable for this embroidery.

CREWEL WOOL comes in a single strand of two plies which cannot be untwisted. However, you may combine plies, a helpful feature when you wish to combine several shades on one needle. Appleton Crewel Wool is one brand name.

MEDICI, a DMC product, is very fine and develops a silky sheen with wear. Combine plies as needed for the size and scale of your project.

BROIDER WUL from Britain is colored with natural dyes that resemble the colors of threads used in needlework before 1850, and has an especially soft hand.

SILK/WOOL BLENDS (50%/50%) are smoother than wool, more substantial than pure silk, and have a lovely hand. Varieties to look for include Impressions from The Caron Collection, Silk and Ivory by Brown Paper Packages, and wool/silk blends from J.L. Walsh and Felicity's Garden.

LINEN

Lighter weights of linen are well suited for embroidery. Individual threads are slightly variable in width within one size; this is part of linen's distinctive character. Take special care to purchase all you need at one time because the dye lots can be irregular. Linen thread sizes are indicated by two numbers: the first is the weight (the higher the number, the finer the thread), the second is the number of plies. Excellent linen threads on the market include Rainbow Linen from Rainbow Gallery, Flax 'n Colors from The Thread Gatherer, Londonderry Linen (in sizes 18/3, 30/3, 50/3, 80/3, and 100/3), and threads from Norsk Engros USA and Ginnie Thompson.

FROM TOP: Appleton's Crewel Wool (1); DMC's Medici (2); Broider Wul (3); Brown Paper Packages' Silk and Ivory (4); J.L. Walsh's wool/silk blend (5); Felicity's Garden wool/silk blend (6); The Caron Collection's Impressions—overdyed (7), solid (8); Rainbow Gallery's Rainbow Linen (9 & 10); The Thread Gatherer's Flax 'n Colors (11 & 12); Londonderry Linen size 50/3 (13), size 30/3 (14), size 18/3 (15 & 16); Norsk Engros USA's Linen Thread (17 & 18); Ginnie Thompson's size 50/2 Linen Thread (19).

COTTON

Less expensive than wool or silk, cotton is washable, easy to work with, and is a popular choice for embroidery.

STRANDED FLOSS (EMBROIDERY FLOSS) is a six-ply cotton with a sheen, available in hundreds of colors. Always separate the plies, then recombine them so the strands can "blossom out" for a fuller look. Use as few plies as one or as many as you wish for the desired effects. The best-known stranded flosses are from DMC and Anchor.

OVERDYED FLOSS is stranded floss dyed by hand for special effects. Colors may be shades within a single color family or several different colors that blend gradually from one to another on the same strand. Look for overdyed floss from Needle Necessities, Weeks Dye Works, and Sampler Threads from The Gentle Art.

PEARL COTTON (*coton perlé*) is twisted, non-separable, and has a lustrous sheen. Most sizes work well for embroidery: Size 3 (thickest), 5, 8, and 12 (finest). Well-known brand names include DMC and Anchor (both available in skeins or balls), as well as Overture from Rainbow Gallery. Watercolours from The Caron Collection is a three-ply cotton with a silky sheen (one ply equals one strand of #5 pearl cotton) and is hand-dyed in variegated colors.

SPECIALTY COTTONS include Flower Thread from Ginnie Thompson, a fine, soft non-divisible thread with a matte finish. Wildflowers from The Caron Collection resembles flower thread.

Floche from DMC is a softly twisted, non-divisible thread with a soft hand.

Brilliant Cutwork and Embroidery Thread is a twisted, non-divisible thread that comes in two sizes (12 and 16) and also works for other categories of embroidery. Coton à Broder is a fine, non-stranded thread with a slight sheen.

Candlewicking thread is especially designed and weighted for this specific technique, and has a matte appearance. A noted brand is Traditional Candle Wicking Cotton from Cascade House (Australia).

SILK RIBBON

Silk ribbons are very thin and flat, soft enough to drape but strong enough to withstand being pulled in and out of fabric. Washing silk ribbon is not recommended. The most common widths are 2mm (less than ⅛"), 4mm (slightly larger than ⅛"), 7mm (about ⁵⁄₁₆"), and 13mm (about ¹¹⁄₁₆"), and other various widths, depending on the manufacturer. One widely available brand of solid colors is from YLI Corp. Overdyed silk ribbons are available from Thread Gatherer (dyed to match other threads in its line) and Petals from Sweet Child of Mine.

FROM TOP: DMC's floss (1 & 2); Anchor's floss (3 & 4); Petals' overdyed floss (5); Weeks Dye Works' floss (6); Sampler Threads' floss (7); Needles Necessity's floss (8); DMC's Floche (9); The Caron Collection's Watercolours (10); DMC's pearl cotton #3 (11), #5 (12 & 13), #8 (14); Anchor's pearl cotton #12 (15); Cascade House's Candlewicking Thread (16 & 17); DMC's Coton à Broder size 16 (18), size 12 (19); YLI's silk ribbon—overdyed 4mm (20), 7mm (21), 4mm (22), 2mm (23).

SILK

Silk, once a rare and expensive commodity, is enjoying renewed popularity and is reasonably affordable although more expensive than cotton. Silk threads come in weights similar to cotton threads. Many stitchers find silk a particular pleasure to work with, for it possesses a beautiful "hand" and glides easily through fabric. It requires dry-cleaning and dry-blocking.

Silk threads fall into two categories. Filament silk is composed of a continuous fiber that is carefully unwound from silkworm cocoons in lengths up to 1,000 yards and possesses exceptional smoothness. Spun silk is produced from shorter staple fibers, and is not as smooth as filament but still possesses silk's desirable properties.

Silks similar in weight to stranded cotton floss include Soie d'Alger from Au Ver a Soie, Silk Mori from Kreinik Mfg. Co., Waterlilies by The Caron Collection, Silk 'n Colors from The Thread Gatherer, and silk from Needlepoint Inc., Madeira, J.L. Walsh, and Gloriana.

Kreinik Mfg. Co. manufactures or imports many other silk threads in many weights and looks. Silk Serica is a three-ply filament silk with a high sheen which can be separated into individual plies or stitched as it comes off the reel. Ping Ling is a low twist, six-strand filament silk with high luster. Soie Gobelins is a two-ply twisted filament silk. Soie Platte is an untwisted filament silk with an extremely high luster. Soie Perlee is a three-ply twisted filament silk. Soie Noppee is a heavy, one-ply spun silk with luster.

Soie Chenille à Broder from Au Ver a Soie resembles a velvet cord ("chenille" is French for caterpillar) and can be used for Satin-stitch embroidery and couching.

Other silks of interest to the embroiderer are Splendor from Rainbow Gallery, Melange from Cascade House, and Soie 1003 from Au Ver a Soie (a tightly twisted, very fine thread).

REAL METALS

Threads made of real gold, silver, and copper are rare and expensive. You can find splendid stitched examples on historic needlework. In many cases, you can substitute synthetic thread for the real thing. For those who desire authenticity, real metals—half a percent of gold on silver-plated copper, known as "gilt"—are available from Kreinik Mfg. Co. and sold in individual strands. Categories available (with the French terms in parentheses) are Rough Purl (*Bullion Matte*), Smooth Purl (*Bullion Brilliant*), Crimped Purl (*Faconnee Brilliant*), Bright Check Purl (*Frieze Brilliant*), Pearl Purl (*Jaceron*) and Russia Braid (*Soutache*); each type comes in several weights. (For books about working with real metals, see the Bibliography.)

FROM TOP: Kreinik's Silk Mori (1 & 2); The Caron Collection's Waterlilies (3); The Thread Gatherer's Silk 'n Colors (4); Needlepoint Inc.'s silk (5); Madeira's silk (6 & 7); J.L. Walsh's silk (8 & 9); Gloriana's silk (10 & 11); Kreinik's Silk Serica (12), Soie Perlee (13), Soie Platte (14), Soie Gobelins (15), Ping Ling (16); Au Ver a Soie's Silk 1003 (17); Rainbow Gallery's Splendor silk (18); Kreinik's Soie Noppee (19), Pearl Purl (20 & 21), Smooth Purl (22), Bright Check Purl (23), Crimped Purl (24), silver-gold combination (25).

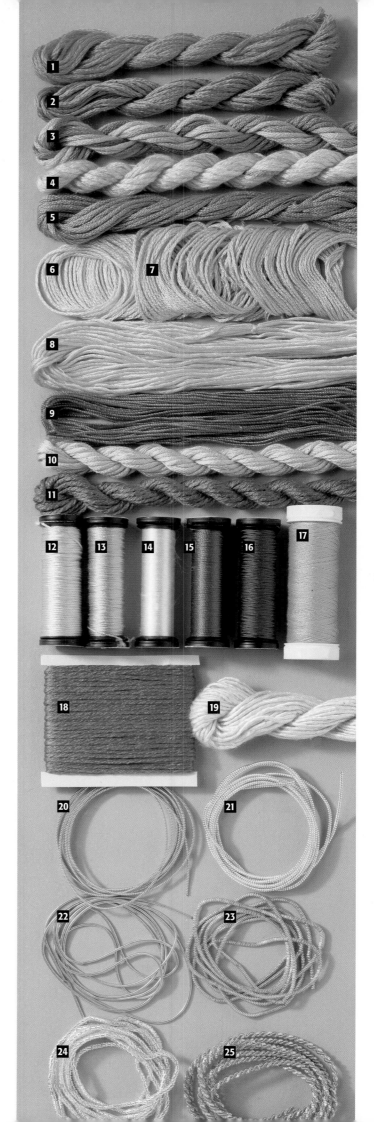

SPECIALTY AND SYNTHETIC FIBERS

Many exciting options are available to the contemporary stitcher as fiber manufacturers develop new fibers for this ever-growing field. It's not possible to list all the currently available novelty threads, but those mentioned here are some of the more versatile and popular fibers which should enjoy popularity for years to come. In most cases it's impossible to specify the number of plies to use, because the threads are intended for special effects which are up to the stitcher's discretion. Listed below are some popular brand names, grouped by type.

METALLICS Metallic Pearl Cotton and Metallic Floss from DMC are metallic and viscose blends that resemble their cotton cousins in weight and have relatively "soft hands" for metallic threads.

Blending Filament (including Hi Lustre) from Kreinik Mfg. Co. can be combined with other fibers, creating sparkling highlights for special effects; available in dozens of colors, including fluorescents.

Japan Thread from Kreinik Mfg. Co. duplicates the look of real metal threads of silver, copper, gold, and dark gold. It's available in three weights: #1 (finest), #5, and #7 (thickest).

Cord from Kreinik Mfg. Co. is a thin, one-ply thread for backstitching and couching, available in 15 colors.

Cable from Kreinik Mfg. Co. is thicker than Cord (above) and comes in silver and gold.

Ribbon from Kreinik Mfg. Co. is a flat metallic ribbon in two widths: ⅟₁₆" and ⅛" wide; available in dozens of colors, including fluorescents.

Braid from Kreinik Mfg. Co. is a flat braid with a bright, metallic sparkle, in five weights: #4 Very Fine, #8 Fine, #12 Tapestry, #16 Medium, #32 Heavy; available in dozens of colors, including fluorescents.

Facets from Kreinik Mfg. Co. is a heavy, three-dimensional thread for couching; it resembles a string of tiny beads; available in six colors.

RAYON Marlitt, a four-stranded floss from Anchor, and six-stranded DMC rayon floss are smooth, silky threads with a radiant shine. They're a bit slippery and can be difficult to work with because they knot and kink easily. (Moistening the thread as you stitch helps eliminate this.) They're less expensive than silk but have a beautiful silk-like sheen.

FROM TOP: DMC's Metallic Pearl Cotton #5 (1 & 2), Metallic Floss (3 & 4); Kreinik's Hi Lustre Blending Filament (5 & 6), Blending Filament (7 & 8), Fluorescent Blending Filament (9 & 10), Japan Threads (11 & 12), Cord (13 & 14), Cable (15 & 16), ⅟₁₆" Ribbon (17 & 18), ⅛" Ribbon (19 & 20), #4 Braid (21 & 22), #8 Braid (23 & 24), #12 Braid (25 & 26), #16 Braid (27 & 28), #32 Braid (29 & 30), Facets (31); DMC's Rayon Floss (32); Anchor's Marlitt (33).

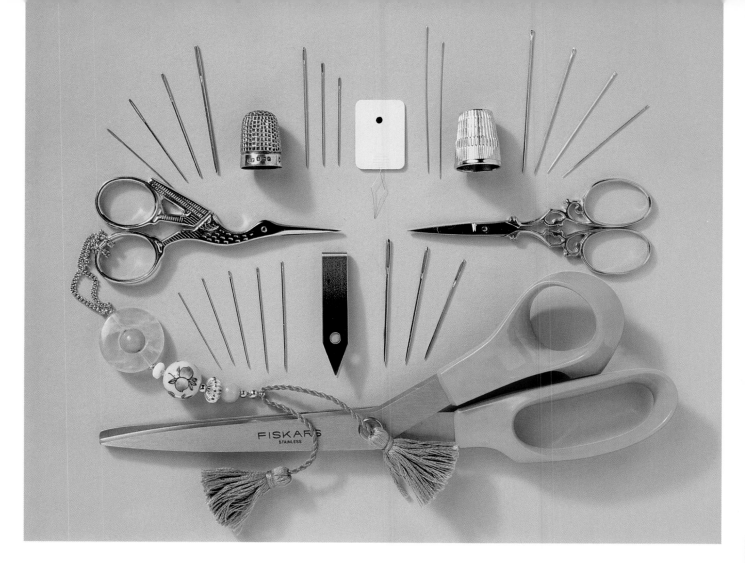

EMBROIDERY NEEDLES

High-quality needles are expensive, but are more than worth the investment, for they will make your work a pleasure. Carelessly made needles have small imperfections that can snag on fabric and threads from previous stitching.

The larger the number, the smaller/finer the needle (milliners are exceptions). If the needle is too large, it's difficult to pass easily through the fabric and may produce sloppy-looking stitches. If too small, it damages the thread—even to the point of breakage—with each stitch you take.

CREWEL (EMBROIDERY) These are the shortest needles used for embroidery, and are sized from 1 (the largest) to 10 (the smallest).

CHENILLE These sharp-pointed needles have large eyes for easy threading, and are sized from 13 (the largest) through 26 (the smallest).

TAPESTRY These blunt-pointed needles will not pierce the fabric sufficiently for most embroidery stitches but are useful when you need to weave an additional thread on the surface of already-completed stitches (for an example, see the Threaded Backstitch on page 111). They're sized the same as chenille needles.

BEADING These narrow needles have very fine eyes which can pass easily through the holes of beads, and are available in both long and short lengths.

MILLINERS These long needles have the same diameter along the entire length; use them to execute Bullion Knots.

SHARPS These general, all-purpose needles are useful for hand-finishing and basting.

NEEDLE THREADERS

These tiny, inexpensive tools (also see pages 21 and 183) are wonderful time-savers; keep one handy as you work.

EMBROIDERY SCISSORS

Reserve your scissors for needlework only and keep them with your other stitching tools. Have them professionally sharpened when they become dull.

EMBROIDERY SCISSORS Use these for clipping threads and removing mistakes. (Never use a seam ripper for the latter.) Use a scissors sheath or case to protect the points and prevent them from stabbing other items in your stitching bag or basket. If you stitch with metallic and synthetic fibers, consider a second pair of embroidery scissors that are old and duller than your fine ones. (If you only have one good pair, don't cut these fibers using the tips of the scissors; cut closer to the base of the blade.)

OTHER TOOLS

TWEEZERS Very useful for picking out threads when you're correcting mistakes.

THIMBLES These embroiderer's aids prevent callused and punctured fingertips, but are a personal preference.

SHEARS Use dressmaker's shears for cutting your fabrics.

ABOVE, CLOCKWISE FROM BOTTOM: Shears, embroidery scissors with decorative fob, tapestry needles, thimble, crewel needles, needle threader, beading needles, thimble, milliners needles, embroidery scissors, chenille needles, tweezers, sharps needles.

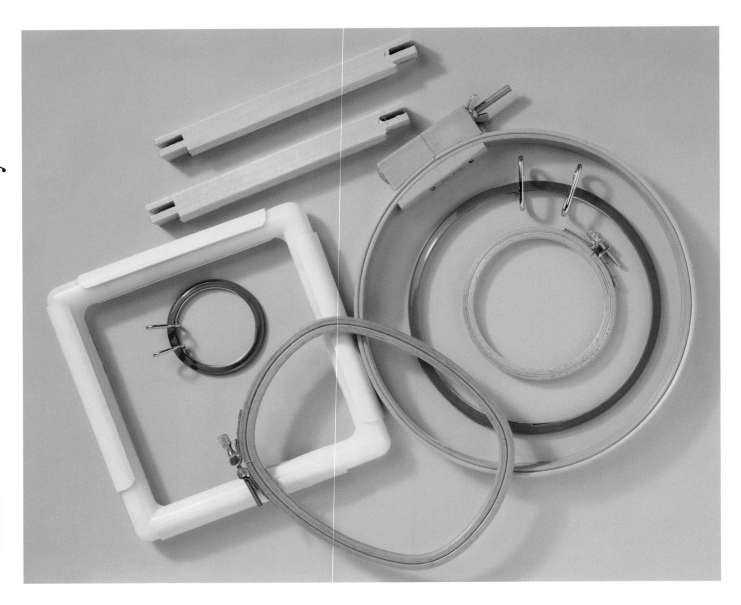

EMBROIDERY FRAMES

Using a hoop or frame enables you to stitch with an even tension and keeps your work area visible. Experiment with a number of different frame systems to see which one works best for your stitching needs (and your body's needs!).

HOOPS These simple round frames, used by embroiderers for centuries, consist of two closely-fitting wood or metal rings. Some hoops rely only on the close fit of the two components to produce tension; other have devices such as metal springs or screws for this purpose. Most hoops intended for embroidery are ⅜" to ½" deep and range from 3" to 8" in diameter; for larger projects, try a quilting hoop; most are 1" deep and offered in many diameters.

STRETCHER BARS Lightweight, easy-to-use, and inexpensive, these modular frames consist of four ¾"-square wood strips that dovetail at the ends to form an open square or rectangle upon which you'll tack your fabric. They're usually sold in pairs; you need to buy one pair for the width of your fabric, and a second pair for the length. If you stitch a lot, you'll eventually have an assortment of lengths that will work together to fit many projects. (These bars are specifically intended for needlework; don't confuse them with stretcher bars for painter's canvas.) Pre-assembled mini stretcher bars are ideal for projects of 4" to 12" dimensions.

Q-SNAPS This modular system consists of four plastic tubes called elbows (in lengths of 6", 8", 11", or 17") that join together to form a square or rectangle. You stretch your fabric over this framework, then snap a plastic clamp (resembling a "C" in cross-section) on each side, and roll the clamps away from the center of the fabric to tighten. As with stretcher bars, you buy the lengths you need to build a frame to suit your project. Like hoops, Q-Snaps are very easy to apply and remove.

CLOCKWISE FROM UPPER LEFT: Stretcher bars, hoops, Q-Snaps.

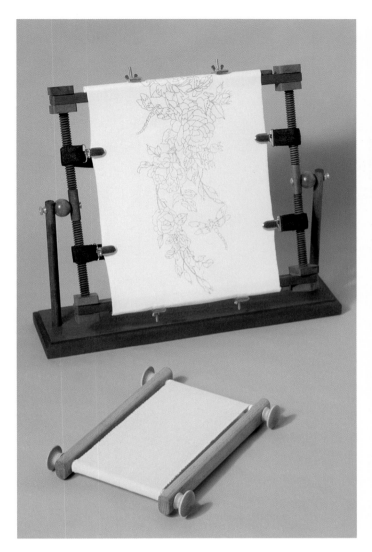

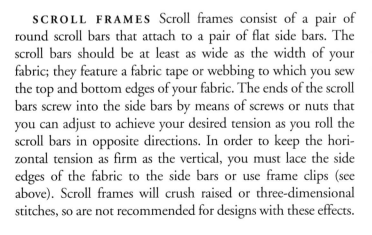

ABOVE: Table frame with frame clips; scroll frame.
RIGHT: Floor stand with hoop.

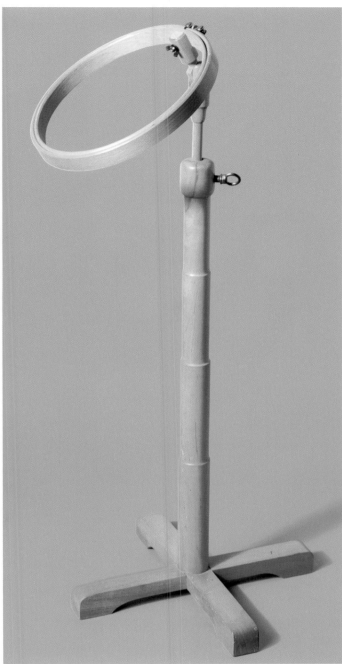

SCROLL FRAMES Scroll frames consist of a pair of round scroll bars that attach to a pair of flat side bars. The scroll bars should be at least as wide as the width of your fabric; they feature a fabric tape or webbing to which you sew the top and bottom edges of your fabric. The ends of the scroll bars screw into the side bars by means of screws or nuts that you can adjust to achieve your desired tension as you roll the scroll bars in opposite directions. In order to keep the horizontal tension as firm as the vertical, you must lace the side edges of the fabric to the side bars or use frame clips (see above). Scroll frames will crush raised or three-dimensional stitches, so are not recommended for designs with these effects.

TABLE AND FLOOR STANDS Table and floor stands free both your hands for stitching (particularly important if your embroidery requires you to use a laying tool) and enable you to stitch in a favorite chair. You can make height and angle adjustments to suit you so stitching is as comfortable as possible. Many come with their own scroll frames, which can be detached for portable stitching, too.

FRAME CLIPS These adjustable clips attach to the sides of scroll frames to ensure that horizontal tension of the fabric equals vertical tension, and eliminate the fuss of lacing, unlacing, and re-lacing by hand as you move to a new area of your fabric.

ADDITIONAL EQUIPMENT FOR EMBROIDERY

LAYING TOOLS When you work with multiple plies on a single needle, you'll need to keep the threads parallel, not twisted, as you stitch. (This is called "laying" the thread.) A variety of laying tools will help you achieve this. The simplest is a large tapestry needle or bodkin. Others specifically designed as laying tools include a stroking tool (also known as a tekobari); one end resembles an awl or stiletto, and the other end is square to prevent it from slipping from your fingers. A trolley needle has a point like a tapestry needle affixed to a metal band that fits on the end of your finger.

PINCUSHIONS Pincushions are useful for stowing threaded needles if you must change colors often. Pincushions come in a variety of sizes and styles; select one that fits in your stitching bag or basket. Many stitchers like to make their own personalized models.

Many manufactured pincushions come with an emery, which looks like a very small pincushion filled with a gritty, sand-like material which keeps needles clean and sharp.

NEEDLEBOOK OR NEEDLECASE With "pages" of soft fabric, a needlebook keeps your pins and needles protected (and protects you from the needles, too) and organized. Each "open page" is designed to store a particular needle type in a range of sizes. As with pincushions, this is an item you can make yourself to show off your stitching talents. (See Rose Basket project on page 284.)

Many stitchers like to store their needles in needlecases, which may be narrow and cylindrical or large and box-like; some of the latter have magnets to keep needles in place.

THREAD PALETTE These plastic, wood or paper palettes have a series of holes along the edges to hold individual colors of threads, which you attach using half-hitch knots.

THREAD ORGANIZER There are many products on the market for storing and identifying threads you accumulate. One of the simplest is small individual plastic bags held together on a metal binder ring. Storage boxes such as those used for hardware and fishing lures work well for thread wound on bobbins. On the other end are wooden boxes or chests that resemble fine furniture.

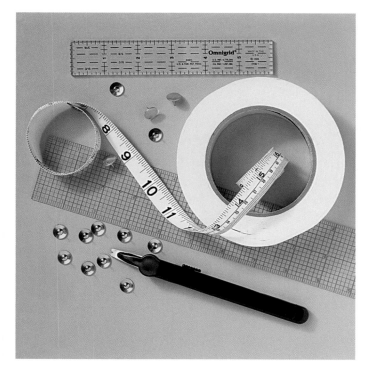

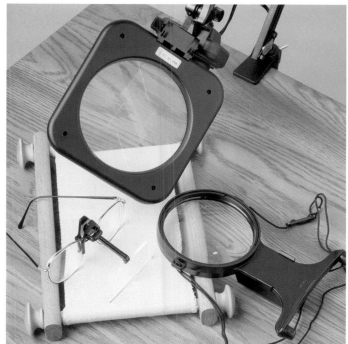

RULER AND TAPE MEASURE Clear plastic rulers calibrated in inches are invaluable and come in a 6" length that fits easily into a stitching bag. For measuring a larger area, a tape measure is useful and takes up little space.

THUMBTACKS AND TACK PULLER Use these to attach fabric to stretcher bars. (Don't use staples to attach embroidery fabric; you'll risk pulling one of the fine threads and spoiling the appearance of the fabric.)

DRAFTING TAPE This tape is less sticky than regular masking tape and helps keep your needlework cleaner. Use it for taping the cut edges of your fabric before mounting it in a stitching frame. Find it at art supply stores.

LIGHTING AND MAGNIFICATION Both your eyesight and your needlework deserve optimal lighting. Choose a light that directs a circle (not a spotlight) of light onto your entire stitching surface. Floor lamps and swivel-arm table lamps (such as an architect's light) are good choices. To avoid casting shadows over the work surface, right-handers will benefit from a light directed over the left shoulder, left-handers from the right.

For very fine work you may want to use a lamp that has a magnifier attached. Other possibilities include magnifiers that hang around the neck, attach to your eyeglasses, or are worn atop the head.

EMBELLISHMENTS Small, decorative accents give your embroidery beauty, whimsy, and individuality. Look for buttons, beads, and charms at your local needlework shop, catalogs, and consumer shows. Find them also in embroidery kits, often as the focus of a design theme.

TOP LEFT: 6" ruler, measuring tape, drafting tape, 18" ruler, tacks and tack puller.
TOP RIGHT: Magnifiers for tabletop, neck, and eyeglasses.
ABOVE: Assorted beads, buttons, and charms by Mill Hill, Porcelain Rose, Just My Imagination, and Creative Beginnings.

CLOCKWISE FROM UPPER LEFT (OPPOSITE PAGE): Pincushion, thread organizer box with paper reels, paper thread palette, bodkins, plastic thread palette, mini pincushion, needlecase, awl.

EMBROIDERY DESIGNS

Design options for embroidery are limitless. The whole world of pictorial art awaits the embroiderer, who may choose pre-printed illustrations and painted backgrounds, or select artwork from another medium to stitch. For those who have illustration talent, embroidery offers the same creative possibilities as painting. Even simple line drawings become gorgeous works of art when filled in with beautiful, colorful threads.

PRE-PRINTED DESIGNS ON FABRIC

PRE-PRINTED OUTLINES Fabric with printed design outlines have been popular for a century or more, and they've served as many a young stitcher's introduction to working with a needle and thread. Often they're sold in kits that contain all the necessary threads as well as a picture with a key to indicate thread colors and specific stitches.

PRE-PRINTED FABRIC This method offers the stitcher painted color blocks for the background of the design; only the actual foreground motifs need be stitched (outlines are provided), not the entire fabric surface. These are usually sold in kits which come with illustrated keys to indicate the thread colors and type of stitches to use.

STAMPED CROSS-STITCH Although we usually think of cross-stitch as a counted thread technique, pre-printed cross-stitch designs are available that indicate cross stitches on a ground fabric. Because it is impossible for the printer to line up the stitches with the grain of the fabric perfectly, the stitcher follows the stamping, not the fabric weave, so the technique falls under the category of embroidery instead of counted thread.

ABOVE LEFT: Pre-printed designs on fabric include designs that require only embroidery accents (top), designs with painted backgrounds only, and designs with outlines only.

ABOVE RIGHT, FROM TOP: Iron-on transfer design, pouncing pad with powder, transfer paper and wheel, various transfer pens and pencils.

DESIGNS YOU TRANSFER ONTO FABRIC

These methods offer you the option of combining your choice of fabric, thread colors, and design.

IRON-ON TRANSFER DESIGNS This method is similar to pre-printed outlines (far left) except you iron the design onto your choice of fabric. Many iron-on transfers are available in a wide range of styles to suit contemporary tastes. A revival of interest in old designs has sparked publishers to re-issue transfers for popular subjects.

TRANSFER PENS AND PENCILS These inexpensive tools enable you either to trace a design onto paper, then iron the design onto your fabric (yielding a mirror image), or to draw directly onto your fabric. Some are designed to wash out of the fabric after stitching. Others leave marks which intentionally fade after a brief period of time (from eight to 48 hours) to use when you know you will have sufficient time to complete the stitching. Manufacturers offer various colors of pencils and pens to enable you to transfer onto both light and dark fabrics.

DIRECT TRACING If the design fabric is light in color and weight, it's often possible to place the fabric over the design outline and draw directly onto the fabric, using a fabric-marking pen. The marks then wash out when the stitching is completed. Always test-wash the fabric before transferring.

DRESSMAKER'S CARBON This allows you to transfer a mirror image of a design onto fabric.

PRICKING AND POUNCING This is one of the oldest methods of design transfer, and requires a sharp needle (the eye end may be inserted into a wine cork to make it easier to handle) or tracing wheel to pierce the design paper and either pounce powder, tailor's chalk, or a fabric-marking pen. This method is popular with quilters, so you can find supplies for this method at quilting shops.

embroidery basics

BEFORE YOU STITCH
PREPARING YOUR FABRIC

ALLOW EXTRA FABRIC FOR FINISHING Always allow at least two or three inches of fabric beyond the design to allow you to finish the project as desired. Always check project instructions to see if you need to allow extra fabric or if the design will be positioned off-center.

PRESHRINK YOUR FABRIC Unless you're using fabric such as silk that must be dry-cleaned, always wash the fabric in warm water and press out all creases.

Overcast the raw edges of your fabric using a zigzag stitch on your sewing machine or an overlock machine. If you prefer, you may make a narrow hem along the edge, hand-sew seam tape to raw edges, or simply hand-overcast the raw edges.

TRANSFERRING YOUR DESIGN

ORIENT YOUR FABRIC Identify the straight grain of the fabric and align it vertically. Apply the design to the fabric using one of the following methods.

USING TRANSFER PENS AND PENCILS Once you've selected a design, copy the linework onto tracing paper. Next, retrace the design on the other side of the paper with a transfer pencil or pen (the latter is available for dark fabrics). Finally, place the transfer side over the fabric and iron the design following manufacturer's instructions. Take care to press the iron in an up-and-down motion to avoid moving the transfer in relation to the fabric. Although most brands guarantee the product will wash out or dissolve in the air, always test the fabric before transferring, washing if necessary.

DIRECT TRACING If the design fabric is light in color and weight, it's often possible to place the fabric over the design outline and draw directly onto the fabric, using a fabric-marking pen (not the same as a transfer pen) that will wash out when the stitching is completed. Always test-wash the fabric before transferring.

PRICKING AND POUNCING This is one of the oldest methods of design transfer, and is performed in two stages. First, use a sharp needle (the eye end may be inserted into a wine cork to make it easier to handle) to prick holes in the design paper, close enough to make the design readable. You may also use a tracing wheel (page 104). Then secure the design over the fabric and "pounce" the design through the pricked holes by using pounce powder (sold in quilt stores), tailor's chalk, or a fabric-marking pen.

MOUNTING THE FABRIC ON A HOOP OR FRAME

Decide which method of framing will work for your project. Hoops are best reserved for small projects in which the design is smaller than the diameter of the hoop. Under no circumstances should you allow the hoop to press down over previous stitching; to do so will crush or distort the stitches.

USING A HOOP Wrap the smaller (bottom) ring with a strip of cloth to protect your fabric. If your hoop has a screw, tighten it so the larger ring fits somewhat snugly over the inner ring, then pull them apart. Place the inner ring under the intended design area of your fabric, then fit the outer ring over the same area. Do not attempt to pull the fabric tighter once both rings are in place. If the fabric is not sufficiently taut, remove the outer ring and adjust screw if necessary. Take care not to stretch the fabric along the four bias edges; it's easy to distort these areas and permanently injure the fabric.

Always remove the hoop after each stitching session. Leaving the hoop in place indefinitely may create permanent creases in the fabric that will never wash and press out.

USING STRETCHER BARS First connect the bars at the corners, tapping them together with a hammer or rubber mallet. Check that the corners are perfectly square.

The outer edges of your overcast fabric should align with the outer edges of the bars. Begin tacking at the midpoint of the top and bottom bars, pulling the fabric reasonably taut. Repeat at the midpoint of the side bars. Work from the midpoints to the corners sequentially in both directions. Place tacks approximately 1" apart, or closer. Your fabric should be completely free of wrinkles or ridges. As you stitch, re-tighten fabric as necessary.

USING A SCROLL FRAME Sew the top and bottom edges of your overcast fabric to the webbing on the scroll bars, using carpet or upholstery thread and firm Backstitches.

To maintain equal tension in the horizontal axis, you'll have to attach the sides of the fabric to the sides of the frame. The easiest solution is to use clips made for this purpose (see page 101) or you may lace the fabric to the side bars, using dental floss, upholstery thread, or pearl cotton. The disadvantage of this method is that you must unlace—then re-lace—the sides every time you scroll to a different area of the fabric. This may be more of a problem with some designs than others.

PLYING THREADS

Some multiple-ply threads such as stranded floss and silk must be separated before stitching, even if you intend to use the same number of plies in your needle at once. Manufacturing and packaging tend to pack the fibers together, twist, or flatten them. Separating them allows them to fluff out, which results in better coverage on the fabric.

Always test the number of plies you need for the visual results you want to achieve. If your thread comes in three plies, but you need to stitch with four plies, cut two lengths of three-ply thread, separate them all, and combine four, reserving the remaining two plies for the next "needleful."

Some threads have nap (direction). Run your fingers first in one direction along the length of the thread, then in the other direction. The smoother direction represents "going with the nap," which is the direction you'll want the thread to enter the fabric, so take note of this as you thread your needle.

MERGING DIFFERENT THREAD DYE LOTS

Because it's often impossible to estimate the amount of thread required for an embroidery design, purchase more than you think you'll need. Even so, you may discover—when you're nearing the midpoint of the design—that you're running out of one or more colors, especially if you've had to rip out stitches. You may be able to find additional thread at your local shop that was dyed in the same lot with the thread you've already used. Unfortunately, the thread you find in the shop may be a slightly different shade than the original, even if the manufacturer labels it with the exact same color name and number. This is simply unavoidable, even by reputable manufacturers, because of the nature of the dyeing process.

How much this affects your project depends on several factors. If the color in question appears in scattered motifs throughout a design that has many colors, the difference in shades may not be noticeable. In this case, just make sure you use only one dye lot within one motif.

If the color in question fills up a large area, you're faced with the problem of a glaring line of demarcation between the two shades. If you're stitching with one ply of thread, there's no simple solution; you can live with the two shades or you can buy enough of the new shade to re-stitch the entire area. However, if you're stitching with multiple plies, there is a solution if you've reserved some of the original shade and haven't stitched more than half of the area in question. The trick is to introduce increasing amounts of the new shade as you stitch. Instead of an abrupt color change, the stitching will gently blend from one shade to the other. Here's an example of how you would accomplish this when stitching with three plies:

1. Stitch with three plies of the original shade.
2. Stitch with two plies of the original shade and one ply of the new shade.
3. Stitch with one ply of the original shade and two plies of the new shade.
4. Stitch with three plies of the new shade.

TO BEGIN STITCHING

STARTING THREADS

In general, use a thread length of approximately 18" long unless specific design instructions state otherwise; some specialty threads, especially metals and metallics, may require a shorter length. Threads longer than 18" may twist, tangle, or knot as you stitch, and disrupt your stitching rhythm. Also, the thread closest to the needle will make so many trips in and out of the fabric that it will become stressed and frayed, and will no longer match the thread at the opposite end.

THE IN-LINE METHOD Determine the direction in which your first line of stitching will proceed. Hold a 2" tail of thread in place on the back of the fabric as you make the first few stitches, checking to see that the backs of the stitches cover the tail.

THE WASTE KNOT METHOD Make a sturdy knot and insert the needle from the right side of the fabric, about four inches from the point you wish to begin stitching. When you're done with that length of thread, clip off the knot, turn the fabric over, then thread the tail into the needle and weave it into the back of the stitches.

THE IN-LINE WASTE KNOT METHOD Plan the direction you'll be stitching, make a knot and insert it (from the top) along that same path. Clip the knot off just before you reach it. This method works for some but not all embroidery stitches; it depends on the pattern of the thread on the back of the stitching.

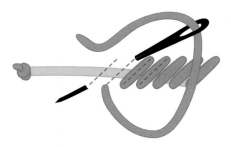

In-line Waste Knot Method

STITCHING TECHNIQUE

TENSION Maintaining consistency of tension within a given stitched area (part or whole of the design, depending on the variety of stitches) is essential for the good appearance of the finished project. Stitching with too tight a tension makes the fabric pucker. Stitching with too loose a tension creates stitches that tend to snag more easily. You may find that longer stitches require slightly more tension than shorter ones, but be sure to test-check first. Each stitch has its own tension requirement; those that are particularly noteworthy are specified in the Embroidery Stitch Gallery, page 110.

THE STAB STITCH If you use a needlework frame (hoop, stretcher bars, or scroll frame) you must stitch using the stab method: Insert the needle and thread into the fabric with your dominant hand, then pull the needle through from the back either with your dominant hand or the less dominant hand (this latter is possible only with a floor or table stand that frees you from having to hold the frame).

Some stitchers prefer to use no frame and stitch using the sewing method, in which you insert and pull up the needle in one continuous motion. Because this affects the tension, this method is not recommended for beginners. It's also not a good idea to use this method when you're stitching with more than one strand of thread or attempting to stitch motifs of Satin stitches that must lie perfectly uniform.

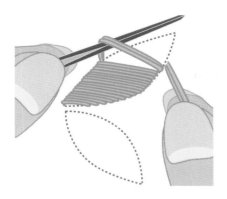

USING A LAYING TOOL When stitching with multiple plies of thread, the plies may twist or lump together. Avoid this by using a laying tool (page 102) and a floor or table stand to free your less dominant hand. Hold the laying tool in your less dominant hand and stroke the threads as you tighten each stitch so the threads lie flat and parallel.

ENDING THREADS To end a thread, weave it in and out of completed stitches on the back of the area you have just stitched. If the stitches are long and loose on the back (as with Satin stitches), double back with a small reversed stitch (or two).

Ending a thread on the back of fabric

Never weave the tail of a dark-colored thread through the back of an area stitched with light-colored thread. This rule also applies to carrying a dark thread from one color block to the next. No matter what the color, avoid carrying the thread between color blocks more than ½" apart.

ADDING SURFACE EMBELLISHMENTS
Beads add texture, dimension, and fine detail to embroidered designs. If the thread you've stitched the design with is too thick to pass through a bead, use fewer plies, a lighter weight thread, or a beading needle (see page 99). Try one of these three attachment methods.

1. with a half-cross stitch   **2. with a cross stitch**

3. in a thread nest

Spangles, sequins, and paillettes add interest and sparkle to embroidery, and have been used to embellish stitchery since the Renaissance. Select one of these four attachment methods depending on the desired look of the finished piece.

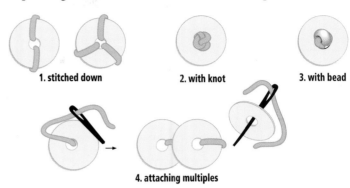

1. stitched down   **2. with knot**   **3. with bead**

4. attaching multiples

Buttons and charms (page 103) add individuality and informality to designs. Attach them with thread through the pre-formed holes. Flat charms with only one hole or ring may require an additional attachment to prevent twisting.

WHEN STITCHING IS COMPLETE
CLEANING THE FINISHED PIECE
The process of stitching practically guarantees that both stitching and ground fabric will be soiled to some degree. It's hard to avoid transferring oils from the fingers to stitching materials, or to protect your work from common house dust, not to mention accidental spills, smudges, and pet hair.

TEST FOR COLOR FASTNESS Before washing the embroidery, test the thread for colorfastness by seeing if swatches of thread bleed when immersed in hot water. If color bleeding occurs, keep running the thread under cooler water until the water runs clear. This will alert you to pay particular attention to areas stitched with colors that bleed.

WASHING AND PRESSING Launder your piece gently, using warm water and mild soap, swishing it through the water long enough for the soap to dissolve any oils and dirt. Avoid rubbing or squeezing the fabric roughly. Rinse thoroughly until you are convinced that the rinse water is clear. Lay the stitchery between two pieces of fabric (linen is excellent) or towels, gently reshaping the fabric if necessary, and allow the stitchery to dry in this manner.

Always press embroidery face down over a clean terry cloth towel. Most specialty threads, especially synthetics, may suffer damage if you iron them directly. Natural fibers can also be flattened and spoiled by the iron. Use a press cloth and an up-and-down motion with the iron.

CLEANING EMBROIDERY THAT CANNOT BE WASHED Never wash silk embroidery, goldwork, or an embroidery that has been painted. Seek the advice of a professional who specializes in cleaning fine needlework. ✺

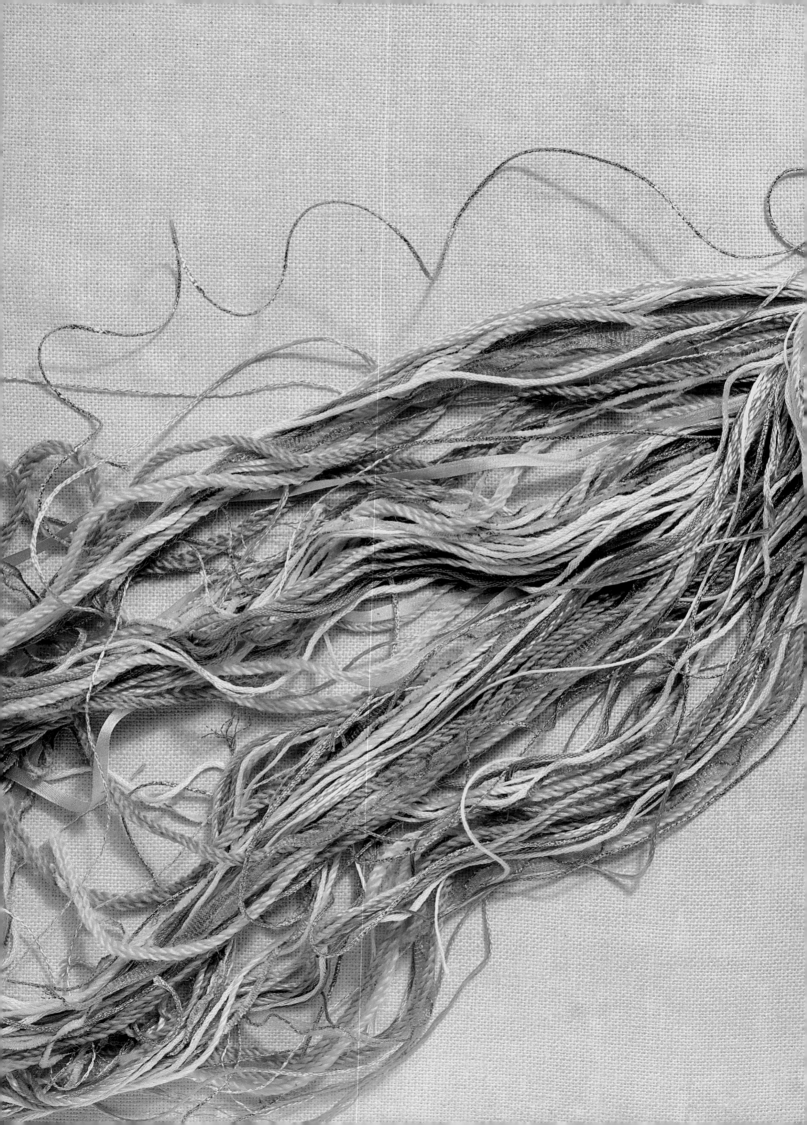

embroidery
stitch gallery

embroidery stitches

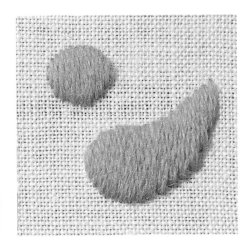

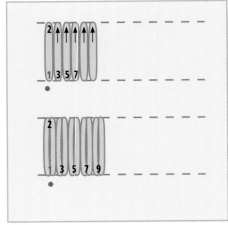
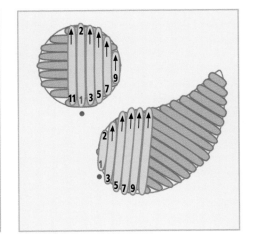

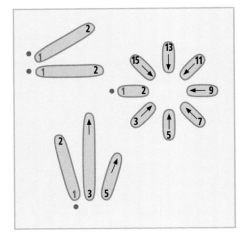

STRAIGHT
Other Name: Stroke

DESCRIPTION
Generally used as a single, individual stitch in any direction.
Length may vary.

HOW TO STITCH
Work from bottom to top, from top to bottom, from left to right or from right to left.
If using more than one strand of thread, keep strands parallel for best results.
Use any type of thread.

SUGGESTED USES
Whiskers, grass spikes, flowers, insect antennae, any small detail that requires a straight line

The red dot in each stitch diagram indicates where to begin stitching.

SATIN

DESCRIPTION
Comprised of a group of Straight stitches stitched very closely together to make a solid filling.
May be stitched vertically, horizontally, or diagonally.
May be stitched perpendicular to the outer edge of the shape (as shown) or slanted.

HOW TO STITCH
Work from bottom to top.
Keep stitches smooth and not twisted (use a laying tool if necessary) with uniform tension.
If using multiple strands on one needle (as in lower diagram), try more than one color.
Use any type of thread.

SUGGESTED USES
Filling for any small or medium shape, bands, borders

PADDED SATIN
Other Name: Raised Satin

DESCRIPTION
Comprised of two solid layers: first a bottom layer of Satin stitches, then a top layer of Satin stitches worked perpendicular (or nearly so) to the bottom layer.
Creates a solidly filled-in, raised area.
Usually both layers worked in one color, but the upper layer may be shaded (see the Jacobean Pomegranate on page 144).
Gives the illusion of a motif positioned in the foreground of a design.

HOW TO STITCH
Decide which direction you want the direction of the top layer to be, then stitch the bottom layer in the other direction.

SUGGESTED USES
Any shape (leaves, flowers) that requires a smooth, raised area

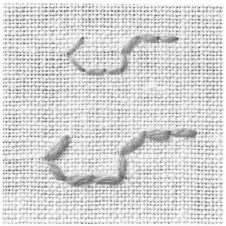
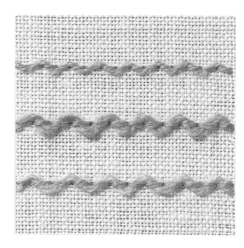

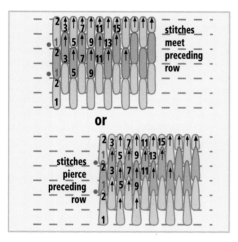
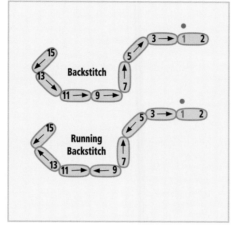

III

LONG-AND-SHORT

DESCRIPTION

Comprised of a series of Straight stitches stitched in a particular arrangement.

The first row of stitches is a series of alternating long and short stitches.

In successive rows, all the stitches are the same length as the long stitch of the first row.

Produces excellent shading effects when stitched in graduated colors.

HOW TO STITCH

When stitching successive rows, either pierce the stitches of the previous row (lower diagram) or make sure stitches meet in the same hole (upper diagram).

Non-fuzzy or slightly twisted threads work best.

SUGGESTED USES

Any medium to large shape (petals, leaves) that requires shading, bands, borders

BACKSTITCH
Other Name: Point de Sable

DESCRIPTION

Comprised of short, even stitches that form an outline or design detail.

HOW TO STITCH

The basic Backstitch requires a specific stitching sequence: take the first stitch "backward," bring up needle two stitch lengths in the direction you'll be traveling, then insert needle in the same hole where the previous stitch began.

The stitching sequence of the *Running Backstitch* is slightly different than the Backstitch to ensure that the thread on the back does not show through the fabric (compare diagrams).

Space the stitches evenly to resemble a line of machine stitching.

Use any kind of thread, but fuzzy or thick threads tend to obliterate the outline or details.

SUGGESTED USES

Outlines, details within motifs, lettering

THREADED BACKSTITCH
Other Name: Laced Backstitch

DESCRIPTION

Comprised of Backstitches woven with a second "threading" thread that does not pierce the fabric.

Makes a heavier line than basic Backstitch.

Effective in one or two colors.

Try two very different types of thread (different in size, texture, etc.)

HOW TO STITCH

First stitch all the Backstitches; then bring up the threading thread at one end of the Backstitches and weave it under the Backstitches from alternating sides without piercing the fabric.

If possible, use a tapestry needle for the threading thread. If using a sharp needle, weave the threading thread by inserting the eye of the needle under the Backstitches.

SUGGESTED USES

Outlines, borders, lettering, stems, tendrils, bands

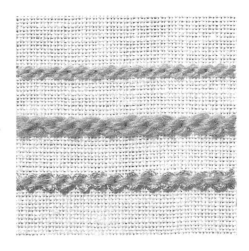

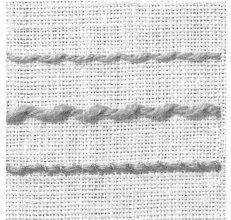

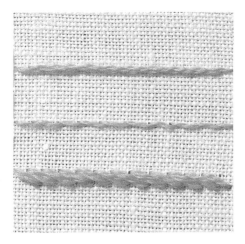

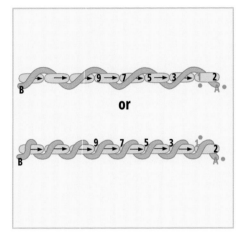

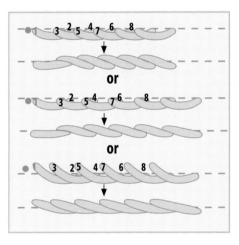

DOUBLE-THREADED BACKSTITCH
Other Name: Interlaced Backstitch

DESCRIPTION

Comprised of a line of basic Backstitches woven with a second and third "threading" threads that do not pierce the fabric.

Creates a broad, textured line.

Effective in one, two, or three colors.

The threading threads look dramatic when stitched with metallic threads.

HOW TO STITCH

First stitch all the Backstitches; then bring up the first threading thread at one end of the Backstitches and weave it under the Backstitches from alternating sides without piercing the fabric. Repeat with the second threading thread, working the side opposite the first.

To obtain the look shown in the diagram, use a somewhat loose tension.

SUGGESTED USES

Outlines, borders, tendrils, lettering, stems

WHIPPED BACKSTITCH

DESCRIPTION

Similar to the Threaded Backstitch except the "whipping" thread weaves under the Backstitches from one side only.

The whipping thread may weave over and under every Backstitch (lower diagram) or every other Backstitch (upper diagram).

Effective in one or two colors.

HOW TO STITCH

First stitch all the Backstitches; then bring up the whipping thread at one end and weave it over and under the Backstitches from one direction only without piercing the fabric.

For a fine line, use short Backstitches and fine thread; for a thicker line, use longer Backstitches and thicker thread.

SUGGESTED USES

Outlines, borders, lettering, tendrils, stems

STEM
Other Names: Crewel, South Kensington

DESCRIPTION

Historical notes and experts disagree over the correct name and stitching method for this stitch; often confused with the Outline stitch (page 113).

HOW TO STITCH

Position the thread below the needle as you stitch.

Snug up each stitch before proceeding to the next.

Work from left to right.

Keep stitches small and uniform.

In the upper two diagrams, Step 3 is half the distance of Steps 1–2; Step 5 shares a hole with Step 2.

In the middle two diagrams, Step 3 is closer to Step 2 than in the top diagrams.

In the lower diagrams, Step 1 is above Step 2, creating a wider stitch line.

SUGGESTED USES

Universal: outlines, filling, lettering

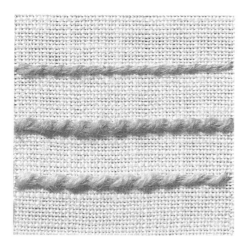
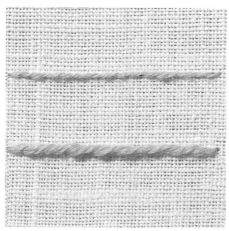

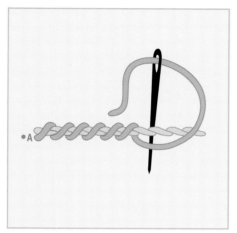
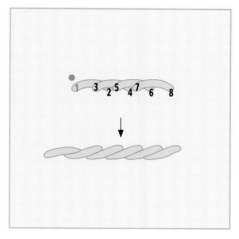
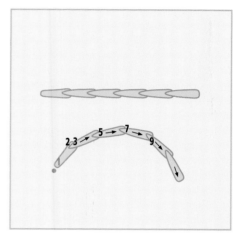

WHIPPED STEM

OUTLINE

SPLIT
Other Name: Kensington Outline

113

DESCRIPTION

Comprised of a line of basic Stem stitches woven with a second, "whipping" thread that does not pierce the fabric.

Makes a heavier line than Stem stitch.

Effective in one or two colors, the same kind of thread or a different one.

HOW TO STITCH

Stitch Stem stitches first.

To keep the whipping thread evenly spaced, position the needle straight down into the overlap of two adjacent Stem stitches (as shown).

If possible, use a tapestry needle for the whipping thread. If using a sharp needle, weave the whipping thread by inserting the eye of the needle under the Backstitches.

SUGGESTED USES

Outlines, borders, stems, tendrils, lettering, bands

DESCRIPTION

Similar to the Stem stitch (page 112) except the thread is positioned above the needle, as you stitch.

HOW TO STITCH

Work from left to right.

Keep stitches the same size; small stitches work best.

Use any kind of thread.

SUGGESTED USES

Outlines, filling, lettering

DESCRIPTION

The working stitch splits the previous stitch.

The placement of the split may vary from the center of the previous stitch to the end closest to the new stitch (as shown).

Works well around curves if stitches are short.

Creates a subtle shading when worked in rows.

HOW TO STITCH

Work from left to right or from right to left.

Take care to split the previous stitch as close as possible to the center of the thread width.

Keep stitches the same size; small stitches work best.

An untwisted thread splits easier than a twisted one.

SUGGESTED USES

Outlines, filling

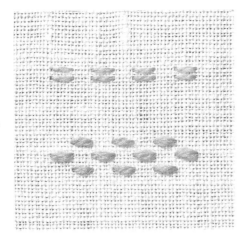

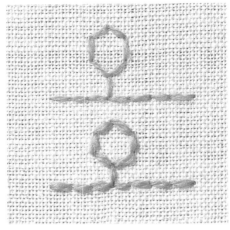

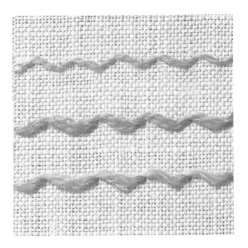

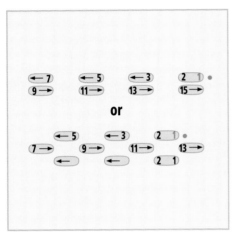

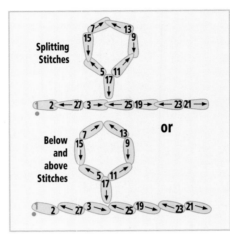

114

RUNNING

DESCRIPTION
The simplest of all stitches.

All stitches are of equal length, both on top and bottom of fabric.

Rows may be grouped in columns, alternating or staggered, to create patterns.

HOW TO STITCH
Work from right to left, or from left to right.

If using multiple strands of thread, keep strands parallel.

Use any kind of thread.

SUGGESTED USES
Soft motif outline (single line), filling, borders, bands

DOUBLE RUNNING
Other Names: Holbein, Chiara,
Two-sided Line, Two-sided Stroke, Stroke

DESCRIPTION
Comprised of one row (journey or pass) of Running stitches which are evenly spaced, followed by a second row (return journey) which fills in the empty spaces.

Usually stitched in one color, but two colors may be used.

HOW TO STITCH
When stitching the return journey, keep the linework as straight as possible by following one of these methods:

1. Split the previous stitch (upper diagram).
2. Bring up and insert the needle above and below the stitches of the first journey (lower diagram). The stitch tension pulls the return-journey stitches into a straight line.

Stitch with a slightly loose tension.

SUGGESTED USES
Borders, meandering motifs, bands

WHIPPED RUNNING
Other name: Cordonnet

DESCRIPTION
Comprised of a line of basic Running stitches woven with a second, "whipping" thread that does not pierce the fabric.

Makes a much heavier line than basic Running stitch.

The thickness of the whipping thread greatly affects the appearance of the finished stitch.

Effective in one or two colors.

HOW TO STITCH
First stitch the Running stitches.

If possible, use a tapestry needle for the whipping thread. If using a sharp needle, weave the whipping thread by inserting the eye of the needle under the Backstitches.

SUGGESTED USES
Outlines, tendrils, bands

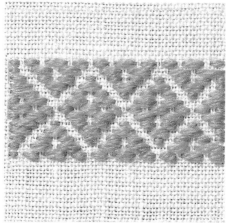

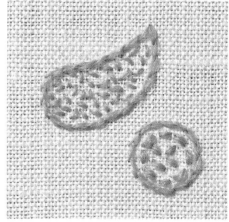

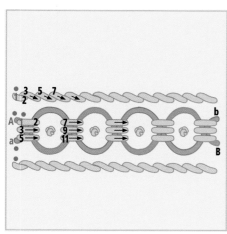

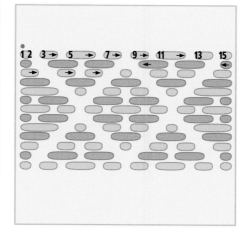

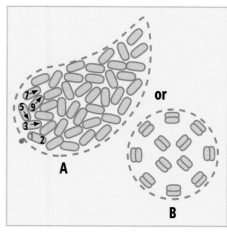

GUILLOCHE

DESCRIPTION
Actually a composite stitch consisting of Satin stitches (page 110) in groups of three or more; two woven threads which pass under the Satin stitches to form circles, and do not pierce the fabric; a border of Stem stitches (page 112) above and below the circles; and French Knots (page 133) in the center of each circle.

Effective in one or more colors.

The name is an architectural term referring to ornamental borders containing two or more undulating and interwoven lines.

HOW TO STITCH
Work from left to right or from right to left.

Keep the woven threads somewhat loose to keep a rounded appearance.

SUGGESTED USES
Borders, bands

DARNING
Other Names: Basting, Damask

DESCRIPTION
Comprised of rows of Running stitches which vary in length and spacing.

Each row is usually in one color, but colors may vary from row to row.

HOW TO STITCH
Work from right to left, then from left to right.

Stitch with a loose tension.

SUGGESTED USES
Filling, background, borders

SEED
Other Name: Dot, Rice Grain, Seeding, Speckling

DESCRIPTION
Comprised of tiny single (A) or double (B) Backstitches of equal length, randomly scattered at various angles (A) or placed in patterns (B).

HOW TO STITCH
Try to keep the spacing between stitches or stitch groups fairly uniform.

SUGGESTED USES
Filling, background

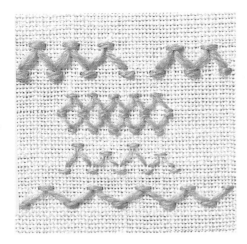

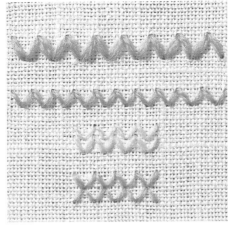

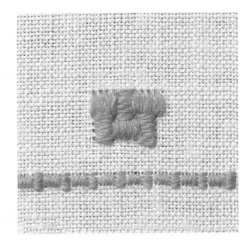

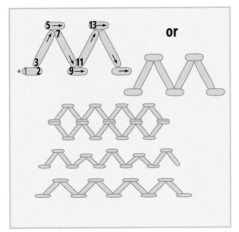

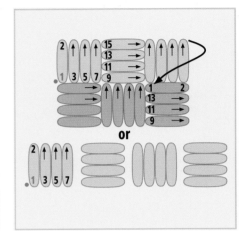

116

CHEVRON

ARROWHEAD

BASKET FILLING

DESCRIPTION

The stitch pattern forms two parallel broken lines (see page 206 for Closed Chevron) connected by pairs of diagonal stitches in the shape of a "V" or chevron.

Most effective if kept relatively small.

The horizontal stitch of Step 5 can lie directly opposite the stitch of Step 2, or they can be spaced apart.

Height of stitches may vary (see diagram, second from bottom).

Rows of Chevron stitches may line up in columns, be staggered, or oppose each other.

HOW TO STITCH

Work from left to right.

Work diagonal stitches alternating between lower and upper lines.

Snug up each leg of the stitch as the needle emerges from the fabric.

SUGGESTED USES

Bands, borders, filling

DESCRIPTION

Comprised of diagonal stitches worked between two parallel (imaginary) lines, or concentric circles, forming "Vs."

Effective when stitched in a circle to create flower heads or sun rays.

Most effective in groups.

HOW TO STITCH

Work from left to right.

Steps 2 and 4 share the same hole, Steps 3 and 5 share the same hole, etc.

Use any non-fuzzy thread.

SUGGESTED USES

Outlines, filling, borders, flowers, bands, sun rays

DESCRIPTION

Comprised of a series of same-length Satin stitches arranged in alternating vertical and horizontal groups of three to six (four is most common).

The Satin-stitch groups may be stitched close together (top) or slightly apart (bottom).

HOW TO STITCH

Keep stitches smooth (use a laying tool if necessary) with uniform tension.

SUGGESTED USES

Baskets, borders, background, bands

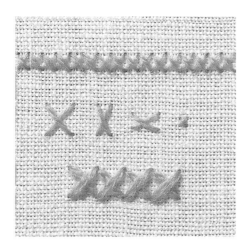

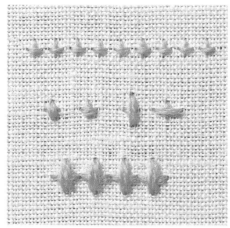

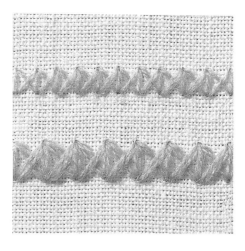

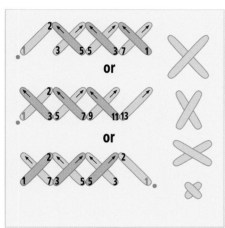

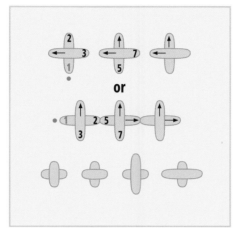

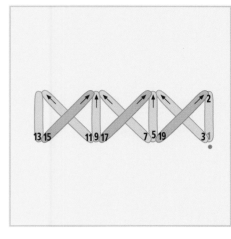

CROSS
Other Names: Sampler, Berlin, Point de Marque, Cross-stitch

DESCRIPTION
One of the oldest and most popular stitches.

Used extensively as a counted thread technique (see page 194).

Most commonly square, but may be stitched tall or squat (above, right).

HOW TO STITCH
You may complete each cross individually (middle diagram) or stitch the first legs of an entire row first, then fill in the second legs on the return journey (upper diagram).

Make sure all the top legs slant in the same direction.

Work from left to right or from right to left (bottom diagram).

When stitching on fabrics other than evenweave, draw parallel lines to keep stitches the same size (use water- or air-soluble marking pen).

SUGGESTED USES
Filling, outlines, bands, motifs

UPRIGHT CROSS
Other Names: St. George's Cross

DESCRIPTION
As its name implies, this upright crossed stitch resembles a plus sign.

HOW TO STITCH
Work from left to right or from right to left.

Make sure all the top legs are oriented in the same direction for a single design, unless otherwise desired. Note difference between upper and middle diagrams.

SUGGESTED USES
Filling, stars, bands

ZIGZAG
Other Name: Cross-stitch with Bar

DESCRIPTION
Comprised of crossed stitches separated by vertical stitches.

HOW TO STITCH
Work from right to left.

On the first journey work all vertical stitches and lower right to upper left diagonal legs, then complete the remaining diagonal legs on the return journey.

SUGGESTED USES
Bands, borders, filling

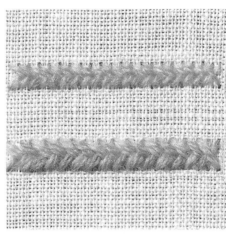

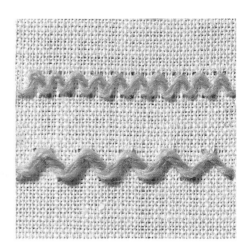

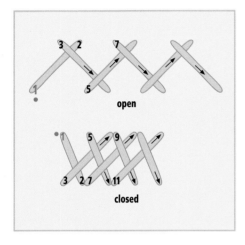

118

HERRINGBONE

Other Names: Catch, Mossoul, Persian, Plaited, Russian, Russian Cross, Witch

DESCRIPTION
A versatile stitch with many variations.
On the back, stitches will resemble two parallel lines of Backstitches or Running stitches.
In the open variation (top), the ends of each stitch do not touch; in the closed variation (bottom) they do.

HOW TO STITCH
Work from left to right.
Keep the spacing and length of stitches uniform; keep similarly angled legs parallel.
If stitching a vertical row, turn fabric 90 degrees.
Keep multiple strands of thread parallel as you stitch.

SUGGESTED USES
Filling, borders, bands

DOUBLE HERRINGBONE

DESCRIPTION
Comprised of two rows of basic open Herringbone in two colors nestling and interlaced together.

HOW TO STITCH
Stitch basic Herringbone in darker color first, then add a second series of basic Herringbone stitches in the lighter color for best results.
Note that the second leg (C–D) of the second row weaves under the second leg (3–4) of the first color; continue this pattern for the entire row.
In another variation, the second series of Herringbone stitches is simply stitched on top of the first series without weaving under one leg of the Herringbone stitches beneath.

SUGGESTED USES
Bands, borders

THREADED HERRINGBONE

DESCRIPTION
Comprised of a line of basic open Herringbone stitches woven with a second "threading" thread that does not pierce the fabric.
Effective in one or two colors as well as in threads of different weights.

HOW TO STITCH
First stitch all the Herringbone stitches; then bring up the threading thread and weave it over and under the Herringbone stitches as shown without piercing the fabric.
Take care not to pull the threading so tight that it distorts the basic Herringbone stitches.
If possible, use a tapestry needle for the threading thread. If using a sharp needle, weave the threading thread by inserting the eye of the needle under the Backstitches.

SUGGESTED USES
Bands, borders

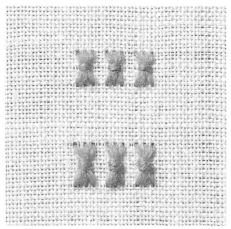

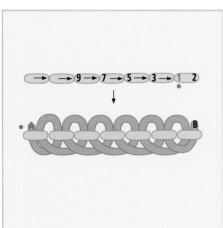

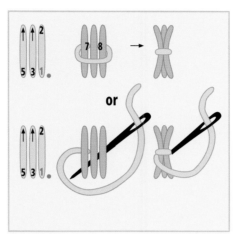

PEKINESE

SHEAF

ERMINE

DESCRIPTION
This textured, interlaced stitch appears in many Chinese embroideries.
Effective in one or two colors.

HOW TO STITCH
First work a line (curved or straight) of somewhat loose Backstitches, from right to left (shown) or from left to right; then add the interlacing thread from left to right without piercing the fabric (as shown).
If possible, use a tapestry needle for the threading thread. If using a sharp needle, weave the threading thread by inserting the eye of the needle under the Backstitches.

SUGGESTED USES
Filling, outline, bands

DESCRIPTION
Resembles a tied bundle of wheat stalks.
Individual sheaves may be arranged in vertical, horizontal, staggered, or interlaced rows.

HOW TO STITCH
Work from right to left (shown) or from left to right.
First stitch the three Straight stitches, then bring the needle up beneath the Straight stitches just to the left of the middle stitch, and wrap the thread snugly around the Straight stitches once (upper diagram) or twice (lower diagram). Then insert the needle to the right of the center stitch, nudging Straight stitches together with thumb.

SUGGESTED USES
Borders, filling, bands

DESCRIPTION
Comprised of three Straight stitches, one vertical and two crossing diagonally at the lower half of the Straight stitch.
When worked in black thread on white fabric, it resembles ermine fur, hence its name.
May be arranged in an orderly fashion or scattered for filling.

HOW TO STITCH
Take care to keep the angle and length of the two diagonal stitches equal.

SUGGESTED USES
Filling, bands

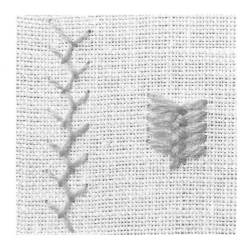

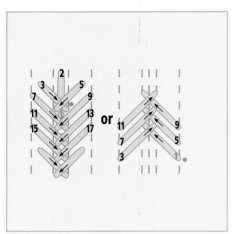

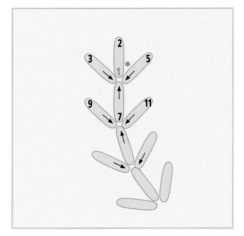

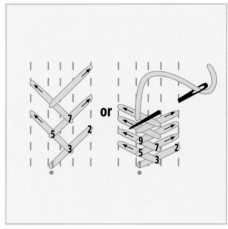

FISHBONE

DESCRIPTION
Resembles the backbone and ribs of a fish; hence its name.

HOW TO STITCH
Draw guidelines (see diagrams) onto fabric before stitching, using a water- or air-soluble pen.

Work from top to bottom or from bottom to top (compare diagrams).

Each time the needle returns to the center, insert it just slightly to the left or right of the central guideline.

To form a leaf or shrub, make the top or bottom few stitches gradually shorter than the other stitches.

SUGGESTED USES
Borders, leaves, small shrubs, architectural finials, wings, feathers, fish bones, bands

FERN

DESCRIPTION
Resembles a fern leaf, hence its name.

Comprised of a series of three Straight stitches of equal length.

The angles of the side stitches may vary.

The central stitches may follow a curve.

HOW TO STITCH
Work from top to bottom.

SUGGESTED USES
Leaves, veins of leaves, fish bones, seaweed

LEAF
Other Name: Fir

DESCRIPTION
The angle of the alternating Straight stitches determines the distance between the stitches.

HOW TO STITCH
Work from bottom to top.

The working stitch always goes over the previous stitch.

SUGGESTED USES
Filling, borders, leaves, vines

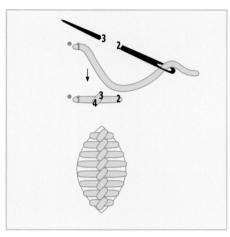

ATTACH SAMPLE
OR PHOTO HERE

ATTACH SAMPLE
OR PHOTO HERE

DIAGRAM

DIAGRAM

ROUMANIAN
Other names; Romanian, Oriental, Antique, Indian Filling, Janina

DESCRIPTION
Comprised of Straight stitches tacked down at the center with a relatively short, slanted stitch.

HOW TO STITCH
Keep the placement of the tack-down stitch centered.

SUGGESTED USES
Filling, borders, leaves and other small shapes

As you find variations or new stitches not illustrated in this book, add them here and on pages 142–143 to personalize the Embroidery Stitch Gallery.

STITCH _____
Other Names: _____

DESCRIPTION
_____
_____
_____
_____
_____
_____

HOW TO STITCH
_____
_____
_____
_____
_____
_____
_____
_____
_____
_____
_____

SUGGESTED USES
_____
_____
_____

STITCH _____
Other Names: _____

DESCRIPTION
_____
_____
_____
_____
_____
_____

HOW TO STITCH
_____
_____
_____
_____
_____
_____
_____
_____
_____
_____
_____

SUGGESTED USES
_____
_____
_____

embroidery stitches

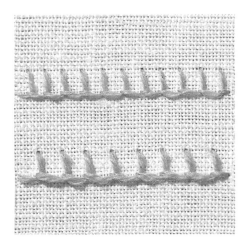

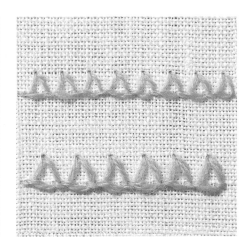

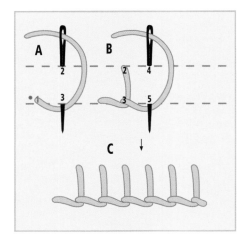

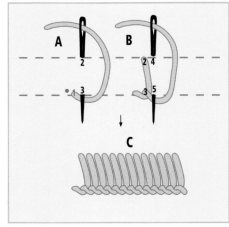

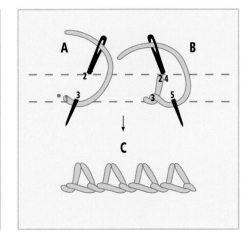

122

BLANKET
Other Name: Spaced Buttonhole

DESCRIPTION
A very versatile stitch, with many variations in size, angle, and arrangement of the vertical legs.

This stitch is sometimes erroneously called the Buttonhole stitch, but in the Blanket stitch the vertical legs are always spaced apart, whereas in the Buttonhole stitch they are always spaced together as closely as possible.

HOW TO STITCH
Work from left to right.
End with a short tack stitch.
Use any type of thread or narrow ribbon.

SUGGESTED USES
Edgings, bands, borders, outlines, filling, flowers (when worked in a circle)

BUTTONHOLE
Other Name: Closed Blanket

DESCRIPTION
This stitch is worked the same way as the Blanket stitch, but the vertical legs have no spaces between them.

HOW TO STITCH
Work from left to right.
End with a short tack stitch.
Use any type of thread, but note that fuzzy threads may obscure the character of the stitch.

SUGGESTED USES
Edgings, borders, flowers, wheels, bands. Used in clothing construction to finish raw edges and buttonholes, and make belt loops. Used in cutwork embroidery.

CLOSED BLANKET
Other Name: Closed Buttonhole

DESCRIPTION
A simple variation of the Blanket stitch. "Closed" means the vertical stitches touch and enclose a certain area.

HOW TO STITCH
Work from left to right.
Use any type of thread.

SUGGESTED USES
Edgings, borders, bands, filling

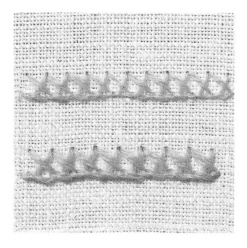

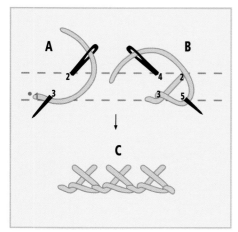

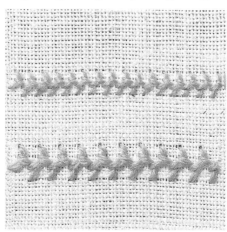

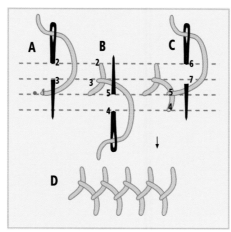

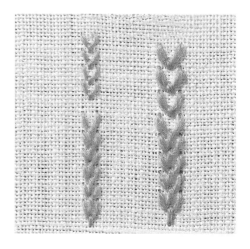

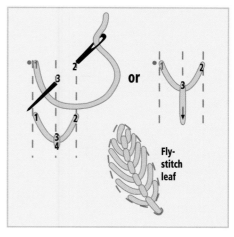

CROSSED BLANKET
Other Name: Crossed Buttonhole

DESCRIPTION
Another simple variation of the Blanket stitch.

The legs of two adjacent stitches cross each other, and may be of equal length (shown) or not.

HOW TO STITCH
Work from left to right.

Use any type of thread.

SUGGESTED USES
Filling, edgings, borders, bands

CRETAN
Other Names: Persian, Quill, Long-armed Feather

DESCRIPTION
A versatile line stitch with a plait along the center.

Works well for straight or curved lines.

Good for filling shapes such as leaves or petals.

May be worked with legs close together or apart (called *Open Cretan* stitch).

May be worked in a straight vertical line (called *Quill* stitch).

Vary the angle of the needle in Steps 2–3, 4–5, etc., to create a very different appearance.

HOW TO STITCH
Work from left to right or from top to bottom.

Use any type of thread.

SUGGESTED USES
Borders, filling, bands

FLY
Other Names: Y, Tied, Open Loop

DESCRIPTION
A versatile and easy stitch.

Resembles an open Detached Chain stitch (page 130).

The length of the tie-down leg can be short or long to give a very different appearance: may resemble a "V" or a "Y."

Can be arranged in vertical, horizontal, or curved rows.

May be worked singly (bird in sky) or in groups to make shapes such as a leaf (see above) or a band.

The length of the legs may be equal or independent of each other (see leaf diagram).

HOW TO STITCH
Work from right to left, from left to right, or from top to bottom.

Use any type of thread.

SUGGESTED USES
Borders, filling, base of flower buds, birds in sky, bands, leaves, petals

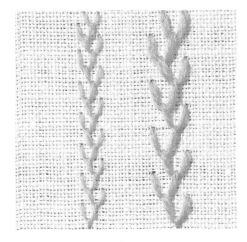

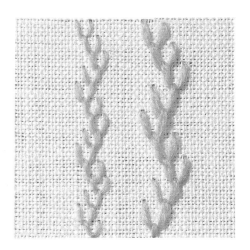

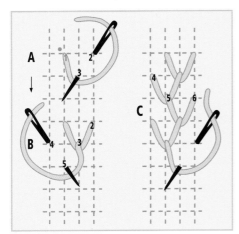
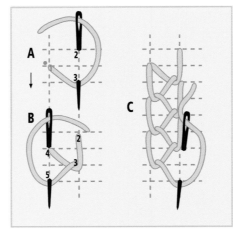
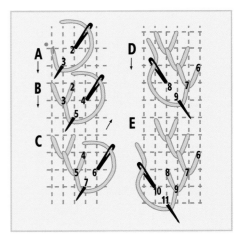

124

FEATHER
Other name: Plumage, Briar

DESCRIPTION
A decorative line stitch used extensively as a smocking stitch and on crazy quilts.
Works well on straight or curved lines.

HOW TO STITCH
Work from top to bottom.
Use any kind of thread.

SUGGESTED USES
Bands, borders, filling, outlines, ferns, trees, vines, shrubs

CLOSED FEATHER

DESCRIPTION
A variation of the Feather stitch.
May be used as a couching stitch for other threads or ribbons.
Works well for straight lines only.

HOW TO STITCH
Work from top to bottom.
Use a thin, round, twisted thread when creating a channel for additional thread or ribbon (so as not to obscure the latter).

SUGGESTED USES
Borders, bands

DOUBLE FEATHER

DESCRIPTION
A wider variation of the Feather stitch.
Makes a feathery, branched decorative line.

HOW TO STITCH
Work from top to bottom.
Use any type of thread.

SUGGESTED USES
Borders, flower stems, branches, bands, shrubs, trees, vines

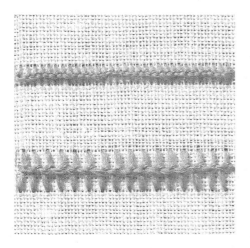
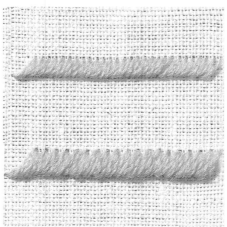
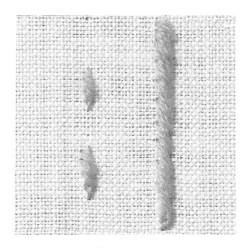

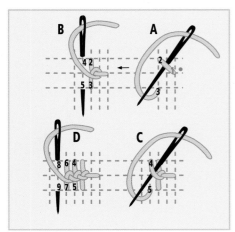
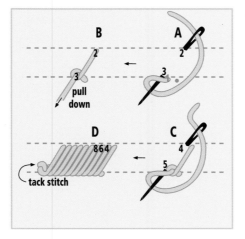
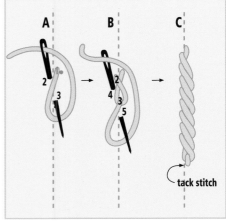

LOOP
Other Names: Centipede

DESCRIPTION
Works well for straight or gradually curved lines.

Creates a raised, plaited center line.

The length of the legs may be equal (shown) or independent of each other.

HOW TO STITCH
Work from right to left.

Good stitched in any type of thread, but a firm, round twisted thread creates the most pronounced raised center line.

Maintain even tension to keep plait well defined and uniform.

SUGGESTED USES
Borders, bands, filling, leaf midribs and veins, fish skeleton, centipedes (fuzzy threads)

BROAD ROPE

DESCRIPTION
Creates a rope-like appearance, but quite different—and wider—than the Narrow Rope stitch (at right).

One side of the stitch is higher than the other, creating a more pronounced three-dimensional appearance.

HOW TO STITCH
Work from right to left.

Make the stitches close together.

Use a firm thread for best results.

SUGGESTED USES
Ropes, outlines, borders, bands

NARROW ROPE

DESCRIPTION
Creates a rope-like appearance, but quite different—and narrower—than the Broad Rope stitch (at left).

HOW TO STITCH
Work from top to bottom.

At the beginning of each new stitch, the needle pierces the fabric to the left of the vertical guideline but emerges along the vertical guideline.

Use your thumbnail to move the previous stitch over to begin the new stitch.

End with a short tack stitch.

Use a firm thread for the best result.

SUGGESTED USES
Ropes, outlines, borders, insect bodies, vines

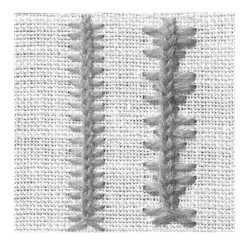

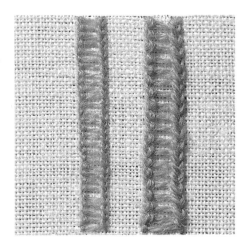

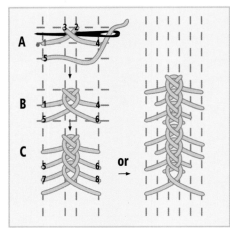

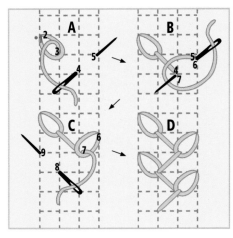

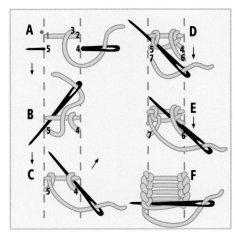

VAN DYKE

DESCRIPTION
A variable-width line stitch with a central raised plait.

The "legs" may vary from long to practically non-existent.

The lengths of the "legs" can be independent of each other (right diagram).

HOW TO STITCH
Work from top to bottom.

Snug up the thread at the central braid to keep the plait well defined.

SUGGESTED USES
Borders, outlines for furry animals, filling, bands

FEATHERED CHAIN
Other Name: Chained Feather

DESCRIPTION
A wide, zigzag line stitch.

Good with almost any type of thread.

Used extensively on crazy quilts.

HOW TO STITCH
Work from top to bottom.

Draw guidelines to keep stitches even in size and spacing with water- or air-soluble pens.

SUGGESTED USES
Borders, bands, vines

LADDER
Other Name: Step

DESCRIPTION
A wide line stitch; width may vary.

The horizontal stitches may be close together or with spaces in between.

Almost any type of thread works well, but a round thread creates more definition at the raised edges.

HOW TO STITCH
Work from top to bottom.

Always keep the ground fabric under tension as you work.

Keep plaited edges as similar in size and shape as possible.

SUGGESTED USES
Filling, borders, a channel for ribbons or other threads, bands

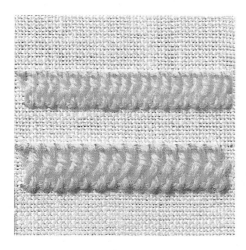

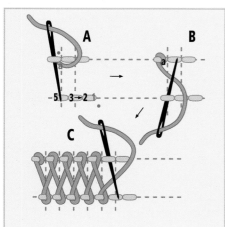

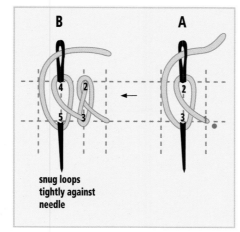

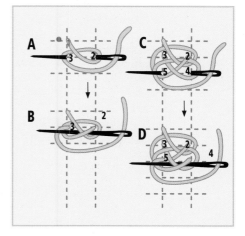

INTERLACED BAND
Other Names: Laced Cretan,
Double Pekinese

DESCRIPTION
Effective in one or two colors, and in one or two types of threads.

The length of the Backstitches determines whether the band will be lacy (long Backstitches) or solid (short Backstitches).

The rows of Backstitches need not be parallel (as shown).

HOW TO STITCH
Work the Backstitches from right to left (as shown) or from left to right; lace from left to right.

Don't pull the lacing threads so tight that the Backstitches become distorted.

SUGGESTED USES
Borders, bands, a channel for ribbons or other threads

BRAID
Other Name: Gordian Knot

DESCRIPTION
Has a flat, braided appearance.

Works well for straight and curved lines.

Works best with twisted thread such as pearl cotton.

HOW TO STITCH
Work from right to left.

The height of the stitches should be ¼" or less, unless thread is thick.

Make stitches small and close together to retain a braided look.

Do not use on items that will be laundered (loops are not stable).

SUGGESTED USES
Borders, bands

PLAITED BRAID

DESCRIPTION
An old stitch, used since the 16th Century, and in metal threads during the 17th Century.

Creates a heavy, flat, rich, complex, plaited band.

Takes a bit of practice to master.

HOW TO STITCH
Work from top to bottom.

Repeat steps C and D until you reach the desired length.

Strive to keep the tension even and the loops uniform.

As you stitch, use a pin to keep loops open.

SUGGESTED USES
Bands, borders

embroidery stitches

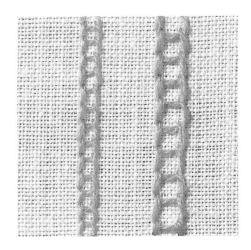

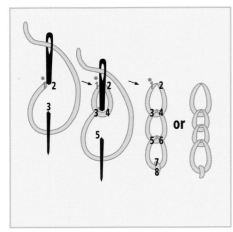
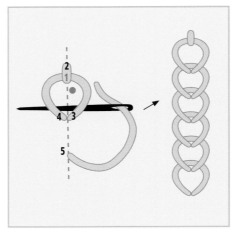
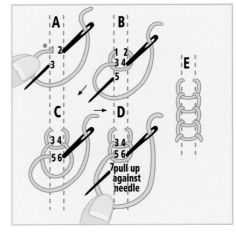

128

CHAIN

DESCRIPTION
One of the easiest, most useful, and versatile embroidery stitches for curved and straight lines.

HOW TO STITCH
After forming the thread loop, snug up the loop gently against the working thread; then form a second loop with the working thread and repeat the first step.

To end, make a small tack stitch over the last loop.

Keep stitches as equal in length as possible, or vary the length for a different effect (far right diagram).

Don't pull the stitches so tight that the fabric puckers.

Use any type of thread, but a firm thread retains the character of the stitch better.

SUGGESTED USES
Outlines, filling, lettering, bands

BROAD CHAIN
Other Name: Reverse Chain

DESCRIPTION
Creates a wider stitch than the basic Chain stitch.

Works well for straight and curved lines.

HOW TO STITCH
Work from top to bottom.

First make a small straight stitch, then continue with modified Chain stitches which slide under the previous stitch.

Keep the stitches somewhat loose.

Use any type of thread, but a firm thread allows the individual stitches to keep their shape.

SUGGESTED USES
Stems, tree trunks, monograms, borders, outlines, bands

OPEN CHAIN
Other names: Square Chain, Ladder, Roman Chain

DESCRIPTION
A common variation of the Chain stitch; stitches may vary in width and depth.

Useful in couching down ribbons, cords, or other threads.

HOW TO STITCH
Hold the thread loop with thumb.

Work from top to bottom.

Use guidelines to keep stitches even.

Anchor the last stitch by a tack stitch at each corner.

Use any type of thread; a fine, firm thread is best when stitching a channel for ribbons or other threads.

SUGGESTED USES
Outlines, borders, bands, roof shingles, caterpillar (fuzzy thread), a channel for ribbons or other threads

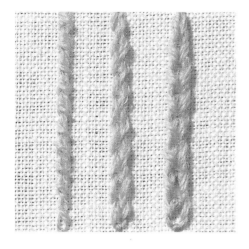

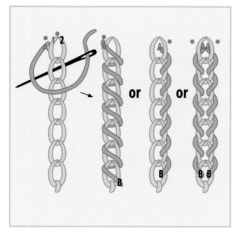

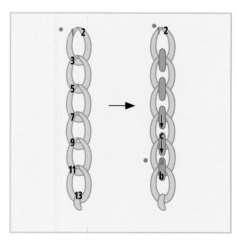

WHIPPED CHAIN

THREADED CHAIN

BACKSTITCHED CHAIN

DESCRIPTION

Comprised of a basic Chain stitch ornamented with one or more "whipping" threads.

Effective in one or more colors, as well as different thread weights and types.

HOW TO STITCH

Complete Chain stitches first.

Bring up the whipping thread at one end of the line of Chain stitches, covering one side, both sides, or the whole chain.

When whipping, do not pierce the fabric except to begin and end the whipping thread.

If possible, use a tapestry needle for the whipping thread. If using a sharp needle, weave the whipping thread by inserting the eye of the needle under the basic Chain stitches.

Use any type of thread.

SUGGESTED USES

Borders, outlines, edgings, bands

DESCRIPTION

Comprised of a basic Chain stitch ornamented with another "threading" thread.

Creates a wider stitch than the basic Chain.

Effective in one or two colors, as well as different thread weights and types.

HOW TO STITCH

Complete Chain stitches first.

Bring up the threading thread at one end of the line of Chain stitches; do not pierce the fabric except to begin and end it.

Threading should be somewhat loose.

If possible, use a tapestry needle for the threading thread. If using a sharp needle, weave the threading thread by inserting the eye of the needle under the basic Chain stitches.

SUGGESTED USES

Borders, outlines, edgings, stems, bands

DESCRIPTION

Adds extra durability to the already-durable Chain stitch; especially good for clothing.

Effective in one or two colors.

HOW TO STITCH

Complete the basic Chain stitches first, then add the Backstitches.

Use different types or weights of thread.

SUGGESTED USES

Outlines, lettering, filling, bands

embroidery stitches

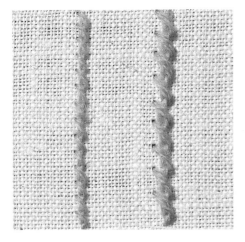

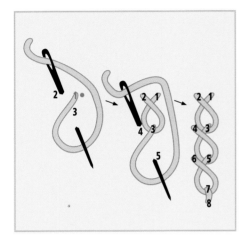
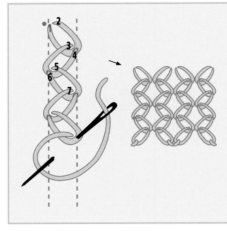
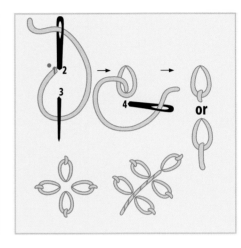

TWISTED CHAIN

DESCRIPTION
Creates a more textured, rope-like line than the basic Chain stitch (page 128).
Close single or multiple rows create an interesting outline.

HOW TO STITCH
Work this like a basic Chain stitch except where the needle inserts at Step 2.
Use a firm, twisted thread for best stitch definition.

SUGGESTED USES
Outlines, filling, lettering, stems, bands

ZIGZAG CHAIN

DESCRIPTION
The angle between the stitches and the stitch size may vary.
Works well for straight and gently curving lines.
Creates an overall pattern when multiple lines are stitched back to back (right diagram).

HOW TO STITCH
Always pierce the previous stitch to prevent it from slipping and turning.
Work from top to bottom.
Use any type of thread; fuzzy threads may obscure the character of the stitch.

SUGGESTED USES
Textured lines, overall pattern, zigzag lines, bands, filling, borders

DETACHED CHAIN
Other Name: Lazy Daisy

DESCRIPTION
Comprised of a single Chain stitch.
This well-known versatile stitch may be grouped to create flowers (as shown), leaves (as shown), sun rays, etc.

HOW TO STITCH
Vary the length of the tack-down stitch if desired (as shown at right).
Use any type of thread.

SUGGESTED USES
Filling, flower petals, flower buds, leaves, bird's beak or eye, sun rays, animal ears

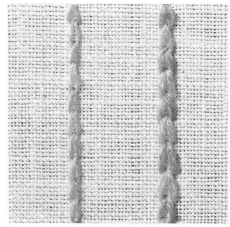

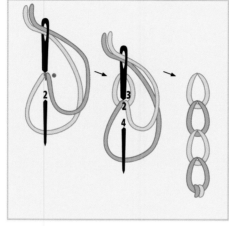
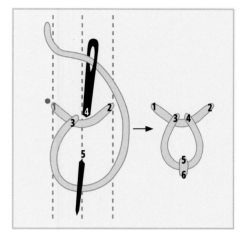

CABLE CHAIN
Other Name: Cable

DESCRIPTION
Resembles separate links of a chain.
This variation of the Chain stitch works well on straight or curvy lines.

HOW TO STITCH
1. Wrap thread around the needle as shown.
2. Insert the needle a short space from where the thread originally emerged from the fabric; this will be the distance of the "cable" between the Chain stitches.
3. Snug the thread wrap around the needle and be sure the working thread goes under tip of needle for the Chain stitch before pulling the needle through the fabric.
4. As you draw the needle through the fabric in Step 3, hold the entire stitch down with your thumb.

Use a firm thread for best results.

SUGGESTED USES
Outlines, filling, chains, necklaces

CHECKERED CHAIN
Other Names: Magic Chain,
Alternating Chain

DESCRIPTION
Two threads of equal size and weight but of contrasting colors are worked in the eye of needle at the same time.
Works well on straight or gently curving lines.

HOW TO STITCH
Loop one color thread under the needle and one color on top of the needle as you make a Chain stitch.
Alternate which color is beneath the needle.
As you pull the loop closed, you may need to pull the other color thread so it disappears behind the newly-formed loop.
Work from top to bottom.
Use a firm, twisted thread for best results.

SUGGESTED USES
Outlines, borders, filling, stems, bands

TÊTE DE BOEUF

DESCRIPTION
The name is French for "bull's head," and the shape of the stitch resembles an animal with horns.

HOW TO STITCH
Begin by stitching a modified Fly stitch (page 123) but make the tack-down stitch a Chain stitch instead of a Straight stitch.
(Stitching literature offers several different methods of stitching; this method seems the least confusing.)
Use a firm thread for best results.

SUGGESTED USES
Filling, borders, base for flower buds, bands

131

embroidery stitches

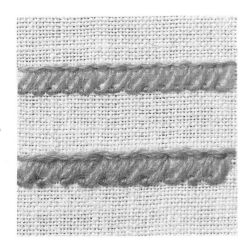

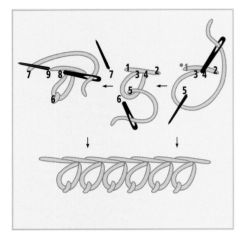

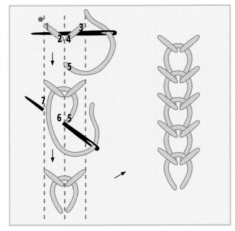

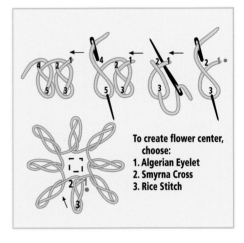

132

PETAL
Other Name: Pendant Chain

DESCRIPTION
Works well for straight, diagonal, and curved lines or circles.

HOW TO STITCH
The chain loop is always on the diagonal because steps 5 and 6 are directly below step 1.

Work from right to left.

Use a firmly twisted thread for best results.

SUGGESTED USES
Borders, flowers (when worked in a circle), leaves, lacy edgings, bands

WHEAT EAR

DESCRIPTION
Works best in straight rows, but may handle gentle curves.

HOW TO STITCH
Work from top to bottom, or from left to right.

Draw guidelines to help you stitch uniform shapes, but the wheat's "ears" (the straight stitches) may graduate in length from top to bottom of a vertical line to resemble an actual head of wheat.

Use a firm thread for best results.

SUGGESTED USES
Textured lines or bands, borders, ears of wheat, bunny heads

ROSETTE CHAIN

DESCRIPTION
Resembles a twisted chain.

Works well for straight or gently curved lines.

When stitched in a circle, forms a daisy-like flower.

Because it's not a stable stitch, it's not suitable for clothing.

HOW TO STITCH
Hold the thread loop with your thumb when working the rest of the stitch.

Pass the needle under the thread near the beginning of the stitch; do not pierce the fabric.

Work from right to left.

Use a stiff, firmly twisted thread for best results; metallic threads work well.

SUGGESTED USES
Bands, flower petals

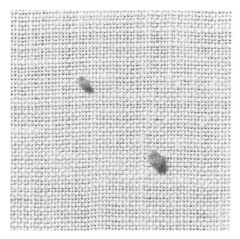

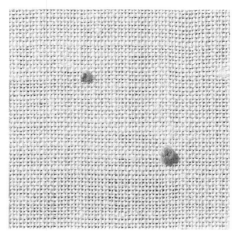

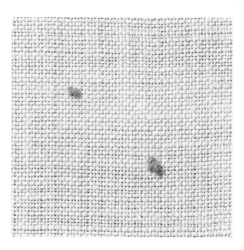

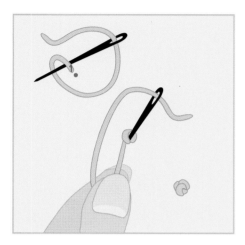

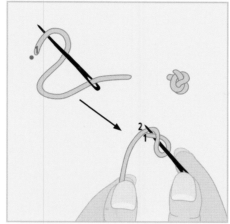

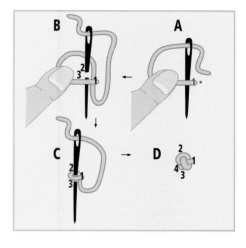

FRENCH KNOT
Other Names: French Dot, Wound, Knotted, Twisted Knot

DESCRIPTION
Has the appearance of a small, spherical, raised knot.

HOW TO STITCH
Wrap the thread around the needle only once or twice.

Keep the thread snug around the barrel of the needle as you complete the stitch.

Insert the tip of the needle a few fabric threads away from the point from which the needle originally emerged.

Works best when the fabric is held taut in a frame or hoop.

If you want a larger knot, increase the plies of thread, not the number of wraps, or make a Colonial Knot (at right).

Use any type of thread.

SUGGESTED USES
Small flowers, flower centers, eyes, curly fur and hair, textured filling

COLONIAL KNOT
Other Names: Candlewick Knot, Figure-8 Knot

DESCRIPTION
Has the appearance of a small, spherical, raised knot, slightly larger than a French Knot (at left) with a slight "dimple" in the center.

HOW TO STITCH
Keep the thread snug around the barrel of the needle as you complete the stitch; note the "figure 8" of thread around the needle.

Insert the tip of the needle a few fabric threads away from the point from which the needle originally emerged.

Works best when the fabric is held taut in a frame or hoop.

Use any type of thread.

SUGGESTED USES
Small flowers, flower centers, eyes, curly fur and hair, textured filling

CHINESE KNOT
Other Names: Peking (Pekin) Knot, Forbidden Knot, Blind Knot

DESCRIPTION
Similar to a French Knot (at left), but with a small "tail."

Typical placement is usually side by side with no space between the knots or between rows of knots.

On the back of fabric, the thread makes a series of short, straight stitches (like a picket fence).

HOW TO STITCH
Snug the thread around the barrel of the needle before you pull it through the fabric.

Work from right to left or from top to bottom.

Use any type of thread, but firm threads retain the distinct character of the knot.

SUGGESTED USES
Outlines, textured filling

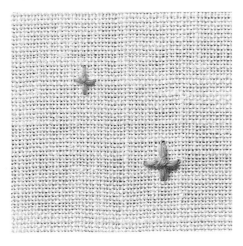

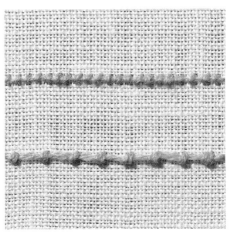

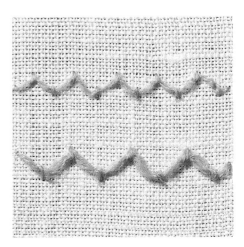

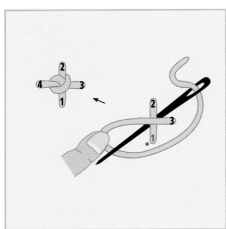

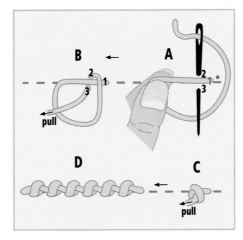

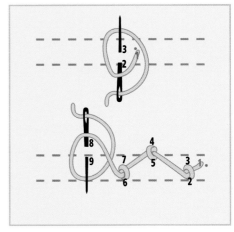

134

FOUR-LEGGED KNOT

DESCRIPTION
Resembles an upright cross with a knot in the center.

This isolated stitch can be grouped or scattered randomly or in a pattern.

The lengths of the legs may vary, but typically are of equal length for any single stitch.

HOW TO STITCH
Pull the thread straight up to tighten the knot before completing stitch.

Use any type of thread.

SUGGESTED USES
Filling, backgrounds (when scattered), borders, stars

CORAL

Other Names: Coral Knot, Beaded Stitch, German Knot, Knotted Stitch, Snail Trail

DESCRIPTION
One of the oldest stitches, used in 17th- and 18th-century English crewel work and German Schwalm work.

Resembles a chain of beads.

Works well for straight or curved lines.

For filling, arrange the rows of knots opposite each other or dovetail them.

HOW TO STITCH
Insert and bring up the needle a short distance apart, so that the knot covers most of this "bite" of fabric.

Insert the needle vertically into the fabric, or at a slight angle.

Work from right to left, or from top to bottom.

For best results, space the knots at short, equal intervals, closer around curves to maintain a smooth line.

Use a firm thread for best results.

SUGGESTED USES
Filling, linework

ZIGZAG CORAL

DESCRIPTION
A decorative zigzag variation of the Coral stitch (at left).

The spacing and angle between the knots may vary.

HOW TO STITCH
Work from right to left or from top to bottom.

To keep the border of equal width, mark two guidelines with an air- or water-soluble pen or thread.

The point of the needle must always face toward the inside of the guidelines.

Use a firm thread for best results.

SUGGESTED USES
Borders, rows, bands

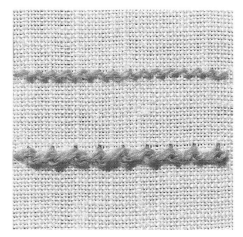

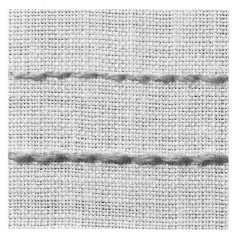

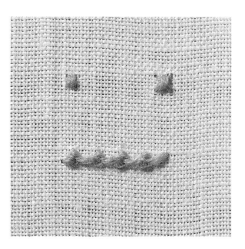

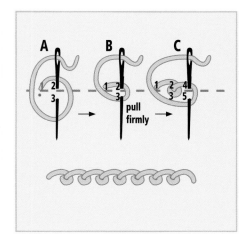

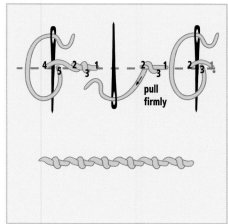

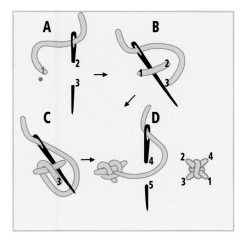

SCROLL
Other Name: Single Knotted Line

DESCRIPTION
This quick and easy stitch creates a line of small wave-like scrolls, each ending in a knot.

The spacing between knots may be close together or widely spaced apart.

HOW TO STITCH
Firmly snug the loop of thread around the needle before pulling needle through to complete stitch.

Work from left to right.

Use any type of thread.

SUGGESTED USES
Borders, filling, outlines, bands, waves or water surface

PEARL

DESCRIPTION
Resembles a string of tiny pearls at evenly spaced intervals.

HOW TO STITCH
To make the "knot" slip to the end of the stitch, pull on the working thread in the direction that the line of stitches is forming.

Work from right to left or from top to bottom.

Use a firm thread for best results.

SUGGESTED USES
Outlines, bands

PALESTRINA KNOT
Other Names: Double Knot, Tied Coral, Old English

DESCRIPTION
Resembles a beaded line (when in a series) or a single squared knot (at lower right).

Works well on curved lines.

HOW TO STITCH
Keep knots evenly and closely spaced.

Note that the needle slides between the knot and the fabric.

Work from left to right (as shown) or from right to left.

Use any type of thread, but a firm thread maintains the character of the stitch.

SUGGESTED USES
Borders, lines, outlines, isolated dots or squares, bands

embroidery stitches

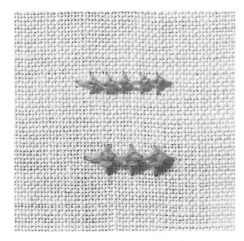

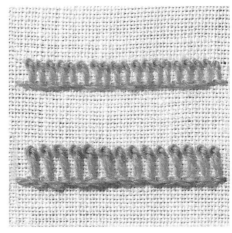

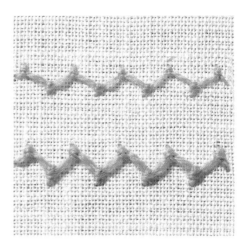

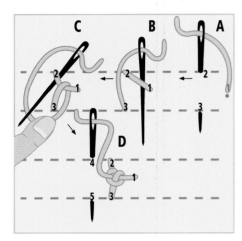

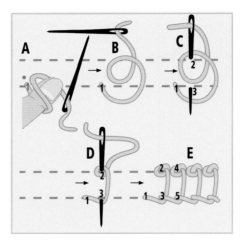

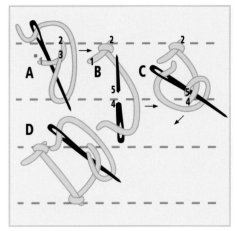

136

BASQUE KNOT
Other Name: Knotted Loop

DESCRIPTION
Don't confuse this highly textured, knotted line stitch with the Loop stitch (page 125) which does not form a knot.

Looks like a reverse Palestrina Knot (page 135) with "wings."

Creates a solid textured filling when rows are dovetailed.

HOW TO STITCH
Snug the first loop against the thread (Step C) before making second loop of the knot.

Hold tension on the thread with your thumb.

Work from right to left.

Use a firm thread for best results.

SUGGESTED USES
Straight and curved bands, filling

KNOTTED BUTTONHOLE

DESCRIPTION
A decorative variation of the Buttonhole stitch (page 122).

The height of the vertical stitch may be even (as shown) or vary.

HOW TO STITCH
Wrap the thread around your thumb once (A); slide loop off thumb (B) and insert the needle through the loop (C).

To keep knots of equal size, snug the thread loop against the needle (D).

Work from left to right.

Use any type of thread.

SUGGESTED USES
Outlines, borders, edgings, bands, flower stamens

KNOTTED INSERTION
Other Name: Knotted Faggot

DESCRIPTION
Decoratively joins two hemmed edges of fabric or creates a decorative zigzag band.

HOW TO STITCH
The needle is always under previously worked legs but over the working thread (steps C and D).

Snug the knot before proceeding to the next stitch.

Use a firm thread for best results.

SUGGESTED USES
Borders, bands, joining pieces of fabric

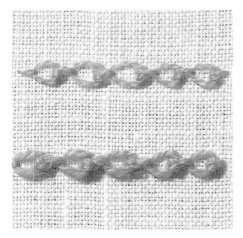

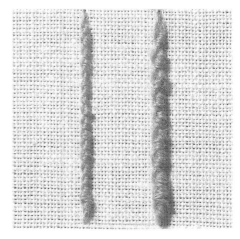

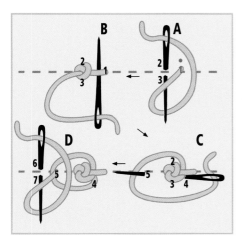
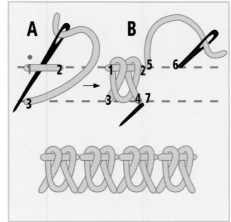
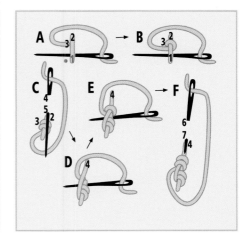

KNOTTED CABLE CHAIN

DESCRIPTION
This decorative combination of the Coral and Chain stitches looks difficult but is quite easy to stitch.

Works well on straight, curved, or angled lines.

HOW TO STITCH
Pierce fabric only at the numbers shown above.

Sliding the needle under the short stitch at the start of the Coral Knot automatically places the knot inside the chain.

Work from right to left.

Use a firm thread to maintain the character of the stitch.

SUGGESTED USES
Lines, borders, bands, necklaces, anchor chains

SORBELLO

DESCRIPTION
Named for the Italian city.

This highly textured square stitch resembles two loops in a square.

Good for filling in geometric designs, similar to Cross stitches.

Works well as a line of stitches that touch, or as isolated stitches.

HOW TO STITCH
Keep the loops loose and the short horizontal stitch straight.

Work from left to right.

Use firm thread to retain the character of the stitch.

SUGGESTED USES
Straight or curved lines, borders, bands, filling

PORTUGUESE KNOTTED STEM

DESCRIPTION
Creates a heavy, knotted, rope-like line.

Works well for straight and curved lines.

HOW TO STITCH
Work from bottom to top (turn fabric if necessary).

Do not pierce fabric when wrapping threads.

The second wrap stitch should always be below the first wrap stitch.

Use any type of thread except fuzzy types.

SUGGESTED USES
Outlines, borders, bands, stems, ropes

137

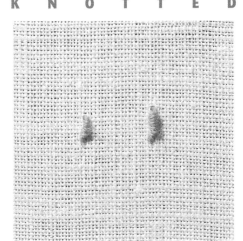

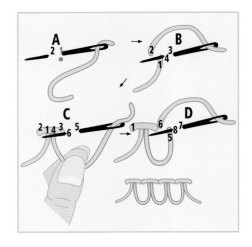

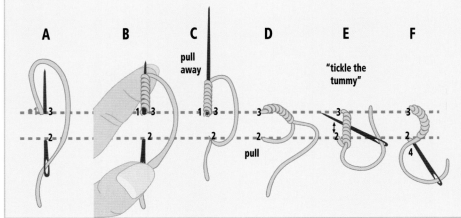

138

TURKEYWORK
Other Name: Plush

DESCRIPTION
Creates a looped or cut pile; cutting the loops produces a shag effect.

The length of the loop determines the depth of the pile.

HOW TO STITCH
Work from the bottom row to the top row.

Tighten each stitch after Step 4.

Use any type of thread.

SUGGESTED USES
Miniature tassels, fringe, animal fur and manes, beards, hair

As you find variations or new stitches not illustrated in this book, add them on pages 142–143 to personalize the Embroidery Stitch Gallery.

BULLION KNOT
Other Names: Caterpillar, Worm, Coil, Knot, Post, Grub, Porto Rico Rose

DESCRIPTION
This versatile stitch resembles a long, coiled knot.

Requires a bit of practice to master.

HOW TO STITCH
1. Wrap thread clockwise around needle (A & B) and hold with finger.
2. Hold wraps with thumb and finger while gently pulling the thread through (C).
3. Tug the wraps away from you (C) then toward you (D).
4. Stroke the underside of the wraps until they look even (E).
5. Insert the needle again at point 2 (F).

The number of thread wraps on the needle is determined by the distance between points 2 and 3; an equal distance will yield a straight knot while more wraps than the distance will yield a curved knot.

Use any type of thread and a milliners needle (page 99).

SUGGESTED USES
Petals, leaves, tips of flower stamens, caterpillars, worms, heavy outlines, insect bodies, roses (when encircled around one or more French Knots), flower buds

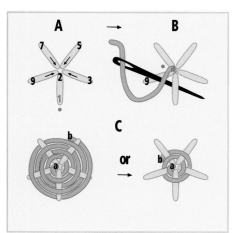
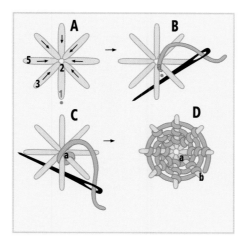
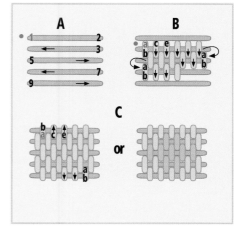

WOVEN SPIDER WEB

DESCRIPTION
Comprised of foundation spokes (usually five) and a second thread woven over and under the spokes.
Effective in one or more colors.

HOW TO STITCH
Begin with a foundation of an odd number of Straight stitches radiating from a central point, like the spokes of a wheel.
The larger the diameter of the design circle, the more spokes are necessary.
If the diameter is small, create the foundation spokes with a single Fly stitch (page 123) and two Straight stitches.
Pull the weaving stitches snugly towards the center for a compact effect or weave somewhat loosely for an entirely different look.
Use any type of thread or ribbon.

SUGGESTED USES
Flowers, spider web, wheels, circles, dots

WHIPPED SPIDER WEB
Other Names: Ribbed or Backstitch Spider Web

DESCRIPTION
Comprised of a series of Backstitches around foundation spokes which resemble a wheel.
Effective in one or more colors.

HOW TO STITCH
Start at center and work clockwise around spokes (backstitch over one spoke, under two spokes, repeat).
The number of spokes may be even or odd.
Pull the whipping stitches snugly towards the center for a compact appearance or space the concentric rings of stitches farther apart to resemble a spider's web.
Use any type of thread.

SUGGESTED USES
Flowers, spider web, wheels, circles, dots

BURDEN
Other Name: Short

DESCRIPTION
Short stitches perpendicular to long, parallel foundation stitches create a woven appearance.
Effective in one or more colors. A darker color works best for the foundation stitches.

HOW TO STITCH
Stitch foundation stitches (horizontal or vertical) using single (shown) or double threads.
For a solid appearance, stitch foundation stitches close together; for a lacy look, space them somewhat apart.
If stitching the short stitches in more than one color, complete each row before proceeding to the next, keeping each thread in a separate needle.
Stitch over the top and bottom foundation stitches last.
Use any non-fuzzy type of thread.

SUGGESTED USES
Filling, baskets, rugs, woven tapestries

embroidery stitches

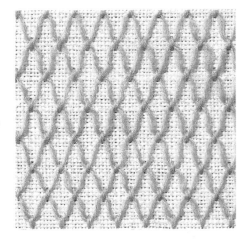
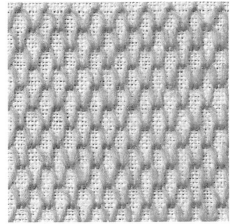
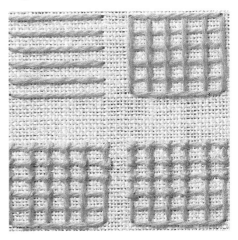

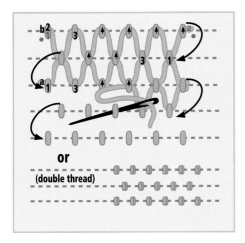
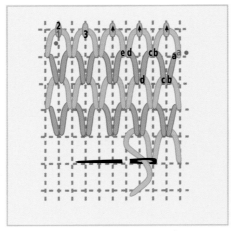
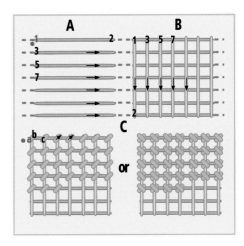

140

CLOUD FILLING
Other Name: Mexican

DESCRIPTION
Comprised of a regularly spaced grid of short vertical stitches woven with a second thread.

Usually stitched in two colors.

HOW TO STITCH
Use a double thread or a thick thread for the short stitches.

Space the short stitches evenly in a checkerboard pattern.

Draw guidelines to help keep stitches even.

Using a tapestry needle, weave the second color thread under the short stitches without piercing the fabric except at the beginning and end of the row.

Use any type of thread.

SUGGESTED USES
Filling

WAVE
Other Name: Wave Filling

DESCRIPTION
Comprised of rows of stitches which loop under the stitches of the previous row.

Most effective when stitches are closely spaced.

Effective in one or more colors.

HOW TO STITCH
Draw guidelines to keep stitches even.

Start at the top of area to be embroidered with a series of short, vertical, evenly spaced stitches.

When stitching the next row, pierce the fabric only at letters (on diagram); do not pierce fabric where the working thread loops under the stitches of the previous row.

Note the compensating stitches at the ends of rows 2 and 4 in diagram.

Don't pull the thread too tightly.

Use any type of thread.

SUGGESTED USES
Filling

SQUARED FILLING
Other Name: Couched Filling

DESCRIPTION
This filling stitch has many variations; all involve long foundation threads held in place by couching threads at the intersections, with various elements added to the empty squares, if desired.

Effective in one or more colors.

Compare to Squared Filling Variations I, II, and III (page 141).

The size of the grid may vary, but keep it consistent within a single area; a larger grid allows more and larger design elements within the grid.

HOW TO STITCH
Stitch horizontal, then vertical stitches for the foundation; couch the foundation at the thread intersections using a diagonal (lower left diagram) or Cross stitch (lower right diagram).

Use any type of thread.

SUGGESTED USES
Filling, borders, bands

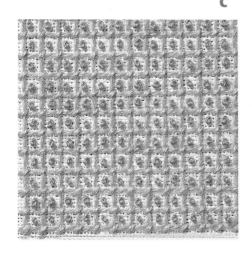

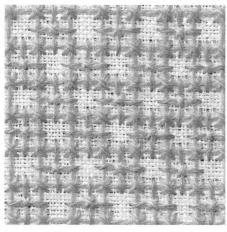

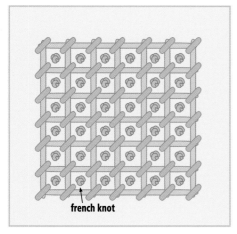
french knot

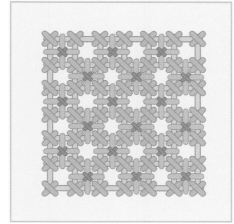

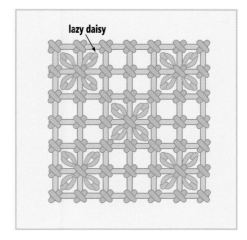
lazy daisy

SQUARED FILLING VARIATION I

DESCRIPTION
This variation of the Squared Filling stitch features diagonal couching threads at the intersections, with French Knots added to the empty squares.
Effective in more than one color.

HOW TO STITCH
As you stitch the foundation, make sure empty squares will be large enough to accommodate the added knots.
Stitch the foundation of basic Squared Filling (page 140); couch the foundation at the thread intersections using a diagonal stitch.
Add French Knots (page 133) centered in the empty spaces.
Use any type of thread.

SUGGESTED USES
Filling

SQUARED FILLING VARIATION II

DESCRIPTION
This variation of the Squared Filling stitch features Cross-stitched couching threads at the intersections, with Upright Cross and Cross stitches added to some of the empty squares in a regular pattern.
Effective in more than one color.

HOW TO STITCH
As you stitch the foundation, make sure empty squares will be large enough to accommodate the added stitches.
Stitch the foundation of basic Squared Filling (page 140); couch the foundation at the thread intersections using a Cross stitch (page 117).
Add Upright Cross stitches (page 117) and Cross stitches to the appropriate empty squares.
Use any type of thread.

SUGGESTED USES
Filling

SQUARED FILLING VARIATION III

DESCRIPTION
This variation of the Squared Filling stitch features Cross-stitched couching threads at the intersections, with Detached Chain stitches added to some of the empty squares in a specific pattern.
Effective in more than one color.

HOW TO STITCH
As you stitch the foundation, make sure empty squares will be large enough to accommodate the added stitches.
Stitch the foundation of basic Squared Filling (page 140); couch the foundation at the thread intersections using a Cross stitch (page 117).
Add Detached Chain stitches (page 130) in the appropriate empty squares.
Use any type of thread.

SUGGESTED USES
Filling

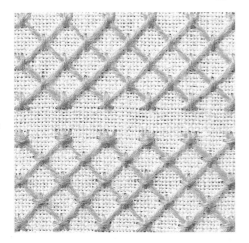

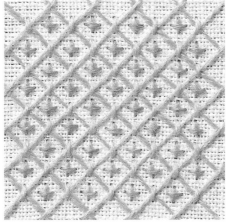

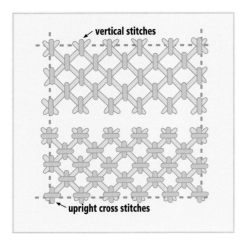

vertical stitches

upright cross stitches

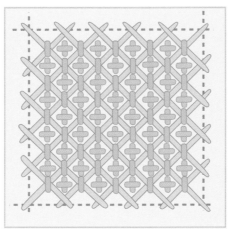

DIAGRAM

142

TRELLIS FILLING
Other Name: Trellis Couching

DESCRIPTION
This filling stitch has many variations; all involve diagonal foundation threads held in place by couching threads at the intersections, with various elements added to the empty diamonds, if desired.
Effective in more than one color.

HOW TO STITCH
As you stitch the foundation, make sure empty diamonds will be large enough to accommodate the added stitches.
Stitch diagonal stitches in both directions for the foundation; couch the foundation at the thread intersections using short horizontal or vertical Straight stitches (upper diagram) or Upright Cross stitches (lower diagram).
Use any type of thread.

SUGGESTED USES
Filling

TRELLIS FILLING VARIATION

DESCRIPTION
This variation of the Trellis Filling stitch features Straight-stitch couching threads at the intersections, with Upright Cross stitches added to the empty squares.
Effective in more than one color.

HOW TO STITCH
As you stitch the foundation, make sure empty diamonds will be large enough to accommodate the added stitches.
Stitch diagonal stitches in both directions for the foundation; couch the foundation at the thread intersections using a short Straight stitch (page 110). Add Upright Cross stitches (page 117) in the empty diamonds.
Use any type of thread.

SUGGESTED USES
Filling

STITCH
Other Names:

DESCRIPTION
_____
_____
_____
_____
_____
_____

HOW TO STITCH
_____
_____
_____
_____
_____
_____
_____
_____
_____
_____
_____
_____

SUGGESTED USES
_____
_____
_____

ATTACH SAMPLE
OR PHOTO HERE

ATTACH SAMPLE
OR PHOTO HERE

ATTACH SAMPLE
OR PHOTO HERE

DIAGRAM

DIAGRAM

DIAGRAM

143

STITCH_____
*Other Names:*_____

DESCRIPTION
_____
_____
_____
_____
_____
_____

HOW TO STITCH
_____
_____
_____
_____
_____
_____
_____
_____
_____
_____
_____
_____
_____

SUGGESTED USES
_____
_____
_____

STITCH_____
*Other Names:*_____

DESCRIPTION
_____
_____
_____
_____
_____
_____

HOW TO STITCH
_____
_____
_____
_____
_____
_____
_____
_____
_____
_____
_____
_____
_____

SUGGESTED USES
_____
_____
_____

STITCH_____
*Other Names:*_____

DESCRIPTION
_____
_____
_____
_____
_____
_____

HOW TO STITCH
_____
_____
_____
_____
_____
_____
_____
_____
_____
_____
_____
_____
_____

SUGGESTED USES
_____
_____
_____

jacobean pomegranate

This faithful adaptation of Jacobean crewel work captures the essence of an ancient symbol of abundance—the pomegranate. In Exodus 39:24 we read: "And they made upon the hem of the robe pomegranates of blue and purple and scarlet and twined linen." As if taking its cue from scripture, this fanciful fruit draws its beauty from the rich tapestry colors of soft wool, with added floss accents and a hint of gold in the dragonfly wings.

DESIGN BY NANCY ROSSI
Finished design size: 10" x 10"
Finished project size: 15½" x 15½"

MATERIALS
½ yd. natural Strathaven linen
Embroidery threads listed in key
Size 9 crewel needle
Two pairs of 18" stretcher bars (or scroll frame with 18" bars)
½ yd. plum-colored fabric (for under-pillow)
17" x 34" polyester clothing-weight fleece
Polyester fiberfill
Beige and plum sewing thread

INSTRUCTIONS
Read Before You Stitch (page 105) and To Begin Stitching (page 106). Select a transfer method; center and transfer the design outline (pages 148–149) to an 18" square of linen fabric. Overcast the edges of the linen and mount it on stretcher bars or a frame.

TO STITCH
Use one strand of wool except where noted in the colored design. See design (pages 146–147) for number of floss strands to use.

To stitch a Woven Picot (page 146), bring up thread and make a loop (A), adjusting it to make a ⅜" picot. Insert a pin (B) over the loop and into the fabric; pass the working threads behind the top of the pin, then slip the needle through the loop. Tighten the stitch gently to form the top of the picot, then weave thread from side to side of the loop (C & D); pull each stitch snug and continue weaving until you reach the ground fabric (E). Secure the end of the thread and remove pin.

TO CONSTRUCT
Use ½" seam allowance.

Trim design fabric to 14½" square, centering design. Cut a second piece of beige fabric and fleece to match. Baste fleece to back of design fabric. With right sides facing, sew design fabric to second beige square, leaving a 4" opening along one side. Trim fleece close to seam, trim corners, turn, and press. Slip-stitch opening closed.

Cut two 16½" squares of plum fabric and one square of fleece. Baste fleece to wrong side of one square of plum fabric. With right sides facing, sew plum fabric squares together, leaving a 4" opening along one side. Trim fleece close to seam, trim corners, turn, and press. Slip-stitch opening closed.

Center and baste wrong side of design unit over under-pillow. Sew together 1¾" from edges of design unit (using a ⅛" stitch length); leave 4" opening for stuffing. Fill lightly with fiberfill, including corners. Sew opening closed.

Designer Nancy Rossi of the Kooler Design Studio uses her experience as an illustrator to create her distinctive needlework designs, which are noteworthy for their inventive, collage-style compositions. Her specialties include needlepoint and crewel work which allow her expertise as a colorist to shine. Also a potter, Nancy studied art at Syracuse University.

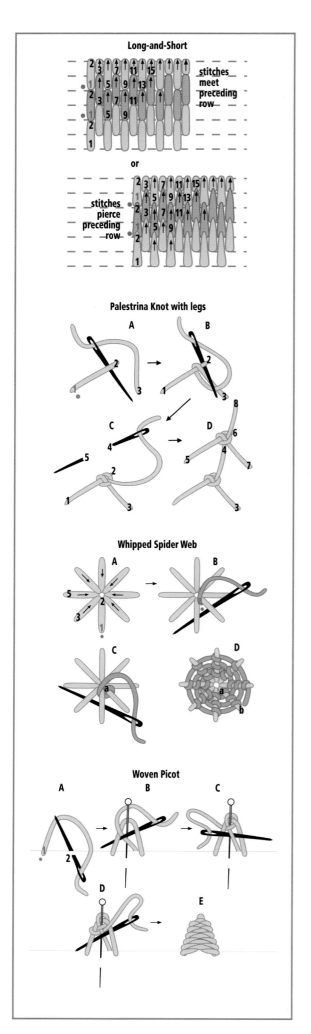

Long-and-Short

2 3 5 7 9 11 13 15
stitches meet preceding row

2 3 5 7 9 11 13 15
1
or

2 3 5 7 9 11 13 15
stitches pierce preceding row

Palestrina Knot with legs

A   B
C   D

Whipped Spider Web

A   B
C   D

Woven Picot

A   B   C
D   E

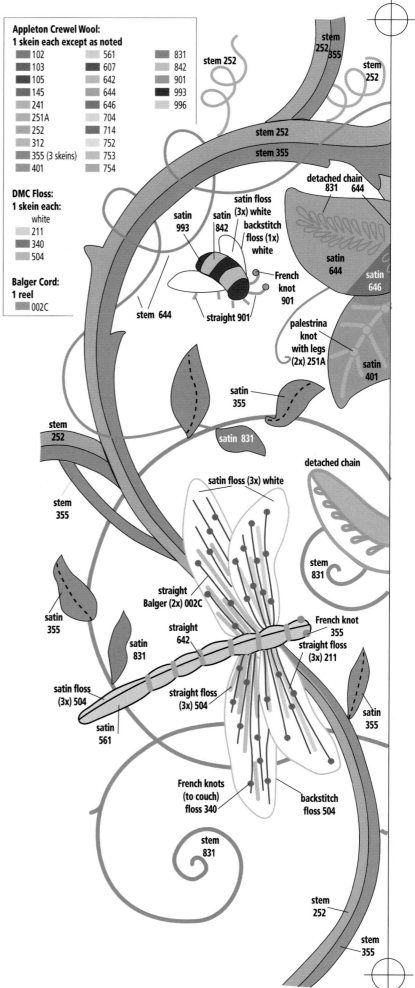

Appleton Crewel Wool:
1 skein each except as noted

102	561	831
103	607	842
105	642	901
145	644	993
241	646	996
251A	704	
252	714	
312	752	
355 (3 skeins)	753	
401	754	

DMC Floss:
1 skein each:
white
211
340
504

Balger Cord:
1 reel
002C

stem 252 355

stem 252

stem 252

stem 252 355

stem 252

stem 355

detached chain 831 644

satin 993

satin floss (3x) white

satin 842

backstitch floss (1x) white

satin 644

satin 646

French knot 901

stem 644

straight 901

palestrina knot with legs (2x) 251A

satin 401

satin 355

satin 831

stem 252

stem 355

satin floss (3x) white

detached chain

stem 831

straight Balger (2x) 002C

satin 355

satin 831

straight 642

straight 504

French knot 355

straight floss (3x) 211

satin floss (3x) 504

straight floss (3x) 504

satin 355

satin 561

French knots (to couch) floss 340

backstitch floss 504

stem 831

stem 252

stem 355

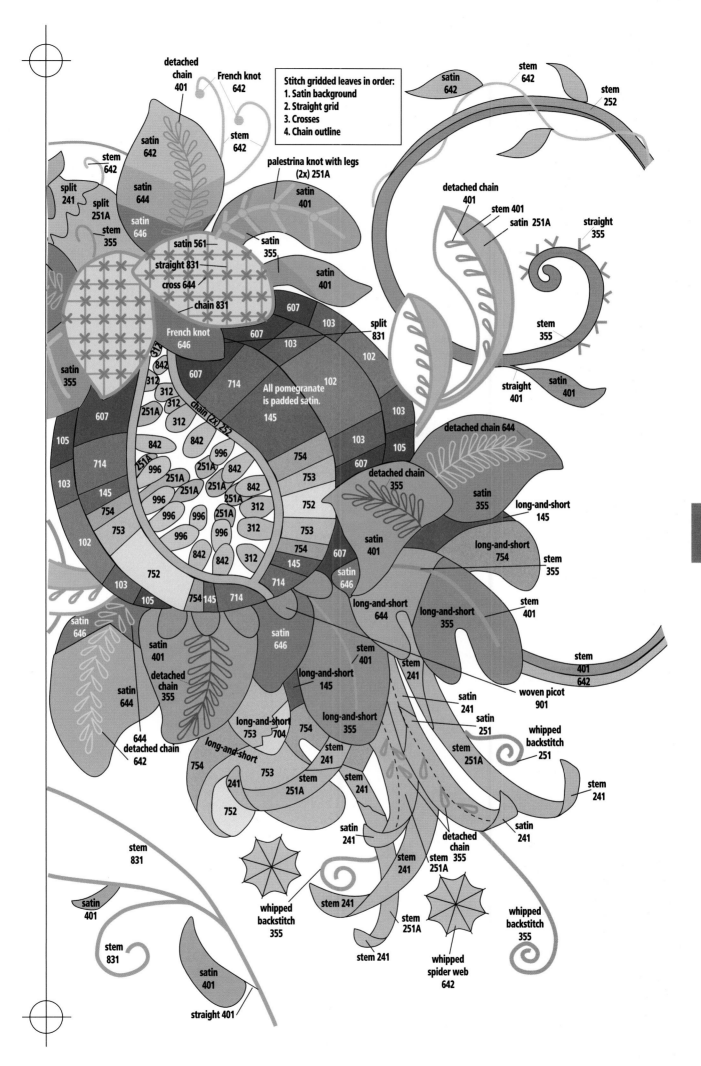

detached chain 401

French knot 642

satin 642

stem 642

stem 642

satin 642

stem 642

stem 252

Stitch gridded leaves in order:
1. Satin background
2. Straight grid
3. Crosses
4. Chain outline

detached chain 401

stem 401

satin 251A

straight 355

split 241

split 251A

stem 355

satin 646

palestrina knot with legs (2x) 251A

satin 401

satin 355

satin 401

satin 561

straight 831

cross 644

chain 831

French knot 646

satin 355

607

607

103

103

102

split 831

straight 355

stem 355

312

842

312

607

312

251A

714

All pomegranate is padded satin.

145

102

103

straight 401

satin 401

842

312

312

chain (2x) 252

103

105

detached chain 644

607

105

714

842

251A

996

842

996

satin 355

103

145

251A

251A

251A

996

251A

842

754

753

detached chain 355

long-and-short 145

754

251A

996

251A

842

312

752

long-and-short 754

753

996

996

996

251A

312

753

satin 401

stem 355

102

753

842

312

607

satin 646

long-and-short 355

stem 401

752

842

842

312

754

satin 646

103

754

145

714

long-and-short 644

satin 646

105

754

145

714

stem 401

satin 401

detached chain 355

satin 241

satin 251

stem 401

stem 241

long-and-short 145

woven picot 901

satin 644

644 detached chain 642

long-and-short 753 704

754

long-and-short 355

stem 241

satin 241

satin 241

stem 251A

whipped backstitch 251

long-and-short 754

753

stem 241

stem 241

stem 241

stem 241

satin 241

detached chain 355 stem 251A

satin 241

stem 241

241

752

stem 831

satin 401

whipped backstitch 355

stem 241

stem 241

stem 251A

whipped backstitch 355

stem 831

whipped spider web 642

satin 401

straight 401

stem 241

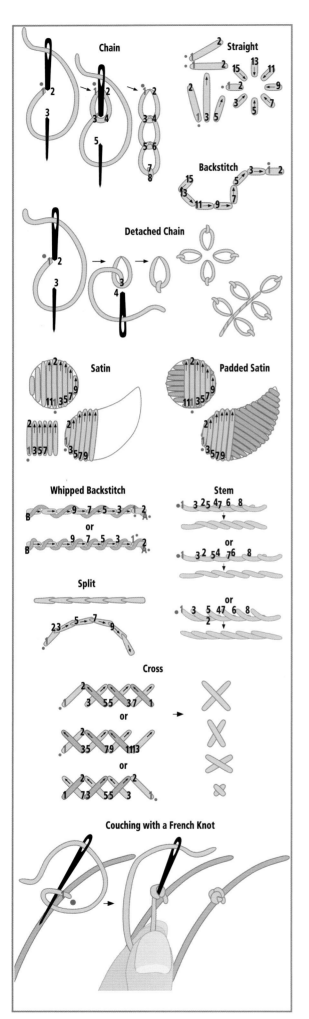

Chain

Straight

Backstitch

Detached Chain

Satin

Padded Satin

Whipped Backstitch

or

Stem

or

Split

or

Cross

or

or

Couching with a French Knot

flight of fancy

A winged beauty spreads its gaudy wings and pauses mid-flight upon a delicate trellis. The setting, hearkening back to an 18th-century garden, is composed of deceptively simple stitches suitable for a beginning embroiderer. The butterfly is essentially composed of satin stitches, allowing the brilliant colors to steal the show on this diminutive boudoir pillow. The trellis and border are an ideal introduction to candlewicking, a favorite American folk art.

DESIGN BY BARBARA BAATZ

Finished design size: 5⅜" x 5⅜"
Finished project size: 9" x 9"

MATERIALS
½ yd. natural muslin
Ecru candlewicking thread
Floss listed in key
8"-sq. polyester fleece
Ecru sewing thread
Polyester fiberfill
Two pairs of 12" stretcher bars (or scroll
    frame with 12" bars)

INSTRUCTIONS
Read Before You Stitch (page 105) and To Begin Stitching (page 106). Select a transfer method and transfer the design outline (page 152) to a 12" square of muslin; center the design. Overcast the edges of the design fabric and mount it on stretcher bars or a frame.

TO STITCH
CANDLEWICKING MOTIFS (trellis and border): Use one strand of candlewicking thread for Padded Satin and Stem stitches, Backstitches, and Colonial Knots.

BUTTERFLY: Use two strands of cotton floss for Backstitches, French Knots, and Satin/Split stitches. Begin Satin stitches along outer edges of wings; when you proceed to the lighter colors, use the Split stitch, splitting the previously made stitches. Complete the light-colored spots last, splitting the stitches that surround them.

Read When Stitching Is Complete (page 107) and wash design fabric.

TO FINISH
Use ½" seam allowance.

Trim design fabric 8" square, centering design. For backing, cut one piece of muslin 8" square.

For ruffle, cut two 4" x 28" pieces of muslin. With right sides facing, join short ends to form a continuous loop. Fold ruffle with wrong sides together (do not press) and fill with small pieces of fiberfill (loose, 1"-dia. bunches, do not pack tightly) as you machine-gather together ½" and ¼" from raw edges. Pull up gathers to fit outer edges of design fabric. Baste to right side of design unit, positioning ruffle seams at sides of design.

With right sides facing, sew backing to design unit, leaving a 4" opening on one side. Trim corners and turn right side out. Fill pillow firmly with fiberfill and slip-stitch opening closed. ✿

Designer Barbara Baatz has been a member of the Kooler Design Studio for nine years. She has earned respect for her work in virtually all disciplines of needlework, including needlepoint, cross-stitch, and embroidery, as well as many other craft projects.

Watercolor quilt courtesy of Whims, Inc.

FLIGHT OF FANCY

Ecru Candlewick Thread		Anchor	DMC Floss
Backstitch:			**Backstitch:**
trellis (1x)		152	939 navy blue - vy dk
Colonial knot:			**French Knot:**
● ● trellis/ borders (1x, 1-wrap)		152	● ● 939 navy blue - vy dk
Padded Satin:			**Satin/Split:**
borders (1x)		50	605 cranberry - vy lt
Stem:		271	819 baby pink - lt
borders (1x)		29	891 carnation - dk
		27	893 carnation - lt
		152	939 navy blue - vy dk
		355	975 golden brown - dk
		119	3746 blue violet - dk
		885	3823 yellow - ultra pale

STITCH DIAGRAMS FOR FLIGHT OF FANCY

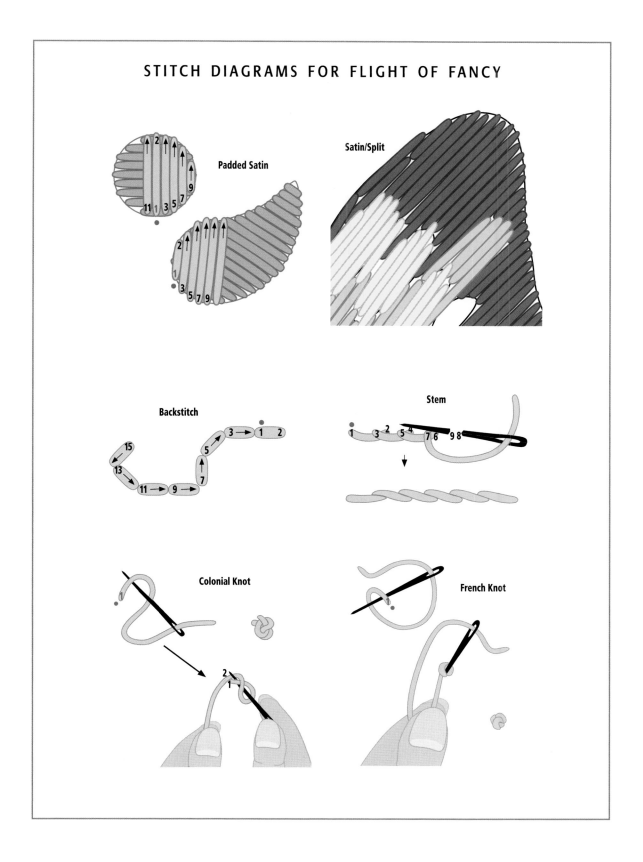

Padded Satin

Satin/Split

Backstitch

Stem

Colonial Knot

French Knot

silk garden

May we agree that silk is the queen of fibers? And flowers the crown jewels of creation? Then what shall we call this royal marriage of silk and blossoms... an artist's vision, a gardener's dream, a stitcher's delight? This opulent botanical garden, reminiscent of floral designs popular in the Elizabethan Age, derives its delicate beauty from fine silk ribbons that capture the essence of petals, vines, and leaves from nature's own designs.

DESIGN BY DEANNA HALL WEST
Finished design size: 9½" x 6"
Finished project size: 38" x 38"

MATERIALS
1¼ yd. green lightweight silk crepe de chine (or purchased 40"-sq. scarf)
Silk ribbon and floss listed in color key
Size 20 chenille needle
Embroidery hoop, 10"-dia. (or wider)
Green sewing thread to match fabric

INSTRUCTIONS
Read Before You Stitch (page 105) and To Begin Stitching (page 106). Overcast the edges of the design fabric. Select a transfer method and transfer the design outline (page 156) to one corner of fabric, 2½" from overcast edges. Mount the fabric on the hoop (make sure inner hoop is wrapped with fabric).

TO STITCH
See color keys for size and color of ribbon, and number of floss strands to use.

TO CONSTRUCT
Trim off overcast edges, making sure that fabric is perfectly square. With right sides facing, fold in half so design corner matches opposite corner. Using ¼" seam allowance, machine-sew raw edges together, leaving a 4" opening for turning. Trim corners, turn right side out, press edges lightly, and slip-stitch opening closed. Topstitch ⅛" from all three edges (both seamed and folded).

If you used a purchased scarf for your ground fabric, it's a good idea to sew it into a triangle to conceal the back of the stitching. Fold the scarf in half along the bias and topstitch or whipstitch the straight edges together. 🌼

Designer Deanna Hall West of the Kooler Design Studio, the Editorial Director of this book, is a needlework editor, teacher, and designer of a series of silk ribbon embroidery books. Knowledgeable in needlework history, techniques, and fibers, Deanna also has an undergraduate degree in biology and a master's degree in botany.

FLOSS STITCHES

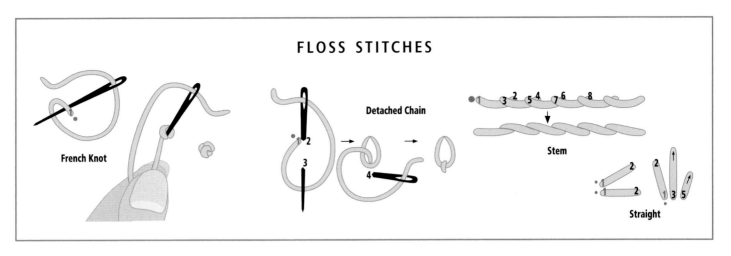

French Knot

Detached Chain

Stem

Straight

SILK GARDEN

Anchor		DMC floss	
French Knot:			
302	○	743	yellow - med
---	●	5282	gold metallic
Detached Chain:			
---	⬭	5282	gold metallic (1X)
Stem:			
266	⠒	3347	yellow-green - med (2X)
266	⠒	3347	yellow-green - med 1X
---	⠒	5282	gold metallic (2X)
Straight:			
266	╱	3347	yellow-green - med (2X)
85	╱	3609	plum - ultra lt
---	╱	5282	gold metallic (2X)
---	╱	5282	gold metallic (1X)

Transfer this pattern to fabric. Use the key at left for floss colors and stitches. Use the key below for ribbon stitches; see drawing on page 157 for ribbon colors.

Ribbon symbols
(refer to color chart for ribbon colors):

○	**Colonial Knot**
●	**French Knot**
⬭	**Detached Chain**
⌐○	**Ribbon**
⊙	**Spider Web Rose**
╱	**Straight**
Ø	**Straight over Colonial Knot**
▽	**Tacked Loop**
✕	**Tacked Straight**

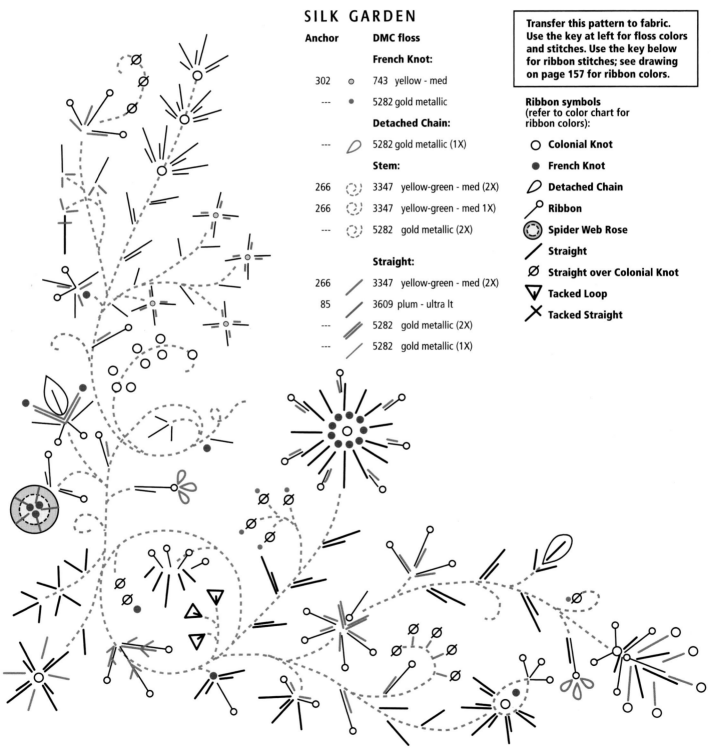

RIBBON STITCHES

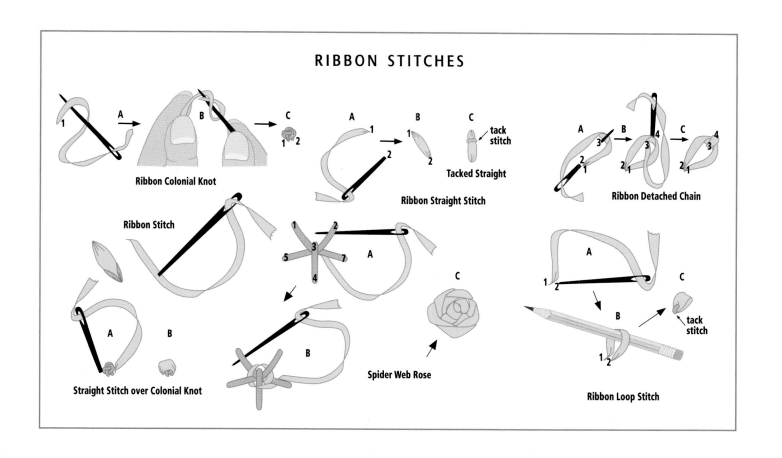

Ribbon Colonial Knot

Ribbon Straight Stitch

tack stitch

Tacked Straight

Ribbon Detached Chain

Ribbon Stitch

Straight Stitch over Colonial Knot

Spider Web Rose

Ribbon Loop Stitch

tack stitch

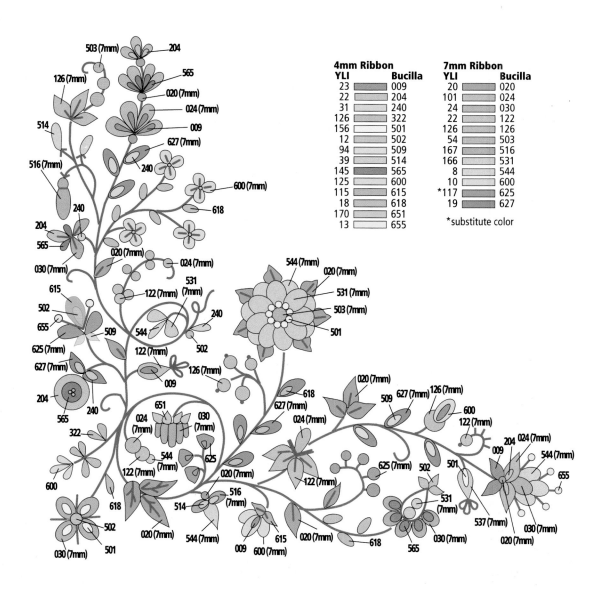

4mm Ribbon			
YLI	**Bucilla**		
23	009		
22	204		
31	240		
126	322		
156	501		
12	502		
94	509		
39	514		
145	565		
125	600		
115	615		
18	618		
170	651		
13	655		

7mm Ribbon	
YLI	**Bucilla**
20	020
101	024
24	030
22	122
126	126
54	503
167	516
166	531
8	544
10	600
*117	625
19	627

*substitute color

rosa blanca

The pristine beauty of white-on-white, drawing its definition from the play of light and shadow, takes shape as a single, elegant rose. In this splendid example of Renaissance cutwork, sturdy buttonhole stitches delineate the design, which will stand out in relief after you cut away the fabric of the background. The result is a gem of a jewelry pouch, worthy of your most precious items of adornment.

DESIGN BY DIANE CLEMENTS
Finished Design Size: 7" x 3"
Finished Project Size: 7" x 5"

MATERIALS
24" x 18" white linen (Ulster)
One ball White Cebelia #30 (DMC)
#8 embroidery needle
Small, thin, curved-blade scissors
Thimble
Light blue chalk pencil
5"-dia. wooden embroidery hoop
Dawn® dishwashing detergent
White sewing thread
¾"-dia. magnetic snap
White, non-woven, heavyweight
   interfacing

INSTRUCTIONS
FABRIC PREPARATION
Preshrink the linen by soaking it in a solution of dishwashing detergent and warm water, then rinsing thoroughly in cool water. Press until completely dry.

For the flap (the design fabric), cut a 12½" x 9½" piece of linen.

Using a light box or other light source, transfer the pattern to the right side of the flap: lay the pattern under the linen, with the outer curve of the design 2" from one long edge of fabric. Trace all lines, including the bars, with the chalk pencil.

TO STITCH
For all stitches, use the sewing method rather than stab method. Do not carry the thread between design lines. Mount the linen in the embroidery hoop.

DESIGN LINE #1 (OUTER SCALLOPED EDGE): Beginning at #1, stitch the padding of uneven Running stitches, one width of the Cebelia inside/above the design line (Fig. 1). Add thread as needed by leaving a tail on the front then slipping through a few padding stitches and continuing with Running stitches. Work the second

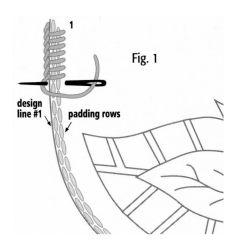

Fig. 1

design line #1   padding rows

row of padding between the first row and the design line in a bricked pattern. Continue with the thread in the needle if it's in very good condition; otherwise start a new thread. Next, beginning at #1, make Buttonhole stitches over the padding and design line (Fig. 1). Clip off the padding tails as the Buttonhole stitches approach them.

design line #1

1

design line #2

2

design line #3

3

5

9

10

11

8

7

6

4

5

3

4

160

Add more thread as needed (Figs. 2a and 2b).

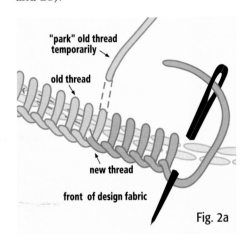

"park" old thread temporarily

old thread

new thread

front of design fabric

Fig. 2a

pull old thread from front and secure under back of new stitches

old thread

new thread

back of design fabric

Fig. 2b

At the inside corners, make the center stitch longer than its neighbors (Fig. 3).

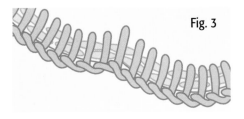

Fig. 3

DESIGN LINE #2 (INNER SCALLOPED EDGE AND BARS): Beginning at #2, work the first row of padding and the Buttonhole bars as they occur (Fig. 4); stitch three taut core

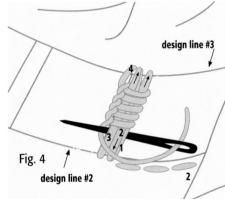

design line #3

4

3 2

2 1

design line #2

2

Fig. 4

threads as shown, then make firm Buttonhole stitches over the core threads, leaving ¹⁄₁₆" unworked between the padding and the first and last Buttonhole stitches on the bar to accommodate Buttonhole stitches to be worked later along the design lines.

To make the Y-shaped buttonhole bars, make three core threads for the long segment, and work Buttonhole stitches to the intersection of the Y (Fig. 5). Make three core threads for the short segment and work Buttonhole stitches back to the intersection. Insert the needle up between the last two stitches on

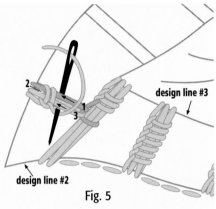

design line #3

2

1

3

design line #2

Fig. 5

the long segment of the Y and continue stitching to the design line (Fig. 6).

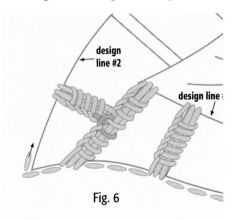

design line #2

design line

Fig. 6

Work the second row of padding, slipping under or through the anchors for the bars. Work Buttonhole stitches over the padding and design line.

DESIGN LINES #3–#11 (LEAVES, PETALS, AND FLOWER CENTER): Work these shapes in the same sequence: padding and then

Buttonhole stitches. For outside corners and circles, see Figs. 7 and 8.

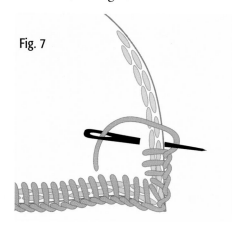

Fig. 7

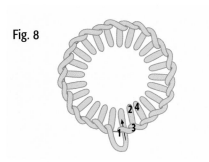

Fig. 8

LEAF VEINS: Use Outline stitches (Fig. 9) to make the center vein first. *Whip on wrong side to a side vein and

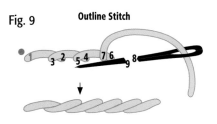

Fig. 9   Outline Stitch

work it from the center vein to the end.* Repeat ** for remaining leaf veins. End off the thread as you complete each leaf.

PETAL DETAIL: Use Backstitches (Fig. 10) to work the longer of the two lines from the center toward the edge of

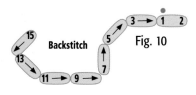

Backstitch   Fig. 10

the petal. Whip on the wrong side to the beginning and carry thread to the second line. Backstitch the second line. End off the thread upon completion of each petal.

TO CLEAN

To remove chalk markings and any spots and stains, soak in a solution of dish-washing detergent and lukewarm water. It will take approximately two hours for the chalk to disappear. Rinse thoroughly in cool water.

While the linen is still wet, press right side down on a white terry towel until completely dry.

TO CUT

Allow a 2" assembly allowance on the top edge of the flap and ⅝" on each side of the 2" allowance (Fig. 11).

From the wrong side of the design, trim closely next to the looped edge of

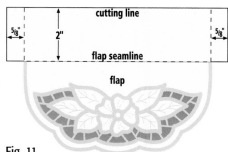

Fig. 11

the Buttonhole stitches along the scalloped edge, using the small, curved scissors. On the right side, cut along the center of the areas to be cut out (black area on pattern) and into each inside corner. Turn to the wrong side and trim closely next to the Buttonhole stitches.

TO FINISH

Cut a 8⅛" x 14" piece of linen (Fig. 12). With right sides facing, sew the flap to one short side of the pouch piece, using a 2" seam.

With wrong sides facing, fold the pouch piece in half, matching the sides and top. Sew a ⅜" seam along each side of the pouch, including the extensions on the flap. Trim to a scant ¼". Press open.

With right sides facing, sew a ¼" seam along each pouch side, enclosing the raw edge, taking care to avoid catching the embroidered area.

Turn under 1" twice on the pouch front, back, and flap. Pin in place.

Cut four 1" x 1½" pieces of interfacing. Slip one piece of interfacing inside

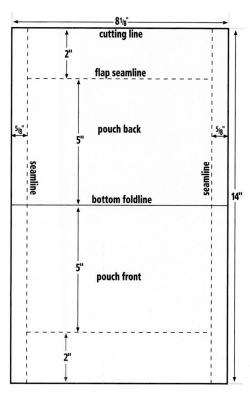

Fig. 12

the folds of front and back as reinforcement for the snap (Fig. 13). Position and insert the magnetic snap halves inside

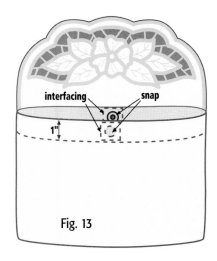

Fig. 13

the pouch. Slip a second piece of interfacing behind the snap to prevent it from showing through to the outside of the pouch. Sew the folded edge down by hand or machine, taking care to avoid catching the embroidered area. ❀

Designer Diane Clements has pursued needlework in a variety of techniques since childhood, with a particular interest in lace-making and whitework. She is an accomplished teacher, needlework judge, and award-winner for her original embroidery.

161

petite fleur

As delicate as a teasing breeze, as subtle as the scent of a night-blooming garden, shadow work works its magic on pure white batiste. A faint tint of color, echoing the outline threads, appears as an illusion. Atop a porcelain treasure box, the beribboned bouquet of forget-me-nots is reminiscent of the fine shadow work popular in the early years of the 20th Century when dainty handwork was fashionable.

DESIGN BY DIANE CLEMENTS
Finished design size: 3½" diameter
Finished project size: 5¼" diameter x 2¾" high

MATERIALS
8"-sq. white batiste
Niagara® Original Spray Starch, Professional Finish
DMC cotton floss # 341, #523, #3823, #3824
One package Mill Hill petite glass beads #40161
Framecraft ivory porcelain bowl w/ 3½"-dia. lid
Clear, transparent nylon thread
#28 tapestry needle
#12 short beading needle
.5mm mechanical pencil with 2H lead
8"-sq. cream-colored moiré taffeta
5"-dia. wooden embroidery hoop (both rings wrapped with white bias tape)
5"-dia. regular-weight quilt batting
Dawn® dishwashing detergent
Double-stick tape

INSTRUCTIONS
TO TRANSFER
Lay the batiste on a white terry towel. Apply spray starch to one side and press dry. Lift the cooled batiste off the towel and lay it on the ironing board, starched side up. Iron back and forth several times to take out the towel impressions.

Note that the printed design (page 165) is already reversed, and that you will be stitching on the wrong side of the fabric. With the starched side (wrong side) of the batiste up, center and place it over the pattern and trace all lines with the mechanical pencil, taking care not to distort the fabric by dragging the pencil.

Center and mount the batiste in the embroidery hoop.

TO STITCH
FLOWER PETALS: Use one strand of #341 floss. Work the most prominent petal first and continue to work the petals in each flower from foreground to background.

Begin on the top line at the base of the petal with an away waste tail (no knot) twice as long as the #28 tapestry needle (Fig. 1). The small Backstitches that show on the right side should be less than 1mm long.

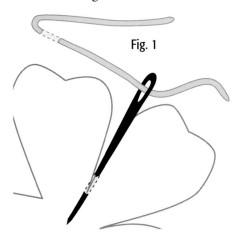

Fig. 1

When moving from the top line to the bottom line, hold the thread above the needle (Fig. 2).

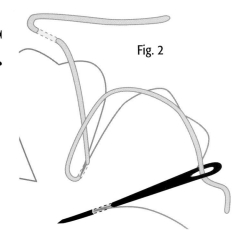

Fig. 2

When moving from the bottom line to the top line, hold the thread below the needle. The needle exits the same hole that the previous stitch entered, sharing the hole (Fig. 3).

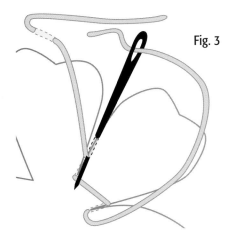

Fig. 3

Continue the Closed Herringbone stitch until you reach the top of the petal (Fig. 4). Six Backstitches will show on the right side of each side of the petal.

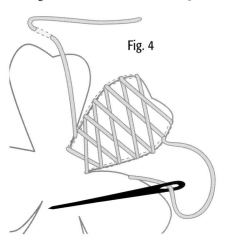

Fig. 4

Turn the work so the petal is oriented as shown in Fig. 5. With the thread above the needle, make the next stitch.

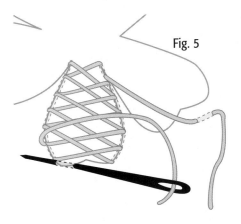

Fig. 5

Hold the thread above the needle and work Outline stitches left to right on the drawn line; the needle exits out of the hole the previous stitch entered (Fig. 6).

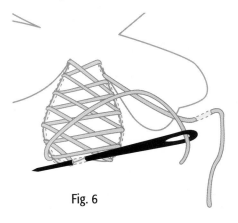

Fig. 6

Outline-stitch to the other side of the petal. Check that the shape has been surrounded by Backstitches on the right side of the fabric.

To end the thread, slip the needle through the stitches along the petal top. End the beginning waste tail by slipping through the stitches on the petal side. Clip off both tails. Keep these tails as close to the edges as possible to maintain the even shadow on the right side.

When stitching a petal that shares a design line with a previously worked petal, avoid a double line of Backstitches on the right side by using the holes made while working the previous petal.

LEAVES: Use one strand of #523. Outline-stitch from the center of the leaf to the base (Fig. 7a). To begin the closed Herringbone stitch on the rounded end,

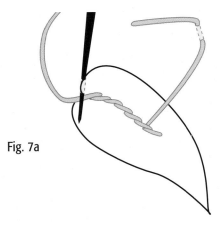

Fig. 7a

make a stitch on each side of the vein (Figs. 7a and 7b) and work to the point

Fig. 7b

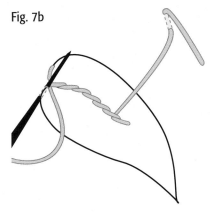

of the leaf. End off the beginning and ending tails.

RIBBON: Use one strand of #3824. This motif is composed of fourteen connected shapes; work them in numerical order, from foreground to background (Fig. 8). Plan to end off a thread upon

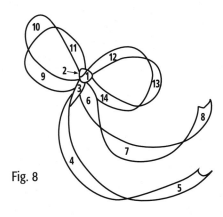

Fig. 8

completion of a shape. Begin another thread in the next shape.

To stitch the knot of the bow, turn the work so the knot is oriented as

PATTERN FOR PETITE FLEUR

shown in Fig. 9. Note that the top line of the shape is longer than the bottom

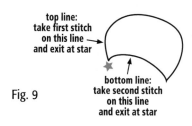

top line:
take first stitch
on this line
and exit at star

bottom line:
take second stitch
on this line
and exit at star

Fig. 9

line, so the stitches on the shorter line must be shorter than those on the longer line to produce a continuous shadow on the right side. Begin any shape with unequal-length lines on the longer line to establish the optimum length stitch.

To move from a shape with a pointed end to a shape with a pointed beginning, make the first stitch in the new shape on the longer line. Keep the thread within the design area to maintain the shape. Four stitches share the hole at the intersection. Finish the tail on shape #5 with two Outline stitches.

FLOWER CENTERS: Use one strand of #3823. Make three Colonial Knots (Fig. 10) in a triangular pattern for each flower.

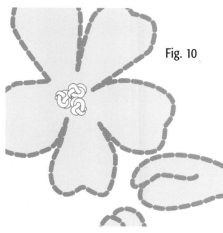

Fig. 10

TO CLEAN

After rubbing a drop of detergent directly on the pencil marks, soak overnight in a solution of dishwashing detergent and lukewarm water. Rinse thoroughly in cool water. Press right side down on a white terry towel.

ADD BEADS: Lay the wrong side of the batiste atop the right side of the taffeta fabric. Baste these two layers together near the edges. (The underlining will add depth of color and mask the thread that trails between the beads.)

Use the transparent nylon thread and make two stitches to hold each bead flat on the fabric (Fig. 11). Refer to the pho-

Attaching a bead

Fig. 11

tograph or position the beads as desired amongst the flowers.

TO FINISH

Cut the embroidered fabric unit into a 6" circle, with the design centered. Baste a line around the circle ¼" from the edge. Lay the embroidery right side down and center the circle of quilt batting atop the wrong side of the embroidery.

Trim the clear acetate (included with porcelain bowl) to 3½" in diameter and place it on top of the batting. Pull on the basting thread to gather the fabric around the batting and acetate. Place design unit inside the edge of the lid. Place the raised side of the metal locking disk toward the gathers and firmly push it into the lid. Use double-stick tape to attach the lid liner to the metal disk. ❀

Designer Diane Clements is a teacher for The Embroiderers' Guild of America, Inc., in her local chapter in Northern California as well as the Greater Pacific and Rocky Mountain regional seminars. Her specialties include fine machine sewing, silk and metal work, Japanese embroidery, canvas embroidery, and quilting.

165

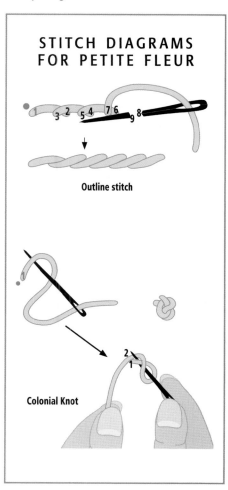

STITCH DIAGRAMS FOR PETITE FLEUR

3 2 5 4 7 6 8

Outline stitch

Colonial Knot

2
1

counted thread

 Of the three groups of needlework presented in this book, COUNTED THREAD is the most diverse. Sharing a common ancestry with needlepoint, the branches of the counted thread family tree reach out in many directions, but share one thing in common: they require the stitcher to count threads of an evenly woven fabric. Appropriate fabric for counted thread is softer and finer than needlepoint canvas, and matches our notion of what true fabric looks like. Counted thread work may entirely fill the fabric, but more commonly leaves portions of the fabric unstitched; in this sense it resembles surface embroidery.

Counted thread offers much variety in its degrees of complexity. Techniques such as cross-stitch and Swedish weaving are easy to learn and master, while complex drawn thread work and advanced Hardanger challenge the stitcher. There is truly something for every level of skill and experience, and certainly a great diversity in appearance.

Pulled thread, drawn thread, and hemstitching are sometimes grouped together under the heading of whitework, meaning they are traditionally worked in white thread on white fabric. Drawn thread, hemstitching, and Hardanger also may be categorized as openwork because they involve cutting away of portions of the ground fabric to create open, lacy effects.

Historical samplers display examples of many of these techniques, and continue to provide contemporary designers with an almost inexhaustible supply of stitches, motifs, and inspiration. It's no accident that the Counted Thread Stitch Gallery is longer than those of the other chapters and has the most subgroups: Sampler, Blackwork, Pulled Work, Hardanger, Drawn Work, Edgings. What a treasure house of stitching history is contained within!

Sampler; Scotland, embroidery on linen. Courtesy of Fine Arts Museums of San Francisco, Gift of Mrs. Hilda R. Nuttall in memory of Magdelina Nuttall, DY52814.

ORIGINS OF COUNTED THREAD

Just as the development of embroidery is linked to the invention of silk textiles, so the emergence of counted thread work coincides with the production of linen cloth. Archeologists have found fragments of tools used to manufacture linen in the sites of Swiss lake dwellers who lived around 8000 BC.

Linen makes a splendid ground fabric for stitching, from the relatively coarse, low thread counts to very fine, high counts that tax the eyesight. The flax fiber looks beautiful even if not bleached or dyed; the variations in color of the natural fibers are subtle and rich. Early linen fabric woven by hand was often not an evenweave, which affected the shape of the stitches, making square stitches appear oblong. The development of modern looms created true evenweaves in which the number of warp threads per inch exactly matched the number of weft threads per inch.

Folk costumes from around the world display geometric stitched designs that are obviously counted thread work. Many cultures stitch their most powerful symbols on ceremonial textiles, whether they be Christian crosses on Cyprus lace or the sacred peyote flower on clothing of the Huichol Indians of Mexico. What's fascinating is that some of the same stitches show up at far-flung locations—the cross stitch, darning stitches, and variations of the Florentine stitch, for instance.

One of the greatest impulses that spurred the development of counted thread work was the desire to mimic expensive bobbin lace. It's impossible to overestimate the importance of lace in fashions from the Renaissance through the Baroque era. Lacemaking was a painstaking process, and well-made lace was worth a fortune, sometimes used as currency and contraband. Aristocrats, clergymen, and wealthy merchants wore lace to proclaim their elevated status much as people today wear costly jewels. The human desire for upward mobility led to the invention of stitching directly onto fabric to re-create the look of true *punto in aria* (Italian for "stitch in the air") lace that was not worked on ground fabric. Pulled thread, drawn thread, Hardanger, and even American "chicken scratch" are all attempts to simulate true lace, and succeed admirably.

Of great interest to modern stitchers is the development of counted thread samplers, which deserves its own story…

SAMPLERS

In recent years, samplers have been rediscovered, assessed anew, and valued as much or more than they were when they were first stitched. Worthy of their own museum shows, learned symposiums, and scholarly treatises, samplers are now considered a fine art, commanding exorbitant prices for antique originals in good condition.

Stitchers and non-stitchers around the world are beguiled by these sometimes imperfect but always intriguing specimens stitched by girls and young women. Some stitchers of today love to duplicate samplers of yesteryear, looking for the right combination of softly aged thread colors and natural linen. Contemporary needlework designers use old samplers as springboards for new designs, borrowing a motif here, an alphabet there, for "new" samplers with vintage appeal.

Archeologists have found samplers in Peru and dated them approximately 200–500 AD; they appear to be compilations of many small motifs. Some of the earliest European samplers were notebooks of designs that stitchers fancied. Favorite motifs would be copied from books or other stitchers' work, "stored" on a sampler known later as a "spot" or band sampler and perhaps used subsequently on another project.

The earliest sampler in existence that bears an actual, stitched date (1598) and name is that of Jane Bostocke, an Englishwoman. Jane's famous sampler is filled with numerous blackwork patterns, a few flowers and a small dog, lettered inscriptions, and decorated with tiny beads and metal threads. Other historical samplers show multiple motifs of various techniques such as drawn thread and darning patterns.

Perhaps the samplers that evoke the greatest emotional resonance for women today are those that were stitched from the 17th through the early 19th Centuries to demonstrate the completion of a young woman's formal education, which was often limited to stitching and music. Samplers from these centuries are as many and varied as the individuals who stitched them, and are composed of almost every type of fiber imaginable, including human hair.

English "band" samplers of the 17th century feature design elements—stitches, techniques, and sometimes just pretty motifs—arranged in bands on long and narrow pieces of linen. Typical are meandering floral motifs in colors, with areas of whitework done in satin stitch, drawn thread, pulled thread, and needleweaving.

English orphanage and charity school samplers, with their variety of letters and numbers stitched in one color, taught poor girls how to stitch monograms and mark linens so they might be employable above scullery-maid level when they reached adulthood. Compared to other samplers, they look somewhat stark and plain, yet nevertheless they are striking in their simplicity.

American samplers of the 18th and early 19th Centuries directly reflect young ladies' education; each school had a sampler

Sampler; New York, stitched by Maria Mimse, c. 1780. Formerly in the collection of Peter Cifelli.

"style" with certain motifs or motif arrangements, which aids historians trying to date and place undated, unsigned pieces. These "schoolgirl" samplers were a way to perfect one's stitching technique and expand one's stitching repertoire. Many of these samplers are full of imperfections. By comparing different parts of the sampler, or later samplers, you can see just how much a stitcher has progressed over her course of study.

American samplers exhibit alphabets, numbers, flowers, houses, figures, and—most charming of all—sayings. Quaintly pious, the sentiments expressed often hinted at resignation over the sorrows of earthly existence and the desire to live virtuously. This saying, stitched by Ann Clair Tinges in 1798, typifies the American sampler in cadence and moral earnestness: *Good natur'd mirth an[d] open heart/And looks unskill'd in any art/There are the charms which ne'er decay/Tho' youth and beauty fade away.*

The beauty and charm of samplers may reside in the fact that, although they may have been stitched in a particular school's style or teacher's design, no two are exactly alike, a quality valued by collectors and admired by all who love authenticity.

Besides displaying a great variety of what we refer to in this book as "sampler" stitches (pages 194–222), historic samplers

contain many stitches from other categories of counted thread such as drawn thread or blackwork.

There's so much more to learn about the history of samplers than we can offer here; if you're yearning for more, browse through the Bibliography for books solely devoted to this topic.

COUNTED CROSS-STITCH

The cross stitch goes back many centuries, and is important in many needlework traditions from the decoration of clothing to portraying images on samplers. One time-honored application, Assisi work, uses cross stitches to create a solidly-filled background, allowing the negative space of unstitched portions of the ground fabric to appear in relief.

Another charming expression is counted cross-stitch on perforated or punched paper, which enjoyed popularity in the late 19th Century, and was used for small items such as bookmarks and covers for books, needlecases, and notebooks. Paper is even more ephemeral than textiles, and most of these small items have vanished. What have remained are the framed "motto" samplers that were enclosed in glass. By the Victorian era, stitched sayings had softened somewhat from the strictly moral and exceedingly pious sayings found on samplers a century earlier, and display sentiments of the "Home Sweet Home," "Welcome," and "When This You See, Remember Me" variety. The most common stitches on perforated paper were full cross and tent stitches, stitched with cotton floss, crewel wool, and even silk.

Stamped cross-stitch—fabric with pre-printed images to stitch—was popular in the late 19th and early 20th Centuries. It was quick and easy to stitch on small linens such as tea towels and pillowcases as well as framed pictures. This incarnation of cross-stitch cannot truly be called counted thread work because the stamping eliminated the need to count threads. Unfortunately, the images were sometimes crudely produced and off-grain, and eventually fell out of fashion, even to the point of ridicule. Cross-stitch was at its lowest point in the mid-1900s until a popular revolution turned things around.

"Modern" counted cross-stitch began in the 1970s and came of age in the 1980s. Stitchers were willing to count fabric threads once again rather than follow a pre-determined outline. Pictorial in nature, counted cross-stitch bears as much relation to 19th-century needlepointed pictures (see related story on page 14) as it does to samplers. Small motifs have always been popular in samplers, but solidly cross-stitched designs are relatively new. The Dutch Treat piece (page 262) is a splendid example of a realistic design "painted" in cross stitches.

The modern cross-stitch designer can now turn to a computer to create designs for publishing. Building an image along a linear grid is a task for which computers are ideally suited, and it's not surprising that the rise of cross-stitch as a favorite needlework coincided with the development of personal computers. Of course, not all printed charts are computer-generated; many designers prefer to draw their charts by hand, as if to mirror the hands-on activity of stitching itself. Nevertheless, computers as an aid to design are here to stay, and enable designers to create ever-more complex designs. The latest twist is to generate computerized charts from scanned photographs, enabling stitchers to stitch a portrait of a loved one or other image of personal significance.

BLACKWORK

We can thank the vanity of aristocrats for providing us with much of what we know about blackwork. One of the most common applications of

Detail of Quaker Sampler; Burlington County, New Jersey, stitched by Elizabeth Sager, c. 1830. Formerly in the collection of Peter Cifelli.

this elegant 16th-century technique was on articles of clothing, which, unlike textiles for other uses, were almost certain to be worn until they fell to pieces. Fortunately, skilled painters were on hand in the courts of Europe to show in detail what their royal patrons wore. Without these portraits, we might have to rely on written descriptions and sketches of blackwork patterns. Instead, such masters as Hans Holbein the Younger, who painted members of England's Henry VIII's court, captured blackwork patterns on their subjects' clothing with almost photographic clarity.

Blackwork evinces a certain formality, and has a delicacy and restraint compared to other more opulent needlework of the time such as crewel and silk work. The patterns of blackwork display arabesques and stylized "eastern" motifs, often resembling iron grillwork. They show a strong Islamic influence, borrowing heavily from Moorish motifs that filtered from Africa through Spain onto the rest of the Continent and the British Isles.

It is commonly assumed that Henry VIII's first wife, Catherine of Aragon, brought the art of blackwork to the English court from her native Spain, but costume historians disagree on its exact introduction to England, many insisting that it predates Catherine's arrival. It was used lavishly on garments—sleeves, bodices, collars, cuffs, and nightcaps, as well as bedspreads and bed draperies. Depending on the stitching method, the finished piece may be reversible. Traditionally

blackwork was stitched in black thread on a white background; sometimes red thread was substituted. Often, glimmering threads of gold added an extra touch of luxury. Fabrics with a thread count of 22 to 36 works best, along with a smooth-textured thread to maintain crisp lines. Modern stitchers now use blackwork in stylized pictorial designs, often as filling for outlined shapes.

Blackwork's foundation is the double running stitch (page 211), which is executed in two trips or journeys. The first "outbound journey" consists of every other stitch of the pattern, plus small details outside the primary design line. The "return journey" takes care of the remaining unstitched spaces. Another name for this wonderfully efficient stitch is Holbein, named for the portrait artist previously mentioned. It's also possible to stitch blackwork patterns using the basic backstitch which is fine for designs that don't need to be reversible, such as framed pieces.

Blackwork may contain gradations of shading within a motif, accomplished in one of two ways. Either the stitcher may work the pattern with progressively thicker thread by adding plies, working from areas of less shading to heavily shaded areas, or the stitcher may vary the actual pattern by eliminating or adding more stitches to vary the complexity and density of the pattern.

Not all blackwork designs exhibit shading. Many beautiful "diaper patterns" feature motifs outlined in other stitches such as stem or chain, but filled in with simple double-running patterns. To provide interest, each motif may be composed of a different pattern—some dense, some light—to bring some motifs forward and make others recede. Cross stitches and Algerian eyelets are common additions to traditional blackwork designs.

Look for two beautiful blackwork patterns—executed in metallic gold and copper threads—surrounding the pictorial oval on the Acorn Sampler (page 266).

PULLED THREAD

Many people initially confuse pulled thread with drawn thread, perhaps because pulled thread "draws" the threads of the ground fabric together. True drawn thread involves cutting threads of the ground fabric (shown on page 252). Once the inexperienced stitcher makes this distinction, it's obvious that pulled thread is the less complex of the two. Because pulled thread requires no cutting, it leaves the fabric stronger than drawn thread does.

Considered a type of whitework, pulled thread is also called Dresden work, Flemish work, Bohemian lace, Tonder embroidery (named for a city in Denmark), or embroidered lace. Like drawn thread work, it's an attempt to mimic expensive lace. Some of the finest historical pulled thread work consists of elaborate pictorial motifs, such as flowers, with each petal worked in a different pattern, to stunning effect.

Pulled thread reached the peak of perfection in northern Germany and Denmark in the 18th Century before it spread to the rest of Europe and America. It can be found on very fine muslin or lawn fabrics (up to 100 threads to the inch) from that era, and used on men's and women's clothing, especially collars and cuffs, petticoat flounces, aprons, and handkerchiefs, often worked by professional embroiderers or in convents. Pulled thread also appears in "peasant embroidery" around the world, most notably the Greek islands, Russia, Turkey, and India, often worked in colors to contrast with the fabric.

The concept behind pulled thread is to stitch with sufficient tension on the working thread to distort the threads of the ground fabric into decorative, lacy patterns. For best results, the ground fabric should be somewhat loose; it will "pull in" more easily. Usually the working thread is the same color as the fabric, or a very close shade, for a practical reason: pulled thread relies on small tack stitches to maintain the correct "pull," and these are best left as invisible as possible. The working thread may be various weights of pearl cotton or cordonnet, and must be strong to withstand the tension. For the lightest, laciest effects, however, the working thread should be no thicker than the fabric threads.

The amount of "pull" may vary for different effects; some patterns require a slight, medium, or tight pull. Some patterns create a denser pattern than others. Pulled thread samplers show this effect best; even when stitched with the same thread, some patterns will appear darker, others lighter. Interestingly, the same pulled stitches that look so fine and beautiful when stitched under tension look quite ordinary when stitched with no tension. Truly, the pulling creates a bit of magic! When recreating antique pulled work, contrasting threads are not a good choice. If a dramatic effect is desired, try backing the monotone pulled work with a colored fabric.

The Rose Basket needlebook project (page 284) displays two pulled thread effects: the basket itself is composed of a densely worked pattern in a thread that contrasts with the fabric; two borders around the basket motifs show off the subtle effect of ecru-on-ecru, allowing the play of light and shadow to create the drama.

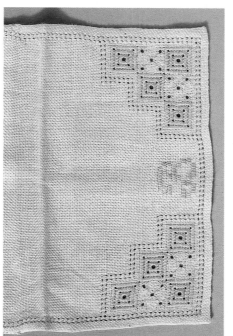

Detail of pulled thread work on a handkerchief holder; pulled satin, eyelet, and four-sided stitches. From the private collection of Deanna Hall West.

One particular style of pulled work is German Schwalm work, in which the stitcher first establishes the outline of a motif—hearts, flowers, doves and other shapes from nature—in coral knots or chain stitches, then fills it in with pulled thread patterns. These outlines are a helpful place to hide beginning and ending threads of the pulled work.

Unfortunately, it's not possible to show both the stitching sequence and the finished pulled effect in the same diagram, but the photographs of the stitched patterns on pages 230–242 of the Stitch Gallery will give you an idea of what to expect.

HARDANGER

Named for a picturesque region in Norway, Hardanger is the most well-known category of *hvitsøm* (the Norwegian word for whitework). Pronounced "har-dung-er," it is traditionally stitched white-on-white or cream-on-cream, or sometimes cream on natural linen with thread counts as high as 50. Now that modern stitchers have embraced it internationally, other colors have become popular, even in high contrasts such as dark thread on white, or pastels on dark fabric.

The aesthetic of Hardanger rests on the balance between mathematically calculated geometric motifs worked in a heavy thread, and light, airy stitches of fanciful loops and dainty picots made in openwork areas in a lighter weight thread of the same color. Along with drawn thread (described in the following story) Hardanger requires the stitcher to cut away threads of the ground fabric in order to fill the open area with stitches, and is another way to imitate true lace. Hardanger is an ideal introduction for intermediate stitchers to take the plunge and try their first drawn thread work (see pages 243–251 in the Stitch Gallery).

The foundation of all Hardanger designs are Kloster Blocks, simple rectangles of (usually) five satin stitches in pairs that oppose each other across the openwork areas. They require the heavier thread, as do the purely decorative satin-stitch motifs that are independent of the openwork, as well as edgings worked in the buttonhole stitch. The satin-stitch motifs are borrowed from Norwegian life. The ship motif, derived from the bow of old Viking vessels, may be arranged in multiples to create tulip flowers. Stars, so important to seafaring folk, appear frequently; when stitched in pure white thread they resemble snowflakes. (Yes, it's true that snowflakes have six points, and Hardanger stars have eight, but that's one of the constraints of geometry.)

Stitches for the openwork areas are worked in a lighter weight thread than the satin motifs. Some, such as needleweaving, bind and decorate the ground threads left uncut. Others "fill in the blanks" with picots, dove's eyes, spider webs, and

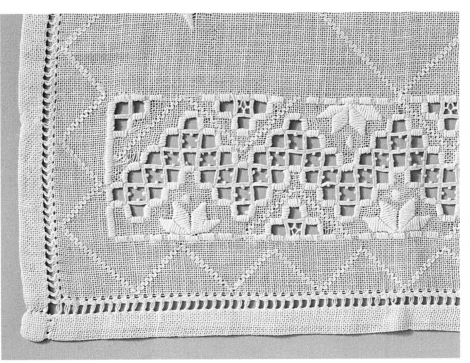

Detail of Hardanger embroidery; c. 1900. From the private collection of Rosalyn Watnemo, Moorhead, Minnesota.

twisted bars, and are responsible for the lacy appearance. Additional touches include a few classic pulled thread stitches such as the cable and four-sided stitch to further enhance the uncut fabric areas.

Historically used by the Norwegians as apron trim and on collars and cuffs for both men's and women's folk costumes, Hardanger reached its greatest popularity from 1650–1850. Since then, it has been adopted for decorative purposes, to add a lacy look to household linens of all kinds—doilies, pillows, table linens, and such. Today it retains as much appeal as ever, so much so that Hardanger is considered a fit subject for framed pictures.

Hardanger's origins are obscure. One theory is that its ancient roots are in the Near East, for needlework experts claim that Hardanger displays Assyrian and Egyptian influences which may be the result of the Vikings' forays in the Mediterranean Sea. The universal symbol of the eight-pointed star is also found in Indian embroidery.

A close relative of Hardanger is Cyprus lace, which springs from the heart of ancient Mediterranean cultures, and hints at their common roots. Cyprus lace uses many of the same stitches as Hardanger: eight-pointed satin-stitch stars, pulled four-sided stitches, eyelets, hemstitches, and drawn thread areas bound with satin stitches and needlewoven with picots. Of note are the many ways to portray Greek Orthodox cross motifs with elaborate flourishes. Traditionally, Cypriot women learn the techniques from other family members and stitch this lace on table linens for their dowries.

DRAWN THREAD AND HEMSTITCHING

Drawn thread falls under the general heading of whitework, and some varieties may also be categorized as needlelace. "Drawn" refers to the withdrawing of threads of the ground fabric, which creates open areas which are later filled with

needleweaving. Once the designated fabric threads are removed, various stitching treatments may be added to contain and finish off the cut areas with a lacy look.

Drawn thread grew in popularity when lace pattern books became available in Europe during the 16th Century. Not only hems but decorative bands appeared on linen clothing, especially shirts and shifts. The shirt that England's Charles I wore to his execution in 1649 (which heroically survived him!) shows beautiful decorative drawn thread work around the neck and on the sleeves. Drawn thread was revived with a passion in the 1880s, used this time for table and bed linens.

Hemstitching, an ancient art, is integral to drawn thread; it organizes and stabilizes the threads immediately adjacent to the cut and withdrawn areas. Used to hem garments ever since humans decided to clothe themselves in textiles, hemstitching may or may not involve removing horizontal fabric threads (cutting a channel). Removing threads probably began as a handy way to make sure one's hemstitches were straight and true. The channel area offers an opportunity for fanciful embellishment, and there are an infinite number of patterns to

Detail of tea cozy with drawn work; England. From the private collection of Deanna Hall West.

fill this purpose. The examples offered in the Counted Thread Stitch Gallery (pages 252–256) provide a good introduction to the types of variations that are possible.

Three other techniques are related to drawn thread work and are usually referred to as needlelaces: reticello, Hedebo, and Ruskin lace, all of which are currently enjoying revived interest.

Reticello (also called reticella), a lacemaking technique from Italy, flourished in the 16th and 17th Centuries. Reticello employs some of the same stitches—buttonhole, satin, four-sided, picots, needleweaving—as Hardanger, and is built upon a fabric ground that is cut away to show off the motifs, which are frequently circular or resemble compass points.

Hedebo bears a strong resemblance to reticello, and can be recognized by its distinctive motifs, many of which were borrowed from motifs carved in 18th-century Danish furniture—natural shapes such as flowers, leaves, fruits, and more abstract motifs such as hearts, semicircles, and crescents. (Incidentally, Hedebo is pronounced "hay-the-bow," from the Danish words for "heather born." The Danes who developed it lived on the heaths of Denmark.)

John Ruskin, a social reformer in Victorian England, spearheaded a revival of the linen industry in the Lake District to relieve poverty in the area. His friend Marion Twelves encouraged local women to produce a needlelace that resembled reticello. Under their efforts a cottage industry sprang up to produce what came to be called Ruskin lace. A great variety of lacy household linens were thus stitched and exported in the late 19th Century.

Coming full circle, drawn thread work is the parent of Teniffe lace, a true *punto in aria* lace without a ground fabric. It evolved to duplicate the corner motifs of drawn thread patterns, where a horizontal and vertical drawn thread band meet, resulting in a square area that could accommodate circular designs worked around spokes.

COUNTED THREAD ON SPECIALTY FABRICS

Several counted thread techniques have evolved to take advantage of the properties of certain textiles. Unpretentious in style, modest in scale, and easy to learn, they are a delight to stitch.

Swedish Weaving—If ever a technique could qualify as "surface embroidery," it is Swedish weaving, in which the needle and thread do not pierce through the fabric but barely skim the surface of a specialty fabric known as huck, or huckaback. It's also known as Swedish darning, Swedish embroidery, huck weaving, and huck embroidery; the Spanish know it as *punto Yugoslavo*, and the East Indians call it *kashida*. This technique has been used for centuries on towels and table linens, and even clothing.

Cotton huck fabric has loose threads called "floats" on one side of the fabric; these are arranged in rows and designed to accommodate a threaded needle. Each stitch is held on the surface of the fabric by the floats, and no working threads show in any form on the back of the fabric. The stitcher slides a threaded needle under the floats in an up/down progression while holding the needle in the same horizontal position for every stitch, creating decorative patterns.

Detail of tea cloth with drawn thread work; reticello square and hemstitching. From the private collection of Deanna Hall West.

Traditional Swedish weaving designs are primarily geometric, although charming design motifs are possible (for an example, see the tulips in Forever Springtime border, page 280). The time-tested thread choices are stranded floss and pearl cotton, but metallic threads offer new possibilities.

Huck fabric is not always easy to find, but you may substitute Aida fabric used for cross-stitch. The top two threads of Aida's four-thread compound "square" may be separated much like the floats of huck fabric. In fact, more designs are now possible using Aida because it has both horizontal and vertical thread floats.

Chicken Scratch—An American folk art as homespun as candlewicking, this "country craft" lets the squares of gingham fabric guide the stitcher in counting. Categorized as needlelace, chicken scratch is an offshoot of Teniffe Lace from the Canary Islands, which in turn is descended from Spanish lacemaking and drawn thread work. It's also known as snowflaking, mountain lace, even "Hoover's lace" during the Depression. (Why shouldn't every women have lace?)

In chicken scratch the counting is simple because gingham provides a ready-made grid, and is easy on the eyes. Worked primarily in white thread over the colored squares of gingham, the look is light and lacy. Sometimes other colors are added as accents only. The stitcher may choose stranded floss, pearl cotton, crochet thread, or candlewicking thread.

Stitches for chicken scratch include Smyrna cross, leaf, detached chain, and eyelets. Simple needleweaving such as spider webs provide lacy detailing. The stitches form geometric patterns which may remain abstract for design elements such as borders, or used to fill an outlined motif. One of the reasons this is a simple lace technique is that it doesn't involve cutting the ground fabric, is easy to see, and quick to stitch. ✦

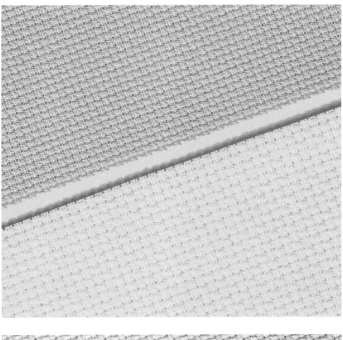

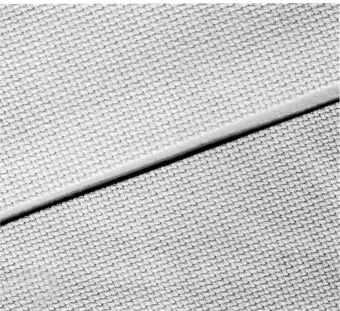

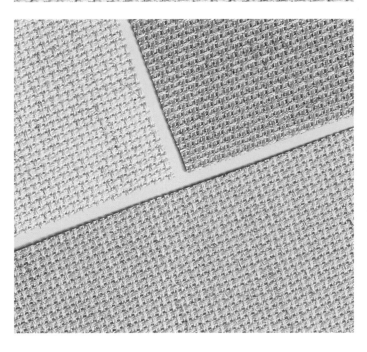

FABRICS FOR COUNTED THREAD WORK

Essential to the success of counted thread work is the ground fabric called evenweave, defined as fabric that has the same number of threads in each direction: the warp (vertical axis) and weft (horizontal axis). As its name implies, "counted thread" means you must count the fabric threads (linen) or thread squares (Aida) as you stitch the design, usually presented as a charted graph.

Evenweave fabric for stitching (such as linen) has a specific count, meaning the number of threads per inch. The higher the count number, the finer (closer) the weave, so the size of your finished design depends on the count of the fabric you choose. Also consider whether you intend to stitch the design over one or two threads of fabric. Higher counts (starting with 25) often require that you stitch over two threads (two warp and two weft) of fabric, although many designs feature stitches over both one- and two-thread units. Stitching over one thread of a high-count fabric enables you to achieve fine details, while stitching over two threads enables you to fill in color blocks more quickly.

Linen has historically been the most popular choice for counted thread work, but the contemporary stitcher can choose from an impressive variety of fabric styles and fiber contents. Specialty weaves such as Aida make counting easier and are excellent for beginning stitchers.

AIDA

Aida fabric's distinctive, complex weave creates small corner holes that make counting easier and enable the stitcher to see exactly where each stitch should be placed. It's possible to execute fractional cross stitches (page 194) on Aida, but more difficult than on linen. (Beginning stitchers would do well to choose a design without fractional stitches.) Aida fabrics are usually chemically sized by the manufacturer to impart stiffness to the fabric; frequent washing dissolves the sizing and makes the fabric softer and more pliable.

Aida from Zweigart and Charles Craft, 100% cotton (except Damask Aida noted below), comes in counts of 8, 11, 14, 16, and 18. Herta is a 6-count fabric with an Aida weave.

Damask Aida (not shown) from Zweigart, a 52% cotton/48% rayon blend with a soft sheen, comes in counts of 11, 14, and 18.

Country Aida (not shown) from Zweigart is a 7-count polyacrylic in white, cream, sand, and black.

Fiddler's Cloth (oatmeal), Fiddler's Lite (light oatmeal), and Fiddler's Colors from Charles Craft, a cotton/polyester/linen blend, comes in counts of 14, 16, and 18, and has a homespun appearance.

Rustico Aida (not shown) from Zweigart is a cotton, rayon, linen blend in counts of 14 and 18, with a homespun appearance, similar to Fiddler's Cloth.

TOP: 14-ct. and 11-ct. Aida from Zweigart.
MIDDLE: 16-ct. and 18-ct. Aida from Zweigart.
BOTTOM: 14-ct. Fiddler's Colors, 14-ct. Fiddler's Lite, and 14-ct. Fiddler's Colors from Charles Craft.

LINEN

Linen has been a popular choice for stitchers for counted thread work throughout the centuries, so it's a natural choice for projects such as samplers which require an authentic look. Besides its appearance, linen enjoys the advantages of strength and longevity. Linens are usually chemically sized by the manufacturer to impart stiffness to the fabric; frequent washing dissolves the sizing and makes the linen softer and more pliable.

As mentioned previously, linen is the best choice of fabric if your chosen design features fractional cross stitches. (See page 194 for a description of how to stitch them.) However, fractional stitches are possible only when you're stitching over two threads of linen; stitching over one thread of linen limits you to designs that feature only full (basic) cross stitches.

Linens from Zweigart include 19-count Cork, 25-count Dublin, 28-count Cashel, 32-count Belfast, 36-count Edinburgh (also spelled Edinborough), and 45-count Fine Linen (actually a cotton/linen blend) in many colors.

Wichelt Imports distributes an extensive line of linens from Permin of Copenhagen in counts of 16, 18, 26, 28, 30, 32, 35, and 40, in many colors.

Charles Craft imports 100% linen in white, cream, tea-dyed, and natural colors in counts of 20, 28, and 32.

R&R Reproductions offers a line of hand-dyed linens to help give your stitchery an antique or unique look.

UPPER LEFT: 25-ct. Dublin Linen and 19-ct. Cork Linen from Zweigart.
UPPER RIGHT: 28-ct. linen from Wichelt Imports, 28-ct. Tea-dyed Linen from Charles Craft, 28-ct. Cashel Linen from Zweigart.
ABOVE: 45-ct. Fine Linen, 36-ct. Edinburgh Linen, 32-ct. Belfast Linen from Zweigart.

175

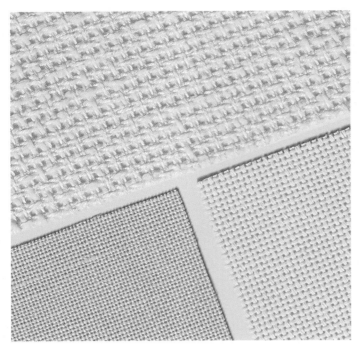

UPPER LEFT: 7-ct. Klostern, 28-ct. Quaker Cloth, and 18-ct. Davosa from Zweigart.

UPPER RIGHT: 25-ct. Lugana from Zweigart, 32-ct. Jobelan from Wichelt Imports, and 28-ct. Jubilee from Zweigart.

ABOVE: 22-ct. linen Hardanger and 22-ct. cotton Hardanger from Zweigart.

SPECIALTY COTTONS AND BLENDS

Fabrics in this category vary in appearance, weight, and drapability, so select them according to your project need.

Jubilee from Zweigart and Jobelan from Wichelt Imports are 28-count cotton plain weaves. Jobelan also comes in 16-, 20-, 25-, and 32-counts.

Davosa from Zweigart is an 18-count cotton plain weave.

Quaker Cloth from Zweigart is a 28-count linen/cotton blend.

Lugana from Zweigart is a 25-count cotton/rayon blend.

Floba (not shown) from Zweigart a rayon/linen blend, comes in counts of 14, 18, and 25.

Klostern from Zweigart, a rayon/cotton blend, is 7-count with a rustic look. The low count creates large stitches that require many plies of thread. It's especially good for children and for adults with less than perfect eyesight.

HARDANGER

This 100% cotton, 22-count evenweave from Zweigart was originally designed for Hardanger work. (The Hardanger technique, however, is also traditionally done on a plain-weave cotton or linen.) This weave features pairs of threads which give it a basketweave appearance. Zweigart imports a linen Hardanger.

Oslo (not shown) from Zweigart, also 22-count, has the same characteristic basketweave appearance as Hardanger but is made of mercerized cotton, which gives it a soft, drapey hand.

PLASTIC CANVAS & VINYL AIDA

These plastic "fabrics" are ideal for projects that require sturdiness such as placemats, jewelry, plant pokes, refrigerator magnets, etc., and may be cut in any shape without raveling. Unfortunately, designs with fractional stitches are not suitable.

PLASTIC CANVAS comes in a translucent white color in counts of 7, 10, and 14.

VINYL AIDA from Charles Craft and Crafter's Pride, 14-count, features the appearance of the Aida weave and is sold in sheets of 12" x 18" and 30" x 36". Vinyl-Weave™ from Daniel Enterprises, also 14-count, comes in sheets of 12" x 18", 13" x 36", and 30" x 2 yards.

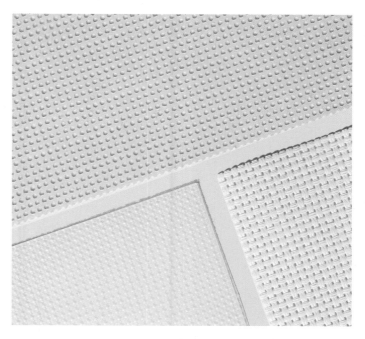

PERFORATED PAPER

Popular in the 19th Century, this punched paper is enjoying a revival. It's ideal for framed stitchery as well as small projects such as bookmarks, Christmas ornaments, and greeting cards. It's somewhat fragile and cannot handle fractional stitches.

SPECIALTY FABRICS

Popular in Europe for table linens and now available in America, these fabrics feature surface interest such as special evenweave areas, either tone-on-tone or with a contrast woven area. They're most frequently used for home decorating, but needlework designers find them useful for many design effects.

A sampling of fabrics with special color patterns include: Hopscotch and Cornerblock from Charles Craft feature colored, woven stripes which form blocks with a 14-count white or natural central area for stitching.

WASTE CANVAS

Also known as Blue Line Canvas, waste canvas is a loosely woven evenweave canvas held together with chemical sizing that dissolves when wet, allowing the canvas to pull apart easily. Made of 100% cotton, it's available in counts of 6.5, 7.5, 8.5, 10, 10.5, 11, 12, 13, 14, and 16.

Use it when you wish to stitch on a non-evenweave fabric such as dress fabric and clothing. Simply baste the canvas over the area to be stitched, stitch the design, wet the canvas, and remove the canvas thread by thread.

SELVAGED BANDS (STITCH BANDS)

These specialty bands from Zweigart and Wichelt Imports have decorative, finished selvage edges either in the same color as the fabric, or in a contrasting color. They're useful for small projects such as bellpulls, chatelaines, basket bands, camera straps, curtain tiebacks, hatbands, etc. Made of cotton, linen, and cotton/rayon blends, they're available in Aida weave in counts of 14 and 16, and in linen weave in counts of 24, 28, and 30 in eleven widths ranging from ¾" to 8".

UPPER LEFT: 14-ct. perforated paper from Yarn Tree, 14-ct. perforated plastic canvas from Darice, 14-ct. Vinyl-Weave™ from Crafter's Pride. MIDDLE: 14-ct. Cornerblock and 14-ct. Hopscotch from Charles Craft. BOTTOM: 13-ct. waste canvas from Zweigart and 23-ct. selvaged band from Wichelt Imports.

PRE-MADE PRODUCTS WITH EVENWEAVE INSERTS

Zweigart, Charles Craft, Daniel Enterprises (Crafter's Pride), M.C.G. Textiles, and other manufacturers make pre-made items with evenweave inserts that free you from having to finish a project when you're through with the stitching. Products include bookmarks, Christmas stockings, tree skirts, gift bags, napkins, placemats, pillows, aprons, jar lid covers, breadcovers, tote bags, baby items such as bibs, bonnets, and blankets, and more. Other pre-made items feature evenweave areas woven in the ground fabric such as hand towels. Also available are satin-stitch-edged Aida shapes to appliqué onto towels, clothing, tote bags, etc.

AFGHAN FABRICS

These fabrics feature woven stripes or borders that create evenweave areas to fill with stitching. They can be easily fringed to spare you the trouble of elaborate finishing. Anne Cloth (18-count, from Zweigart), Hearthside (14-count, from Zweigart), and Lady Elizabeth Afghan (14-count, from Charles Craft) feature windowpane squares. Gloria (14-count) from Zweigart features a large central area for stitching, surrounded by a border. Abby Cloth from Zweigart (18-count) offers borders to stitch around a woven pattern in the central area.

ABOVE: Placemat from Crafter's Pride, infant bibs from Charles Craft (upper) and Crafter's Pride (lower), baby booties from M.C.G. Textiles, Showcase huck towel (left) from Charles Craft, Velour Fingertip Towel (right) from Charles Craft, Patchmates appliqués (with colored borders) from Zweigart, Additions appliqués (with self-colored borders) from Crafter's Pride, and Anne Cloth (background) from Zweigart.

THREADS FOR COUNTED THREAD WORK

Stitchers today enjoy an array of threads to suit an endless variety of designs. Choosing the colors and fibers of threads is one of the most exciting tasks that you will undertake as a stitcher. The look of the piece, as well as the experience of stitching it, will depend on the choices you make.

Different threads offer varying degrees of shine, thickness, firmness, and texture. Depending on the type of thread and the particular stitches you choose, you may need to use a laying tool (pages 23, 102, and 183) to obtain the results you desire.

COTTON

Less expensive than wool or silk, cotton is washable, easy to work with, and is the most popular choice for many kinds of counted thread work.

STRANDED FLOSS (EMBROIDERY FLOSS) is a six-ply cotton thread with a sheen, and available in hundreds of colors. Always separate the plies, then recombine them so the strands can "blossom out" for a fuller look. Use as few plies as one or as many as you wish for the desired effects. The best-known stranded flosses are from DMC and Anchor.

OVERDYED FLOSS is stranded floss dyed by hand for special effects. Colors may be shades within a single color family or several different colors that blend gradually from one to another on the same strand. Look for overdyed floss from Needle Necessities, Weeks Dye Works, Petals from Sweet Child of Mine, Sampler Threads from The Gentle Art, and Bravo from Rainbow Gallery.

PEARL COTTON *(coton perlé)* is twisted, non-separable, and has a lustrous sheen. Most sizes work well for counted thread work: Size 3 (thickest), 5, 8, and 12 (finest). Well-known brand names include DMC and Anchor (both available in skeins or balls), as well as Overture from Rainbow Gallery. Watercolours from The Caron Collection is a three-ply cotton with a silky sheen (one ply equals one strand of #5 pearl cotton) and is hand-dyed in variegated colors.

SPECIALTY COTTONS include Coton à Broder, a twisted, non-divisible thread with a subtle sheen. It comes in two sizes (12 and 16) and works well for counted thread work.

Flower Thread is a soft, fine, non-divisible cotton thread with a matte finish. Look for this thread from Ginnie Thompson, Danish Flower Thread, and Wildflowers from The Caron Collection.

Floche from DMC is a softly twisted, non-divisible mercerized thread with a silky sheen, and is both washable and dry-cleanable.

FROM TOP: Stranded floss from Anchor (1) and DMC (2); Petals' overdyed floss from Sweet Child of Mine (3); Weeks Dye Works (4) and Sampler Threads (5) overdyed floss; Rainbow Gallery's Bravo (6 & 7); Needle Necessities' overdyed pearl cotton (8); DMC's #3 (9) and #5 (10) pearl cotton, Anchor's #12 (11) pearl cotton; DMC's #5 (12) and #8 (13) pearl cotton; The Caron Collection's Watercolours (14); Rainbow Gallery's Overture (15); DMC's Coton à Broder #16 (16) and #12 (17); The Caron Collection's Wildflowers (18); Ginnie Thompson's Flower Thread (19, 20, 21); DMC's Floche (22).

SILK RIBBON

Silk ribbons are very thin and flat, soft enough to drape but strong enough to withstand being pulled in and out of fabric. Washing silk ribbon is not recommended.

The most common widths are 2mm (less than ⅛"), 4mm (slightly wider than ⅛"), 7mm (about ⁵⁄₁₆"), and 13mm (about ⁹⁄₁₆"), and other various widths, depending on the particular manufacturer. These include YLI Corp., The Thread Gatherer (Silken Ribbons), and Sweet Child of Mine (Petals). Overdyed silk ribbon is available in 2mm, 4mm, and 7mm widths.

Several brands of synthetic ribbon are available which can be substituted for silk.

WOOL AND WOOL BLENDS

Several lightweight wool threads are suitable for counted thread work.

CREWEL WOOL comes in a single strand of two plies which cannot be untwisted. However, you may combine plies, a helpful feature when you wish to combine several shades on one needle. Appleton Crewel Wool is a well-known brand name.

MEDICI, a DMC brand name, is very fine and develops a silky sheen with wear. Combine plies as needed for the size and scale of your project.

BROIDER WUL from England is made with natural dyes that resemble the colors of threads used in needlework before 1850, and has an especially soft hand.

SILK/WOOL BLENDS (50%/50%) are smoother than wool, more substantial than pure silk, and have a lovely hand. J.L. Walsh and The Caron Collection (Impressions) manufacture beautiful wool/silk blends.

LINEN

Linen thread comes in various weights; the lighter weights such as 10/2 are well suited for counted thread work. (The size of linen threads is expressed by two numbers: the first denotes the weight, the second the number of plies.) Individual threads are slightly variable in width within one size; this is part of linen's distinctive character. Take special care to purchase all you need at one time because the dye lots can be irregular. Three excellent linen threads are Rainbow Linen from Rainbow Gallery, Flax 'n Colors from The Thread Gatherer, and Londonderry Linen (five sizes: 18/3, 30/3, 50/3, 80/2, 100/3).

RAYON

Marlitt, a four-stranded floss from Anchor, and six-stranded DMC Rayon Floss are smooth, silky threads with a radiant

FROM TOP: YLI 4mm (1), 7mm (2), 2mm (3) silk ribbon; The Thread Gatherer's 7mm (4) and 4mm (5) Silken Ribbon; Sweet Child of Mine's Petals (6); Appleton's Crewel Wool (7); DMC's Medici (8); Broider Wul (9); J.L. Walsh's wool/silk blend (10); The Caron Collection's Impressions (11 & 12); Londonderry's size 18/3 (13 & 14), 30/3 (15), 50/3 (16) Linen Thread; The Thread Gatherer's Flax 'n Colors (17); Rainbow Gallery's Rainbow Linen (18, 19, 20); DMC's Rayon Floss (21); Anchor's Marlitt (22); Rainbow Gallery's Neon Rays (23, 24, 25).

shine. They're a bit slippery and can be difficult to work with because they knot and kink easily. (Moistening the thread as you stitch helps eliminate this.) They're less expensive than silk but have a beautiful silk-like sheen.

Neon Rays from Rainbow Gallery is a shiny rayon ribbon which spreads out or compresses, depending on the size of the stitch.

Ribbon Floss is a ⅛"-wide, flat, flexible, shiny rayon thread, used to showcase specialty stitches.

SYNTHETIC FIBERS

Many exciting options are available to the contemporary stitcher as fiber manufacturers develop new fibers for this ever-growing field. It's not possible to list all the currently available novelty threads, but those mentioned here are some of the more versatile and popular fibers which should enjoy popularity for years to come. Because they're used for special effects, it's up to the stitcher's discretion to select the number of plies to use. Listed below are some popular brand names, grouped by type.

Metallic Pearl Cotton and Metallic Floss from DMC are metallic and viscose blends that resemble their cotton cousins in weight and have relatively "soft hands" for metallic threads.

Blending Filament (including Hi Lustre) from Kreinik Mfg. Co. can be combined with other fibers, creating sparkling highlights for special effects; available in dozens of colors, including fluorescents.

Japan Thread from Kreinik Mfg. Co. duplicates the look of real metal threads of silver, copper, gold, and dark gold. It's available in three weights: #1 (finest), #5, and #7 (thickest).

Cord from Kreinik Mfg. Co. is a thin, one-ply thread for backstitching and couching; available in 15 colors.

Cable from Kreinik Mfg. Co. is thicker than Cord (above) and comes in silver and gold.

Ribbon from Kreinik Mfg. Co. is a flat metallic ribbon in two widths: 1/16" and ⅛"; available in dozens of colors, including fluorescents.

Braid from Kreinik Mfg. Co. is a flat braid with a bright, metallic sparkle, in five weights: #4 Very Fine, #8 Fine, #12 Tapestry, #16 Medium, #32 Heavy; available in dozens of colors, including fluorescents.

Fyre Werks from Rainbow Gallery is a flat metallic ribbon in a polyester/nylon blend; colors include hologram gold and silver.

Facets from Kreinik Mfg. Co. is a heavy, three-dimensional thread that resembles a string of tiny beads and is used for couching; available in six colors.

FROM TOP: DMC's Metallic Floss (1 & 2) and Metallic Pearl (3); Kreinik Mfg. Co.'s Blending Filament (4 & 5), Hi Lustre Blending Filament (6 & 7), Fluorescent Blending Filament (8 & 9), Japan Threads (10 & 11), Cord (12–15), #4 Braid (16), #8 Braid (17), #12 Braid (18), #16 Braid (19), #32 Braid (20), 1/16" Ribbon (21–23), ⅛" Ribbon (24 & 25), Ombre (26–31), Facets (32 & 33); Rainbow Gallery's Fyre Werks (34 & 35).

181

SILK

Silk, once a rare and expensive commodity, is enjoying renewed popularity and is reasonably affordable although more expensive than cotton. Silk threads come in weights similar to cotton threads.

The molecular structure of the silk fiber enables it to reflect light in a distinctive way. Many stitchers find it a particular pleasure to work with, for it possesses a beautiful "hand" and glides easily through canvas. It requires dry-cleaning and dry-blocking.

Silks similar in weight to stranded cotton floss include Soie d'Alger from Au Ver a Soie, Silk Mori from Kreinik Mfg. Co., Waterlilies by The Caron Collection, Silk 'n Colors from The Thread Gatherer, and silk from Needlepoint Inc.

Silk Serica from Kreinik Mfg. Co. is a three-ply filament silk with a high sheen which can be separated into individual plies or stitched as it comes off the reel for a thicker look. Also from Kreinik are Soie Gobelins (a two-ply twisted filament silk) and Soie Perlee (a three-ply twisted filament silk).

Other silks of interest are Splendor from Rainbow Gallery, Melange from Cascade Yarns, and Soie 1003 from Au Ver a Soie (a tightly twisted, fine silk), and silk threads from J.L. Walsh and Gloriana.

NEEDLES & ACCESSORIES FOR COUNTED THREAD WORK

High-quality needles are expensive, but more than worth the investment, for they will make your work a pleasure. Carelessly made needles have small imperfections that can snag on fabric and threads from previous stitching.

The larger the number, the smaller/finer the needle (milliners are exceptions). If the needle is too large, it's difficult to pass easily through the fabric and may produce sloppy-looking stitches. If too small, it damages the thread—even to the point of breakage—with each stitch you take.

TAPESTRY NEEDLES have blunt points which prevent splitting the threads of the fabric as you stitch. The large eye makes the job of threading easier. Select the needle size according to the number of stitches per inch. Of course, you must take the thickness (or number of strands) of the thread into consideration, too, but this should not be a problem if you've selected the right thread for the stitch count.

CURVED TAPESTRY NEEDLES are useful in repairing stitches or adding missing stitches on items that are already finished (framed pictures, for example).

FROM TOP: Au Ver a Soie's Soie d'Alger (1 & 2); Au Ver a Soie's 1003 silk (3 & 4); Kreinik's Silk Serica (5 & 6), Silk Mori (7), Soie Perlee (8, 9, 10), Soie Gobelins (11 & 12); Needlepoint Inc.'s silk (13); J.L. Walsh's silk (14 & 15); Rainbow Gallery's Splendor (16 & 17); The Thread Gatherer's Silk 'n Color (18); Gloriana's silk (19); The Caron Collection's Waterlilies (20); Cascade Yarns' Melange (21).

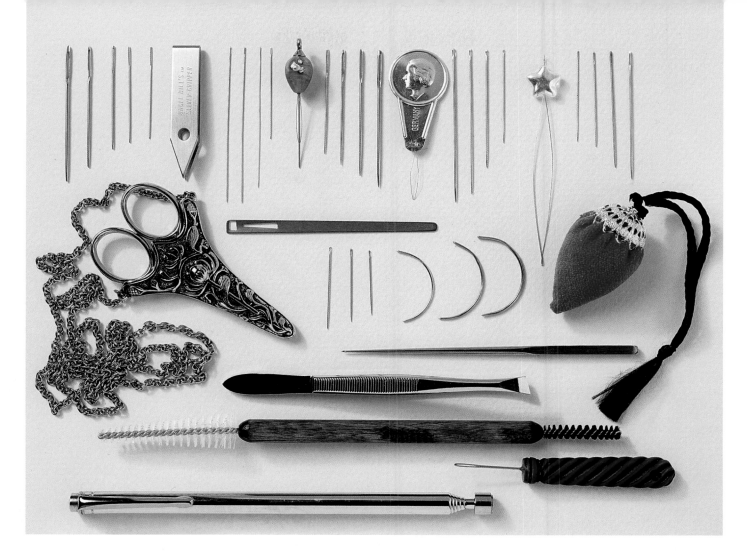

QUILTING (BETWEENS) NEEDLES are short and sharp, with large eyes, and used to secure thread ends because they can pierce the threads on the wrong side of the stitching. Sizes 9 and 10 work well for this purpose.

CREWEL (EMBROIDERY) NEEDLES are short-eyed and used for very fine couching threads and sometimes for double-running patterns when you need to pierce the thread of the previous stitch.

BEADING NEEDLES are long and narrow with very fine eyes which can pass easily through the holes of beads. Look for short beading needles which are newly available.

MILLINERS These long needles have the same diameter along the entire length; use them to execute Bullion Knots.

NEEDLE THREADERS These tiny, inexpensive tools are wonderful time-savers and will spare you much aggravation. Keep one handy as you work so you don't have to search for it every time you need it.

EMERY An emery looks like a very small pincushion and is filled with a gritty, sand-like material which keeps needles clean and sharp.

TWEEZERS Use to pick out threads when you're correcting mistakes.

LAYING TOOLS When you work with multiple plies on a single needle, you'll need to keep the threads parallel, not twisted, as you stitch. (This is called "laying" the thread.) A variety of laying tools will help you achieve this. The simplest is a large tapestry needle, bodkin, awl, or stiletto. Others specifically designed as laying tools include a stroking tool (also known as a tekobari); one end resembles an awl or stiletto, and the other end is square to prevent it from slipping from your fingers. A trolley needle has a point like a tapestry needle affixed to a metal band that fits on the end of your finger.

THREAD CATCHER This tool is designed to help you repair individual stitches and handle the working thread when it's too short to work in a regular needle.

MAGNETIC WAND This telescoping wand with a magnet enables you to pick up needles, pins, and scissors from the floor or between sofa and chair cushions.

BOO-BOO STICK This tool with brushes on each end removes fiber residue from fabric after you've ripped out stitches.

STITCH COUNT	NEEDLE
6–9 stitches per inch	Size 22
11–14 stitches per inch	Size 24 or 26
16–22 stitches per inch	Size 26 or 28

ABOVE, FIRST ROW, FROM LEFT: Tapestry needles, tweezers, beading needles, needle threader, chenille needles, needle threader, milliners needles, thread catcher, crewel/embroidery needles.

SECOND ROW, FROM LEFT: Embroidery scissors in sheath, bodkin, quilting needles, curved tapestry needles, emery.

THIRD ROW (TOP TO BOTTOM): laying tool, tweezers, Judy's Boo-boo Stick, thread catcher, magnetic telescoping rod.

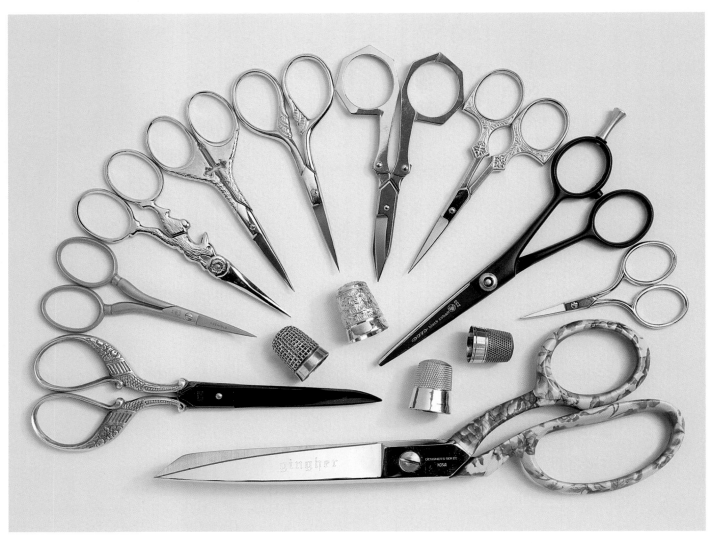

SCISSORS FOR COUNTED THREAD WORK

Reserve your scissors for needlework only and keep them with your other stitching tools. Have them professionally sharpened when they become dull.

EMBROIDERY SCISSORS Use these for clipping threads and removing mistakes. (Never use a seam ripper for the latter.) Use a scissors sheath or case to protect the points and prevent them from stabbing other items in your stitching bag or basket. If you stitch with metallic and synthetic fibers, consider a second pair of embroidery scissors that are old and duller than your fine ones. (If you only have one good pair, don't cut these fibers using the tips of the scissors; cut closer to the base of the blade.)

Note in the photograph above that the scissors second from the left have curved points, useful for ripping out mistakes.

THIMBLE Whether or not to stitch with a thimble is a strictly personal preference. Spending the time to master using a thimble is well spent if it saves your fingertips, especially if you stitch a lot.

SHEARS Use dressmaker's shears for cutting your fabric.

ABOVE: Embroidery scissors, thimbles, and shears.
RIGHT: Buttons, charms, and beads to embellish your stitchery.

EMBELLISHMENTS Small, decorative accents give your stitchery beauty, whimsy, and individuality. Look for buttons, beads, and charms at your local needlework shop, catalogs, and consumer shows. Find them also in counted thread kits, often as the focus of a design theme.

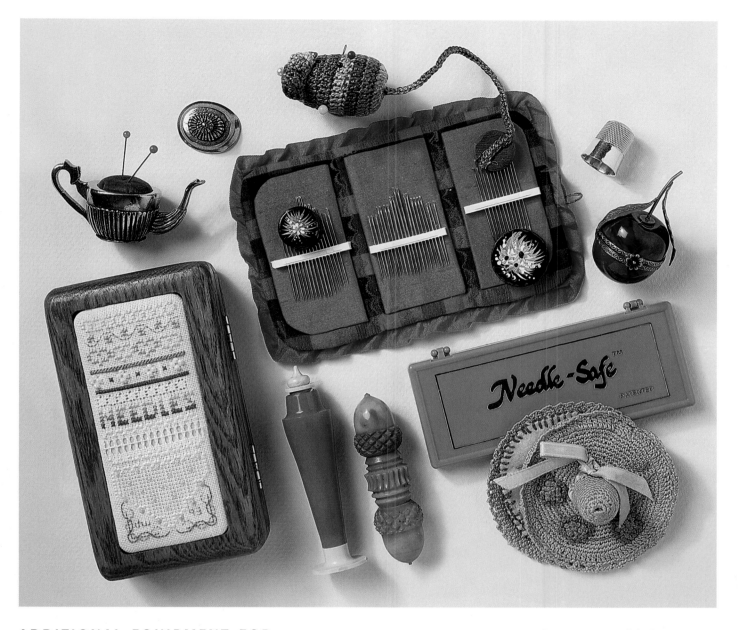

ADDITIONAL EQUIPMENT FOR COUNTED THREAD WORK

NEEDLEBOOK OR NEEDLECASE With "pages" of soft fabric, a needlebook keeps your needles protected (and protects you from the needles, too) and organized. Each "open page" is designed to store a particular needle type in a range of sizes. As with pincushions, this is an item you can make yourself to show off your stitching talents.

Many stitchers like to store their needles in needlecases, which may be narrow and cylindrical or large and box-like (also called needle safes); some of the latter have magnets to keep needles in place.

PINCUSHIONS Pincushions are useful for stowing threaded needles if you must change colors often. Many stitchers like to keep pins handy, especially to mark the fabric as they stitch to help in counting threads. Pincushions come in a variety of sizes and styles; select one that fits in your stitching bag or basket. Many stitchers like to make their own personalized models.

MAGNETS A pair of magnets that attach to each other from both sides of the fabric are handy to hold needles and small embroidery scissors to the fabric so they're in easy reach.

CLOCKWISE FROM UPPER LEFT: Pewter teapot pincushion, needlebook with magnets and crocheted mouse pincushion, thimble, thimble case, needle safe, antique needlebook (hat) with thimble holder, two antique needlecases, needlecase.

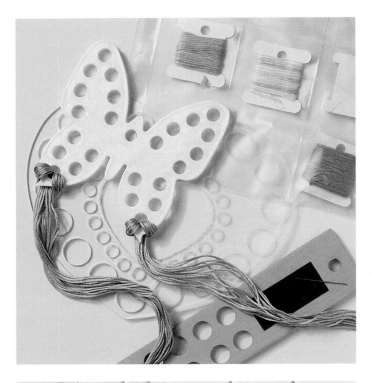

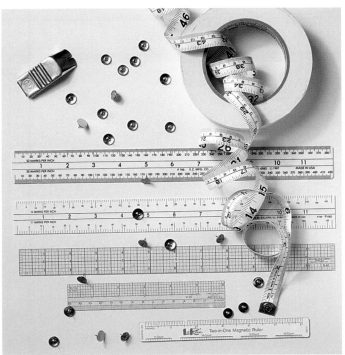

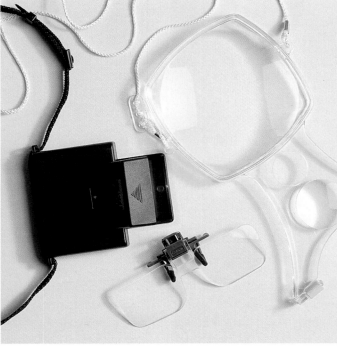

THREAD PALETTE These plastic, wood or paper palettes have a series of holes along the edges to hold individual colors of threads, which you attach using half-hitch knots.

THREAD ORGANIZER There are many products on the market for storing and identifying the threads you accumulate. Two of the simplest are individual plastic bags held together on a metal binder ring or divided plastic sheets for a three-ring binder. On the other end are wooden boxes or chests that resemble fine furniture.

RULER AND TAPE MEASURE Clear plastic rulers calibrated in inches are invaluable and come in 6" lengths that fit easily into a stitching bag. Plastic rulers calibrated to thread counts (for both Aida and linen fabrics) are of particular value to the counted thread stitcher. For measuring a larger area, a tape measure is useful and takes up little space.

THUMBTACKS AND TACK PULLER Use these to attach fabric to stretcher bars. (Avoid using staples, which may damage the fabric.)

DRAFTING TAPE This tape is less sticky than regular masking tape (which may also be used). To prevent the fabric from raveling, tape the cut edges of your fabric before mounting it in a stitching frame. You can find both drafting and masking tape at art supply stores.

LIGHTING AND MAGNIFICATION Both your eyesight and your needlework deserve optimal lighting. Choose a light that directs a circle (not a spotlight) of light onto your entire stitching surface. Floor lamps and swivel-arm table lamps (such as an architect's light) are good choices. To avoid casting shadows over the work surface, right-handers will benefit from a light directed over the left shoulder, left-handers from the right.

For very fine work you may want to use a lamp that has a magnifier attached. Other possibilities include magnifiers that hang around the neck, are worn atop the head, or attach directly to your glasses.

STITCHER'S GLOVES Elastic gloves massage your hand muscles as you stitch and help minimize hand fatigue. Several styles and sizes are available

UPPER LEFT: "Floss Keeper" thread organizer, three styles of thread palettes.

UPPER RIGHT: Tacks and tack puller, measuring tape, drafting tape, two rulers with thread-count calibrations, three rulers with inch calibrations.

LOWER LEFT: Neck light, neck magnifier, eyeglass magnifier.

FRAMES FOR COUNTED THREAD

Using a frame enables you to stitch with an even tension and keeps your work area visible. Experiment with a number of different frame systems to see which one works best for your stitching needs (and your body's needs!).

STRETCHER BARS Easy-to-use and inexpensive, these modular frames consist of four ¾"-square wood strips that dovetail at the ends to form an open square or rectangle upon which you'll tack your fabric. They're usually sold in pairs; you need to buy one pair for the width of your fabric, and a second pair for the length. If you stitch a lot, you'll eventually have an assortment of lengths that will work together to fit many projects. (These bars are specifically intended for needlework; don't confuse them with stretcher bars for painter's canvas.) Mini stretcher bars are ideal for projects of 4" to 12" dimensions; some come pre-assembled.

Q-SNAPS This modular system consists of four plastic tubes called elbows (in lengths of 6", 8", 11", or 17") that join together to form a square or rectangle. You stretch your fabric over this framework, snap a plastic clamp (resembling a "C" in cross-section) on each side, and roll the clamps away from the center of the fabric to tighten. As with stretcher bars, you buy the lengths you need to build a frame to suit your project. Like hoops, Q-Snaps are very easy to apply and remove. (Don't place clamps over previously stitched areas.)

SCROLL FRAMES Scroll frames consist of a pair of round scroll bars that attach to a pair of flat side bars. The scroll bars should be at least as wide as the width of your fabric; they feature a fabric tape or webbing to which you sew the top and bottom edges of your fabric. The ends of the scroll bars screw into the side bars by means of screws or nuts that you can adjust to achieve your desired tension as you roll the scroll bars in opposite directions. In order to keep the horizontal tension as firm as the vertical, you must lace the side edges of the fabric to the side bars or use frame clips (see below). Scroll frames will crush raised or three-dimensional stitches, so are not recommended for designs with these effects.

TABLE AND FLOOR STANDS Table and floor stands free both your hands for stitching (particularly important if your stitchery requires you to use a laying tool) and enable you to stitch in a favorite chair. You can make height and angle adjustments to suit you so stitching is as comfortable as possible. Table and floor stands usually can accommodate scroll frames, stretcher bars, or Q-Snaps with available accessories. Many stands come with their own scroll frames, which can be detached for portable stitching, too.

FRAME CLIPS These adjustable clips (pages 22 and 101) attach to the sides of scroll frames to ensure that horizontal tension of the fabric equals vertical tension, and eliminate the fuss of lacing, unlacing, and re-lacing as you move to a new area of your fabric.

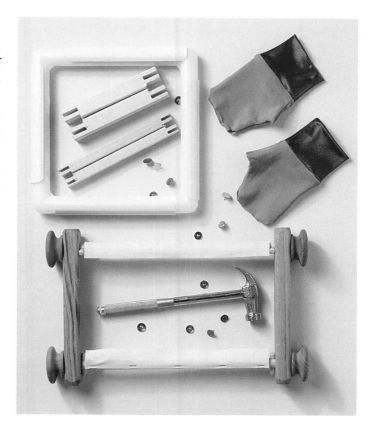

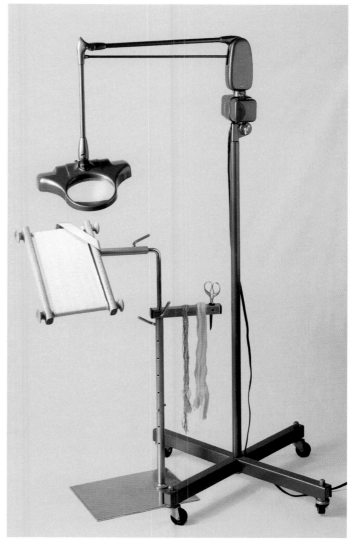

UPPER RIGHT, CLOCKWISE: Q-Snaps and stretcher bars; stitcher's gloves; scroll frame, hammer, and tacks.
LOWER RIGHT: Floor stand with scroll frame attached; Dazor floor light with magnifier.

DESIGNS FOR COUNTED THREAD WORK
CHARTED DESIGNS

"Counted thread" means exactly that! This style of needlework requires you to count individual fabric threads or distinctly woven squares (in Aida fabric), following a printed chart presented on a grid that indicates the fabric weave. Usually the designer has already chosen the color palette for the design, and may offer an alternate color palette. Of course, if the design is not part of a kit, you may make your own color or design changes (not recommended for a beginner).

A chart may be printed in colors that best match the threads or with black and white symbols that represent the various colors (or a combination of both), explained in a separate key. The key also indicates the particular stitches to use for the design, and often the number of strands to use and order in which to stitch. In magazines and leaflets it's common to see individual specialty stitches diagrammed separately.

Counted thread offers you the opportunity to experiment with making design changes and use various design elements from several sources. To design your own counted thread work, experiment with drawing your own chart on graph paper, using colored pencils. You can lay lightweight graph paper over an illustration to help you achieve the shapes you want.

CHART-READING ACCESSORIES

Several accessories make chart reading easier. Colored, transparent Line-A-Timers® use static electricity to adhere to the chart, helping you follow rows on a chart; they can be repositioned as you progress. Magnetic strips serve the same purpose. The Bugz-Eye retractable magnifier allows you to read chart details easily up close.

DESIGNS ON COMPUTER AND CROSS-STITCH SOFTWARE PROGRAMS

Needlework may be an ancient art, but it benefits from advances in computer technology. Hundreds of charted designs can be stored on a single CD-ROM that you can purchase. Because you print out only the designs you intend to stitch, you'll eliminate paper clutter and storage problems. If you're inclined to chart your own designs, you may wish to investigate the many cross-stitch charting programs. (Most of the printed charts you buy were probably charted by computer.)

TOP: Color and black-and-white charted designs, Mini Bugz-Eye magnifier with retractor (left), magnetic board, ruler and magnet strip (top), Line-A-Timer® highlighter (bottom).

BOTTOM: CD-ROM of charted designs; Pattern Maker™ cross-stitch design program (as well as a CD of cross-stitch clip art designs) for the personal computer.

counted thread basics

BEFORE YOU STITCH
MOUNTING THE FABRIC ON A FRAME

ALLOW EXTRA FABRIC FOR FINISHING Always allow at least two or three inches of fabric beyond the design on all sides to allow you to finish the project as desired. Check project instructions to see if you need to allow extra fabric or if the design will be positioned off-center. You may find it helpful to sew a running-stitch outline of the design perimeter.

ORIENT YOUR FABRIC FOR STITCHING If possible, identify the warp and align it vertically (the selvage edge is parallel to the warp). If your fabric does not have a selvage edge, remove a thread in each direction; the warp threads will show slightly more ridges than the weft threads.

PREVENT THE EDGES OF YOUR FABRIC FROM FRAYING Machine-zigzag or hand-overcast the raw edges. Another option is to tape the raw edges using drafting or masking tape. Always cut away these taped edges before framing or otherwise finishing your project.

IF USING STRETCHER BARS First connect the bars at the corners, tapping them together with a hammer or rubber mallet. Check that the corners are perfectly square.

The outer edges of the fabric should reach the edges of the bars or fold over the edges slightly. Begin tacking at the midpoint of the top and bottom bars, pulling the fabric reasonably taut. Work from the midpoints to the corners. Repeat for the side bars. Place tacks approximately 1" apart, or closer. Your fabric should be completely free of wrinkles or ridges. As you stitch, re-tighten fabric as necessary.

IF USING A SCROLL FRAME Sew the top and bottom edges of your fabric to the webbing on the scroll bars, using pearl cotton or carpet thread and firm Backstitches.

To maintain equal tension in the horizontal axis, you'll have to attach the sides of the fabric to the sides of the frame. The easiest solution is to use clips made for this purpose. The alternative is to lace the fabric to the side bars, using carpet thread, dental floss, or pearl cotton. The disadvantage of this method is that you must unlace—then re-lace—the sides every time you scroll to a different area of the fabric. This may be more of a problem with some designs than others.

Many stitchers like to stitch the design "inside the well" of the stretcher bars or frame, designating the side of fabric that wraps around the bars or rods the "wrong" side of the design. This helps keep the right side of the design fabric cleaner.

If you like to carry your stitching to places other than your primary stitching area, always carry your work in a protective covering such as a plastic bag or pillow case. You can also buy stitching bags designed for this purpose.

ESTIMATING THREAD AMOUNTS

Most charted designs today specify the amount of thread the design will require. However, if this is not the case, or if you're designing your own needlework, then you must calculate the thread requirements.

When stitching designs that will be solidly filled in with Cross (or other) stitches, be alert for areas to be stitched in one color. It's important to use thread from one dye lot for each color block to avoid possible color variations between dye lots. The most accurate method to estimate how much thread you'll need for a solidly stitched project is to stitch one square inch using

- the intended thread in the correct number of plies
- the fabric of the same thread count you plan to use
- the stitch(es) you plan to use.

From this sample you'll be able to calculate how much thread to buy; you'll also be able to determine if your chosen thread has the coverage you desire and whether you'll have to increase the number of plies. Please note that different colors of the same fiber may vary slightly in thickness depending on how the particular dyes affected them.

As you "stitch your inch" pay close attention to the amount of thread you use. Next calculate (you may have to estimate) approximately how many square inches you'll need for each color of thread. Multiply the square inches of the color times the amount you used for your sample. If you're unsure of your calculations, ask a knowledgeable shop owner for assistance.

For specialty stitches, stitch two inches of repeats in linear fashion instead of a square, noting thread use. After you determine the total length of repeats in the design, you can then calculate the amount of thread you'll need.

PLYING THREADS

Some multiple-ply threads—cotton and silk floss, for example—must be separated before stitching, even if you intend to use the same number of plies in your needle at the same time. Manufacturing and packaging tend to pack the fibers together, twist, or flatten them. Separating them allows them to fluff out, which results in better coverage on the fabric.

Always test the number of plies you need for a particular fabric. If your thread comes in three plies, but you need to stitch with four plies, cut two lengths of three-ply thread, separate them all, and combine four, reserving the remaining two plies for the next "needleful."

Some threads—wool in particular—have nap (direction). Run your fingers first in one direction along the length of the thread, then in the other direction. The smoother direction represents "going with the nap," which is the direction you'll want the thread to enter the fabric, so take note of this as you thread your needle.

MERGING DIFFERENT THREAD DYE LOTS

In an ideal world you'll always buy enough thread at one time to complete your project. Naturally, this will not always be the case! Maybe you'll discover—when you're nearing the midpoint of the design—that you're running out of one or more of the colors, especially if you've had to rip out stitches. If you're lucky, you'll find additional thread at your local shop that was dyed in the same lot with the thread you've already used. If you're not so lucky, the thread you find in the shop may be a slightly different shade than the original, even if the manufacturer labels it with the exact same color name and number. This is simply unavoidable, even by reputable manufacturers, because of the nature of the dyeing process.

How much this affects your project depends on several factors. If the color in question appears in scattered motifs throughout a design that has many colors, the difference in shades may not be noticeable. In this case, just make sure you use only one dye lot within one color block.

If the color in question fills up a large area—as a solidly-filled background, for example—you're faced with the problem of a glaring line of demarcation between the two shades. If you're stitching with one ply of thread, there's no simple solution; you can live with the two shades or you can buy enough of the new shade to re-stitch the entire area. However, if you're stitching with multiple plies, there is a solution if you've reserved some of the original shade and haven't stitched more than half of the area in question. The trick is to introduce increasing amounts of the new shade as you stitch. Instead of an abrupt color change, the stitching will gently blend from one shade to the other. Here's an example of how you would accomplish this when stitching with three plies:

1. Stitch with three plies of the original shade.
2. Stitch with two plies of the original shade and one ply of the new shade.
3. Stitch with one ply of the original shade and two plies of the new shade.
4. Stitch with three plies of the new shade.

TO BEGIN STITCHING
READING A CHART

Charts are arranged so that squares on the grid (negative space) corresponds to intersections of the fabric threads. This concept baffles some beginners; the initial tendency is to imagine the lines on the chart represent the fabric threads. (Adding to the confusion is the fact that the fabric threads shown in the diagrams of individual stitches look like a grid.) Allow yourself time for this idea to "click" in your mind; once it does you'll have it for life!

 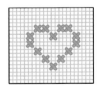

Charted Design   Stitched Design

Many stitchers like to sew lines of running stitches from top to bottom and side to side to divide the fabric into quarters. These lines serve as guidelines as you read a chart. If your chart doesn't indicate the center of each axis, draw the lines yourself with a pencil.

Where on the fabric do you begin stitching? It varies, depending on the design itself: the shape of the design elements, the number of color changes, etc. The obvious choices may be the top of the design, a particularly bold border, or some other dominant area of the design.

When you've completed a few color blocks of a design, check the number and placement of stitches you've stitched against the chart. The small amount of time you spend

checking and rechecking throughout the project may be particularly well-spent if it saves you from ripping out and re-stitching larger areas later on.

STARTING THREADS

In general, use a thread length of approximately 18" long unless design instructions specify otherwise; some specialty threads may require a shorter length. Threads longer than 18" may twist or tangle as you stitch, and disrupt your stitching rhythm. Also, the thread closest to the needle will make so many trips in and out of the holes in the fabric that it will become stressed and frayed, and will no longer match the thread at the opposite end.

IN-LINE METHOD Determine the direction in which your first line of stitching will proceed. Hold a 2" tail of thread in place on the back of the fabric as you make the first few stitches, checking to see that the back of the stitches covers the tail.

WASTE KNOT (away-waste knot) **METHOD** Make a sturdy knot and insert the needle into the front of the fabric, about four inches from the point you wish to begin stitching. When you're done with that length of thread, clip off the knot, turn the fabric over, then thread the tail into the needle and weave it into the back of the stitches. Use this method for blackwork and drawn and pulled work.

Combine both methods for efficiency—Plan the direction you'll be stitching, make a knot and insert it (from the front) along that same path. Clip the knot off just before you reach it; there's no need to hold the thread in place and check for coverage, and no need to rethread and weave later. (This method won't work for blackwork or drawn and pulled work.)

In-line Waste Knot Method

STITCHING TECHNIQUE

TENSION Maintaining consistency of tension within a given stitched area (part or whole of the design, depending on the variety of stitches) is essential for the good appearance of the finished project. Stitching with too tight a tension makes the fabric buckle. Stitching with too loose a tension yields a fabric that looks sloppy with stitches that tend to snag more easily. Some counted thread stitches require a looser or tighter than average tension; this will be noted in the individual stitch descriptions in the Counted Thread Stitch Gallery. (Pulled thread stitches, an entire category of counted thread stitches, usually require a very firm tension to achieve the desired effect.) You may find that longer stitches require slightly more tension than shorter ones, but be sure to test-check first.

STAB STITCH If you use a needlework frame (stretcher bars, scroll frame) you must stitch using the stab method: Insert the needle and thread into the fabric with your dominant hand, then pull the needle through from the back either with your dominant hand or the less dominant hand (this latter is possible only with a floor or table stand that frees you from having to hold the frame).

Some stitchers prefer to use no frame and stitch using the sewing method, in which you insert and pull up the needle in one continuous motion. Because this requires you to bend the fabric as you stitch and affects the tension, this method is not recommended for beginners. Working with fabric not under tension causes threads to twist more easily, making them harder to control.

USING A LAYING TOOL When stitching with multiple plies of thread, the plies may twist or lump together in an unsightly manner. Avoid this by using a laying tool (and a floor or table stand to free your less dominant hand). Hold the laying tool in your less dominant hand and stroke the threads with each stitch so they lie flat and parallel.

"CLEAN" AND "DIRTY" HOLES This is stitchers' slang for fabric holes that are yet-unstitched (clean) and those that already contain one or more stitched threads (dirty). You'll

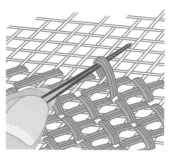

obtain the best results when you choose to bring your needle up through a clean hole whenever possible. If your working thread must share a hole with another stitch, it's preferable that the subsequent stitch be inserted from the front of the fabric, not brought up from the back, which goes against the nap of the previous stitch. (See the Algerian Eyelet, page 217, for a dramatic example.)

COMPENSATING STITCHES As you study the stitch diagrams you will notice that some show compensating stitches, which are small "fill-in" stitches not technically part of an individual stitch unit. Their purpose is to fill in small or oddly shaped areas which do not accommodate a perfect stitch unit. Expect to encounter this situation as you stitch. The usual solution is to first place full stitch units, then later fill any open areas with compensating stitches. They should appear to be a complete stitch unit that is partially obscured by surrounding design elements or the edge of the design area.

ENDING THREADS To end a thread, weave it in and out horizontally or vertically (never diagonally) on the back of the area you have just stitched. If the stitches are long and loose on the back, double back with a small stitch (or two) or use a small, sharp needle to pierce the threads on the back.

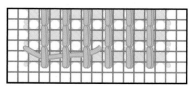

Ending a thread on the back
of the fabric

Never weave the tail of a dark-colored thread through the back of an area stitched with light-colored thread. This rule also applies to carrying a dark thread from one color block to the next. No matter what the color, avoid carrying the thread between color blocks more than ½" apart.

WORKING WITH BLENDING FILAMENT AND OTHER SPECIALTY THREADS

Blending filament (see page 181) and certain other synthetic threads are naturally slippery and require special handling. Whether you're stitching with several plies of blending filament or combining these specialty threads with stranded floss, you'll have an easier time if you tie the slippery thread to the needle. To use two strands of filament, cut a length twice as long as needed and fold it in half; insert the loop through the eye of the needle. Pull the loop over the point of the needle, then tighten the loop at the end of the eye. Add floss (if needed), using a needle threader if necessary.

For an uneven number of strands (any combination), cut a length twice as long as needed; thread needle normally. Then cut a second length 2" longer than needed; tie it to the needle (one end will be very short). When the loop of the second thread is tightened, it will secure all strands to the needle.

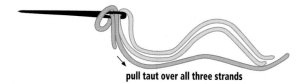

pull taut over all three strands

ADDING SURFACE EMBELLISHMENTS

Beads add texture, dimension, and fine detail to designs. If the thread you've stitched the design with is too thick to pass through a bead, use fewer plies, a lighter weight thread, or a beading needle (see page 183). Try one of these three attachment methods.

1. with a half-cross stitch

2. with a cross stitch

3. in a thread nest

Spangles (paillettes, sequins) add interest and sparkle to designs, and have been used to embellish stitchery since the Renaissance age. Select one of these four attachment methods depending on the desired look of the finished piece.

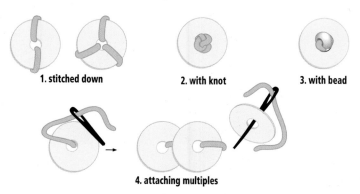

1. stitched down　　**2. with knot**　　**3. with bead**

4. attaching multiples

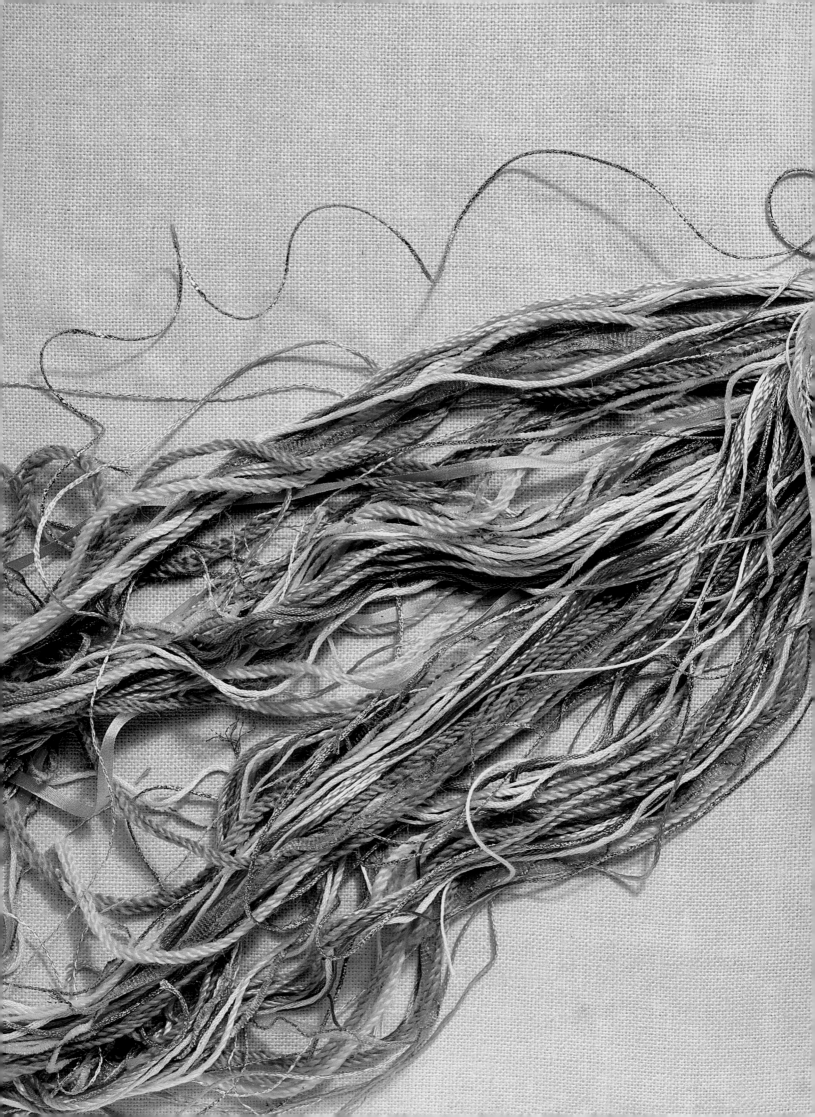

counted thread
stitch gallery

counted thread stitches

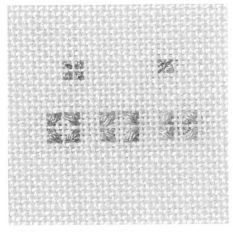

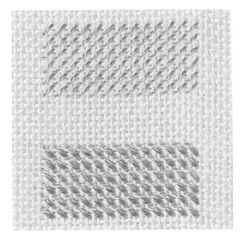

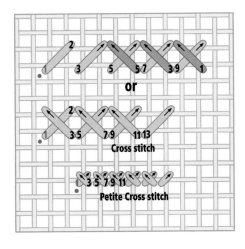

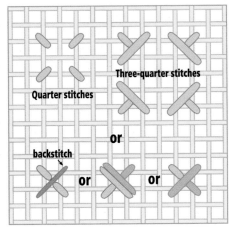

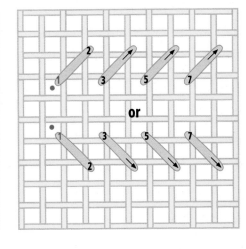

CROSS

Other Names: Cross-stitch, Point de Croix, Point de Marque, Sampler, Berlin, Counted Cross, Petite Cross

DESCRIPTION
One of the simplest and most versatile stitches; practiced around the world.
Cross-stitch embroidery adorns clothing (esp. regional costumes), home furnishings, and church vestments.
Known as a *Petite Cross* (lower diagram) when stitched over one intersection.

HOW TO STITCH
Choose one of two methods of stitching:
  1. Complete each Cross stitch individually (middle diagram), or
  2. Stitch a row of half Cross stitches, then complete each stitch on the return journey (top diagram).
Top "leg" must always cross in the same direction.

SUGGESTED USES
Universal: pictorial designs, samplers, clothing, home and church furnishings, filling (Petite Cross: alphabets, samplers, facial features)

FRACTIONAL CROSS

Other Name: Partial Cross

DESCRIPTION
In pictorial cross-stitch, Fractional Cross stitches help create smoother and more realistic shapes and outlines than basic, square-shaped Cross stitches would.
Several configurations are possible: a quarter stitch with a three-quarters stitch, two three-quarters stitches, or one three-quarters stitch with one corner left unstitched.

HOW TO STITCH
Combinations include two Quarter Crosses plus Backstitch (lower left), two Three-quarters Crosses (lower center), and one Quarter and one Three-quarters Cross (lower right).

SUGGESTED USES
Facial features, minute details, outer edges of a cross-stitched shape

HALF CROSS

DESCRIPTION
One half of a Cross stitch.
May slant in either direction.

HOW TO STITCH
Because it's only half as dense and thick as a full Cross stitch, it gives the illusion of being behind or in back of the full Cross stitches; it's useful for shadows, wispy clouds, or objects in the distance.
Work from left to right (shown), from right to left, from top to bottom, or from bottom to top.

SUGGESTED USES
Bands, filling, shadows, lacy or background effects

194

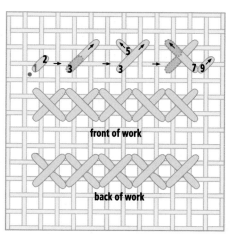

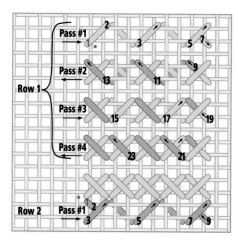

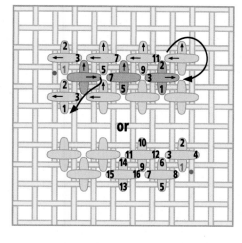

REVERSIBLE CROSS I
Other Names: Brave Bred,
Marking Stitch, Two-sided Cross,
Double-sided Cross

DESCRIPTION
This Cross stitch also makes a Cross
stitch on the backside of the fabric.

Good for stitched items which will be
seen on both sides, such as towels,
table linens, napkins, and clothing.

In the stitched example the upper block
shows the Cross stiches on the front
of the fabric and the lower block
shows the back of the fabric.

HOW TO STITCH
There are several ways to stitch a
reversible stitch (see variation at
right); this version is somewhat
quicker to stitch.

SUGGESTED USES
Towels, napkins, clothing, samplers,
alphabets

REVERSIBLE CROSS II

DESCRIPTION
This Cross stitch also makes a Cross
stitch on the backside of the fabric.

Good for stitched items which will be
seen on both sides, such as towels,
table linens, napkins, and clothing.

In the stitched example the upper block
shows the Cross stiches on the front
of the fabric and the lower block
shows the back of the fabric.

HOW TO STITCH
Each line of Cross stitches for this second version requires four journeys,
so it's somewhat more time-
consuming than the version shown
at left.

The top leg of the Cross stitch of the last
stitch of each row slants in the
opposite direction.

SUGGESTED USES
Towels, napkins, clothing, samplers,
alphabets

UPRIGHT CROSS
Other Name: Straight Cross,
St. George's Cross

DESCRIPTION
This very old and simple stitch, seen on
old samplers, is useful for small areas
or small-scale motifs.

HOW TO STITCH
Usually worked from left to right; if
worked from right to left, reverse
stitching direction of leg 3–4.

May be worked diagonally (bottom
diagram).

SUGGESTED USES
Samplers, bands, filling

The red dot in each stitch diagram
indicates where to begin stitching.

195

counted thread stitches

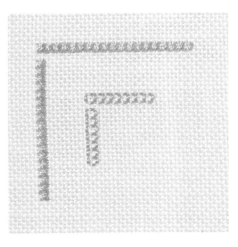

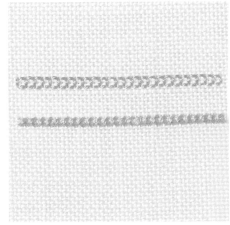

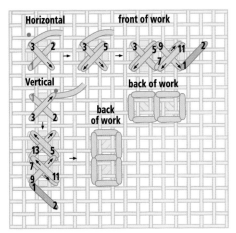

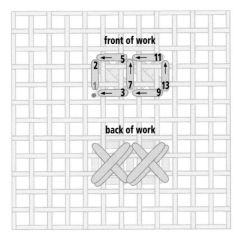

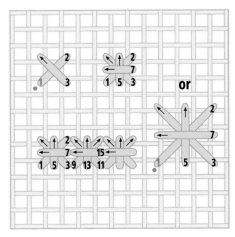

196

MARKING
Other Name: Sampler

DESCRIPTION
Originally used to mark household linens and clothing with initials for owner identification, and numbers for washing rotation.

All variations of Marking stitches are reversible.

There are two ways to stitch Marking stitches: a three-legged Cross stitch reversible to a Four-sided stitch (most popular, above), or the reverse (at right).

HOW TO STITCH
Work from left to right or from top to bottom.

Weave starting tails into stitches on the back, following the stitch pattern.

Some letters require compensating stitches (re-crossing or weaving around previously worked threads).

SUGGESTED USES
Alphabets, numbers, bands, borders

MARKING VARIATION

DESCRIPTION
A Four-sided stitch reverses to a three-legged Cross stitch.

Compare to a three-legged Cross stitch reversible to a Four-sided stitch (at left).

Marking thread ("marking cotton") was manufactured in the early 19th Century specifically to be used for marking linens and clothing.

HOW TO STITCH
Work from left to right, using an away-waste knot.

Weave starting tails into stitches on the back, following the stitch pattern.

Some alphabet letters require compensating stitches (re-crossing or weaving around previously worked threads) when stitching.

SUGGESTED USES
Alphabets, numbers, bands, borders

SMYRNA CROSS
Other Names: Double Cross, Leviathan, Railway, Double Straight Cross

DESCRIPTION
A combination stitch comprised of a Cross covered by an Upright Cross.

Usually stitched over two-by-two or four-by-four threads of fabric.

HOW TO STITCH
Work from left to right, from right to left, or vertically.

Note the numbering of the top stitch when traveling from left to right; reverse this sequence when traveling from right to left.

SUGGESTED USES
Bands, borders, filling, corners, finials, "one-stitch" eyes, alphabets, samplers

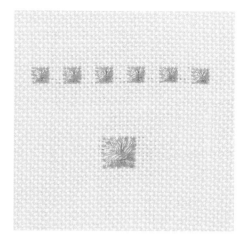

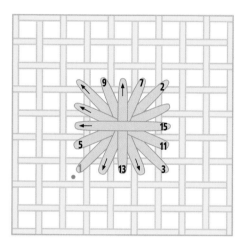
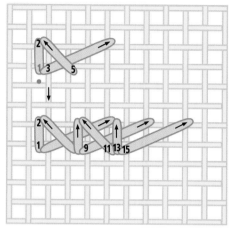
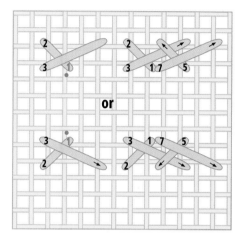

DOUBLE LEVIATHAN

DESCRIPTION
This large, textural, square stitch is larger and more complex than the Smyrna Cross (page 196).

HOW TO STITCH
If stitching multiples, make sure the final (top) stitch lies in the same directions for all stitches.

SUGGESTED USES
Bands, borders, corners, finials, isolated motifs, samplers

MONTENEGRIN
Other Names: Montenegrin Cross, Two-sided Montenegrin Cross

DESCRIPTION
This three-step stitch creates a braid-like appearance with upright bars.

Traditionally decorates the regional costumes of Slavic countries; derives its name from the Montenegro region of Yugoslavia.

Used on antique English and American samplers.

The vertical upright stitch differentiates this stitch from the Long-arm Cross (at right).

Reversed, it displays a row of Cross stitches with a vertical upright stitch between each Cross.

HOW TO STITCH
Work from left to right in rows.

The size of the stitch may vary, but the ratio of stitch length and height (2:1) should stay the same.

SUGGESTED USES
Samplers, bands, borders, clothing, filling, backgrounds

LONG-ARM CROSS
Other Names: Plaited Slav, Long-leg Cross, Portuguese Twist

DESCRIPTION
This two-step stitch is one of the oldest embroidery stitches.

Creates a petite braid-like appearance.

Used as the background in early Italian Assisi embroidery.

HOW TO STITCH
Work from left to right in horizontal rows.

The size of the stitch may vary, but the ratio of stitch length and height (2:1) should stay the same.

See the Acorn Sampler project on page 268 for traditionally used compensating stitches.

SUGGESTED USES
Samplers, bands, filling, borders, backgrounds

197

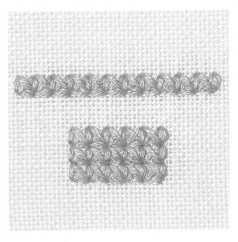

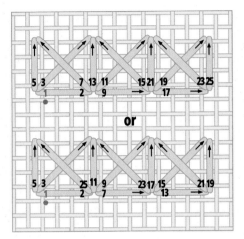

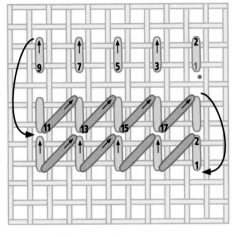

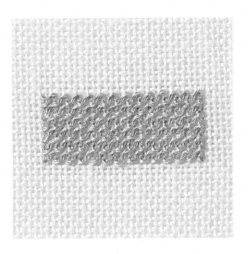

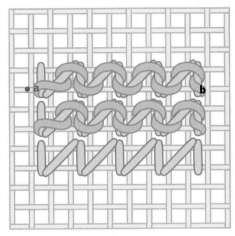

TWO-SIDED ITALIAN CROSS

Other Names: Italian, Italian Cross, Arrowhead Cross

DESCRIPTION

This reversible stitch can be worked in one journey or two; each appears the same on the front but slightly different on the back.

1. One journey (upper diagram) creates a three-legged Cross stitch on the back with a Straight stitch at the base.

2. Two journeys (lower diagram) creates a three-legged Cross stitch on the back with a Straight stitch at the base and side, similar to the stitch on the front.

A preferred stitch in 16th-century Italy; used as a background stitch for early Assisi embroidery (later supplanted by the Cross stitch).

HOW TO STITCH

Work from left to right in row.

SUGGESTED USES

Bands, filling, Assisi embroidery, samplers, backgrounds

BOSNIA

Other Names: Bosnian, Fence, Yugoslav Border, Zigzag Holbein, Barrier

DESCRIPTION

This one-color, two-journey, reversible stitch originated in Yugoslavia.

Closely related to the Barrier stitch (page 199) and misnamed as such, except the angle of the stitch between the upright stitches is different; for the Bosnia stitch, the diagonal stitch angles from the lower left to the upper right.

When stitched in a line, called the *Yugoslav Border* stitch.

HOW TO STITCH

Can be worked right to left or the reverse.

SUGGESTED USES

Bands, borders, filling, samplers

THREADED BOSNIA

DESCRIPTION

Comprised of a line of basic Bosnia stitches woven with a second "threading" thread that does not pierce the fabric.

Effective in one or more colors.

HOW TO STITCH

Thread the second thread around top and bottom pairs of Bosnia stitches.

Different rows of Bosnia stitches may be threaded with different thread colors for subtle shading.

SUGGESTED USES

Bands, borders, filling, samplers

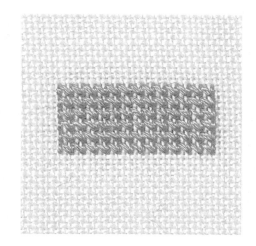

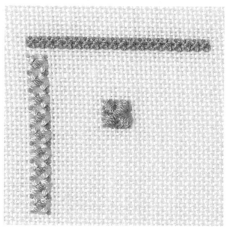

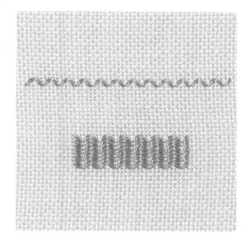

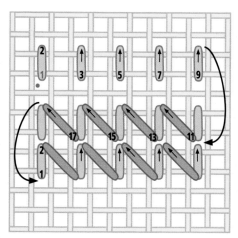

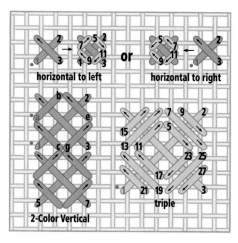

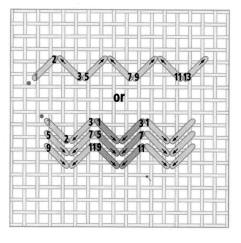

BARRIER
Other Name: Fence

DESCRIPTION
This two-journey, reversible stitch is closely related to the Bosnia stitch (page 198) and is considered to be the French version of the Bosnia.

The diagonal leg of this stitch is angled from the lower right to the upper left.

HOW TO STITCH
Work from left to right or from right to left.

If the fabric is not under tension, you may stitch it using a sewing motion.

SUGGESTED USES
Bands, borders, filling, samplers

RICE
Other Names: Crossed Corners Cross, William and Mary

DESCRIPTION
A popular stitch since the 16th Century.

Effective in one or two colors, and in one or two different thread types or weights (usually heavier or darker thread is the bottom Cross stitch).

Many variations are possible by enlarging the basic Cross stitch and adding more legs (lower right diagram).

HOW TO STITCH
Work from left to right, from right to left, or vertically.

SUGGESTED USES
Bands, borders, filling, alphabets, samplers

ARROWHEAD
Other Name: Double-sided Italian

DESCRIPTION
This is a flat, zigzag stitch which can be arranged in rows or columns.

Individual pairs of stitches may be placed in an isolated, scattered manner (called powdering) to fill a motif.

HOW TO STITCH
Work from left to right, or vertically in pairs of stitches.

To create a less dense filling, space the rows or columns of stitches apart.

Use any type of thread.

SUGGESTED USES
Bands, filling, samplers, backgrounds

199

counted thread stitches

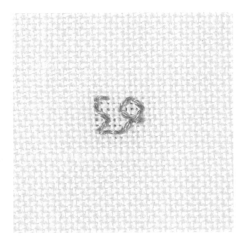

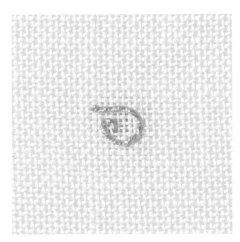

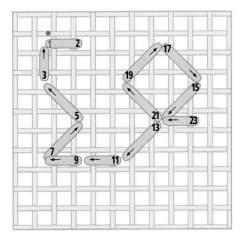
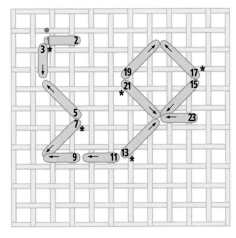
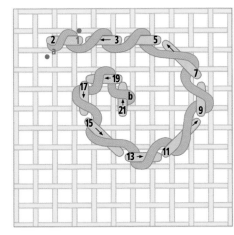

BACKSTITCH
Other Name: Point de Sable

RUNNING BACKSTITCH

WHIPPED BACKSTITCH

DESCRIPTION

This basic and utilitarian stitch may be worked over any number of threads, most commonly over two, three, or four threads; should be consistent within a single stitched piece.

Commonly used to outline motifs.

Provides a foundation stitch for other stitches: Whipped Backstitch (at right), Threaded Backstitch (page 111), and more.

HOW TO STITCH

Work from left to right, from right to left, vertically, or diagonally.

Use any type of thread.

SUGGESTED USES

Outlines, borders, accents within and beyond motifs

DESCRIPTION

A combination of a Running stitch and Backstitch.

Prevents the thread on the back from showing through the fabric as a shadow (compare to the basic Backstitch, at left).

HOW TO STITCH

Carefully note the direction of each stitch at asterisks (*); stitches on the back must follow the same shape as the outline on top.

SUGGESTED USES

Outlines, borders, accents for motifs

DESCRIPTION

Comprised of a line of basic Backstitches woven with a second "threading" thread that does not pierce the fabric, creating a thicker outline than Backstitches.

If the whipping thread is a second color, it creates a bi-colored line resembling a candy cane.

HOW TO STITCH

Stitch a foundation of Backstitches first.

Work from left to right, from right to left, or vertically for either the Backstitches or whipping thread.

Use a tapestry needle for the whipping thread to avoid piercing the Backstitches or the fabric.

SUGGESTED USES

Stems, tendrils, branches, insect antennae, or anywhere a thicker or bi-color Backstitch is appropriate

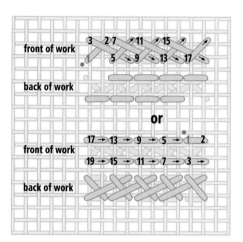

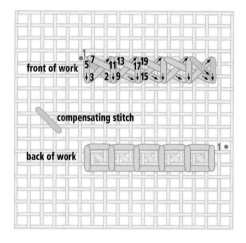

DOUBLE BACKSTITCH

Other Names: Crossed Backstitch,
Point Croise

DESCRIPTION

An old stitch used on antique samplers.
A reversible stitch: a double row of
    Backstitches forms on one side and
    a Closed Herringbone on the other.
The second version (lower diagram) is
    used in shadow work (see Petite
    Fleur project, page 162).

HOW TO STITCH

Work from left to right if you want the
    Closed Herringbone side to be on
    the fabric front. Work from left to
    right, from right to left, or vertically
    if you want the double row of
    Backstitches to be on fabric front.

SUGGESTED USES

Shadow work, bands, borders, samplers

ALTERNATING DOUBLE
BACKSTITCH

DESCRIPTION

Common on antique English samplers,
    this stitch reverses to the same
    appearance on the back of the fab-
    ric, alternating Closed Herringbone
    stitches and a double row of
    Backstitches.
This stitch usually alternates between
    three Double Backstitches that
    show on the front and three Double
    Backstitches that show on the back.

HOW TO STITCH

The easiest method is to first stitch three
    Double Backstitches, then turn the
    fabric to the back and stitch three
    more Double Backstitches on this
    side; by alternating the fabric from
    front to back, you can maintain the
    same stitching sequence.
Or, follow the sequence diagrammed.

SUGGESTED USES

Bands, borders, samplers

DOUBLE BACKSTITCH
WITH BARS

Other Name: Double Backstitch
Variation

DESCRIPTION

The Double Backstitch with Bars
    reverses to a row of Four-sided
    stitches (lower diagram).
Because the upright stitches are on top
    of the other stitches, they create a
    distinctively identifiable band.

HOW TO STITCH

Work from left to right.

SUGGESTED USES

Bands, borders, samplers

counted thread stitches

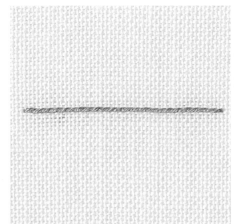

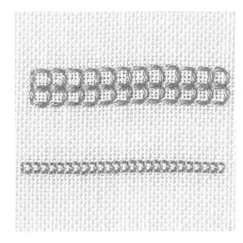

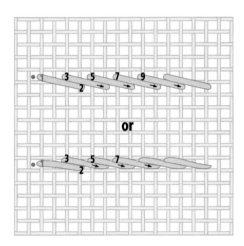

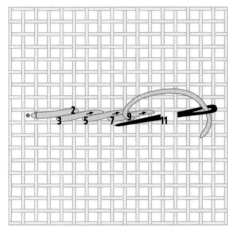

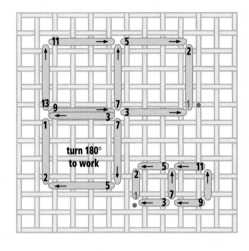

STEM
Other Names: Crewel, Stalk, Outline, South Kensington, Encroaching Stem

DESCRIPTION
One of the most well-known and most-used stitches.

This simple line stitch works well around curves, creating a narrow rope-like appearance.

Stitch length may vary but should remain somewhat short.

HOW TO STITCH
Stitch from left to right, or from bottom to top.

To vary width of stitch, insert needle at slight angle (upper diagram); this is called the *Encroaching Stem* stitch.

Keep stitches of roughly equal length; may be shorter around curves.

Keep the working thread to the bottom of needle (when working horizontally), or to the right of needle (when working vertically).

Use any type of thread.

SUGGESTED USES
Outlines, filling

OUTLINE
Other Name: Stem

DESCRIPTION
Similar to the Stem stitch (at left) except that working thread is above the needle for each stitch.

This simple line stitch works well around curves, creating a narrow rope-like appearance.

Sometimes misnamed a Stem stitch.

HOW TO STITCH
Keep the working thread to the left of needle (when working vertically) or to the top of needle (when working horizontally).

Keep stitches of roughly equal length; may be shorter around curves.

Use any type of thread that fits the even-weave fabric.

SUGGESTED USES
Outlines, filling

FOUR-SIDED
Other Names: Square Openwork, Four-sided Openwork

DESCRIPTION
This old stitch can be a pulled stitch to create a lacy effect (page 235), or not pulled.

Reverses to a three-legged Cross stitch on the back.

HOW TO STITCH
Worked from right to left or from left to right.

Note that the vertical legs are not doubled when stitching a horizontal row; leg 7–8 is leg 1–2 of next stitch.

Multiple rows produce doubled horizontal threads.

SUGGESTED USES
Bands, borders, filling, alphabets, samplers

202

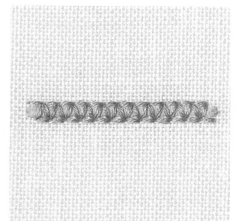
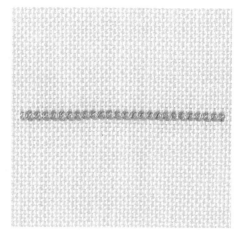
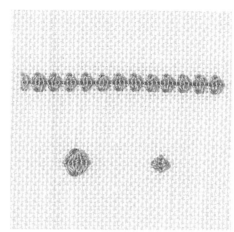

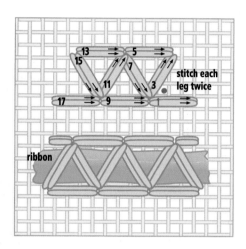
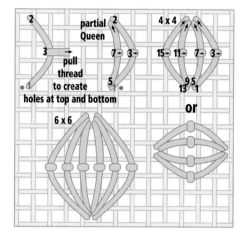

THREE-SIDED
Other Names: Point Turc, Turkish, Lace, Bermuda Faggoting

DESCRIPTION
This flat triangular stitch can be worked on either evenweave or non-even-weave fabrics in straight or gently curved lines.

This old stitch can also be worked as a pulled stitch.

Used to join two fine fabrics together (*Bermuda Faggoting*), lace to fabric (*Lace*), or for ribbon insertion (lower diagram).

HOW TO STITCH
Work from right to left and stitch each leg twice.

Keep the sides of the triangle equal.

Regardless of whether the stitch is pulled or not, use a fine thread and large needle to create holes.

SUGGESTED USES
Bands, filling, samplers, joining two fabrics together, channel for lace or ribbon

ZIGZAG
Other name: Cross-stitch with Bar

DESCRIPTION
This two-journey stitch is commonly found on antique and modern samplers.

HOW TO STITCH
Work first pass from right to left, then from left to right for final pass, noting that the vertical legs are doubled.

SUGGESTED USES
Bands, borders, filling

QUEEN
Other Name: Rococo

DESCRIPTION
Appears on 17th-century English samplers and American Colonial items such as folded pocketbooks, pincushions, and pinballs.

Used for geometric or stylized floral or fruit patterns.

Because vertical legs are pulled, tiny holes form at the top and bottom of stitch, creating a distinctive pattern.

Usually worked in groups of four, but groups of two or six are possible.

HOW TO STITCH
Work individual stitches from right to left.

Work groups of stitches diagonally.

Pull each vertical leg fairly tightly to create tiny holes at top and bottom of stitch.

Tack down each vertical stitch by a short horizontal stitch.

SUGGESTED USES
Geometric shapes, bands, flowers, fruit

203

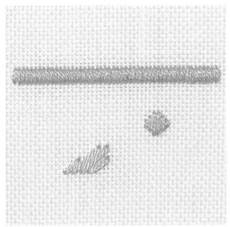

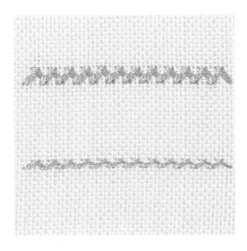

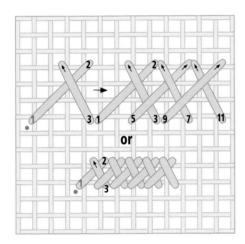

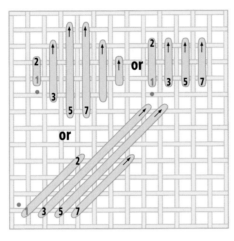

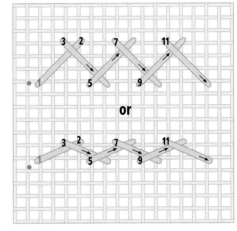

204

PLAIT
Other Name: Spanish

DESCRIPTION
Commonly found on early American samplers.

Creates a braid-like appearance with vertical straight stitches on back.

Sometimes confused with the Long-arm Cross stitch (page 197) which has its long stitch twice as long as its height, and a double row of horizontal stitches on back.

HOW TO STITCH
Work left to right in horizontal rows.

SUGGESTED USES
Bands, outlines, filling

SATIN
Other Names: Flat, Damask

DESCRIPTION
One of the oldest, easiest, and most versatile stitches.

Comprised of a series of Straight stitches worked closely together across a designated shape.

May be of any length and in any direction (vertically, horizontally, or diagonally).

HOW TO STITCH
Work from left to right (shown) or from right to left.

Work from bottom to top of stitch, or the reverse.

For best results, work with fabric held under tension by a frame or hoop.

SUGGESTED USES
Lines, filling, bands, borders, small motifs

OPEN HERRINGBONE
Other Names: Cat, Catch, Persian, Plaited, Russian, Russian Cross, Witch, Fishnet, Mossoul

DESCRIPTION
This old sampler stitch creates a lacy zigzag line.

Actually an evenly spaced variation of a Cross stitch which crosses off-center.

Many variations are possible.

HOW TO STITCH
Work from left to right.

SUGGESTED USES
Bands, borders, filling, foundation for other stitches

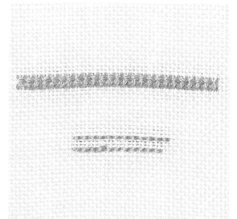
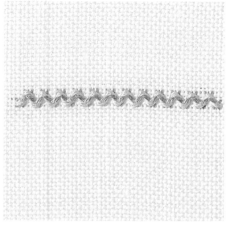
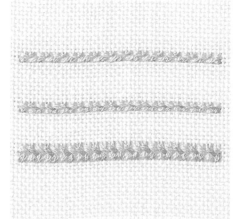

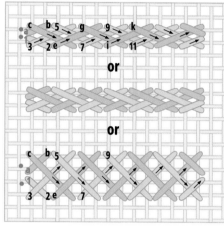
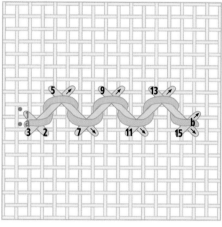

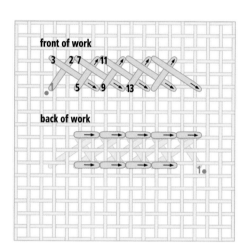

CLOSED HERRINGBONE
Other Names: Shadow Stitch, Close Herringbone

DOUBLE HERRINGBONE
Other Name: Indian Herringbone

THREADED HERRINGBONE
Other Name: Barred Witch

205

DESCRIPTION

Formed like the Open Herringbone stitch (page 204), except the diagonal stitches touch at the top and bottom, making the row of stitches more dense.

Creates a channel for enclosing a ribbon, flat braid, or threads.

When worked on the reverse side of a sheer fabric (usually organdy), forms Backstitches on the front; the Herringbone stitches create a shadow within the Backstitch lines, and is known as shadow work (see Petite Fleur project, page 162).

HOW TO STITCH

Work from left to right.

SUGGESTED USES

Borders, bands, filling, shadow work

DESCRIPTION

This two-journey stitch is a variation of the Open Herringbone.

Effective in one or two colors.

HOW TO STITCH

Work from left to right.

Work the second journey over the first journey (top diagram) or interlace it with the first journey (bottom two diagrams).

This stitch can be expanded to incorporate up to six journeys (in six different colors) by increasing the spacing between the legs in the first journey.

SUGGESTED USES

Borders, bands

DESCRIPTION

Comprised of a line of basic Open Herringbone stitches woven with a second "threading" thread that does not pierce the fabric.

May be worked in one color but more effective if worked in two colors or two different thread types (especially metallics).

HOW TO STITCH

Work from left to right.

First stitch the foundation row of Open Herringbone stitches, then add the threading stitches.

SUGGESTED USES

Bands, borders, lacy filling

counted thread stitches

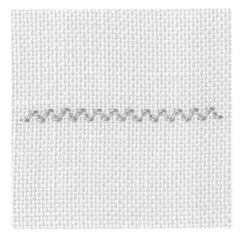

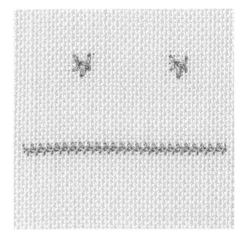

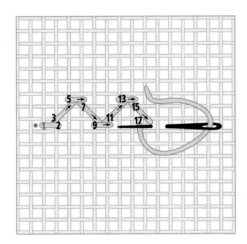
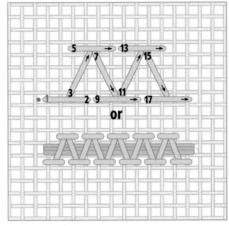
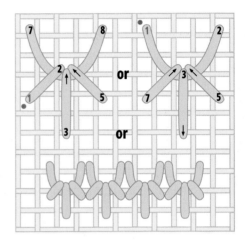

206

OPEN CHEVRON

DESCRIPTION
This flat stitch creates a zigzag line.
May vary in height and width.
When stitched in rows of mirror images and used as a filling, the parallel stitches will be doubled (see page 116).
Useful as a channel for ribbon or thread insertion.

HOW TO STITCH
Work from left to right (as shown) or from top to bottom between two parallel lines.

SUGGESTED USES
Bands, filling, smocking, borders, samplers

CLOSED CHEVRON

DESCRIPTION
The upper horizontal legs of a row share the same fabric holes with their neighbors, as do the lower horizontal legs.
Height and width of stitch may vary.
Useful as a channel for ribbon, cord, or thread insertion (lower diagram and lower stitched example).

HOW TO STITCH
Work from left to right.

SUGGESTED USES
Bands, borders, background, lattice filling

CROWN

DESCRIPTION
May be stitched in rows or arranged in an isolated, scattered manner (called powdering) to fill a motif.

HOW TO STITCH
To stitch in horizontal or vertical rows, choose one of two methods:
1. Work three straight bottom stitches and then weave leg 7–8 under these (upper left diagram).
2. Work the Fly stitch (page 123) first, then the two remaining lower straight stitches (upper right diagram).
Use any type of thread.

SUGGESTED USES
Scattered filling, borders, bands

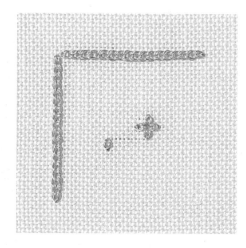
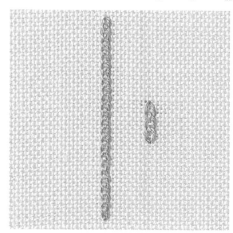
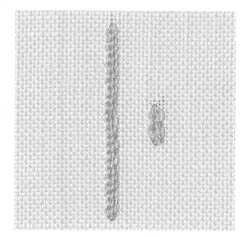

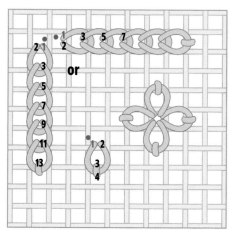
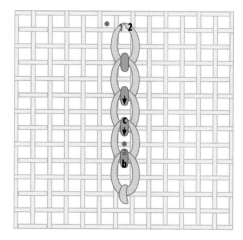
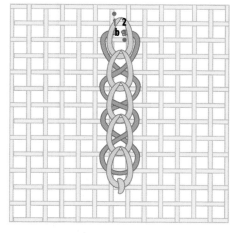

CHAIN
Other Names: Kensington, Tambour, Point de Chainette

DESCRIPTION
One of the oldest and most widely used stitches for canvas work, surface embroidery, and counted thread.

Has many variations (see pages 128–132) which can be worked on evenweave fabrics.

A single Chain stitch (lower middle diagram) is called a *Detached Chain* or *Lazy Daisy* stitch.

HOW TO STITCH
Work in any direction or over any number of threads.

Don't pull loops too tightly; let them resemble a petal, not a straight line.

Use any type of thread.

SUGGESTED USES
Bands, filling, outlines

BACKSTITCHED CHAIN

DESCRIPTION
Comprised of a foundation of Chain stitches further embellished by Backstitches.

A sturdy stitch, especially good for clothing.

HOW TO STITCH
Effective in one or two colors, types, or weights of thread.

SUGGESTED USES
Outlines, lettering, bands

THREADED CHAIN

DESCRIPTION
Comprised of a foundation of Chain stitches ornamented with another "threading" thread.

Enlarges the width of the chain stitches.

The second thread pierces the fabric only at the beginning and end of its journey.

HOW TO STITCH
Effective in one or two colors, types, or weights of thread.

SUGGESTED USES
Outlines, bands, borders

207

counted thread stitches

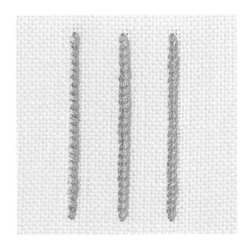

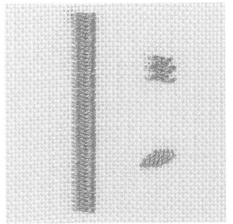

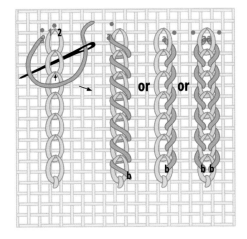

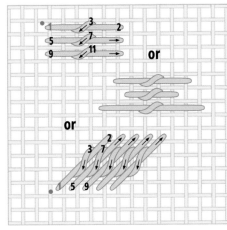

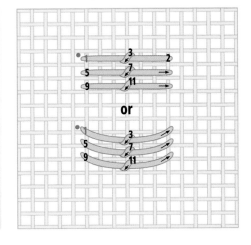

208

WHIPPED CHAIN

DESCRIPTION
Comprised of a foundation of basic Chain stitches ornamented with additional "whipping" thread(s).

The whipping thread pierces the fabric only at the beginning and end of the Chain stitches.

The whipping thread can encompass entire Chain stitch, one side, or both sides.

HOW TO STITCH
Effective in one or two colors, types, or weights of thread.

SUGGESTED USES
Outlines, bands, borders

ROUMANIAN
Other Names: Oriental, Antique, Indian Filling, Janina or Ianina, Romanian

DESCRIPTION
Compare the length of the crossing stitches with the Roman stitch (at right); the tack-down or crossing stitch (3–4) of the Roumanian stitch is usually slightly longer and more slanted.

The length of long stitch may be the same or vary to follow the particular shape of a leaf or other motif.

Effective when stitched closely together to create a solid filling.

Effective in one color.

HOW TO STITCH
Work vertically or diagonally.
Always center the tie-down stitch.
Stitch the long stitch somewhat loosely.

SUGGESTED USES
Borders, bands, filling for stems, leaves, or long narrow spaces

ROMAN
Other Name: Branch

DESCRIPTION
Similar to Roumanian stitch except the tack-down or crossing stitch is shorter.

The tack-down stitch may gently shape the long stitch into a curve.

Effective when spaced closely to make a solid filling, or when spaced apart.

HOW TO STITCH
Work vertically, horizontally, or diagonally.

Work from left to right or from top to bottom.

Always center the tie-down stitch.

SUGGESTED USES
Borders, bands, filling for motifs, stems

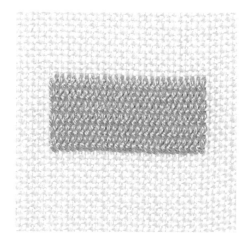

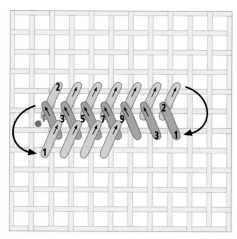
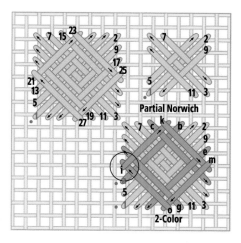
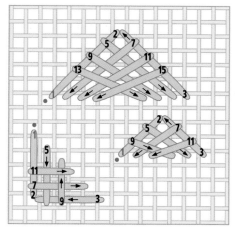

PLAITED GOBELIN
Other Name: Gobelin Plait

DESCRIPTION
Each row overlaps the previous row and slants in opposite direction to create an overall plaited appearance.

May encompass any number of fabric threads (see page 59).

Effective in one or more colors.

HOW TO STITCH
Work in horizontal rows from left to right, then from right to left.

Always position needle in a vertical position on the back of fabric.

Turn fabric 90 degrees to stitch vertical rows.

SUGGESTED USES
Bands, filling, borders, backgrounds

NORWICH
Other Names: Waffle, Southern Cross, Plaited Interlaced

DESCRIPTION
A large, decorative, highly textured, square stitch with a raised diamond center.

A partial Norwich stitch forms a Cross stitch with a woven center.

Effective in one, two, or more colors.

HOW TO STITCH
Must be worked over a square consisting of an uneven number of threads (five, seven, nine and eleven are the most common).

For best results, secure the ground fabric on scroll frame or stretcher bars.

Use almost any type of thread, but fuzzy threads tend to obscure the stitch pattern.

SUGGESTED USES
Corners, bands, borders, samplers

SPRAT'S HEAD

DESCRIPTION
This textured stitch was originally a tailoring stitch used to strengthen fabric at a stress point, such as a pocket or a pleat.

"Sprat" is a type of herring.

HOW TO STITCH
A shiny thread such as stranded cotton, stranded silk, pearl cotton or rayon shows off the woven features of this stitch best.

SUGGESTED USES
Corner motifs, triangular motifs, bands, trees (when stacked upon one another)

209

counted thread stitches

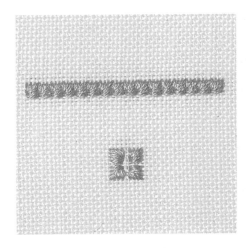

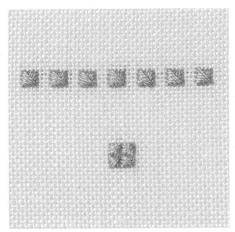

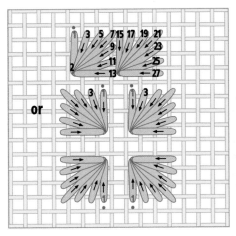

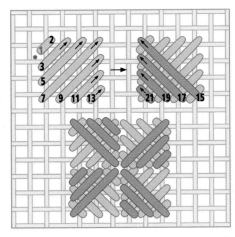

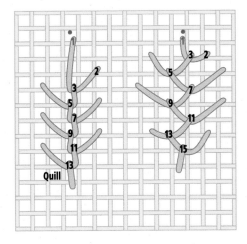

RAY
Other Names: Fan Stitch, Square Ray

DESCRIPTION
This square stitch may be arranged in four different directions.
May be used as a pulled stitch.

HOW TO STITCH
Use any type of thread, but shiny threads enhance the play of light on the angled threads.
Work from left to right, from right to left, or vertically.

SUGGESTED USES
Backgrounds, corners, motifs, bands, borders

CROSSED CORNERS CUSHION

DESCRIPTION
This square stitch may be arranged in four different directions, and the blocks may be arranged alternately.
The diagonal base stitches usually number five or seven.

HOW TO STITCH
Use any type of thread, but shiny threads show off the angled stitches best.

SUGGESTED USES
Bands, filling, borders

CRETAN
Other Names: Persian, Long-armed Feather, or Quill

DESCRIPTION
Appears frequently on regional costumes on the island of Crete, hence its name.
Also found on Persian embroideries, hence its alternate *Persian* name (used by the French).
The appearance is altered considerably by varying the distance between the stitches and the width of the overlap (see page 123).
Also called *Quill* stitch when worked in straight line (left diagram).

HOW TO STITCH
Stitch from top to bottom or from left to right.
Use any type of thread.

SUGGESTED USES
Bands, filling for leaves or petals

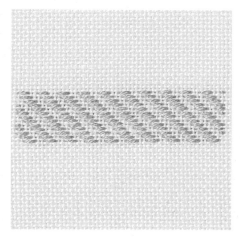
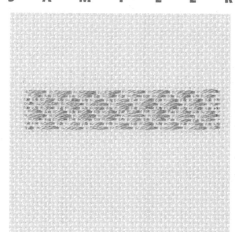

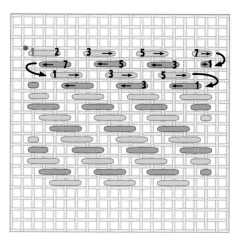
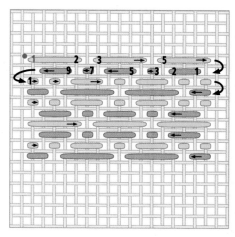
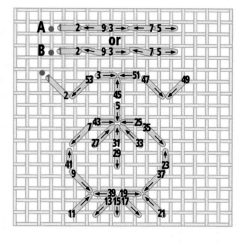

DARNING
Other Names: Pattern Darning, Basting

DARNING VARIATION

DOUBLE RUNNING
Other Names: Holbein, Line, Two-sided Line, Chiara, Italian, Two-sided Stroke, Stroke

DESCRIPTION
Comprised of a series of Running stitches of equal (shown above) or unequal (right) lengths that create woven patterns.

A favored stitch of the Greek islands and Eastern Europe.

Many patterns are possible (see page 47).

Effective in one or more colors.

HOW TO STITCH
Use thread of similar weight and thickness of fabric thread for best results.

Stitch somewhat loosely to prevent puckering; also leave small loop of thread at ends of each row on the wrong side of the fabric.

SUGGESTED USES
Borders, filling, backgrounds, bands

DESCRIPTION
Compare to diagram at left.

HOW TO STITCH
Use thread of similar weight and thickness as fabric threads for best results.

Stitch somewhat loosely to prevent puckering; also leave small loop of thread at ends of each row on the wrong side of the fabric.

SUGGESTED USES
Borders, filling, backgrounds, bands

DESCRIPTION
Comprised of Running stitches over two (usually) or three threads.

This reversible stitch requires two journeys: Make the first journey by stitching every other stitch and all side motifs; complete the second journey by filling in the missing stitches.

Many patterns are possible (see page 114).

Effective in one or two colors.

HOW TO STITCH
Keep the straight lines straight and corners angled correctly by using one of these stitching methods:
1. Split the threads at beginning and end of each stitch (see A, above).
2. Stitch below, then above previous stitches (see B, above).

SUGGESTED USES
Bands, borders, filling, backgrounds

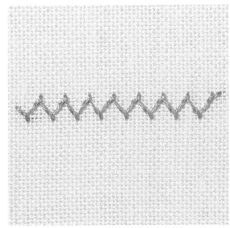

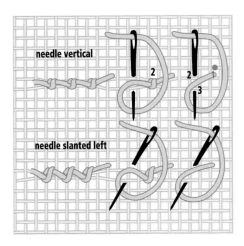

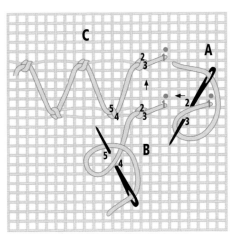

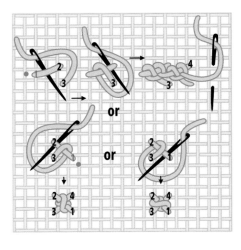

212

CORAL

Other Names: Coral Knot, Beaded, German Knot, Snail Trail, Knotted, Knotted Outline

DESCRIPTION
Produces a line of surface knots, resembling a string of beads.

An old international stitch (Chinese, Spanish, English, Irish, German and Italian embroiderers used this stitch at various times).

Extensively used on Jacobean crewel work.

HOW TO STITCH
Work from right to left.

Hold the needle vertically (upper diagram) or slanted (lower diagram).

Common spacing for knots is approximately ⅛" apart.

Tighten knot by bringing needle and thread straight up, perpendicular to fabric.

SUGGESTED USES
Outlines, filling, leaf veins

ZIGZAG CORAL

DESCRIPTION
A series of Coral Knots create a zigzag line with knots at the top and bottom points.

HOW TO STITCH
Work horizontally from right to left, or vertically from top to bottom.

The point of the needle always faces toward the inside of the two imaginary parallel lines where the knots are formed.

When making the knot, the thread always goes over the needle and then under its point.

Use a medium-weight, lightly twisted thread.

SUGGESTED USES
Bands, borders

PALESTRINA

Other Names: Palestrina Knot, Double Knot, Tied Coral, Old English Knot. Single Knot: Squared Palestrina; Isolated, Single, Small or Reversed Palestrina

DESCRIPTION
Resembles the Coral stitch except it's larger, has more texture, and looks "knottier."

A single Palestrina Knot is a square stitch with a horizontal or vertical top stitch (see lower diagrams).

A series of knots creates a line with a beaded appearance.

HOW TO STITCH
Work from left to right (as shown) or from right to left.

Pull thread taut at each step.

Space knots evenly, either nearly touching or with a small distance apart to show the connecting thread.

Firm twisted threads show off the knots best.

SUGGESTED USES
Outlines, linear designs, filling, bands, lettering, accents (single knots)

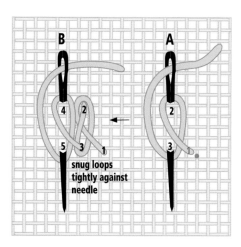

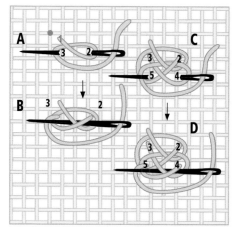

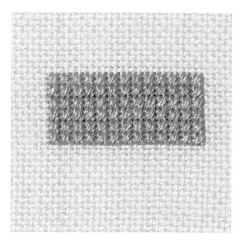

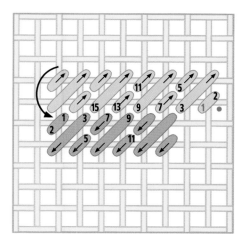

BRAID
Other Name: Gordian Knot Stitch

PLAITED BRAID

MOSAIC
Other Name: Diagonal Hungarian

DESCRIPTION

This popular stitch from 17th-century English samplers has the appearance of a flat braid.

Works well for straight lines or gently curved lines.

The size of the stitch may vary, but close, small-to-medium stitches look best.

HOW TO STITCH

Work from right to left.

A twisted or metallic thread works well.

SUGGESTED USES

Bands, borders, wide stems

DESCRIPTION

Used on samplers, clothing, and furnishings since the early 16th Century; often worked in metal threads.

Creates a complex, wide-line, plaited stitch well worth the practice needed to perfect it.

The size of the stitch may vary and is usually wider than diagrammed.

HOW TO STITCH

Work from top to bottom, turning fabric if necessary.

Maintain an even tension and keep loops of equal size.

Try using pins to help keep loops open.

Most stitchers find a stiff, round thread works best.

SUGGESTED USES

Bands, borders, straight stems

DESCRIPTION

Comprised of a three-stitch group of diagonal stitches forming a small square.

Found on some antique samplers; used today by linen and canvas stitchers (see page 35).

Effective in one or more colors; different colors can be arranged in alternate blocks or in horizontal or vertical stripes.

HOW TO STITCH

Work horizontally from right to left, or diagonally from left to right.

See page 35–36 of the Needlepoint chapter for additional ways to work this stitch and its variations.

SUGGESTED USES

Filling, stems, bands, borders

counted thread stitches

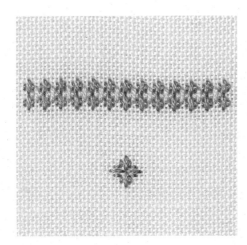

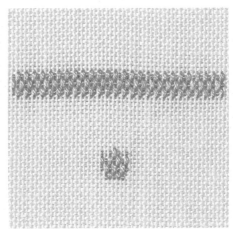

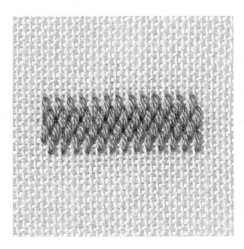

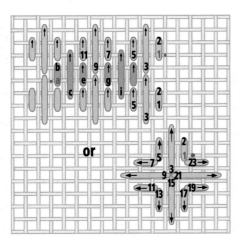

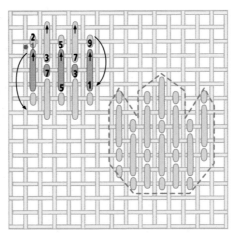

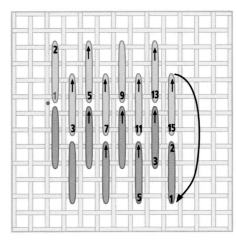

214

HUNGARIAN
Other Name: Point d'Hongrie

DESCRIPTION
A three-stitch group of straight stitches creates a small diamond shape.

Each succeeding row dovetails into previous row.

Individual stitches can be arranged into different motifs (lower diagram).

Effective in one or more colors (in rows); can create subtle shading.

Also a popular canvas stitch (see page 46).

HOW TO STITCH
Work horizontally from left to right or from right to left.

SUGGESTED USES
Filling, bands, borders, motifs

PARISIAN

DESCRIPTION
Comprised of alternating long stitches (usually three threads tall) and short stitches (usually one thread tall).

Also a popular canvas stitch (see page 49).

Each row dovetails into the previous row.

HOW TO STITCH
Work from right to left or from left to right.

Use two colors either in alternate rows, or in one color for the long stitches and another for the short stitches.

Use stranded floss or silk for good coverage.

SUGGESTED USES
Filling, bands, borders

BRICK
Other Name: Alternating

DESCRIPTION
Comprised of stitches of equal length which stair-step up and down, usually worked over two or four threads (as shown; also see page 43).

A good choice to use for subtle shading, with each row stitched in a darker or lighter shade of the same color, or in a different color entirely.

HOW TO STITCH
Most non-fuzzy threads will work as long as the threads cover the fabric; stranded cotton or silk work well.

SUGGESTED USES
Bands, borders, filling

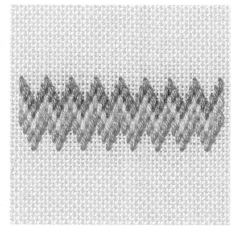

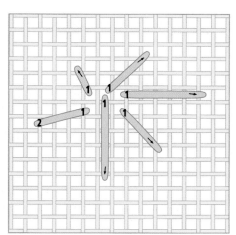

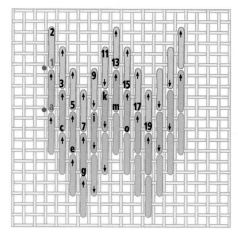

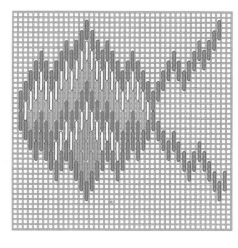

STRAIGHT
Other Name: Stroke

DESCRIPTION
A single straight stitch worked in any direction over any number of threads.

Creates details in or around stitched motifs, such as eyelashes, lettering, or fringe; often stitched on top of other stitches.

HOW TO STITCH
Use any type of thread as long as it suits the fabric.

SUGGESTED USES
Motif accents, details

FLORENTINE
Other Names: Bargello, Flame, Irish, Hungary, Cushion, Hungarian Point

DESCRIPTION
A popular stitch for several centuries, favored by Colonial American embroiderers (see the page 14 for story, page 45 for stitch).

Composed of vertical straight stitches, usually over four or six threads, which form a zigzag (or variation of a zigzag) pattern in an orderly sequence.

Subsequent rows are usually stitched in different colors; endless combinations are possible.

HOW TO STITCH
The numbering shown in the diagram provides best coverage on back for durability.

SUGGESTED USES
Bands, filling; use on upholstery, fire screens, cushions, pocketbooks, pincushions

FLORENTINE VARIATION
Other Name: Carnation Pattern

DESCRIPTION
This is a good example of the stylized pictorial effects possible with variations of this stitch.

HOW TO STITCH
Follow this sequence: for downward steps, stitch from bottom to top; for upward stitches, stitch from top to bottom; this creates long stitches on the back, for better coverage.

SUGGESTED USES
Bands, filling; use on upholstery, fire screens, cushions, pocketbooks, pincushions

215

counted thread stitches

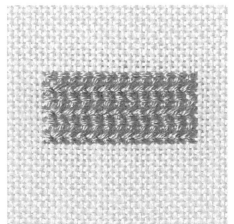

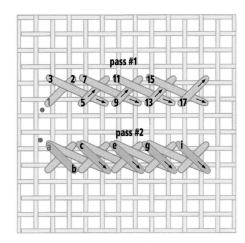

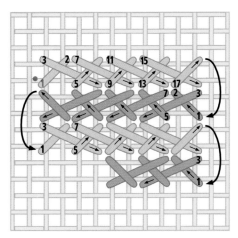

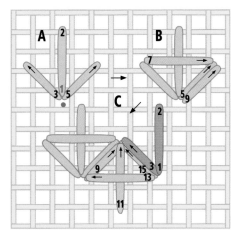

WILLIAMSBURG

DESCRIPTION
Indigenous to United States, this stitch was first found on a 17th-century sampler in Williamsburg, Virginia.

Basically a Double Backstitch with an additional slanted stitch added in the second journey.

The slanted stitch can be the same or a different color for added decoration.

This reversible stitch forms a Four-sided stitch on the back.

HOW TO STITCH
Work from left to right.

Stitch the first journey (foundation row) and end thread at the end of the row; begin second journey at the left again.

SUGGESTED USES
Bands, borders

GREEK CROSS

DESCRIPTION
The first row and every other row after is actually a Double Backstitch (page 201), except that the return row faces the opposite direction.

The slant of the top stitch is in the opposite direction on succeeding rows.

HOW TO STITCH
Work in horizontal rows from left to right and then from right to left.

SUGGESTED USES
Bands, borders, filling

LOARA STANDISH

DESCRIPTION
Indigenous to the United States, this stitch appeared on the oldest known American sampler (Massachusetts, c. 1640) stitched by Loara Standish, daughter of Myles Standish.

This stitch has been found only on the antique sampler mentioned above, but present-day sampler designers use it in their designs.

This reversible stitch looks the same on the front and back.

HOW TO STITCH
Work from left to right.

SUGGESTED USES
Bands, filling

216

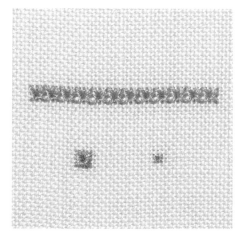

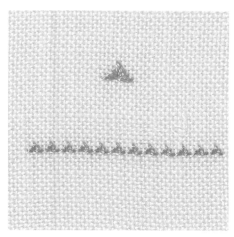

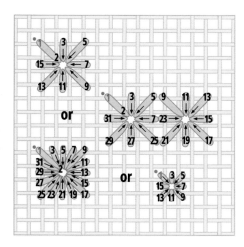

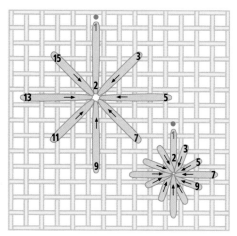

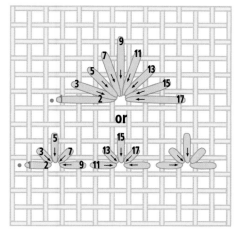

ALGERIAN EYELET
Other Names: Eyelet, Star Eyelet, Star

DESCRIPTION
This square stitch is usually worked over two, four, or six threads.

Can be pulled to create a central hole for an open, lacy appearance.

Historically, used to create alphabet letters on antique samplers.

HOW TO STITCH
Always stitch into the center to keep the hole "clean."

For a pulled stitch, pull the thread as you bring the needle up at the perimeter of the stitch (holes around the perimeter are not desirable).

To stitch horizontal rows, stitch all the top halves of the stitches first, then the bottom halves on the return journey.

See pages 64, 241, 246, and 272 for additional Algerian Eyelets.

SUGGESTED USES
Alphabets, bands, borders

DIAMOND EYELET
Other Name: Star Eyelet, Star

DESCRIPTION
This eyelet stitch (also see page 241) creates the shape of a diamond.

Many variations are possible, including as a pulled stitch.

HOW TO STITCH
Work in a clockwise direction; an alternate method is to stitch the legs at 12:00, 3:00, 6:00, and 9:00, and then fill in the remaining stitches.

For a pulled stitch, pull only when the thread is at the perimeter; this opens the center hole only, not the perimeter.

SUGGESTED USES
Stars, bands, filling; lacy look if pulled

DIAMOND EYELET VARIATION

DESCRIPTION
One-half (either top, shown, or bottom) of a whole Diamond Eyelet.

Many variations are possible, including as a pulled stitch.

HOW TO STITCH
Work from left to right (shown), or from right to left.

For a pulled stitch, pull only when the thread is at the perimeter; this opens the center hole only, not the perimeter.

SUGGESTED USES
Bands, filling; lacy look if pulled

counted thread stitches

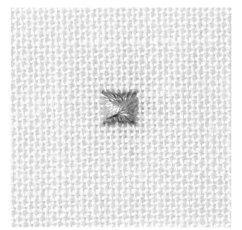

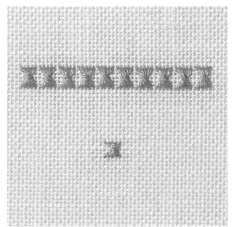

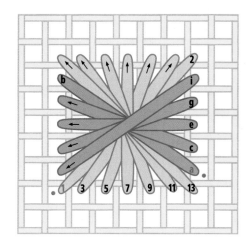

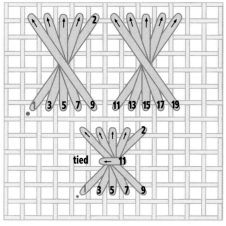

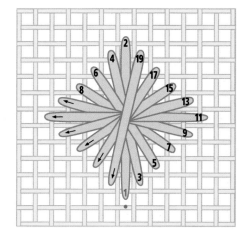

RHODES

DESCRIPTION

This highly textured, square stitch is named after Mary Rhodes, a British needlework designer.

Can be worked over a square of any number greater than three threads of fabric, but fewer than five threads doesn't show the stitch's character.

Effective in one or more colors.

The topmost stitches may snag.

HOW TO STITCH

Work in counterclockwise pattern.

Use smooth thread for best results.

If desired, tie the top stitch at its center (see Half Rhodes, at right).

Work with fabric held under tension by a frame or hoop.

If you want the diagonal stitch (lower left to upper right) to be topmost, then start on stitch to the right and make the 3–4 stitch the first stitch.

SUGGESTED USES

Corners, borders, architectural or geometric features

HALF RHODES
Other Name: Partial Rhodes

DESCRIPTION

Half of a full Rhodes stitch(at left) forms a horizontal or vertical hourglass shape.

Most effective in one color.

Can be a tied stitch (see page 67); the tie may be stitched in a second color.

HOW TO STITCH

Work horizontally, diagonally, or as a half drop (see page 67).

Work with fabric held under tension by a frame or hoop.

SUGGESTED USES

Bows, bands, borders

RHODES DIAMOND

DESCRIPTION

Worked on the same principle as the Rhodes stitch (far left), except for the shape.

Most effective in one color.

HOW TO STITCH

Work in a counterclockwise pattern.

Work with fabric held under tension by a frame or hoop.

If you want the upright vertical stitch to be topmost, then start on stitch to the right and make the 3–4 stitch the first stitch.

SUGGESTED USES

Dimensional architectural accents, clothing accents, finials, stars

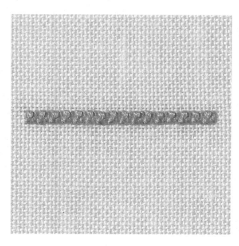

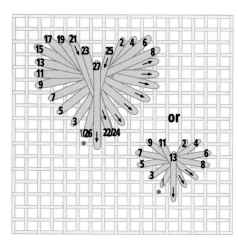

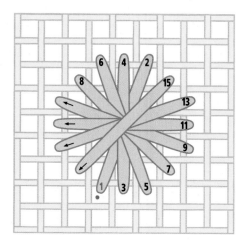

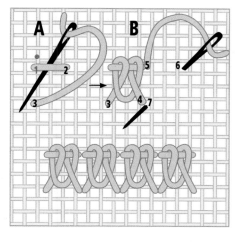

RHODES HEART

DESCRIPTION
This Rhodes stitch variation takes the shape of a textured heart.

May require compensating stitches (note legs 23–24 and 25–26 in the diagram of the larger heart).

Effective in one color.

Most symmetrically shaped hearts can be stitched as a Rhodes Heart.

HOW TO STITCH
Work in a counterclockwise pattern.

Work with fabric held under tension by a frame or hoop.

SUGGESTED USES
Dimensional accents on clothing, finials on fence posts and houses, jewelry (lockets), filling

RHODES OCTAGON

DESCRIPTION
Another shape variation of the Rhodes stitch.

May vary in size.

Effective in one color.

HOW TO STITCH
Work in a counterclockwise pattern.

Work with fabric held under tension by a frame or hoop.

SUGGESTED USES
Flowers, dimensional architectural accents, finials, balls

SORBELLO

DESCRIPTION
This textured, square, knotted stitch is popular on embroideries from Sorbello, Italy.

Works up fairly quickly.

HOW TO STITCH
Work from left to right.

Keep loops loose so that stitch creates a square shape.

SUGGESTED USES
Borders, bands, straight or curved lines, filling

219

counted thread stitches

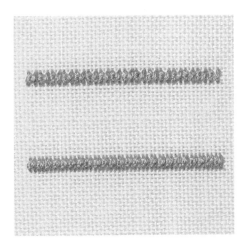

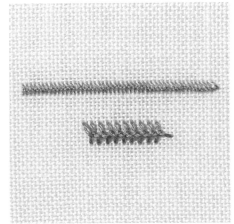

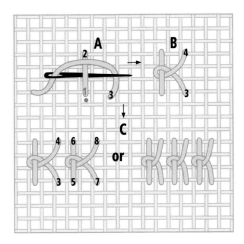

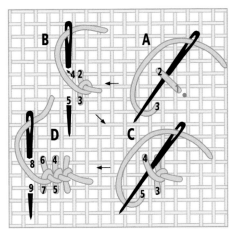

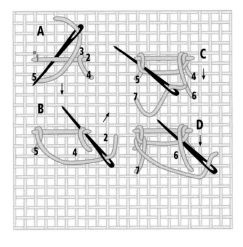

SIENNESE

LOOP
Other Name: Centipede

LADDER

DESCRIPTION
This looped line stitch resembles the letter "K."

Effective in a straight line.

Stitches may be close together or spaced apart.

The looped leg of this stitch may be pulled tightly or left loose.

HOW TO STITCH
Work from left to right.

Keep stitches of equal height and tension.

SUGGESTED USES
Bands, borders, filling

DESCRIPTION
This line stitch with a raised center works well for straight or curved lines.

The length of the side legs may vary.

HOW TO STITCH
Work from right to left.

SUGGESTED USES
Bands, borders, filling, leaf midrib and veins, centipede

DESCRIPTION
This wide line stitch appears on old samplers; line may be straight, undulating, or of variable widths.

Spacing between stitches may vary, as may the width.

HOW TO STITCH
Work from top to bottom.

A round thread produces more depth at the stitch edges, but almost any thread, including metallic, will work.

SUGGESTED USES
Bands, borders; channel for ribbon, threads, or braid

220

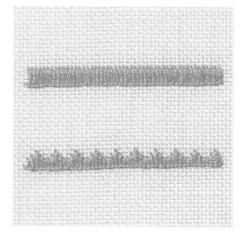

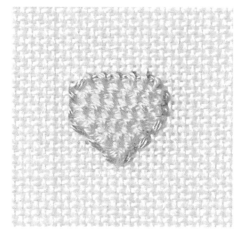

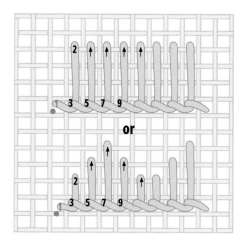

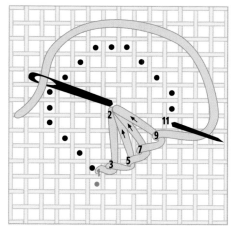

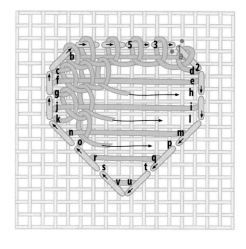

BUTTONHOLE
Other Name: Closed Blanket

DESCRIPTION
A universally used stitch (see pages 158, 144, 156, and 276); found on antique samplers, Hardanger work, cutwork, and clothing (edging for buttonholes).

The vertical legs should be close enough to touch (if there are spaces, then the stitch is called a *Blanket* stitch; see page 122).

Height of the vertical legs may vary (lower diagram).

HOW TO STITCH
Use practically any type of thread.

SUGGESTED USES
Edgings, bands, borders, outlines, filling, motifs, channel for ribbons or thread

BUTTONHOLE WHEEL
Other Names: Buttonhole Circle, Buttonhole Ochka, Wheel, Blanket Pinwheels

DESCRIPTION
Comprised of a series of Buttonhole stitches worked in a circle with or without a common central hole.

May vary in size.

Popular in Elizabethan and Ukrainian embroidery.

HOW TO STITCH
If desired, pull the stitch slightly to enlarge the central hole.

SUGGESTED USES
Round motif for flowers, wheels, circles

DETACHED BUTTONHOLE

DESCRIPTION
Used in Elizabethan (and other) samplers and raised embroidery, this stitch creates a raised motif on top of the fabric.

Effective in one or more colors.

You may introduce shading with each new line of Buttonhole stitches.

HOW TO STITCH
Backstitch (shown) or Chain-stitch around motif first if motif is to be completely stitched down to fabric.

Backstitch only at the top if motif (petal or leaf) is to be loose and anchored only at the base and tip.

A firm, twisted thread creates the best results.

Strive to maintain uniform loops and tension.

SUGGESTED USES
Filling stitch for leaves, petals; raised motifs, flower centers

counted thread stitches

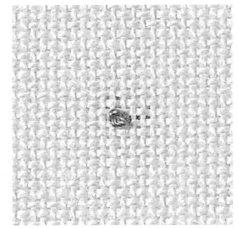

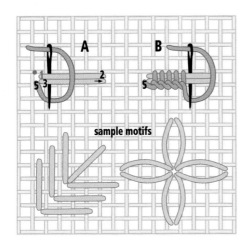

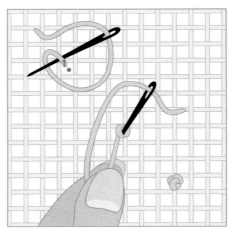

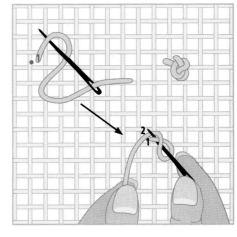

222

BUTTONHOLE BAR

DESCRIPTION
This textured stitch appears on 17th-century whitework samplers, cutwork, and textured embroidery. Effective in one color.

HOW TO STITCH
Use two (shown) or three straight foundation stitches.

The individual Buttonhole stitches do not pierce fabric except at beginning and end of row.

To keep foundation threads straight for some motifs (see lower left diagram) stitch enough Buttonhole stitches to just cover foundation threads.

To curve (bow out) foundation threads (see lower right diagram) pack the foundation threads with more Buttonhole stitches until they curve.

Use firmly twisted thread for best results.

SUGGESTED USES
Textured motifs, channel for ribbon or cord (multiple bars), samplers

FRENCH KNOT
Other Names: French Dot, Wound, Knotted, Twisted Knot

DESCRIPTION
Has the appearance of a solitary, raised knot.

HOW TO STITCH
Wrap thread around needle only once or twice.

For larger or thicker French Knots, increase number of thread strands or weight of thread.

Keep thread snug around barrel of needle when completing stitch.

When finally inserting needle back into the ground fabric, move one linen thread (or a partial Aida square) over from where needle originally emerged to keep the knot from slipping through the fabric to the back.

Use any type of thread or ribbon.

Work with fabric held under tension by a frame or hoop.

SUGGESTED USES
Flowers, eyes and eye highlights, fur and hair, outlines, filling

COLONIAL KNOT
Other Names: Candlewick Knot, Figure-8 Knot

DESCRIPTION
This solitary, raised knot stitch is slightly larger than a French Knot (at left).

HOW TO STITCH
Keep thread snug around barrel of needle when completing stitch.

When finally inserting needle back into the ground fabric, move one linen thread (or a partial Aida square) over from where needle originally emerged to keep the knot from slipping through the fabric to the back.

Use any type of thread or ribbon.

Work with fabric held under tension by a frame or hoop.

SUGGESTED USES
Same as for French Knot: flowers, eyes and eye highlights, fur and hair, outlines, filling

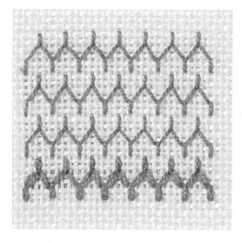

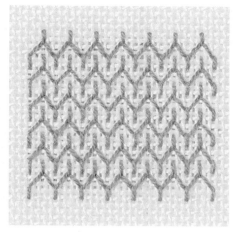

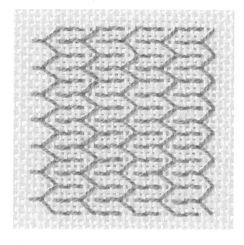

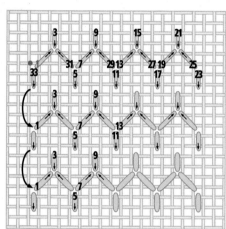

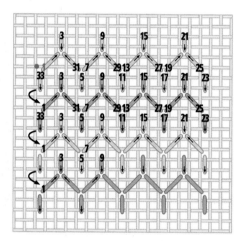

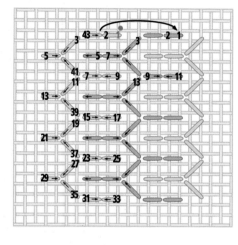

WISHBONE PATTERN I

WISHBONE PATTERN II

WISHBONE PATTERN III

223

DESCRIPTION

A simple, reversible blackwork pattern. Compare to Wishbone Patterns II and III.

Each succeeding row may be stitched using one more fiber strand than its predecessor (one strand for Row 1, two strands for Row 2, three strands for Row 3); design becomes denser with added strands (see lowest row of stitched example, above).

HOW TO STITCH

Stitch using the Double Running stitch as diagrammed. For further information on the Double Running stitch, see page 211.

SUGGESTED USES

Filling, backgrounds, bands, borders

DESCRIPTION

This variation of the basic reversible Wishbone pattern has the same stitch configuration, but these stitches are closer to one another.

Has a denser appearance than Wishbone Pattern I.

Compare to Wishbone Patterns I and III.

HOW TO STITCH

Stitch the same as Wishbone Pattern I, but space the rows closer together.

SUGGESTED USES

Filling, backgrounds, bands, borders

DESCRIPTION

This variation of the basic reversible Wishbone pattern is turned 90 degrees and the (now) horizontal legs are one stitch longer.

Compare to Wishbone Patterns I and II.

HOW TO STITCH

Stitch the same as Wishbone Pattern I, but stitch in vertical rows, and add an extra stitch to each leg, except for first and last rows.

SUGGESTED USES

Filling, backgrounds, bands, borders

The red dot in each stitch diagram indicates where to begin stitching.

counted thread stitches

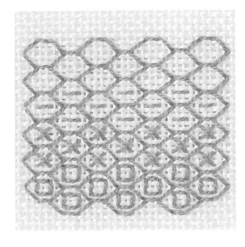

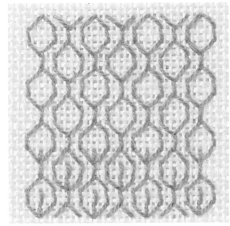

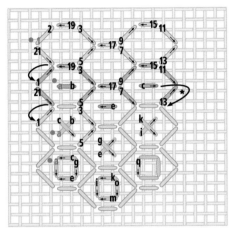
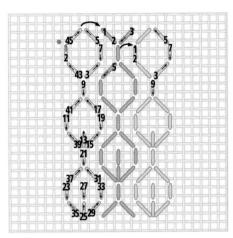
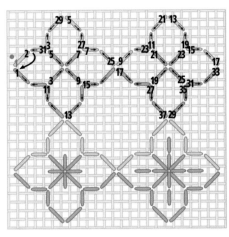

LOZENGE PATTERN I & VARIATIONS

DESCRIPTION
Comprised of a basic six-sided Lozenge Pattern which may accommodate increasingly more dense internal motifs (note progression in photo).

HOW TO STITCH
Stitch using the Double Running stitch as diagrammed or see page 211.

For the example shown here, add the internal motifs after the lozenge pattern is complete.

For all internal motifs, keep the traveling thread on back of fabric moving in the same direction (entering and exiting the lozenge shape in a similar pattern). For the horizontal straight stitch, carry the traveling thread horizontally on the fabric back and tack behind already-completed stitches (at star) to avoid having long threads on fabric back or visible shadow lines on the front.

SUGGESTED USES
Filling, backgrounds, bands, borders

LOZENGE PATTERN II & VARIATIONS

DESCRIPTION
A variation of the basic Lozenge Pattern, arranged vertically with additional threads separating each lozenge.

The simple Lozenge Pattern (top of stitched example) can stand on its own or be embellished (middle and lower examples).

Each succeeding column may be stitched using one more fiber strand than its predecessor to create an increasingly more dense effect.

HOW TO STITCH
Stitch using the Double Running stitch as diagrammed or see page 211.

Stitch these specific internal motifs as part of the same sequence with the basic lozenge design.

SUGGESTED USES
Filling, backgrounds, bands, borders

LOZENGE PATTERN III & VARIATIONS

DESCRIPTION
A variation of the basic Lozenge Pattern, with the lozenges arranged around a central point to form "floral" clusters which create an open area which can accommodate another full floral cluster.

Many variations are possible; adding stitches to the interior of each floral cluster creates more complex and dense motifs.

HOW TO STITCH
Stitch using the Double Running stitch as diagrammed or see page 211.

Begin each row separately.

SUGGESTED USES
Filling, backgrounds, isolated motifs (medallion)

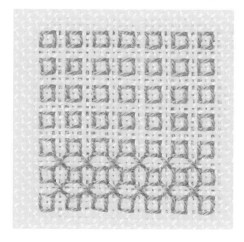

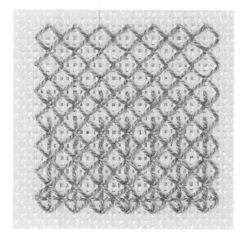

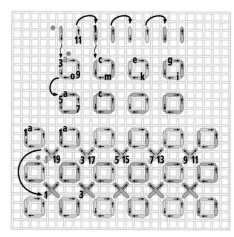

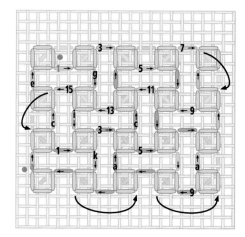

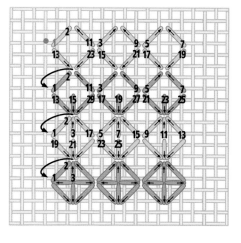

SQUARE PATTERN I & VARIATION

DESCRIPTION

Use this basic Square Pattern "as is" or embellish it further to create variations (see lower half of diagram for an example).

HOW TO STITCH

The top three rows diagram the basic Running stitch pattern for the squares only.

Stitch the vertical stitches in ascending and descending vertical rows.

Stitch the horizontal stitches in rows from left to right and reverse.

SUGGESTED USES

Filling, backgrounds, bands, borders

SQUARE PATTERN II

DESCRIPTION

This embellished variation of the basic Square Pattern (at left) creates an intriguing basketweave pattern.

HOW TO STITCH

Stitch the foundation of small squares first (see Square Pattern I, at left), then stitch the remaining horizontal stitches, and finally the remaining vertical stitches.

SUGGESTED USES

Filling, backgrounds, bands, borders

TRELLIS PATTERN & VARIATIONS

DESCRIPTION

Use the basic Trellis Pattern "as is" or add stitches in varying amounts to make the pattern darker and/or denser.

HOW TO STITCH

Stitch using the Double Running stitch as diagrammed or see page 211.

If you stitch with the fabric turned 90 degrees, the orientation of the internal stitching may change (see the variation in the middle of the diagram).

SUGGESTED USES

Filling, backgrounds

counted thread stitches

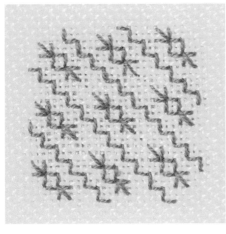

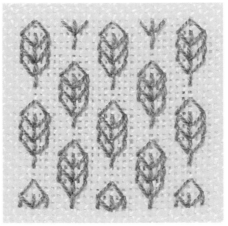

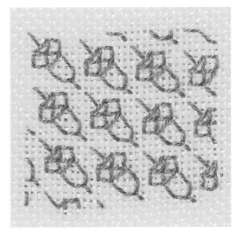

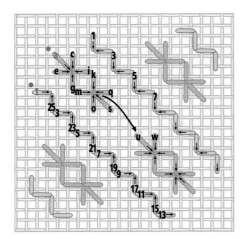

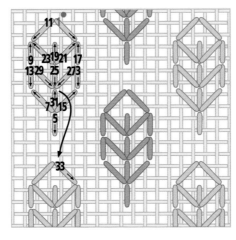

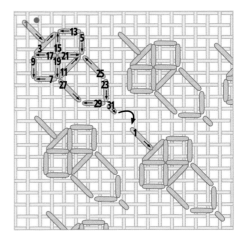

GEOMETRIC FILLING PATTERN

DESCRIPTION
This simple filling pattern is comprised of diagonal bands, with the isolated motif offset one thread to the left in adjacent bands.

HOW TO STITCH
Stitch using the Double Running stitch as diagrammed or see page 211.

Work the zigzag borders first, then work the isolated motifs diagonally, traveling on the back of the fabric to the next motif.

SUGGESTED USES
Filling, backgrounds

LEAF FILLING PATTERN

DESCRIPTION
In this pattern, an object motif (a leaf) creates an overall vertical pattern.

Many variations are possible; any small, simple outlined shape may serve as a pattern.

HOW TO STITCH
Stitch using the Double Running stitch as diagrammed or see page 211.

Work the pattern in vertical rows which may or may not dovetail, traveling on back of fabric to next motif.

SUGGESTED USES
Filling, backgrounds

ACORN FILLING PATTERN

DESCRIPTION
In this pattern, an object motif (an acorn) creates an overall diagonal pattern.

Many variations are possible; any small, simple outlined shape may serve as a pattern.

Each new row line "steps down and over" one thread to the right (does not line up horizontally or vertically).

HOW TO STITCH
Stitch using the Double Running stitch as diagrammed or see page 211.

Work the pattern in diagonal rows traveling behind fabric to next motif.

SUGGESTED USES
Filling

226

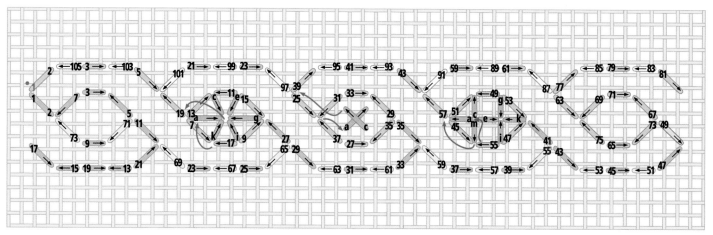

BORDER PATTERN I & VARIATIONS

DESCRIPTION

This basic cable Border Pattern may be stitched without the internal variations (as shown).

Cable pattern may be further embellished with other internal as well as external elements (see Border Patterns II, III, and IV, page 228).

HOW TO STITCH

Stitch using the Double Running stitch as diagrammed above or see page 211.

Work the border in two passes; the first is shown in blue and white, the second in pink and white.

Add interior motifs (green) in the first pass.

SUGGESTED USES

Borders, bands

227

counted thread stitches

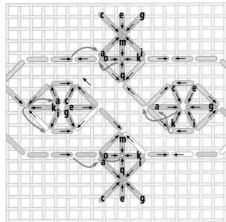
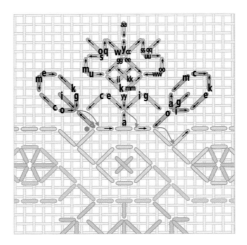
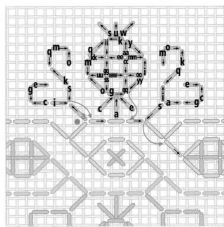

BORDER PATTERN II

DESCRIPTION
Border Pattern II adds a few external elements to the basic Border Pattern I with internal elements (page 227), giving it more contrast with an open cable, dense internal "holes" and additional external motifs.

HOW TO STITCH
Stitch using the Double Running stitch (as diagrammed above or see page 211).

To stitch cable Border Pattern I, see page 227.

Complete the extra motifs at the same time as the basic Border Pattern.

Complete the center and top side motifs with the first (blue) pass, the rest with the second (pink) pass.

Note that only the first internal element is stitched with the second pass; all the others are stitched with the first pass.

SUGGESTED USES
Borders, bands

BORDER PATTERN III

DESCRIPTION
This border expands the basic Border Pattern I by adding floral elements to the top and bottom and an "X" in the center hole (see page 227).

HOW TO STITCH
Stitch using the Double Running stitch (as diagrammed above or see page 211).

To stitch cable Border Pattern I, see page 227.

Complete the floral motif during the first (blue) pass.

To complete the border (second pink pass), turn chart and repeat the floral motif on other side. (The numbering won't be correct, but the stitches follow the same sequence and traveling order).

SUGGESTED USES
Filling, wide borders, bands

BORDER PATTERN IV

DESCRIPTION
This border expands the basic Border Pattern I by adding floral elements (different than those in Border Patterns II and III) to the top and bottom and an "X" in the center hole (see page 227).

HOW TO STITCH
Stitch using the Double Running stitch (as diagrammed above or see page 211).

To stitch cable Border Pattern I, see page 227.

To stitch the floral motif on the top of the border, turn chart and stitch during first (blue) pass. (The numbering won't be correct, but the stitches follow the same sequence and traveling order.)

Complete blue pass back to beginning; then work the pink pass for a border with symmetrical sides.

SUGGESTED USES
Borders, bands

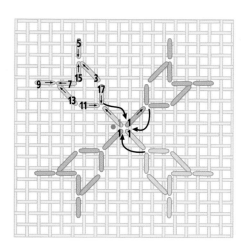
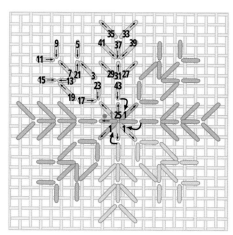
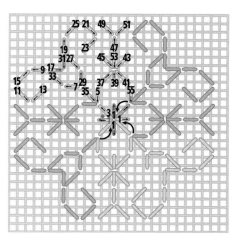

MEDALLION PATTERN I

DESCRIPTION
This simple medallion pattern may be used alone or spaced in rows and/or columns to create a filling pattern.

HOW TO STITCH
Stitch using the Double Running stitch (as diagrammed above or see page 211).

Work each medallion separately.

Work each medallion from the center out, traveling around one arm then back to the center to start the next arm.

SUGGESTED USES
Filling, isolated motifs, bands, borders

MEDALLION PATTERN II

DESCRIPTION
This medallion pattern is an expansion of Medallion Pattern I, with four additional "arms."

HOW TO STITCH
Stitch using the Double Running stitch (as diagrammed above or see page 211)).

Work each medallion separately.

Work each medallion from the center out, traveling around one arm then back to the center to start the next arm.

SUGGESTED USES
Filling, borders, isolated motifs, bands

MEDALLION PATTERN III

DESCRIPTION
This medallion pattern is a variation of Medallion Pattern I, with additional arm extensions.

As a filling, this pattern creates lacy, positive spaces that contrast with the eight-point star negative area of the fabric between individual medallions.

HOW TO STITCH
Stitch using the Double Running stitch (as diagrammed above or see page 211).

Work each medallion separately.

Work each medallion from the center out, traveling around one arm then back to center to start the next arm.

SUGGESTED USES
Filling, wide borders, isolated motifs, bands

229

counted thread stitches

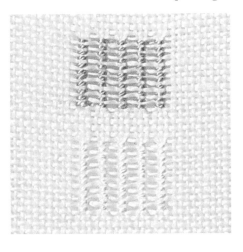

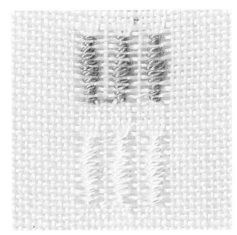

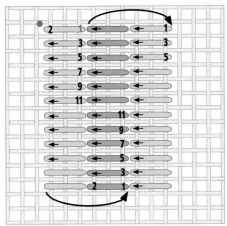
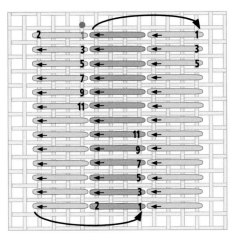
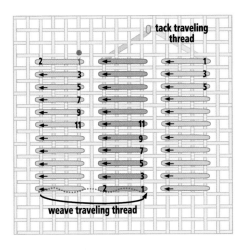

NARROW SATIN
Other Names: Pins, Cord, Rope

230

DESCRIPTION
Comprised of a single row or rows of pulled Satin stitches, usually over two or three fabric threads.

HOW TO STITCH
Pull thread tightly and evenly.
Work in horizontal or vertical rows (vertical shown).

SUGGESTED USES
Borders, bands, filling

Pulled work is usually done with threads the same color as the ground fabric so the tack stitches and traveling threads are not visibly obvious. If you're using thread that is a different color than the ground fabric, bury the threads in previously worked stitches.

SATIN VARIATION I

DESCRIPTION
Stitched in same sequence as Narrow Satin (at left), but with varying tension on the working thread.
Usually covers four or more fabric threads, with no unstitched fabric threads between rows.

HOW TO STITCH
Work vertically or horizontally (diagram shows vertical).
Alternate pulled areas with areas of looser tension to produce a "fat, thin, fat, thin" pattern.

SUGGESTED USES
Borders, bands, filling

SATIN VARIATION II

DESCRIPTION
Stitched in same sequence as Narrow Satin (at far left), but with varying tension on the working thread.
Usually covers four or more fabric threads, with one thread left unstitched between the rows.

HOW TO STITCH
Travel between rows by mimicking weave of fabric (illustrated at lower part of diagram), or use a tack (illustrated at upper part of diagram).

SUGGESTED USES
Borders, bands, filling

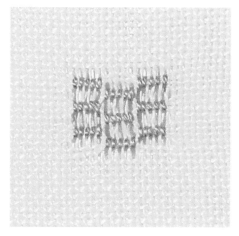

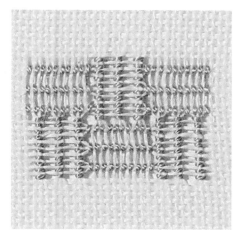

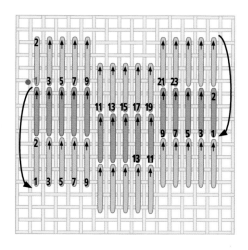
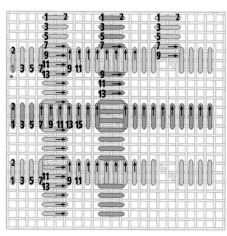
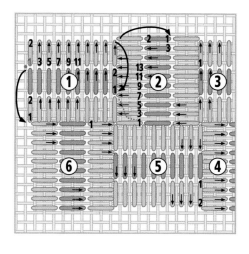

ALTERNATING SATIN

DESCRIPTION
Comprised of pulled Satin-stitch units offset from one another, which creates an overall "netting" effect.

HOW TO STITCH
Stitch with a tight and even pull.

Work a horizontal group of vertical stitches over four threads; move down two fabric threads below first group, and work another horizontal group.

Move up two fabric threads and work another horizontal group.

Continue across row, alternating groups.

Follow this up-and-down sequence for remaining rows.

SUGGESTED USES
Borders, filling

BASKET FILLING
Other Name: Open Basket

DESCRIPTION
Comprised of horizontal and vertical rows of pulled Satin-stitch groups.

HOW TO STITCH
Stitch with a tight and even pull.

For first horizontal row, start with four compensating pulled Satin stitches. Skip three fabric threads, then stitch ten vertical stitches; repeat sequence to end of row.

For second horizontal row, stitch ten vertical stitches, skip three fabric threads; repeat sequence to the end of the row.

For vertical rows, start with a group of ten Satin stitches, skipping over previously stitched bars; repeat to end of row.

For second vertical row, stitch a group of four stitches, skip over previously stitched bars, then continue to stitch groups of ten stitches.

SUGGESTED USES
Filling

CHESSBOARD

DESCRIPTION
The first block is comprised of three horizontal rows of ten pulled Satin stitches each; the second block follows the same pattern as the first, but is arranged perpendicular to the first; this arrangement is for both horizontal and vertical directions.

Most effective in an area large enough to show off the large pattern repeat.

Pattern resembles a plain weave.

HOW TO STITCH
Stitch with a tight and even pull.

SUGGESTED USES
Filling

The red dot in each stitch diagram indicates where to begin stitching.

counted thread stitches

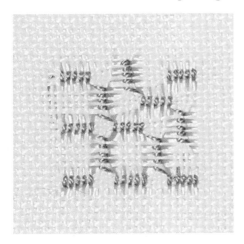

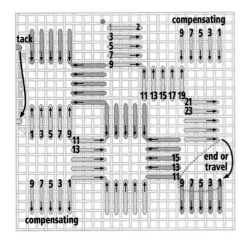

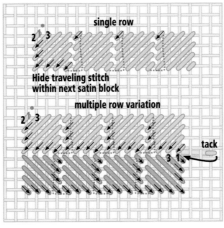

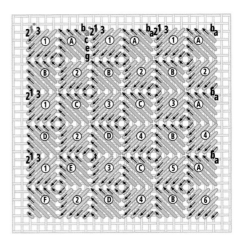

STEP

DESCRIPTION
Comprised of groups of five pulled Satin stitches, worked diagonally and with successive groups perpendicular to one another, creating an overall diagonal zigzag pattern.

HOW TO STITCH
Stitch with a tight and even pull.

Work in diagonal rows.

To travel between rows, try these options:

1. End each diagonal row in previously-stitched Satin stitches.

2. Travel diagonally, then weave the traveling thread into the fabric (shown as a horizontal, red dotted line); the traveling thread will be partially concealed by the group of Satin stitches worked over it.

3. When bordered by an outline (such as Chain stitches), hide the traveling thread within the outline.

SUGGESTED USES
Filling, diagonal border

DIAGONAL SATIN
Other Name: Pulled Scotch

DESCRIPTION
Comprised of blocks of pulled, diagonal Satin stitches (page 204) stitched in the same direction across each row, then alternating direction for the second row. Each group of Satin stitches resembles a leaf.

HOW TO STITCH
For each Satin-stitch block, pull the first two stitches tightly, then gradually relax the tension as stitches get wider, then pull tightly for the last two stitches of this group; this creates an attractive, elongated diamond shape.

Travel on the back to the top of the second block, covering the traveling thread with the next group of Satin stitches as diagrammed.

Use a tack stitch (as shown) to begin the second row.

SUGGESTED USES
Borders, bands, filling

DIAGONAL SATIN FILLING
Other Name: Pulled Scotch

DESCRIPTION
Comprised of blocks of diagonal Satin stitches that alternate direction, creating four-petalled floral motifs.

HOW TO STITCH
For each Satin-stitch block, see *How to Stitch* at left.

For a two-row pattern: Complete the first block; move down diagonally to the second block; move up horizontally to third; diagonally to fourth; and so on. Catch the traveling thread in the Satin stitches of the new block. Fill in remaining areas in like fashion.

For filling: Work the blocks diagonally in one direction first (numbered rows). Secure working thread at end of each diagonal row. Then fill the adjacent rows with the stitches perpendicular to the previous stitches (lettered rows).

SUGGESTED USES
Borders, bands, filling

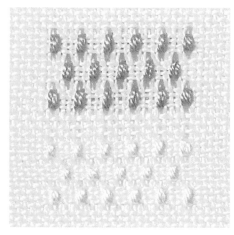
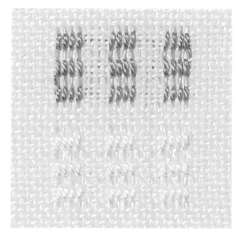
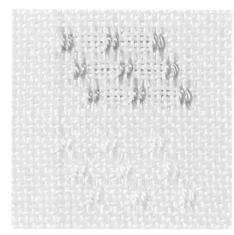

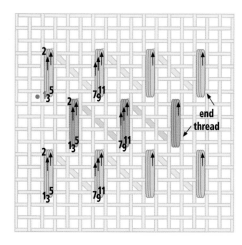
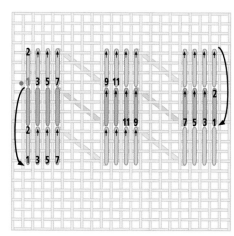
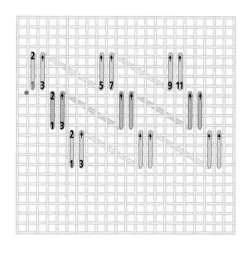

COIL FILLING

DESCRIPTION

Comprised of a group of three vertical Satin stitches in the same fabric holes, with an even number of fabric threads left between each cluster (diagram shows four threads).

The second row alternates so the stitch cluster falls between and below the first row.

HOW TO STITCH

Stitch with a medium-to-tight, even pull.

Work over four threads.

Secure the working thread at end of each row.

SUGGESTED USES

Filling, bands, borders

SPACED SATIN FILLING

DESCRIPTION

Comprised of groups of Satin stitches with unstitched areas between groups (diagram shows five threads).

Many variations are possible by changing the number of threads covered, the number of stitches in each group, and the number of threads between groups; alternating subsequent rows may be offset.

Compare Spaced Satin Filling Variation I (at right) and II (page 234).

HOW TO STITCH

Stitch with a medium and even pull.

Weave down to next row or end the thread in the back of previous Satin stitches.

SUGGESTED USES

Filling, bands, borders

SPACED SATIN FILLING VARIATION I

DESCRIPTION

Comprised of pairs of Satin stitches with unstitched areas between groups (diagram shows six threads); subsequent rows are offset, creating a diagonal pattern (compare with Variation II, page 234).

HOW TO STITCH

Stitch with a medium and even pull.

Secure the working thread at the end of each row.

SUGGESTED USES

Borders, bands, filling

233

counted thread stitches

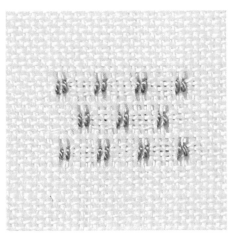

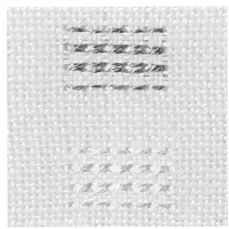

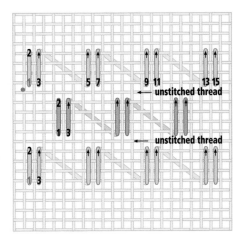
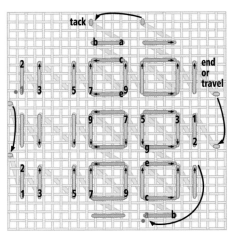
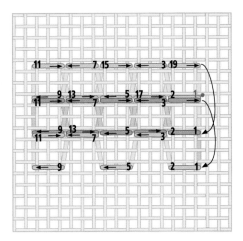

SPACED SATIN FILLING VARIATION II

DESCRIPTION

Comprised of pairs of Satin stitches with unstitched areas between groups (diagram shows five threads); subsequent rows are evenly offset and one thread is left unstitched between the rows (compare with Variation I, page 233).

HOW TO STITCH

Stitch with a medium and even pull.
Secure the working thread at the end of each row.

SUGGESTED USES

Borders, bands, filling

COBBLER FILLING

DESCRIPTION

Comprised of a grid of horizontal and vertical rows of pulled Satin-stitch groups.

HOW TO STITCH

Stitch with a tight and even pull.
Work a pair of stitches two threads apart, skip four threads; repeat this pattern to the end of the row.
Secure the working thread at the end of the row or travel to start the second and subsequent rows using tack stitches (shown); change stitching direction of the stitches for the second row to maintain the same stitch slant on the front.
For the third row, pull in the direction of the first row, or start each row anew, working like first row.
Turn work 90 degrees to work vertical rows.

SUGGESTED USES

Filling, bands

PEBBLE FILLING

DESCRIPTION

This wave pattern creates close horizontal rows of holes and dense clusters of threads.
Each row consists of two passes.
Subsequent rows share holes.

HOW TO STITCH

Stitch with a tight and even pull.
Work in horizontal rows over three threads.
Work stitch over three horizontal threads, travel vertically up three threads, then across three, under three, in a wave pattern to the end of row.
For return pass, fill in the spaces left open in the upper and lower levels of the first pass.
In the second row, the upper level of stitches share the same spaces as the lower level of the first row.

SUGGESTED USES

Borders, bands, filling

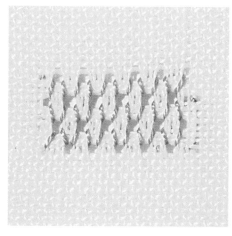

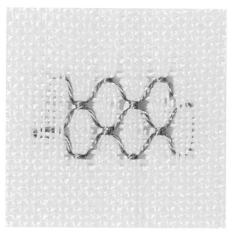

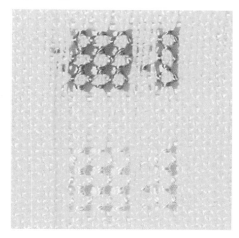

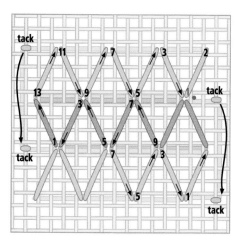

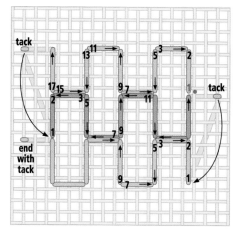

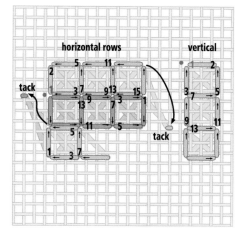

WAVE

DESCRIPTION
Creates a subtle trellis pattern.

The slanted stitch on the front of the fabric straightens when pulled.

Always worked over an even number of threads.

HOW TO STITCH
Stitch with a tight and even pull.

To maintain the pull at the end of the row, make a tack stitch three threads beyond the stitching (as shown); travel down to the next row, make a tack stitch and come up at the second 1 to begin second row.

Be careful not to pull the tack stitches.

SUGGESTED USES
Filling, bands

HONEYCOMB

DESCRIPTION
Creates a bold trellis pattern.

The vertical stitches slant when pulled.

Most effective when stitched with a thick thread.

HOW TO STITCH
Stitch with a tight and even pull.

At end of the first row, make a tack stitch three threads beyond the stitching (as shown).

To start the second half of the honeycomb, you may turn work 180 degrees to work back to the beginning of the first row; end with tack stitch or travel down and continue pattern.

SUGGESTED USES
Borders, filling for large areas

FOUR-SIDED FILLING
Other Names: Square, Punch

DESCRIPTION
One of the most popular stitches in pulled thread work.

May be stitched in either horizontal or vertical rows (for diagonal rows, see Diagonal Pulled Four-sided, page 236).

HOW TO STITCH
Stitch with a tight pull.

The needle always travels diagonally on the back, creating "Xs" except when traveling row to row.

To travel to the next row, take a tack stitch three threads away (as shown) and proceed to the next row.

SUGGESTED USES
Entire designs and alphabets, borders, bands, filling

235

counted thread stitches

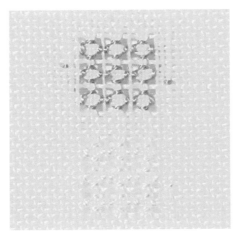

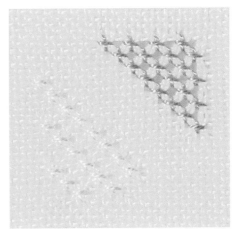

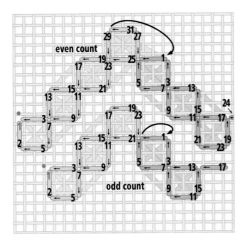

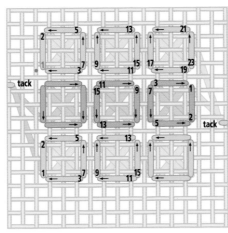

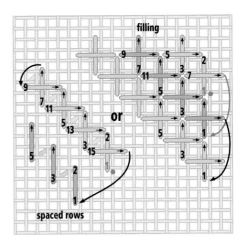

236

DIAGONAL PULLED FOUR-SIDED
Other Name: Square

DESCRIPTION
Comprised of individual squares in the basic Four-sided sequence, but the position of the first stitch of each Four-sided stitch changes with each diagonal step.

HOW TO STITCH
Stitch with a tight and even pull.

Travel on the diagonal between squares, except at the turning square on odd-numbered borders where it travels horizontally. (Diagram shows both odd and even turns; note difference in sequential numbering.)

SUGGESTED USES
Borders

PULLED FOUR-SIDED FILLING VARIATION
Other Name: Barred Four-sided

DESCRIPTION
Comprised of individual Four-sided squares with an unstitched fabric thread between the horizontal and vertical rows, creating an overall pattern of holes with single vertical and horizontal fabric threads delicately highlighted in a fairly large hole.

HOW TO STITCH
Stitch with a tight pull.

Work one Four-sided stitch, skip one thread, work one Four-sided stitch, repeat across row.

To travel to subsequent row, use tack stitches (as shown) to maintain correct pull.

Remember to skip one thread between rows of stitches.

SUGGESTED USES
Filling, borders, bands

DIAGONAL RAISED FILLING
Other Names: Diagonal Cross Filling, Diagonal Raised Band

DESCRIPTION
Comprised of diagonal rows of straight stitches, completed in two passes, to form an upright cross, creating dominant diagonal bands of holes and raised stitches.

Each stitch must be over an even number of fabric threads; over four or six threads is most common.

HOW TO STITCH
Stitch with a tight and even pull.

You may stitch with a sewing motion after first pass is complete and the holes have been established.

SUGGESTED USES
Individual or spaced-apart diagonal bands, filling (when rows share the same holes)

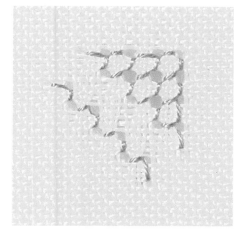

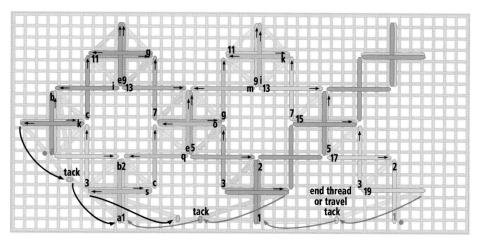

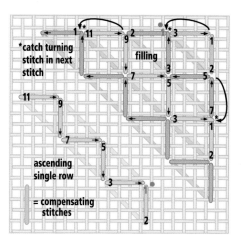

DIAGONAL RAISED FILLING VARIATION
Other Name: Open Trellis

DESCRIPTION
Comprised of two sets of diagonal, raised rows worked in opposite directions, creating a large trellis pattern.

Diagonal rows create a double stitch at the crossing point (see diagram).

HOW TO STITCH
Stitch using a tight, even pull.

Work all bottom-right-to-top-left diagonal rows first (as shown), tacking between rows.

To complete pattern, turn work 90 degrees and work bottom-left-to-top-right rows.

The distance between rows is equal to the size of the stitch: four-by-four stitches are four threads apart, six-by-six stitches are six threads apart, etc.

You may stitch with a sewing motion after first pass is complete and the holes have been established.

SUGGESTED USES
Filling, borders, bands

FAGGOT

DESCRIPTION
May be enjoyed from the right side of the fabric (as diagrammed) or from the back (Reverse Faggot, page 238); the stitch threads on the front are horizontal and vertical, those on the back are diagonal.

The word "faggot" means a bundle of firewood; here it implies a bundling of threads to form a pattern.

Stitches may be worked over two, three, four, five, and even six threads.

May pucker tightly woven fabric.

HOW TO STITCH
Work diagonally with a tight, even pull.

Rotate the diagram to start in different corners.

Whenever a stitch covers a hole on the back (see *), follow with a perpendicular stitch to pull this covering thread away from the hole.

SUGGESTED USES
Filling, diagonal bands or borders

237

counted thread stitches

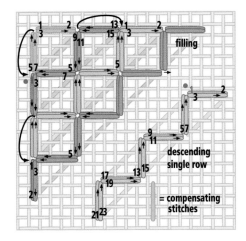

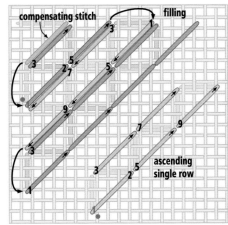

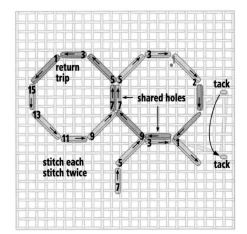

238

DOUBLE FAGGOT

DESCRIPTION
Resembles basic Faggot stitch except that each stitch is worked twice, which gives a more tightly squared-grid appearance.

May be worked over two to six threads (four threads shown).

HOW TO STITCH
Stitch using a tight, even pull.

The stitching sequence is the same as the basic Faggot (page 237).

SUGGESTED USES
Filling, diagonal bands or borders; combines well with other stitches for composite patterns

REVERSE FAGGOT

DESCRIPTION
Identical to the back of the basic Faggot stitch, but worked from the front.

May be worked over three to six threads (four threads shown).

HOW TO STITCH
Stitch using a tight, even pull.

For filling, begin with a waste knot in the opposite direction of the first stitch to maintain the correct pull.

To develop a rhythm, remember to alternate between the right and left sides of each row.

SUGGESTED USES
Filling, diagonal borders and bands

RINGED BACKSTITCH

DESCRIPTION
Comprised of Backstitches over three threads, which form a series of octagons, worked in two journeys.

Where rows overlap, four stitches occupy the same holes.

HOW TO STITCH
Stitch using a tight, even pull.

Work each Backstitch twice, unless you use a thick thread; if so, try using a tighter pull and make only one Backstitch pass.

Work each octagon in a figure-8 pattern.

Subsequent rows share holes.

Make tack stitches between rows.

SUGGESTED USES
Filling, borders, bands

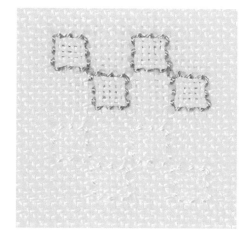

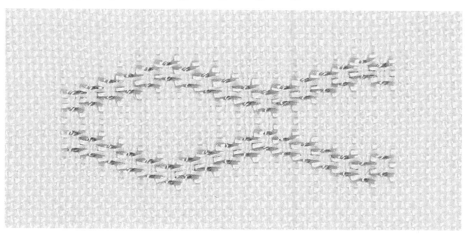

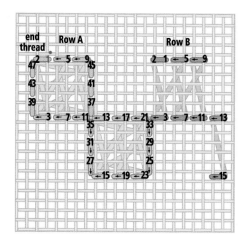

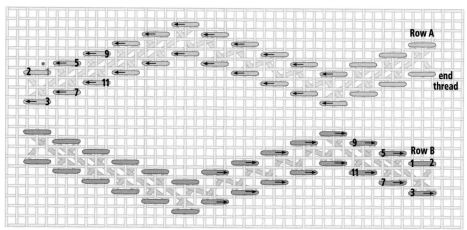

SQUARE

DESCRIPTION

Comprised of Backstitches over two threads which form a series of diagonal squares.

The square can be groups of three-by-three Backstitches (shown), four-by-four, etc.

When stitched in the same color as the ground fabric, the build-up of thread on the reverse side creates a padded stitch with a lighter value than the ground fabric.

HOW TO STITCH

Stitch using an even, medium-to-tight pull.

Complete the tops and bottoms of all the squares in a diagonal pattern before reversing diagonal direction to complete the sides of these squares.

When the diagonal row is complete, end the working thread.

SUGGESTED USES

Filling, diagonal bands and borders

DIAMOND FILLING

DESCRIPTION

Comprised of pairs of stepped Backstitches (actually Double Backstitches, page 201) in two rows that form undulating lines.

The Backstitches may be worked over two or more threads (three shown).

HOW TO STITCH

Stitch using a tight, even pull.

Once you master the sequence, try varying the size of the diamonds by making the undulations shorter or longer.

SUGGESTED USES

Filling, border

239

As you find variations or new stitches not illustrated in this book, add them to pages 242, 251, and 260–261 to personalize the Counted Thread Stitch Gallery.

counted thread stitches

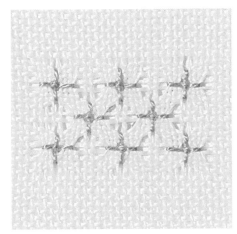

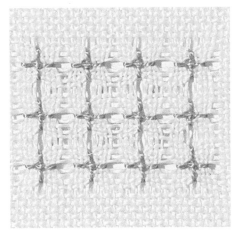

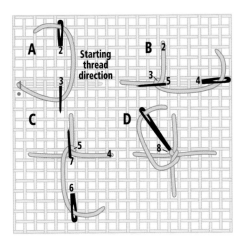

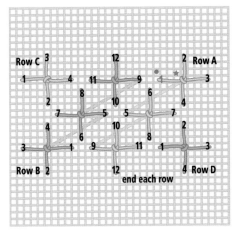

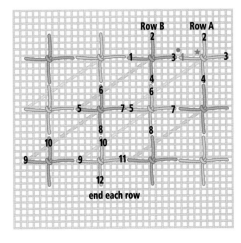

240

GREEK CROSS
Other Name: Lacy Filling

DESCRIPTION
Each stitch is worked around a center hole.

The working thread forms four loops, each similar to a Buttonhole stitch.

The four-loop group is tacked down into the center hole.

The stitch legs may be worked over three to six threads; four (shown) is most common.

HOW TO STITCH
Stitch using a tight, even pull.

Master the individual stitch first before using it for fillings (at right).

Pull the thread tight after each leg of the stitch.

All legs and the tack stitch use the same center hole.

Work on fabric under tension for best results.

SUGGESTED USES
Filling; combined with other stitches in a composite pattern; stars

GREEK CROSS FILLING VARIATION I
Other Name: Lacy Filling

DESCRIPTION
Comprised of basic Greek Cross stitches (at left) in a pattern to create a filling that resembles a trellis.

HOW TO STITCH
Stitch with a tight, even pull.

Refer to Greek Cross (at left) to learn the basic stitch. The star indicates that the center knots are not included in the sequential numbering, but must be stitched.

For a filling, work diagonally from the upper right corner for Row A; for Row B, work from the bottom left to the upper right; repeat sequence for additional rows. This allows you to start the pattern in any corner and travel to the next cross (diagonal rows C and D show this).

Secure the working thread at end of each row.

SUGGESTED USES
Filling, bands, borders

GREEK CROSS FILLING VARIATION II

DESCRIPTION
Comprised of basic Greek Cross stitches (at far left) in a pattern to create an illusion of circles.

HOW TO STITCH
Stitch with a tight, even pull.

Refer to the Greek Cross (at far left) to learn basic stitch.

The star indicates that the center knots are not included in the sequential numbering, but must be stitched.

Work each row diagonally from the upper right to the lower left.

Begin a new thread at the beginning of each row.

SUGGESTED USES
Filling, bands, borders

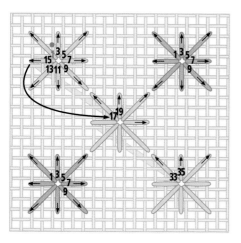

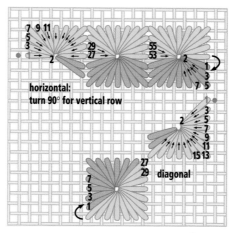

STAR EYELET

ALGERIAN EYELET
Other Name: Square Eyelet

DESCRIPTION

This pulled stitch may be used individually, in rows, or in groups.

Makes an attractive border pattern when individual eight-legged eyelets form diagonal rows (shown).

The length of the legs may or may not be equal (page 217).

HOW TO STITCH

Stitch using an even, medium to tight pull.

Always pull the thread when it's at the perimeter of the stitch to open the central hole (holes along the perimeter are not desirable).

To make the center holes consistent in size, use an awl or stiletto.

The central hole should always be open and not covered on the back by a traveling thread.

SUGGESTED USES

Borders, bands, filling, stars

DESCRIPTION

This pulled stitch may be used individually, in rows (as shown), or in groups.

This stitch makes an attractive border pattern when individual multiple-legged eyelets are worked in straight rows. See pages 64, 217, 246, 272, and 289 for additional Algerian Eyelets.

Usually worked over four to eight threads.

HOW TO STITCH

Stitch using an even, slight to medium pull.

Always pull the thread when it's at the perimeter of the stitch to open the central hole.

For horizontal rows, stitch around the top half of a square (pulling a little more at the corners), travel to the second eyelet and stitch as the first; continue to end of row (as shown).

To return, complete an entire eyelet; repeat to complete the rest of the row.

For vertical rows, turn diagram and fabric, and work as for horizontal eyelets.

For diagonal rows, stitch around half of the first square until you reach opposite corner stitch, travel to second eyelet and stitch like the first eyelet; continue to end of diagonal row. To return, complete a square, then travel to next eyelet; complete the rest of the squares.

For a variation, you may stitch a diagonal row of half-eyelets, which looks like a series of joined triangles.

To make the center holes consistent in size, use an awl or stiletto.

Use a thin thread to avoid congestion in the center hole.

SUGGESTED USES

Borders, bands, individual motifs, filling, sampler alphabets

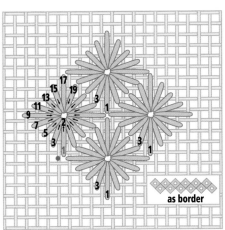

as border

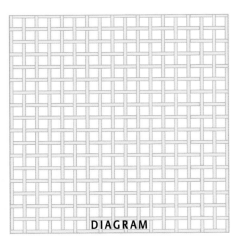

DIAGRAM

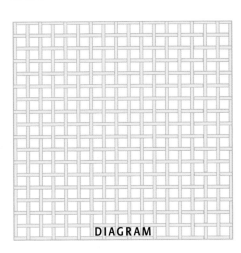

DIAGRAM

242

DIAMOND EYELET

STITCH_____
*Other Names:*_____

STITCH_____
*Other Names:*_____

DESCRIPTION

This pulled stitch may be used individually, in rows, or in groups (as shown).

Makes an attractive border pattern when worked in diagonal rows (inset).

Usually worked over 8 to 12 threads.

See page 217 for additional Diamond Eyelets.

HOW TO STITCH

Stitch using an even, slight to medium pull.

Always pull the thread when it's at the perimeter of the stitch to open the central hole.

Stitch in diagonal rows when possible; complete each row separately.

Make sure the traveling thread is covered by subsequent stitches.

Use an awl or stiletto to make the center holes consistent.

SUGGESTED USES

Filling, borders, bands, motifs

DESCRIPTION
_____
_____
_____
_____
_____
_____
_____

HOW TO STITCH
_____
_____
_____
_____
_____
_____
_____
_____
_____
_____
_____
_____

SUGGESTED USES
_____
_____

DESCRIPTION
_____
_____
_____
_____
_____
_____
_____

HOW TO STITCH
_____
_____
_____
_____
_____
_____
_____
_____
_____
_____
_____
_____

SUGGESTED USES
_____
_____

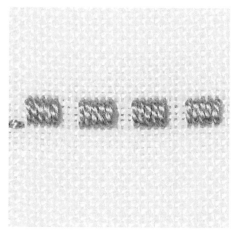

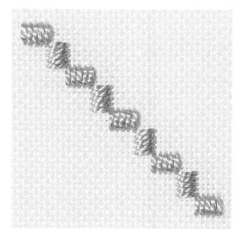

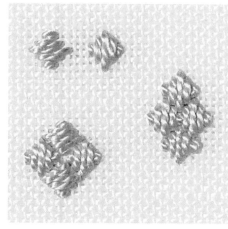

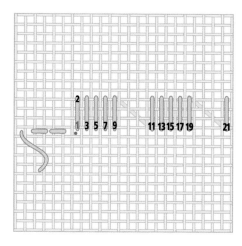

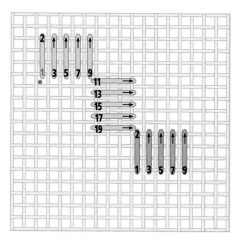

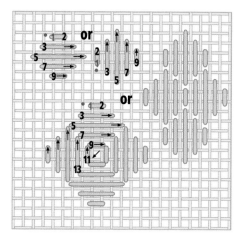

KLOSTER BLOCKS, WORKED HORIZONTALLY

Other Name: Satin Stitch Blocks

DESCRIPTION

Comprised of a rectangular block of Satin stitches which run parallel to the fabric threads.

Each Kloster Block must contain an odd number of Satin stitches (usually five, sometimes seven).

Satin stitches usually cover four perpendicular threads (sometimes six).

Size of Kloster Block remains constant throughout a single piece.

HOW TO STITCH

Start the first Kloster Block with an away-waste knot or a tail of several inches anchored with a few Backstitches; reweave tail later into back of formed stitches.

Generally, use a thicker thread for Kloster Blocks than for the rest of a Hardanger design.

SUGGESTED USES

Foundation stitching for cutwork

KLOSTER BLOCKS, WORKED DIAGONALLY

DESCRIPTION

Comprised of a series of Kloster Blocks at right angles to one another.

Each Kloster Block must contain an odd number of Satin Stitches (usually five).

HOW TO STITCH

Note that adjoining Kloster blocks share a common hole and the traveling thread does not travel diagonally from block to block.

Generally, use a thicker thread for Kloster Blocks than for the rest of the Hardanger design.

SUGGESTED USES

Foundation stitching for cutwork

The red dot in each stitch diagram indicates where to begin stitching.

DIAMOND MOTIF

DESCRIPTION

This small, versatile, diamond-shaped, Satin-stitch motif may be arranged horizontally or vertically in many combinations.

Additional stitches may be added to make a larger motif or other variations.

May be combined with other Satin-stitch motifs.

HOW TO STITCH

Use the same size thread as for Kloster Blocks.

SUGGESTED USES

Isolated single or grouped motifs; combine with different motifs

counted thread stitches

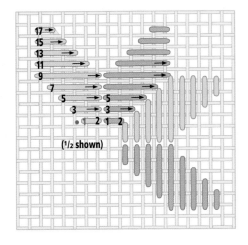

(½ shown)

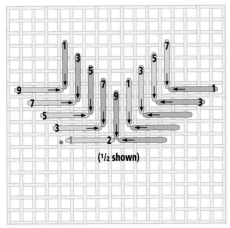

(½ shown)

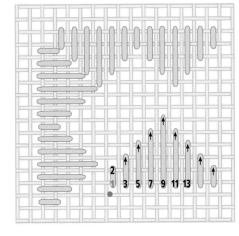

244

STAR MOTIF
Other Name: Snowflake Motif

DESCRIPTION
This commonly used, star-shaped, Satin-stitch motif in Hardanger embroidery usually has eight points (stitched example).
Use entire star motif or partial star motif for other variations.
Similar designs appear on Scandinavian knitwear.

HOW TO STITCH
Use the same size thread as for Kloster Blocks.

SUGGESTED USES
Isolated single or grouped motifs

STAR MOTIF VARIATION

DESCRIPTION
A commonly used, star-shaped, Satin-stitch motif.
Compare to Star Motif (at left).
Use partial or entire eight-pointed motif.

HOW TO STITCH
Use the same size thread as for Kloster Blocks.

SUGGESTED USES
Isolated single or grouped motifs

SATIN FRINGE MOTIF

DESCRIPTION
This versatile, Satin-stitch motif may be used to create bands, corners, or as an isolated triangular motif.
Variations include varying the height and number of stitches, orientation, and combination.

HOW TO STITCH
Use the same size thread as for Kloster Blocks.

SUGGESTED USES
Bands, isolated single or grouped motifs, corners, borders

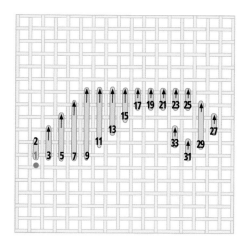

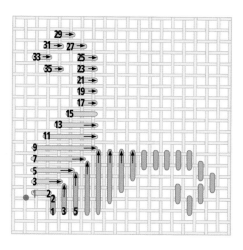

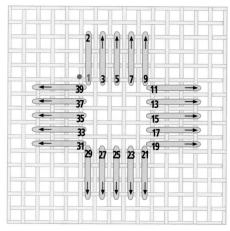

SHIP MOTIF

DESCRIPTION

This Satin-stitch motif resembles the bow of an ancient Viking ship.

May be arranged and combined in many ways to produce various motifs.

A popular variation is the Tulip Motif (at right).

Creates a scroll-type border or band when arranged in a line.

HOW TO STITCH

Use the same size thread as for Kloster Blocks.

SUGGESTED USES

Isolated single or grouped motifs, bands

TULIP MOTIF

DESCRIPTION

A pair of perpendicular Satin-stitched Ship Motifs resembles a tulip blossom.

Four Tulip Motifs joined at the base make an attractive and substantial center motif for a design.

Various motifs may be added to the Tulip Motif such as the Diamond Motif (page 243).

HOW TO STITCH

Use the same size thread as for Kloster Blocks.

SUGGESTED USES

Isolated motifs

FLORAL MOTIF

DESCRIPTION

Comprised of four Kloster Blocks arranged so as to spotlight a central square.

A pulled Algerian Eyelet (also see pages 64, 217, 241, 246, 272, and 289) makes an attractive and common treatment for the center open square.

HOW TO STITCH

Use the same size thread as for Kloster Blocks.

SUGGESTED USES

Isolated motifs, bands

245

counted thread stitches

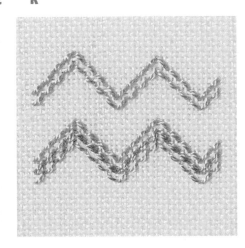

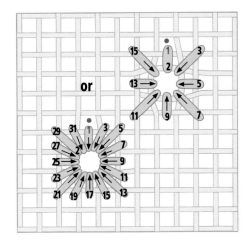

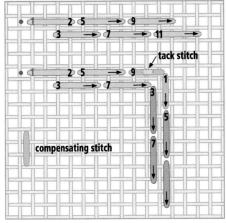

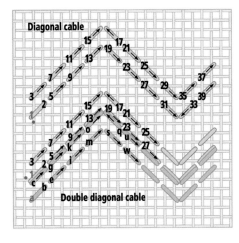

246

ALGERIAN EYELET

DESCRIPTION
This pulled version of the basic Algerian Eyelet (pages 64, 217, 241, 272, and 289) is often added between the Buttonhole Edge and Kloster Blocks in Hardanger designs.

Makes an attractive center for Star (page 244) or Floral Motifs (page 245).

Usually encompasses a four-thread square, but may be larger.

HOW TO STITCH
Always insert the needle into the center hole.

Pull the working thread when it's at the perimeter of the stitch to open the central hole

Use the same size thread as for Kloster Blocks.

SUGGESTED USES
Bands, borders, individual design motifs

CABLE STITCH
Other Name: Faggot

DESCRIPTION
Provides a linear design element to Hardanger embroidery.

May or may not be worked as a pulled stitch.

HOW TO STITCH
Work from left to right.

When making a 90-degree corner, note that the outer two stitches are only three threads long (shown in pink); the first stitch of the new direction emerges from the same hole where the last stitch ended.

Hide a small tack stitch behind the last stitch before turning the corner.

Use finer thread than that used for Kloster Blocks.

SUGGESTED USES
Design motifs or areas, isolated design elements, bands, borders

DIAGONAL CABLE, DOUBLE DIAGONAL CABLE
Other Name: Reversed Faggot, Double Reversed Faggot

DESCRIPTION
A single row of Diagonal Cable stitches (upper diagram) creates two actual rows of stitches.

May or may not be a pulled stitch.

HOW TO STITCH
Note change in stitch direction at each peak.

For a Double Diagonal Cable (lower diagram), stitch the Diagonal Cable pattern a second time; note that the middle row of stitches is doubled.

Use finer thread than that used for Kloster Blocks.

SUGGESTED USES
Design motifs or areas, isolated design elements, bands, borders

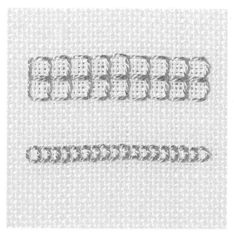

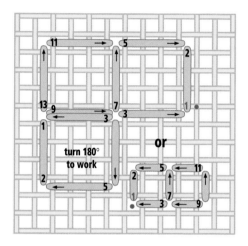
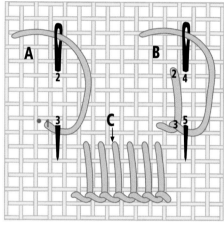
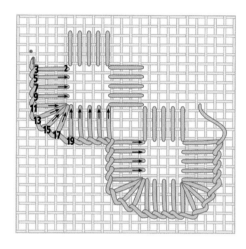

FOUR-SIDED
Other Names: Square Openwork, Four-sided Openwork

BUTTONHOLE
Other Name: Closed Blanket

BUTTONHOLE EDGING
Other Name: Closed Blanket

DESCRIPTION
This old stitch reverses to a three-legged cross.

May or may not be a pulled stitch.

HOW TO STITCH
Work from left to right (lower right diagram) or from right to left (upper diagram)

Note that when you're stitching a row, the vertical legs are not doubled; leg 7–8 becomes leg 1–2 of the next stitch.

The horizontal threads are doubled when multiple rows are stitched (upper diagram).

SUGGESTED USES
Bands, borders, motifs

DESCRIPTION
Creates a band or border; gives an "appliqué look" around a design.

Also see page 221 for an additional Buttonhole stitch variation.

HOW TO STITCH
Work from left to right.

End with a small tack stitch.

SUGGESTED USES
Borders, bands, motifs

DESCRIPTION
A traditional and sturdy method to finish the edges of a Hardanger design.

May be used by itself or with Kloster Blocks (shown) as an edging.

Stitch usually covers four fabric threads.

The Buttonhole stitches prevent the fabric threads from raveling.

HOW TO STITCH
Work from left to right.

To begin, use an away-waste knot; do not start at an inside or outside corner.

End with a small tack stitch, then bury the tail in previously worked Buttonhole stitches.

Maintain an even, tight tension.

Carefully cut fabric close to raised edge of stitch, then trim away any remaining fabric nubs.

SUGGESTED USES
Edgings, design elements

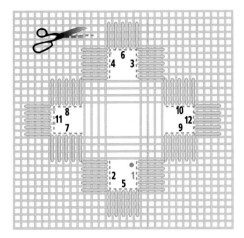

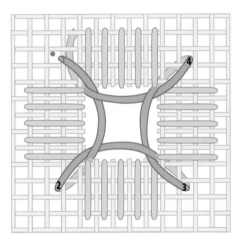

248

CUTTING TECHNIQUE

DESCRIPTION
Cutting and removing ground threads create holes in the ground fabric which provide open areas to fill with various "lacy" stitches.

HOW TO CUT
Every Kloster block must have an opposing Kloster block across the motif; always double-check before cutting.

Begin cutting only after all Kloster blocks, Buttonhole stitches, and Eyelets are complete. (There are exceptions, but this a good general rule to follow.)

You will need two essential tools: small, very sharp, fine-pointed embroidery scissors, and tweezers to remove cut threads.

Cut only those threads perpendicular to the long Satin stitches of the Kloster Blocks; never cut parallel to these Satin stitches.

Always cut with the scissors held to the left side of the Kloster Block.

Insert the tip of the scissors into the fabric hole shared by the first stitches of adjoining Kloster Blocks, then gather four ground threads onto the blade of the scissors and bring scissors' point back through the fabric to front. (These four threads are enclosed by the Kloster Block; working in this manner ensures that only four threads are cut.)

Snug the scissors' blades close to the end of the Kloster block stitches and cut the four threads on the blade. Now cut the same four threads from the opposing Kloster block.

Proceed, cutting the threads with the shortest distance and then the remaining (note numbers on diagram) or in a clockwise pattern. Rotate the fabric as needed.

Cut all ground threads for a single motif before withdrawing or withdraw thread groups as they are cut.

SQUARE FILET
Other Name: Square Filet Filling, Corner Filet

DESCRIPTION
This lacy filling stitch is used with Kloster Blocks (shown), Wrapped Bars (page 249), or Woven Bars (page 250).

HOW TO STITCH
Finish all sides of the Kloster Block square before stitching Square Filet.

Stitch clockwise or counterclockwise (as shown).

Stitch all Square Filets in one design in same direction.

Use a finer thread than used for Kloster blocks.

SUGGESTED USES
Lacy filling for cutwork area

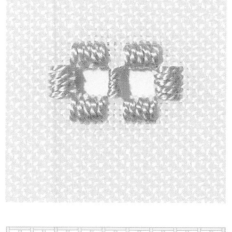

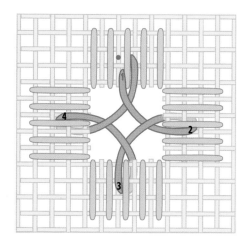

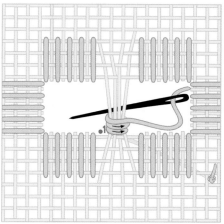

DOVE'S EYE
Other Name: Dove's Eye Filling

DESCRIPTION
This lacy filling stitch may be worked on Kloster Blocks (shown), Wrapped Bars, Woven Bars, or any combination of these.

HOW TO STITCH
Three-and-one-half sides of a cut square must already be wrapped or woven, or all four Kloster Blocks finished (as shown), before beginning a Dove's Eye. (After completing Dove's Eye, finish the remaining Wrapped or Woven Bar.)

Work clockwise (shown) or counterclockwise; be consistent throughout a single design.

Cross all four sides of the Dove's Eye in the same direction.

Strive to keep all Dove's Eyes the same size throughout the design; you may need to gently manipulate the open area because squares with Kloster blocks on one side are usually slightly smaller than those with Bars.

Don't pull so tightly that you distort or re-align the Wrapped or Woven Bars.

Use a finer thread than for Kloster blocks.

SUGGESTED USES
Filling for cutwork area

WRAPPED BARS
Other Name: Overcast Bars

DESCRIPTION
One of several ways to embellish remaining ground fabric threads in cutwork areas.

HOW TO STITCH
Wrap bar evenly from left to right.

Wrap tightly to create a "lacier" look.

To ensure smooth wrapping, make sure that each wrap sits next to the previous stitch, not on top of it.

Use a finer thread than for Kloster blocks.

SUGGESTED USES
Foundation bars

counted thread stitches

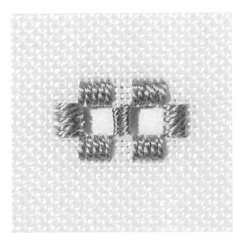

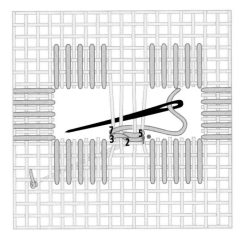

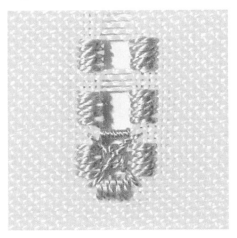

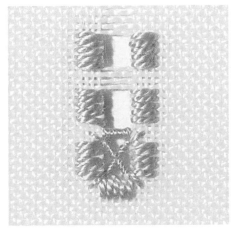

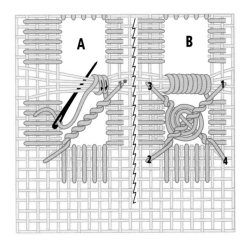

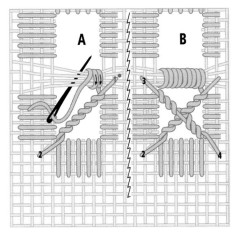

250

WOVEN BARS

DESCRIPTION
One of several ways to embellish remaining ground fabric threads in cutwork areas.

HOW TO STITCH
Anchor the thread behind the Kloster Blocks and begin weaving on the right side of bar.

Always insert needle down into the middle of the bar.

Use medium tension when wrapping bars.

Don't distort the bars by pulling too tightly; the sides of each bar should remain straight.

Cover the bars as evenly as possible with the weaving thread.

Use a finer thread than for Kloster blocks.

SUGGESTED USES
Foundation bars

TWISTED BARS

DESCRIPTION
A diagonal filling for cutwork areas.

HOW TO STITCH
Three or four sides of a cutwork area must already be wrapped or woven, or all four Kloster Blocks finished, before beginning a Twisted Bar.

When wrapping the diagonal thread, place the needle under the diagonal thread for the first wrap; wrap three or four times across bar.

If the fourth side is finished, then run thread under back of stitches and come up at 3; if the fourth side is not finished, then wrap or weave bar and come up at 3 (as shown).

Leg 3–4 crosses over the previously Twisted Bar; on the return, insert the twisting thread under the intersection to stabilize the threads.

End thread behind Kloster Blocks or proceed to next open square.

SUGGESTED USES
Filling for cutwork area

SPIDER WEB FILLING

DESCRIPTION
A diagonal filling for any cutwork area; may be added to Wrapped or Woven Bars or Kloster Blocks.

HOW TO STITCH
Work foundation threads as for Twisted Bars (at left), but when the second leg is half wrapped to the intersection of crossing threads, begin weaving around the intersection several times.

The size of central woven area (number of times circling the intersection) is a personal choice (the diagrams shows two circles), but maintain consistency throughout a project.

A Spider Web in a square bordered by Kloster Blocks will be closer to the sides than one in a square bordered by Woven or Wrapped Bars.

Use a finer thread than for Kloster blocks.

SUGGESTED USES
Filling for cutwork area

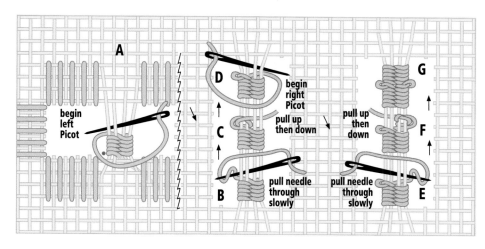

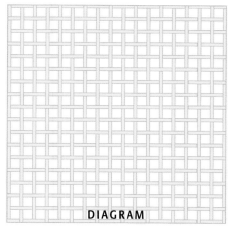

DIAGRAM

PICOT
Other Names: Picot Loop, Picot Knot

DESCRIPTION
Add these small open knots as you weave Woven Bars to further embellish the filling.

Use alone or with other filling stitches as long as the open square doesn't become too crowded.

HOW TO STITCH
After weaving one-half of a Woven Bar, stop and begin the Picot on the same side of the bar on which you began; slide the needle down the middle of the bar, facing left (A).

Pull thread under the needle and then wrap thread around needle once "under, over, under" (B). Lay the thread back towards the eye of the needle, parallel with the needle (B).

Holding the small loop with thumb and forefinger, gently pull needle through loop and then down and level with fabric (C).

Insert the needle in the middle of the bar, pull thread up gently and then down to "seat" the knot (C).

Complete a second Picot on the right side of the Woven Bar (D–F), mirroring the same sequence.

Complete the Woven Bar (G).

Picots take some practice to master!

SUGGESTED USES
Decorative addition to Woven Bars

As you find variations or new stitches not illustrated in this book, add them here and on pages 242, and 260–261 to personalize the Counted Thread Stitch Gallery.

STITCH_____
Other Names:_____

DESCRIPTION
_____
_____
_____
_____
_____
_____

HOW TO STITCH
_____
_____
_____
_____
_____
_____
_____
_____
_____
_____
_____
_____

SUGGESTED USES
_____
_____
_____

counted thread stitches

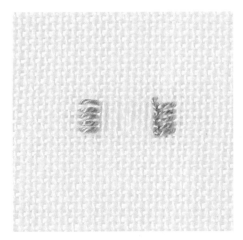

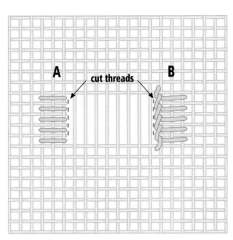

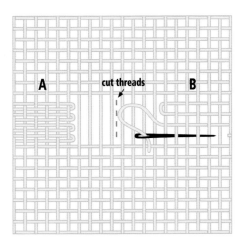

PREPARING THE CHANNEL, METHOD I

HOW TO STITCH

In both variations, stitch the sides of the channel before cutting the fabric threads.

In variation A, stitch Satin stitches at the end of the channel, making sure there is one stitch beyond the top and bottom fabric threads to be cut.

In variation B, stitch Buttonhole stitches at the end of the channel, making sure there is one stitch beyond the top and bottom fabric threads to be cut.

Use either variation A or B (not both).

HOW TO CUT

Using sharp scissors, cut horizontal fabric threads adjacent to the completed stitches at both ends of the channel.

To avoid cutting threads other than those to be withdrawn, "load" the lower scissors blade with the threads you want to cut (four threads shown).

Withdraw cut threads one at a time.

PREPARING THE CHANNEL, METHOD II

HOW TO CUT

In both variations, cut the fabric threads of the channel first, and re-weave the cut threads into the fabric at the ends of the channel.

Using small, sharp scissors, cut the horizontal fabric threads one at a time at the midpoint of the intended channel (if the channel is long, cut threads about three or four needle lengths from the end of the channel). Check and re-check that you're cutting the correct threads. Withdraw one thread carefully until you reach the end of the channel and reweave it into the channel end. Repeat procedure for other end of channel before handling the next fabric thread.

HOW TO SECURE FABRIC THREADS

For variation A (lower stitched example), thread the first withdrawn thread onto a tapestry needle and re-weave it into the fabric at the channel end. Note that there will be pairs of threads with the same weave in this area, and that the re-woven area is denser than the surrounding fabric.

For variation B (upper stitched example), withdraw every other fabric thread beyond the channel width to the edge of the fabric or to the length of the cut channel thread (whichever is the shortest distance). Thread one of the cut channel threads onto a tapestry needle and re-weave it into one of the empty lines created by the previously withdrawn fabric threads.

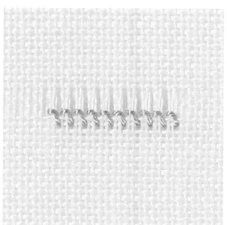

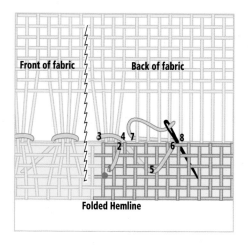

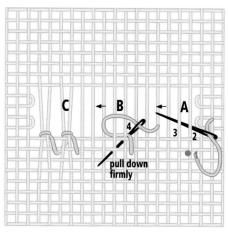

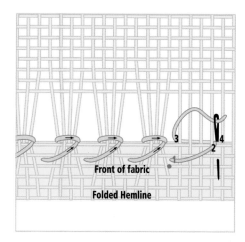

ANTIQUE HEMSTITCH

DESCRIPTION

This variation of the basic Hemstitch (at right) creates a line of small horizontal stitches on the fabric front.

Use to join a hem (as shown) or decorate a drawn thread channel.

HOW TO STITCH

Withdraw only two to four threads for the channel for a hem (shown); withdraw more threads if you'll be adding additional stitching to both channel edges.

Stitch on the back of the fabric.

Work from left to right.

Firmly pull the working thread to bundle the vertical fabric threads tightly at the edge of the channel.

If hemming, fold the hem up so that the folded edge meets the channel (as shown) and baste in place; slip needle between fabric and folded hem.

SUGGESTED USES

Hems for table, bed, and bath linens; ornaments; samplers; clothing

HEMSTITCH

DESCRIPTION

Secures and decorates a hem or drawn thread channel.

From two to six vertical fabric threads may be bundled together (two threads shown).

HOW TO STITCH

Select a method to prepare the channel (page 252).

Withdraw two or more threads (four shown).

Stitch on the front of the fabric.

Work from right to left (shown) or from left to right.

After the first stitch (at 4), pull firmly down with the thread to tighten the bundle and "seat" it with the horizontal fabric threads.

SUGGESTED USES

Decorative hem for table, bed, and bath linens; ornaments; samplers; clothing

HEMSTITCH VARIATION

DESCRIPTION

Secures and decorates a hem or drawn thread channel.

From two to six vertical fabric threads may be bundled together (four threads shown).

HOW TO STITCH

Select a method to prepare the channel (page 252).

Withdraw two or more threads.

Stitch on the front of the fabric.

If hemming, fold the hem up so that the folded edge meets the drawn thread channel (as shown) and baste in place.

Catch all three layers of fabric as you stitch.

If the fabric on the inside of the hem is same length as the hem, this prevents a ridge of fabric from showing.

SUGGESTED USES

Decorative hems for table, bed, and bath linens; ornaments; samplers; clothing

counted thread stitches

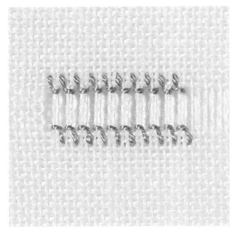

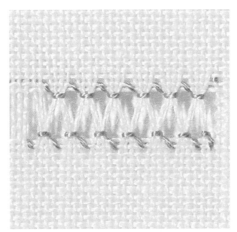

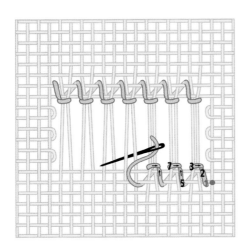

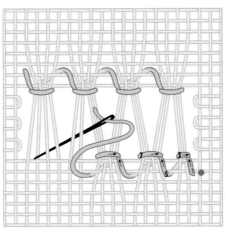

LADDER HEMSTITCH

DESCRIPTION

Bundles the same threads on both sides of the channel to form a ladder-like pattern; may also secure a hem.

May bundle from two to six vertical fabric threads (two shown).

Withdraw as few as three or four fabric threads, or more.

HOW TO STITCH

Prepare channel (Method II, page 252).

Stitch on the front of the fabric.

Work from right to left.

Stitch one edge of the channel first, using the basic Hemstitch or Hemstitch Variation (page 253), then rotate fabric 180 degrees and repeat stitching on this second side, bundling the same threads as for the first edge to form parallel bundles.

SUGGESTED USES

Decorative band or hem for table, bed, or bath linens; samplers; clothing

ZIGZAG HEMSTITCH

Other Names: Serpentine Hemstitch, Trellis Hemstitch

DESCRIPTION

This variation of the Hemstitch decorates both edges of a channel, and may also secure a hem.

Regroups the vertical fabric threads to create diagonal bundles (compare to the Ladder Hemstitch, at left).

May bundle from two to six vertical fabric threads (two/four shown), but must be an even number.

Usually has a wider channel than either the Hemstitch or Antique Hemstitch; withdraw as few as three or four fabric threads, or more.

HOW TO STITCH

Prepare channel (Method II, page 252).

Stitch on the front of the fabric.

Work from right to left.

Stitch one edge of the channel first, using the basic Hemstitch or Hemstitch Variation (page 253), gathering together bundles of two, four, or six threads.

Rotate fabric 180 degrees and repeat stitching on this second side; divide the first bundle in half as you hemstitch. As you form bundles on the second edge, make sure half the vertical threads are from one opposite bundle, and half from its adjacent bundle, to form a zigzag across the channel.

Note that the upper bundles are in groups of four threads, but lower bundles start with only two threads.

SUGGESTED USES

Decorative band or hem for table, bed, and bath linens; ornaments; samplers; clothing

The red dot in each stitch diagram indicates where to begin stitching.

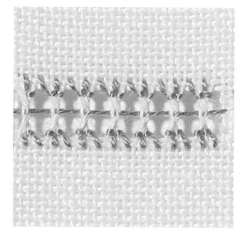

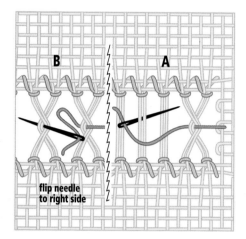

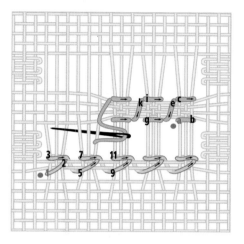

INTERLACED HEMSTITCH

ITALIAN HEMSTITCH
Other Names: Double Hemstitch,
Roumanian Hemstitch, Italian Hemstitch

DESCRIPTION

An added embellishment to the Ladder Hemstitch (page 253) with the vertical, fabric-thread bundles decoratively re-organized.

HOW TO STITCH

Prepare channel (Method II, page 252).

Stitch on the front of the fabric.

Work from right to left.

Stitch both sides of the channel, using the Ladder Hemstitch (page 254), gathering together bundles of two (shown), three, or four threads.

Anchor the interlacing thread securely to the sides of the channel by weaving it among the vertical fabric threads.

Work the interlacing in this sequence:

1. Bring needle and thread to front of fabric at a midway point in the finished edge at the right side of the drawn thread channel.

2. Carry the working thread across two bundles of threads, insert the needle facing right under one bundle and over the next (A).

3. Flip the needle so that it is now facing left (B). This will "flip" these two bundles, one over the other. Draw the working thread firmly through these two bundles.

Repeat Steps A and B across the channel.

Strive to keep the working thread in middle of the channel.

SUGGESTED USES

Decorative band or hem for table, bed, and bath linens; ornaments; samplers; clothing

DESCRIPTION

Comprised of two drawn thread channels on either side of an embellished, uncut horizontal row.

HOW TO STITCH

Prepare channel (Method II, page 252).

Create two channels; leave three or four threads between channels.

Stitch on the front of the fabric.

Work from right to left.

Withdraw the lower channel first and complete the hemstitching, (page 253), gathering together bundles of two, four, or six threads. Then withdraw the threads for the second channel, and hemstitch that edge (not shown).

Work the stitches for the central area.

Group the vertical fabric threads in parallel bundles.

SUGGESTED USES

Samplers; bed, bath, and table linens; ornaments

counted thread stitches

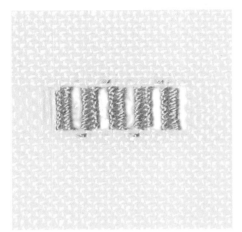

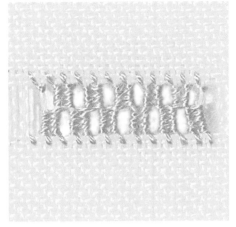

ATTACH SAMPLE
OR PHOTO HERE

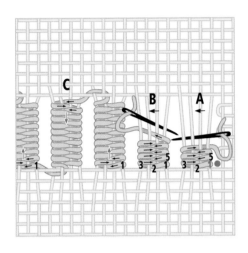

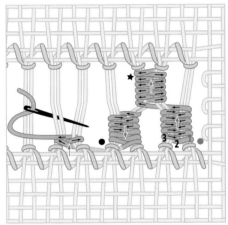

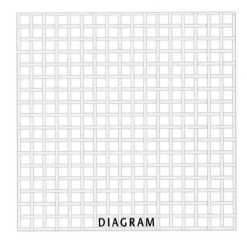

DIAGRAM

NEEDLEWOVEN HEMSTITCH
Other Name: Woven Hemstitch

DESCRIPTION
Numerous variations and combinations are possible; this diagram shows the most basic.

May or may not be pulled.

As a variation, the Hemstitch or Hemstitch Variation (page 253) may be used to bundle vertical threads together for certain variations (see variation at right).

HOW TO STITCH
Prepare a channel of four or more fabric threads first (Method II, page 252).

Work from right to left (as shown) or from left to right.

Needleweave bundles of four vertical fabric threads in parallel bars; strive to keep the same number of wraps and same tension for each bundle.

At each edge of the drawn thread channel, take a small tack (as shown)

SUGGESTED USES
Samplers; bed, bath, and table linens; clothing; ornaments

NEEDLEWOVEN HEMSTITCH VARIATION

DESCRIPTION
The variation of the Needlewoven Hemstitch (at left) splits the needle-woven bundles in a zigzag effect.

The Hemstitch or Hemstitch Variation (page 253) may be used to bundle vertical threads together (shown).

HOW TO STITCH
Stitch as for the Needlewoven Hemstitch (at left) but halfway up the first needlewoven bar, "jump" to the next two vertical fabric threads, leaving the first two threads unstitched past the halfway point.

Occasionally the working thread must travel through the back of the needleweaving to reach the next stitching location (* on the diagram).

The • in the diagram indicates a tack stitch through back of hemstitches.

SUGGESTED USES
Samplers; bed, bath, and table linens; clothing; ornaments

STITCH_____
Other Names:_____

DESCRIPTION
_____
_____
_____
_____
_____
_____
_____

HOW TO STITCH
_____
_____
_____
_____
_____
_____
_____
_____
_____
_____
_____
_____
_____

SUGGESTED USES
_____
_____
_____

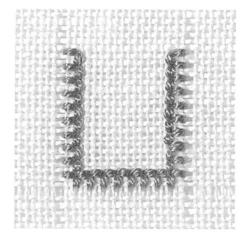

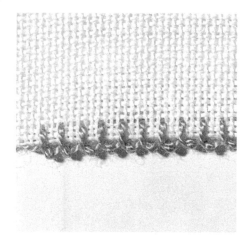

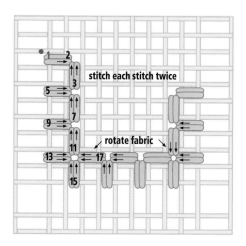

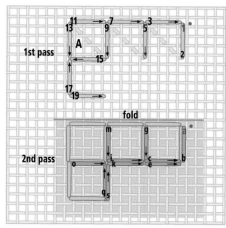

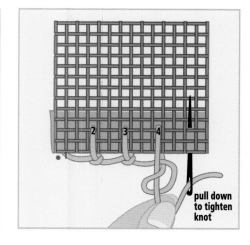

NUN'S EDGING

DESCRIPTION

This tightly pulled stitch easily finishes a raw edge on evenweave or non-evenweave fabrics.

Stitched by convent nuns in Europe to finish the edges of lingerie for the retail market.

Usually covers two (shown), three, or four threads.

HOW TO STITCH

Work each stitch twice before proceeding to the next stitch.

Stitch from top to bottom, rotating fabric to turn corners.

For ease, remove the ground thread immediately to the left of the Nun's Edging (as shown) before stitching and cutting.

Cut the fabric adjacent to the outside stitches.

SUGGESTED USES

Bath, bed, and table linens; ornaments; needlebook pages

SQUARED EDGING

DESCRIPTION

This two-journey, pulled stitch is usually worked on evenweave fabrics.

Produces four layers of fabric at corners.

HOW TO STITCH

Work from right to left or from top to bottom, over two, three, or four fabric threads.

After completing first journey, fold fabric along upper edge of horizontal stitches and stitch second journey through both layers of fabric using a tight tension.

Carefully trim excess fabric on back and adjacent to double line of stitching.

SUGGESTED USES

Bath, bed, and table linens; bellpulls; samplers; needlework accessories

ARMENIAN EDGING

DESCRIPTION

This decorative edging of small loops and knots may be used on evenweave or non-evenweave fabrics.

The vertical legs may be evenly spaced close together or apart.

HOW TO STITCH

Work from left to right.

Start the thread at the fold of fabric.

Insert the needle into the hem at the fold, twist thread into a loop, insert the needle into hem from the back through both layers, then thread it through the loop to form a knot.

Tighten the knot by pulling down on working thread before beginning the next stitch.

Add extra rows by stitching through the loops of the previous row.

A smooth thread works best.

Trim excess fabric on back.

SUGGESTED USES

Bath, bed, and table linens; clothing; hankies

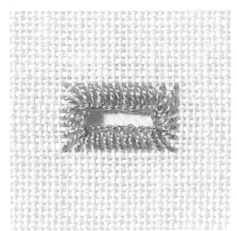
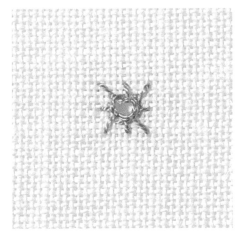

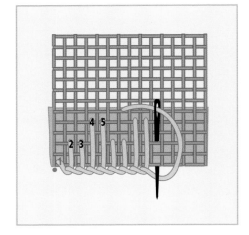
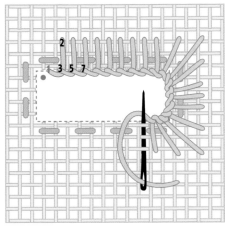
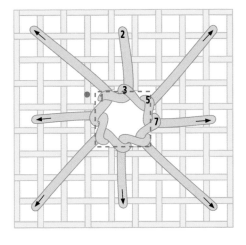

BUTTONHOLE EDGING, FOLDED HEM

DESCRIPTION
Finishes the edges of many different types of embroidery on evenweave as well as non-evenweave fabrics.

HOW TO STITCH
Insert the needle into the hem at the fold; stitch a series of Buttonhole stitches (page 221) along the fold.

The vertical legs should be close enough to nearly touch (if vertical legs are far apart, this is called *Blanket Stitch Edging*).

Height of the vertical legs may vary.

Trim excess fabric on back.

Use any type of strong thread.

SUGGESTED USES
Hemmed edges for bath, bed, and table linens; needlework accessories

BUTTONHOLE EDGING STITCH, OPENWORK

DESCRIPTION
Commonly used for internal cutwork areas (shown) as well as eyelets (at right) and folded or non-folded edges (see Hardanger, page 248; cutwork, page 160).

HOW TO STITCH
For internal areas and fabric edges which tend to fray, use a Running-stitch outline (pink lines in stitched example) before stitching the Buttonhole stitches (cutwork, page 158).

Work from left to right, but don't start in a corner.

The length of the Buttonhole legs may vary; when practical, loop the last stitch under the first stitch.

Use small sharp embroidery scissors for cutting.

SUGGESTED USES
Samplers; clothing; bath, bed, and table linens; cutwork and drawn work

BUTTONHOLE EDGING, EYELET

DESCRIPTION
Sturdily finishes the edges of holes for garment lacings or drawstring bags.

HOW TO STITCH
Height of the legs may vary.

For internal areas which tend to fray, use a Running-stitch outline before stitching the Buttonhole stitches.

Use a stiletto or awl to open and round the cut hole before stitching Buttonhole stitches.

SUGGESTED USES
Reinforces holes for drawstring bags and garment lacings, etc.

As you find variations or new stitches not illustrated in this book, add them to pages 242, 251, and 260–261 to personalize the Counted Thread Stitch Gallery.

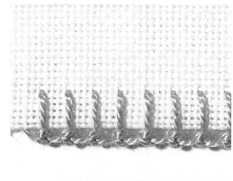

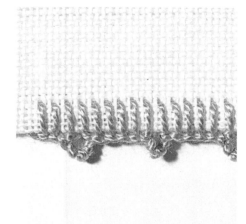

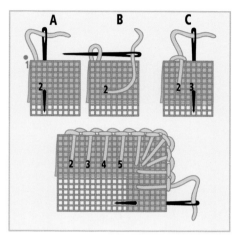

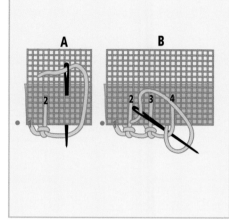

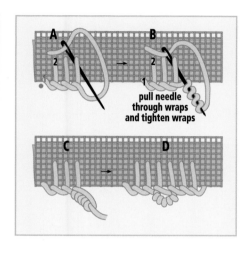

259

HEDEBO BUTTONHOLE EDGING

DESCRIPTION
Works well on evenweave and non-evenweave fabrics.

The stitches may be touching one another or slightly apart.

HOW TO STITCH
Fold and trim fabric so that fabric on back is greater than the stitch length (as shown).

Work from left to right.

Bring thread through fabric at fold; begin about one inch from a corner. Insert the needle from the fabric back and through both layers of fabric; pull thread through, leaving a small thread loop. Insert needle through loop from the back and pull up, tightening loop against folded edge.

To end thread, bury tail in fabric fold. Trim excess fabric on back.

SUGGESTED USES
Bath, bed, and table linens; clothing; hankies; needlework accessories

ANTWERP EDGING
Other Names: Knot, Knotted, Blanket

DESCRIPTION
This decorative edging is comprised of a Buttonhole stitch and an additional knot.

Works well on evenweave and non-evenweave fabrics.

Additional rows of stitches create a wider, lacy edging.

HOW TO STITCH
Work from left to right.

Start thread at the fold of fabric.

Add extra rows by stitching through the loops of the previous row.

Use any thread; a round, thick thread like pearl cotton works best.

Trim excess fabric on back.

SUGGESTED USES
Bed, bath, and table linens; clothing; hankies; needlework accessories

BULLION PICOT EDGING

DESCRIPTION
Comprised of Buttonhole stitches with an added small picot formed at regular intervals along the edging.

HOW TO STITCH
Work from left to right.

Stitch several Buttonhole stitches (keep this number consistent throughout a project) and then add a Bullion Picot stitch by inserting the needle behind the vertical leg of the last Buttonhole stitch (A). Wrap thread four to six times around the needle (B). Hold Bullion Picot between thumb and forefinger and gently pull needle and thread through the wraps. Tighten the wraps (C) and secure the Bullion Picot by stitching the next Buttonhole stitch (D).

Strive for uniformly sized Picots.

Trim excess fabric on back.

SUGGESTED USES
Bath, bed, and table linens; clothing; hankies; bellpulls

ATTACH SAMPLE
OR PHOTO HERE

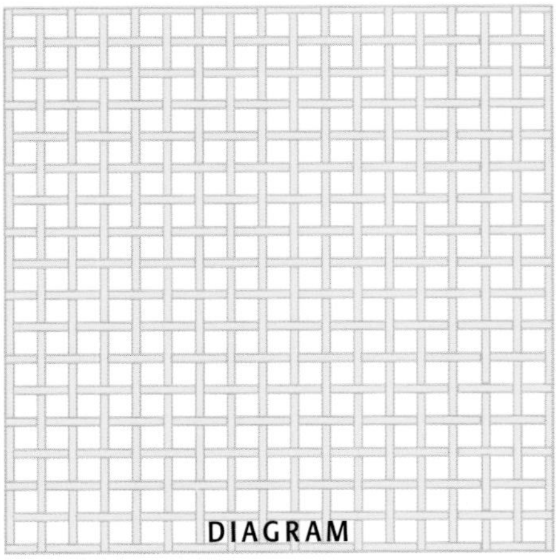

ATTACH SAMPLE
OR PHOTO HERE

ATTACH SAMPLE
OR PHOTO HERE

DIAGRAM

DIAGRAM

DIAGRAM

260

STITCH_____
*Other Names:*_____

DESCRIPTION

HOW TO STITCH

SUGGESTED USES

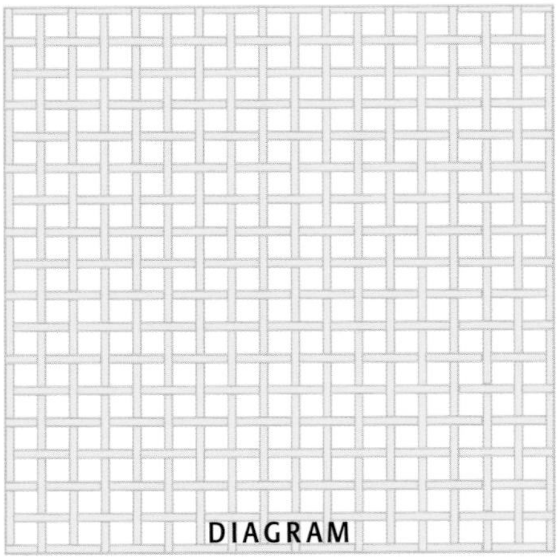

STITCH_____
*Other Names:*_____

DESCRIPTION

HOW TO STITCH

SUGGESTED USES

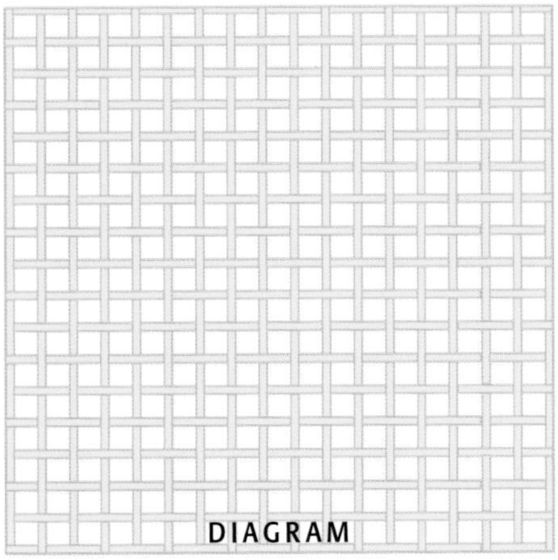

STITCH_____
*Other Names:*_____

DESCRIPTION

HOW TO STITCH

SUGGESTED USES

ATTACH SAMPLE OR PHOTO HERE	ATTACH SAMPLE OR PHOTO HERE	ATTACH SAMPLE OR PHOTO HERE

DIAGRAM **DIAGRAM** **DIAGRAM**

STITCH_____
*Other Names:*_____

DESCRIPTION
_____
_____
_____
_____
_____
_____

HOW TO STITCH
_____
_____
_____
_____
_____
_____
_____
_____
_____
_____
_____

SUGGESTED USES
_____
_____
_____

STITCH_____
*Other Names:*_____

DESCRIPTION
_____
_____
_____
_____
_____
_____

HOW TO STITCH
_____
_____
_____
_____
_____
_____
_____
_____
_____
_____
_____

SUGGESTED USES
_____
_____
_____

STITCH_____
*Other Names:*_____

DESCRIPTION
_____
_____
_____
_____
_____
_____

HOW TO STITCH
_____
_____
_____
_____
_____
_____
_____
_____
_____
_____
_____

SUGGESTED USES
_____
_____
_____

dutch treat

*Pause for a cup of tea and enjoy the flowers!
Traditional blue and white Delft porcelain—an art form born in
China, borrowed and popularized by the Dutch—creates a
complementary backdrop for the warm natural hues of fruits and
sunflowers. Composed of full cross stitches and backstitches, this
project is truly a treat—easy enough for a beginner, yet attractive
enough to catch an experienced stitcher's fancy.*

DESIGN BY LINDA GILLUM
Finished design size: 9⅜" x 9⅞"
Finished project size: 13⅞" x 14½"

MATERIALS
15"-sq. White Aida fabric, 14-ct.
Floss listed in key (page 265)
Size 24 or 26 tapestry needle
12¼" x 12⅞" white frame
Blue mat with 9⅝" x 10¼" opening
Red mat with 9⅜" x 10" opening
18"-W scroll frame or four 15"
    stretcher bars

INSTRUCTIONS
TO STITCH
Read Before You Stitch (page 189) and
To Begin Stitching (page 190). Mount
the Aida fabric on a scroll frame or
stretcher bars.

Each square on the chart (pages
264–265) represents one square of Aida
fabric. Center and stitch design using
three strands of floss, except one strand
for DMC #3747. Use one strand of floss
for Backstitches, except two strands for
cherry stems.

TO FINISH
To frame your stitchery, see Framing
Your Needlework on page 290. ❁

Designer Linda Gillum, the Executive Vice
President of Kooler Design Studio, Inc., uses
her background as a fine artist in watercol-
ors, oil painting, and pastels to create
award-winning needlework designs, with an
emphasis on counted cross-stitch. She is
well-known for her animal and baby designs.

Shaded rows indicate where chart areas overlap.

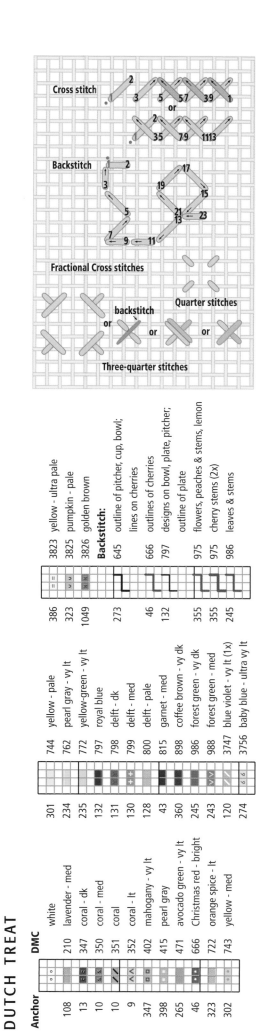

Cross stitch / **Backstitch** / **Fractional Cross stitches** / **Quarter stitches** / **Three-quarter stitches**

backstitch or — or — or

DUTCH TREAT

Backstitch:

Anchor	DMC		Description
386	3823		yellow - ultra pale
323	3825		pumpkin - pale
1049	3826		golden brown
273	645		outline of pitcher, cup, bowl; lines on cherries
46	666		outlines of cherries
132	797		designs on bowl, plate, pitcher; outline of plate
355	975		flowers, peaches & stems, lemon
355	975		cherry stems (2x)
245	986		leaves & stems

Anchor	DMC	Description
301	744	yellow - pale
234	762	pearl gray - vy lt
235	772	yellow-green - vy lt
132	797	royal blue
131	798	delft - dk
130	799	delft - med
128	800	delft - pale
43	815	garnet - med
360	898	coffee brown - vy dk
245	986	forest green - vy dk
243	988	forest green - med
120	3747	blue violet - vy lt (1x)
274	3756	baby blue - ultra vy lt

Anchor	DMC	Description
	white	white
108	210	lavender - med
13	347	coral - dk
10	350	coral - med
10	351	coral
9	352	coral - lt
347	402	mahogany - vy lt
398	415	pearl gray
265	471	avocado green - vy lt
46	666	Christmas red - bright
323	722	orange spice - lt
302	743	yellow - med

acorn sampler

The verse about the venerable old oak growing from a tiny acorn evokes the image of building a grand sampler, stitch by stitch, from threading the first needle to completing the final touches. This blending of pictorial cross-stitch and specialty stitches with the tradition of English band samplers includes four different stitch treatments for acorns and will give you a taste of working on linen with metallic threads. Your stitching knowledge, like a sapling oak, will grow in small, measurable steps until you reach mastery.

DESIGN BY SANDY ORTON
Finished design size: 6" x 12"
Finished project size: 11½" x 17½"

MATERIALS
15" x 21" Light Sand Cashel Linen,
    28-count (Zweigart)
Floss and specialty threads listed in key
    (pages 270–271)
Size 24 & 26 tapestry needles
9" x 15" faux burl frame with
    gold beading
18"-W scroll frame or pairs of 15" & 21"
    stretcher bars

INSTRUCTIONS
TO STITCH
Read Before You Stitch (page 189) and To Begin Stitching (page 190). Mount the linen fabric on a scroll frame or stretcher bars.

Each square on the main chart (pages 268–269) equals two threads of fabric. Each square on the detail charts (page 273) equals one thread of fabric. Use three strands of floss for full Cross stitches, and one strand for Petite Cross stitches; see key for number of strands to use for other stitches. Use the alphabet (page 273) to personalize your sampler.

TO FINISH
To frame your sampler, see Framing Your Needlework on page 290. ✤

Designer Sandy Orton of Kooler Design Studio, Inc., has established her reputation with her original designs based on antique samplers, and is especially fond of English band samplers. She is equally adept in pictorial designs, including translations of fine art paintings. Her background in illustration and teaching serve her well in her work.

The Acorn Sampler Chart continues on page 269.

Shaded rows indicate where chart areas overlap.

Petite Cross area—see separate chart on page 273.

Petite Cross personalization
See alphabet on page 273.

Petite Cross personalization
See alphabet on page 273.

ACORN SAMPLER

Anchor		DMC Cross Stitch (3x)	
370		301	mahogany - med
117		341	blue violet - lt
347/890		402(2x)/436(1x)	blended; tan/mahogany - lt
265/264		471(1x)/472(2x)	blended; avocado green - lt
878		501	blue-green - dk
876		503	blue-green - med
859		523	fern green - lt
8581		647	beaver gray - med
900		648	beaver gray - lt
275		746	off white
360		838	beige-brown - vy dk
341		918	red copper - dk
844		3012	khaki green - med
870		3042	antique violet - lt
887		3046	yellow-beige - med
846		3051	green-gray - dk
262		3363	pine green - med
928		3761	sky blue - vy lt
122		3807	cornflower blue
373		3828	hazelnut brown
375		3862	mocha beige - dk
---		002HL	#8 metallic braid (Kreinik) (1x)
---		1300	woodland fantasy (Needle Necessities overdyed floss. See note.)

Petite Cross (1x):

Anchor			
360		838	saying, personalization
---		1420	grecian olive (Needle Necessities overdyed floss. See note.)

Smyrna Cross (3x):

Anchor			
373		422	border acorn tops
360		838	border acorn tops
375		3862	border acorn tops

Mosaic (2x):

Anchor			
265/264		471(1x)/472(1x)	blended; border acorns
275		746	border acorns
175		794	background of capital "T"
844		3012	border acorns
870		3042	background of capital "T"
928		3761	background of capital "T"

Long-arm Cross (2x):

Anchor			
375		3862	some band separations

Note: When using overdyed floss, complete each stitch individually.

Anchor		DMC	

Rice:

| 373 | | 422 | side border bottom stitch (3x) |
| 375 | | 3862 | side border top stitch (2x) |

Four-sided (2x):

| 375 | | 3862 | some band separations |

Queen (2x):

360		838	acorn tops in "medallion" at top and bottom
373		3828	acorn tops in "medallion" at top and bottom
375		3862	acorn tops in "medallion" at top and bottom

Rhodes (3x):

| --- | | 1300 | woodland fantasy (Needle Necessities overdyed floss) acorns in center band (3x) |

Satin (4x):

| --- | | 1420 | grecian olive (Needle Necessities overdyed floss) acorns in "medallion" at top and bottom (4x) |

Padded Satin (2x):

370		301	acorn tops in middle band
347/890		402(1x)/436(1x) blended; acorn tops in middle band	
341		918	acorn tops in middle band

Algerian Eyelet:

| 275 | | 746 | centers of acorn "medallions" at top and bottom (3x) |
| 360 | | 838 | letter form of capital "T" (2x) |

Irish (4x)

370		301	lower band
347		402	lower band
347		472	lower band
175		794	lower band
341		918	lower band
844		3012	lower band
846		3051	lower band
928		3761	lower band
122		3807	lower band (work this color first)

Double Running (1x):

---		002 #4 braid (Kreinik); top wishbone filling pattern	
---		202HL #4 braid (Kreinik); bottom wishbone; part of acorn & leaf band	
---		150V #4 braid (Kreinik); border leaves; part of acorn & leaf band	

Backstitch:

| --- | | 150V #4 braid (Kreinik); "T" leaves & acorns (1x) | |
| 375 | | 3862 | fence posts & rail, edge of roof & house, top border (2x) |

Straight:

| 360 | | 838 | fence posts, large cow's head, windows, tips of satin-stitched acorns (over three threads) (2x); edge of fence posts (1x) |
| 341 | | 918 | tails, ears & legs of cows (2x) |

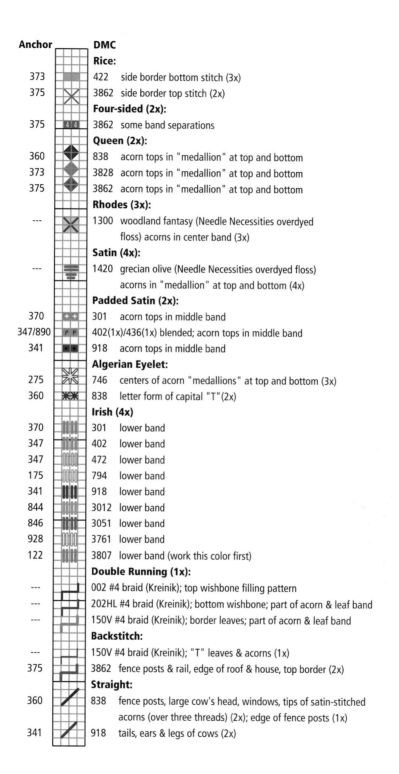

271

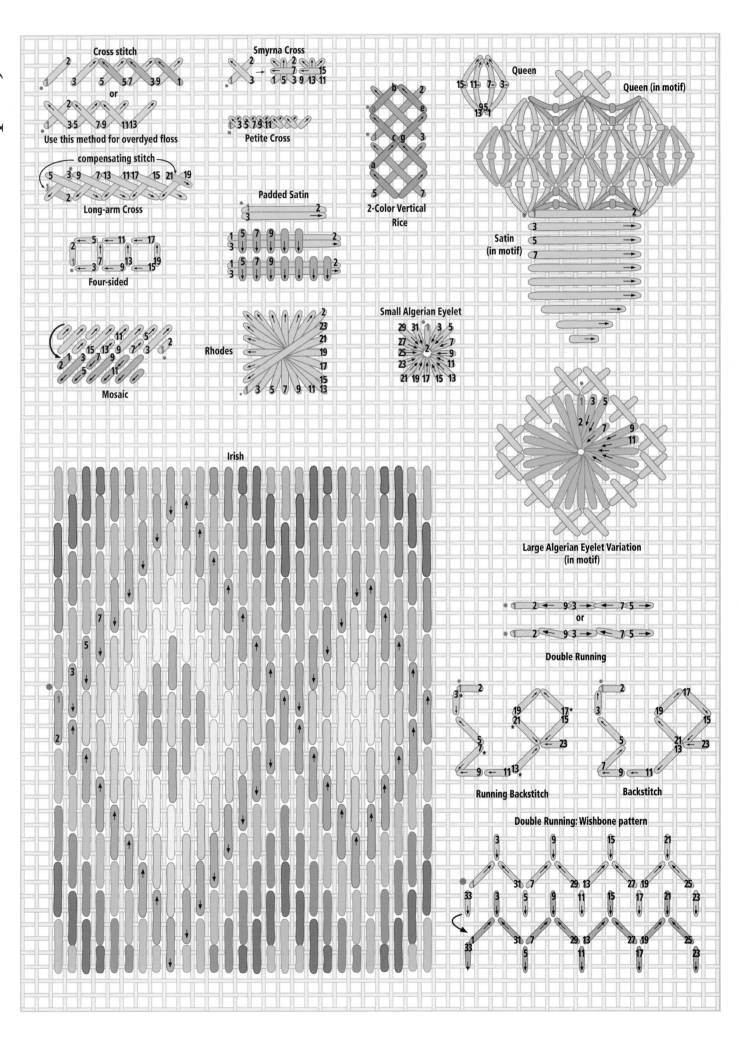

Cross stitch

or

Use this method for overdyed floss

compensating stitch

Long-arm Cross

Four-sided

Mosaic

Smyrna Cross

Petite Cross

Padded Satin

Rhodes

2-Color Vertical Rice

Small Algerian Eyelet

Queen

Queen (in motif)

Satin (in motif)

Large Algerian Eyelet Variation (in motif)

Double Running

Running Backstitch

Backstitch

Irish

Double Running: Wishbone pattern

SMALL DETAIL CHART: Saying

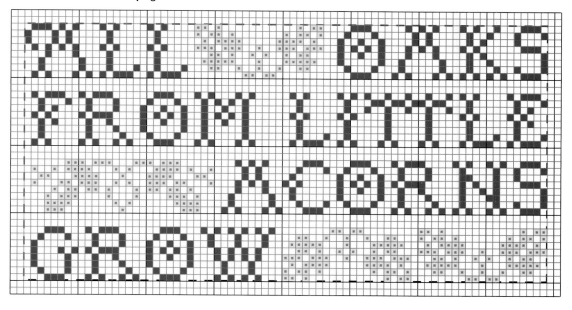

SMALL DETAIL CHART: Alphabet and Numbers for Personalizing

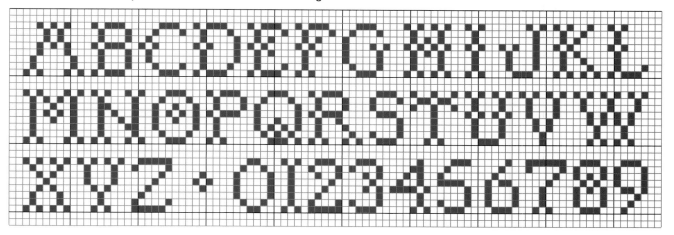

These charts are for petite cross-stitch. Stitch over one thread intersection.

Use one strand of floss and stitch each Petite Cross individually before proceeding to the next stitch.

simple elegance

Like a new snowfall that dusts the trees and rooftops, light-colored pearl cotton adds a fanciful frosting to natural linen in this elegant Hardanger masterpiece. Orderly geometry takes an aesthetic turn in an elongated doily full of lacy details and cutwork, a beautiful introduction to this old Norwegian needlework technique. This project makes an ideal beginner's sampler, a lesson in elementary drawn-thread work, and a worthy family heirloom-to-be.

DESIGN BY LINDA ABEL

Finished design size: 12" x 5⅝"
Finished project size: 12" x 5⅝"

MATERIALS

9" x 15" 18-count Natural Cork Linen
   (Zweigart)
Two balls #5 Ecru pearl cotton
One ball #8 Ecru pearl cotton
Size 22 & 24 tapestry needles
Small, sharp scissors

INSTRUCTIONS

Read Before You Stitch (page 189) and To Begin Stitching (page 190). Fold linen in half lengthwise and finger-press a crease down the center fold.

Use #5 pearl cotton and size 22 needle for Kloster Blocks, Star Motifs, and Buttonhole Edging. Use #8 pearl cotton and size 24 needle for Algerian Eyelets, Woven Bars with Picots, and Dove's Eyes.

Read about Kloster Blocks, Star Motifs, Buttonhole Edging, Algerian Eyelets, Picots, Dove's Eyes, and Cutting on pages 278–279.

TO STITCH

Begin stitching Kloster Blocks along the inner and outer design borders where indicated by red dot on chart (close to the center crease).

Stitch Kloster Blocks and Star Motifs in inner design areas.

Stitch Buttonhole Edging along outer perimeter.

Stitch Algerian Eyelets just inside the Buttonhole edging.

Cut fabric threads where indicated on chart, and withdraw threads.

Stitch Woven Bars, adding Picots as you reach them; add Dove's Eyes when you reach the halfway point of the fourth side of a Woven Bar.

Trim off excess fabric along Buttonhole Edging.

TO FINISH

Wash and press doily (see Cleaning the Finished Piece, page 107); any little fabric nubs left beyond the Buttonhole stitches will shrink into the design. ❀

Designer Linda Abel is a recognized expert in Hardanger technique. Her designs have been published in books and many nationally known magazines, and she teaches Hardanger classes at consumer trade shows, The Embroiderers' Guild of America, Inc., workshops, and needlework shops.

start here

SIMPLE ELEGANCE

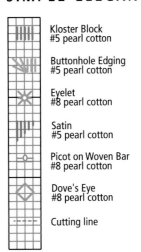

Kloster Block
#5 pearl cotton

Buttonhole Edging
#5 pearl cotton

Eyelet
#8 pearl cotton

Satin
#5 pearl cotton

Picot on Woven Bar
#8 pearl cotton

Dove's Eye
#8 pearl cotton

Cutting line

Finished size: 4¼" square

COASTER INSTRUCTIONS

You will need a 9" square of 18-ct. Natural Cork Linen, one ball each of #5 and #8 Ecru pearl cotton, size 22 and 24 tapestry needles, and small, sharp scissors.

Follow instructions for the Doily (page 274) and stitch one diamond-shaped motif from either the top or bottom of the chart (page 276). When stitching the Buttonhole-stitch border, continue the Buttonhole stitches along the outer edge of the Kloster-Block diamond.

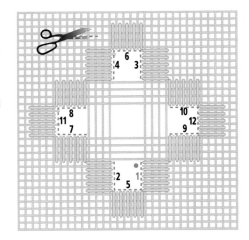

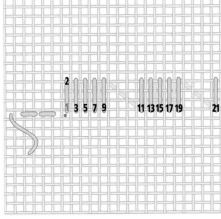

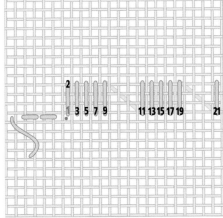

CUTTING TECHNIQUE

Every Kloster block must have an opposing Kloster block across the motif; always double-check before cutting.

Begin cutting only after all Kloster blocks, Buttonhole stitches, and Eyelets are complete. (There are exceptions, but this a good general rule to follow.)

You will need two essential tools: small, very sharp, fine-pointed embroidery scissors, and tweezers to remove cut threads.

Cut only those threads perpendicular to the long Satin stitches of the Kloster Blocks; never cut parallel to these Satin stitches.

Always cut with the scissors held to the left side of the Kloster Block.

Insert the tip of the scissors into the fabric hole shared by the first stitches of adjoining Kloster Blocks, then gather four ground threads onto the blade of the scissors and bring scissors' point back through the fabric to front. (These four threads are enclosed by the Kloster Block; working in this manner ensures that only four threads are cut.)

Snug the scissors' blades close to the end of the Kloster block stitches and cut the four threads on the blade. Now cut the same four threads from the opposing Kloster block.

Proceed, cutting the threads with the shortest distance and then the remaining (note numbers on diagram) or in a clockwise pattern. Rotate the fabric as needed.

Cut all ground threads for a single motif before withdrawing or withdraw thread groups as they are cut.

KLOSTER BLOCK, WORKED HORIZONTALLY

Start the first Kloster Block with an away-waste knot or a tail of several inches anchored with a few Backstitches; reweave tail later into back of formed stitches.

Generally, use a thicker thread for Kloster Blocks than for the rest of a Hardanger design.

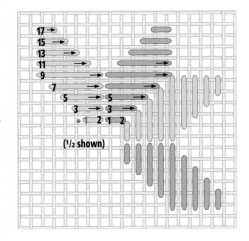

STAR MOTIF

Use the same size thread as for Kloster Blocks.

KLOSTER BLOCK, WORKED DIAGONALLY

Note that adjoining Kloster blocks share a common hole and the traveling thread does not travel diagonally from block to block.

Generally, use a thicker thread for Kloster Blocks than for the rest of the Hardanger design.

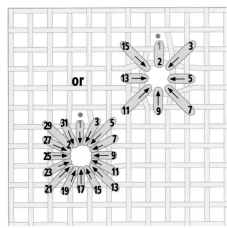

ALGERIAN EYELET

Always insert the needle into the center hole.

Pull the working thread when it's at the perimeter of the stitch to open the central hole

Use a finer thread than for Kloster blocks.

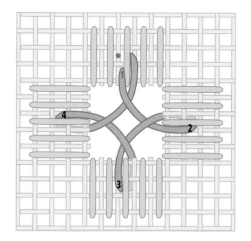

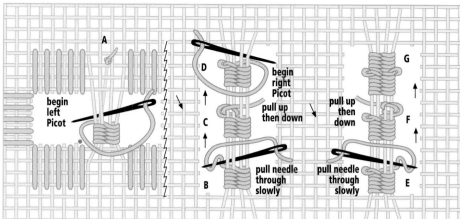

DOVE'S EYE

Three-and-one-half sides of a cut square must already be wrapped or woven, or all four Kloster Blocks finished (as shown), before beginning a Dove's Eye. (After completing Dove's Eye, finish the remaining Wrapped or Woven Bar.)

Work clockwise (shown) or counter-clockwise; be consistent throughout a single design.

Cross all four sides of the Dove's Eye in the same direction.

Strive to keep all Dove's Eyes the same size throughout the design; you may need to gently manipulate the open area because squares with Kloster blocks on one side are usually slightly smaller than those with Bars.

Don't pull so tightly that you distort or re-align the Wrapped or Woven Bars.

Use a finer thread than for Kloster blocks.

PICOT

After weaving one-half of a Woven Bar, stop and begin the Picot on the same side of the bar on which you began; slide the needle down the middle of the bar, facing left (A).

Pull thread under the needle and then wrap thread around needle once "under, over, under" (B). Lay the thread back towards the eye of the needle, parallel with the needle (B). Holding the small loop with thumb and forefinger, gently pull needle through loop and then down and level with fabric (C).

Insert the needle in the middle of the bar, pull thread up gently and then down to "seat" the knot (C).

Although the diagram illustrates a woven bar with 2 picots, this design has only 1 picot per bar.

Complete the Woven Bar (G).

Picots take some practice to master!

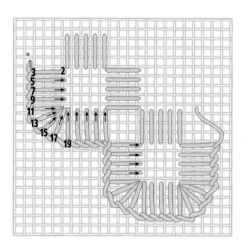

BUTTONHOLE EDGING

Work from left to right.

To begin, use an away-waste knot; do not anchor in previously stitched Kloster Blocks; do not start at an inside or outside corner.

End with a small tack stitch, then bury the tail in previously worked Buttonhole stitches.

Maintain an even, tight tension.

Carefully cut fabric close to raised edge of stitch, then trim away any remaining fabric nubs.

springtime borders

A carefully cultivated row of bright pink tulips ensure it's forever springtime… Soulful waves of blue define a truly blue horizon… These idyllic images come by way of Swedish weaving, an old technique that's easy and fun to do. Try it on these towels made of traditional huck fabric, specially woven for this delightful form of needlework.

DESIGNS BY MARY POLITYKA BUSH
Finished design size: 19" x 1⅞"
Finished project size: 19" x 25"

MATERIALS

For each towel:

¾ yd. of 19"-W White Linen Huck toweling*

One skein each #5 pearl cotton (DMC) in colors listed on page 282

One reel #001 Silver #12 Tapestry Braid (Kreinik Mfg. Co.)

Size 24 tapestry needle

Small, sharp needle (for hemming)

White sewing thread

For Truly Blue Horizons only: 20" of ⅜"-W light green satin ribbon

*You may substitute 20"-W x 27"-L cotton huck fabric. Be sure to trim fabric even with the floats in horizontal rows. Turn and stitch ¼" hems on sides after weaving is complete.

INSTRUCTIONS

GENERAL INSTRUCTIONS

Zigzag-stitch or hand-overcast raw edges of toweling.

Identify the right side of the fabric; it will display pairs of thread "floats" which resemble a number "11" when oriented correctly.

Cut each thread the length specified in the box on page 282. Work each thread of the design from the center outward, beginning with the left side of the design. Work rows in numerical order. Do not trim thread ends.

STITCHING TECHNIQUE

Begin with Row 1, about 5½" from bottom cut edge; the starting point (shown as arrows on the charts) at the exact center should be between two pairs of floats. (If there's only one pair at this point, move up one row.) Slide the threaded needle under these two pairs of floats and pull half the length of the thread through. Pin the other half aside.

Hold the needle horizontally as you work and keep fabric as flat as possible. For straight rows, slide the needle under all pairs of floats in a straight line. Make sure you catch only the floats; check the wrong side of the toweling to make sure you do not pierce the fabric itself.

Maintain a fairly relaxed tension as you weave. Never pull thread so tight that the fabric puckers.

For rows that are not straight, move the needle down to lower rows or up to upper rows of floats as shown on chart.

Rows 2 and 12 of Truly Blue Horizons and Rows 8, 13, 17, and 18 of Forever Springtime feature crossover loops; slide the crossovers from left to right (Fig. 2, page 282), then continue the rest of the row from right to left.

Note that although Rows 11 and 13 of Truly Blue Horizons and Rows 16–18 of Forever Springtime are straight lines, the thread skips some floats.

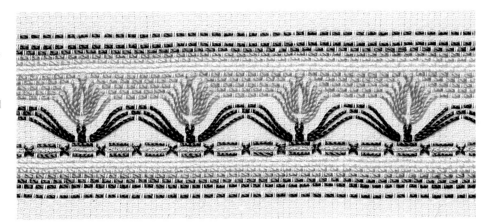

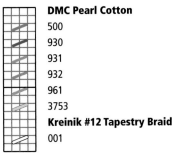

DMC Pearl Cotton

500
930
931
932
961
3753

Kreinik #12 Tapestry Braid

001

When two or more rows share the same pair of floats, take care to "stack" the threads side by side under the pair of floats. To avoid piercing these floats or any threads already in place, wiggle the needle gently as you slide it under the floats to make room for additional threads.

When the entire left half of the design is complete, turn fabric and chart upside down and complete rows as mirror images.

Secure thread ends by weaving the working thread back into the same last few floats as shown in Fig. 1. This hides the cut thread ends on the fabric front. See Fig. 2 for finishing the herringbone rows hiding the working thread's cut end under a previous stitch. Clip tails close to nearest pair of floats.

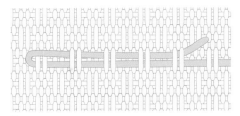

Fig. 1

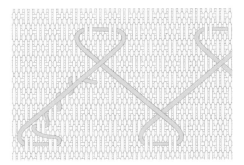

Fig. 2

TO FINISH

For Truly Blue Horizons, use a bodkin to thread ribbon through the herringbone channel. Turn ends under and secure with tiny stitches.

To hem, turn under ½" on raw edges; turn again and slip-stitch along pressed edges. 🧵

Designer Mary Polityka Bush has been stitching and designing since childhood. Her interest and talent in designing Swedish weaving, which she considers her specialty, has helped spark renewed interest in this technique. Other areas of her expertise include needlepoint and designing with specialty threads.

Row	Color	Cut
1, 2, 24, 25	500 pearl cotton	27"
3, 23	930 pearl cotton	27"
4, 22	931 pearl cotton	27"
5, 21	932 pearl cotton	27"
6, 7, 19, 20	3753 pearl cotton	27"
8, 9, 10, 11, 12	961 pearl cotton	48"
13, 14, 15	500 pearl cotton	48"
16	001 Tapestry Braid (#12)	27"
17 & 18	930 pearl cotton	36"

TRULY BLUE HORIZONS

Row	Color	Cut
1, 18, 19	500 pearl cotton	27"
2	500 pearl cotton	48"
3, 4	930 pearl cotton	48"
5, 6	931 pearl cotton	48"
7, 8	932 pearl cotton	48"
9, 10	3753 pearl cotton	48"
11, 13	001 Tapestry Braid (#12)	27"
12	500 pearl cotton	68"
14	3753 pearl cotton	27"
15	932 pearl cotton	27"
16	931 pearl cotton	27"
17	930 pearl cotton	27"

DMC Pearl Cotton

500
930
931
932
3753

Kreinik #12 Tapestry Braid

001

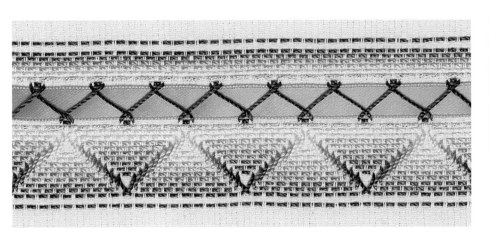

Forever Springtime

Truly Blue Horizons

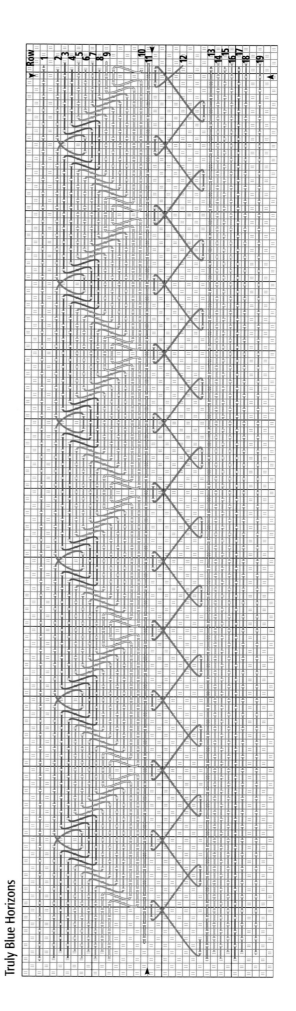

rose basket

Tiny, dainty stitches of linen and silk threads adorn a needlebook that could have been made two hundred years ago by an accomplished needleworker. The open, lacy look is the result of highly textured, pulled-thread stitches that are delightfully easy to execute. If fine needlework has seriously caught your fancy, treat yourself to this small masterpiece—both beautiful and practical—which will stand the test of time.

DESIGN BY RAE IVERSON
Finished design size: 6" x 3⅜"
Finished project size: 3" x 3⅜" (closed)

MATERIALS

10" x 8" Cream Milan Linen, 28-ct. (Norden Craft)
Silk threads listed in key (Needlepoint Inc.)
Londonderry linen thread, size 50/3, Ivory
7" x 5" ivory fabric (interlining)
7" x 5" lightweight fusible interfacing
6" x 3½" moss green synthetic suede (lining)
6" x 3½" ivory wool felt (for one pair of pages; use multiples if desired)
⅜ yd. of ⅛"-W ivory satin ribbon
Ivory and light blue sewing thread
Size 24 & 28 tapestry needles
Scroll frame with 10" scroll rods
For tassel: 2" x 3" heavy cardboard

INSTRUCTIONS
TO STITCH

Read Before You Stitch (page 189) and To Begin Stitching (page 190). Mount the linen fabric on the scroll frame, lacing or clipping sides of fabric to the side bars. Using light blue sewing thread, sew a line of Running stitches along the vertical center of the linen to indicate the spine/fold.

Each square on the charts (pages 286 and 287) equals one thread of linen. Use one strand of floss. Work the stitches in the following order, referring to the charts for placement, key (page 288) for thread type and stitch diagrams (page 288). For photo of opened needlebook, see page 289.

PULLED THREE-SIDED: Work each stitch twice, pulling thread tight enough to pull the fabric threads together but not pucker the fabric; don't pull thread as tightly at corners.

SATIN (also called Pins): Pull fabric thread lightly. Note there is only one fabric thread between rows of Satin stitches on right half of the design.

PADDED SATIN: For base of basket motif, pad the Satin stitches by first working two long horizontal stitches the length of the Satin-stitch areas, then stitch Satin stitches atop them.

PULLED ITALIAN CROSS: Start at bottom of basket, working the first row from left to right; work the second row from right to left, etc.

PETITE CROSS VARIATION: Work the legs of both "journeys" like tent stitches (see diagram). Stitch initials on the left side of the design using the separate alphabet chart (page 289).

BROAD CHAIN: Do not pull this stitch. Bury the thread tails under previous Petite Cross stitches.

PULLED THREAD EYELET: Work each stitch twice, pulling thread; texture and tension should match Three-sided stitches.

LONG UPRIGHT CROSS (this pattern is called **FRENCH DIAGONAL**): Not a true pulled stitch, but stitch the horizontal stitches with slightly more tension than the vertical to create a hint of texture.

If you desire, you may stitch the next two stitches without the frame.

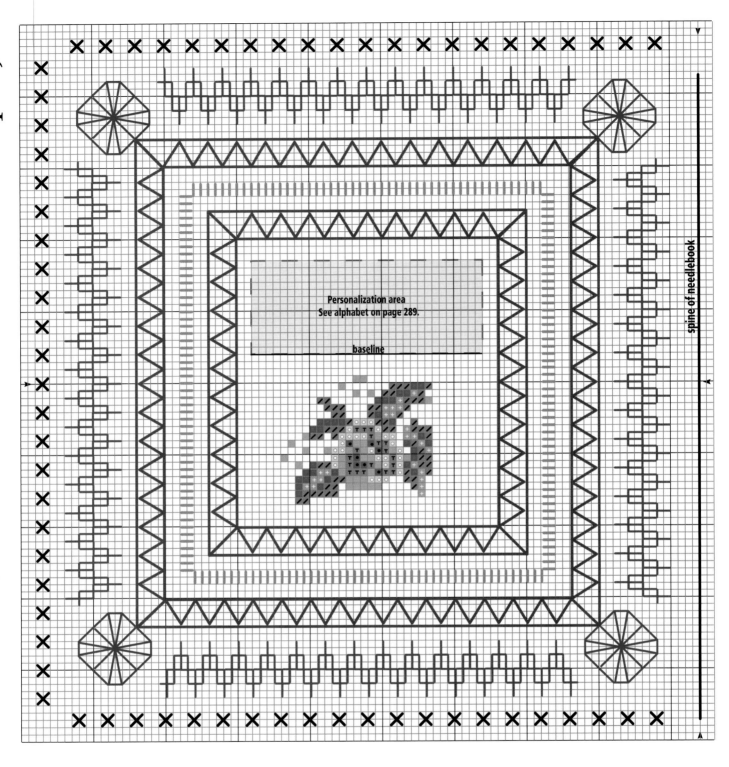

Personalization area
See alphabet on page 289.

baseline

spine of needlebook

PALESTRINA KNOT: Shown as Xs on the chart; these fall along the same lines as the outer folded edges of the needlebook. Work from right to left.

NUN'S EDGING: Placement is not shown on chart; allow eight fabric threads unstitched between Palestrina Knots and Nun's Edging. Use linen thread.

TO FINISH

Trim design fabric along the outer edge of Nun's Edging. Spray the wrong side of the design fabric with water and press with a warm iron, checking that the borders are square. Let cool.

Trim interfacing to fit the dimensions of the design fabric inside the Palestrina-Knot border. Following manufacturer's instructions, fuse interfacing to back of ivory fabric. With right side of interlining unit to wrong side of design, miter at corners (Fig. 1a) the folded edges of the design fabric to the inside, overcasting at mitered seams (Fig. 1b). Lightly stitch Nun's Edging to interfacing using a Herringbone stitch (Fig. 2), making sure not to catch the front of the design fabric.

To make the twisted cord, cut four 8" lengths of the darkest green floss; separate and recombine strands. Twist

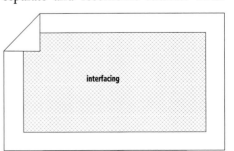

interfacing

Fig. 1a

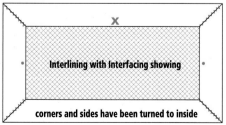

Fig. 1b

tightly, bring both ends together, and allow the strands to twist together. Matching the folded end of the cord with the bottom of the needlebook spine, lay the cord along the spine and

over to the inside at top edge; tack only the raw edge of the cord at the pink X (Fig. 1b), trimming cord if necessary.

To make tassel, wrap the darkest green floss (from design) around the shorter dimension of the cardboard rec-

Fig. 2

```
    3 2      7
   ↘    ↘      ↘
   1      5
```

Herringbone

tangle 20 times. To make the tassel hanger, thread a needle with two strands of floss and slip it under the wrapped floss along one long edge of cardboard. Tie off securely and remove cardboard. Using a separate length of floss, bind the tassel threads together ¼" below hanger tie and conceal thread ends. Trim loops at bottom of tassel. Thread the hanger tails onto a needle and attach tassel to the folded end of the twisted cord. Pin the cord and tassel out of the way.

ROSE BASKET

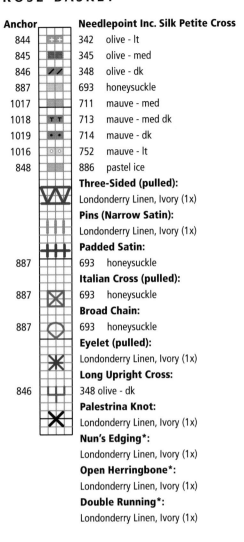

Anchor		Needlepoint Inc. Silk Petite Cross	
844	+ +	342	olive - lt
845		345	olive - med
846	/ /	348	olive - dk
887		693	honeysuckle
1017		711	mauve - med
1018	T T	713	mauve - med dk
1019	• •	714	mauve - dk
1016	○ ○	752	mauve - lt
848		886	pastel ice

Three-Sided (pulled):
Londonderry Linen, Ivory (1x)

Pins (Narrow Satin):
Londonderry Linen, Ivory (1x)

Padded Satin:
887   693   honeysuckle

Italian Cross (pulled):
887   693   honeysuckle

Broad Chain:
887   693   honeysuckle

Eyelet (pulled):
Londonderry Linen, Ivory (1x)

Long Upright Cross:
846   348 olive - dk

Palestrina Knot:
Londonderry Linen, Ivory (1x)

Nun's Edging*:
Londonderry Linen, Ivory (1x)

Open Herringbone*:
Londonderry Linen, Ivory (1x)

Double Running*:
Londonderry Linen, Ivory (1x)

*Not charted; used for finishing

Cut ribbon in half and tack at pink dots (Fig. 1b, page 286)

Trim synthetic suede ⅛" smaller on all sides than design unit. Center over wrong side of design unit and attach using Herringbone stitch (page 287) in the darkest green thread from design.

Trim felt ⅛" smaller on all sides than suede; use pinking shears, if desired. (You may make more than one pair of pages.) Center over suede and attach to spine using a Double Running stitch (Fig. 3) and ivory linen thread, stitching through all layers. Using green thread, tack cord to spine of needlebook. 🌣

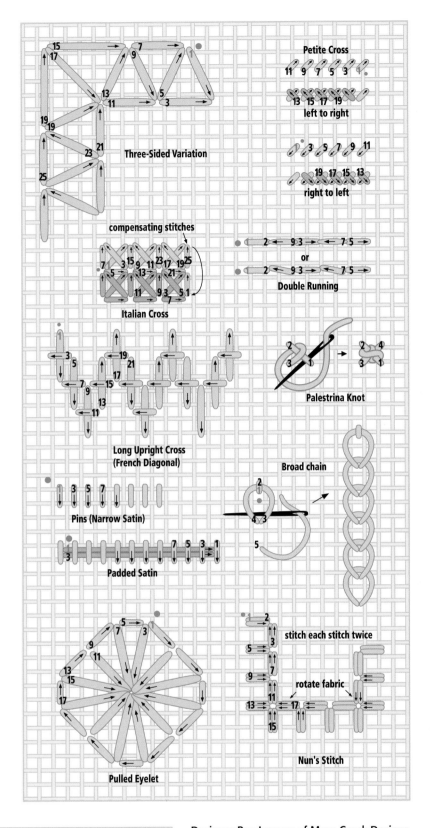

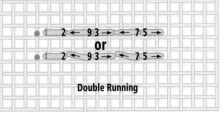

Fig. 3

Designer Rae Iverson of Moss Creek Designs, has a background in art and needlework, including calligraphy, charcoal pencil work, photography, sewing, knitting, and writing. Her specialty is using antique motifs and sampler stitches in her original designs. As a teacher, she emphasizes the historical aspects of needlework.

FRAMING YOUR STITCHERY

Skillful framing makes the difference between a project that looks amateurish and one that looks professional. Doesn't your stitchery deserve the best treatment you can afford? Commercial framing can be expensive, but you can learn the tricks of the trade and spend the savings on fabric and threads for your next project!

Whenever possible, use standard-sized frames and mats that you can purchase ready-made. Professional framing establishments are often willing to custom-make a frame to the dimensions of your project, with the understanding that you will lace and mount the stitchery yourself (these steps are usually the most costly procedure in the framing process).

Whether or not to use glass is controversial. Glass can trap moisture inside the frame, create glare over the stitchery, or crush the stitches. On the other hand, glass protects the stitchery from dust, cooking aromas, grease, and smoke. If you choose to use glass, be sure to use a mat or spacers of balsa wood or mat board in the corners to prevent the glass from touching the stitchery.

TOOLS AND MATERIALS

FRAME AND MOUNT BOARD You may find these sold together or separately. If your frame comes without a mount board, have one cut from mount board stock sold at art supply or frame stores.

MAT(S) Optional; the desired look of the finished project will guide you.

RULER, PENCIL, AND PAPER Use to measure and note sizes and dimensions.

SCISSORS, PINS, AND LARGE-EYED STRAIGHT OR CURVED NEEDLE Use to trim, position, and lace fabric. Small T-pins work better than standard dressmaker's pins.

FLEECE Glued to the mount board, cotton batting or polyester fleece cushions and "rounds out" your design fabric; find it in fabric and craft stores. Use white craft glue to join fleece to the corners of the mount board.

HEAVY THREAD OR TAPE The best choice for heirloom-quality designs is to lace the edges of the design fabric on the back of the mount board. Dental floss, upholstery or carpet thread, or nylon thread work well. Another option is to tape the fabric edges to the back of the mount board with acid-free linen or plastic tape.

DECORATIVE PAPER Optional, it's a nice touch to add to the back of the framed piece to ensure a finished appearance. Wrapping paper offers appealing patterns; brown paper works as well.

GLAZIER POINTS OR BRADS Use to secure covered mount board in the frame. Find these at hardware stores; use a small hammer or blunt knife (such as a dinner knife) to insert them. If you do a lot of framing, you may want to purchase a time-saving brad gun.

HANGER OR WIRE For small designs, use a sawtooth hanger; these are usually packaged with the requisite nails. For frames larger than 16" x 20", use hanger wire and screw eyes. Find these at hardware stores.

FRAMING INSTRUCTIONS

Read When Stitching Is Complete (page 29 for needlepoint, page 107 for embroidery, page 191 for counted thread) and launder your stitchery (dry-clean silk) if necessary.

CALCULATING FRAME AND MAT SIZES The suggestions here are general; your project may require special proportions or considerations.

To calculate the size of the mat opening, add ½" to 1" to all sides of a small design; for a large design, add 1" to 2" to all sides. (The example shown illustrates a mat that is flush with the top and sides of the design; this will not always be the case.)

To calculate the outer dimensions for mat and/or frame, add 2" to 3" on all sides for a medium-size design, 4" for large designs. Include the rabbet area (the recessed edge of the frame) in these measurements.

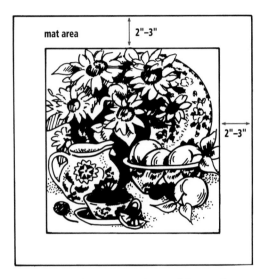

Calculate the mat opening and frame size.

MOUNTING THE DESIGN ON THE MOUNT BOARD If you're using fleece, glue the fleece to the corners of the mount board.

If you're not using a mat, center the design over the mount board, aligning the grain of the fabric with edges of the board. Trim fabric so it extends 1" to 1½" beyond all edges of the mount board. Machine-zigzag or hand-overcast raw edges.

On the back of the mount board, mark the center on all four sides with a pencil. On the design fabric, sew a short (1"-long) running-stitch line to mark the center on all four sides.

Mark centers of fabric and mount board edges.

If you're using a mat (see previous diagram), center the mat over the design and mark the window opening on four sides by pinning into the fabric, following the grain. Remove the mat and measure out from the pins equal to the depth of the mat. Mark these outside edges with running stitches, following the grain. Trim the fabric so it extends 1" to 1½" beyond the marked line. Machine-zigzag or hand-overcast raw edges. Position the fabric over the fleece side of the mount board, aligning the stitched outline with the edges of the board; turn the unit over (design side down) and match the center marks.

Pin the fabric into the edges of the mount board, following the marked outline and working from the center of each side to the corners, spacing pins ½" apart. Pull the fabric snug so the marked outline rolls slightly over the mount board edges to the back. When all sides are pinned, check if the fabric sags or looks loose. If so, re-pin along a new thread line of the fabric (inside the original line) until the fabric is stretched very taut over the mount board. Miter the corners of the fabric by folding the points in first, then the sides; pin in place.

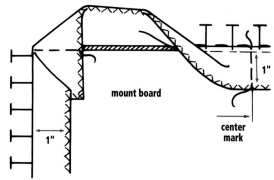

Fold fabric to the back and pin, mitering at corners.

Secure the fabric to the back by lacing: Thread the large-eyed needle with enough thread to complete the lacing for one side. Stitch the laces tightly, about ½" apart, from the centers of each side outward; lace the longer sides first, then the shorter sides. After every three or four lacings, re-tighten the thread. Before securing each thread, check that the laces are as tight as you can reasonably make them.

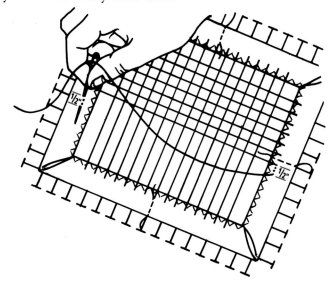

Lace the edges of the fabric.

Finish the lacing process by sewing the mitered corners in place.

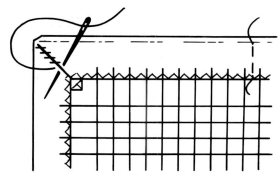

Stitch mitered corners in place.

Insert the design unit (including mats) into the frame and secure using glazier points or brads.

Secure design unit in frame using glazier points.

FINISHING TOUCHES Cut the backing paper ⅛" smaller on all sides than the frame, and glue to the back edges of the frame, keeping the paper as taut as possible. Mist the paper with water; as it dries it will shrink to fit tightly.

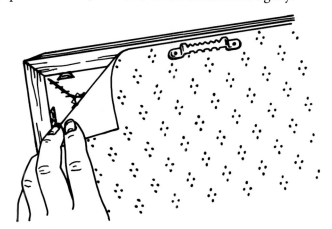

Attach backing paper and sawtooth hanger.

If using a sawtooth hanger, position it at the center top and nail it in place. For a wire hanger, measure one-third the distance from the top of the frame on both sides and screw in the screw eyes at these points. Attach wire to the eyes, allowing a small amount of slack in the wire. ✪

DMC	ANCHOR	DMC	ANCHOR	DMC	ANCHOR	DMC	ANCHOR	DMC	ANCHOR	DMC	ANCHOR
White	2	352	9	517	162	646	8581	758	868	827	160
Ecru	387	353	6	518	1039	647	1040	760	1022	828	9159
208	110	355	1014	519	1038	648	900	761	1021	829	906
209	109	356	5975	520	862	666	46	762	234	830	277
210	108	367	217	522	860	676	891	772	259	831	277
211	342	368	214	523	859	677	886	775	128	832	907
221	897	369	1043	524	858	680	901	776	24	833	907
223	895	370	855	535	401	699	923	778	968	834	874
224	893	371	854	543	933	700	228	780	309	838	1088
225	1026	372	853	550	102	701	227	781	308	839	1086
300	352	400	351	552	99	702	226	782	307	840	1084
301	1049	402	1047	553	98	703	238	783	306	841	1082
304	1006	407	914	554	96	704	256	791	178	842	1080
307	289	413	236	561	212	712	926	792	941	844	1041
309	42	414	235	562	210	718	88	793	176	869	944
310	403	415	398	563	208	720	326	794	175	890	218
311	148	420	374	564	206	721	925	796	133	891	35
312	979	422	943	580	281	722	323	797	132	892	33
315	1019	433	358	581	280	725	305	798	131	893	28
316	1017	434	310	597	1064	726	295	799	136	894	27
317	400	435	1046	598	1062	727	293	800	144	895	1044
318	399	436	1045	600	59	729	890	801	359	898	360
319	218	437	362	601	57	730	845	806	169	899	52
320	215	444	290	602	63	731	924	807	168	900	333
321	9046	445	288	603	62	732	281	809	130	902	897
322	978	451	233	604	55	733	280	813	161	904	258
326	59	452	232	605	1094	734	279	814	45	905	257
327	100	453	231	606	334	738	361	815	43	906	256
333	119	469	267	608	332	739	387	816	1005	907	255
334	977	470	267	610	889	740	316	817	13	909	923
335	38	471	266	611	898	741	304	818	23	910	229
336	150	472	253	612	832	742	303	819	271	911	205
340	118	498	1005	613	831	743	302	820	134	912	209
341	117	500	683	632	936	744	301	822	390	913	204
347	1025	501	878	640	903	745	300	823	152	915	1029
349	13	502	877	642	392	746	275	824	164	917	89
350	11	503	876	644	830	747	158	825	162	918	341
351	10	504	1042	645	273	754	1012	826	161	919	340

DMC	ANCHOR	DMC	ANCHOR	DMC	ANCHOR	DMC	ANCHOR	DMC	ANCHOR	DMC	ANCHOR
920	1004	975	355	3345	268	3760	169	3821	305	3859	914
921	1003	976	1001	3346	267	3761	928	3822	295	3860	1018
922	1003	977	1002	3347	266	3765	170	3823	386	3861	1017
924	851	986	246	3348	264	3766	167	3824	8	3862	375
926	850	987	244	3350	59	3768	779	3825	323	3863	378
927	848	988	243	3354	74	3770	1009	3826	1049	3864	376
928	274	989	242	3362	263	3772	1007	3827	311	3865	2
930	1035	991	1076	3363	262	3773	1008	3828	373	3866	390
931	1034	992	1072	3364	260	3774	778	3829	901		
932	1033	993	1070	3371	382	3776	1048	3830	5975		
934	862	995	410	3607	87	3777	1015	3831	42		
935	861	996	433	3608	86	3778	1013	3832	39		
936	269	3011	846	3609	85	3779	1012	3833	38		
937	268	3012	844	3685	1028	3781	904	3834	94		
938	381	3013	842	3687	68	3782	899	3835	92		
939	152	3021	905	3688	66	3787	273	3836	90		
943	188	3022	8581	3689	49	3790	393	3837	100		
945	881	3023	1040	3705	35	3799	236	3838	131		
946	332	3024	397	3706	33	3801	1098	3839	121		
947	330	3031	905	3708	31	3802	1019	3840	120		
948	1011	3032	903	3712	1023	3803	972	3841	159		
950	4146	3033	391	3713	1020	3804	63	3842	170		
951	1010	3041	871	3716	25	3805	62	3843	410		
954	203	3042	870	3721	896	3806	62	3844	1089		
955	206	3045	888	3722	1027	3807	122	3845	433		
956	40	3046	887	3726	1018	3808	1068	3846	1090		
957	50	3047	852	3727	1016	3809	1066	3847	879		
958	187	3051	681	3731	76	3810	1066	3848	1076		
959	186	3052	262	3733	75	3811	1060	3849	1070		
961	76	3053	261	3740	873	3812	188	3850	188		
962	75	3064	883	3743	869	3813	875	3851	187		
963	73	3072	847	3746	1030	3814	1074	3852	307		
964	185	3078	292	3747	120	3815	877	3853	1003		
966	206	3325	129	3750	1036	3816	876	3854	1002		
970	316	3326	36	3752	1032	3817	875	3855	311		
971	316	3328	1024	3753	1031	3818	923	3856	868		
972	298	3340	329	3755	140	3819	278	3857	352		
973	297	3341	328	3756	1037	3820	306	3858	1007		

ANCHOR TO DMC FLOSS COLORS

ANCHOR	DMC	ANCHOR	DMC	ANCHOR	DMC	ANCHOR	DMC	ANCHOR	DMC	ANCHOR	DMC
1	B5200	55	604	110	208	164	824	234	762	290	444
2	White	57	601	111	208	167	598	235	414	291	444
2	3865	59	326	112	550	168	807	236	3799	292	3078
6	353	60	3688	117	341	169	806	238	703	293	727
8	3824	62	603	118	340	170	3765	239	702	295	726
9	352	63	602	119	333	170	3842	240	966	297	973
10	351	65	3350	120	3747	175	794	241	989	298	972
11	350	66	3688	120	3840	176	793	242	989	300	745
13	817	68	3687	121	793	177	792	243	988	301	744
19	304	69	3687	121	3839	178	791	244	987	302	743
20	816	70	3685	122	3807	185	964	245	700	303	742
22	814	72	902	123	791	186	959	246	986	304	741
23	818	73	963	127	939	187	958	253	772	305	725
24	776	74	3354	128	775	187	3851	254	472	306	3820
25	3716	75	962	129	3325	188	3812	255	907	307	783
26	894	76	961	130	809	188	3850	256	906	307	3852
27	894	77	3350	131	798	189	991	257	905	308	782
28	893	78	3803	131	3838	203	954	258	904	309	781
29	891	85	3609	132	797	204	913	259	772	310	434
31	3708	86	3608	133	796	205	911	260	3364	311	3827
33	3706	87	3607	134	820	206	564	261	3053	311	3855
35	3705	88	718	136	799	208	563	262	3052	313	742
36	3326	89	917	137	798	209	912	263	3362	314	741
38	335	90	554	139	797	210	562	264	3348	316	971
38	3833	90	3836	140	3755	211	562	265	3348	323	722
39	309	92	553	142	798	212	561	266	471	324	721
39	3832	92	3835	143	824	213	504	267	469	326	720
40	956	94	552	144	800	214	368	268	937	328	3341
41	893	94	3834	145	3755	215	320	269	936	329	3340
42	309	95	554	146	322	216	367	271	819	330	947
42	3831	96	554	147	312	217	367	273	645	332	946
43	815	97	554	148	311	218	319	274	928	333	900
44	815	98	553	149	336	225	703	275	746	334	606
45	814	99	552	150	336	226	702	276	543	335	606
46	666	100	327	152	939	227	701	277	830	336	3779
47	321	100	3837	158	747	228	700	278	3819	337	922
48	3689	101	550	159	827	229	910	279	734	338	921
49	3689	102	550	159	3841	230	909	280	733	339	920
50	957	103	3609	160	827	231	453	281	732	340	919
52	899	108	210	161	813	232	452	288	445	341	918
54	956	109	209	162	517	233	451	289	307	342	211

ANCHOR	DMC	ANCHOR	DMC	ANCHOR	DMC	ANCHOR	DMC	ANCHOR	DMC	ANCHOR	DMC
343	3752	393	3790	868	3856	914	3859	1011	948	1050	3781
347	402	397	3024	869	3743	920	932	1012	754	1060	3801
349	301	398	415	870	3042	921	931	1013	3778	1062	598
351	400	399	318	871	3041	922	930	1014	355	1064	597
352	300	400	317	872	3740	923	699	1015	3777	1066	3809
352	3857	401	413	873	3740	924	731	1016	3727	1068	3808
355	975	403	310	874	834	925	721	1017	316	1070	993
357	433	410	995	875	3817	926	712	1017	3861	1070	3849
358	433	410	3843	876	3816	928	3761	1018	3726	1072	992
359	801	433	996	877	3815	933	543	1018	3860	1074	3814
360	898	433	3845	878	501	936	632	1019	315	1076	991
361	738	590	712	879	500	939	794	1020	3713	1076	3848
362	437	681	3051	879	3847	940	793	1021	761	1080	842
363	436	683	500	880	951	941	792	1022	760	1082	841
365	435	778	3774	881	945	942	738	1023	3712	1084	840
366	739	779	3768	882	758	943	436	1024	3328	1086	839
367	738	820	437	883	3064	944	869	1025	347	1088	838
368	437	830	644	884	920	945	834	1026	225	1089	995
369	402	831	613	885	739	956	613	1027	3722	1089	3844
370	434	832	612	886	677	968	778	1028	3685	1090	996
371	400	842	3013	887	3046	969	316	1029	915	1090	3846
372	738	843	3012	888	3045	970	3627	1030	3746	1092	964
373	3828	844	3012	889	610	972	3803	1031	3753	1094	605
374	420	845	730	890	729	975	828	1032	3752	1096	3753
375	869	846	3011	891	676	976	3752	1033	932	1098	3801
375	3862	847	3072	892	225	977	334	1034	931	4146	950
376	3774	848	927	893	224	978	322	1035	930	5975	3830
376	3864	849	927	894	224	979	312	1036	3750	8581	646
378	841	850	926	895	223	1001	976	1037	3756	9046	321
378	3863	851	924	896	3721	1002	977	1038	519	9159	828
379	840	852	3047	897	221	1002	3854	1039	518	9575	758
380	838	853	372	898	611	1003	922	1040	647		
381	938	854	371	899	3782	1003	3853	1041	844		
382	3371	855	370	900	648	1004	920	1042	504		
386	3823	856	370	901	680	1005	816	1043	369		
387	Ecru	858	524	903	3032	1006	304	1044	895		
388	842	859	523	904	3790	1007	3772	1045	436		
390	822	860	522	905	3021	1007	3858	1046	435		
390	3866	861	935	906	829	1008	3773	1047	402		
391	3033	862	520	907	832	1009	3770	1048	3776		
392	642	868	3779	914	407	1010	951	1049	301		

YARDS TO METERS

YARDS	METERS	YARDS	METERS	YARDS	METERS	YARDS	METERS	YARDS	METERS
⅛	0.11	2⅛	1.94	4⅛	3.77	6⅛	5.60	8⅛	7.43
¼	0.23	2¼	2.06	4¼	3.89	6¼	5.72	8¼	7.54
⅜	0.34	2⅜	2.17	4⅜	4.00	6⅜	5.83	8⅜	7.66
½	0.46	2½	2.29	4½	4.11	6½	5.94	8½	7.77
⅝	0.57	2⅝	2.40	4⅝	4.23	6⅝	6.06	8⅝	7.89
¾	0.69	2¾	2.51	4¾	4.34	6¾	6.17	8¾	8.00
⅞	0.80	2⅞	2.63	4⅞	4.46	6⅞	6.29	8⅞	8.12
1	0.91	3	2.74	5	4.57	7	6.40	9	8.23
1⅛	1.03	3⅛	2.86	5⅛	4.69	7⅛	6.52	9⅛	8.34
1¼	1.14	3¼	2.97	5¼	4.80	7¼	6.63	9¼	8.46
1⅜	1.26	3⅜	3.09	5⅜	4.91	7⅜	6.74	9⅜	8.57
1½	1.37	3½	3.20	5½	5.03	7½	6.86	9½	8.69
1⅝	1.49	3⅝	3.31	5⅝	5.14	7⅝	6.97	9⅝	8.80
1¾	1.60	3¾	3.43	5¾	5.26	7¾	7.09	9¾	8.92
1⅞	1.71	3⅞	3.54	5⅞	5.37	7⅞	7.20	9⅞	9.03
2	1.83	4	3.66	6	5.49	8	7.32	10	9.14

INCHES TO MILLIMETERS (MM) AND CENTIMETERS (CM)

INCHES	MM	CM	INCHES	CM	INCHES	CM
⅛	3	0.3	9	22.9	30	76.2
¼	6	0.6	10	25.4	31	78.7
⅜	10	1.0	11	27.9	32	81.3
½	13	1.3	12	30.5	33	83.8
⅝	16	1.6	13	33.0	34	86.4
¾	19	1.9	14	35.6	35	88.9
⅞	22	2.2	15	38.1	36	91.4
1	25	2.5	16	40.6	37	94.0
1¼	32	3.2	17	43.2	38	96.5
1½	38	3.8	18	45.7	39	99.1
1¾	44	4.4	19	48.3	40	101.6
2	51	5.1	20	50.8	41	104.1
2½	64	6.4	21	53.3	42	106.7
3	76	7.6	22	55.9	43	109.2
3½	89	8.9	23	58.4	44	111.8
4	102	10.2	24	61.0	45	114.3
4½	114	11.4	25	63.5	46	116.8
5	127	12.7	26	66.0	47	119.4
6	152	15.2	27	68.6	48	121.9
7	178	17.8	28	71.1	49	124.5
8	203	20.3	29	73.7	50	127.0

bibliography

GENERAL

A–Z of Embroidery Stitches. Country Bumpkin Publications. Kent Town, South Australia, 1997. 144 pp.

Arthur, Liz. *Embroidery 1600-1700 at the Burrell Collection.* John Murray Publishers, Ltd., London, 1995. 127 pp.

Bath, Virginia Churchill. *Needlework in America.* Viking Press, NY, 1979. 336 pp.

———. *Embroidery Masterworks, Classic Patterns and Techniques for Contemporary Application.* From the Textile Collection of the Art Instiute of Chicago. Henry Regnery Company, Chicago, IL, 1972. 225 pp.

Beck, Thomasina. *Gardening with Silk and Gold, a History of Gardens in Embroidery.* David & Charles, Devon, Great Britain, 1997. 160 pp.

———. *The Embroiderer's Story.* David & Charles, Devon, Great Britain, 1995. 160 pp.

———. *The Embroiderer's Flowers.* David & Charles, Devon, Great Britain, 1992. 160 pp.

———. *The Embroiderer's Garden.* David & Charles, Devon, Great Britain, 1988. 192 pp.

Bolton, Ethel Stanwood and Eva Johnston Coe. *American Samplers.* Dover Publications, Inc., NY, 1973. 416 pp.

Brittain, Judy. *The Bantam Step-by-Step Book of Needle Craft.* Bantam Books, NY, 1980. 512 pp.

Brown, Pauline. *The Encyclopedia of Embroidery Techniques.* Viking Studio Books, NY, 1994. 176 pp.

———. *Embroidery, a Complete Course in Embroidery Design and Technique.* Villard Books (Random House), NY, 1987. 239 pp.

Caulfield, Sophia Frances Anne and Blanche C. Saward. *The Dictionary of Needlework.* L. Upcott Gill, London, 1882. Facsimile produced by Arno Press, NY, 1972. 528 pp.

Clabburn, Pamela. *The Needleworker's Dictionary.* William Morrow & Co., NY, 1976. 296 pp.

de Dillmont, Thérèse. *Encyclopedia of Needlework.* DMC Library, Mulhouse, France, 1880. 804 pp.

Eaton, Jan. Mary Thomas's *Dictionary of Embroidery Stitches, New Revised Edition.* Trafalger Square Publishing, North Pomfret, VT, 1998. 208 pp.

Feltwell, Dr. John. *The Story of Silk.* St. Martin's Press, NY, 1990. 233 pp.

Hirst, Irene (editor). *The Complete Book of Needlework.* Taplinger Publishing Co., Inc., NY, 1963. 320 pp.

Marein, Shirley. *Stitchery, Needlepoint, Applique, and Patchwork.* The Viking Press, Inc., NY, 1974. 207 pp.

Petersen, Grete and Elsie Svennas. *Handbook of Stitches.* Van Nostrand Reinhold Co., NY, 1966. 79 pp.

Reader's Digest. *Reader's Digest Complete Guide to Needlework.* Reader's Digest Association Inc., Pleasantville, NY, 1979. 504 pp.

Ring, Betty. *American Needlework Treasures.* E.P. Dutton, NY, 1987. 112 pp.

Snook, Barbara. *Spinnern Needlework Stitches.* Crown Publishers, Inc., NY, 1963. 127 pp.

Swan, Susan Burrows. *Plain & Fancy: American Woman and Their Needlework, 1700-1850.* Holt, Rinehart and Winston, NY, 1977. 240 pp.

———. *Winterthur Guide to American Needlework.* Winterthur/Rutledge Books. Crown Publishers, NY, 1976. 140 pp.

Swift, Gay. *The Batsford Encyclopedia of Embroidery Techniques.* B.T. Batsford Ltd., London, 1984. 240 pp.

Synge, Lanto. *The Royal School of Needlework, Book of Needlework and Embroidery.* Collins, London, 1986. 256 pp.

———. *Antique Needlework.* Blandford Press, London, 1982. 202 pp.

Thomas, Mary. *Mary Thomas's Embroidery Book.* Dover Publications, NY, 1983 (originally 1936). 304 pp.

van Wyk, Hetsie. *Embroider Now.* Perskor Publishers, Johannesburg, South Africa, 1977. 286 pp.

Vincent, Margaret. *The Ladies' Work Table, Domestic Needlework in Nineteenth Century America.* Allentown Art Museum. Distributed by University Press of New England, London and Hanover, 1988. 140 pp.

Warner, Pamela. *Embroidery, a History.* B.T. Batsford Ltd., 1990. 208 pp.

bibliography

NEEDLEPOINT

Ambuter, Carolyn. *Carolyn Ambuter's Even More Complete Book of Needlepoint.* Harper & Row, NY, 1987. 192 pp.

Beinecke, Mary Ann. *Basic Needlery Stitches on Mesh Fabrics.* Dover Publications, Inc., NY, 1973. 64 pp.

Blackburn, Rev. Robert E. Jr. *Father B's Book of Stitches.* Father B's Bag, Ltd., Lansing, IL, 1994. 245 pp.

Christensen, Jo Ippolito. *The Needlepoint Book (Revised Edition).* Fireside (Simon & Schuster), NY, 1999. 428 pp.

———. *The Needlepoint Book.* Fireside (Simon & Schuster), NY, 1976. 384 pp.

Driskell, Linda. *Favorite Stitches for Linen and Canvas.* Needlecrafts Unlimited Co., Gadsden, AL, 1997. 67 pp.

———. *Favorite Stitches for Linen and Canvas. Volume II.* Needlecrafts Unlimited Co., Gadsden, AL, 1997. 75 pp.

———. *Favorite Stitches for Linen and Canvas. Volume 3.* Needlecrafts Unlimited Co., Gadsden, AL, 1997. 73 pp.

Hanley, Hope. *101 Needlepoint Stitches and How to Use Them.* Dover Publications, Inc., NY, 1986. 111 pp.

Harlow, Eve. *The New Anchor Book of Canvaswork Stitches and Patterns.* David & Charles, Devon, Great Britain, 1989. 128 pp.

Hart, Brenda. *Favorite Stitches.* Self-published, Tucson, AZ, 1994. 109 pp.

Hickman, Julia. *Decorative Needlepoint, Tapestry and Beadwork.* Reader's Digest Association, Inc., Pleasantville, NY, 1993. 128 pp.

Higginson, Susan. *The Madeira Book of Needlepoint Stitches.* A & C Black Ltd., London, 1989. 112 pp.

Howren, Suzanne and Beth Robertson. *More Stitches For Effect.* Shear Creations L.L.C., Alexandria, VA, 1997. 79 pp.

———. *Stitches For Effect.* Shear Creations L.L.C., Alexandria, VA, 1996. 65 pp.

Ireys, Katherine. *The Encyclopedia of Canvas Embroidery Stitch Patterns.* Thomas Y. Crowell Company, NY, 1972. 160 pp.

Lantz, Sherlee. *A Pageant of Pattern for Needlepoint Canvas.* Atheneum, NY, 1973. 510 pp.

Murphy, SuZy. *SuZy's Small Stitches.* Self-published, Cheyenne, WY, 1998. 162 pp.

Parry, Linda (editor). *A Practical Guide to Canvas Work, from the Victoria and Albert Museum.* The Main Street Press, Pittstown, NJ, 1987. 72 pp.

Pearson, Anna. *The Complete Needlepoint Course.* Chilton Book Company, Radnor, PA, 1991. 176 pp.

Pester, Ann E. *Dictionary of Needlepoint Stitches.* Golden Press, NY, 1978. 192 pp.

Proctor, Molly. *Victorian Canvas Work, Berlin Wool Work.* B.T. Batsford Ltd., London, 1972. 160 pp.

Rhodes, Mary. *The Batsford Book of Canvas Work.* B.T. Batsford Ltd., London, 1983. 240 pp.

Rome, Carol Cheney and Georgia French Devlin. *A New Look at Needlepoint.* Crown Publishers, Inc., NY, 1972. 229 pp.

Zimmerman, Jane. *An Encyclopedia of 375 Needlepoint Stitch Variations.* Self-published, Richmond, CA, 1973. 121 pp.

EMBROIDERY

Carter, Virginia. *A Handbook of Metal Threads for the Embroiderer.* Self-published, St. Louis, MO, 1975. 48 pp.

Clarke, Gary. *Candlewicking & Beyond.* Aussie Publishers, Victoria, Australia, 1997. 53 pp.

Coss, Melinda. *Reader's Digest Complete Book of Embroidery.* Reader's Digest Association, Inc., Pleasantville, NY, 1996. 192 pp.

Davis, Mildred J. *The Art of Crewel Embroidery.* Crown Publishers, Inc., NY, 1962. 224 pp.

Dawson, Barbara. *The Technique of Metal Thread Embroidery.* B.T. Batsford Ltd., London, 1982. 97 pp.

Eaton, Jan. *The Complete Stitch Encyclopedia.* Barron's Educational Series, Inc., Woodbury, NY, 1986. 131 pp.

Enthoven, Jacqueline. *The Stitches of Creative Embroidery.* Van Nostrand Reinhold, NY, 1964. 212 pp.

Fitzwilliam, Ada Wentworth and A. F. Morris Hands. *Jacobean Embroidery.* B.T. Batsford Ltd., London, 1990 (originally 1928). 57 pp.

Gostelow, Mary. *Mary Gostelow's Embroidery Book.* E.P. Dutton, NY, 1978. 247 pp.

Harlow, Eve (compiled by). *The Anchor Book of Crewelwork Embroidery Stitches.* David & Charles, Devon, Great Britain, 1989. 128 pp.

Lampe, Diana. *Embroider A Garden.* Sally Milner Publishing Pty. Ltd., Rozelle, NSW, Australia, 1993. 106 pp.

————, and Jane Fisk. *Embroidered Garden Flowers.* Sally Milner Publishing Pty. Ltd., Rozelle, NSW, Australia, 1991. 106 pp.

Marsh, Christina. *Anchor Complete Embroidery Course.* David & Charles, Devon, Great Britain, 1998. 128 pp.

Montano, Judith Baker. *Elegant Stitches, an Illustrated Guide & Source Book of Inspiration.* C & T Publishing, Lafayette, CA, 1995. 177 pp.

Pyman, Kit. *Gold & Silver Embroidery.* Search Press, Tunbridge Wells, Great Britain, 1987. 112 pp.

Rodgers, Sandy. *Silk and Metal Threads on Canvas.* The Yarn Cellar Publishing Co., Medina, OH, 1989. 54 pp.

Saunders, Sally. *Royal School of Needlework Embroidery Techniques.* With designs by Anne Butcher & Debra Barrett. B.T. Batsford Ltd., London, 1998. 160 pp.

Snook, Barbara. *The Creative Art of Embroidery.* Hamlyn Publishing Group Ltd., London, 1972. 176 pp.

Wark, Edna. *Metal Thread Embroidery.* Kangaroo Press Pty. Ltd., Kenthurst, Australia, 1989. 80 pp.

Williams, Elsa A. *Heritage Embroidery.* Van Nostrand Reinhold, NY, 1967. 112 pp.

Wilson, Erica. *Erica Wilson's Embroidery Book.* Charles Scribner's Sons, NY, 1973. 374 pp.

————. *The Craft of Crewel Embroidery.* Charles Scribner's Sons, NY, 1971. 96 pp.

COUNTED THREAD

Altherr, Ilse. *Pulled Thread Sampler.* Self-published, Lancaster, NH, 1992. 26 pp.

————. *Mastering the Art of Pulled Thread Embroidery.* Self-published, Lancaster, NH, 1989. 133 pp.

————. *Blackwork & Holbein Embroidery.* Book 2. Self-published, Lancaster, NH, 1981. 105 pp.

————. *Reversible Blackwork.* Book 1. Self-published, Lancaster, NH, 1978. 70 pp.

Ambuter, Carolyn. *The Open Canvas, an Instructional Encyclopedia of Openwork Techniques.* Workman Publishing, NY, 1982. 271 pp.

Barnett, Lesley. *Blackwork.* Search Press, Tunbridge Wells, Great Britain, 1996. 48 pp.

Bennett, Eileen. *A Note Book of Pulled Thread Stitches.* Self-published, Jenison, MI, 1999. 69 pp.

————. *A Note Book of Sampler Stitches, Book Two.* Self-published, Jenison, MI, 1993. 26 pp.

————. *A Note Book of Sampler Stitches.* Self-published, Grandville, MI, 1990. 32 pp.

Buell, Karen R. *Blackwork from Threads and Things.* Self-published, Hoyt Lake, MN, 1985. 26 pp.

Campbell, Etta. *Linen Embroidery.* B.T. Batsford Ltd., London, 1957. 72 pp.

Cave, Oenone. *Cut-work Embroidery and How to Do It.* Dover Publications, Inc., NY, 1982. 90 pp.

Christie, Mrs. Archibald. *Samplers & Stitches, a Handbook of the Embroiderer's Art.* B.T. Batsford Ltd., London, 1920. 150 pp.

Colby, Averil. *Samplers.* B.T. Batsford Ltd., London, 1964. 266 pp.

Don, Sarah. *Traditional Samplers.* Viking Penguin, Inc., NY, 1986. 144 pp.

Driskell, Linda. *Favorite Stitches for Linen and Canvas.* Needlecrafts Unlimited Co., Gadsden, AL, 1997. 67 pp.

————. *Favorite Stitches for Linen and Canvas.* Volume II. Needlecrafts Unlimited Co., Gadsden, AL, 1997. 75 pp.

————. *Favorite Stitches for Linen and Canvas.* Volume 3. Needlecrafts Unlimited Co., Gadsden, AL, 1997. 73 pp.

————. *Heirloom Whitework Sampler.* Needlecrafts Unlimited Co. Gadsden, AL, 1991. 27 pp.

————. *Miniature Drawn Thread Sampler.* Needlecrafts Unlimited Co. Gadsden, AL, 1991. 17 pp.

————. *Heirloom Drawn Thread Sampler, an Introduction to Hemstitching.* Needlecrafts Unlimited Co. Gadsden, AL, 1990. 34 pp.

————. *Romantic Reversible Blackwork, a Collection of Patterns.* Needlecrafts Unlimited Co. Gadston, AL, 1990. 16 pp.

Drysdale, Rosemary. *The Art of Blackwork Embroidery.* Charles Scribner's Sons, NY, 1975. 160 pp.

Eaton, Jan. *The Complete Stitch Encyclopedia.* Barron's Educational Series, Inc., Woodbury, NY, 1986. 131 pp.

Fangel, Esther; Ida Winckler, and Agnete Wuldem Madsen. *Danish Pulled Thread Embroidery (Sammentrækssynung).* Dover Publications, Inc., NY, 1977. 100 pp.

Fawdry, Marguerite and Deborah Brown. *The Book of Samplers.* St. Martin's Press, NY, 1980. 157 pp.

Finseth, Claudia Riiff. *Scandinavian Folk Patterns for Counted Thread Embroidery.* Pacific Search Press, Seattle, WA, 1987. 184 pp.

Fry, Mary. *Pulled Thread Workbook.* Self-published, Summit, NJ, 1978. 200 pp.

Geddes, Elizabeth and Moyra McNeill. *Blackwork Embroidery.* Dover Publications, Inc., NY, 1976. 115 pp.

Geldens, Janny. *The Complete Book of Hardanger.* Little Hills Press Pty. Ltd., Crow's Nest, NSW, Australia, 1994. 107 pp.

Goldberg, Rhoda Ochser. *The New Dictionary of Counted-Thread Embroidery Stitches.* Random House, NY, 1998. 194 pp.

Gostelow, Mary. *Blackwork*. Van Nostrand Reinhold, NY, 1976. 160 pp.

Harlow, Eve (compiled by). *The Anchor Book of Counted Thread Embroidery Stitches*. David & Charles, Devon, Great Britain, 1987. 128 pp.

Huish, Marcus B. *Samplers and Tapestry Embroideries*. Longmans, Green & Co., NY, 1913. (Reprinted by B.T. Batsford Ltd., London, 1990.) 176 pp.

King, Donald. *Samplers, Victoria and Albert Museum*. Her Majesty's Stationery Office, London, 1960. 80 pp.

Lofthouse, Kate S. *A Complete Guide to Drawn Fabric*. Sir Issac Pitman & Sons, Ltd., London, 1933. 47 pp.

Love, Janice. *Fundamentals Made Fancy*. Love 'N Stitches. Athens, GA, 1993. 60 pp.

———. *Hardanger. Basics and Beyond*. Love 'N Stitches. Athens, GA. 1990. 52 pp.

McNeill, Moyra. *Drawn Thread Embroidery*. Henry Holt and Co., NY, 1989. 144 pp.

———. *Pulled Thread Embroidery*. Taplinger Publishing Co., NY, 1971. 207 pp.

Meier, Susan L. and Rosalyn K. Watnemo. *Advanced Charted Hardanger Embroidery with Complete Instructions*. Nordic Needle, Fargo, ND, 1982. 20 pp.

———. *Beginner's Charted Hardanger Embroidery with Complete Instructions*. Nordic Needle, Fargo, ND, 1980. 24 pp.

Miller, Suzann. *Resource Book of Needlework Stitches*. Material handouts from needlework classes. Volumes I–V. Self published, Waukee, IA, 1994-99.

Müller, Barbara. *Florentine Embroidery*. Lacis Publications, Berkeley, CA, 1993. 95 pp.

O'Steen, Darlene. *The Proper Stitch*. Symbol of Excellence Publishers, Inc., Birmingham, AL, 1994. 144 pp.

Pascoe, Margaret. *Blackwork Embroidery, Design & Technique*. B.T. Batsford Ltd., London, 1986. 144 pp.

Petersen, Grete. *Stitches and Decorative Seams*. Van Nostrand Reinhold Company, NY, 1983. 95 pp.

Reader's Digest. *Jo Verso's Complete Cross Stitch Course*. Reader's Digest Association, Inc., Pleasantville, NY, 1996. 120 pp.

Scoular, Marion. *Why Call It Blackwork?* Self-published, Duluth, GA, 1993. 37 pp.

Sebba, Anne. *Samplers: Five Centuries of a Gentle Craft*. Thames & Hudson, NY, 1979. 160 pp.

Shipp, Mary. *Stitches for Counted Thread Embroidery. Volume I, Flat Stitches*. HGSystems, Inc., Bath, NY, 1995. 303 pp.

———. *Stitches for Counted Thread Embroidery. Volume II, Dimensional Stitches*. HGSystems, Inc., Bath, NY, 1995. 331 pp.

Steinacker, Henriette. *Weißstickerei*. Otto Maier Ravenburger, Germany, 1989. 64 pp.

van Zandt, Eleanor. *Complete Book of Cross Stitch and Counted Thread Techniques*. Reader's Digest Association, Inc., Pleasantville, NY, 1994. 160 pp.

Verso, Jo. *Jo Verso's World of Cross Stitch*. David & Charles, London, 1992. 128 pp.

———, Jane Greenhoff, and Brenda Keyes. *The Embroiderers' Guild Making Samplers*. David & Charles, London, 1993. 144 pp.

Whiting, Sue (compiled by). *The Anchor Book of Hardanger Embroidery*. David & Charles, Devon, Great Britain, 1997. 128 pp.

Zimmerman, Jane. *The Art of English Blackwork*. Self-published, Richmond, CA, 1996. 187 pp.

———. *Pulled Thread Embroidery Stitches*. Self-published, Richmond, CA, 1988. 74 pp.

———. *Blackwork Patterns (Revised Edition)*. Self-published, Richmond, CA, 1985. 98 pp.

Access Commodities (Distributor: Appleton and Broider Wul yarns, Au Ver a Soie silk, hoops, threads, fabrics)
PO Box 1995
Rowlett, TX 75030
1-972-412-5253

Anne Brinkley Designs (porcelain boxes)
12 Chestnut Hill Lane
Lincroft, NJ 07738
1-800-633-0148

Anne Powell Ltd. (scissors, needlework accessories)
PO Box 3060
Stuart, FL 34995
1-561-287-3007
Web: www.annepowellltd.com
email: apowell@annepowellltd.com

Berroco, Inc. (Handeze massage gloves)
PO Box 367
Uxbridge, MA 01569
1-800-343-4948
Web: www.berroco.com
email: berroco@ix.netcom.com

Big Eye Lamp (lights and magnifiers)
133 Yellowbrook Road
Farmington, NJ 07727
1-732-938-2490
Web: www.big-eye.com
email: info@big-eye.com

Brown Paper Packages (threads)
18 Grand Lake
Ft. Thomas, KY 41075
1-606-441-4421

Bugz Eye International Corp. (magnifiers)
PO Box 19990
Denver, CO 80219
1-888-284-7393

Caron Collection Ltd., The (threads)
55 Old South Avenue
Stratford, CT 06615
1-800-862-2766
Web: www.caron-net.com
email: mail@caron-net.com

Carson Optical (magnifiers)
200-5 East 2nd Street
Huntington Station, NY 11746
1-800-967-8427
Web: www.carson-optical.com
email: info@carson-optical.com

Cascade House (candlewick yarns, silk thread)
475 North Road
Langwarrin 3910
Victoria, Australia
613-977-5852

Charles Craft (evenweave fabrics, premades)
PO Box 1049
Laurinburg, NC 28352
1-800-277-1009
Web: www.charlescraft.com
email: surf@nconline.com

Coats & Clark (Anchor threads, threaders)
30 Patewood Drive, Suite 351
Greenville, SC 29615
1-864-234-0331
Web: www.coatsandclark.com

Colonial Needle Co. (needles)
1150 Yonkers Avenue
Yonkers, NY 10704
1-914-237-6434
Web: www.colonialneedle.com
email: jcollingham@worldnet.att.net

CompuStitch (stitch catcher)
PO Box 157
Syracuse, NY 13206
1-800-445-3661

Creative Beginnings (charms)
PO Box 1330
Morro Bay, CA 93442
1-800-367-1739
Web: www.creativebeginnings.com

Daniel Enterprises: Crafter's Pride (vinyl Aida, premades)
306 McKay Street
Laurinburg, NC 28352
1-910-277-7441
Web: www.crafterspride.com
email: denterprise@carolina.net

Darice (plastic canvas)
21160 Drake Road
Strongsville, OH 44136
1-440-238-9150
Web: www.darice.com

Dazor Manufacturing Corp. (lights and magnifiers)
4483 Duncan Avenue
St. Louis, MO 63110
1-800-345-9103
Web: www.dazor.com
email: info@dazor.com

DMC Corporation (threads, yarns, needles)
Port Kearny Building, #10A
South Hackensack Avenue
South Port Kearny, NJ 07032
1-973-589-0606
Web: www.dmc-usa.com

Dovo (German scissors)
4705 S. Honeymoon Bay Road
Freeland, WA 98249
1-360-331-1354

DJV Designs (wooden needlecases, floss storage systems)
27488 Enterprise Circle, W#2
Temecula, CA 92590
1-909-693-5299
Web: www.djvdesigns.com
email: info@djvdesigns.com

Edroy Products Company, Inc. (magnifiers)
245 N Midland Ave.
PO Box 998
Nyack, NY 10960
1-914-358-6600
email: nyack1@aol.com

Felicity's Garden (threads)
Distributed by High Country West
114 N. San Francisco Street, Suite 201
Flagstaff, AZ 86001
1-520-779-2900

Fleur De Paris Corporation (Distributor: canvas, yarns, threads, scissors)
5835 Washington Blvd.
Culver City, CA 90230
1-800-221-6453

Gay Bowles Sales, Inc. (beads, buttons)
PO Box 1060
Janesville, WI 53547
1-608-754-9466
Web: www.millhill.com
email: millhill@inwave.com

Gentle Art, The (Sampler Threads hand-dyed cotton floss)
4081 Bremo Recess
New Albany, OH 43054
1-614-855-8346
email: gentleart@aol.com

Gingher, Inc. (scissors, tweezers)
322-D Edwardia Drive
Greensboro, NC 27409
1-336-292-6237
Web: www.gingher.com

Gloriana (silk threads)
4011 - 39th Avenue
Oakland, CA 94611
1-510-531-8749

HobbyWare, Inc. (Pattern Maker software)
PO Box 501996
Indianapolis, IN 46250
1-800-768-6257
Web: www.hobbyware.com

JCA, Inc. (Paternayan yarn)
35 Scales Lane
Townsend, MA 01469
1-800-225-6340

JHB International Inc. (buttons)
1955 S Quince Street
Denver, CO 80231
1-303-751-8100
Web: www.buttons.com
email:sales@buttons.com

J. L. Walsh Silk (threads)
4338 Endgewood
Oakland, CA 94602
1-510-530-7343

Just My Imagination (buttons)
924 Wheat Ridge Drive
Troy, IL 62294
1-618-667-8531

K's Creations (floor stands, table frames, scroll frames)
PO Box 161446
Austin, TX 78746
1-800-727-3769
Web: www.kscreation.com
email: kscreation@aol.com

Kreinik Manufacturing Company, Inc. (metallic, metal, and Au Ver a Soie silk threads, paillettes, needles)
3106 Timanus Lane, Suite 101
Baltimore, MD 21244
1-800-354-4255
Web: www.kreinik.com
email: kreinik@kreinik.com

L.C. Kramer Company (Distributor: fabrics, threads, lights, scissors, working frames)
2525 Burnside Street
Portland, OR 97214
1-503-236-1207
email: kramer@aracnet.com

Lacis (Ulster linen, books)
3163 Adeline Street
Berkeley, CA 94703
1-510-843-7178
Web: www.lacis.com
email: staff@lacis.com

LoRan/Dal-Craft, Inc. (thread storage and needlework accessories)
PO Box 61
Tucker, GA 30085
1-800-521-7311
Web: www.lorancrafts.com
email: info@lorancrafts.com

Madeira Threads (threads)
9631 NE Colfax
Portland, OR 97220
1-503-252-1452
Web: www.madeirathreads.com
email: scs@madeirathreads.com

MagEyes (magnifiers)
222 Sidney Baker South, Ste. 204
Kerrville, TX 78028
1-800-210-6662

Mardina Enterprises (threaders and needles)
PO Box 2247
LaGrange, GA 30241
1-888-627-3462
Web: www.mardina.com

Marie Products (stretcher bars, lap frames, floor stands, hoops, blocking boards)
PO Box 78000
Tucson, AZ 85703
1-800-421-4567

M.C.G. Textiles (fabrics, premades)
13845 Magnolia Ave.
Chino, CA 91710
1-909-591-6351

Needle in a Haystack (full-service retail shop)
1340 Park Street
Alameda, CA 94501
1-510-522-0404
Web: needlestack.com
email: haystack@needlestack.com

Needle Necessities Inc. (threads)
7211 Garden Grove Blvd., #BC
Garden Grove, CA 92841
1-800-542-7300
Web: www.needlenecessities.com
email: needlenec@msn.com

Needlepoint Inc. (silk threads)
275 Post Street
San Francisco, CA 94108
1-800-345-1622

Nordic Needle (retail mail-order catalog for needlework supplies)
1314 Gateway Drive
Fargo, ND 58103
1-800-433-4321
Web: www.nordicneedle.com
email: needle@corpcomm.net

Norsk Engros USA, Inc. (linen thread)
217 W. Water Street
Decorah, IA 52101
1-319-382-9431

Omnigrid Inc. (rulers)
1560 Port Drive
Burlington, WA 98233
1-360-757-4743
email: 40mni@sos.net

Ott-Lite Technology (lights and magnifiers)
1214 West Cass Street
Tampa, FL 33606
1-800-842-8848
Web: www.ott-lite.com
email: debbij@ott-lite.com

Porcelain Rose (buttons)
PO Box 7545
Long Beach, CA 90807
1-562-424-9728
email: gdolce19@ldt.net

Q-Snap Corporation (working frames)
PO Box 68
Parsons, TN 38363

R and R Reproductions (hand-dyed evenweave fabrics)
5386 Kemps River Drive, Suite 108-6
Virginia Beach, VA 23464
1-800-921-3299
email: wedye4you@aol.com

Rainbow Gallery (threads)
7412 Fulton Avenue, Suite 5
North Hollywood, CA 91605
1-800-522-6827
Web: www.rainbowgallery.com
email: rainbowthr@aol.com

Ramco Arts Inc. (magnifiers)
2616 Gravel Drive
Ft. Worth, TX 76118
1-817-284-1996

SeldenCraft, Inc. (lights and magnifiers)
660 Main Street South - 8A
Woodbury, CT 06798

Simply Needlepoint (retail shop)
433 Front Street
Danville, CA 94526
1-925-820-1442

Sudberry House, Inc. (wooden needlework boxes, trays, footstools, thread palettes)
Box 895, 12 Colton Road
Old Lyme, CT 06371
1-800-243-2607
Web: www.sudberry.com
email: sales@sudberry.com

Sulky of America (threads, transfer pens and pencils)
3113 Broadpoint Drive
Harbor Heights, FL 33983
1-941-629-3199
email: sulkyofamerica@mindspring.com

Susan Clarke Designs (buttons)
653 Jackson Street
Red Bluff, CA 96080
1-916-527-1383
email: randy@tco.net

Sweet Child of Mine (hand-dyed silk ribbons, threads)
137 E Fremont Avenue
Sunnyvale, CA 94087
1-408-720-8426

The Flower Thread Company (Ginnie Thompson linen thread)
PO Box 3024
Sumter, SC 29151
1-803-499-2105
Web: www.flowerthread.com

Thread Gatherer, The (hand-dyed silk ribbons and threads)
2108 Norcrest Drive
Boise, ID 83705
1-208-387-2641

Unicorn Books (books)
1338 Ross Street
Petaluma, CA 94954
1-707-762-3362

Weeks Dye Works (hand-dyed cotton floss)
404 Raleigh Street
Fuquay Varina, NC 27526
1-919-557-7186
email: weesdyewk@mindspring.com

Whims, Inc. (watercolor quilt kits)
36453 Bohlken Drive
Lebanon, OR 97355
1-541-451-6776
email: whims@continet.com

Wichelt Imports, Inc. (evenweave fabrics, bellpull hardware)
162 N. Hwy 35
Stoddard, WI 54658
1-800-356-9516
Web: www.wichelt.com
email: wichelt@centuryinter.net

YLI Corporation (silk ribbon, threads)
161 W. Main Street
Rock Hill, SC 29730
1-800-296-8139
email: ylicorp@rhtc.net

Yarn Tree (perforated paper)
PO Box 724
Ames, IA 50010
1-800-247-3952
Web: www.yarntree.com
email: info@yarntree.com

Zweigart (evenweave fabrics and canvas, premades)
262 Old New Brunswick Road
Piscataway, NJ 08354
1-732-562-8888
Web: www.zweigart.com
email: info@zweigart.com

index

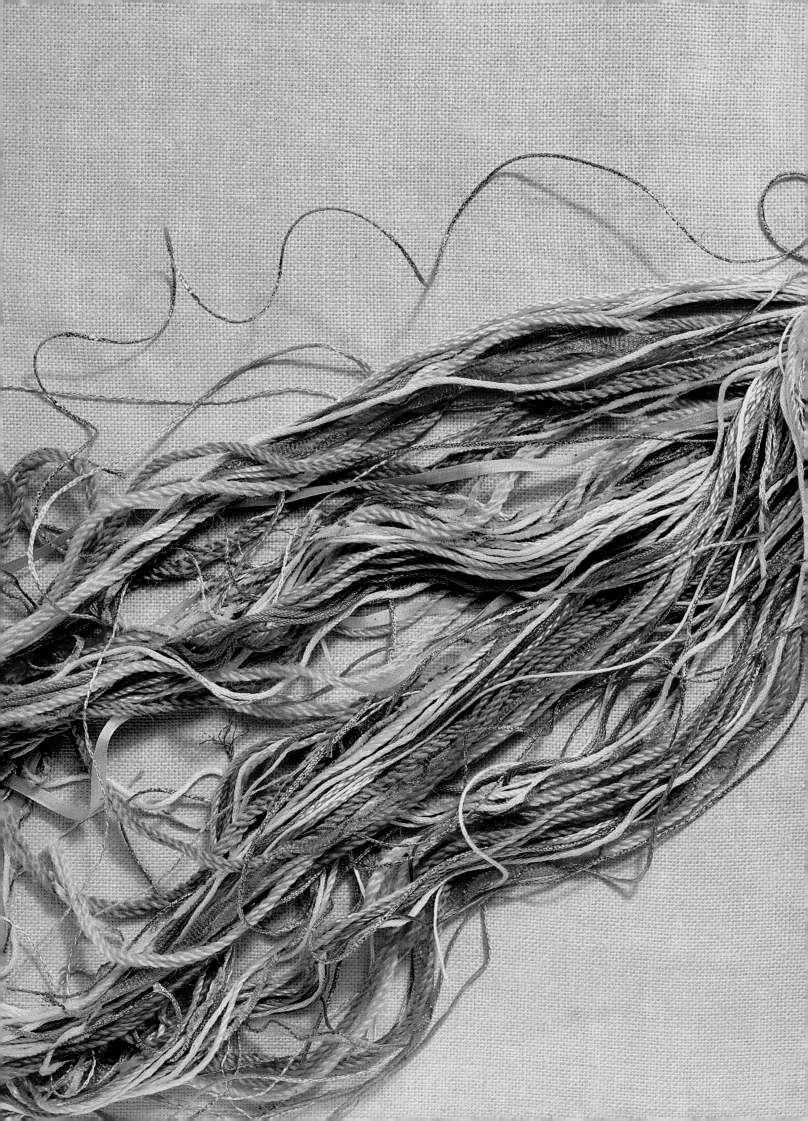

stitch
index

Diabetes Meal Planning & Nutrition

FOR DUMMIES®

A Wiley Brand

by Toby Smithson, RDN, CDE, with Alan L. Rubin, MD

FOR DUMMIES®

A Wiley Brand

Diabetes Meal Planning & Nutrition For Dummies®

Published by **John Wiley & Sons, Inc.**, 111 River Street, Hoboken , NJ 07030-5774 www.wiley.com

Copyright © 2014 by John Wiley & Sons, Inc., Hoboken, New Jersey

Published simultaneously in Canada

For general information on our other products and services, please contact our Customer Care Department within the U.S. at 877-762-2974, outside the U.S. at 317-572-3993, or fax 317-572-4002.

For technical support, please visit www.wiley.com/techsupport.

Wiley publishes in a variety of print and electronic formats and by print-on-demand. Some material included with standard print versions of this book may not be included in e-books or in print-on-demand. If this book refers to media such as a CD or DVD that is not included in the version you purchased, you may download this material at http://booksupport.wiley.com. For more information about Wiley products, visit www.wiley.com.

Library of Congress Control Number: 2013947507

ISBN 978-1-118-67753-7 (pbk); ISBN 978-1-118-67733-9 (ebk); ISBN 978-1-118-67748-3 (ebk); ISBN 978-1-118-67751-3 (ebk)

Manufactured in the United States of America

SKY10041274_011323

Contents at a Glance

Table of Contents

Foreword

Proper nutrition is one of the foundations of good diabetes care, along with exercise and medication, if necessary. In type 1 diabetes, proper nutrition serves to balance the effect of the insulin that must be administered as well as exercise, so that the blood glucose remains as close to normal as possible. In type 2 diabetes, proper nutrition helps to reduce weight if overweight, thus preventing complications like heart, eye, kidney, and nerve disease and providing energy for the tasks of daily living.

For too long, people with diabetes have thought that proper nutrition means loss of freedom to eat the things they enjoy. As this book shows, such an idea is a myth. You can enjoy almost all the foods you grew up with, but if they raise the blood sugar or the cholesterol or the blood pressure, you must eat them in moderation. It is very important that proper nutrition be based on your needs. If it is not, you will be reluctant to follow the recommendations of your doctor or dietitian. Proper nutrition can never be found on a pad of paper called a "diabetic diet."

No one is more qualified to teach you about proper nutrition than Toby Smithson. Toby has lived with type 1 diabetes since she was a young girl. She is a professional dietitian who has been recognized by her peers for her excellent work and is a certified diabetes educator. She is a spokesperson for the American Dietetic Association, has received the Outstanding Dietitian in Illinois Award in 2009 from the American Dietetic Association, and she recently served as president of the Illinois Dietetic Association. Toby's website, www.Diabeteseveryday.com, is a treasure chest of information about nutrition as well as many other aspects of diabetes.

This book, *Diabetes Meal Planning & Nutrition For Dummies*, distills decades of knowledge in an easily readable form. It starts by providing a basic understanding of diabetes. It proceeds by teaching you about nutrients like carbohydrates, proteins, and fats and the best way to prepare them. It continues with meal planning and ends with a menu of seven delicious days of food.

Studies have shown that proper nutrition can have a significant effect toward lowering the hemoglobin A1c, a measure of diabetic control that correlates with diabetic complications. You are taking a major step in that direction by reading this book and applying its concepts to your diabetes.

Alan L. Rubin, M. D.

Introduction

The most recent semi-official estimate of the number of people with diabetes in the United States was released in January 2011, and the tally was 25.8 million — 8.3 percent of the entire population. But, with more than 150,000 new cases each month, that number is outdated even before it's released. You can add 1.9 million for 2011, 1.9 million for 2012 (and so on) if you enjoy playing with big numbers, but it's more likely the number you're most concerned about is 1 — yourself, or a loved one. Coincidentally, this book has exactly the same concern.

You can see by the title that the main subject is food — the words *meal* and *nutrition* are the giveaway. But, food and diabetes health can't be separated, and with the exception of essential insulin for people with type 1 diabetes, the food you eat every day is as important — maybe even more important — than your diabetes medicine. Food is the simplest, least expensive, most available, and most immediate treatment option for diabetes health. Not special food — plain old food you walk past every time you're in a grocery. Yet, most people with diabetes struggle to adopt healthier eating habits, many to the point of giving up. There is a simple solution that can end the struggle.

If the word *planning* in the title seems like the least important (even least interesting) subject in the pages ahead, you are in for an amazing surprise — maybe even an epiphany. See, the struggle with healthy eating doesn't come from your stomach, your pancreas, or an uncontrollable hand that sneaks unhealthy food into your mouth when you're not looking. Your struggle with healthy eating is a struggle between your incredible brain, and your primitive survival chemistry, and when it comes to food, chemistry often wins. You're about to learn how planning can tip the balance, and make healthier eating your newest accomplishment.

About This Book

Diabetes Meal Planning & Nutrition for Dummies zeros in on the important relationship between diabetes and food, and helps you make choices that benefit your long-term health and satisfy your eating preferences. The book's focus is on which foods you can, and should, eat to improve your health with diabetes, and not on what you shouldn't eat. There is no doubt, by the way, that how you choose to eat when you have diabetes can have a remarkable effect on your health — this book helps ensure that effect is a positive one.

The book acknowledges and explains some of the barriers you may have experienced to adopting healthier eating habits, and how your best intentions can be sabotaged. And, you see how the power of making eating decisions in advance — planning — can get you beyond those barriers and keep you there. More than 80 percent of people with type 2 diabetes are overweight or obese, and many have made attempts to change eating habits without success. This discussion on planning may be just the advice you need.

The target audience is people already diagnosed with type 1 or type 2 diabetes, but the concepts and practical advice for managing diabetes with diet apply to gestational diabetes, and to those with prediabetes. This book doesn't substitute for medical nutrition therapy from a registered dietitian, but should help you put your personalized diabetes meal plan into action.

Diabetes Meal Planning & Nutrition for Dummies does discuss diabetes as a disease, but if you're new to diabetes you may want to grab one of Dr. Rubin's other books, *Diabetes for Dummies* or *Type 1 Diabetes for Dummies*, for a more detailed discussion. Food is an important part of managing diabetes over the long term, but there's a lot more you need to know.

Diabetes often occurs with medical conditions, like celiac disease or lactose intolerance, that limit food choices. And, diabetes can promote health conditions, like kidney failure, that trigger very specific dietary requirements which are significantly different than general recommendations for a diabetes meal plan. Your doctor and a registered dietitian can advise you in these cases, but advice in this book may not always apply.

You should know that you don't have to read this book from front to back. All *Dummies* books are written so that each chapter will make sense on its own. It's not necessary that you remember anything either — a detailed table of contents helps you find what you need whenever you need it. This book is meant to be a reference; there will be no final exam to test your memorization skills.

Here are a few other tidbits that may answer your questions before you have to ask:

- ✔ Blood glucose is often casually called *blood sugar*. Blood glucose is the correct terminology and is used exclusively in the book. In common usage, the terms mean the same.

- ✔ Blood glucose is measured in milligrams per deciliter (mg/dl) in the United States, but many countries use the International System of Units measure of millimoles per liter (mmol/l). The same is true for cholesterol and triglycerides. Where this book only gives U.S. units, refer to Appendix C for conversion factors.

- ✔ Nutritional information is given in metric measures — grams, milligrams, and micrograms. Appendix C provides conversion factors to U.S. measures, but frankly there's no need to convert these. The number of carbohydrate grams in a particular food is unrelated to the total weight of the food, so converting to U.S. measures doesn't really clarify anything.

✔ The recipes in Chapter 18 are offered with common U.S. measures and Fahrenheit cooking temperatures. The exchange list in Appendix A also gives food portions in U.S. measures. Appendix C provides conversions for U.S. food measures and cooking temperatures to metric and imperial units. Note that U.S. measures of dry ingredients don't necessarily correspond well with metric measures of dry ingredients by weight.

✔ Healthy eating is no less important for people with type 1 diabetes, but insulin does provide a more direct way to control blood glucose. Some discussion about managing food amount and timing may be less relevant to people with type 1 diabetes when rapid acting insulin is used.

✔ The term *diabetic* is not used to refer to a person with diabetes. Diabetes is not who you are; it's a condition you have.

✔ This book does not spend much time addressing the particulars of insulin dosing, insulin-carbohydrate ratios, or insulin correction factors. These are very individualized and must be worked out with your doctor or diabetes educator.

Foolish Assumptions

Your authors have some preconceived notions about you, and thought you might be interested in knowing what those are. This book assumes the following:

✔ You have diabetes, or have an interest in someone who has diabetes. It's OK if neither is true, by the way.

✔ You realize that effectively managing diabetes for better health includes managing what and how you eat. Maybe you've been advised about the importance of diet, or maybe you learned from previous experience with diabetes.

✔ You are not expecting a miracle answer that requires no further thinking or effort from you.

✔ Even though you are not expecting a miracle, you appreciate advice that makes healthy eating for diabetes easier.

Icons Used in This Book

Throughout *For Dummies* books you find icons that call your attention to something especially important, or something technical. This book includes the following icons:

A tip often suggests you try something or check something out. A tip usually leads to something surprising about food or nutrition.

A warning is exactly what it sounds like. It's often a caution to avoid jumping to conclusions, or to make unwarranted assumptions.

The Remember icon might re-emphasize something discussed earlier in the section, or it may be a reminder to follow specific advice when you put what you've learning in practice.

Technical stuff is beyond what's key to the book's message, but something some curious readers might find interesting. You may skip over technical stuff.

In some places Dr. Rubin has added special insight from his expertise and experience.

Beyond the Book

There is much more information available from your authors, and from the *For Dummies* brand, for your learning pleasure. Check out these resources to learn more about diabetes, diabetes self-management nutrition, nutrition, or to find some great recipes:

- ✔ Find the *For Dummies Cheat Sheet* for this book at `www.dummies.com/cheatsheet/diabetesmealplanningandnutrition`. The cheat sheet gives you a quick reference for 15 gram portions of carbohydrate foods you'll eat often, as well as a list of nutrients that are extra special for diabetes, and the foods you can eat to get them.

- ✔ *For Dummies* online articles are available at `http://www.dummies.com/WileyCDA/redirect/extras/diabetesmealplanningandnutrition`, and these short articles offer a little more detail on some very important concepts.

- ✔ You can meet your authors face to face, literally, on their respective websites. You can find Dr. Rubin at `www.drrubin.com` and Toby Smithson at `www.DiabetesEveryDay.com`, both on video so you can get an idea of who's giving you the wonderful advice in the book.

✔ And, although this book includes 22 diabetes-friendly recipes, you can use what you learn about choosing diabetes friendly dishes from other resources. Some excellent places to start would be *Diabetes Cookbook For Dummies*, *Glycemic Index Cookbook For Dummies*, *Mediterranean Diet Cookbook For Dummies*, and *Hypertension Cookbook For Dummies,* all published by John Wiley and Sons.

Where to Go From Here

You can start anywhere with *For Dummies* books, but there's a logic to beginning at the beginning. If that's not in your personality, consider starting on Chapter 10 to see why healthy eating, diabetes or not, is so difficult in this society. Chapter 14 reviews how some popular diet plans will fit with effective diabetes self-management, and if you're not sure what diabetes self-management means, try Chapter 3.

Chapter 11 addresses how you can stay motivated, and offers some simple tricks that usually bring big rewards. If you're heading straight to the buffet or bar, check Chapter 15; the grocery can be found in Chapter 12.

Some final advice is don't get in such a rush. Diabetes will still be there, and changes often come slowly. Take your time, try different approaches to eating healthier, and be patient about seeing real improvements in your lab work. Most importantly, follow the advice that Sir Winston Churchill gave the graduating class of Harrow School in 1941, when all he said in his commencement address was, "Never give up, never give up, never give up."

The nine word Churchill commencement address is an excellent example of an urban legend. His speech was short, but considerably longer than nine words. However, the advice is so incredibly appropriate to anyone living with diabetes, it's possible to imagine that's exactly what Churchill would have said were he addressing the subject.

Part I

Diabetes and Food: An Intimate Connection

getting started with

diabetes meal planning

web extras

Visit www.dummies.com for great Dummies content online.

In this part...

- ✔ Learn that it's important to watch every bite of food you put in your mouth, and how each bite contributes to a healthy glucose level.

- ✔ Become an active partner in your body's metabolism. The better the helper you are, the less damage you experience from the diabetes.

- ✔ Understand what diabetes is, and know the difference between type 1 and type 2.

- ✔ Know how to test your blood glucose levels at home, especially with type 1 diabetes. With so many different ways to test, you no longer have to guess your blood glucose level.

- ✔ Learn about the different types of healthcare professionals that you might want to see . . . from your family physician to an endocrinologist, from a registered dietician to a certified diabetes educator.

- ✔ Read up on the different kinds of medication currently offered for diabetes type 1 and type 2. Some are oral meds; some are injectable meds. These medications can be used in combination, and it's important that you take them according to your doctor's instructions.

Chapter 1

Having Your Diabetes and Eating, Too

In This Chapter

▶ Realizing that food is effective medicine for diabetes

▶ Considering your essential role in preserving your health

▶ Keeping your brain working for you

▶ Impacting your health by how you choose to eat

Hippocrates, sometimes called the father of modern medicine, once said "let food be thy medicine, and medicine be thy food." When it comes to diabetes, Hippocrates was absolutely correct. It would be difficult to think of another serious medical condition that's so intimately and immediately connected to food. Yes, there are drugs for diabetes — eight different classes of diabetes drugs, numerous formulations of insulin, drugs that help other drugs work better, and a few drugs that seem to benefit diabetes by accident — and diabetes drugs are extremely important. Without insulin, people with type 1 diabetes could not live. Putting your confidence in drugs alone is insufficient to keep diabetes from affecting your long-term health, and you don't have to rely on advice that's more than 2,300 years old to believe that.

The definitive 800-page resource book for diabetes-specialized healthcare professionals in the 21st century, *The Art and Science of Diabetes Self-Management Education (American Association of Diabetes Educators)* begins its chapter on diabetes drugs by reminding professionals and patients that, "*any pharmacologic treatment for type 2 diabetes is only a supplement to lifestyle changes.*" Lifestyle is more important than drugs when it comes to type 2 diabetes. How you choose to eat is the most important, and perhaps the most challenging, lifestyle issue that people with diabetes face, and is just as important for people with type 1 diabetes as for those with type 2. With diabetes, food really is medicine.

Chances are you already have a least a vague idea that what you eat is important to diabetes, and this book will give you the whole story on just how the food choices you make can work to preserve your long-term health. But knowing and doing are two different things, and it's doing that really counts.

In this chapter you learn about your key role in your own health care, see how overcoming emotion and impulse can help you actually do what you know is best for your health, and get a five-point plan for adding healthy and active years to your life.

Accepting Your Role in Diabetes Management

Whether you have type 1 diabetes or type 2 diabetes, you share one crucial responsibility from your diagnosis going forward — doing your part. In simple terms, you must now become an active helper in your body's metabolism, and the better helper you become, the less likely you are to experience the damage that diabetes can do to your body.

Type 1 diabetes results when your capacity to produce insulin is lost. Type 2 diabetes is related more to your natural insulin being unable to do its job effectively. If you were a car and insulin was gasoline, type 1 diabetes is having an empty tank, and type 2 diabetes is more like lost efficiency from clogged fuel injectors. Managing type 1 diabetes requires constantly adding gasoline; type 2 diabetes requires that you get your fuel injectors to work better. The real story is a little more complicated.

Losing glucose homeostasis

Your body needs to keep a certain concentration of glucose circulating in your blood — a normal blood glucose level. Glucose is the favorite fuel of your trillions of cells, and some really important cells — your brain cells — can't get their energy from anything else. Glucose in your bloodstream is all about energy — it's delivered right to the doorstep of every cell that needs it.

Because glucose enters your blood after you eat carbohydrate foods, causing your blood glucose levels to rise, your body has a way to return those levels back to normal by storing the excess for later. The stored glucose can be released back into the blood when glucose levels drop between meals, keeping a constant supply available for your brain. This kind of balance in a biological system is called *homeostasis*.

The hormone responsible for escorting glucose into storage is insulin, and insulin is automatically released from special cells on your pancreas when blood glucose levels are going higher after eating. If insulin isn't available or isn't working properly, blood glucose can't be stored, and blood glucose levels remain high. High blood glucose levels not only upset glucose homeostasis, but begin to damage cells and tissue.

Chronic high blood glucose levels is diabetes — literally. It's important that you understand diabetes, and Chapters 2 and 3 include a more in-depth explanation. In the simplest terms, having diabetes means your blood glucose levels go up after eating and don't come down to normal levels in a normal amount of time.

Type 1 diabetes results when insulin production capacity is destroyed, and no insulin is available to facilitate glucose homeostasis. Type 2 diabetes begins when the cells that normally store excess glucose stop responding to insulin. So, even though insulin may be available, blood glucose levels remain high. The long-term damage caused by high blood glucose, in either case, can progress to very serious consequences like heart attack, stroke, vision loss, nerve damage, kidney failure, and more. These secondary conditions are called *complications of diabetes*, and avoiding these outcomes is one reason that lowering blood glucose levels is so important.

High glucose levels not only mean that excess glucose can't get into cells to be stockpiled, but glucose can't get into cells to properly fuel energy needs. That means your microscopic cells, like the muscle cells you need to move, don't have access to their favored fuel, and must turn to plan B or plan C for generating energy. Plan B and plan C are ordinarily temporary plans for times of shortage — generating energy without glucose is inefficient, and even produces toxic waste products. Diabetes upsets your entire energy balance.

Taking your place in glucose metabolism

Treating diabetes is not like treating an infected cut, where the problem goes away after a week or two. In fact, diabetes treatment is called *diabetes management*, hinting at a responsibility that requires continuous oversight. And, that's exactly what diabetes management is — continuous oversight. Managing diabetes is like managing a company, or a sports team, or a lawn, or anything else where the goal is to achieve and sustain a certain level of performance. The manager works to provide the best environment and materials for success, looks at performance indicators, sets priorities, makes adjustments to improve efficiency, tries to avoid disruptions, and always keeps a focus on surviving and prospering over the long term.

Effective management is a key to success in business, sports, lawn care, and diabetes. But, while the management responsibilities for businesses, sports teams, and even lawn care can be delegated to professional experts, the extraordinarily important job of managing your diabetes has suddenly fallen on you — diabetes self-management. Not only that, you've inherited responsibility for the equivalent of a business that's failing, a sports team with all its stars on injured reserve, and a lawn that's been overcome by weeds — and the stake is your long-term health.

Fortunately, if you're willing to take this responsibility seriously, there is a proven plan that can turn you into a successful manager of your body's metabolism. And, as daunting as this might sound, with some dedication and practice you'll be managing your metabolism like a pro, and enjoying the rest of your life's activities even more than before. How's that? Well, like any good manager, success is a little bit of participating, but a whole lot of setting up a system where success is possible.

You can't actually fix your glucose metabolism. You can, however, provide the best environment and materials for success, look at performance indicators, set priorities, make adjustments to improve efficiency, try to avoid disruptions, and always keep a focus on surviving and prospering over the long term. That sort of management strategy lets your natural metabolism work as well as it possibly can, and that's effective diabetes self-management at its best. And, you can do it.

Eating a healthy diet and managing your carbohydrate consumption is essential to your long-term health with diabetes. Taking your medication as directed, exercising regularly, getting adequate rest, reducing stress, and not smoking also have important, sometimes critical, roles in your long-term health, but there's no separating diabetes health from food. Although you may think this challenging part of managing diabetes effectively mostly involves your pancreas, your stomach, or some other food related organ, you might be surprised.

Understanding Your Brain

Right between your ears is your incredible and mysterious brain, and your brain plays essential roles in managing diabetes. But, the different roles your brain plays in diabetes management aren't always in your best interests, and more often than you might imagine messages from your brain make managing diabetes more difficult.

On the surface, literally and anatomically, it's obvious that your brain helps you to understand diabetes, to remember what your healthcare team has advised you to do, to schedule your time, to decide what you're going to eat, and to comprehend what you read in this book. The part of your brain doing your thinking, the outer *cerebral cortex* layer, is an amazing problem solver that has never been duplicated biologically or electronically. Your thinking brain can evaluate hundreds of variables, look at issues from every direction, factor in previous experience, apply concepts that are only abstract, project future outcomes, and come to solidly logical conclusions. When your thinking brain is in charge, it's hard to go wrong. And, if things do go wrong, your thinking brain will figure out exactly why, and make sure the same thing doesn't go wrong again.

But, guess what? Your thinking brain isn't always in charge. At times, the well thought recommendations from your marvelous thinking brain get outvoted. At other times, your thinking brain takes too long to make decisions, allowing another part of your brain to beat it to the punch. There's nothing abnormal about this — in fact some completely illogical behaviors, like risking personal safety to assist another person, make humans human. But recognizing how your thinking brain can be nullified in diabetes management can lead to more success — you can change the circumstances and give power back to that part of your brain best suited for management.

Seconding that emotion

It's easy to see how your thinking brain gets overruled if you think about emotions. Everyone makes emotional decisions, sometimes to feel a positive emotion, and sometimes to avoid a negative one. Emotional decisions are often completely conscious — you know the decision may not be completely logical, but you're willing to accept that. There's really no way to avoid some emotional decisions, and seeking or avoiding an emotion in a specific circumstance has an emotional benefit. An illogical decision now and then about diabetes is unavoidable.

It's when a particular pattern of emotional decision making becomes a way of life that problems can arise, and when diabetes is involved illogical emotional behavior can be dangerous. Chapter 10 gives you some important insight of how emotion and eating are tied together, but here are some common emotional patterns that really interfere with self-care:

- Anger and resentment are common, and completely understandable, among people with type 1 diabetes. Type 1 diabetes is a virtually random and completely life-changing event which happens suddenly, mostly to young and otherwise healthy individuals. And, the management responsibilities are more complex than with type 2 diabetes and are unending. But, when natural anger and resentment at fate turns into a defiant refusal to give in to the management responsibilities of type 1 diabetes, serious consequences can result. Anger and resentment are natural emotions — defiance is not.

- Guilt can play a similar role in type 2 diabetes because type 2 diabetes usually develops slowly, and in many cases could have been prevented. Guilt is anger, but directed at oneself rather than at fate. Guilt about type 2 diabetes can lead to thinking you deserve the worst diabetes can offer, and that emotion is incompatible with managing diabetes to preserve your health.

- Viewing illness as a personal weakness keeps people, more often men, from even acknowledging diabetes, or has them looking to challenge diabetes to a strength contest. Ironically, the greatest strength is acknowledging the reality of diabetes, and taking self-management responsibilities seriously.

- Misplaced selflessness is an emotional reaction more common among women. Managing diabetes effectively does require prioritizing your own health, and taking time for exercise or changing a family's eating patterns can take a back seat to what's perceived as caring for others.

These emotional patterns usually impact the whole range of diabetes management, not just eating. With some self-analysis, maybe helped by counseling, misdirected emotional responses to diabetes can be changed for the better. Ultimately, emotions are recognizable, but your brain also messes with your efforts to eat healthier in secret, unrecognizable ways. It takes some planning to outsmart your impulsive brain.

Exposing impulsive eating

If you're like most people, you probably have some digital photographs stored on your computer. To you, these photos are colorful and represent pleasant memories. But in computer language, your photos are just a series of black and white ones and zeros — it's a secret language, but looking at millions of ones and zeros won't stimulate any pleasant memories for you. Your body has a secret language, too — a chemical language. Although you don't consciously understand this chemical language any more than the ones and zeros on your computer, this chemical language stores vivid memories, especially about food, and you can understand those memories very, very well.

It's an amazing system that has helped humans survive the toughest times. For an overly simplistic explanation, consider that the part of your brain responsible for survival doesn't trust your thinking brain with some very important responsibilities. Your thinking brain could be so wrapped up evaluating something logically that it might forget to eat when food is available. And, in tough times, you have to grab food whenever you can. So this part of your brain gives you a fabulous chemical reward when you remember to eat — a chemical that brings a comforting feeling of well-being. It's a chemical reward that's so satisfying that you'll remember to eat no matter what your thinking brain is preoccupied with. And to make double sure you won't miss an eating opportunity, your brain gives you a little boost even if you think about food, or see a picture of food. Eventually, impulsive eating when food is available is second nature and completely unconscious. Most importantly, in the contest between your impulse to eat and your thinking brain, impulse usually wins.

This amazing biological system is, however, obsolete in a society where food is constantly available, and is running on overload when images of food surround you everywhere you look. It does not, however, have an off switch. Chapter 10 explains how being surrounded by food and food images triggers unhealthy impulses, and if managing diabetes effectively depends upon managing food effectively, impulsive eating is public enemy number one.

That's where meal planning comes in. Planning ahead puts your thinking brain in charge, and it's your thinking brain that understands how important what you eat today and tomorrow can be to your health ten years from now. Your thinking brain may not be good for making spur-of-the-moment decisions, but when you give it time, without standing in front of an open refrigerator or watching a waiter deliver food to the next table, you win.

That is precisely what makes diabetes meal planning so crucial. Taking emotion and impulse out of your eating decisions means better decisions, and better decisions about food can have a direct and immediate benefit to your health.

Deciding What to Eat

So, if you're going to put your logical brain in charge of planning your meals, it needs facts. A significant portion of this book is dedicated to giving you the nutrition facts your thinking brain wants to put in a spreadsheet, so a broad overview in this first chapter is only fair. One caution — your impulsive brain would rather be in charge of eating, and you may find yourself resistant to thinking about food in an analytical way. Just take a break, and remind yourself how important it is to understand healthy eating — don't believe that it isn't important.

Forgetting "diabetic diet"

Diabetic diet is a phrase you'll hear constantly, and what could be more discouraging than to imagine yourself sentenced to an eating plan that's so restrictive only people with diabetes have to subject themselves to it? The truth is almost the complete opposite. An eating plan that works for diabetes would be an appropriate eating plan for nearly anyone. It's a balanced eating plan with two clear objectives as follows:

- ✔ Help your body manage blood glucose levels as effectively as possible.
- ✔ Provide adequate nutrition with a focus on reducing recognized risks for heart disease.

Other medical conditions, including common *comorbidities* like celiac disease or complications caused by long-term poorly controlled diabetes, may lead to adding an emphasis to other dietary concerns, too. Without any pressing health issues other than diabetes, however, the story is pretty simple.

The specific focus for accomplishing those two objectives is managing carbohydrates and managing dietary fat. Be assured, however, that managing does not mean eliminating. An effective diabetes eating plan commonly recommends that 50 percent of daily calories come from carbohydrates, and 30 percent of daily calories come from fat. It won't shock you to learn that whole-grain pasta primavera with a little olive oil is a better option to satisfy this calorie distribution than a frosted donut. It may shock you to learn that pasta is allowed at all.

Forbidden pasta is only one of the inaccurate pieces of unsolicited advice you can get freely on line, from friends, or from perfect strangers. How about getting the real story? Chapters 12, 13, and 14 help you create your own eating plan, adopt popular and commercial diets for diabetes, and even eat healthy away from home. It's all about knowing what's most important.

Considering carbohydrates

Earlier in this chapter you read a short discussion of glucose homeostasis — glucose balance. Glucose is a sugar, and carbohydrates are made of glucose molecules bound together in chains. That is a drastic oversimplification — other sugars join glucose to form some carbohydrates, too, but glucose is the most prominent, and the most relevant, to diabetes.

Carbohydrates have a prominent role in this book, and Chapter 8 is devoted to understanding carbohydrates in your diet. Carbohydrates are sugars, starches, and fiber, and if you can digest them (some fiber you can't), glucose molecules are unchained and absorbed directly into your blood. The glucose in table sugar is indistinguishable from the glucose in potatoes or milk or an orange. That does not mean these foods are equivalent, but only that a glucose molecule is a glucose molecule.

Glucose is your body's favorite fuel and the only fuel your brain can use. When you eat carbohydrates, your blood glucose levels go higher, whether you have diabetes or not. High blood glucose levels stimulate insulin secretion; low blood glucose levels stimulate another hormone, glucagon. Insulin and glucagon work together to lower, or to raise, blood glucose so a normal level is maintained.

Insulin reduces high blood glucose levels by signaling muscle, fat, and liver cells to pull glucose into the cells, and pack it into a unique starch molecule called *glycogen* until it's needed for energy. As explained earlier in this chapter, diabetes results when sufficient insulin isn't available, or when cells don't respond normally to insulin. Your body can compensate for having no glucose available inside of cells for energy production, but only for a short time. The life expectancy of people with type 1 diabetes before treatment was available could be extended by starving them of carbohydrates, but not for long. Carbohydrate — glucose — is necessary.

Fortunately, injectable insulin is available for treating type 1 diabetes, and it works much like natural insulin to move glucose into cells. And, while type 2 diabetes is a loss of the natural response to insulin, it's not a total loss — glucose will still move into cells, albeit slowly. People with diabetes must eat carbohydrate foods to provide energy.

The amount of carbohydrate, the timing of carbohydrate consumption, and the quality of carbohydrate in the food can either help your body and medication manage blood glucose levels, or complicate the issue. If you eat a lot of carbohydrate at one time, and eat carbohydrate that is digested and absorbed into your blood quickly, blood glucose levels go up very quickly and can overtax your capacity to bring levels down. Even when injecting insulin doses matched to your carbohydrate intake, managing the amount, timing, and quality of carbohydrates pays off. Your personal diabetes meal plan will map this out for you.

So, what about sugar? In some ways, sugar is not much different than any other carbohydrate, and there's a common and dangerous misconception that to manage diabetes one only needs to avoid sugar. You now know that all carbohydrates raise blood glucose levels, and managing carbohydrates, rather than avoiding them, is the best strategy. But sugar does deserve some extra scrutiny. There's mounting evidence that too much sugar is unhealthy for anyone — if sugar causes metabolic disruptions in healthy people, it certainly should be consumed in serious moderation with diabetes. Also, sugar breaks down very quickly during digestion and spikes blood glucose levels — low blood glucose levels can be raised quickly with candy, for instance. Finally, sugar often comes in foods that offer no nutritional value — empty calories and carbohydrates. It's always best to eat carbohydrates that have secondary benefits.

Some of you realize that fruit and milk contain simple sugars — fruit even contains free glucose that can be absorbed directly. But Mother Nature has a way, and even though fruit raises blood glucose fairly quickly, the sugar from fruit, which is delivered with fiber and other nutrients, doesn't have the same long-term negative impact on health that refined sugars have.

Keeping your heart healthy

Most people know that diet can contribute to unhealthy cholesterol levels, and those unhealthy cholesterol levels raise the risk for heart disease. A heart healthy diet can do more than improve cholesterol levels, and a heart healthy diet is especially important for people with diabetes.

Heart health is so important to diabetes because diabetes itself raises the risk of heart attack or stroke two to four times higher than the risk for people without diabetes. Having high LDL cholesterol, high triglycerides, and high blood pressure along with diabetes multiplies the risk even more. High blood pressure, called hypertension, and diabetes together are double trouble for kidney function, too — the two leading causes of kidney failure working together. Heart disease, however, is by far the greatest threat to a person with diabetes.

Your eating habits can contribute to that risk or can work to reduce the threat. You probably know that saturated fat, and especially trans fat, contributes to heart disease, and a healthy diabetes eating plan emphasizes limiting saturated fat. Excess body weight, common among people with type 2 diabetes, is an independent risk factor for heart disease. But, eating a heart healthy diet is as much about what you should be including in your meals, as what you shouldn't. Consider the following:

✔ Soluble fiber, like the fiber in oats and beans, sweeps unhealthy LDL cholesterol from your system.

✔ The Dietary Approaches to Stop Hypertension (DASH) eating plan developed by the National Institutes of Health, which emphasizes eating whole grains, fruits and vegetables, and getting high levels of calcium, magnesium, and potassium from food, can lower blood pressure within two weeks.

✔ Eating foods consistent with the Mediterranean diet, including fruits and vegetables, whole grains, fish, and olive oil, can reduce insulin resistance, reduce general inflammation, and reduce the risk of heart attack or stroke.

✔ People with diabetes seem to excrete vitamin B_1, thiamine, at a higher than normal level, and the lowered thiamine levels may contribute to the accelerated formation of blockages in arteries among people with diabetes. Whole grains are a source of thiamine.

✔ Plant compounds called *flavonoids*, found in green tea, cocoa, and citrus fruits, are antioxidants that improve cholesterol levels, and work to prevent the formation of plaques that can block arteries.

The list of how foods benefit heart health, and diabetes too, often by improving sensitivity to insulin, goes on and on, and in some cases it's clear the compounds can't come from supplements. There simply is no substitute for a balanced diet, rich in whole grains, fruits and vegetables, and healthy fats. You get specific information on how foods can directly benefit your health in several chapters later in the book. Most importantly, a healthy diabetes eating plan includes foods you are pleased to eat. In fact, if you've fallen into poor eating habits for the convenience, you will be amazed how satisfying real food will be to your tastes.

Doing It Yourself

If you're looking for an easy way out, there isn't one. Managing diabetes well is a commitment that has to be followed by action, but there aren't many commitments of your time and attention that could possibly have a bigger payoff. And, if you honestly look at where you invest your time and efforts now, you can surely justify that little more be devoted to your health — Chapter 11 is devoted to strategies that will keep you motivated. The life expectancy of people with diabetes is something like ten years shorter on average, but it's not diabetes itself that steals those years — it's indifference to self-management responsibilities. If doing diabetes management well every day can give you those ten years, and it can, then for every two days you attend to diabetes, you get one extra day of living in return if your diagnosis was at age 50. Nothing is guaranteed, of course, but even if your diagnosis was at an earlier age, the return on investment is unbeatable.

What's required of you to get such as deal? Here's the plan for success:

✔ See your doctor regularly, ask questions, get your lab work done when requested, and ask to see a registered dietitian and a certified diabetes educator for a personalized meal plan, and for continuing education. If your doctor doesn't take diabetes seriously, find another doctor.

✔ Take your medication as prescribed, and test your blood glucose often to see what's going on. If you have type 1 diabetes, that could mean four or five injections, and eight or ten blood glucose tests each day, but an insulin pump and continuous glucose monitor can make those much less burdensome. Insulin can be the best choice for type 2 diabetes as well — if your doctor suggests insulin, don't refuse without serious consideration.

✔ Make time for 150 minutes of moderate exercise, like walking, each week — only 30 minutes a day, five days a week, and the 30 minutes can be done in 10- or 15-minute segments.

✔ Stop smoking, get seven or eight hours of sleep each night, and find a way to reduce chronic stress (exercising will help immensely).

✔ Adopt healthy eating habits.

This book is dedicated to that last bullet, and changing old habits for new ones is always tricky. But, there should be no doubt that you can adopt new eating habits. Don't expect to become an expert in one week, and don't let imperfection discourage you. The target for evaluating effective blood glucose control is called A1C, and A1C measures your average blood glucose over a couple of months. Averages leave plenty of room for imperfection.

The chapters that follow review diabetes in more detail, explain the importance of nutrition, give you the in-depth story on carbohydrates, walk you through meal planning and shopping, discuss the pitfalls of eating out, and give you one week of meals and some marvelous recipes to start your collection.

Ultimately, nobody can actually do this for you. Everyone's different, and everyone starts from a different place. What's difficult for you will be a breeze for someone else. Diabetes self-management works, healthy eating works, and it can work for you.

Don't forget that help is available. Registered dietitians, certified diabetes educators, and supervised support groups can be a huge source of encouragement and positive feedback. The real burden with diabetes can be the feeling that nobody really understands. Don't let feelings like that fester — find the support you need.

Chapter 2

Understanding Diabetes

In the past 30 years, the number of adults and children with diabetes in the United States has increased by five fold, from less than 6 million people in 1980 to more than 30 million estimated in 2013. The story is much the same worldwide. Diabetes is epidemic. In the United States, one in every three people you meet has diabetes or its first cousin *prediabetes*, and the economic costs run in hundreds of billions of dollars.

Diabetes results from the inability to properly process carbohydrate food, specifically the sugar glucose that's set free from carbohydrates during digestion. Glucose is so important that it's delivered by express to virtually every cell in your body. When the delivery can't be completed for one reason or another, an important balance is lost, and diabetes becomes part of your life.

For the overwhelming majority of you (with type 2 diabetes discussed later in this chapter), your current condition is probably related to a less-than-healthy lifestyle over many years, especially how and what you've been eating. But changing how and what you eat can go a long way in minimizing the long-term and life-threatening health effects of diabetes. Adopting better habits is even more important now that you have diabetes than before, when diabetes may have been preventable. Understanding diabetes and the connection between diabetes and lifestyle are important first steps in taking control of your diet and your health.

Defining Diabetes Mellitus

Diabetes mellitus is defined simply as having higher than normal levels of glucose in your blood too often, a condition called hyperglycemia. Blood glucose is sometimes called *blood sugar*, but glucose is a very special sugar when it comes to diabetes, as you learn later in this chapter. For the sake of accuracy, *blood glucose* is the correct terminology, and the term used throughout this book.

The actual words *diabetes mellitus* are Greek and Latin, loosely translated to mean constantly flowing sweet urine. Frequent urination is a common symptom of diabetes as your body works to remove excess blood glucose through your kidneys, and it's reasonable to assume that urine would be sweet. In fact, tasting urine to detect the sweetness of excess blood glucose was a diagnostic test that doctors would perform in the days before the chemistry was well understood. Fortunately, there are now better ways to detect hyperglycemia than urine tasting.

Whereas there are several different ways a person can acquire diabetes — injury or damage by toxins for example — type 1 and type 2 diabetes are the most common "natural" forms. This book's focus is, therefore, on type 1 and type 2 diabetes and variations of those two conditions.

Explaining the role of glucose

Glucose is a sugar; in chemistry terms, a "simple" sugar or monosaccharide. There are many chemical varieties of sugars; for example, you've probably heard of fructose and lactose. But glucose is especially important because it's your body's favorite fuel to provide the energy needed for activity like muscular movement, body heat, and, most importantly, brain function.

You may see your brain as mostly important for thinking, but there are many really important activities that depend on signals from your brain that happen with no thinking required. Your brain accounts for 20 percent of your energy use, some of which goes to support rather important activities like automatically breathing.

Sugars are unique chemical compounds. Glucose and fructose, for instance, have exactly the same chemical formula with 6 carbon atoms, 12 hydrogen atoms, and 6 oxygen atoms — $C_6H_{12}O_6$ — but differ remarkably because the chemical bonds between the carbon atoms and other elements are very different. Fructose is much sweeter in taste and doesn't raise blood glucose levels except slightly from a small amount of fructose that is converted to glucose in the liver.

Your body doesn't have a central location where glucose is burned for energy, like a roaring fireplace or the cylinders of a car's engine. Instead, glucose is converted to energy on a microscopic level inside trillions and trillions of the individual cells that make up you.

You can understand how this works by thinking about muscles. When you raise your fist toward your shoulder, your bicep muscle gets shorter; it contracts to bend your elbow and pull the lower arm upward. You can actually measure the difference in bicep muscle length, first with your arm extended straight out and again with your arm bent toward your shoulder. The contraction of your bicep muscle is actually the contraction in unison of millions of individual muscle cells that go together to make a bicep — the cells themselves contract. Movement requires energy, and each individual muscle cell is burning glucose to provide that energy. If you add a 20 pound dumbbell to your muscle movements it's easy to feel the increasing energy requirement, the heat given off, and eventually the depletion of fuel as the muscle becomes exhausted. The real action to generate this energy takes place inside of individual cells.

Cells come in all shapes and sizes, but most are way too small to see without a microscope. The different kinds of materials and structures that make a cell, including your DNA, are contained within what's called a cell membrane. It's tempting to think of a cell membrane as something like a plastic freezer bag — you can see what's in there, but it can't escape even if it's liquid. Likewise, you can't put something else in through the plastic without making a hole where liquid can leak out. In reality, cell membranes aren't completely impermeable like the freezer bag and can be influenced to let materials come into or leave the cell through the membrane. And if glucose is converted to energy inside of your cells, it's apparent that glucose found its way into those cells somehow.

Simplifying insulin

Although not always the case, many important cell types including muscle cells won't allow glucose to freely pass through the cell membrane without a mediator. That's where insulin becomes so important.

Insulin is a hormone produced by specialized cells in your pancreas called *beta* cells or islet cells. Hormones are chemicals released from one location within a body that affect cells in other parts of the body. In the case of insulin and glucose, it's insulin that signals individual cells to allow glucose passage through the cell membrane. This process is often illustrated with insulin as a key unlocking a door that glucose can use to enter the cell, and in many ways this picture is accurate. Both glucose and insulin circulate in your blood to deliver fuel to almost every cell that requires energy to perform its duty.

A more detailed discussion of glucose and insulin comes in the next chapter, and for even more information consult Dr. Rubin's book *Diabetes For Dummies* (Wiley). The main issue here, to define diabetes, is to understand that if the marvelous and precise ability of insulin to convince cells to open the door and take glucose inside is lost or diminished, glucose remains in the bloodstream.

This means cells needing, or at least greatly preferring, glucose for energy don't have any. This also means glucose levels in your blood remain higher than normal, even as your kidneys slowly try to remove the excess. This abnormal state is hyperglycemia, and if this abnormal state becomes your "normal" state, then you have diabetes.

People who know someone with diabetes may associate low blood glucose, hypoglycemia, as a symptom of diabetes. Hypoglycemia deprives the brain of adequate energy, so the signs of low blood glucose are obvious, mimicking alcohol intoxication and leading to unconsciousness. However, hypoglycemia is a result of diabetes treatment, with injected insulin or other medications that stimulate natural production of insulin from islet cells, not diabetes. It's high blood glucose levels, hyperglycemia, that defines diabetes, and this condition can be unnoticeable.

Exploring Type 1 Diabetes and LADA

Type 1 diabetes, formerly known as juvenile diabetes and as insulin-dependent diabetes, is what many people think of as real diabetes. The familiar image is one of an exceptionally thin child taking insulin injections, and that's a fairly accurate image. Type 1 diabetes does tend to occur at a younger age (your author Toby Smithson's age of onset was eight), and insulin injections are a routine part of having type 1 diabetes. Type 1 is relatively rare compared to type 2, accounting for less than 10 percent of diabetes cases worldwide.

Type 1 diabetes also commonly shows itself suddenly, frequently diagnosed only following a life-threatening emergency as the capacity to produce insulin is lost. In retrospect, the signs of type 1 diabetes mellitus — constantly flowing sweet urine along with an unquenchable thirst and a never ending appetite — would have been obvious for weeks. Still, an onset with symptoms building for a week or a month is far more acute than the onset of type 2 diabetes.

Recently, doctors have recognized a variation of type 1 diabetes occurring in adults that doesn't involve the sudden and drastic need for insulin injections.

Losing the capacity to produce insulin

Your immune system protects your body's internal workings from intruders, whether the intruder is a splinter or a disease causing virus or bacteria. The appearance of an intruder stimulates all-out war. Your immune system can mobilize blood cells immediately with names like killer T-cells and begin manufacturing antibodies specifically designed to target the intruder and finish the job over a period of a few days. Your immune system has probably saved your life many times.

Sometimes, because an intruder contains substances in common with body tissue, this awesome firepower is directed both at an intruder and also at essential parts of the same body the immune system is supposed to protect. When damage is caused by one's own misguided immune system, the condition is called an *autoimmune* disorder. In rheumatoid arthritis, for example, the immune system attacks and damages certain tissue in joints, deforming fingers as a result. In type 1 diabetes a confused immune system attacks and destroys the insulin producing *beta* cells of the pancreas. The destruction of pancreatic *beta* cells means that eventually no insulin is naturally produced, and the body can't move glucose into cells.

That typical sudden and violent onset of type 1 diabetes is not quite as sudden as it seems. The emergency is actually the climax to *beta* cell destruction that progresses over a period of weeks or months as insulin-producing capacity is steadily depleted. Cells begin to starve for glucose fuel, even as blood glucose levels go higher. Sensing that cells need glucose, hunger hormones stimulate appetite, but additional food only sends blood glucose higher again. Eventually, as blood glucose levels rise to many times normal levels, dehydration from excreting glucose constantly in urine and a buildup of waste products called *ketones* from cells burning fat (an emergency alternative to glucose) cause a condition known as *diabetic ketoacidosis* (DKA). DKA is an urgent medical emergency, and this first DKA event begins what is for all intents and purposes a lifetime of daily insulin injections necessary for survival.

The major practical difference between type 1 and type 2 diabetes mellitus is the universal requirement for insulin, by injection or some other method, in type 1 diabetes. Patients with type 2 diabetes usually do not require insulin at the beginning of their illness.

Prior to the mid 1920s when insulin was first isolated, people with type 1 diabetes simply didn't survive. Now, however, medical advances in insulin quality, insulin delivery systems (insulin pumps), and real-time blood glucose monitoring allow people with type 1 diabetes to effectively control blood glucose levels for a lifetime. Dr. Rubin's book *Type 1 Diabetes For Dummies* (Wiley) provides a complete guide to this unique condition and is a must read for parents, spouses, friends, and people with type 1 diabetes.

Looking for a cure for diabetes is proceeding on many fronts. Some of the more promising directions include the following:

- ✔ A vaccine against the substance that promotes the development of autoantibodies that kill beta cells
- ✔ Use of oral insulin to "quiet" the immune system
- ✔ Use of intranasal insulin to stimulate protective immune cells
- ✔ Development of drugs that block the immunity that kills beta cells
- ✔ Regeneration of beta cells with drugs or stem cells (cells that form many other cells)

This is a partial list and should give you cause for celebration if you have type 1 diabetes. It should encourage you to control your diabetes as well as you possibly can so that you will be free of complications of diabetes when the cure arrives.

Latent autoimmune diabetes of adults (LADA) has more in common at the start with type 2 diabetes than with type 1 diabetes with one key exception: a berserk immune system. LADA does not come on dramatically like typical type 1 diabetes. In fact, diagnosis and treatment almost always begins as if the patient has developed type 2 diabetes, which doesn't involve autoimmune destruction of *beta* cells, as explained later in this chapter. DKA doesn't typically occur, insulin therapy is not required, and oral medications with lifestyle changes can often manage blood glucose levels effectively for a time. LADA is so different from type 1 in these regards that some call LADA type 1.5 diabetes. However, what puts LADA in the type 1 diabetes category is the presence of *beta* cell antibodies, and the resulting destruction of these insulin producing cells, albeit ever so slowly. Adults with LADA tend to require insulin therapy for blood glucose control sooner than adults with type 2 diabetes, and antibody studies of patients diagnosed as type 2 suggest that more than 10 percent (in some studies nearly 30 percent) are LADA instead.

In some circles type 1 diabetes is referred to as "bad diabetes," hinting that type 2 diabetes must be "good diabetes." Type 1 diabetes does require more attention than type 2 because DKA is always possible, as is low blood glucose with insulin injections. But the tools available to control blood glucose levels in type 1 can make that constant attention pay off. Type 2 diabetes can be, and too often is, ignored because the consequences of inattention are often not immediate. But just because you're ignoring diabetes doesn't mean diabetes is ignoring you, and the complications of diabetes discussed later in this chapter aren't concerned with which type diabetes you have.

Puzzling over the causes of type 1

The primary cause of type 1 diabetes is clear — destruction of insulin producing *beta* cells by the patient's own immune system. The cause of this misguided immune system response is not clear.

There is a genetic component that increases the risk for developing type 1 diabetes, but studies of identical twins, who are literally identical in a genetic sense, demonstrate that genetics doesn't cause type 1 diabetes. Having an identical twin with type 1 diabetes increases the twin's risk of developing type 1 diabetes only to something like 30 percent.

Certain viral infections seem to be a promising suspect in triggering the autoimmune response, but there is no smoking gun. Some researchers have proposed that type 1 and type 2 diabetes are essentially the same disease expressed in different ways. Population data hints that inadequate vitamin D is to blame, that persistent organic pollutants like dioxin might play a role, or that excessive hygiene has contributed to an overactive immune system. A long-term study known as TRIGR (which stands for Trial to Reduce IDDM in the Genetically at Risk) is monitoring more than 2,000 babies on three continents to look at a potential connection between some cases of type 1 diabetes and cow's milk or certain infant formulas.

The bottom line is that the cause or causes of the autoimmune response leading to type 1 diabetes is still unknown at this time.

Analyzing Type 2 and Gestational Diabetes

Type 2 diabetes, formerly known as adult-onset diabetes and as noninsulin-dependent diabetes, is by far more common than type 1, accounting for more than 90 percent of diabetes cases. Type 2 diabetes does tend to occur at a more advanced age than type 1, and the onset is slow and steady over a period of years with correspondingly mild, even unnoticeable, symptoms. The American Diabetes Association produces statistics every few years revising the estimated number of Americans with diabetes, and the numbers always show about 25 percent of the total cases as "undiagnosed." None of the undiagnosed cases of diabetes could possibly be type 1.

Type 2 diabetes is often called a lifestyle disease, and there is ample evidence demonstrating that type 2 is preventable with diet and exercise alone. Still, nearly 2 million new cases arise each year in the United States, and the trend is still heading higher.

Following the progression of type 2

Type 2 diabetes doesn't begin as a problem with insulin production like type 1 diabetes. In fact, the *beta* cells at the insulin factory are often working overtime. The high blood glucose levels that define type 2 diabetes result from a problem getting glucose into the cells that need it. Remember the insulin-as-a-key-that-unlocks-the-cells image discussed earlier? With type 2 diabetes some of the locks have been changed, and the key (insulin) doesn't work. Type 2 diabetes begins with what's called insulin resistance — normal or above normal levels of insulin finding unresponsive cells leaves excess glucose stranded in the blood.

But this all begins in slow motion. In fact, there is a recognized condition known as prediabetes (or impaired glucose tolerance) that can be ringing the warning bell for years. Prediabetes is when blood glucose levels are higher than normal, but not high enough to be officially diagnosed as diabetes. A famous study called the Diabetes Prevention Program (DPP) found that people with prediabetes who adopted a healthier diet, lost a modest amount of weight, and exercised regularly reduced their odds of progressing to type 2 diabetes by a whopping 58 percent. The results were even better for participants who were over 60 years of age, and the lifestyle changes were more effective at holding off diabetes than the very effective diabetes medication metformin. Prediabetes is commonly one component of what's called metabolic syndrome, a condition that also includes abnormal blood cholesterol levels.

Type 2 diabetes begins and progresses slowly, often without symptoms. If you're overweight, don't exercise, have a family history of diabetes, or belong to certain ethnic groups like African-Americans, Latinos, Asian-Americans or Native Americans, annual testing for diabetes is a must.

So, why don't more people put a stop to type 2 diabetes before it starts? One reason is because they don't get regular medical checkups that always include a blood glucose level; they don't know there's a problem. But even those who know aren't reminded by symptoms. The symptoms of modest hyperglycemia can be unnoticeable, especially because some like frequent urination or fatigue tend to be a natural age-related inconvenience.

In time, however, insulin resistance may increase, and the pancreatic *beta* cells just get tired of trying to produce enough insulin and wear out. Many people with type 2 diabetes go through a range of medications targeting different pathways for reducing blood glucose levels, and some will eventually end up taking the same kinds of insulin injections as people with type 1. Type 2 diabetes is considered, as this overview suggests, a progressive condition, where progressive actually means getting worse all the time.

It is essential, however, that you understand this progression (regression) to poorer and poorer health is not inevitable. Just as diet and exercise was amazingly effective at preventing diabetes among participants with prediabetes in the DPP study, so too can diet and exercise along with diabetes medication improve blood glucose control after the diagnosis. Adopting and sticking with a healthy lifestyle can have a profound effect on insulin sensitivity and blood glucose balance. Type 2 diabetes, unlike type 1, can be put into remission.

Weighing the role of body mass

It wouldn't take Sherlock Holmes to figure out that body mass and type 2 diabetes are closely linked. One clue would be that 85 percent of people with type 2 diabetes fall into the overweight or obese range (or higher) on the Body Mass Index (BMI) scale. An above normal weight is something shared by the great majority of people with type 2 diabetes.

Too, just as the average BMI has steadily risen over the past 20 years or so, where more than two-thirds of the U.S. adult population now falls into or beyond the overweight BMI range, the incidence of type 2 diabetes has risen at almost exactly the same rate. In fact, plotting the lines on a graph shows a nearly identical incline, and these trends are illustrated in Figure 2-1, beginning in 1980 as the type 2 obesity epidemic began. Even more telling, and more concerning, is that rising obesity among children and adolescents has caused type 2 diabetes, once nearly unheard of in this age group, to become relatively common. In the years 2000 to 2005, type 2 diabetes represented almost one-third of new diabetes cases among youth 10 to 19 years old, with a rate of almost nine cases of type 2 per 100,000 youth.

Also, modest weight loss of from 5 to 7 percent of body weight in people with prediabetes can return blood glucose levels to normal. That would be a weight loss of only 10 to 14 pounds for a 200 pound person.

Scientists are zeroing in on the culprit where excess weight and diabetes are linked, and one hint has been body shape. It seems that weight carried in the midsection of the body, as opposed to legs and posterior for example, increases the risk of type 2 diabetes substantially. Sometimes referred to as an apple shape (where the posterior focused weight is called a pear shape), weight around the midsection represents internal fat deposits, too. This "visceral" fat sends chemical signals that promote insulin resistance, and is much more associated with type 2 diabetes than subcutaneous — under the skin — fat. Visceral fat explains why people of Asian origin acquire type 2 diabetes at a normal BMI, because body scans have shown they accumulate visceral fat at lower body weight than other ethnic groups. The role of visceral fat also explains why losing a modest amount of weight can have such a striking impact on insulin resistance. Visceral fat, fortunately, is the first to go in a diet and exercise weight loss effort, and the exercise part is especially effective at eliminating these dangerous internal fat deposits.

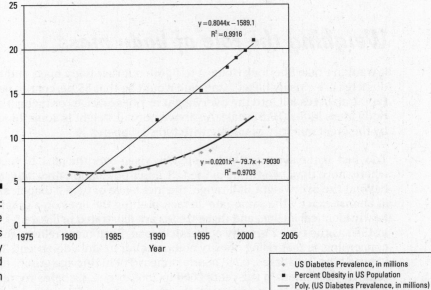

US Prevalence of Diabetes and Obesity v. Time

Figure 2-1:
Prevalence of diabetes and obesity in the United States from 1980 to 2001.

Considering ethnicity, genetics, and age

Ethnicity and genetics are associated to some degree, and both have a relationship to type 2 diabetes. There are genetic variations that increase the risk for, or make people susceptible to type 2 diabetes. In fact, the risk that a child will develop type 2 diabetes if a parent has type 2 diabetes is a stronger link than for a parent with type 1 having a child with type 1. But overall, specific genes that are strongly associated with type 2 diabetes have been elusive, even though more than 30 genes have been identified as contributing to an increased risk.

There is nothing elusive about the risk differences associated with ethnicity, however. Whereas again the specific reasons aren't known, essentially every other ethnic group has a higher risk for type 2 diabetes when compared to non-Hispanic whites. Even more troubling, the occurrence and severity of diabetic complications (discussed later in this section) is greater among those groups, too. It's difficult to separate other risk factors such as weight and culture from the data, but researchers who evaluated records on women from the long-term Nurses' Health Study made adjustments for BMI. Following more than 78,000 nurses who didn't have diabetes over a 20-year period saw 3,800 cases of type 2 diabetes develop. In the unadjusted data the risk for type 2 diabetes was 120 percent higher for African- Americans, 76 percent higher for Hispanics, and 43 percent higher for Asians than for whites. However, adjusting for BMI changed the order making risk 126 percent higher for Asians, 86 percent higher for Hispanics, and 34 percent higher for African-Americans. This suggests that BMI is the greatest risk for Asians and a lower risk for African-Americans. The rates of type 2 diabetes are also higher in Native American populations and Pacific Islanders.

It's important to point out that the so-called Western diet, high in calories and fat, clearly plays a part in the higher incidence of type 2 diabetes in some ethnic groups. Migrating to the United States is actually a risk factor for type 2 diabetes, and as Western culture and dietary habits spread to other countries, like India, the type 2 diabetes incidence increases there, too. One piece of good news from the Nurses' Health Study, however, hinted that a healthy diet cut the risk of developing type 2 diabetes more for other ethnic groups than for whites. That suggests that a healthy diet can do more to control the course of diabetes in these groups where diabetic complications are so common.

Aging increases the risk for type 2 diabetes in all ethnic groups and both genders. Some of the reasons may be exceptionally complicated biochemical changes having to do with insulin output and glucose transport. But there is a clear relationship with a couple of simple and familiar reasons — diet and exercise.

Senior citizens tend to be overweight, and often that weight is carried in the midsection, suggesting visceral fat with its negative effects on insulin sensitivity. Adults in the 45 to 70 age group have the highest rates of obesity on the BMI scale, more than 30 percent, and weight is a defined risk factor for type 2 diabetes. Not coincidentally, the age groups 65 to 74 and 75+ have the highest rates of type 2 diabetes, more than 20 percent of that population.

Beyond the excess weight, which is likely related to both diet and reduced physical activity, the natural loss of muscle mass that comes with aging could have a role in insulin resistance. Muscles play an important part in getting glucose out of the bloodstream, and fewer muscle cells means fewer places glucose can go. Maintaining muscle mass with age has many benefits, and preserving insulin sensitivity may be one. Studies measuring insulin sensitivity while building muscle mass with resistance exercise (weight lifting) have shown positive results, and resistance training has become a standard recommendation for aging adults. You don't need to take up serious pumping iron workouts to get the benefit resistance exercises offer, but feel free if you are so inclined.

Lifestyle changes (weight loss, improved diet, and exercise) have proven to be even more effective than drugs in preventing the progression of prediabetes to diabetes.

Developing diabetes during pregnancy

Some women without diabetes develop a condition called *gestational diabetes* during pregnancy. Gestational diabetes is almost always a temporary loss of blood glucose balance, and levels return to normal after giving birth. Gestational diabetes isn't the same thing as having diabetes before a pregnancy. Dr. Rubin's book *Diabetes For Dummies* thoroughly addresses pregnancy with pre-existing type 1 or type 2 diabetes.

New diagnostic criteria increases the percentage of women considered to have gestational diabetes from less than 5 percent of pregnancies to more than 18 percent, according to the American Diabetes Association. The new criteria are intended to add emphasis to the issue of blood glucose management during pregnancy, and most women are able to resolve the risks with a focus on lifestyle, especially diet. Of course, women with gestational diabetes should be under the watchful eye of their physician.

Having gestational diabetes during a pregnancy increases the likelihood that you will have gestational diabetes in later pregnancies. Having gestational diabetes also increases the risk for developing type 2 diabetes later, especially where other risk factors like excess body weight are in play. Even though gestational diabetes usually goes away after the birth, follow-up screening is recommended to be certain that the abnormal blood glucose levels weren't caused by the coincidental onset of type 1, LADA or type 2 diabetes during pregnancy.

Summing Up the Potential Complications of Diabetes

Dr. Rubin's book *Diabetes For Dummies* (Wiley) devotes three chapters and 65 pages to a detailed explanation of the many potential complications of diabetes. The attention and effort you're asked to give to managing blood glucose levels with medication, testing your blood, physical activity, and especially diet is to reduce your risk for these complications.

In everyday life you probably use the word *complication* to describe something that disrupts your plans slightly, but can be resolved with a minor adjustment or two. A flat tire, unannounced guests, or a power outage all qualify as a complication in everyday life. Used in a medical context for describing the potential health effects of diabetes, the word has a much more serious meaning. Don't be fooled by the innocent word complication — in diabetes, the stakes are literally life and limb.

In general, the complications of diabetes can be separated into short-term complications and long-term complications. Short-term complications are related to the level of your blood glucose right now. Long-term complications are related to your success managing blood glucose levels and overall cardiovascular health markers, like blood pressure, over many years. This book is aimed at reducing your risk for long-term complications.

There are only two short-term complications — very low blood glucose levels (hypoglycemia), and very high blood glucose levels (hyperglycemia).

✔ Hypoglycemia is a complication of diabetes treatment, but it can be extremely serious so deserves some emphasis. When insulin levels are too high compared to blood glucose, your brain runs low on fuel. Hypoglycemia can result from too much injected insulin, too little food to match medications that stimulate natural insulin release from the pancreas, or from alcohol consumption. Symptoms may mimic intoxication, and accidents are common on account of disorientation. But hypoglycemia can progress to coma and death without treatment.

✔ Hyperglycemia results when there is not enough insulin available to reduce blood glucose levels. DKA was explained earlier in this chapter's description of the typical onset of type 1 diabetes, but DKA remains a risk for anyone with type 1 for a lifetime. DKA is a toxic state and can be fatal if untreated. People with type 2 diabetes don't ordinarily experience blood glucose levels high enough to develop DKA, but a similar condition called *hyperosmolar syndrome* can be a life threatening risk. Usually hyperosmolar syndrome is triggered by dehydration associated with another illness like norovirus, sometimes called stomach flu.

The long-term complications develop where diabetes is poorly controlled over the years, and this is where lifestyle choices like committing to a healthy diet play such a crucial role in preserving health. The damage that excessive blood glucose levels cause over time can have debilitating and deadly consequences, but are preventable in large part.

✔ Heart attack and stroke are much more common in people with diabetes, two to four times more likely. And, people with diabetes have a higher death rate, and are more likely to have another event if they survive the first. The risk for heart disease is often increased by abnormal cholesterol levels and high blood pressure related both to high blood glucose, and to excess weight and a less-than-healthy lifestyle. Treating and managing diabetes with lifestyle must include treating and managing these related risks for heart disease.

✔ Kidney disease affects up to 5 percent of people with type 2 diabetes, and up to 30 percent of people with type 1. In fact, diabetes is the leading cause of kidney failure in the United States that eventually may require dialysis treatment or a kidney transplant.

Toby says anyone who's frustrated following a diabetes-friendly diet to better manage blood glucose should try the renal diet for dialysis patients just for comparison. A renal diet restricts fluid, protein, sodium, phosphorus, and potassium, and in her view is the most restrictive diet in medical nutrition therapy.

✔ Neuropathy describes conditions resulting from damage to nerves, and is a very common complication of diabetes affecting some 60 percent of patients. Neuropathy can result in pain or numbness of extremities (especially the feet), the inability of some muscles to move, digestive problems called *gastroparesis*, urinary difficulties, sexual dysfunction, and a range of other difficulties.

✔ Vision is threatened from an increased risk of cataracts, glaucoma, and especially diabetic retinopathy. Retinopathy is another example of how high blood glucose levels can damage small blood vessels.

✔ Diabetic foot disease is the leading cause of non-traumatic amputations in the United States, and the progression of foot ulcers is often complicated by the absence of sensation due to neuropathy (and a neglect of routine self examination of the feet).

Many people with diabetes assume these terrible outcomes are simply part of the normal course of diabetes, but that assumption is dangerously wrong. Controlling blood glucose levels and adopting a healthy overall lifestyle can greatly reduce your risk for all of these long-term complications, and it's never too late to start.

Chapter 3

Managing Diabetes and Blood Glucose

Your body is remarkable in many ways. Chapter 6, for instance, shows how you recycle the complex components of the food you eat to use again as building blocks for your own cells, or as the ingredients of various biochemical recipes. Here's another incredible process you're familiar with, even if you don't realize it — *homeostasis*. Homeostasis means maintaining stable conditions. For example, your body has a complex control system to maintain a relatively constant body temperature of 98.6° Fahrenheit, and you hardly ever have to think about it. But, if your temperature goes much higher or lower than normal you've got potentially serious problems, and you need to help your body regain temperature homeostasis.

You've got another amazing system of checks and balances for maintaining homeostasis with blood glucose levels. Glucose is your favored source of energy — your brain's only source of energy — and it travels around in blood to reach cells everywhere. Blood glucose is a little like the porridge Goldilocks was searching for — everything's best when it's just right. Having diabetes, however, means blood glucose levels aren't just right, and your body needs a little help from you to regain and maintain homeostasis. Fortunately, you have the ability to do just that.

In this chapter you see why the normal balance of glucose is so important to health, and how diabetes disrupts that crucial balance. More importantly, you see how you can help recover blood glucose homeostasis, and who can help you along the way.

Getting Glucose In and Out of Your Blood

Glucose is a simple sugar that is extremely important to you as a source of energy. It's the key ingredient in a biochemical recipe that produces a powerhouse molecule *adenosine triphosphate*, best known by its initials ATP. ATP is your fuel, the source of the energy you use to move or to think or, for that matter, to generate the heat needed to remain a steady 98.6° Fahrenheit.

The conversion of glucose to energy via ATP takes place inside of the cell membranes of trillions and trillions of individual cells, most all of which are properly equipped to prepare the recipe for ATP in structures called *mitochondria.* And, because blood already visits cells in your farthest outreaches to deliver oxygen and remove wastes, blood also conveniently brings glucose right to the doorstep of cells that need it to make energy. Your body can convert other ingredients to energy if necessary, but glucose is the first choice.

You get glucose from food, and you eat a lot more glucose than you might think, even if you don't have an overactive sweet tooth. Actually, glucose isn't that sweet anyway. Virtually all of the glucose you eat is locked in chains with other sugars or more glucose — *polysaccharides*. If the chains are small the molecule is still considered a sugar — table sugar (sucrose) is one molecule of glucose and one fructose — a *disaccharide*. If the chains are longer, even to hundreds or thousands of glucose molecules, the molecules are *starch* or *fiber*. Taken together, sugars, starches, and fiber are *carbohydrates*, a word you're surely familiar with if you have diabetes.

Most dietary carbohydrates come from plants. Plants are constructed in large measure of the carbohydrate cellulose, and cellulose can include thousands of linked glucose molecules. As a carbohydrate, cellulose is definitely in the fiber category and not a very digestible fiber at that. If humans could easily digest cellulose, you might have a favorite old-family recipe for cotton ball sauté or cedar planked plank. Fortunately, plants also make more digestible and more flavorful carbohydrates.

 The only dietary carbohydrate you get from animals is lactose, or milk sugar. Lactose in mother's milk is how infants (and puppies and calves) get carbohydrates for energy, but the ability to digest lactose diminishes in most humans after infancy. As a result, an estimated 65 percent of the human population is lactose intolerant to some degree.

Glucose as a single molecule is liberated from its chain gang polysaccharides by various digestive processes, starting right in your mouth with saliva. By the time your food passes through your stomach, small intestine, and maybe the first portion of your colon all of the easily digestible carbohydrate has been broken apart by specific enzymes, finally freeing the individual glucose molecules. At that point, glucose is ready to be captured.

Just because fiber is less digestible and may not surrender its glucose easily doesn't mean it isn't a very important part of a healthy diet. In Chapter 6 you'll see the many benefits of "fantastic fiber."

Within your intestinal tract are millions of fingerlike projections called *villi,* which are especially rich in blood supply. Before liberated glucose can escape through the colon as waste material, the molecules are absorbed directly into your bloodstream through small capillaries in a process called active transport. Much glucose absorption occurs in the first part of your small intestine, and absorption is very efficient due to the vast surface area of millions of villi. The process is also relatively quick, so eating carbohydrate food results in a surge of glucose entering the bloodstream. Rising blood glucose levels are a serious insult to homeostasis. You won't be surprised to learn that your body has a solution to that problem.

Finding an escort — insulin

Specific cells, located among in cell clusters in your pancreas known as the Islets of Langerhans, can sense rising blood glucose levels, and these cells — called beta cells — are capable of doing something about it. Beta cells produce insulin, and they do their producing in earnest when blood sugar levels are on the rise. High blood glucose levels are an abnormal state, and insulin lowers blood glucose levels simply by helping put the glucose somewhere else — inside of cells.

You already know that glucose goes toward producing ATP inside of cells, but without insulin as an escort many cells aren't so anxious to invite glucose inside. Insulin is the key that unlocks doors in cell membranes, allowing glucose to pass into your cells and out of your blood.

As blood glucose levels begin to drop, the *beta* cells sense this favorable change and suppress their release of insulin. In healthy individuals this process is incredibly precise, and blood glucose homeostasis is achieved in a few hours. But, getting glucose into cells and out of the blood is only part of the blood glucose homeostasis story.

Storing glucose for later

If you're following the glucose story carefully, and of course you are, you have two very insightful questions.

- ✔ If all your excess glucose is escorted into cells to create energy, what happens if you don't need energy at that particular time?

- ✔ If you use all of your glucose for energy during the Iron Man Triathlon, why doesn't your blood glucose level drop to zero unless you eat constantly?

Wow — you have asked two excellent questions! It's true that at times you don't need much energy even if you've just eaten and have glucose surging through your system. At other times, as you have pointed out, you need a lot of energy with no food in sight. And, it is true that during those times you need a lot — your triathlon — glucose is drawn into muscle cells from your blood glucose even when your blood glucose levels are normal.

The solution to this problem is storage. Your cells are able to convert excess glucose into a storage molecule called *glycogen*, and to restore this secret stash back to glucose whenever energy as ATP needs to be whipped up. Glycogen stored in your muscle cells provides energy to those muscles when you're working hard and not eating; however, glucose stored in a muscle cell stays in that muscle cell. So, when muscle glycogen is depleted during your triathlon, and your muscle cells are pulling additional glucose from your blood, what keeps your blood glucose stable? In other words, what maintains homeostasis when blood glucose levels should be going down?

The answer is important to understanding diabetes — it "ain't chopped liver," as they say. It is, however, *your* liver. One special place where glucose is stashed as glycogen is in liver cells — your liver is a warehouse for extra glucose. Glycogen in liver cells isn't obliged to remain in liver cells as it is with muscle cells. Liver cells can release glucose back into your bloodstream.

As blood glucose levels begin to dip, another group of special cells in the pancreas' Islets of Langerhans, this time *alpha* cells, spring into action. *Alpha* cells secrete a hormone called *glucagon* which stimulates your liver to release stored glucose back into your bloodstream. Glucagon is so effective that people with type 1 diabetes sometimes carry a dose of this hormone for an emergency injection when their blood glucose levels go dangerously low. The injection can bring levels up much faster than eating even pure glucose. Glucagon's action to raise blood glucose answers the triathlon question.

It's important to note that insulin and glucagon are secreted more or less constantly to maintain blood glucose homeostasis, even when the circumstances are somewhere in between sedentary and extreme exertion. Like a tightrope walker leaning a little left and then a little right, in normal metabolism these hormones maintain a beautiful blood glucose balance.

The storage capacity for glucose in muscle cells and the liver is fairly limited. When you consume excess calories, including carbohydrates, insulin will also facilitate glucose storage in fat cells, not as glycogen but as glycerol and triglycerides. Fat molecules store a lot of energy and contribute to energy needs as glycogen is depleted, which explains how exercise really does reduce fat.

Losing the Glucose Balance

Diabetes, however, is a state of blood glucose *imbalance* related to insulin. As explained more thoroughly in Chapter 2 (and in exquisite detail in Dr. Rubin's books *Diabetes for Dummies* and *Type 1 Diabetes for Dummies*), in type 1 diabetes insulin production capacity is completely lost, and in type 2 diabetes cells become resistant to insulin. In both cases, blood glucose levels after eating carbohydrate foods do not come down to normal levels in a normal way.

It's fair to say that what defines a normal level of blood glucose in humans is the level preferred by your brain. Your brain is very important to your existence, is a glucose hog, does not require insulin to absorb glucose, and usually gets whatever it wants or needs. But your brain is more concerned about operating with low blood glucose levels than about higher levels. High blood glucose causes problems in other ways.

What is a normal level for blood glucose? In common measure about 1 teaspoon of glucose dissolved in your 1½ gallons of blood is perfect. In laboratory measure that's 4,000 milligrams (4 grams) of glucose in your 50 deciliters (5 liters) of blood equaling 80 milligrams per deciliter, or 80 mg/dl. Milligrams per deciliter, mg/dl, is the standard measure used in the United States and some other countries, but an alternative unit *millimoles per liter* (mmol/l) is the international standard measure for blood glucose levels, used commonly in many countries, too. The difference in units is not relevant, but mg/dl can be easily converted to mmol/l by dividing by 18. Therefore, 80 mg/dl and 4.44 mmol/l represent the same concentration when measuring blood glucose.

International diagnostic standards actually set a normal blood glucose range at between 60 and 99 mg/dl. This standard is for *fasting blood glucose*, which is your level after having no food or drink for 8 hours. A fasting blood glucose level from 100 to 125 mg/dl is known as *impaired glucose tolerance*, commonly called prediabetes. A fasting blood glucose level higher than 126 mg/dl is considered diagnostic for diabetes if that result occurs on more than one fasting blood glucose test.

Another test more representative of a realistic response to food is conducted. Called an *oral glucose tolerance test* (OGTT), this test measures blood glucose response after ingesting glucose (usually 75 grams) over a two or three hour period by testing fasting blood glucose level before the test, and testing at hourly intervals after the oral dose of glucose. A normal result is blood glucose below 200 mg/dl after one hour, and below 140 mg/dl after two hours. If the two hour result is higher than 140 mg/dl but lower than 200 mg/dl, it represents impaired glucose tolerance or prediabetes. A result higher than 200 mg/dl after two hours is diagnostic for diabetes. A blood glucose level higher than 200 mg/dl on any random test is diagnostic for diabetes.

A variation of the OGTT is recommended for all pregnant women to test for gestational diabetes. The test, given between the 24th and 28th week of pregnancy, uses either a 50 gram or 100 gram oral dose of glucose, and a normal response is a blood glucose level below 140 mg/dl after one hour (50 gram dose) or after three hours (100 gram dose).

These carefully set diagnostic standards measure the extent of blood glucose imbalance. Rarely necessary for diagnosing type 1 diabetes, where blood glucose levels can exceed 500 mg/dl at its sudden onset, people with type 2 diabetes may have a long history of routine lab tests charting the loss of blood glucose balance over many years. When a diabetes diagnosis is made, testing and evaluating blood glucose levels should become a routine part of daily life.

Measuring Blood Glucose

Most people living with diabetes in the 21st century won't fully appreciate being able to test blood glucose levels anytime, anywhere, and with an instrument you can carry in your pocket. But, prior to the early 1980s, blood glucose levels were measured only in medical labs, and estimating blood glucose levels at home involved matching colors of a paper strip dipped into urine. The lab result was, obviously, never a real-time result, and the urine test only signaled approximate levels of hyperglycemia. Glucose doesn't generally appear in urine until blood glucose levels approach 200 mg/dl. In short, people with diabetes 30 years ago, almost exclusively type 1 diabetes, were doing a lot of estimating (guessing) about blood glucose levels, its response to food, and insulin dosing. How things have changed.

Testing blood glucose at home

Guessing about blood glucose levels is completely unnecessary. Now, it's possible to draw a very small amount of blood from your finger or other location (with some meters), and get a relatively accurate measure of blood glucose in ten seconds. Blood glucose meters today also store historical information, which can be downloaded to a computer or transmitted to a physician's office. More and more people with type 1 diabetes are wearing *continuous glucose monitors,* which sense glucose levels through a small wire inserted into the fluid just beneath the skin. Although not fully approved for use in making treatment decisions, these monitors provide blood glucose levels anytime and can be programmed to alert the users when levels are trending higher or lower. Having an approved closed-loop system, where these monitors and an insulin pump work together to balance blood glucose levels without human involvement, is probably only a few years away.

Testing blood glucose levels is extremely important for people with type 1 diabetes because they must make real-time self-treatment decisions about food and insulin dosing based upon the result. People with type 1 should test before every meal and approximately two hours after meals with some frequency, a time frame referred to as *postprandial.* They should test before exercising, before bedtime, and anytime they might sense high or low blood glucose levels. They should test anytime someone who knows them asks suggests they may "be low" — often they lack self awareness of hypoglycemia clues that are obvious to others. They should also test if consuming alcohol in excess, because alcohol can trigger hypoglycemia, and hypoglycemia can resemble alcohol intoxication.

Testing with type 2 diabetes usually follows a less stringent schedule — maybe only once or twice a day. More testing is recommended if low blood glucose levels are a potential side effect of medication (insulin or a few different kinds of pills), and Dr. Rubin provides guidelines in *Diabetes For Dummies*.

Many people with type 2 diabetes wouldn't think of testing more often than their doctor prescribes, but one of the great values of home blood glucose testing is looking for patterns. For instance, you can bet there are certain foods that have a dramatic impact on your blood glucose levels, but you can't know which ones without doing some self-experimentation by testing. Most type 2 medications aren't appropriate for resolving incidental hyperglycemia like insulin can, but you can certainly change your behavior to compensate in the future. If you find by some extra testing that Grandma's recipe for rice pudding sends your blood glucose to 320 mg/dl, you could stop eating Grandma's rice pudding. Your doctor may give you a funny look, but think about asking for a few more testing strips each month so you can take advantage of this remarkable technology to better control blood glucose levels.

Getting the averages

Daily blood glucose testing can give you an excellent look at your status at one moment of the day, and that can be essential, especially for people with type 1 who are making treatment decisions. But, in the big picture your success with diabetes is a long distance race — you hope a long, long, long distance race. Minimizing your risks for complications is much less about your blood sugar level at 6:45 AM on August 7th than it is about your average blood glucose levels in August, and July before, and June before that.

Fortunately, there's a very important blood test that can give you a big picture view of your blood glucose control. Your doctor will order a test for *hemoglobin A1C*, sometimes called HbA1C or simply A1C, at least once a year to evaluate your average blood glucose levels over a two or three month period. In technical terms, A1C is a measure of glycated (or interchangeably, glycosolated) hemoglobin — what percentage of your blood hemoglobin has reacted with glucose. Dr. Rubin's book *Diabetes for Dummies* offers a detailed explanation for you scientists.

The important point is that A1C is an excellent predictor of your overall blood glucose control, and consequently of your risk for diabetes-related complications.

The A1C test gives a weighted average, meaning your blood glucose control the month of the test has slightly more influence on the result than your control the month before, and so on. This variation is related to the limited life span of hemoglobin. A normal A1C, in individuals without diabetes or prediabetes, would be something lower than 6 percent (A1C is expressed as a percentage of hemoglobin that is glycated). Target values for people with diabetes have been established by both the American Diabetes Association (ADA) and the American Association of Clinical Endocrinologists (AACE) at less than 7.0 percent and less than 6.5 percent, respectively.

Two important studies have supported the relationship between A1C and diabetes-related complications — the *Diabetes Control and Complications Trial* (DCCT) in the United States and Canada, and the *United Kingdom*

Prospective Diabetes Study (UKPDS) in the United Kingdom. The DCCT involved more than 1,400 people with type 1 diabetes, and the UKPDS included more than 5,000 people newly diagnosed with type 2 diabetes. Both studies demonstrated clear and convincing reductions in the incidence of diabetes-related complications with better control of blood glucose (lower A1C). The UKPDS of type 2 diabetes projected a 37 percent decrease in eye, kidney, and nerve complications for every 1 percent reduction in A1C, and an 18 percent reduction in the risk for heart attack. The downside in both studies was the risk for low blood glucose episodes. Clearly, consistent blood glucose control, as indicated by the A1C, is an important goal for anyone with diabetes, and a main reason meal planning and nutrition is so critical.

Continuous glucose monitoring is a procedure which is useful for identifying blood glucose patterns from hour to hour over a period of several days, and is becoming a more common test for averages over a short time span as technology improves. This procedure records a blood glucose level every few minutes, although the data is not usually available in real time except to people with type 1 diabetes who wear monitors routinely. Still, downloading data gives a graphic picture of exactly how blood glucose levels rose and fell during the monitoring period, and comparing the graph with the timing of meals, exercise, and medication can be revealing.

Toby's first experience with continuous glucose monitoring was to investigate a pattern of low blood glucose levels occurring regularly at lunchtime. Expecting to see a slow decline in levels through the morning, the continuous data showed a sharp rise in mid-morning blood glucose levels to near 300 mg/dl instead, followed by a steep drop to the low level she thought was the real issue. This data allowed adjustments in morning insulin dosing to compensate for the steep variations.

Following Doctor's Orders

Since an estimated 25 percent of people with diabetes remain undiagnosed, it's pretty clear that a significant number of people with diabetes don't get regular medical care. However, studies of patients under medical care, such as the *Diabetes Attitudes, Wishes and Needs* study (DAWN), have shown a troubling level of adherence to taking medication, self monitoring of blood glucose, diet and exercise, and keeping appointments for medical care. Avoiding the serious complications of diabetes requires a multidimensional approach directed at both prevention and intervention. There are many resources available to help you keep your diabetes from exploding into really serious health problems, and the most important resource is you.

Choosing a "which" doctor

You may be inclined to think you can't actually choose a doctor or health care team, but like many other responsibilities for diabetes care, it's up to you to know what's necessary and to make some demands if you're not getting the support you need.

Dr. Rubin's book *Diabetes for Dummies* (Wiley) gives a detailed overview of medical care in one of the chapters, but here's a quick listing of medical resources you can take advantage of:

- **Primary physician**: Most people with type 2 diabetes work with a primary physician, who prescribes medication and routinely monitor for signs of diabetes-related complications in physical exams and laboratory work. A primary physician may or may not have access to in-house diabetes-related support resources like a registered dietitian, certified diabetes educator, or an organized patient support group. Your primary physician should, however, be willing and anxious to recommend or formally refer you elsewhere for these very important support services.

- **Endocrinologist or diabetologist:** These specialized physicians are most likely working with people with type 1 diabetes, or people with type 2 diabetes who have poorly controlled blood glucose or diabetes-related complications. They are the experts in diabetes treatment and will likely have in-house health professionals to help with diet, exercise, blood glucose monitoring, and emotional support.

- **Registered dietitian:** Because food and eating habits are so closely connected with weight, blood glucose, and the risk for heart disease, seeing a registered dietitian, an expert in *medical nutrition therapy*, is very important. Because this book is about food and diabetes, the advantages to seeing a registered dietitian are discussed in detail later in this section.

- **Pharmacist:** Your pharmacist is perhaps your best resource for education about medications, not only those prescribed for diabetes, but also those prescribed for other conditions. Most important, your pharmacist knows how your variety of medications could interact. Diabetes is so prevalent now that many pharmacists are diabetes educators.

- **Certified diabetes educator:** A wide range of health care providers — physicians, registered nurses, registered dietitians, pharmacists, clinical psychologists, podiatrists, and others — have studied and taken a comprehensive certification examination to provide a broad range of education and support to people with diabetes. Spending time with a certified diabetes educator, individually or in a group, for diabetes self-management education (DSME) can be helpful in tying together the many medical and lifestyle responsibilities patients struggle to balance.

✔ **Podiatrist:** Getting regular foot exams and early treatment of potential problems by a podiatrist can literally be a limb saver. The loss of sensation and circulation problems makes your feet an easy target for minor infections that can become difficult to control. Anyone with neuropathy (nerve damage) should see a podiatrist regularly.

✔ **Dentist:** Diabetes can increase the risk of gum disease, so regular visits to your dentist for examination and cleaning are very important.

✔ **Mental health professional:** Diabetes can be overwhelming, and people with diabetes are significantly more likely to experience depression than the general population. Diabetes can be distressing. More than 41 percent of the participants in the DAWN study, mentioned earlier in this chapter, reported "poor well being" even decades beyond their diagnosis. Distress at diagnosis is much higher. Depression and stress deserve attention in their own right, but need particular focus where diabetes is concerned because feeling depressed can diminish with self-care behaviors. Only 10 percent of the DAWN study participants reported ever having sought psychological treatment — don't hesitate to get help with the emotional stresses diabetes can bring.

Make sure each of your resources sends a report to your primary physician so that she knows what's being done for you.

Minding your medications

If you're controlling your diabetes with only lifestyle changes, hooray for you! More than likely you've been prescribed one or more medications to help control blood glucose levels, and maybe even medications for blood pressure, cholesterol, or other conditions completely unrelated to diabetes and its potential complications. Rule number 1 is to take your medications as prescribed. Various studies, including DAWN, have shown adherence to medication schedules among people with diabetes range somewhere between 65 percent and 95 percent, often depending upon the complexity (including more than one daily dose) of the schedule. The goal should be 100 percent.

Insulin is the most effective controller of blood glucose levels, and the most complicated and burdensome. Insulin is the only option for treating type 1 diabetes, but can be effective in controlling blood glucose levels in type 2 also. Insulin therapy is discussed in the next section.

Most people with type 2 diabetes begin therapy with oral medications — pills. The market for specific diabetes medications is so active, with new additions and, unfortunately, removal for unacceptable side effects, it would be useless to offer a list here and call it current. Plus, there are both brand names and generics for many available medications, and some newer medications are not pills, but non-insulin injections. Rather than even listing the various classes, which generally include more than one drug and an unpronounceable name like *thiazolidinediones*, here's how diabetes medications work to control blood glucose:

✔ Some oral medications coax pancreatic *beta* cells to produce more insulin. These meds require that *beta* cells are still working well, and low blood glucose levels — hypoglycemia — can be a dangerous side effect.

✔ Other oral medications, including the most common medication prescribed at diagnosis, *metformin*, work to decrease glucose output from liver cells and increase insulin sensitivity in muscle cells. Hypoglycemia is not a side effect of these drugs.

✔ One group of drugs helps insulin work better with muscle and fats cells, and decreases glucose output from the liver. Some drugs in this class of pills have been removed from the market due to an increased risk for heart problems.

✔ A couple of medications interfere with carbohydrate digestion, reducing the efficiency of glucose absorption, thereby reducing blood glucose spikes after meals.

✔ A fairly new category of drugs work in different ways to increase the action of a hormone called *GLP-1*. This natural gut hormone slows stomach emptying, increases insulin secretion, and reduces glucose output by the liver. In people with diabetes, secretion of natural GLP-1 is impaired, and disappears quickly due to the action of an enzyme called DPP-4. One class of type 2 diabetes drugs works to block the action of DPP-4, allowing natural GLP-1 to stay active longer. A second class of injectable drugs is a compound that mimics GLP-1, but lasts longer. Neither class increases the risk for hypoglycemia because the stimulation of insulin secretion is dependent upon blood glucose levels.

✔ A drug called an *amylin analog* is taken by injection by some people who are also taking insulin. This drug slows digestion and decreases glucose output from the liver to help smooth blood glucose spikes after eating.

✔ The newest class of diabetes drugs, approved just as this book was completed, are called *sodium glucose co-transporter 2 inhibitors* (SGLT2 inhibitors) These drugs increase the excretion rate of excess blood glucose through the kidneys by lowering the blood glucose level at which the kidneys naturally begin to remove glucose from your system.

Many of these medications can be given in combination. All of these medications should be taken as prescribed. Whether you take medication or not, you will benefit from a healthy diet and exercise.

Explaining insulin therapy

In January, 1922 a young Canadian boy lying near death from type 1 diabetes was injected with insulin from the pancreas of a calf. This moment marked the successful beginning to one of the greatest medical stories of all time, when researchers working at the University of Toronto isolated and purified (to some extent) the secret hormone that would lower blood glucose, and save dying children. Insulin has been saving children (and adults) ever since.

In 1982, purified human insulin became commercially available, and insulin formulations and delivery techniques have improved remarkably over the years. Insulin, which is your body's exact response to rising blood glucose levels, is the most effective treatment for diabetes, but is rarely introduced as an option for type 2 diabetes early on.

Insulin must be taken by injection (an inhaled option has been commercially available, but is not at this time), some formulations require frequent blood glucose testing to be effective, and insulin therapy comes with a clear risk for hypoglycemia. One common myth holds that insulin causes complications, and more than 70 percent of participants in the DAWN study thought the effectiveness of insulin therapy is low, and that insulin would not help them. This study also found some physicians using insulin therapy as a threat to motivate better adherence to diet and exercise recommendations. Whatever the difficulties and misconceptions, insulin therapy remains essential for people with type 1 diabetes, and an underused option for people with type 2 diabetes. Common misconceptions and scare tactics are unfortunate.

The most immediate use for insulin is counteracting rising blood glucose levels after eating carbohydrate foods, and the formulations intended for this purpose are called *rapid* or *short* acting. Rapid formulations begin to act on blood glucose levels quickly, reach peak activity within one to two hours, and are no longer active in four to six hours. Short-acting regular insulin is slower to act, slower to peak, and endures for two to four hours. Rapid- or short-acting insulin is taken at mealtime in a dose matched to the amount of carbohydrate to be consumed. The *insulin to carbohydrate ratio* is specific to the patient and may vary from meal to meal. Two concentrations of insulin are available in the United States — U100 (100 milligrams of insulin per milliliter of injection solution) is more common than U500, which is five times more concentrated for individuals requiring especially large doses.

Intermediate or *long-acting* insulin formulations are intended to provide a steady *basal* rate, or background rate, of insulin throughout the day in the same manner that your *beta* cells secrete a background level. For people with type 1 diabetes who are already taking injections, intermediate-acting *NPH* can be mixed with doses of regular. NPH is active as a basal level for 10 to -18 hours. Long-acting insulin formulations are usually effective when injected only once each day, and provide a basal level for up to 24 hours. Long-acting insulin, Levimir or Lantus, is the most likely first step for people with type 2 diabetes beginning insulin therapy.

Insulin pumps are becoming more common for people with type 1 diabetes. An insulin pump delivers rapid-acting insulin from a reservoir through a tube inserted beneath the skin. A control device allows the user to initiate a meal-time dose, called a *bolus*, by selecting the desired dose and then pressing a start button. Because the tube remains inserted, an insulin pump can deliver the appropriate basal rate of insulin with rapid-acting formulations. The location of the tube insertion, the *infusion set*, is changed routinely, generally every three days, but that one operation replaces as many as 15 separate injections. Insulin pumps give the user much greater control, much greater flexibility, and greater comfort.

Seeing a Registered Dietitian

Adopting and sticking with eating habits that maximize blood glucose control and heart health is, perhaps, the biggest challenge diabetes presents. First, for most people this represents a significant change. Second, misconceptions abound regarding what a diabetes-friendly diet includes, or more accurately doesn't include — no sugar, no carbohydrates, no this, and none of that. Some give up without ever trying. But, a skillful registered dietitian not only knows medical nutrition therapy to account for your weight, blood glucose control and medications, but also knows that enjoying food doesn't have to be surrendered. The DAWN study showed only about one third of participants adhered to their eating plan — a registered dietitian can help you embrace this crucial lifestyle change by providing a balanced, personalized meal plan for you.

Toby avoids using the phrase *diabetic diet* because it sounds so restrictive. With the minor exception of accounting for carbohydrates, there is nothing about an eating plan for diabetes that's different from a heart healthy diet for virtually anyone.

Losing body weight

More than 80 percent of people with type 2 diabetes are overweight or obese. There are lots of great reasons for losing weight — better mobility, improved sleep apnea, higher self-esteem, lower blood pressure, and a reduced risk for several cancers to name a few. But, where type 2 diabetes is concerned, losing only a modest amount of weight — 5 to 7 percent of body weight — improves insulin sensitivity and blood glucose control. That means an improved A1C, and a reduced risk for diabetes-related complications. Responsible and steady weight loss eases the burden on an overworked pancreas, helps diabetes medications work more effectively (including insulin for people with type 1 diabetes), and can greatly improve your quality of life as well.

A registered dietitian customizes an eating plan to help you lose weight, while making certain your food and medication remain appropriately matched. An excellent registered dietitian also works to achieve your weight loss goals by focusing on foods you can eat, not by declaring groups of foods as off limits.

Reducing risk for heart disease

Heart disease is the leading cause of death among the many diabetes-related complications, and heart disease is linked with diet even in the absence of diabetes. So, you can anticipate that your registered dietitian focuses as much on reducing your risk for heart disease as on controlling blood glucose levels. A standard set of health indicators for diabetes, known as the ABCs, includes A1C as the A, blood pressure as the B, and cholesterol as the C. The target values are A1C less than 7 percent, blood pressure less than 140/80, and cholesterol LDL (bad cholesterol) less than 100 mg/dl with HDL (good cholesterol) greater than 40 mg/dl or 50 mg/dl for men and women, respectively. Note that two of the three, blood pressure and cholesterol, are independent of diabetes as risks for heart disease and stroke in the general population (although poor blood glucose control worsens the risks).

Reducing heart disease risk in your diet includes

- Replacing saturated fats from meat and full fat dairy products with lower fat foods, fish, and healthy unsaturated fats
- Replacing refined grains like bread and rice and pasta with whole grains
- Adding more fruits and vegetables
- Replacing sodium with spices, and avoiding sodium in prepackaged or canned foods

Getting to know carbohydrates

Managing carbohydrates — not eliminating carbohydrates — is a key to controlling blood glucose levels, and reducing your risk for diabetes-related complications. And, carbohydrates are everywhere. Your registered dietitian helps you learn where to find carbohydrates, identifies healthier carbohydrate foods you can enjoy, and balances your intake of carbohydrate foods throughout the day in your personalized meal plan.

Carbohydrates are so important to diabetes that Chapter 8 is completely devoted to taking a detailed look at this group of foods in your diet. Still, routinely meeting with a registered dietitian help you gain confidence in your ability to eat freely while controlling your diabetes.

You may find a registered dietitian associated with your medical provider, a local hospital, in private practice, or available through your local department of public health. You can search for a registered dietitian in your local area on the website of the Academy of Nutrition and Dietetics, www.eatright.org. Find a registered dietitian who is also a certified diabetes educator by looking for the CDE notation in their title, or by searching the website of the American Association of Diabetes Educators (www.diabeteseducator.org) and look for the RD or RDN designation. A registered dietitian/certified diabetes educator has an advanced understanding of diabetes and nutrition.

Starting Your New Management Job

If you haven't already gotten the hints through these first three chapters, it's time you hear it directly. You have a new job. The good news is that it's a high-level management position with lots of freedom, and the power to make important decisions daily. Even better, the long-term benefits for a job well done may include an extra ten healthy years of living. If you're 50 years old now that could mean every day you do this job well adds an extra half day later. It's hands down the best deal you'll ever see.

Is there bad news, too? It all depends on your attitude. Diabetes self-management — you would be the self in that phrase — requires your attention and commitment to act. This responsibility for self care on a daily basis is somewhat unique to diabetes. Effective diabetes self-management involves not only faithfully taking your medication and monitoring blood glucose, but also adopting a healthy lifestyle, which includes a focus on diet and exercise.

Unfortunately, too many people with both type 1 and type 2 diabetes either don't get the message, or the message doesn't sink in. Adherence to diet and exercise recommendations tend to be less than 40 percent, and the percentage of people with diabetes meeting all of the ABCs targets is closer to 10 percent. If you want to thrive with diabetes, and you certainly can, here are three commitments that will keep you on the road to success:

- **Embracing reality:** There is, of course, the terrible reality of diabetes-related complications that must be acknowledged, but turn your focus on the motivating reality that you have an incredible opportunity to directly affect the quality of your future health every day. The inconvenience of doing diabetes self-management effectively, and there are inconveniences, is a small price to pay for the extraordinary benefits.

- **Prioritizing your attention and time:** Proactive diabetes self-management behaviors, like preparing healthy food and making time for exercise, can't be the last thing on your list of priorities. You undoubtedly have much competition for your time and attention, but diabetes self-management should get the nod more often than not.

- **Learning:** You're already on the right track to using your brain by reading this book, but don't give up. You never have to be a diabetes expert, but you must be open to learning new things.

Your relationship with diabetes and diabetes self-management is long term, and you can choose in great measure how it goes. The medical professionals and medications you can have as part of your management team are powerful partners. But, in the tug-o-war with diabetes for control of your long-term health, your team can't win unless you choose to do some tugging, too.

Chapter 4

Doing More to Manage Diabetes

It may seem like you've got a lot stacked against you when you're confronted with diabetes, and anyone who's completely unconcerned about the potential negative health effects is either uninformed, or refusing to face reality. But the important point is that diabetes only has the potential for negative health effects — negative health effects are absolutely not inevitable. And, it's you who has the most to say about it.

It is perfectly possible to lead a normal, healthy, and active life with diabetes — to thrive with diabetes. If you're taking your medication as prescribed, that's step one. Follow the advice on healthy eating for diabetes you get throughout this book, and you are well on your way to thriving. Now it's time to explore how to put the finishing touch on your triumph.

This chapter reviews the incredible benefits of a healthy lifestyle that embraces physical activity, rejects tobacco use, and sheds stress. And, to send you on your way, you see the importance of adopting an attitude that makes your long-term health a real priority.

Adopting a Healthy Diabetes Lifestyle

Lifestyle is a word without much meaning by itself. But, add something to it — rural lifestyle, casual lifestyle, modest lifestyle, or lifestyles of the rich and famous — and a clear picture pops into your mind. So, what pops into your mind when you hear *healthy lifestyle*? Maybe a lunch of carrot juice and vitamin pills after a midmorning five-mile run? Or, how about hanging upside down by the ankles to improve circulation? Is your idea of healthy something extreme?

If so, it's time to bring your idea of a healthy lifestyle back to earth so you can see it as something that's right for you. Adopting a healthy lifestyle isn't about training for the Iron Man Triathlon. It's about making small decisions that fit better choices into your other lifestyle. And, just like pennies make dollars, small decisions can have big results.

Getting physical activity

You could make a long list of reasons why many children and adults get less physical activity now than in days gone by — technological, social, environmental, entertainment, demographic, development planning, and safety are a few. A recent study caused something of an uproar when data from The American Heritage Time Use Study showed that women in 2010 expended an average of 360 fewer calories daily than women in 1965, primarily because of significantly less time spent on physical housework. The statistics are virtually the same, of course, for men.

The fact that it's less likely you'll get physical activity during the course of your normal day doesn't make physical activity less important. It simply makes it less likely you'll get the incredible benefits of regular activity unless you're convinced it's worth the effort to find opportunities. With what you've learned about diabetes, and the importance of blood glucose control and cardiovascular health, see if you're not convinced making a commitment to exercise is worth the effort when you hear the full story.

Physical activity offers the following benefits to your immediate and your long-term health:

- Exercise lowers blood glucose, and boosts insulin sensitivity. Higher insulin sensitivity can persist for 24 to 72 hours after exercising

- Exercise reduces dangerous visceral fat — fat deposited around internal organs, which is associated with insulin resistance and type 2 diabetes — more effectively than diet

- Exercise helps prevent high blood pressure and helps lower blood pressure even among people diagnosed with hypertension

- Exercise prevents plaque buildup (atherosclerosis) in arteries and vessels, reducing the risk for heart attack or stroke by lowering bad LDL cholesterol and triglyceride levels, and raising good HDL cholesterol

- ✔ Exercise helps arteries retain flexibility, reducing the potential for plaque buildup

- ✔ Vigorous exercise helps prevent some cancers, including colon and postmenopausal breast cancers

- ✔ Exercise improves balance, and along with adequate calcium and vitamin D increases bone strength, both reducing the likelihood of a fall and reducing the risk of fracture in a fall

- ✔ Exercise may reduce the risk of dementia

- ✔ Exercise improves sleep, reduces the symptoms of stress and depression, enhances sexual enjoyment, improves mobility, and extends lifespan.

That's an impressive list, and you must be anxious to know exactly what you need to do now to get these benefits for yourself. Current recommendations are for 150 minutes per week of moderate activity, like walking, or 75 minutes of vigorous activity. Lately, resistance exercise — lifting weights would be the most obvious example — has been getting more and more attention for health benefits that are complimentary to aerobic activity like walking or biking. A review of data from the National Health and Nutrition Examination Survey III concluded that every 10 percent increase in muscle mass corresponded with an 11 percent reduction in insulin resistance. Because insulin resistance is a key cause of type 2 diabetes, the advantages to increasing muscle mass with resistance exercise are obvious.

Some examples of aerobic exercise include walking, biking, dancing, tennis, golf, swimming, shadow boxing or martial arts, and aerobics. Resistance training can be effective not only with weights, but also with stretch bands, a gallon or half gallon of milk, rowing, or by doing pushups.

Making time for exercise is always the barrier people identify when challenged to get more physical activity. However, you can increase your activity levels almost by accident if you change habits. For instance, make it a point to park a good distance from the door at the mall or grocery, and take the stairs instead of an elevator or escalator. Recent research is finding that too much time sitting is a special risk beyond not getting exercise, and taking five minutes just to stand or stroll every hour has some benefit. Finally, any activity is better that none at all. The American College of Sports Medicine guidelines acknowledge that exercise of less than ten minutes duration may have health and fitness benefits, especially for sedentary individuals.

Be certain to consult with your doctor before changing your activity patterns. Foot health is extra important, so wear comfortable shoes and avoid blisters. But, make it a point to get whatever physical activity you can.

Weight-training (resistance) exercise may be as important — possibly more important — than aerobic exercise for controlling your blood glucose. The government guidelines recommend doing resistance exercise on two or more days a week involving all the major muscle groups: the chest, back, shoulders, hips, abdomen, and upper and lower legs.

Extinguishing the smokes

In January 1964, the U.S. Surgeon General released a report entitled *Smoking and Health: Report of the Advisory Committee to the Surgeon General.* The report was quickly followed by congressional action requiring health warnings on cigarette packaging, and an advertising ban for cigarettes on television and radio that became effective in 1970. Since the initial report, the percentage of adult smokers has declined in the United States from 42 percent to less than 20 percent.

Still, smoking remains a leading cause of preventable death in the United States, although it's notable that contending for the top spot is the group of obesity-related health threats like high blood pressure and diabetes. The combination of smoking and diabetes is a double whammy on your cardiovascular system, when having diabetes has already multiplied your risk.

Smoking damages the lining of arteries and blood vessels, promoting the buildup of waxy plaque (atherosclerosis), and increases the risk for peripheral arterial disease (PAD) and stroke. Smoking reduces levels of good HDL cholesterol, and increases blood pressure and heart rate. Smoking also reduces the flow of oxygen to your heart muscle and reduces your capacity for exercise.

You can simply stop smoking, even though it may not be easy. Give it a try and don't hesitate to get help. Don't let smoking cancel out the gains from all of the attention you're ready to give to managing diabetes.

If you can't do it alone or return to cigarettes the first time you try to stop, don't despair! There's plenty of help available to you, and most smokers don't break this tough habit on the first try. Keep at it. The benefits are enormous.

Shedding stress

Everyone experiences stress because some stress is natural and unavoidable. Start with what's called the *fight or flight* response — pounding heart, dry mouth, perspiration, muscle tension, shaking, lightheaded, and heightened awareness. These responses are an instinctive physical reaction to a perceived threat, even if the threat is a job interview, roller coaster ride, or public speaking assignment. A rush of adrenaline increases breathing and heart rate, raises blood pressure and blood glucose levels, and can even impair logical decision making and thinking. Fortunately, the extreme physical response to these states of extreme stress is usually temporary.

Lower levels of stress over the long term can have the same physical effects. The intensity of your response is not as noticeable, but over time chronic stress has a more negative effect on health. A 2010 study in Israel looked at the levels of the stress-related hormone cortisol in matched groups of hospitalized men, one group hospitalized for heart attack, and the other hospitalized for other reasons. Rather than testing for cortisol in urine, blood, or saliva for a measure of real time stress, the researchers measured accumulated levels in hair, reflecting chronic stress over a period of months. Comparing the two groups for cardiovascular risk factors, cortisol levels in hair was a stronger predictor of heart attack than any other factors, including smoking and weight.

It's not possible to eliminate all stress from your life — having diabetes is stressful, as are families, jobs, 24-7 news on television, travel, finances, and hundreds of other circumstances. You can reduce stress, however, by practicing the following simple suggestions:

- Don't sweat the small stuff.

- Make time for leisure — it really is good for your health.

- Get enough sleep — most adults need seven to eight hours each night, and sleep deprivation has negative effects on your health, too.

- Exercise regularly — it's a healthy way to release pent up tension.

- Avoid excess caffeine and don't smoke.

- Don't make perfection your goal — you'll be forever frustrated.

- Seek professional help with severe stress or depression.

Want another reason to learn how to shed stress? Stress impedes your ability to make wise decisions about diet, and making wise decisions about diet can be an excellent path to losing your stress over having diabetes. It's a circular benefit.

Prioritizing Your Health

Nobody can promise you that diabetes absolutely won't affect your health in some negative way — there are too many variables, including how long your blood glucose levels have been compromised. But, you can be sure that dedicating some time and effort to following through on the responsibilities of diabetes self-management will have a definite positive impact. And, the sooner you prioritize your health into action, the better off you'll be.

Making the commitment

There's nothing about diabetes self-management that's impossible for you to accomplish. In fact, it's not terribly difficult, as really difficult things go. Inconvenient would be a better description. Yet, way too many people with diabetes simply don't commit to the effort. Maybe the absence of attention-getting symptoms in type 2 diabetes has them doubting that diabetes is really all that serious. Perhaps they have an opposite view — no matter what they do, there's nothing that will keep the complications away. In both cases, those people haven't made the effort to learn the truth. Learning about diabetes, and the opportunity you have for thriving with this condition, is surely an important commitment. And, making commitments to seize control of your health is what diabetes self-management is all about. Your first commitment should be to acknowledging the realities of diabetes, and diabetes self-management.

The first reality, this is a serious condition. For those with type 1 diabetes, dangerous low and high blood glucose levels are always possible, and avoiding danger requires awareness, and blood glucose monitoring. The risks directly related to blood glucose levels are less common with type 2 diabetes, but still possible depending upon medication (for low blood glucose levels) and overall health (for very high levels). But, for anyone with diabetes the greatest danger is from the increased risks, related to persistent high blood glucose levels, for heart attack, stroke, damage to your eyes, kidney failure, loss of sensation, unmanageable infections, sexual dysfunction, digestive problems, and more. It's not something that should completely occupy your mind, but it is important to understand what's at stake. Even if you're feeling fine, or think you're feeling fine, your A1C tells the real story — believe what it's telling you.

The more important reality, these risks can be reduced significantly by the lifestyle decisions you make every day — how you eat, whether you take your medication as prescribed, how much you're willing to prioritize exercise. The challenge to effective diabetes self-management is mostly a mental one — a promise you make to yourself and keep. If you commit to meeting the challenge and to tolerating the certain inconveniences, you can have a remarkable impact on your health. It's really that simple.

Learning new tricks

One of the great inconveniences you confront with diabetes self-management is learning to really think about food — before you eat. It's just something that most people resist. Yet, living a normal and healthy life with diabetes simply demands that you learn to do this abnormal thing regularly. Carbohydrates have a direct affect on your blood glucose levels, and it is essential that you learn how to manage carbohydrates in your diet. And, that means not only learning to recognize carbohydrate foods, but also how to measure and count them.

In reality, it's as easy as pie. And, if you know that pie is likely a source of the carbohydrates you need to be counting, you're ahead of the game already. Nevertheless, intelligent people are often rendered helpless in the face of the advanced second grade math required for tracking carbohydrates in their diet. This is a mental block you too may encounter, as the impulsive part of your brain works to keep your thinking brain out of food-related decisions.

Don't believe the old dog, new tricks adage. You can learn to think analytically about food, and after a little practice, evaluating your meals becomes second nature. That doesn't mean you need to know the carbohydrate content of every food ever prepared. There are excellent, pocket-sized books that can help you manage your diet like a professional. Again, it's about your commitment — where there's a will, there's a way.

Valuing prevention

The long-term health risks associated with diabetes are a result of years of accumulated damage, which can be occurring day by day with virtually no symptoms. Managing those risks means making commitments and accepting inconveniences day to day and year to year, sometimes with little positive feedback. That is the challenge of valuing prevention — trusting the evidence even when the payoff isn't immediately obvious.

Studies show that diabetes can cut the life span of middle-aged adults by 8 to 12 years if the condition isn't managed effectively. But, at diagnosis those missing years are still 10 or 15 years away. Trusting that what you do today and tomorrow can have a profound benefit to your health many years down the road is best viewed as an investment — an investment in the quality of your future. And, prevention is the best investment you'll ever make.

So, remind yourself regularly why you're making the healthy choices you make and take some time to celebrate the payoff that you can't see yet. Birthdays are a great time to celebrate diabetes management success. If you value prevention and make everyday choices with your future in mind, the time will come when you realize it has paid off.

Carefully managing your diabetes, whether Type 1 or 2, has a bigger payoff than you may think. There is a "legacy effect" that results from keeping your blood glucose close to normal, especially early in the disease. Even when your control slips a bit later on, your risk for a heart attack or stroke years later is significantly less that the person who never made the effort to adopt those habits that keep blood glucose as close to normal as possible.

Part II
Nutrition with Purpose

Top 5 Reasons to Monitor Your Blood Glucose Levels

Food has a tremendous impact on your physical body, whether you have diabetes or not. It fuels the body; it provides comfort; and food can just simply be fun. But where diabetes is concerned, food is medicine. The choices you make every day about the foods you eat have a tremendous impact on the quality of your future.

1. **You get to know your levels.** Managing diabetes is all about balance, and those with diabetes have to balance food, medication, and exercise to keep blood sugar levels in an acceptable range because their bodies can no longer do it for them. Some foods and activities can influence blood glucose, and it's good to know which situations will put blood sugar out of the acceptable range.

2. **Good monitoring keeps away potential problems.** Consistently high blood sugar causes complications in the eyes, kidneys, and the extremities such as hands and feet. The longer the blood sugar is high, the more severe the damage. Keeping your blood glucose in check keeps you healthy.

3. **You know the effectiveness of your medications.** By keep close tabs on your blood glucose levels, you can see how effective your medication or insulin is. If it's not working as well as it could, it's time to change meds. Talk to your doctor if you feel a switch in medication would be beneficial.

4. **Monitoring your blood glucose put you in charge.** It helps you see the trends and patterns in your blood glucose levels, such as lower when you exercise or higher when you've eaten. All this information helps you work with your doctors to find the best combination of meds, exercise, and foods for you.

5. **It helps your heart.** There is an increased risk of heart disease for people diagnosed with diabetes. To save your heart, keep your blood sugar in control to the best of your ability. Frequent blood glucose monitoring is the best tool for the job.

Learn about the metric system and how it works to your advantage in the article "Metric . . . or Not" at www.dummies.com/extras/diabetesmeal planningandnutrition.

In this part...

✔ Ease into the deeper waters of nutrition, but keep the focus squarely on the practical relationship between food and diabetes — especially carbohydrates.

✔ Learn about the advantages of regular exercise and how it lowers your blood glucose and increases your insulin.

✔ Understand how stress (or lack of it) is a huge factor in keeping your blood glucose level consistent. Do your best to lose the stress, and always make time for a little rest and relaxation. You'll be healthier for it.

✔ Learn how to incorporate protein, fat, and carbs into your diet. These can work to keep your blood glucose in check, or they can cause some serious problems.

✔ Check out all the kitchen tools and gadgets that make your life easier, from really cool electronic kitchen scales to oil misters. And while you're stocking your kitchen with tools, don't forget to read about stocking your pantry, too.

Chapter 5

Explaining Nutrition Requirements for Diabetes

....

In This Chapter

▶ Learning the diabetes ABCs

▶ Aiming for an above average A1C

▶ Deflating high blood pressure

▶ Bringing down HDL cholesterol

▶ Adjusting to special situations

....

*W*here diabetes is concerned, food is medicine.

Diabetes, both type 1 and type 2, is all about food. At the most basic level, diabetes is defined by losing the capacity to process carbohydrate food in a normal way. But, food is also the key to living healthy with diabetes, helping you control blood glucose levels and reduce your risk for diabetes complications.

This chapter describes how a nutrition plan for diabetes can keep food working for you, and details the importance of aiming to reach certain targets set for specific health markers. These targets are known as the diabetes ABCs — A1C, Blood pressure, and Cholesterol. But even though these targets are clearly associated with better outcomes, a 2004 study of people with diabetes found only 7.3 percent met target values for all of the diabetes ABCs.

This chapter gives you the outline for living in good health with diabetes, but you should see a registered dietitian personally, not only for the most precise eating plan possible for you, but also for the support and encouragement these medical professionals can offer as you make changes to protect your long-term health.

Targeting Blood Glucose Control

Before you had diabetes there were two participants working in tandem to manage your blood glucose levels. First, carbohydrate-containing food, which supplies the glucose that feeds into your bloodstream as it becomes liberated from sugar or starch molecules during digestion. Second, your pancreas, which has *beta* cells that release insulin to lower high levels of blood glucose, and *alpha* cells that release glucagon to raise low levels of blood glucose. This remarkable system kept adequate supplies of glucose stored away in muscle, fat, and liver cells for energy needs, and kept your blood glucose levels balanced in the normal range whether you had eaten recently or not.

After diabetes, this amazing system requires another participant — you. Whether you have type 1 diabetes or type 2 diabetes, your natural system for maintaining blood glucose balance needs help, and unless you're very young or otherwise incapacitated, that help has to come from you. And, taking your medication, including insulin if necessary, is an important but incomplete approach to controlling blood glucose. The main reference book for certified diabetes educators declares that patients need reminding that pharmaco- logic treatment for type 2 diabetes is only a supplement to lifestyle changes.

Matching medication and food

It's possible, with an early diagnosis and a strong commitment to lifestyle, to manage type 2 diabetes without medication. This course, however, isn't commonly the case, and type1 diabetes can't be managed without insulin. So, keeping blood glucose levels in balance almost always involves matching medication to your ingestion of carbohydrate foods. And both the volume and the timing of eating carbohydrate foods are important.

Everyone's blood glucose levels go higher after eating carbohydrate foods because it takes time to release insulin and for insulin to do its work. The objective of managing diabetes medications and food is to blunt sharp rises in blood glucose levels, and to get levels back down in a way that's close to a normal response.

When your diabetes treatment includes rapid acting or short acting (regular) insulin taken before a meal, matching medication with food can and should be done with some precision. That means people with type 1 diabetes, or those with type 2 who are taking these formulations of insulin, must know carbohy- drates. Chapter 8 addresses *carb counting*, and with some experience and care you will be able to control blood glucose levels very nicely much of the time.

The relationship between insulin and carbohydrate food is best illustrated by your specific *insulin to carbohydrate ratio* (I:C ratio). That figure is usually expressed as 1 unit of insulin to compensate for a certain number of carbohy- drate grams — 1:15, for instance, means 1 unit of insulin for every 15 grams of carbohydrate. A meal that includes 45 grams of carbohydrate would require 3 units of insulin if 1:15 is your insulin to carb ratio. However, your insulin to carb ratio is very much an individual number for you, and your I:C ratio may be different than the I:C ratio for someone else, and may even be different for your breakfast than for your lunch or dinner.

Treating diabetes with rapid or short-acting insulin also requires adjustments. If your blood glucose level is in the normal range at mealtime, your I:C ratio is all you need. But, if your blood glucose is higher than normal, whether at mealtime or not, you need to apply a correction factor. Your correction factor represents how much your blood glucose levels will drop — how many milligrams per deciliter (mg/dl) in the United States — if you take one unit of insulin without food. The number differs from person to person, and may be different according to the time of day.

The individualized numbers are never perfect, but where these insulin formulations are part of your treatment, matching the dose to your food is fairly accurate and extremely flexible.

Matching food and insulin always requires knowing your blood glucose level before you take the insulin. Overdosing results in dangerous low blood glucose levels (*hypoglycemia*), and under dosing leaves blood glucose above normal. Testing blood glucose before every meal and testing again two hours after your meal — called postprandial — helps you keep your I:C ratio and correction factors zeroed in.

Matching food and medication with this kind of precision doesn't apply to other diabetes medications, including *intermediate acting* or *long acting* insulin formulations. Even diabetes pills that are taken at mealtime aren't dose-adjusted based upon what you're eating at that meal. However, it's important to control carbohydrate consumption in a different way for optimal blood glucose control.

Your diabetes meal plan allocates your daily carbohydrate foods evenly, more or less, to each meal so that your daily dose of glucose from food doesn't all come at the same time. Your meal plan also emphasizes that you get your carbohydrates from foods that are slowly digested, like beans and fruit, rather than from added sugars that can cause blood glucose levels to spike soon after eating. Ultimately, the goal is to help you keep your blood glucose under control, and the benefits of blood glucose control are profound.

Keeping A1C in range

A1C, sometimes called hemoglobin A1C or HbA1C, is the A of the diabetes ABCs. Your doctor orders a lab test of your *hemoglobin A1C* periodically; diabetes professionals pay careful attention to this number. Dr. Rubin explains A1C in perfect detail in *Diabetes for Dummies* (John Wiley and Sons), but here are two important facts you should know now:

✔ A1C measures your average blood glucose levels over the 60 to 90 day period before the test. Even though yesterday's blood glucose level influences the A1C value more than your level 6 weeks ago — a weighted average — A1C gives the clearest picture of blood glucose control hour to hour, day to day, and week to week. This test is especially important for people with type 2 diabetes who do not frequently test their blood glucose levels at home.

✔ A1C values are closely correlated with your risk for many diabetes-related complications, like heart disease and kidney failure. In that regard, the target values set for blood glucose control by the American Diabetes Association (ADA) or the American College of Clinical Endocrinologists (ACCE) are numbers with real meaning. The ADA target is an A1C less than 7 percent, and the ACCE target is less than 6.5 percent.

Table 5-1 shows the correlation between the A1C level and weighted average blood glucose in milligrams per deciliter (mg/dl) and in millimoles per liter (mmol/l). Remember that a normal fasting blood glucose level is 99 mg/dl (5.5 mmol/l) or lower, but levels rise after eating for everyone. The A1C target values represent the level of blood glucose control those organizations view as being both achievable, and effective at minimizing the risk for complications. Highly respected studies, including the *Diabetes Control and Complications Trial* (DCCT) in the U.S. and the *United Kingdom Prospective Diabetes Study* (UKPDS), demonstrated striking reductions in the risk for complications with improved A1C values. The DCCT showed each 1 percent reduction in A1C represented a 37 percent decrease in the risk for complications of the eye, kidneys, and nerves. A recent study in Sweden tracked 12,000 people with diabetes who all began with A1C values averaging 7.8 percent. Over time, researchers grouped subjects into those with improving A1C (who eventually averaged A1C 7 percent), and those with A1C that remained the same or went higher (averaged A1C 8.4 percent). The group that gained control of blood glucose and improved their A1C showed a 40 percent decrease in the risk for cardiovascular complications and death.

Table 5-1	A1C and Average Blood Glucose Level	
A1C Value Corresponds To	*Blood Glucose mg/dl*	*Blood Glucose mmol/l*
5.0%	101 mg/dl	5.6 mmol/l
6.0%	136 mg/dl	7.6 mmol/l
6.5%*	154 mg/dl	8.6 mmol/l
7.0%**	172 mg/dl	9.6 mmol/l
8.0%	207 mg/dl	11.6 mmol/l
10.0%	279 mg/dl	15.6 mmol/l
12.0%	350 mg/dl	19.5 mmol/l

* recommended target of the American College of Clinical Endocrinologists

** recommended target of the American Diabetes Association

Controlling blood glucose levels consistently, and achieving the A1C targets, is incredibly important to your long-term health. The choices you make every day about the foods you eat will have the greatest impact on your A1C and on the quality of your future.

Losing to Win — Weight Loss

Excess weight is a distinct risk factor for type 2 diabetes, and more than 80 percent of people with type 2 diabetes are, in fact, overweight or obese. The characteristic insulin resistance associated with excess weight can complicate treatment for type 1 diabetes as well, requiring larger and larger doses of insulin, and leaving blood glucose elevated for longer periods waiting for injected insulin to take effect. A nutrition plan for effective diabetes management addresses weight loss if necessary, and modest success in this effort can bring huge rewards for blood glucose control.

Weight status is measured on a scale known as the *Body Mass Index*, or BMI for short. For most adults, BMI is an accurate representation of body fatness, and it is excess fat, for all intents and purposes, that leads to metabolic disorders like diabetes. The BMI takes both height and weight into account, and mathematically is your weight in kilograms divided by your height in meters squared — Kg/M^2. Using English measures, BMI can be calculated by taking weight in pounds divided by height in inches squared, and multiplied by 703 to account for converting to the metric basis. Therefore, for a man or woman 5'7" tall (67") weighing 200 pounds, the calculation is as follows:

$$200/ (67)(67) = 200/4489 = .0446 \times 703 = 31.35$$

On the BMI scale, values between 18.5 and 24.9 are considered normal, or healthy, weights. A value between 25 and 29.9 is considered overweight, and any value higher than 30 places the individual into an obese category. A BMI value greater than 40 is often referred to as *morbidly obese*. A 5'7" man or woman weighing 256 pounds would have a BMI value of 40.1.

More than two-thirds of the U.S. adult population falls into the overweight or obese categories, and, alarmingly, one-third of children and adolescents. And, studies consistently show that people underestimate their BMI category, suggesting that the trend toward a heavier population is affecting perception.

Excess weight is mostly the weight of excess fat, which is stored in fat cells called *adipocytes* as energy reserves. Excess calories are stored as fat, whether the calories come from protein, carbohydrate, or dietary fat, and losing weight requires that one begins drawing calories for daily living from that stored fat. In general terms, that means you must burn more calories than you consume by consuming fewer calories, burning more calories, or both. There is really no alternative strategy.

The standard formula is that a 3,500 calorie deficit is equal to one pound, so adjusting diet and activity to make a 500 calorie withdrawal from stored calories every day would lead to one pound weight loss every week. In reality, losing weight is more complicated than this simple formula, and metabolic changes can result in plateaus where weight loss tapers off.

Where diabetes is concerned, the most important thing is to get started, because a loss of only 5 to 7 percent of body weight can make a major difference in blood glucose control. The morbidly obese 5'7", 256-pound subject mentioned previously may hope for a BMI in the normal range by losing 100 pounds, but losing just 18 pounds could improve insulin sensitivity enough to make real improvements in A1C. These improvements are likely related to losing dangerous visceral fat, which accumulates around vital organs, and is the chief suspect for spreading insulin resistance from cell to cell. Visceral fat, however, goes first when a diet and exercise strategy creates a demand for stored calories.

It's worth noting that certain ethnicities, especially people of Asian descent, deposit visceral fat, and develop type 2 diabetes, at BMI values in the normal range. In these cases, weight management becomes important without regard for the standard BMI scale.

The sample week's menu provided in Chapter 17 offers options for 1,300 or 1,700 calories per day. For many people this is a diet suitable for modest weight loss, but weight management is so important to diabetes, for improving blood glucose control and preserving mobility for physical activity, that professional assistance is highly recommended. Again, a registered dietitian can make weight management an element of your medical nutrition therapy and offer the advice and encouragement you need for steady success.

Monitoring Cardiovascular Risks

Having diabetes makes you at least twice as likely as someone who does not have diabetes to have heart disease or a stroke, and you're likely to develop heart disease or have strokes at an earlier age than other people. Some studies suggest that if you've developed type 2 diabetes when middle-aged, your chance of having a heart attack is as high as someone without diabetes who has already had one heart attack. Women who have not gone through menopause usually have less risk of heart disease than men of the same age, but diabetes cancels the protective effects of being a woman in her child-bearing years. People with diabetes who have already had one heart attack run an even greater risk of having a second one. Heart attacks in people with diabetes are more serious and are more likely to result in death. Cardiovascular disease is by far the number one cause of death in people with diabetes — 65 percent of people with diabetes will die from heart attack or stroke. This is very serious stuff. The reasons for this elevated risk are many. Persistent high blood glucose levels damage the inside wall of arteries, making plaque buildup more likely. Excess weight and a sedentary lifestyle, common with type 2 diabetes, increase the risks for high blood pressure, high cholesterol levels, and high blood triglycerides. Arteries lose their flexibility, and the characteristics of the lipoproteins that carry cholesterol may even be more prone to building up on artery walls than similar particles in people without diabetes.

Both regular aerobic exercise and weight training exercise can reverse the increased cardiac risk associated with diabetes. The effect of both together is greater than the sum of the effect of each individually.

Eating habits can play a huge role in improving your increased risk for cardiovascular disease, and meal planning for diabetes management should always have heart health as one goal. Getting regular physical activity, not smoking, and reducing stress is also essential elements of an effective diabetes management lifestyle, not only for better blood glucose control, but also to further reduce cardiovascular risks.

Normalizing high blood pressure

Blood pressure is the B of the diabetes ABCs. Your circulatory system is something like the waterlines that run through your town or city, pushing water through large and small pipes with enough pressure for you to have an invigorating shower. Your arteries, veins, and tiny capillaries deliver materials, like glucose and oxygen, to cells all over your body under the pressure provided when your powerful heart muscle contracts. Water pressure is measured in pounds per square inch, but your blood pressure is measured in millimeters of mercury with a *sphygmomanometer*, and you may have seen devices that actually have a tube of mercury. Blood pressure always includes two numbers — your *systolic* pressure over your *diastolic* pressure. The *systolic* pressure is the pressure against the wall of your arteries when your heart pumps. The *diastolic* pressure is the pressure in your arteries between heart beats. A normal blood pressure is less than 120/80, and the target blood pressure for people with diabetes is 130/80 or lower.

Chronic high blood pressure, when blood pressure measures 140/90 or higher most of the time, is called *hypertension*, and hypertension is a major risk factor for heart attack, stroke, heart failure, aneurysms, peripheral artery disease, and kidney failure. These are many of the same problems that can be caused by diabetes, too, so high blood pressure added to diabetes is a real double whammy.

Dr. Rubin's book *High Blood Pressure for Dummies* (John Wiley and Sons) gives you a comprehensive review of high blood pressure, including causes and treatment, and it's likely that your doctor will prescribe medication to help control your high blood pressure if you have diabetes. However, just as lifestyle choices play a major role in managing diabetes, those same choices can have a major impact in improving your blood pressure. Exercise, not smoking, and what you choose to eat make a real difference.

The effectiveness of eating habits to reduce high blood pressure has been most effectively demonstrated in clinical trials conducted by the National Institutes of Health beginning in 1992. From those studies came an eating plan known as DASH — dietary approaches to stop hypertension — and following the DASH eating plan clearly has a direct impact in improving blood pressure. The DASH eating plan is discussed in Chapter 14, but the main ideas behind the plan are perfectly consistent with managing blood glucose — DASH concepts can fit into your diabetes eating plan. The main highlights of the DASH eating plan as follows:

- ✔ The DASH plan emphasizes lots of whole grains, vegetables, fruit, and low-fat dairy products to maximize your intake of potassium, magnesium, and calcium. DASH limits meat consumption to 6 ounces of lean protein per day.

- ✔ The DASH plan limits dietary sodium, and the more effective follow-up to original DASH studies found that a daily goal of no more than 1,500 milligrams lowered blood pressure even more. Not surprisingly, this is the same maximum sodium intake recommended for anyone with diabetes.

Of course, your use of the salt shaker adds sodium to your diet, so replacing salt with other spices is one key to reducing blood pressure with diet. But, the real secret to limiting sodium is to read nutrition facts labels, because most dietary sodium is likely to come as added salt from prepackaged or canned foods. Look for no-salt-added packaged foods.

Grains, vegetables, fruits, and low-fat dairy should definitely be part of your diabetes meal plan, but except for the nonstarchy vegetables and cheese these foods are carbohydrates. That doesn't mean you should avoid these foods — it means make these whole foods your mealtime carbohydrate choices, to control your blood glucose and your blood pressure all at once. For fabulous recipes consistent with the DASH plan, check *Hypertension Cookbook for Dummies* (John Wiley and Sons), which also provides the nutrition information for each recipe necessary to manage your carbohydrates at each meal.

Remember that nonstarchy vegetables are both incredibly healthy and very low in carbohydrate. Including lots of nonstarchy vegetables in your meal planning keeps you healthy and full.

Lowering LDL cholesterol

Cholesterol is the C in the diabetes ABCs, but this subject can be a little complicated. Cholesterol is essential for a number of cellular functions, playing important roles in building and maintaining cell membranes, synthesizing bile for fat digestion, manufacturing vitamin D, and building certain hormones. Cholesterol is ferried around in your bloodstream by special carriers called *lipoproteins*, and these lipoproteins come in assorted varieties. Low-density lipoproteins, abbreviated LDL (and commonly called bad cholesterol), circulate in the blood to deliver necessary cholesterol to cells around your body. There's nothing bad about that; however, there's a limit to how much cholesterol your cells require, and when that limit is reached your cells close down the receiving department. When cells won't take delivery of more cholesterol, LDL cholesterol continues circulating in the bloodstream where an inflammatory immune response can make it more likely that LDL particles accumulate inside of artery walls, forming waxy plaques. This process is called *atherosclerosis*, and it's the principal cause of heart and cardiovascular disease.

High-density lipoproteins, HDL (commonly called good cholesterol), seem to collect excess cholesterol from your blood, thereby reducing the risk for atherosclerosis. Target cholesterol values aimed at reducing your risk for heart disease, therefore, look at both LDL and HDL. Your medical team looks to lower your LDL while raising HDL levels with medication, exercise, and diet. With diabetes, these cholesterol targets are as follows:

- ✔ LDL levels less than 100 mg/dl (often less than 70 mg/dl if other risk factors are elevated)

- ✔ HDL levels greater than 40 mg/dl for men, and greater than 50 mg/dl for women

- ✔ Triglycerides, another blood fat, should be less than 150 mg/dl

Similar to blood glucose control and high blood pressure, lifestyle choices, like regular physical activity and not smoking, go a long way in keeping your LDL lower and your HDL higher. Diet plays a key role as well, and you should be seeing a consistent pattern by now about how these same lifestyle choices preserve your health on several fronts.

Objective number one for controlling cholesterol is to reduce saturated fat in your diet and eliminate trans fat. That's why healthy diets, including the eating plan that help you manage blood glucose levels, encourage lean cuts of meat and healthy cooking methods like baking, broiling, grilling, or steaming, which don't add fat. Highly processed meats that are high in fat should be eaten in moderation, and trans fats should be avoided because they raise LDL and lower HDL.

Healthy eating isn't completely about what you shouldn't eat, but is equally about what you should eat. For cholesterol management, eat soluble fiber, like the fiber in oats, beans, and barley, and eat lots of fruits and vegetables, especially the leafy greens. Unless there's a reason your doctor says you shouldn't, have alcohol in moderation to help raise HDL. And fish, which is high in omega-3 fatty acids, can raise HDL and make an enviable dinner.

Insulin resistance (including type 2 diabetes), high blood pressure, and high levels of LDL cholesterol are key elements of a broadly defined medical condition known as the *metabolic syndrome*. Although people with metabolic syndrome may not have diabetes, these and other abnormalities associated with metabolic syndrome — such as an increased tendency to form clots and evidence of increased inflammation — are all associated with increased heart attacks. Improvement in lifestyle with a better diet and more exercise is the first step in reversing metabolic syndrome, just as it is for diabetes.

Considering Some Special Circumstances

People with diabetes are people first, so they span the entire spectrum of what people are, from babies to the elderly, from Olympic athletes to the sedentary, and virtually everything else you can imagine. Some circumstances may deserve special consideration when it comes to diet, however. These common scenarios should be addressed individually with a specialized medical team, but a broad overview may interest you.

Children

Type 1 diabetes can strike children at almost any age, and type 1 diabetes always requires insulin injections matched with carbohydrate intake to balance blood glucose levels. Although the foundation of maintaining long-term health in spite of diabetes is *self-management*, young children are unable to take on that responsibility. Therefore, with type 1 diabetes in children, parents or other caretakers must play the primary role in balancing food and insulin, and experts suggest that some parental oversight is important into the teen years as well.

The biggest concern with children taking insulin, and especially young children, is severe hypoglycemia, or low blood glucose. There is evidence that hypoglycemic events can do permanent damage to young, developing brains, and avoiding such occurrences may require frequent blood glucose monitoring, and eating on demand — getting toddlers to do anything on demand can be challenging. Unpredictable activity levels can make blood glucose control even more challenging.

Ultimately, kids and adolescents are growing, and it takes adequate food with adequate nutrients to support this rapid growth. Because tight blood glucose control is so difficult, A1C targets for children and adolescents are set higher than for adults. For children under six, where hypoglycemia can be so dangerous, an A1C less than 8.5 percent is considered satisfactory. The

A1C target is gradually brought in line with the recommendation for adults as teens become adults.

Type 2 diabetes in children has become much more common in recent years as childhood obesity rates have risen sharply, and these children may also have high blood pressure and high cholesterol levels. Because children have unique dietary requirements to support growth, it's extra important that a diet and exercise program for diabetes self-management involve a medical team with a registered dietitian. A recent study, conducted by the National Institute of Diabetes and Digestive and Kidney Diseases, compared the effectiveness of common type 2 diabetes pills for controlling blood glucose levels in children 10 to 17 years of age. The results showed that these medications were much less effective in children, suggesting that insulin therapy early in the course of type 2 diabetes in children may be the most effective long-term option for preserving health.

Recommendations are that diabetes management support when children are involved must include the entire family, and should include frequent contact with the family and patient to assure that a satisfactory pattern of diabetes management is adopted.

Elderly

The incidence of type 2 diabetes is highest in the senior population, as high as 20 percent of the population over 65, and managing diabetes in seniors does present its own set of challenges. Plus, management is important because people aged 65 have the potential for 20 or more additional years of quality living. Diabetes complications can certainly develop in that span of time, plus seniors with diabetes may well bring other risk factors, like high blood pressure and elevated cholesterol, into the mix.

Effective diabetes management for healthy seniors is not terribly different than for younger adults, keeping a focus on controlling blood glucose, blood pressure, and cholesterol with medication, exercise, and diet. Adequate calcium and vitamin D are necessary for bone health, and seniors do need to manage weight. Typically, a loss of muscle mass and added body fat comes with aging, and added fat can increase insulin resistance.

Preparing healthy meals at home is something seniors may tend to do less often, and eating out frequently makes healthy eating a special challenge. Seniors diagnosed later in life also find that selecting carbohydrate choices from an exchange list, where specific foods and serving sizes are detailed, is easier than carbohydrate counting. Appendix A provides an exhaustive list of exchanges.

Treating diabetes in elderly adults who are frail or mentally impaired is the greatest challenge, complicated by multiple health conditions and drugs, an undependable memory, a lack of mobility for beneficial exercise, changes in normal metabolism, and inconsistent help by caregivers. Treatment decisions often aim primarily at avoiding the potential for low blood glucose, and dietary concerns may require a greater focus on malnutrition than on blood glucose control.

Individualizing treatment is especially important for seniors. The ADA sets a goal of a hemoglobin A1C in order to prevent long-term complications. Because these may take 20 years to develop, intensive measures to get A1C to target levels may be unnecessary. The increased hypoglycemia that accompanies treating to a hemoglobin A1C of 7 is unnecessary in that individual.

Athletes

Exercise is a crucial element of effective diabetes self-management, and something most people with diabetes don't do enough. The case with athletes, however, is the opposite — more than normal levels of exercise. And, the dietary challenge is in balancing the calorie and carbohydrate requirements for energy with safe blood glucose levels, both during athletic activity, and in between training or competition. Maintaining safe blood glucose levels means avoiding both extremely low and extremely high blood glucose levels, both of which are risks.

A low blood glucose level, called hypoglycemia, can occur when exercise depletes glucose stored in muscle and liver cells, and insulin is still available. A high blood glucose level, called hyperglycemia, can happen when there is inadequate insulin available to move glucose into cells. Both conditions can be dangerous. Excessively low blood glucose deprives the brain of the glucose it needs to manage everything that goes on in your body. High blood glucose levels require muscle cells to burn fat, and the buildup of waste products called ketones can turn blood dangerously acidic in athletes with type 1 diabetes. Intense exercise can affect blood glucose levels not only during activity, but for hours afterwards.

The key to balancing blood glucose and carbohydrates in athletes is monitoring blood glucose levels frequently — before, after, and, if possible, during intense activities. Blood glucose monitoring during normal activities as well helps establish routine energy needs necessary to support the more extreme activity level.

Celiac and gluten sensitivity

Like type 1 diabetes, *celiac disease* is an immune system glitch, where a person's own immune system attacks the lining of the small intestine in response to a protein found in grains called *gluten*. Damage to the intestinal lining can interfere with the normal absorption of vitamins and minerals, and even carbohydrates needed for energy. Having type 1 diabetes increases the likelihood of having celiac disease, or a less severe gluten sensitivity, with estimates putting the risk at 5 to 10 times higher than the general population.

Celiac Disease for Dummies (John Wiley and Sons) provides a comprehensive review of this autoimmune condition, but the challenge for people with diabetes and celiac is diet — specifically, grains. The only effective treatment for celiac disease is strictly following a gluten-free diet, and even though the market for gluten-free products is rapidly expanding, balancing two different eating plans can be burdensome. The best choices for whole grains when managing diabetes and celiac disease, or an unspecified gluten sensitivity, are brown rice, quinoa, amaranth, or gluten-free oats. Support from a registered dietitian can be helpful in establishing an eating plan for effectively managing both conditions.

Gastroparesis

Gastroparesis means stomach paralysis, but in practical terms it's a potential complication of diabetes resulting from damage to the nerve that controls stomach emptying — gastroparesis is an *autonomic neuropathy* which causes your stomach to empty slowly. The general problem where gastroparesis is concerned is the disruption of normal eating patterns, and the potential for inadequate calories, insufficient macronutrients, vitamin and mineral deficiencies, and even dehydration from lack of fluids. Food high in fiber, like grains, fruits, and vegetables, can be especially difficult to eat, (digest) and so are meats and high-fat foods.

Managing gastroparesis can include eating smaller, but more frequent, meals, getting some essential nutrients from liquids, and eating pureed food. It's essential to balance these dietary changes with diabetes medication, and the nutrition requirements for blood glucose control. Again, guidance from a registered dietitian is critical.

Kidney failure

Poorly controlled diabetes is the leading cause of kidney failure, followed closely by high blood pressure, also too common among people with type 2 diabetes. Your kidneys filter waste products from your blood, including excess glucose, and high blood glucose levels over time cause kidney damage that reduces their filtration capacity. This damage is referred to as the complication *nephropathy*. Controlling blood glucose levels can help prevent nephropathy from advancing to kidney failure, but when the filtration rate (called GFR for *glomuler filtration rate*) of your kidneys is degraded to a point considered to be kidney failure, a special diet is necessary to delay progression.

In the earlier stages of kidney disease it's likely that your diet limits protein amounts and provides only high-quality protein. This diet also assures adequate fat and carbohydrates provide for your energy needs so that protein is not metabolized for energy.

When kidney disease progresses to end stage, where dialysis or a kidney transplant is necessary, your diet restricts fluids, phosphorous, sodium, potassium, and protein. This diet requires a registered dietitian with input from a specialized kidney doctor called a *nephrologist*. Dr. Rubin's book *Diabetes for Dummies* (John Wiley and Sons) gives a complete overview of this long-term complication, but the take home message about kidney failure is that controlling blood glucose, blood pressure, and LDL cholesterol from the early stages of your diabetes can go a long way in saving you from confronting this very difficult complication.

Chapter 6

Meeting the Macronutrients — Protein, Fat, and Carbohydrates

The term *macro* means big, and macronutrients are certainly of big importance. But the term *macro* is used when referring to protein, fat, and carbohydrate primarily because you need them in big amounts. The macronutrients are what build you, protect you, and fuel your many activities. And the macronutrients store energy you know as calories.

In this chapter you learn why protein, fat, and carbohydrates are so important, and how your body has a specialized demolition crew ready to deconstruct each of the three macronutrients into its absorbable components so you can build what you need from the pieces.

The quality and quantity of macronutrients is important to diabetes, and to overall health. And, because you get the majority of your macronutrients from food, your meal planning lessons in this chapter gives you a little what and why, as well as the where, which, and how much about each of these three essential nutrients.

Building with Protein for Diabetes Management

Proteins are extraordinarily complex, and the blueprint for assembling all of the proteins you require is coded into your DNA. Protein molecules are primarily chains of amino acids, and the chains can include many thousands of amino acid molecules, making some proteins very large. One of the most interesting points about proteins, however, is their *secondary* and *tertiary* structure (the specific sequence of different amino acids is a protein's *primary* structure). Secondary structures are loops and turns in the amino acid chain, and a tertiary structure is sometimes called by the more descriptive word *folding*. The shape of protein molecules given by these complex geometric shapes equips the molecules for their particular functions.

zroteins are the jacks of all trades in human biology. Proteins are especially efficient in binding tightly to other molecules, often assisted by pocket-shaped depressions in the protein molecule created by its special folding pattern. The following describes some of the more important functions and roles of protein in your body:

✔ Protein is necessary for growth, critical for children, teens, and pregnant women, but important to everyone in this regard for tissue repair.

✔ Protein provides structure, both on a cellular level to help maintain cellular shape and on a whole body scale where protein makes up hair, nails, tendons, and ligaments.

✔ Special *motor* proteins are responsible for the contraction of muscle cells. Muscles are the largest accumulation of proteins in your body, and remember that it's specialized muscles that pump your blood and move air into and out of your lungs — important stuff, to say the least.

✔ Proteins called *enzymes* speed up chemical reactions, and include the digestive enzyme pepsin, which works specifically to break down protein. The function of enzymes to facilitate and accelerate chemical reactions is crucial to life, and as many as 4,000 enzyme involved biochemical reactions have been identified.

✔ Proteins serve as transporters and messengers. Antibody proteins, part of your immune system, capture and hold foreign bodies, including bacteria and viruses, and hemoglobin transports oxygen to cells around the body. Important protein hormones, like insulin, send signals to cells — insulin signals cells to allow glucose molecules to pass through the cell membrane, and it's a pretty important function with diabetes.

That's an impressive list of responsibilities, and gives a glimpse into why protein in your diet is so important. It's necessary to have all the right raw materials available to keep all of your working proteins in production. A diabetes-focused diet typically recommends 20 percent of calories from protein — that's about 75 grams per day for a 1,500-calories-per-day eating plan.

Researchers looking for the infectious agent in Creutzfeldt-Jakob disease, the human form of what's more popularly known in cattle as Mad Cow disease, were puzzled by being unable to detect any of the genetic material common to disease causing agents like bacteria or virus, which allows them to replicate themselves. Eventually, the cause of this group of diseases was determined to be a mis-folded protein now called a *prion*. This brain disease, which is 100 percent fatal, seems to progress not by self replication of the prion, but rather when the mis-folded prion protein influences other normal proteins to mis-fold as well.

Recycling amino acids from food

Amino acid molecules are what characterize proteins. Amino acids primarily consist of carbon, hydrogen, and oxygen like most *organic* compounds, but always include nitrogen in what's called an amino group. Many of the proteins in your body turn over rapidly, degrading into their amino acid constituents. An average adult may turn over 250 grams of protein every day, mostly from muscle. Some of the amino acids are reincorporated into new protein, and some is burned as energy (protein stores 4 calories of energy per gram). The nitrogen becomes a waste product from protein burned for energy, and is excreted in urine as *urea*. This constant turnover is why protein is such an important part of your diet — new amino acids are always necessary to build new protein. Your dietary protein recommendations are calculated to resupply amino acids for rebuilding protein that has been burned for energy, or otherwise lost.

Hundreds of specific amino acids have been identified, but only 20 are specifically coded into human DNA for inclusion in protein assembly. Other amino acids do play important roles in metabolism, however. Your body can actually produce some of the 20 protein coded amino acids from other amino acids, or from protein degradation products. But you cannot produce 9 of the 20, and these are, therefore, called *essential amino acids*. These amino acids must be acquired from food.

Table 6-1 lists the nine essential (indispensable) amino acids, nine nonessential (or dispensable) amino acids, and two conditionally nonessential amino acids. These two amino acids can normally be assembled from available materials, but under some circumstances cannot. The categorization in Table 6-1 represents the requirements for adults.

Table 6-1	Essential and Nonessential Amino Acids
Essential Amino Acids	**Nonessential Amino Acids**
Isoleucine	Alanine
Leucine	Arginine
Lysine	Aspartic acid
Methionine	Asparagine
Phenylalanine	Glutamic acid
Threonine	Glutamine
Tryptophan	Glycine
Valine	Proline
Histidine	Serine
	Cysteine*
	Tyrosine*

* Conditionally nonessential

Managing diabetes with diet includes getting an adequate intake of high quality protein in your diet to maintain important muscle mass, and to keep important metabolic functions humming along. The highest quality protein has amino acids which are readily available, and easily absorbed, during digestion. Some foods, called *complete protein* foods, contain all of the essential amino acids in sufficient amounts. Foods that don't contain all nine essential amino acids are called *incomplete*, and the missing essential amino acids are called the *limiting* amino acid. Lysine, threonine, and tryptophan are the most common limiting amino acids.

Finding animal sources of protein

Nutrition researchers can give protein sources a score, based upon the abundance of essential amino acids, relative abundance of nonessential amino acids, the digestibility of the protein food, and the presence of allergens or compounds that inhibit amino acid accessibility. In the scoring contest, animal sources of protein win, hands down.

Using a measure known as *relative biological value,* eggs, fish and shellfish, chicken, beef, and milk are all the overachievers. But virtually all sources of animal protein can be considered high quality, strictly looking at the protein component. Animal sources of protein tend to be of higher quality, complete with respect to essential amino acids, and digestible, because we share similar metabolic processes. One notable exception is gelatin, which is typically made from bones, hide, or connective tissue, and does not include the essential amino acid tryptophan.

Harvesting plant sources of protein

As a rule, plant proteins are not complete proteins, containing all of the essential amino acids in suitable amounts. Plant protein also tends to be less accessible in digestion, ultimately scoring lower on scales rating biological value or amino acid content. It's perfectly possible to get all the necessary amino acids in a vegetarian (vegan) diet, but generally requires consuming complementary foods over the course of the day, where one food provides an adequate source of the amino acid that is deficient in the other. There is one notable exception to that generalization, however — soy.

The soy bean, often served green as edamame or prepared as tofu, is a high-quality and complete protein. Four ounces of edamame or tofu will give you 14 grams of high quality protein, twice the protein of a large egg or 8 ounce glass of milk. Incorporating soy into a vegetarian or vegan diet can assure that all essential amino acids are consumed in sufficient amount.

Many other plant sources of protein are available as well. Beans and other legumes, nuts, and grains all can contribute to daily protein requirements. The grain quinoa offers 6 grams of protein in a ¼ cup (dry) serving, for instance, and a healthy diet should always include plant sources of protein. Vegetarians who do not consume eggs or milk and vegans do need to get protein from a variety of complementary sources to assure they get a complete range of essential amino acids, or learn to love soy.

Leaning toward lean — a diabetes priority

Here's the thing about animal sources of protein — they almost always come with a dose of unhealthy saturated fat, plus some dietary cholesterol. And, because diabetes significantly increases your risk for heart disease, eating in a heart-healthy way by limiting saturated fats and cholesterol is an important assignment for maintaining your overall health. Fat, as a macronutrient, is discussed in more detail in the next section.

You can reduce the fat content of the meat and dairy products you eat by making simple choices. For example, remove the skin from poultry, select leaner cuts of beef and pork (and trim excess fat), buy 90 percent lean ground beef or ground turkey, use low-fat or nonfat milk, cheese, and other dairy products, and eat especially fatty meats like bacon and pastrami only in moderation. Balancing the rich source of protein in meat and dairy products with saturated fat is one reason to look for some of your protein from plant sources, and your grocery will offer a variety ever-improving of meat substitutes from soy, flavored and textured for uses reserved for meat.

Figuring Out Fats for Heart Health

Dietary fat is kind of complicated. To start with, the proper terminology would be *lipids* — lipids include both oils and solid fats. But lipid is a technical term not used too often in dietary jargon, so just remember that the term fat includes oils, too (remember lipid, however, for a discussion about fat imbalance later).

You may be under the impression that fat should be eliminated completely from your diet, but if you could do that, and it wouldn't be easy, you would soon find that you're having skin problems, weakened bones, vision issues, and maybe even trouble thinking. Fats are an essential part of your diet, and with diabetes it's likely your meal plan recommends that you get 25 to 35 percent of your calories from fat. Too much of the wrong kind of fat, however, has clearly negative health implications.

Most of the fat you get from foods comes in the form of *triglycerides*, which is glycerol chemically bound to three individual fatty acids. Fats are *hydrophobic*, meaning they don't mix with water, and you probably know that already, having looked at salad dressings where the oil has separated. This property makes fat digestion a little tricky, but the enzyme bile works to break fat globs into smaller bit so *lipase* can detach the fatty acids. Fat digestion and absorption takes place primarily in the small intestine, and the free fatty acids are absorbed into the blood stream of the lymph system, depending upon the molecule size.

You may already know *glycerol*, the molecule that binds the fatty acids as triglycerides in your diet, from your soap, shaving cream, or other personal care products. It often goes by the alias *glycerin* in its more glamorous roles.

Fats, or fatty acids, are chained, organic molecules with the typical carbon and hydrogen elements, and depending upon how many hydrogen atoms are included, a fat is either saturated (with hydrogen) or unsaturated. Saturated fats are solid at room temperature, whereas unsaturated fats are liquid, and unsaturated fats are generally healthier in your diet.

Going beyond insulation

Most people have a good idea where some of the fats from food go when they've been absorbed into the body. *Adipocytes* (fat cells) store fat in layers beneath your skin for cushioning and insulating your entire body, and you've likely noticed that some people have more fat in storage than others. Men and women also tend to accumulate stored fat in different areas, giving adults distinctly different shapes.

But fat is doing a lot more than just lounging around looking cuddly. Adipose cells actually release some hormones, including *leptin*, a hormone that signals the brain when you've had enough to eat. Key vitamins, including vitamins A, D, E, and K, are *fat soluble* and transported to cells by fat molecules. Your brain is about 60 percent fat, and fat in the material that insulates nerves, called *myelin*, helps protect the electrical signals from interference. Fats constitute a part of every cells membrane, and fat can segregate toxins.

Fat also stores energy, and the role of fat for producing energy is relevant to diabetes. You have already heard in previous chapters how glucose, a carbohydrate, is your body's favored fuel for energy production. But you store a relatively limited amount of glucose in muscle, fat, and liver cells. When glucose isn't available, your cells can convert fat into energy. Fat molecules store 9 calories per gram of fat, more than twice as much energy, twice as many calories per gram, as either carbohydrate or protein. The byproduct of burning fat, however, is compounds called ketones, and if the concentration of ketone wastes becomes too great, blood can turn dangerously acidic. *Ketoacidosis* from excess ketones can be fatal, and is a risk for people with type 1 diabetes where glucose isn't available to cells because insulin concentrations are insufficient. Ketoacidosis is common at diagnosis, when natural insulin production suddenly stops, and therapeutic insulin has not been initiated, but can occur anytime blood glucose levels get very high due to an imbalance of blood glucose and insulin.

Highlighting unsaturated fat

Most all fat containing foods are a mixture of saturated and unsaturated fats, but if less than one third of the fats are saturated, the fat or oil can be considered unsaturated. Monounsaturated fats and polyunsaturated fats are healthier fats in your diet than saturated fats, and it's recommended that two thirds of your daily fat consumption be from unsaturated fats. Unsaturated fats include the well-known omega-3 fatty acid, which means a double carbon bond is on the third carbon in the fatty acid chain.

The health benefits related to unsaturated fat are both in the reduction of the risk for cardiovascular disease, and for diabetes management. Unsaturated fats improve the ratios between bad LDL cholesterol and good HDL cholesterol (see discussion of cholesterol in the next section), and polyunsaturated fat is associated with improved insulin sensitivity. The health benefits of unsaturated fats first gained attention from the Seven Countries Study, which is described in Chapter 14's section on the Mediterranean diet.

Table 6-2 provides a list of dietary sources for unsaturated fat, and notes whether the food is predominately a source of monounsaturated or polyunsaturated fatty acids.

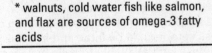

Table 6-2	Dietary Sources of Monounsaturated and Polyunsaturated Fats	
Monounsaturated Fatty Acids	*Polyunsaturated Fatty Acids*
Olive oil	Soybean oil
Almonds, peanuts	Walnuts*
Canola oil	Corn oil
Avocado	Salmon*
Sesame seeds	Flax*
* walnuts, cold water fish like salmon, and flax are sources of omega-3 fatty acids	

Some research hypothesizes that an imbalance between unsaturated omega-6 fatty acids and omega-3 fatty acids can actually increase general inflammation and chronic disease risk. Although both are polyunsaturated fatty acids, the so-called Western diet tends toward more than a ten-fold higher intake of omega-6 fats over the omega-3 fats. The difference is attributed to some extent to the high consumption of omega-6 fats from corn oil and soybean oil in processed and convenience foods. The jury is still out.

Watching out for saturated fat and cholesterol

Saturated fats are carbon chains with no double bonds between the carbon atoms, therefore the molecule is saturated with hydrogen bonds. *Trans fats* result when unsaturated fats are *hydrogenated*, making the fat saturated. Saturated fats are generally solid at room temperature, and hydrogenation of food products like stick margarine was specifically for this purpose.

Current recommendations are to limit saturated fats less than 7 percent of daily calories, and to strictly limit trans fat to less than 1 percent of daily calories. The reservations about saturated fat relate historically to the relationship of elevated blood cholesterol level to cardiovascular disease, especially to the buildup of waxy plaque in arteries (atherosclerosis). More recently, the focus on your total cholesterol level has evolved.

Cholesterol is a type of fat called a *sterol*, and it has several crucial and necessary roles in your biology including roles in the production of vitamin D, testosterone, and estrogen. Cholesterol is manufactured in your cells, but can also be a taken in, along with saturated fat, from foods of animal origin. Where the total cholesterol level was formerly viewed as the measure most significant to heart disease risks, the focus now is redirected at the difference between the particles which ferry cholesterol around in the blood — lipoproteins. In that regard, references to bad LDL cholesterol and good HDL cholesterol actually refers to the *low density lipoprotein* or *high density lipoprotein* particles transporting cholesterol, not to cholesterol itself. And, from the perspective of heart disease risk, it is the levels of LDL, and the ratio of LDL to HDL that seem most significant. Saturated fats, and especially the manufactured trans fats, raise LDL levels and lower HDL levels, and LDLs tend to form arterial plaques whereas HDLs actually remove plaque forming materials.

The research on these issues is always ongoing, and inconsistencies always show up in complicated studies of human diet and health, often related to the difficulty in excluding other potential health factors unrelated to diet. There is solid agreement on the dangers of trans fat, which clearly raises LDL and lowers HDL. There is general agreement that reducing saturated fat is beneficial, but especially beneficial if the calories are replaced by adding monounsaturated fat, like olive oil, instead of adding additional carbohydrates.

With diabetes, polyunsaturated fats have a favorable impact on insulin sensitivity, and trans fats are especially unfavorable. Interestingly, regular consumption of red meat is associated with an increased risk for type 2 diabetes, and the risk is even greater for processed red meat.

Finally, *hyperlipidemia* (there's the lipid word) is the medical term describing abnormally high levels of lipids (fats) in blood — hyperlipidemia is an element of metabolic syndrome. Managing your level of blood lipids is important for managing the risk for diabetes complications. Current target values are LDL lower than 100 milligrams/deciliter (mg/dl), HDL higher than 40 mg/dl for men and 50 mg/dl for women, and triglycerides lower than 150 mg/dl. Triglycerides are a blood fat not as specifically related to fat in the diet.

Energizing with Carbohydrates — The Foundation of a Diabetes Diet

Carbohydrates, specifically molecules of the carbohydrate glucose, are your body's favored fuel, and even though your cells can, and do, extract energy from protein and fat, glucose is choice numero uno. Glucose enters your bloodstream after you eat carbohydrates through absorption sites in your small intestine, and the rising glucose level in your blood signals special *beta* cells in the pancreas to release the hormone insulin. Insulin stimulates cells, especially muscle, fat, and liver cells, to allow glucose molecules to pass through cell membranes where it can be stored inside of these cells for fuel when needed.

Cells store glucose in a molecule called *glycogen*, and glycogen is ready at a moment's notice to jump into a metabolic cycle that spits out the power pack molecule *adenosine triphosphate* (ATP), the real fuel for everything requiring energy. Glycogen is your most accessible source of energy, and carbohydrates in your diet keep the supplies ready when needed.

The role of carbohydrates in your body is not limited to energy, by the way, although diabetes tends to focus attention on that role. Glycolipids (glucose plus lipids) are a component of cell membranes, glycoproteins help protect your sensitive tissues with mucus, and the five carbon sugar ribose is a component of DNA. The sugar lactose is produced in the milk of nursing mothers, and helps humans and animals get the energy needed for growth, temperature regulation, and strenuous activity like crying.

Milk sugar is the only significant carbohydrate component of your diet that is from an animal source, however, and most adults lose the ability to digest lactose. Plants are your carbohydrate factories, and you can thank plant carbohydrates for the wood that built your house, and for the fuel you need every day to run your body. And many plant foods that contain carbohydrates also happen to come along with essential vitamins, minerals, antioxidants, and other compounds that work to keep you healthy.

Carbohydrate stores 4 calories of potential energy per gram, and excess carbohydrate in your diet is stored as fat. Excess consumption of carbohydrate, especially fructose, can also act to raise levels of low density lipoproteins, the so-called bad LDL cholesterol, and blood triglycerides.

High-fructose corn syrup gets its share of bad press, but in reality the fructose content of the most common formulation of this commercial sweetener, used in soft drinks, is only 5 percent higher than table sugar. Sucrose, table sugar, is one molecule of glucose bound to one molecule of fructose — 50 percent fructose.

Beyond being an important macronutrient for energy and nutrients, dietary carbohydrates are overwhelmingly the macronutrient most related to blood glucose levels. And, whether your love for carbohydrates and the calories they provide was important in contributing to your risk for diabetes or not, carbohydrates are certainly important now. Both type 1 and type 2 diabetes are characterized by blood glucose levels that don't come back into normal balance after eating carbohydrate foods.

In type 1 diabetes your body loses the capacity to produce insulin, whereas in type 2 diabetes the cells needed for glucose storage become resistant to the influence of insulin. In both cases, your normal processes for converting food to energy are disrupted. A certain level of blood glucose is necessary to supply cells that don't store glucose, like brain cells, with fuel whenever it's needed. But over time, persistently higher-than-normal levels of blood glucose damage tissues and significantly raise the risk for heart attack, stroke, nerve damage, vision loss, kidney failure, and other negative health impacts, innocently called complications. Controlling blood glucose with diabetes is a balancing act, and you're the acrobat.

Your task after a diabetes diagnosis is to manage your intake of carbohydrates is a way that keeps those variations in blood glucose levels close to normal. Your meal plan recommends you get as much as 50 percent of your daily calories from carbohydrate foods, but not all *carbs* are created equal. Carbohydrates include simple sugars like glucose, and also sugar molecules joined in chains that form starches and fiber. Depending on how quickly the carbohydrates you eat are broken down during digestion and on the mix of carbs with other macronutrients when you eat, blood glucose can rise very rapidly or very slowly. Managing your diabetes means managing carbohydrates.

Sugar and diabetes — sweet or sour?

In one way it would make more sense to talk about sugar last in this discussion about carbohydrate, because the story of carbohydrate in your diet often doesn't start with sugar, but that's where the story usually ends. But, because diabetes has a prominent part in the story, starting at the end might work better.

Virtually everyone knows that sugar has something to do with diabetes — sugar diabetes, the sugar, or a touch of the sugar are all colloquial phrases that mean diabetes in some communities. *Blood sugar* is a common phrase substituted for the more precise *blood glucose*. Sugar affects diabetes, but sugar's role in diabetes may not match what you think of when you hear the word *sugar*.

To you, sugar most likely means common table sugar. To biologists and chemists, the word *sugar* describes a particular kind of organic molecule belonging to a category of similar molecules called *carbohydrates*. Carbohydrates — the word actually means carbon with water — often follow the formula $C-H_2O$, and the numbers of carbons and hydrogens and oxygens can go into many thousands when joined together. Sugars are the simplest carbohydrates, and in the world of food, the simplest of the simple sugar molecules are called *monosaccharides*. Glucose and fructose are two monosaccharides that may be familiar to you.

Disaccharides, which are two monosaccharides joined together, include *sucrose*, common table sugar, the milk sugar *lactose*, and *maltose*, a sugar familiar to beer drinkers. Table sugar is one molecule of glucose, and one molecule of fructose. *Oligosaccharides*, containing up to ten monosaccharides in a chain, are common in legumes like beans.

Carbohydrate digestion works to break chains of sugar molecules into their monosaccharide building blocks. In your diet, simple sugars and disaccharides can be absorbed rapidly, and the glucose component can have an immediate effect on blood glucose levels. When sugars are not naturally packaged in their original state like an apple or a beet — added sugars like sucrose — sole nutritional benefit is in the calories. But, in an affluent society, added sugars usually add up to excess calories, and with diabetes in the equation the rapid rise in blood glucose levels makes control more difficult.

Even among individuals without diabetes, this spiking of blood glucose and insulin levels seems to have long term consequences. And diets high in excess, added sugar clearly contribute to obesity and increase the risk for diabetes and heart disease.

The bottom line on sugar is that it's best eaten in its natural form, for example from fruit, instead of as a refined, added sweetener. Longer-chained saccharides, like the oligosaccharides in legumes, are another excellent dietary source of sugars. And, another carbohydrate group that you're familiar with can be an important contributor to the glucose you need for energy.

Making a chain — complex carbohydrates

As the number of chained together molecules of simple sugars gets longer, the carbohydrate foods are sometimes called complex. Starches are where plants store their excess glucose, and the chemical bonds connecting the simple sugars in starch are easily broken by your digestive system.

Whereas starches can be refined and isolated from their source for dietary purposes like sugar, its use is usually limited to thickening agents like corn starch. You are much more likely to get your dietary starch from the whole food, because starch itself is relatively tasteless. Starches are prevalent in potatoes, corn, peas, beans, lentils, hard shell squashes, quinoa, rice, wheat, barley, oats, and the flours and refined products from grains. Because starches are packaged with protein, fat, and fiber, and because the chain length of simple sugars is more complex, starches often have a less dramatic impact in blood glucose levels.

The *glycemic index* of foods, discussed in Chapter 8, compares the impact of various carbohydrate foods on blood glucose levels using a scale where pure glucose equals a value of 100. Foods with a value exceeding 70 have what's considered a high glycemic index, where foods with a value lower than 55 are assigned a low glycemic index value. Table 6-3 compares the glycemic index of common foods.

Table 6-3	Glycemic Index Value of Selected Carbohydrate Foods
Food	**Glycemic Index Value**
Glucose	100
Baked potato	85
White bread (wheat flour)	72
Lentils	29
Edamame (green soy beans)	18

It's apparent from Table 6-3 that not all starches impact blood glucose modestly. A baked potato and refined wheat flour give up their glucose quickly. But some starches are more resistant to digestion, and foods that also include protein, fat, or fiber slow the digestive process as well. Some diabetes medications, in fact, work in inhibiting the absorption of glucose during digestion, reducing the impact of all carbohydrates on blood glucose.

In your diet, starches must be managed. The glycemic index values are derived from the blood glucose response of individuals without diabetes, and, therefore, take into account the timing and effectiveness of a natural insulin response. But foods that impact blood glucose more modestly in healthy people will also make blood glucose levels easier to control in people with diabetes. Plus, starchy foods bring a range of tastes, texture, and color to your diet, along with vitamins and other essential nutrients you can't go without. Starchy foods also bring important fiber, which is not only important to you, but also to an army of beneficial microorganisms that call your digestive system home.

It's important to mention nonstarchy vegetables in this discussion about complex carbohydrates. Nonstarchy vegetables contain much less carbohydrate than the starchy ones, and in that regard are essential parts of diabetes management by contributing volume without fat, and by having a reduced impact on blood glucose. Greens of all varieties, peppers, cucumber, summer squashes, green beans, carrots, broccoli, cauliflower, artichoke, turnips, fennel, and asparagus are a few of the nonstarchy vegetables that can color your plate and deliver vitamins and healthy phytonutrients to your body.

Fantastic fiber

Fiber is the most complex of carbohydrates, often forming the structural elements of plants. Fiber is relatively indigestible by humans, but is still an extremely important part of your diet. Insoluble fiber provides bulk, which helps to move food residues through your digestive system. But some fiber — soluble fiber — also has beneficial physiological effects. The most accepted benefit of soluble fiber is in lowering bad LDL cholesterol levels — oat bran is well recognized for this benefit, and beans are a tasty source of soluble fiber, too.

Specific benefits to health from the fiber component of your diet are challenging to isolate because foods that offer fiber are also rich in biologically active phytochemicals and antioxidants. But having adequate fiber in your diet may lower blood pressure, reduce the risk for some colorectal and breast cancers, improve your immune system, and improve blood glucose control.

Americans typically consume only about 15 grams of fiber per day, but the recommended daily consumption is 25 grams for women between 19 and 50 years of age, and 38 grams per day for men in that age range. The recommended amount decreases for both men and women over 50, but the more the merrier. While a huge volume of fiber could lead to digestive irritation, if you can tolerate more fiber, get more fiber.

Fiber only comes with plant-based foods, but you can increase your fiber consumption by making different choices. For instance, white bread from refined flour only contains one third the fiber of whole wheat bread — brown rice contains almost six times more fiber as white rice. Oatmeal, beans, and peas are excellent sources of fiber too. Remember that grains, beans, and peas are also starchy, and need to be accounted for in your diet to control blood glucose.

Nonstarchy vegetables, while not necessarily high in fiber, are very low in carbohydrate, and come with a load of assorted nutrients as well. These foods can, and should, be eaten liberally for their nutrition content, their modest effect on blood glucose due to their low carbohydrate content, and for adding more fiber to your daily intake.

Chapter 7

Reading the Fine Print: Micronutrients

You've heard the phrase *big things come in small packages* — that would be a perfect description for micronutrients. *Micro* comes from the Greek word *mikrós*, which means small, as in microscopic. In nutrition, the word *micronutrients* refers to vitamins and other compounds that are essential to your health, but only in very, very small amounts. Where your dietary needs for the macronutrients protein, fat, and carbohydrates are calculated in grams per day, the daily requirements for micronutrients is in milligrams (mg) or even micrograms (mcg or µg). There are 1,000 milligrams or 1,000,000 micrograms in one gram.

If you're not familiar with metric measures, however, these are just abstract numbers. Even 1 gram is smaller than most familiar English measures — there are 28.35 grams in one ounce. To visualize the relative scale of micronutrient requirements, imagine for a minute that a 15,000-pound bull African elephant, standing more than 10 feet tall at his shoulders, weighed exactly one gram. On this scale, a 15-pound bowling ball would be equivalent to one milligram, and one shiny nickel would be slightly less than one microgram. So, while your daily recommendation for carbohydrate consumption might be to eat a large herd of 200 gigantic African elephants, your daily requirement for vitamin B_{12} would be to eat less than $0.15 worth of nickels — 2.5 µg.

This vast difference may have you thinking that micronutrients are insignificant, but don't be fooled. A failure to get adequate vitamin B_{12}, even in this unimaginably small amount, can lead to severe disorders of the nervous system, including dementia. Big things really do come in small packages.

In this chapter you see how important these powerful compounds are to your health and to diabetes management. More importantly, you see how you can be certain you're getting enough, or not getting too much, of the micronutrients that keep the machinery of your marvelous body humming along.

Introducing Versatile Vitamins

Vitamin is a word you probably already know, maybe from chewable supplements shaped like prehistoric cartoon characters. In biology, a vitamin is an organic compound required in small amounts as a vital nutrient, which can't be produced by you in sufficient quantities. Vitamins, therefore, are compounds you must get from food, or from another external source.

Currently, compounds recognized as vitamins are grouped as vitamins A, B, C, D, E, and K — there are 13 different vitamins within these major groups. Here are some interesting facts about vitamins:

✔ The vitamin letter can represent several different compounds, some that are simply the raw material you need to make the actual vitamin compound. Vitamin A, for example, can be retinol, retinal, or any of four different *carotenoids,* including beta carotene.

✔ The six vitamin groups haven't always been the same. There were once vitamins F, G, H, J, L, M, N, O, P, S, and U. Some compounds were reclassified into the B complex (there are currently eight different B vitamins recognized), and scientific advances showed that others could be manufactured by your body.

✔ The discovery of different vitamins has often come from studying the symptoms of a particular vitamin deficiency. In the mid-1750s a Scottish doctor proposed that the disease *scurvy,* a terrible and deadly illness that plagued long ocean voyages, could be prevented by eating lemons and limes. Although vitamin C wasn't actually identified until 1920, the association of this certain illness with deficiencies of certain foods saved the lives of many British sailors, who had been nicknamed *limey.*

Humans need vitamins from conception, for healthy growth and development, and throughout life for the maintenance of cells, and, most importantly, for properly using the energy provided by the macronutrients protein, fat, and carbohydrate — *metabolism.* Since diabetes is a metabolic disorder, you might imagine that getting adequate vitamins would be an important part of diabetes management — you would be absolutely correct.

Give me a "B" (vitamin or two)

There are eight different vitamins grouped into what's called the vitamin B complex — B_1, B_2, B_3, B_5, B_6, B_7, B_9, and B_{12}. Some you will know better by their actual names — thiamine (B_1), riboflavin (B_2), and niacin (B_3). Others, like pyridoxine (B_6) and cobalamin (B_{12}) you're more likely to know by the number. The B vitamins are important in diabetes management for two reasons.

First, all of the B vitamins participate in chemical reactions taking place in your cells to harvest the energy from fats, protein, and carbohydrates, the energy that fuels everything from muscle movement to body heat to transporting glucose from your small intestine into your bloodstream during digestion. That's not all the B vitamins do for you, but that's pretty important stuff.

The second reason B vitamins are important to diabetes management relates to where you find them and how to make the healthiest choices. Most likely you recognize thiamine, riboflavin, and niacin because a long-standing Food and Drug Administration bread enrichment program requires the addition of these B vitamins to refined (white) flours and bread products. Why? Because refining whole grains by removing the bran and germ also removes the natural B vitamins you could have gotten by choosing whole grains in the first place. Choosing carbohydrate foods like grains is an important part of managing diabetes in your daily eating, and getting naturally occurring B vitamins along with your carbohydrate choices is one reason choosing whole grains is so important.

Beriberi, a sometimes deadly condition that damages the nervous and cardiovascular systems, is caused by a deficiency in thiamine, vitamin B_1. This condition was commonly observed among poorer Asians who lived on a diet of virtually nothing except polished rice. Experimenters eventually discovered that adding back the bran and germ, which contain the thiamine, could prevent beriberi. Pellagra, caused by a deficiency of niacin, vitamin B_3, spread across Europe after the introduction of corn from the Americas as a staple food. Researchers eventually learned that the native Americans and Mesoamericans treated their corn (maize) with alkali, like wood ashes or lime, making the niacin in corn available for digestive absorption, and explaining why pellagra was unknown among the native cultures.

Table 7-1 lists the eight B vitamins, their function, and the best dietary sources for getting these essential nutrients.

Table 7-1		A Review of the B Vitamins	
Vitamin and Daily Amount	**Compound**	**Function**	**Source**
B_1 (1 -1.5 mg/day)	Thiamine	Central role in extracting energy from carbohydrates, production, and cell metabolism DNA	Whole grain and enriched grain products, pork, liver
B_2 (1.1-1.3 mg/day)	Riboflavin	Helps produce energy in cells, supports cell growth, helps regulate metabolism	Beef liver, milk and yogurt, spinach
B_3 (14-16 mg/day)	Niacin	Energy production and cell growth, facilitates glucose and fat metabolism, helps enzyme function	Turkey breast, peanut butter, beans, and yogurt
B_5 (5 mg/day)	Pantothenic	Helps produce energy in cells, involved in synthesizing amino acids, fatty acids, neurotransmitters, and antibodies	Yogurt, salmon, sweet potato, corn, egg, whole grains
B_6 (1.3-1.7 mg/day)	Pyridoxine	Helps synthesize amino acids, helps immune system, helps produce hemoglobin, antibodies and insulin	Potato, banana, garbanzo beans, fish
B_7 (30 µg/day)	Biotin	Helps produce energy in cells, regulates hormone synthesis, key role in metabolizing fats, protein, and carbohydrate	Egg, cottage cheese, peanuts, whole grain
B_9 (400 µg/day)	Folate	Makes new cells, helps form hemoglobin, reduces risk for heart disease, crucial to fetal development	Spinach, beans, whole grains, avocado
B_{12} (2.4 µg/day)	Cobalamin	Makes red blood cells, helps form protective sheath for nerves, crucial role in cell division	Salmon, beef, yogurt, shrimp, no plant sources

It should be noted that the daily recommendations for these vitamins vary between men and women, and generally are significantly greater during pregnancy. Folate is especially important during pregnancy for preventing neurological birth defects.

It's also important to point out that vitamin B_{12} is not provided by any plant sources of food. That makes this crucial compound a challenge for vegans to acquire, even in the tiny amount necessary. Strict vegetarians have to consume foods fortified with vitamin B_{12}.

The consistent role of B vitamins in cell metabolism and energy production is related to their involvement with the biochemical cycle that produces the energy molecule *adenosine triphosphate* (ATP) from carbohydrates, fats, and protein. The members of this group of vitamins are participants in the formation of co-enzyme A, NAD, NADP, and other participants in this energy cycle, which is unnecessary to explain in detail, but absolutely essential for life.

Recent research has focused on thiamine, vitamin B_1, as being especially important to diabetes health — thiamine is a key component of normal carbohydrate metabolism. A 2007 study (*Thiamine deficiency in diabetes mellitus and the impact of thiamine replacement on glucose metabolism and vascular disease*) found that a sample of people with both type 1 and type 2 diabetes showed blood levels of thiamine 75 percent lower than normal because they were excreting thiamine in urine at a higher than normal rate. A 2011 study (*High prevalence of low plasma thiamine in diabetes linked to a marker of vascular disease*) suggested that the metabolism of carbohydrates when thiamine levels are low produces by-products that may contribute to serious complications of diabetes, including arterial plaque buildup and neuropathy. A small Pakistani study published in 2009 (*High-dose thiamine therapy for patients with diabetes and microalbuminuria*) improved kidney function among a group with type 2 diabetes by adding thiamine supplements to their diet.

The jury is still out as to whether thiamine supplementation is directly beneficial to diabetes health, and, if so, at what level. However, it seems clear that working plenty of thiamine-rich foods into your diet is a wise strategy. Whole or enriched grain products, lean meats (especially pork), fish, nuts, seeds, and beans are great dietary sources of thiamine.

A sunny day with vitamin D

Discussing vitamin D means beginning with an asterisk (*). It's entirely possible that vitamin D should have gone the way of vitamins F, G, H, J, L, and the others that experts eventually decided weren't really vitamins at all. Dr. Rubin gives a detailed explanation of this asterisk, and a comprehensive review of the importance of vitamin D, in his book *Vitamin D For Dummies* (Wiley). For now, the designation of vitamin D as a vitamin will stick, asterisk or not.

Vitamin D is unique in that you can, and in how you can, make your own. Remarkably, exposure to sunlight turns a form of cholesterol stored in your skin into a precursor of the active form of vitamin D. However, the advertised dangers of overexposure (or any exposure) to direct sunlight keeps many people from getting sufficient exposure for adequate vitamin D production year round. Plus, other factors, like where you live, the color of your skin, and how much body fat you store (body fat captures and holds vitamin D) make consistently adequate production of vitamin D by exposure to sunlight nearly impossible for many people.

Nevertheless, getting adequate vitamin D is crucial to bone health because vitamin D is essential for adequate absorption of calcium and may have many more benefits to your health. For the purpose of this book the following two aspects of vitamin D are most important:

✔ Beyond its crucial role working in tandem with calcium and phosphorous for bone health, evidence that vitamin D has much broader positive impacts on your health is growing. Vitamin D appears to help regulate your immune system and reduce inflammation responses, may work to prevent several cancers, seems to reduce the buildup of dangerous plaques in arteries and help reduce blood pressure, may work to prevent the metabolic syndrome, which is often associated with type 2 diabetes, and may even reduce the risk for both type 1 and type 2 diabetes.

The relationship between low levels of vitamin D and metabolic syndrome (or type 2 diabetes) are confounded by the fact that fat cells tend to capture vitamin D, keeping blood levels depressed. Lower vitamin D levels may simply be a result of obesity, which could be the real culprit behind these related conditions, and there's not much evidence that vitamin D helps control blood sugar levels after diabetes is diagnosed. Inadequate levels of vitamin D, however, does suppress insulin production, and the potential positive effect of adequate levels of vitamin D on heart health and general inflammation would suggest that maintaining adequate levels of vitamin D could help reduce the risk for diabetes complications. Excess weight, however, works against your efforts to increase levels of vitamin D.

✔ It's very difficult to get adequate vitamin D from food. Because vitamin D is a *fat soluble* vitamin, fatty fish like salmon and mackerel tend to be the best natural sources, and animal sources contain the most active form of vitamin D, called D_3. Non-animal sources of vitamin D are a different, less active, form known as D_2, but mushrooms exposed to ultraviolet light can provide significant amounts of D_2. Plant-based foods supply virtually no significant vitamin D (mushrooms are a fungus). Many foods, like milk and orange juice, are fortified with vitamin D, but you may have to drink six cups of milk each day to reach the daily recommended intake for people 1 to 70 years of age of 600 international units (an IU for vitamin D equals .025 μg, so the daily recommendation is for 15 micrograms). The daily recommendation rises to 800 IUs at age 70.

The daily recommended intake for vitamin D is targeted to achieve a minimum blood level of 20 nanograms per milliliter (ng/ml) of 25-hydroxyvitamin D (the active compound that should be measured in the lab). Ultimately, the cautions and challenges with getting adequate sun exposure, coupled with the relative difficulty of consuming an adequate dose of vitamin D from food, makes vitamin D supplementation necessary for many people to maintain an appropriate blood level. Although overdosing on vitamin D is possible, unless you spend a lot of time outside in the sun without sunscreen, and take high doses of supplements too, it is highly unlikely. Most instances of vitamin D toxicity are related to accidental consumption of huge doses. For adults, the upper limit for recommended daily intake is of vitamin D is 4,000 IUs. Dr. Rubin's book *Vitamin D For Dummies* (Wiley) provides a thorough discussion of everything about vitamin D, including the many options available for supplementation.

Your authors both take vitamin D supplements regularly.

Finding Marvelous Minerals

You've probably heard the words *vitamins* and *minerals* spoken together since childhood, but *mineral* is actually a term from geology. The truth is that the nutrients discussed in this section — calcium, chromium, magnesium, potassium, sodium, and zinc — are basic chemical elements like oxygen, gold, or uranium. Each of these is listed on what's called the periodic table of elements, and technically they're all metals. In fact, pure elemental sodium is not only a metal, it's explosively reactive when mixed with water. Calcium is a soft, gray metal that's slightly harder than lead, and magnesium is a metal that burns so brightly it's used in fireworks and flares.

So, why don't you spontaneously erupt into bright white flames as soon as you step into the shower? Because when basic elements combine with other basic elements, they can become stable and even lose the typical metal appearance. Sodium, an explosively reactive metal, combines readily with chlorine, a poisonous gas, to form table salt — sodium chloride. Chemistry is amazing, and biochemistry even more amazing as you will soon see. These important metals play crucial roles in your metabolism, and you find them in the foods you eat.

Calcium — more than strong bones

Most everyone knows that calcium is a necessary nutrient for bone health, and getting adequate calcium in your diet is very important for maintaining bone health as you age — even more so for women than for men. Calcium and phosphorous work together to form bone, and vitamin D plays a crucial role in managing calcium in your body. The process of bone building never ends, because calcium and phosphorous are removed from bone and re-deposited regularly.

Your body works to maintain consistent levels of calcium in your blood. Approximately 99 percent of the calcium in your body is stored in bones and teeth, but if dietary calcium is too low, processes remove calcium from bones so it's always available for other important functions. What could be so important to sacrifice bone strength? How about the following:

- Calcium plays a key role in normal brain and nerve function, specifically in the release of chemicals that allow nerve signals to travel.
- Calcium keeps you moving and keeps your heart beating by helping muscle cells contract.
- Calcium is essential for proper blood clotting.
- Calcium helps to control blood pressure.
- Calcium works to make cells receptive to taking glucose inside of the cell membrane.

It should be obvious that getting enough calcium is important. The current recommended daily intake, or recommended dietary allowances (RDA), ranges from 700 milligrams per day (mg/d) for children aged 1 to 3, 1,000 mg for children 4 to 8, 1,000 mg/d for everyone aged 19 to 50, 1,200 mg daily for women aged 51 and above and men older than 70, and 1,300 mg per day for rapidly growing kids ages 9 to 18.

How do you get your recommended calcium from food? Dairy products like milk, yogurt, and cheese are the richest sources of dietary calcium — one cup of milk or yogurt contains as much as 300 milligrams — check the nutrition facts label for the exact number. Some tofu is processed with calcium, and many foods or drinks are fortified with calcium as well. Canned sardines or salmon can provide significant calcium, but only if you eat the bones along with the fish. Frankly, for strict vegetarians or people with significant lactose intolerance, getting 1,000 or more milligrams of sodium per day can be challenging. Once again, the importance of getting adequate calcium in your diet may require taking a calcium supplement.

It's possible to get adequate calcium from non-dairy, non-fortified foods with careful planning. A lunch of two bean and vegetable burritos in corn torti-llas, diced avocado and salsa, a leafy green salad with raw broccoli, and a poached pear would add 380 milligrams of calcium to your daily quest.

Calcium supplements come in many varieties, including, by the way, calcium/vitamin D combinations. Calcium supplements should be taken with meals for better absorption, but there's a catch on dosing. Your body cannot properly absorb more than 500 milligrams of calcium at one time, and that includes calcium from both food and your supplement. If your intake of calcium containing foods is almost always very low, you still need to take more than one supplement to get your daily requirement and stay under 500 milligrams per dose. Taking a 1,000 milligram dose is wasting the money you spent on the supplement. If your meals often include calcium, purchase smaller doses of calcium supplement, maybe 250 milligram formulations, so you stay under the 500 mg per dose limit when you include the calcium in your meal. Finally, look for supplements that provide calcium in the form of calcium citrate, which is the most readily absorbed calcium compound.

Chromium — from the Emerald City

Chromium is an interesting element. Elemental chromium is used industrially in making stainless steel and for chrome plating, and variations of the chromium element (called isotopes) give rubies their red color and emeralds their characteristic greenness. In your biology, however, chromium plays a role in helping insulin regulate glucose levels, and one compound containing chromium has been designated as *glucose tolerance factor*.

There's agreement that chromium is essential in trace amounts, but research regarding beneficial effects on blood glucose from increasing chromium intake have been inconsistent. Recent research conducted on rats with diabetes in Israel, and published in the British Journal of Nutrition, concluded that glucose tolerance factor, which was extracted from brewer's yeast, has a significant insulin-potentiating effect. In layman's terms, the addition of chromium-containing glucose tolerance factor improved the action of insulin in rats that were insulin deficient.

At this point there is not enough evidence to recommend chromium levels greater than the current *adequate intake* recommendation, which ranges between 20 and 35 µg per day for adults, depending upon age and gender. An adequate intake level is established when there is not sufficient research for an official recommended dietary allowance. Proponents of chromium supplementation, usually with *chromium picolinate*, generally speak in ranges between 200 and 1,000 micrograms per day, and there is general agreement that these ranges are safe.

In general, the amount of chromium in food is small, but only a small amount is necessary for healthy people. Foods which provide chromium include whole eggs (chromium is in the yolk), whole grains, beef, liver, cheese, black pepper, wine, broccoli, and brewer's yeast.

Magnesium matters

If you've ever had, or longed for, *mag wheels* on your car, or powdered your hands before mounting the uneven parallel bars, you're already a magnesium lover. But aside from hundreds of industrial and pharmaceutical uses (for example, milk of magnesia), magnesium is essential to health and life.

Magnesium, for instance, works hand in hand with more than 300 enzymes to facilitate biochemical reactions, including those that create *adenosine triphosphate*, the energy molecule made from carbohydrates and the other macronutrients, and in assembling DNA, the molecule that carries the instructions for building and operating you. Adequate levels of magnesium play a role in controlling blood pressure, too, and increasing dietary intake is a key element of the Dietary Approaches to Stop Hypertension (DASH) eating plan, described in detail in Chapter 14.

Low levels of magnesium have been associated with type 2 diabetes and metabolic syndrome, and low levels may contribute to the formation of calcium plaques in arteries, a risk for heart attack. Having diabetes can result in an increased excretion of magnesium as well, so getting enough magnesium should be a clear priority.

The recommended dietary allowance for magnesium is 320 milligrams per day (mg/d) for women, and 420 mg/d for men, and surveys tend to show that American adults don't get enough magnesium in their diets. White fish, dark greens, broccoli, beans of all varieties, almonds, pumpkin seeds, artichokes, rice and barley, and wheat bran or whole wheat flour are all rich in magnesium. Eating a balanced diet of whole foods provides the appropriate level of magnesium for most people. The upper limit for magnesium from supplements has been set at 350 mg/d, but unless diabetes is poorly controlled supplementation is probably not necessary. Your doctor should decide whether you need a magnesium supplement or not, and that may depend upon medication, other conditions such as Crohn's disease, alcohol abuse, infections, or the status of calcium and potassium levels in your blood.

Potassium — too much, or too little

Potassium is an essential element of fertilizer for plants, particularly with heavy crop production. Its chemical symbol *K* is the third number listed for fertilizers containing nitrogen, phosphorous, and potassium — 15-30-10 fertilizer has 10 percent potassium in the bag (the remaining 45 percent is inert ingredients), and it's often listed as potash on the label. Plants tend to accumulate potassium in their cells, and that might lead you to speculate that plants are a good source of dietary potassium. You would be correct.

Potassium plays key roles in your body by regulating fluid and nutrient balance inside and outside of cells, by facilitating nerve signals, by helping muscles contract, and by counteracting sodium to help maintain normal blood pressure. Potassium is an *electrolyte,* participating in the electrical communication between nerves throughout your body. Studies have shown that low potassium levels negatively impact blood glucose control as well.

Almost 75 percent of adults with diabetes also have high blood pressure, and increasing potassium intake is another objective of the DASH eating plan. Most Americans don't consume enough potassium in their diets — the Recommended Dietary Allowance for adolescents and adults is 4,700 milligrams per day — but this key nutrient is not one that should be ignored. So, regarding the title of this section — too much, or too little — it's almost a certainty that you're getting too little potassium in your diet. There's one circumstance, however, where only a little is too much — a renal diet prescribed for kidney failure. It's ironic that choosing not to eat the kinds of foods that are beneficial to diabetes and high blood pressure now may result in having them virtually eliminated from your diet for dialysis. Don't forget, diabetes and high blood pressure are the number 1 and number 2 causes of kidney failure.

So, maybe you should think about increasing potassium in your diet right now by increasing your intake of potassium rich foods. White beans, edamame (green soy beans), potatoes and sweet potatoes, salmon, canned tomatoes, dates and raisins, spinach and greens, Brussels sprouts, hard shell squashes, yogurt, banana, and cantaloupe are all foods that can add more potassium to your diet today. Note that many of these are carbohydrate foods, illustrating why it's important to plan your carbohydrates carefully, and focus on whole foods in your daily eating.

Your preconceived notions about food may not always be accurate. Bananas have a legendary reputation as a potassium powerhouse, but a plain, boring, white potato has almost twice the potassium ounce for ounce.

Sodium — a little goes a long way

It's appropriate that this discussion of micronutrients puts sodium and potassium together, because they work together in your body in many ways. And both are dietary concerns — potassium because you almost certainly get too little, and sodium because you almost certainly get too much. This variation actually tells the story of the so-called Western diet, because although you could be getting sufficient potassium from vegetables and fruits, instead you're likely getting significantly excess sodium from — well, nearly everything else. In fact, of the more than 4,000 milligrams of sodium the average American consumes each day, only 10 percent or less comes from the sodium chloride in your salt shaker; maybe another 15 percent is naturally occurring in the foods you eat. That leaves 75 percent that's added by someone else, like a food processor or a restaurant. In an interesting turn, therefore, this discussion about sodium doesn't focus on how you can find more, but rather on how you can reduce your daily intake.

So, what good is sodium anyway, how much do you need, and how much is recommended for people with diabetes? Remember, 75 percent of people with diabetes also have high blood pressure, so much of the story of sodium focuses on that other significant risk for heart attack, stroke, and kidney failure.

Sodium, like potassium, is an electrolyte, facilitating the transmission of electrical messages throughout your nervous system, participating in the balance of fluids in your body, and helping in the transport of other compounds through cell membranes. So, sodium is essential, and a deficiency of sodium can be very serious. A sodium deficiency, called *hyponatremia,* usually occurs as a result of fluid retention, where the amount of sodium is not affected, but the concentration of sodium is reduced by excess bodily fluids. It's possible to lose too much sodium through perspiration, but this is something that would most likely be seen in marathon runners or other extreme endurance athletes. It's the concentration of sodium that's important, and maintaining your normal concentration of sodium requires only about 200 to 300 milligrams of sodium per day from diet — most Americans get 20 times more sodium than necessary.

Excess sodium in your diet, especially when potassium is deficient, is closely associated with high blood pressure, called hypertension. Excess sodium contributes to high blood pressure by requiring more blood volume to keep sodium concentration in a normal range. Moving more fluid through the same-sized arteries requires more pressure, and when other lifestyle factors promote narrower arteries by the accumulation of arterial plaques (atherosclerosis) and less flexibility of the arteries, blood pressure can skyrocket. Consistently high levels of sodium, high blood pressure, and diabetes eventually cause kidney damage.

For years the daily recommendation for sodium intake was set at 2,300 milligrams per day (mg/d) for anyone under 51 except in the case of existing high blood pressure. Recently, recognizing the dual risk of diabetes and high blood pressure, a 1,500 mg/d limit was set by the United States Department of Agriculture's Center for Nutrition Policy and Promotion in its the 2010 Dietary Guidelines for Americans for anyone with diabetes. And while salt (sodium chloride) is your most likely source of dietary sodium, preservatives and additives like sodium nitrate can add to the load.

Reducing sodium in your diet can be challenging, but because your most likely sources come from foods in the grocery or at a restaurant you have the information you need, in most cases, from a nutrition facts label, or from the restaurant's website. You just need to be sure to use the information that's available, and don't just look at foods you perceive as salty — sodium is virtually everywhere, and it all adds up. Fortunately, food manufacturers have focused on producing low sodium formulations of many foods in response to public health concerns.

You can find discussions about sodium throughout this book, and a detailed discussion about the DASH eating plan in Chapter 14. The effectiveness of this clinically tested diet at reducing blood pressure almost immediately is one of the best examples of how food can be medicine.

Insulin and zinc — two peas in a pancreas

Zinc is the grayish metal that coats roofing nails, the key ingredient in the white paste you may see on lifeguards' noses, and may even help to dampen the symptoms and duration of the common cold. And zinc is an essential micronutrient.

Zinc is crucial to your immune system, it enhances your senses of smell and taste, is involved in the metabolism of the macronutrients, promotes tissue growth and cell reproduction, is an antioxidant working to protect cells from damage, and is involved with hundreds of enzymes. And zinc plays a very important role in your body's production, storage, and use of insulin, the hormone that lowers high blood glucose levels.

Zinc in pancreatic beta cells binds to several insulin molecules, six to be exact, forming what's called an insulin *hexamer* for storage. In fact, long acting insulin formulations for injection — NPH or Lantus, to name two — contain zinc so that the insulin is bound in hexamers that convert to the active insulin *monomer* (a single insulin molecule) slowly.

Several studies have shown that high blood glucose levels increase the excretion of zinc in urine, and zinc deficiency seems to promote insulin resistance. A study in Finland found that heart disease fatalities and heart attacks in a study group of people with diabetes were more likely in the subjects with lower blood zinc levels. Recent research shows that zinc manages the behavior of *amylin*, a protein also secreted by pancreatic beta cells to help slow carbohydrate absorption. Unmanaged amylin, according to research published in the *Journal of Molecular Biology*, can form clumps that interfere with insulin secretion in type 2 diabetes (where insulin is still produced by the pancreas).

There is not sufficient evidence to suggest getting more than the recommended dietary allowance of zinc brings additional benefits to blood glucose management, and excess zinc can cause imbalances with copper and other micronutrients. It seems prudent, however, t to include foods or a multivitamin that puts adequate zinc into your diet. The current RDA is 8 mg/d for adult women and 11 mg/d for adult men — the RDA varies for children, adolescents, and pregnant or nursing women.

Foods that contain zinc include oysters (the richest source), crab, beef, beans, yogurt, cheese, oatmeal, and almonds. The absorption of zinc from many plant sources is inhibited by phylates, which are also present in the grain, so the bioavailability may be less than zinc from animal sources.

Analyzing Some Antioxidants and Herbal Remedies

How can you keep a sliced apple from turning brown? You can add an antioxidant like the vitamin C in lemon juice. Antioxidants are compounds that can help reduce the cell damage caused by the byproducts of reactions in your cells that use oxygen. These byproducts are called *free radicals,* and they are looking to steal electrons, often from the fats that are present in cell membranes. Vitamins A, C, and E function as antioxidants, but there are other compounds you can get from foods that also work to limit cell damage from free radicals. Some are beneficial to diabetes, and complications of diabetes, and some, perhaps, have an inflated reputation.

Many antioxidant containing foods have been lab tested, and assigned an oxygen radical absorbing capacity (ORAC) score. In fact, the U.S. Department of Agriculture had provided a database of these scores for the comparison of various food products, but the website listing has been removed. In summary, the USDA now states that laboratory measured antioxidant capacity doesn't translate to *in vivo* (in your body) activity for these compounds, that the antioxidant capacity of foods often can't be positively connected with the health benefits or separated from the potential benefits of non-antioxidant mechanisms, and (most importantly) that ORAC scores were "routinely misused by food and dietary supplement manufacturing companies to promote their products and by consumers to guide their food and dietary supplement choices."

Alpha lipoic acid and neuropathy

Alpha lipoic acid is a unique antioxidant because it is soluble — it dissolves — in both water and fat. The molecule was identified in the early 1950s from what had been previously known as *potato growth factor,* an extract from potatoes necessary for some bacteria to grow. Alpha lipoic acid is also involved in the energy cycle, where the energy molecule adenosine triphosphate is produced, and seems to help regenerate the vitamin antioxidants.

Alpha lipoic acid has been examined in relation to diabetes from several different angles. Since many facets of diabetes, and the common complications of diabetes, have a foundation in oxidative stress, this powerful antioxidant has been a candidate for improving insulin sensitivity, damage to arteries and blood vessels, and damage to nerves. Some studies have, in fact, shown improvements to insulin sensitivity, glucose uptake into cells, and to A1C levels in patients treated with higher dose of alpha lipoic acid. The clearest benefit, however, has been in reducing the symptoms of diabetic neuropathy, or nerve pain. In Germany, for instance, high doses of alpha lipoic acid are routinely used as a treatment for neuropathy. Unfortunately, improvements to diabetes-related issues are most effective when the compound is administered intravenously, and less effective when taken as a pill.

Foods containing alpha lipoic acid include potatoes, tomatoes, broccoli, spinach, Brussels sprouts, red meat, liver, and brewer's yeast. Your body can make alpha lipoic acid, and there is no established recommended daily intake from food or supplements. Unless your doctor recommends a supplement, or concurs with your intentions to supplement with this antioxidant, your best strategy, as always, is to eat a diet which includes a wide variety of foods, especially vegetables.

Fenugreek for better blood glucose control

Fenugreek is a plant whose seeds provide a characteristic maple-like flavor to Indian cuisine, but its leaves are edible as well, and can be eaten as salad greens, or dried for use as an herb. Fenugreek has long been used as an herbal medication as well, said to improve milk production in nursing mothers, ease stomach upset, cure baldness, and increase libido (sexual interest) in men. Fenugreek has also been used for many years as a natural remedy for lowering blood glucose levels — but is it effective?

Studies have shown some improvements in blood glucose control, and even reduced bad LDL cholesterol, among subjects with diabetes who were given fenugreek extracts. All in all, these studies have been very small, often over a short time frame, and not well controlled, however. There is a possibility that fenugreek, which is rich in fiber and contains several alkaloids, can work to slow the absorption of carbohydrates, possibly making blood glucose levels easier to manage. Also, some have proposed that an amino acid in fenugreek may stimulate insulin production.

Fenugreek is a delicious addition to food and may have some mildly beneficial impact on blood glucose control. Fenugreek is not a treatment for diabetes, however, and the danger with such a notion could come from declining to seek appropriate medical care on the assumption that this herb will effectively manage blood glucose, and prevent the complications of hyperglycemia, over the long term.

Cinnamon, minus the bun

Who doesn't love the powerful fragrance of cinnamon? This derivative of tree bark has been a food enhancer, and a natural remedy for ailments, for thousands of years. In the United States, you may think of apple pie, or that kiosk in the mall that draws your attention to the cinnamon sweets from any distance.

Cinnamon does contain many active compounds, including *cinnamaldehyde*, which stimulates an antioxidant reaction, especially in the colon. Cinnamaldehyde also seems to work against harmful clotting and exhibits an anti-inflammatory effect. In addition, a few studies have suggested that cinnamon can be helpful in managing blood glucose levels. A study in Pakistan showed people with type 2 diabetes improved fasting blood glucose, blood triglycerides, and bad LDL cholesterol levels after 40 days. A Chinese study showed essentially the same results in 66 patients monitored in a controlled study environment. An analysis of studies involving diabetes and cinnamon, however, found no statistical improvements in blood glucose control from cinnamon supplementation.

The story with cinnamon, therefore, is much like the story with fenugreek. Adding cinnamon to your diet in modest amounts is unlikely to cause a problem, unless, of course, you add your cinnamon on a big sweet roll. Depending upon this unproven herbal remedy as an effective treatment for diabetes, however, would be profoundly unwise.

Garlic — just a breath enhancer?

Vampires (and loved ones) beware — garlic is on the menu. But is garlic actually beneficial to diabetes?

Garlic, as you may guess, is in the onion family and is another food with an interesting history spanning thousands of years. Garlic is also another food that has been touted for its inherent medicinal properties, and the active ingredient is thought to be *allicin*, a sulfur containing compound with antioxidant properties.

Garlic has been shown in studies to exert a modest effect in lowering blood pressure, and seems to reduce atherosclerosis. Both effects may be by increasing the flexibility of arteries. Some cancers may be reduced by eating garlic but not garlic supplements, and regular consumption of garlic over a period of several months is positively associated with reduced tick bites.

However, in spite of the fact that the Internet is awash with websites testifying to the benefits of garlic to diabetes, no reputable studies have been able to demonstrate any beneficial effect to blood glucose control. Garlic is, however, a wonderful flavor enhancer and condiment that may help you reduce sodium, and even fat, in your diet. See Chapter 21 for a tip on incorporating roasted garlic into your eating as a replacement for butter or margarine.

It won't do much good to try and freshen your breath after eating garlic. The chemical that gives your breath that special odor, allyl methyl sulfide, actually moves through your bloodstream to your lungs. So, the problem is not in your mouth, but actually in the air you exhale.

Considering Phytonutrients

A *phytochemical* is a term that simply describes chemical compounds that occur naturally in plants, and history is filled with drug discoveries that resulted from isolating these compounds. Aspirin, for example, was synthesized based upon the properties of the chemical salicin, which occurs naturally in the bark of willow trees. When phytochemicals have nutritional value, they're often referred to as phytonutrients. And the foods which contain phytonutrients are sometimes called functional foods, meaning the phytonutrients offer health benefits beyond the nutritional value of the food.

In nature, phytochemicals are produced by plants to protect them from viruses, fungi, insects, the sun, and even drought, and there are thousands of different chemicals remaining to be studied. It's estimated that 2,000 phytochemicals are plant pigments, making fruits and vegetables favorite subjects for artists who try and match the amazing variation. It's probably worth emphasizing again, in case you missed it, that these compounds are exclusive to plants, and their benefits certainly reinforce dietary recommendations to eat lots of fruit and vegetables. If your diet doesn't currently include a broad selection of fruits and vegetables, and many Americans don't get enough, it's never too late to start.

Colorful carotenoids

Carotenoids are plant pigments, and there are hundreds identified. In plants, carotenoids absorb sunlight for photosynthesis, the process by which plants build carbohydrates from sunlight, water, and the carbon dioxide you exhale every few seconds. The pigments also protect chlorophyll in the plant cells from sunlight damage. Carotenoids are divided into two groups — one group that includes oxygen called *xanthophylls*, and a group that does not include any oxygen called *carotenes*. The carotenes' class label is taken from the compound carotene itself, the pigment that gives carrots their characteristic bright orange color.

The class of xanthophylls includes *zeaxanthin* and *lutein*, and the pigmentation is generally yellow. Xanthophylls give egg yolks their yellow color, but the compounds aren't produced by the chicken — they come from plant materials in chicken feed. In humans, these carotenoids accumulate in the eye, where they absorb damaging ultraviolet light, and protect the retina from damage. One large study that included lutein in a mix of other nutrients showed that this carotenoid along with vitamins C and E, zinc, and copper, slowed the progression of macular degeneration, a leading cause of blindness in seniors. The richest food sources for the xanthophylls are dark leafy greens like kale, spinach, Swiss chard, and turnip and collard greens. Zucchini, broccoli, Brussels sprouts, pistachios, and kiwifruit also contain these carotenoids compounds.

The carotene pigments tend toward orange and red, and include *beta carotene* and *lycopene*. Beta carotene is rapidly converted to vitamin A in the small intestine, and functions in your eyes to improve night vision and color vision. Vitamin A also is essential for your immune system, works in transcribing instructions from DNA, maintains normal skin, and has antioxidant properties. Beta carotene seems to protect pre-menopausal women from breast cancers, slow the progression of (but does not prevent) osteoarthritis, and prevents exercise-induced asthma attacks.

Good sources of beta carotene tend to be orange or dark green fruits and vegetables — carrots, apricots, winter squashes, cantaloupe, sweet potatoes, pumpkin, dark greens like kale and spinach, and herbs like basil and parsley. For some foods, lightly steaming them can improve beta carotene absorption, but in most cases prolonged cooking or the canning process reduces the concentration of available beta carotene. Fat soluble carotenes are also better absorbed if the foods are eaten at meals that include some dietary fat.

Beta carotene supplementation should be done only under the supervision of your doctor. Fat soluble vitamins, like vitamin A, can accumulate to toxic levels over time. And in a study to look at the potential benefits of beta carotene supplementation for smokers, supplementation actually increased the risk of lung cancer, where intake from natural food sources did not.

Lycopene is a carotenoid associated with bright red colors, and tomatoes serve as the standard bearer for the group. Lycopene is an effective antioxidant, and has been studied extensively for a potential benefit in reducing the incidence of cancers, particularly prostate cancer. Much of the evidence for lycopene's possible effect in reducing or improving cancers comes from population studies of cancer incidence among people who eat lots of tomatoes, or have high lycopene blood levels. Unfortunately, much of the evidence is inconsistent, and many of the more positive results suggest that tomatoes are more effective than lycopene alone. That could mean that lycopene has no beneficial role, or that its effectiveness is also related to other compounds, like vitamin C, also found in tomatoes. But the absence of compelling evidence from controlled clinical trials doesn't mean lycopene isn't beneficial to health. A recent study suggested that a variation in a gene called XRCC1 may influence whether lycopene can influence prostate cancer risks. Other research hints that lycopene may reduce the risk of non-alcoholic fatty liver disease. Research on lycopene is ongoing.

Foods rich in lycopene include tomatoes, pink grapefruit, watermelon, pink guava, and papaya. Unlike carotenoids, cooking increases the availability of lycopene, especially with the addition of a monounsaturated fat like olive oil. The concentration of lycopene in canned tomatoes, tomato sauce, or ketchup might be ten times that in a raw tomato. Lycopene is nontoxic, and is the source of the food coloring registered as E160d in the United States.

Gac, a fruit native to Southeast Asia, has the highest concentration of both beta carotene and lycopene of any fruit or vegetable. Gac has 10 times the beta carotene of carrots, and 20 times the lycopene of tomato sauce. Gac fruit also includes fat, which helps the absorption of both carotenoids. Unfortunately, gac only fruits one time each year, and it's relatively short season doesn't facilitate export other than juice supplements.

Chocolate covered flavonoids

Flavonoids are functional plant compounds, like carotenoids, once labeled vitamin P. They are often responsible for providing the color to flowers, help filter ultraviolet light from the sun, and in legumes flavonoids attract a beneficial root infection by cooperative bacteria which supply nitrogen to the plant by converting nitrogen in the air to ammonium.

In general, flavonoids are antioxidants, and often seem to work with vitamin antioxidants, like vitamins C and E, to enhance the function of both compounds. There are more than 4,000 flavonoids, broadly divided, without unanimous agreement, into *flavonols, flavones, flavanones, isoflavones, catechins, anthocyanidins and chalcones.* Flavonoids have been reported to reduce the incidence of coronary heart disease, have anti-bacterial, anti-viral, anti-tumor, anti-inflammatory, antiallergenic effects, and help improve the flexibility of arteries. As with the other phytonutrients, research on flavonoids is complex, and complicated by the range of other nutrients in flavonoids containing foods. Some specific flavonoids of note include the following:

- ✔ *Anthocyanins* are active compounds found in blueberries, blackberries, cranberries, cherries, and the pigment in the fruit of blood oranges and the peel of eggplant. These compounds have been shown to exhibit anti-aging properties, reduce inflammation, and have promise in preventing and treating certain cancers. Black raspberries, a rich source of anthocyanins, have been shown to increase the death rate of cancer cells, inhibit the formation of blood supplies to tumors, and minimize DNA damage. Cancer research involving anthocyanins is an active field.

- ✔ *Hesperidin* is a flavonoid found abundantly in citrus fruits, such as oranges and lemons. Because herperidin may improve blood vessel health, it's used to treat internal hemorrhoids and small leg ulcers caused by poor circulation. Hesperidin is also touted as a treatment for varicose veins, but the jury is still out on whether it's effective for that purpose.

- ✔ *Catechins* might remind you of an informal get together with friends — tea, a little wine, and some chocolate. But this class of flavonoids has some impressive potential health benefits. Unfermented green tea is the winner for total catechin content, and green tea has amassed some pretty strong evidence of benefits for heart disease, some cancers, and even Alzheimer's dementia. People who regularly drink green tea have less heart disease, fewer `strokes`, lower total and `LDL cholesterol`, and recover from heart attacks faster. Some evidence suggests that tea may help fight ovarian and breast cancers, as well. Catechins are anti-inflammatory, and a review of the effectives of weight loss supplements found that green tea had a statistically significant benefit to weight loss.

✔ *Epicatechin*, a specific catechin found naturally in dark chocolate, reduced the brain damage caused by strokes in mice, and an observational study of heavy cocoa drinkers in Panama found striking reductions in that group's risk for heart failure, stroke, diabetes, and cancer. A recent study published in the *Journal of Neurovirology* found that epicatechins protected brain cells from damage by the human immunodeficiency virus (HIV) in AIDS patients. Also, a small study of profoundly ill patients administered epicatechin-enriched cocoa noted improved muscle cell function, and indicators that muscle cells were producing new mitochondria (the structures where macronutrients are converted to energy).

Quercetin, a flavonoid in vegetables, fruit skins, and onions, exhibited the highest antioxidant properties in preventing the oxidation of low density lipoprotein, LDL cholesterol, in the laboratory. The oxidation of LDL in your body is a reaction known to promote arterial plaque buildup. However, coming in a close second place were two flavonoids contained in hops, a key flavoring ingredient of beer — xanthohumol and isoxanthohumol.

Genistein, a flavonoid in soy called an isoflavone, is a powerful antioxidant as well, and has been shown to inhibit arterial plaque formation.

Resveratrol — fruit of the vine

You have probably seen, or at least know of, the famous movie *The French Connection*, but have you heard of the French paradox? The French paradox describes observations that captured public attention in the 1990s showing that despite their higher consumption of saturated fat, the French seem to have a lower incidence of heart disease than people in the United States. When a 1991 story on the television news show *60 Minutes* left an impression that red wine was the key to the French paradox, red wine consumption in the United States increased by more than 40 percent. Eventually, the public's attention turned to *resveratrol*, a natural plant phenol found in the skin of red grapes.

Resveratrol slowly became recognized as an anti-aging substance, based to some extent on reports that doses of this compound extended the life expectancy of yeast cells, nematode worms, and eventually a short-lived fish — in some cases the doses were equivalent to 30,000 milligrams per day for a human. Resveratrol has been cited as beneficial for heart disease, diabetes, cancer, and Alzheimer's dementia, and is said to be anti-viral, able to increase testosterone levels, an anti-aging miracle for skin, and a treatment for acquired tolerance to opiates in people with chronic pain.

Clouding any assessment of resveratrol's potential health benefits is the fact that a prominent resveratrol researcher was cited for nearly 150 counts of fabricating and falsifying data. Moreover, most research has been in lab dishes, or on animals. Noting the relatively low levels of resveratrol in wine, one group of researchers is looking at a different group of polyphenols in wine — *oligomeric procyanidins*. Still others have proposed other explanations for the French paradox, including miscalculation of the data showing lower rates of heart disease among the French in the first place.

With respect to resveratrol, unless you're a short-lived fish hoping to add another five weeks to your average nine weeks lifespan, there aren't likely any miracles for you. Still, most phytonutrients seem to offer cumulative benefits to human health, and small, but pleasant, doses of this compound in a glass of red wine has its own rewards anyway.

If you're visualizing a resveratrol supplement as just another way to have a relaxing glass of wine, your mental image might be a fantasy. The resveratrol in some supplements is derived from the unpurified extract from Japanese knotweed, and may include emodin, a compound that can have a laxative effect. Relaxation is not usually associated with a laxative effect.

Sorting Out Supplements

Someone could write an entire book on supplements. Wait, someone did with *Vitamins For Dummies* (Wiley). Dietary supplements are a complex issue, but registered dietitians have a simple, two word starting point — food first.

That doesn't mean that supplements of one kind or another aren't suitable, or even necessary for you. It means that taking supplements as a substitute for a healthy, balanced diet is no way to achieve good health, and it's certainly no way to prioritize diabetes management. In the previous sections of this chapter you saw time and again how research hints at profound benefits for a particular nutrient, but the effect of that particular nutrient can't easily be separated from everything else that comes in its natural packaging. It could be that another active compound, or something as simple as fiber, gives nutrients like phytochemicals the key to their effectiveness. In some cases, beneficial effects were seen only from the natural, whole food, and specifically not from the nutrient supplement.

The bigger issue is that your focus on micronutrients can't divert your attention away from your primary objectives with diabetes management — blood glucose control, and heart health. Discounting how a healthy diet and overall lifestyle can help resolve diabetes-related concerns is failing to see the forest for the trees. Many of these micronutrient compounds work to prevent health problems, not to cure them. Plus, poorly controlled blood glucose levels inhibit the activity of some micronutrients, and accelerate your excretion of others. With vitamin D, you even learned how excess weight stored as body fat can capture the active compound so it's not even available to exert its powerful influence on your health.

Getting your micronutrients from food first when you have diabetes is one specific and practical example that meal planning pays off. The essential nutrients and powerful phytochemicals that come from dairy products, whole grains, beans, starchy vegetables, and fruit also come along with carbohydrates. Working these foods into your daily eating means making sure your daily carb choices include a wide and varied selection of these healthy options. Appreciating the importance of natural micronutrients in healthy carbohydrate foods can help you make wiser choices too, like when you're tempted to dedicate 25 percent of your daily carb choices to a sugar-sweetened soft drink.

So, who needs supplements? There is relatively general agreement in the medical community that supplementation of one kind or another may be appropriate for the following circumstances:

- Women who may become pregnant should get folic acid daily from fortified foods or a supplement, in addition to eating foods that contain folate, to prevent certain birth defects.

- Pregnant women should take a prenatal vitamin that includes iron, or an iron supplement daily. For women who experience heavy bleeding during their menstrual cycle, an iron supplement may be advised.

- Women nursing an infant may require supplemental vitamins, and their infants need a vitamin D supplement as well.

- Children and adolescents who can't, or don't, drink milk need a vitamin D supplement during seasons they can't get sufficient sun exposure, or if direct sun exposure isn't advised.

- People with lactose intolerance, food allergies, or who are on a very strict diet limited to 1,600 calories per day, or less, may need appropriate supplements.

- People who can't properly absorb vitamins, as a result of bariatric surgery or a digestive disorder like Crohn's, celiac, or other inflammatory bowel disease, may need supplements, sometimes by injection.

- Vegans may require supplemental vitamin B_{12}, calcium, and vitamin D.

- People on medications that require additional nutrients may need to take a supplement.

✔ People over age 50 need additional vitamin B$_{12}$ from fortified foods, or from supplements.

✔ People with an identified vitamin deficiency or with a condition (such as macular degeneration) that is treated with vitamins will likely need a supplement.

You may notice that most all of these circumstances would, or should, involve a physician's care for the underlying condition. So, in these cases you're likely to get specific instructions on which vitamins or nutrients, and how much, you should take.

If you are taking supplements, or planning to take supplements, without specific instructions from your medical provider, at least discuss your daily intake with your doctor and your pharmacist. It's important that your medical providers assess your particular health issues, and evaluate potential interactions with any other prescription or over-the-counter drugs you're taking.

Drug interactions with vitamin supplements can take many forms. Niacin in combination with statins to lower cholesterol can cause serious muscle problems. Calcium supplementation can prevent the proper absorption of certain antibiotics if taken together. And some prescription drugs for acne or psoriasis are chemically similar to vitamin A and pose a risk for vitamin A toxicity if used while taking a supplement.

The likelihood of vitamin toxicity is fairly small unless you're taking doses of the fat soluble vitamins A, E, D, or K, that are significantly beyond the amount your body needs. These compounds are stored in fat, and can accumulate in your body because you excrete excess amounts slowly. The water soluble vitamins, all of the B vitamins and vitamin C, are more easily excreted when you consume amounts in excess of your needs. Of course, that means excessive doses in a supplement are literally flushing your money away.

If this section on supplements sounds like it's all caution and no cheerleading it's because the scientific evidence for mega doses of vitamins and other nutrients rarely supports the popular claims. But dietary supplements are not held to the same kinds of rigid regulatory standards as pharmaceuticals, and manufacturers' claims can push the limits of verifiable results. Plus, consumers are irresistibly attracted to the possibility of a simple solution to good health, and are ever more willing to invest billions of dollars every year on products with completely unsubstantiated promises. The National Institutes of Health, Office of Dietary Supplements, maintains a webpage that provides a world of information on supplements at `http:/ods.od.nih.gov/`.

That said, there are two specific supplements that many people should consider — vitamin D and calcium. And you can probably get both in one. The purpose and function of both is discussed earlier in this chapter.

Vitamin D is a fat-soluble vitamin that lighter skinned people can make with direct exposure to the sun on their skin, but concerns about sun overexposure, living in northern locations, an excess of body fat, not spending time outdoors, and having dark skin all can make getting an adequate amount of vitamin D in this unique fashion difficult. Plus, vitamin D is not easily acquired from foods, especially for vegetarians or people who can't drink milk (which is fortified with vitamin D). The recommended dietary allowance for vitamin D is 600 international units (IUs) per day for anyone age 1 to age 70, and 800 IUs per day after age 70. The upper limit considered safe is 4,000 IUs per day for those older than age 9, and a lower amount for younger children. While vitamin D is a fat-soluble vitamin with a risk for toxicity, your body manages your blood serum level pretty effectively. It's not possible, for example, to accumulate toxic levels of vitamin D from sun exposure alone because your body simply stops making more when a high level is achieved. Adding supplemental vitamin D when levels are already high can be a problem. Very few people, however, would be at risk with supplemental doses of 500 or 1,000 IUs per day.

Calcium is not easy to get from diet alone in adequate amounts either, and for strict vegetarians or those with lactose intolerance getting enough calcium is extremely difficult. The recommended dietary allowance ranges from 700 milligrams per day (mg/d) for children aged 1 to 3, 1,000 mg for children aged 4 to 8, 1,000 mg/d for everyone aged 19 to 50, 1,200 mg daily for women aged 51 and above and men older than 70, and 1,300 mg per day for rapidly growing kids ages 9 to 18. Dairy products are the best sources of calcium, and one of the difficulties in getting adequate calcium on a daily basis is related to your body's capacity to absorb large amounts at one time. Generally speaking, you can only absorb 500 milligrams from any source, food and supplement combined, at any single time. To get your daily dose of calcium from milk could require 6 cups a day, and with diabetes you can't forget that milk is also carbohydrate — and 6 cups may be more than half of your daily carbohydrate budget. Because it's important to get your daily carbohydrates from a variety of sources, setting aside 50 percent of your choices for dairy is not a good strategy. (And who could drink six cups of milk each day anyway?) Calcium citrate is the most readily available form of calcium in supplements, and don't forget to manage your intake at any one time to less than 500 milligrams from both your food and your supplement.

Because vitamin D and calcium are both related intimately with bone health, you can find supplements that combine the two. These are a good choice, and if you're left with an uncomfortable feeling after reading this section, or if you simply will not eat a variety of wholesome foods, talk to your doctor about a simple multivitamin — chances are you can keep your peace of mind.

Chapter 8

Revisiting Carbohydrates

There's a certain risk in talking about carbohydrates too much — guilt by association. Chances are that every time you start snooping around for answers about diabetes, this carbohydrate guy's name keeps popping up. Where there's smoke, there's fire. If it quacks like a duck — you get the picture. This carbohydrate guy must be guilty of something, right?

Not necessarily. It's true that when you have diabetes, carbohydrates become very important to treatment and blood glucose management — there's no separating diabetes and carbohydrates. And recent studies are pointing an accusing finger at added sugar in the amounts some people consume them in the so-called Western diet typical in the United States; however, most carbohydrates played no unique role in causing diabetes.

So, carbohydrates as a food group weren't your enemy before diabetes, and carbohydrates aren't your enemy now. In fact, carbohydrates are still your body's favored and your brain's only source of fuel. Diabetes does mean you need to pay more attention when you're adding fuel to the tank now than you did before. And effective diabetes meal planning and nutrition involves identifying healthy carbohydrates and working them into your diet in a way that best controls your blood glucose.

This chapter helps you identify carbohydrates, determine the best portion sizes, and help you get the right carbohydrates on your plate.

Deciphering Carbs

Carbohydrates are sugars. Chemists often use the word *saccharide*, from the Greek word *sákkharon*, which means, coincidentally, sugar. When learning about carbohydrates it's important to take a chemist's view for a few minutes because your definition of sugar and her definition of sugar are probably different. Where you see a sugar as something sweet tasting, she sees a sugar as a chemical molecule containing only carbon, oxygen, and hydrogen, with hydrogen always in a 2-to-1 ratio with oxygen (like water, H_2O). To your chemist friend, the common names of saccharides end with "ose." Fructose is fruit sugar, lactose is milk sugar, and deoxyribose is a component of DNA (deoxyribonucleic acid).

Sugar molecules often join together in long chains. Unconnected single molecule sugars, like fructose and lactose, are called *monosaccharides*. When two sugar molecules join, as with common table sugar sucrose, it's a *disaccharide*. Chains of from three to ten molecules are referred to as *oligosaccharides*, and longer chains (even to more than 1,000) are *polysaccharides*. A big player in diabetes, as you probably know, is the monosaccharide glucose. Glucose is especially fond of joining together in chains. All of these combinations of sugar molecules, from the singles to the longest chains of cellulose, are carbohydrates. Sugars are small chains, starches are longer chains, fiber is the longest chains.

Finding carbohydrates

In dietary terms, there are two places you can find carbohydrates — mother's milk and plants. Of course, mother's milk for adults usually means mother cows, goats or sheep. Plants, on the other hand, are carbohydrate factories. Plants manufacture carbohydrates from carbon dioxide (CO_2) pulled from the air and water (H_2O) drawn in through roots, using energy from sunlight in a process called *photosynthesis*. Plants are in large measure literally built of carbohydrates.

If you notice, putting CO_2 and H_2O together results in two hydrogens and three oxygens; however, carbohydrates are defined by having twice as many hydrogens in its molecules as oxygens. The extra oxygen is released from plants as waste, but oxygen is hardly a waste product to humans — it's what we must have to breathe. We owe plants both for the air we breathe and the food we eat, although we do help supply plants with carbon dioxide when we exhale.

Because your blood glucose is directly affected by eating carbohydrates, it's important to know where you'll find them in food. Managing your blood glucose levels is about finding a balance between the following:

✔ The carbohydrate foods you eat, which raise your blood glucose level

✔ Your capacity to naturally lower blood glucose by producing and responding to insulin (having diabetes means this process is compromised)

✔ Medications you may need, including insulin, to either help lower blood glucose levels, reduce or slow down the appearance of glucose in your blood, or both

Knowing where you're getting carbohydrates in food is Diabetes 101, however — you can't possibly manage your blood glucose if you don't know which foods have an effect on blood glucose levels in the first place.

The basic list is easy to remember and is detailed in the following table:

Food Group

Dairy products (read the following paragraph)

Any food that comes from plants

OK, it's not quite that simple, but this is an excellent place to start. So many people think it's only sweets — sugar — that can affect blood glucose. Blood glucose is affected by much more than just sweets. If you start with this simple, two item list — dairy products and anything plant — your learning process from here on becomes discovering which foods in these groups don't affect blood glucose levels as much as others. For example, cheese has been mostly relieved of its carbohydrate in the cheese making process. Even though cheese is definitely a dairy product, there's not too much carbohydrate remaining.

Deciding to "carb" or not to "carb"

It's a natural instinct with diabetes to think about eliminating carbohydrates from your diet. After all, carbohydrates are what make your blood glucose levels go high, and high blood glucose levels are best avoided. Wouldn't it make perfect sense to stop eating carbohydrates?

Folklore in Wisconsin says that the last words ever spoken by snowmobilers are often, "hold my drink and watch this." Some ideas seem better than they really are, and eliminating carbohydrates from your diet is one of those. Here are some excellent reasons:

- Your body prefers glucose as a fuel, and your brain requires glucose as a fuel. Carbohydrates in diet are the only reasonable source of that glucose.

- Getting all of your calories from protein and fat is simply not healthy, and will deprive you of important nutrients.

- Depriving yourself completely of any food, much less any food group, is the perfect way to learn to hate your diet. You can't enjoy life when you hate your diet.

- You love carbohydrates — it's biological.

Rather than taking the drastic and virtually impossible step of trying to eliminate carbohydrates, isn't it better to learn how to manage carbohydrates as an important part of a healthy diet?

Evaluating glycemic index/glycemic load

In the previous section, you got the simplest possible explanation of where to find carbohydrates in your diet. The conclusion of that section said that after you know where to look, the focus can turn to which carbohydrate-containing foods affect your blood sugar more than others. Fortunately, someone has already figured that out for you, but there are some important qualifications when diabetes is part of the picture.

The *glycemic index* of carbohydrate containing foods was originally developed in 1981 at the University of Toronto. Recognizing that different foods affect blood glucose differently, researchers fed carbohydrate foods to fasting volunteers and monitored their fasting blood glucose response over the following two hours. The blood glucose response to eating pure glucose serves as a benchmark, affecting levels more quickly and more profoundly, and a little math produces a GI number which compares other foods to glucose. The GI number of glucose is set at 100, and GI values between 70 and 100 are labeled as high, between 56 and 70 as medium, and values of 55 and below are considered low. You can learn more about the glycemic index from *Glycemic Index For Dummies* by Meri Reffetto (Wiley).

Figure 8-1 illustrates the blood glucose response of a high GI index food, and a low GI Index food. Note with the higher GI food blood glucose levels not only go higher, but also begin to rise more quickly.

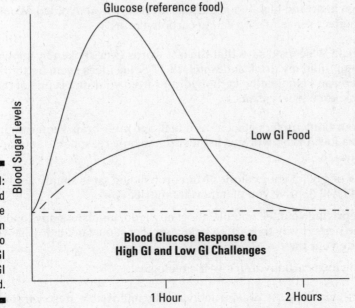

Figure 8-1:
Blood glucose levels in response to both high GI and low GI food.

The following table shows the GI value of common foods, but before you look at that comparison, consider why these numbers vary so much. The impact of a food on blood glucose depends upon the speed of digestive processes, how efficiently free glucose is absorbed into the bloodstream, and how quickly insulin begins to help move glucose out of the bloodstream and into cells. High fiber content, longer chain carbohydrates, how starch molecules are entrapped within the food, whether a food contains both carbohydrate and fat, and unknown factors can slow stomach emptying, slow the liberation of glucose from carbohydrate chains, or interfere with glucose absorption in the small intestine to impact the blood glucose response. Your insulin status is a key issue when evaluating what the glycemic index means to you.

Food	*Glycemic Index Value*
Glucose	100
Baked potato	85
Instant white rice	87
Watermelon	72
White bread	72
Pineapple	66
White spaghetti	64
Ice cream	61
Banana	54
Skim milk	32
Lentils	29
Grapefruit	25
Edamame (green soy beans)	18
Lettuce and cabbage	10

There are two issues to consider about the practical use of the glycemic index. First, different foods contain different amounts of carbohydrate. The blood sugar response of volunteers is measured after eating a particular food in an amount that contains 50 grams of carbohydrate. For glucose this would be 50 grams (about 4 tablespoons), because it's all glucose. For cabbage, getting 50 grams of carbohydrate would mean eating 10 cups of shredded cabbage, or about 800 grams (the GI of cabbage was probably estimated). There is simply not nearly as much glucose in cabbage as there is in glucose.

A second calculation takes this variation in the amount of carbohydrate in the same weight or volume of different foods into account. *Glycemic load* is designed to estimate how much a certain amount of a certain food raises blood glucose compared to eating 1 gram of glucose. Here's where using glycemic index, and by extension glycemic load, in your daily life could become a problem.

Glycemic index numbers, like those in previous table, reflect both the blood glucose response and the insulin response of volunteers who don't have diabetes. If you have diabetes, these numbers don't reflect your insulin response. The inferred precision of glycemic load is taking this information too far if you have diabetes.

To be clear, knowing the glycemic index of foods gives you a great tool. Eating foods with a low glycemic index value, that gradually release glucose into the bloodstream, may allow your abnormal response to insulin to still keep pace with rising blood glucose levels when you have type 2 diabetes. If you take insulin by injection or through an insulin pump, knowing the GI of foods can be useful in timing your injections or bolus. Just be extremely cautious about taking glycemic index and glycemic load as absolute numbers. *Glycemic Index Cookbook For Dummies* (Wiley) includes about 150 delicious recipes to help you incorporate low GI foods into your diet.

Because different foods affect the absorption of carbohydrates differently, the glycemic index also varies according to the accompanying food. It's not an exact science, but lower glycemic foods are generally better for your blood glucose control than higher glycemic foods.

Counting Carbs

Without getting into the deep water of randomized control trials and statistical meta analyses, it's fair to say that managing the total carbohydrate content of meals is still considered the most effective tool for diabetes meal planning. You're probably familiar with *carb counting*, at least with the concept. But, if you're not taking it seriously yet, it's time to start. Your carbohydrate management plan is a component of *medical nutrition therapy*, and managing your carbohydrates in some ways is as important as taking your medication.

Counting to 15 grams

Carbohydrate counting (carb counting for short) doesn't have you count each gram of carbohydrate one by one. Instead, carbohydrates are packaged into 15 gram *carb choices*; one carb choice for a particular food always includes approximately 15 grams carbohydrate.

The counting part is easy. If your meal plan calls for four carb choices at your evening meals, you simply include a total of four carbohydrate foods, each in a serving size that equals approximately 15 grams of carbohydrate. You can eat four different carb choices, you can have two 15 carbohydrate gram servings of the same food (along with two more carb choices of different foods), or you could have four carb choice servings of the same food too, although variety is best. Your meal plan will make a recommendation for a specific number of carb choices at every meal, and probably a carb choice snack or two wedged in somewhere. Just imagine that every morning you find that a fairy has left 12 or 13 tokens on your dresser, each one good for a 15 gram carbohydrate serving during the day — 4 grams for breakfast, 4 grams for lunch, 4 grams for dinner, and 4 grams for a snack. That couldn't be any easier.

Comparing carb choices

Now for the harder part — not hard, just harder. The measure of carbohydrate containing foods — dairy or plant — that includes your 15 grams of carbohydrate is not the same from food to food. Table 8-1 shows the weight, volume, or size of one carb choice for some different foods.

Table 8-1	Measuring a 15 Gram Carb Choice
Food	*One Carb Choice*
Maple syrup	1 tablespoon
Oatmeal	¼ cup, dry
Beans	⅓ cup cooked
Rice or pasta	⅓ cup cooked
Unsweetened cereal	½ cup
Milk	1 cup*
Yogurt	1 cup
Baked potato	3 ounces
French fries	10 fries
Bread	1 slice
Bagel	½ small bagel
Popcorn	3 cups popped

(continued)

Table 8-1 *(continued)*

Food	One Carb Choice
Apple	1 medium sized
Banana	½ medium banana
Raspberries	1 cup
Honeydew melon	1 cup
Nonstarchy vegetables	1½ cups cooked
Nonstarchy vegetables**	3 cups raw

* 1 cup milk is actually 12 grams carbohydrate, but is considered 1 carb choice

** Nonstarchy vegetables include asparagus, artichoke, beets, green beans, broccoli, cabbage, carrots, cauliflower, cucumber, greens, jicama, mushrooms, okra, pea pods, peppers, radishes, rutabaga, spinach, tomato, turnips, yellow and zucchini squash, and many more.

Knowing which portion size of a food you'll eat to get each 15 gram carb choice is really necessary if you're serious about blood glucose control. You may feel unnatural thinking so much about food. Yes, it would be nice if one carb choice for all carbohydrate foods was the same serving size, but there's a big difference between a tablespoon of sugar and 3 cups of shredded cabbage. If the serving size on nutrition labels always equaled 15 grams of carbohydrate it would help, but every can of beans gives nutrition information for ½ cup, and that's 22 grams of carbohydrate. And what about those recipes or restaurant meals where one serving of the dish has 60 grams of carbohydrate?

There's no need to panic. First, this isn't rocket science, as the saying goes. Anyone who's managed type 1 diabetes for a while, where you can carefully match grams of carbs and a precise dose of insulin, already knows that the variations in both food and your metabolism put perfection way out of reach. What's most important is knowing what you need to know. Remember, the all-important A1C is about averages.

There's one final calculation that's like a discount coupon for you with some carbohydrate foods. *Dietary fiber* and *sugar alcohols* are carbohydrates that are not efficiently digested — you can find the grams of these listed on nutrition labels under total carbohydrate. Anytime the dietary fiber or sugar alcohol amount is 5 grams or more you can deduct one half of the amount from total carbohydrate. Often the deduction isn't much — kidney beans have 22 grams total carbohydrate and 7 grams fiber in the ½ cup nutrition label's serving size, so you can deduct 3½ grams from the 22 grams for an adjusted total carbohydrates of 18½ grams per ½ cup. Likewise, a ½ cup serving of a particular *no sugar added* ice cream has 17 grams total carbohydrate and

8 grams sugar alcohol. Because the sugar alcohol is 5 grams or more, deduct one half, 4 grams, from total carbohydrate to get net carbohydrate in the ½-cup serving of 13 grams.

Memorizing the one carb choice portion for foods you eat all the time is easy enough, but nobody can know everything. A good starting place is to practice visualizing the correct measurements of foods for one carb choice while you are at home. To help you with carb food choices you may not eat as often make yourself a cheat sheet, buy a pocket-sized carb counting reference, or download a carb counting app to your smart phone. If you're determined to be successful, easy solutions are available for you.

Insulin bolus dosing

Everyone with type 1 diabetes takes insulin with meals to compensate for the carbohydrate total of the meal. You may take an injection, or you may initiate a bolus from your insulin pump. Some people with type 2 may take insulin injections related to food also, although it's much more common that type 2s take long acting insulin which is unrelated to meals. If you take short or fast acting insulin before meals, there are a few things that need consideration.

- ✔ You need to know your current blood glucose level.
- ✔ You need to estimate how many grams of carbohydrate you intend to eat.
- ✔ You need to know your insulin to carb ratio — one unit of insulin will account for how many grams of carbohydrate?
- ✔ You need to know how to correct for your current blood glucose — less insulin if your blood glucose level is on the low side, and more insulin if blood glucose is elevated.

That is a bunch of need-to-knows. If you're using an insulin pump, your insulin to carb ratio and correction factor should be programmed into the control.

A book on meal planning for diabetes is not a good place to give you your insulin to carb ratio or your correction factor. In fact, no book is a good place to give you that information, not even Dr. Rubin's *Type 1 Diabetes For Dummies* (Wiley). These numbers are unique to you. Your doctor will start you with dosages based upon your size and age, and together you can fine tune based on trial and error. Eventually, your dosages for eating or correcting blood glucose may be different depending on the time of day. The key where meal planning is concerned is you won't know where you're going if you don't know where you're starting — test your blood glucose before meals.

Putting Carbs on Your Plate

You're going to find a common theme about carbohydrates in your diet running throughout this book. Actually, it would be a similar theme for any discussion about healthier eating, but when diabetes is involved everything about healthy eating becomes even more important. Ready? Read carefully because some explanation is necessary.

Eat more whole foods. *Whole foods* is a term often defined as unrefined and unprocessed foods, or foods that are refined or processed as little as possible before consumption. Frankly, terms like *processed*, *natural*, *organic*, and even *whole* can be confusing, and because you hear them used in many different ways it's best to think about examples.

This recommendation to eat more whole foods is absolutely not about special or exotic foods. It's about making simple choices that add up over time to better nutrition, better blood glucose control, and better cardiovascular health. Some excellent and simple examples would be as follows:

- ✔ **Choose whole grains.** Whole grains contain everything that makes up the grain, which is the *bran*, the *germ, and the endosperm*. Refined grains generally only contain the endosperm. Choosing whole grains simply means choosing whole grain breads, crackers and pastas, or whole grains such as oatmeal, barley, quinoa, and brown rice instead of the alternatives — a different package in your regular grocery.

- ✔ **Choose whole fruit.** Whole fruit contains healthy dietary fiber, and no added sugar. You don't have to choose fresh fruit, by the way. Canned or frozen fruit is excellent as long as there are no added sugars (packed in syrup). The no added sugar warning goes for fruit drinks too, of course, but you may be surprised to know that eating the fruit itself is a better choice than 100 percent fruit juice.

- ✔ **Eat lots of vegetables.** Vegetables are especially important to diabetes because of their low carbohydrate content, and rich nutrient content. Again, frozen or canned vegetables are excellent if you avoid added sugar, fat or sodium. Always choose the *no salt added* option for canned vegetables. Pick a wide variety of textures and colors, and avoid adding sugar, fat, or sodium at home with salt, butter, and margarine, or add-ons like salad dressings.

- ✔ **Limit sweets.** Added sugar not only pours concentrated carbohydrates into your diet, but also delivers no nutrients to make it a fair trade. There's no need for you to confuse yourself with the debates about sweeteners like high fructose corn syrup. Simply resolve to minimize sweets, and look for sugar hiding in packaged food so you can avoid that too.

You have to admit that these simple choices look pretty easy on paper. But in practice it takes some effort to get beyond old habits. There's nothing here that says never, ever eat white rice or white bread again — they aren't poison. When it comes time to put carbs on your plate, however, and that time rolls around several times every day, the more often you make the better choice the more your health will benefit.

You don't have to give up the foods you grew up on in order to follow a diabetes-friendly meal plan. Just limit the total carbs to the quantity you and your dietitian have decided is right for you.

Managing staple carbs

Every culture has a carbohydrate food which has sustained it through time, usually a food that stores well, grows locally, is inexpensive, and shows up on the table frequently. Potatoes, bread, rice, pasta, yams, poi, taro, corn, and beans would be a few culturally significant starches.

In an impassionate nutrition assessment these are simply carbohydrate containing foods that can easily be portioned into 15 carbohydrate grams choices — 3 ounces of potato, ⅓ cup rice or pasta or taro, 1 slice bread, or two 6-inch corn tortillas — and worked into your meal plan. In the real world, where your order of General Tso's chicken comes with 10 or 12 cup carb choices of white rice compressed into a bucket, this isn't always so easy.

Managing staple carbohydrates can be one of the most difficult challenges of diabetes management because these are everywhere. They are everywhere, by the way, because we love them. A large order of French fries at a famous fast food drive-through is four carb choices. The five cheese ziti al forno in a popular Italian chain gives you a whopping eight carb choices for the entrée alone. And the mountain of rice you get with an order of saffron peas pulao at your favorite Indian restaurant defies measuring.

There aren't many ways around this challenge — it's one you have to plow through. The measures of these foods that constitute one carb choice is just considerably smaller than what you, and your family, are accustomed to having. Here are a few suggestions that will help you have your staple carbs, and eat them too:

- Add vegetables in volume to rice or pasta, and add spices to liven up the flavor.
- Try mashed potato recipes that add cauliflower or artichoke, foods lower in carbohydrate with similar texture and relatively neutral taste.
- Try one manufacturer's pasta, which is treated in a patented process to make some of the carbohydrates less digestible, having a lesser effect on

blood glucose. Use your blood glucose meter to check your individual response after eating this brand.

✔ Have a salad or low-sodium broth before your meal to help moderate your appetite, and reduce your cravings for staple carb foods.

✔ Fill your plate and stomach with nonstarchy vegetables. These foods are low carbohydrate, nutritious, and filling.

Following your meal plan

If you don't have a meal plan for managing your diabetes, get one. If your meal plan didn't come from a registered dietitian, see one. These two not-so-subtle recommendations are especially crucial if you're not controlling your blood glucose well. Your meal plan builds a framework that can include your favorite foods as much as possible, and sets your daily recommendations for carbohydrate.

There's an overabundance of diet-related information everywhere you look, but the most effective strategies for managing blood glucose and heart health are well established and proven. Nobody is keeping secrets, nobody wants you to do poorly, and nobody is looking to take away everything you love to eat. Your meal plan should be flexible and loaded with an abundance of choices.

The phrase *diabetic diet* is one you've probably heard. It sounds specific, and it sounds restrictive. In reality, nothing could be farther from the truth. A meal plan for effective diabetes management will focus on the amount, and the timing, of carbohydrate foods because carbohydrates affect blood glucose levels directly. Otherwise, it's an eating plan that anybody would be better off following for its emphasis on cardiovascular health, and foods that reduce the risk of other diseases like some cancers.

Chapter 17 gives you a sample diabetes meal plan for one week. Your meal plan looks at total calories relative to weight management concerns, carbohydrates, protein, fat, and sodium. Your meal plan may look at other dietary concerns related to your specific health status, and to your medications.

If you make a personal commitment to follow your meal plan, your health will be better for the effort. But don't hesitate to bring your concerns back to your dietitian. Usually, there's flexibility to make changes that work better for you and your family.

What and when you eat can make a huge difference in how you feel, and in how diabetes affects your life as time passes. Carbohydrates get a lot of unfair blame where diabetes is concerned, but you and your carbohydrates can live together in peace when you learn how to best fit them into your daily life.

Chapter 9

Equipping Yourself For Success

- -

In This Chapter

▶ Preparing your kitchen for a healthier lifestyle

▶ Understanding nutrition information

▶ Finding foods you can love

▶ Reviewing the variety of foods you can eat

- -

*I*n 1966 the comedian, country singer Roger Miller released a whimsical song with the title lyrics, "You can't roller skate in a buffalo herd . . . but you can be happy if you've a mind to." Maybe that song was before your time or not in line with your musical tastes, but it makes an excellent point with an odd choice of words — some things are simply beyond possible, but what is possible often requires only a little willingness. Have no doubts, you can eat great food and manage your diabetes like a pro if you've a mind to — and, by the way, are prepared.

The importance of healthy eating when diabetes is part of your life can't be overstated. Managing what goes into your mouth is an essential part of diabetes self-management, and you are chief of the security detail — no food goes in without your approval. Food gets intimate access to your most sensitive inner workings, so reviewing its résumé and checking out trusted references are steps every good security chief should take.

And, after you're satisfied with the qualifications, be prepared to take full advantage of everything healthy food has to offer. Ultimately, enjoying food that's satisfying and flavorful goes a long way toward keeping your willingness willing.

Stocking Your Diabetes Kitchen

Preparation for diabetes meal planning and nutrition starts with a very minor, but very important, makeover of your kitchen. You want your kitchen set up for ease of food preparation, and that includes everything from measuring cups and scales to the right ingredients.

Preparing food at home more often than not simply makes diabetes management easier, so your kitchen should make food preparation convenient. Of course, you're able to enjoy eating out or food-related social events occasionally, but having drive-through or delivery food on a regular basis makes healthy eating extraordinarily challenging.

Remember that you should have healthier staple foods on hand. It's fun and can be easy to throw together a spontaneous breakfast, lunch, dinner, or snack that fits your diabetes meal plan perfectly by having the best food choices close at hand. These include frozen fruits and vegetables, dried or low-sodium canned beans, frozen lean meats or tempeh, whole grains like oatmeal, brown rice, or quinoa, and low-fat milk or yogurt.

Measuring your food is a necessity — not just for recipes, but also for eating. This is a difficult habit to adopt for many, but the portion size of any food is what determines the nutrient and, importantly, carbohydrate content. Getting the appropriate serving size of different foods that contain 15 grams of carbohydrate — one carb choice — is the foundation of healthy eating for blood glucose control.

Pour your normal bowl of dry breakfast cereal and then measure what you've poured. A 15-gram carb choice for most unsweetened cereals is ¾ cup — how'd you do?

Gathering tools and gadgets

If you don't own an egg cuber, razor-sharp pizza shears, a culinary torch, a Swiss corn zipper, and a truffle shaver, you will never make the cut as an Iron Chef. Fortunately, the equipment standards for a Diabetes Meal Champion are considerably less complicated and way less costly.

Measuring tools are the most essential devices for healthy eating. Americans suffer from what nutrition professionals call *portion distortion*, where years of super-sizing and ever-larger dinner plates have contributed to eating the wrong amounts of the wrong foods. It's simply necessary to measure the weight or volume of the food going into your mouth. You measure what goes into a recipe so the final product is what you want. Think of your meals as a recipe for the blood glucose levels you want.

Later in this chapter you learn some estimating tricks, but when you're at home, estimating shouldn't be necessary. The following sections describe what you really must have in your kitchen.

Kitchen scale

A kitchen scale is how you weigh appropriate portions of protein foods like fish or chicken, and carbohydrate foods, like potatoes, that don't fit into a measuring cup. Kitchen scales don't directly measure grams of protein or carbohydrate in a particular food, although there is at least one model that allows the user to enter a specific code assigned by the manufacturer to produce a nutrition facts label for any of the coded foods. Instead, you learn that a 3-ounce piece of white potato is 1 carb choice, giving you 15 grams carbohydrate. It's the 3 ounces of a white potato that needs to be weighed.

Kitchen scales range from less than $10 to more than $50. Some are simply mechanical and have a dial; but the battery-operated scales have an electronic or digital display. You can find affordable food scales online, at large retailers, at specialty culinary shops, and maybe even at your grocery. Whichever scale fits best into your budget or décor is perfect — managing diabetes with diet only requires some sort of kitchen scale.

Another great way to ensure that you eat just one serving is to get a kitchen scale with a tare feature. You put your bowl on the scale and press the tare button. The scale returns to zero and you can measure your one serving.

Measuring cups, scoops, and spoons

Measuring cups are essential tools that you probably already have in your kitchen. If not, you may want to read *Cooking Basics For Dummies* (Wiley). Measuring cups allow you to portion cooked grains like rice, starchy vegetables like peas and corn (you have liberated from its cob with your corn zipper), and dairy products such as milk or yogurt.

Measuring scoops are more convenient, and less messy, for getting to foods in a larger container like oatmeal or dry cereal. Measuring scoops have a handle just like regular scoops, but they're sized to scoop a specific measure.

Of course, a set of measuring spoons is a must have too, although you'll be glad to know that very few food portions are measured by the spoonful.

Other tools

There are a few kitchen utensils that just make healthy eating more convenient. These aren't must-haves for diabetes self-management like measuring devices, but there's a lot to be said for convenience. Here's a sampling:

- **Oil mister:** An oil mister not only let's you make your own nonstick spray for a fraction of the cost of the store-bought kind, but more importantly reduces added fat to foods that need an oil coating, like roasted vegetables. Simply fill the mister container with oil, and you can pump to spray a fine mist over food or on cooking surfaces.

- **Salad spinner:** A salad greens spinner is the most efficient way to wash and dry salad fixings. Chopped greens go into a slotted bowl, and you can run water liberally over the mixture. Then, the slotted bowl fits into a gear in a larger, closed bowl equipped with a lawn-mower-like rope pull that spins excess water off of the greens. Even if you don't particularly mind wet greens in the first place, spinning the bowl is kind of fun.

- **Food and cheese graters:** A variety of graters come in handy for adding shredded cheese or vegetables to dishes. And, a microplane grater is great for fabulous flavor additions like fresh ginger or lemon zest.

- **Steamer baskets:** Using either a stovetop or microwave steamer basket is the quickest and most flavor-preserving way to prepare fresh or frozen vegetables. Steaming your vegetables, as opposed to boiling them, preserves more of the nutrients because steaming uses less water. Microwave cooking had been under suspicion in this regard after a 2003 study found flavonoids depleted in microwave-cooked broccoli, but more recent results from Spain showed baking and microwave cooking preserves more nutrients than water-based cooking.

- **Vegetable peeler:** A good vegetable peeler takes the work out of preparing fresh vegetables and fruits. Vegetable peelers come in a variety of space age designs, but the truth is the old fashioned metal one with a slightly pointed end for digging out potato eyes has never been topped.

- **Sharp knives:** You don't need an expensive set of cutlery to do basic food preparation, but a few knives, kept sharp, can make a huge difference in the work involved. A 10-inch, curved-blade chef's knife is best for chopping, mincing, and slicing through tough foods, and the one knife where spending a little extra money and purchasing a sharpener can pay off. A small paring knife gets the assignment for smaller or finer work, like peeling fruit or trimming the extra fat from cuts of meat. You can top off your knife collection with a long serrated knife, perfect for slicing bread and for vegetables like tomatoes that bruise easily.

- **Food thermometer:** Every kitchen should have a metal-stem food thermometer on hand for food safety. The U.S. Centers for Disease Control and Prevention estimate that 48 million Americans are sickened every year by food. Cooking *potentially hazardous foods*, like meat products, to the proper temperature can help reduce your risk for illness.

Planning the pantry

One trick to eating healthier is keeping healthier choices around — how simple is that? The truth is that even the most detailed plans, including your menu, need to be adjusted sometimes, even if it's only because you don't feel like preparing what's on today's plan. You can fight the urge to hit the fast-food drive-through and whip up a convenient and healthy breakfast, lunch, dinner, or snack if you keep the right foods handy. Your list of healthy items to keep on hand should include all six food groups, and the following sections offer suggestions for keeping healthy foods at arm's reach.

Grains and starchy vegetables

Grains and starchy vegetables are excellent sources of carbohydrate and fiber. Keep 100 percent whole wheat or rye bread, low-carbohydrate/high-fiber tortillas, and whole grain crackers around for sandwiches, rollups, or spreads. Whole grain pasta, brown rice, and potatoes or sweet potatoes are common staple starches, and consider trying quinoa, a whole grain that includes protein. Whole grain dry cereal or oatmeal make a super breakfast, and for healthy snacking keep some low-fat popcorn or baked chips around, but watch your portion sizes. Some fresh starchy vegetables keep well — potatoes, sweet potatoes, and hard-shell squashes are good examples — and frozen peas or corn can be ready for the table in a jiffy.

Nonstarchy veggies

Nonstarchy vegetables are the foundation for healthy eating and should occupy half of your plate. Again, fresh, frozen, or canned are equally good for you, but watch for added fat and especially sodium. Frozen or canned vegetables like green beans, carrots, broccoli, cauliflower, Brussels sprouts, and stir fry mixtures can be scooped up when on sale so you always have a selection ready at a moment's notice. Always keep salad greens on hand for a quick and healthy meal and for some fun with your salad spinner.

Fruits

Fruits are the healthiest way to enjoy sweetness, and fresh, frozen, or canned are equally nutritious as long as there is no added sugar. Keeping fresh fruit in plain sight can go a long way toward changing your snacking habits for the better. Just remember, all fruit includes carbohydrate, and the 15-carbohydrate-gram portion size varies somewhat from fruit to fruit. The portion size for dried fruit like raisins is only two tablespoons, for instance. You can find a comprehensive list of fruit portion sizes in Appendix A and B.

Healthy proteins

Healthy protein choices should include canned tuna or salmon (canned in water), peanut or almond butter, low-fat cheeses and cottage cheese, eggs or egg substitute, tofu or other meat substitutes like tempeh, frozen fish fillets (not breaded), and low-fat meats and ground meats like 96 percent lean ground beef, ground turkey, pork tenderloin, and beef filet or flank steak.

Low-fat dairy

Low-fat dairy products would include 1 percent or skim milk, and no-fat regular or Greek yogurt. Remember that milk products include carbohydrate, and adding fruit to yogurt increases the carb content.

Healthy fats

Healthy fats are an important part of a healthy diet, protecting your organs, insulating nerves, transporting some vitamins, and forming cell membranes. Healthy fats include healthy oils like olive and canola oil, vegetable nonstick cooking spray, low-fat salad dressings, spray or tub margarines, nuts, and avocados. The objective is to limit saturated fats and to avoid *trans fat*. You can find that information on the nutrition facts label, which is discussed in the section "Understanding Nutrition Facts Labels."

Spices and seasonings

Spices and seasonings are not a food group, but using a variety of flavorings not only enhances your eating pleasure, but also can help you avoid adding salt. Garlic and garlic powder, onions and onion powder, cinnamon, oregano, rosemary, thyme, cumin and chili powder, vinegars, and low-sodium broths can all add pizzazz to your food.

Understanding Nutrition Facts Labels

In the United States as well as in many other countries, nutrition facts labels are required on all packaged foods, and this is a good thing. The information included on the nutrition facts labels tells you everything you need to know about the labeled food product. To be honest, the label also tells you a lot that you don't really need to worry about too much. In fact, the information you don't really need to worry over can look so complicated that it may scare you away from using this valuable resource altogether. Understanding nutrition facts labels for diabetes meal planning and nutrition starts with ignoring some of the information. A typical nutrition facts label is illustrated in Figure 9-1.

For starters, don't worry too much about those values with a percent (%) mark, which are all related to the percentage of daily recommended values for certain nutrients in a 2,000 calories per day diet. (On some labels this becomes even more complicated than on the label illustrated.) Generalities are always too broad, but the issue here is that each label refers to only one serving of only one food. So, unless you're anxious to keep a detailed account of every serving of every food you eat each day (or are living on nothing but linguine salad), this information is more confusing than helpful.

There is an informal rule called the 5/20 rule which says look for less than 5 percent of nutrients you want to avoid, like sodium and cholesterol, and look for more than 20 percent of nutrients you want to find. In this case, one half cup of the linguine and tomato salad gives 60 percent of the daily recommendation for vitamin C, and that's good. But the same salad's 530 milligrams sodium is 22 percent of the daily 2,300 milligram sodium recommendation (it would be 35 percent of the reduced recommendation of 1,500 milligrams per day for people with diabetes), so how bad is that? It depends on how much sodium you get from other sources during a day, and that can be the confusion with the 5/20 rule.

Nutrition Facts

Serving Size 1/2 cup (140g)

Amount Per Serving	
Calories 240	Calories From Fat 130

	% Daily Value *
Total Fat 15g	23%
Saturated Fat 2g	**11%**
Trans Fat 0g	
Cholesterol 0mg	0%
Sodium 530mg	22%
Total Carbohydrate 24g	8%
Dietary Fiber 1g	5%
Sugars 5g	
Protein 3g	

Vitamin A 15%	•	Vitamin C 60%
Calcium 2%	•	Iron 6%

* Percent Daily Values are based on a 2,000 calorie diet.

Figure 9-1: Nutrition facts label for pre-packaged linguine and tomato salad.

The information most important to managing your diabetes is serving size, calories, fat (total, saturated, and trans fat especially), total carbohydrate, dietary fiber, sugar alcohols (not an ingredient in the linguine salad), and sodium. Notice sugar isn't singled out as something that needs your special attention, even though sugar, dietary fiber, and sugar alcohols are listed as subcategories of total carbohydrate on the labels. That's because total carbohydrate includes carbs from sugar, carbs from fiber, and carbs from sugar alcohols. Total carbohydrate is the number that impacts blood glucose, and both fiber and sugar alcohol may deserve your attention because any time these exceed 5 grams you can subtract one half of the amount from total carbohydrate. Both fiber and sugar alcohol digest more slowly (or not at all), so glucose absorption from those is less efficient. These adjustments are mostly important when calculating insulin doses related to foods containing a lot of fiber or sugar alcohols.

Calories

Calories are the units used to describe the energy stored in food, and it's a word used in the sciences as a unit of heat. The term *calorie* as commonly applied to food is actually 1,000 of the heat units — a *kilocalorie*. Calorie has taken on the meaning of kilocalorie when speaking of food.

The calorie as a unit of heat is the amount of heat necessary to raise the temperature of 1 gram of water by 1 degree Celsius. It has been replaced in the International System of Units by the *joule.* One calorie is equal to 4.184 joules. How would a 7,113-joules-per-day diet plan sound to you?

You need food in part because you need the calories of stored energy to keep your body operating, and the more active you are the more calories you need. Calories in excess of what you need result in weight gain because your body stores the excess as body fat to provide energy in times of calorie shortages. Fat is the most efficient way to store calories, which explains why dietary fat gives you more than twice the calories in your food as the same measure of either protein or carbohydrate. Fat stores 9 calories of energy per gram, but protein and carbohydrates store only 4 calories per gram. Alcohol, by the way, stores 7 calories per gram.

Your calories can come from sources that provide no significant amount of other nutrients, like calories from sugars or alcohol. These calories are called *empty* calories. Your calories can also come from foods that provide nutrients along with energy. Calories coming from foods that also provide other nutritional benefits are called *nutrient dense* calories. Healthy eating seeks to maximize nutrient dense calories.

Losing excess body fat means reducing the calories you get from food to fewer calories than you use each day, so you are drawing from calories stored as excess fat. Many people with diabetes, especially type 2 diabetes, need to lose excess weight by reducing calories. Excess body weight, and particularly fat accumulating around vital organs, is at least partially responsible for the insulin resistance that characterizes type 2 diabetes. If you need to lose weight and you have diabetes, see a registered dietitian. It's possible to calculate your daily energy needs and reduce your calorie intake to less than your requirements on your own. Check out *Nutrition For Dummies* (Wiley) to find the equations for calculating your daily energy needs.

But are you willing to add the 240 calories you got from ½ cup linguine salad to the calorie content of every other food you consume every day? And, do you know how much you should reduce your calorie consumption, or how to be certain you aren't eliminating foods beneficial to diabetes management?

You are far better off getting a personalized meal plan from a registered dietitian who can competently account for the requirements of diabetes and weight control, and incorporate medical nutrition therapy for other medical conditions you may have. As a general rule, your diabetes meal plan provides about 50 percent of your calorie needs from nutrient-dense carbohydrates, 20 percent from lean protein, and 30 percent from mostly healthy fats. It's just too important to not get it right.

Grams and milligrams

Food nutrition information is given in metric weight measures, grams, and milligrams, and if you're from the United States, unless you're a scientist, you may have no idea how a gram compares to measures you're more familiar with. There are 28.3495 grams in one ounce, and there are 1,000 milligrams in a gram (28,349.5 milligrams per ounce). But don't get your calculator out.

In some ways it's not that important. You don't have to understand grams and milligrams as related to units you know, but only that your diet should include certain amounts of various nutrients which are measured in these units. A 3-ounce portion of white potato contains 15 grams carbohydrate, 3 grams protein, and no fat. The 18 grams of nutrient weight is only slightly more than 20 percent of the total 3-ounce potato weight, however. And, weighing another carbohydrate food gives you a different percentage between total weight and carbohydrate grams — math doesn't always work here.

Instead, you can rely on memory, nutrition facts labels when available, a reference book, a cheat sheet, a website or app, or your personal assistant to find the grams of the nutrients in different foods. It's not as difficult as it sounds (especially if you actually have a personal assistant). Your main focus should be on carbohydrates, and the one number you may eventually be seeing in your sleep is 15 grams.

Serving sizes

The serving size listed on a nutrition facts label is the weight or volume of the specific food that contains the nutrients listed. For the linguine salad label in Figure 9-1 the stated serving size is ½ cup, and ½ cup of the salad contains 240 calories, 15 grams total fat, 24 grams total carbohydrate, and so on. Nutrition facts label serving sizes vary significantly by product, from 1 tablespoon for vegetable oil to 1 cup for macaroni and cheese, as examples.

A food's stated serving size is not necessarily the appropriate portion size for healthy eating or for blood glucose control. The value of knowing the serving size related to nutrient content is that it usually gives you enough information to calculate or estimate the right portion size for you.

Recipes usually provide the serving size information as "makes 4 servings" or "yield is 8 servings." Just as with nutrition facts labels, the nutrition information applies to one serving of that recipe.

Calculating Food Choices

Remember when math class had you muttering to yourself, "When will I ever need to use this?" Well, the time has come, but don't worry. This math is simple, the answers don't have to be exact, and you can always fall back on your personal assistant for help. In all seriousness, there is more than one way to come up with the correct portion sizes for your meal plan. The real obstacle is convincing yourself to think about food in an analytical way before you start eating. After all, that's what meal planning is all about.

A balanced, 1,700 calories per day meal plan (illustrated in Chapter 17) includes about 85 grams of protein, 55 grams of fat, and 210 grams of carbohydrate. How does that translate into actual food? Read on.

Sizing up your food — portion sizes

Most foods are a mixture of the macronutrients — protein, fat, and carbohydrate. Lean meats contain 7 to 9 grams of protein per ounce, but also contain fat. One cup of 2 percent milk contains 12 grams carbohydrate, 8 grams protein, and 5 grams fat. You get the picture.

For diabetes-related nutrition the emphasis is on 15-gram portions of total carbohydrate, also known as a carb choice, or a starch, milk, or fruit exchange. Carbohydrates have a direct effect on blood glucose levels, and your intake of carbohydrates affects how well your diabetes medication works, too. Your meal plan specifies how many carb choices, or how many grams of carbohydrate, you should have at each meal, most likely three to five carb choices (45 to 75 grams) depending on your calorie requirements. From there you can easily put together the carbohydrate portion of your meals.

You can estimate/calculate a 15-gram-carbohydrate choice from nutrition facts labels by manipulating the label's serving size into a 15-carbohydrate-grams portion size. The linguine salad in Figure 9-1 has 24 grams carbohydrate in the ½ cup serving size. Estimating, you could say that if ½ cup is 24 grams then

¼ cup is 12 grams, and 15 grams is slightly more than ¼ cup. Calculating, you can multiply 24 grams by 2 to find the total carbohydrate in a one cup serving is 48 grams. Dividing 48 grams by 15 grams equals 3.2 carb choices (about 3) per cup, so ⅓ cup would be very close. In fact, 48 grams per cup divided by 3 equals 16 grams carbohydrate per ⅓ cup portion. The label *serving size* is ½ cup, but the 15 gram carb portion is about ⅓ cup. You may be glad to know that ¼ cup works just as well.

If your head hurts you'll be glad to know that measuring appropriate portions of carbohydrate is really easier, but it does require knowing what measure of which food equals 15 carbohydrate grams. Here's where memory, reference books, cheat sheets, experience, or that personal assistant come in. One tablespoon of pure maple syrup is considered a carb choice, but you can measure about 3 full cups of raw, nonstarchy vegetables (cucumbers, broccoli, bell peppers, green beans, and so on) before you get one 15-gram-carb choice (that's why healthy eating includes lots of vegetables). Table 9-1 shows a quick guide to common carbohydrate-containing foods to get you started.

Table 9-1	One Carbohydrate Choice for Common Foods
Food Description	*Measure*
Sugar or concentrated syrups	1 tablespoon
Oatmeal, dry	¼ cup
Grains (rice, barley, etc.), cooked	⅓ cup
Pasta, cooked	⅓ cup
Beans and peas (starchy vegetables)	½ cup
Fresh fruits	½ to 1¼ cup
White potato	½ cup or 3 ounces
Bread	1 slice
Milk	1 cup
Yogurt	¾ cup
Nonstarchy vegetables cooked	1½ cups

Common carbohydrate foods like those in Table 9-1 are easy to remember with experience, but a nutrition facts label or a pocket-sized carbohydrate reference book is an absolute must for deciphering food like the linguine salad in Figure 9-1 if you intend to manage diabetes well.

Portion sizes for protein and fat share one thing in common. Both should be smaller than what most Americans picture. A healthy meal plan for diabetes management may recommend 4 to 6 ounces of protein food (lean meat, tofu, cheese, nuts, and eggs) per day, equaling about one-half of the daily protein recommendation (85 grams for the 1,700 calories per day plan). The rest of your daily protein comes from low-fat dairy (milk and yogurt) and from carbohydrate foods containing protein.

You're also likely to get much of your recommended fat from other foods, including meat, nuts, low-fat dairy, cheese, and carbohydrate foods. Some of this dietary fat is the unhealthier saturated variety, but a healthy diet focuses on sources of healthier *unsaturated* fat. Sources of fat not included in another food group include oils, butter and margarine, and salad dressings. In general, choose low-fat versions of food, and use oils sparingly.

Estimating tricks

When you don't have access to nutrition facts labels or your measuring tools, you have to estimate portion sizes. Estimating is not a replacement for more accurate determinations of portion size, but all in all it works pretty well.

The broadest estimating trick looks at how you fill your whole plate. You should allocate a quarter of your plate to a lean protein and half of your plate to nutritious nonstarchy vegetables, which you remember are very low in carbohydrate. The final quarter of your plate is reserved for your meal plan's three to five carb choices. (See Chapter 13 for the diabetes version of the USDA's MyPlate.)

You can estimate portion sizes by using your hand and your imagination. One ounce of cheese is the size of a domino, 3 ounces of meat matches a deck of cards, 1 tablespoon of margarine resembles half of your thumb, 1 cup of vegetables makes a fist, and a medium apple is equal to a baseball.

Referencing the Right Resources

Healthy eating to manage blood glucose and the risks for diabetes-related complications requires some thinking and preparation. Fortunately, there are credible resources that can help immensely. A pocket-sized reference book can be your best pal, but other resources work just as well.

Searching websites and apps

It may be debatable whether there is too much information available on the web, and now even on your mobile phone or tablet, but it's hard to deny that these technologies can be very handy. An Internet search for "carb counting" returns more than 1 million results, and there are literally hundreds of websites and apps where the nutrition information for specific foods is available.

For individual food items the U.S. Department of Agriculture has a resource at `http://ndb.nal.usda.gov/`, with searchable nutrition information on thousands of specific foods. Other nongovernment websites have similar functions, many of which also include commercial raw products and restaurant items. Nutrition apps for mobile devices are plentiful as well, and some will even scan a product's bar code and display the nutrition facts label.

Be cautious about websites or apps that offer dietary advice, or promote specific diets or products. It's much better that you learn for yourself what healthy eating and effective diabetes self-management requires. That way, you can take advantage of the valuable information and pass on the advice.

Collecting recipes

Enjoying food is absolutely essential, and if you're going to eat more often at home so you have better control of your diabetes — and we did agree that you are — you want wonderful recipes to draw from. Of course, with a market exceeding 20 million people in the United States, alone there are many diabetes cookbooks available. But, you don't have to get your recipes from diabetes cookbooks when you know what to eat. All you need are recipes that include nutrition information and serving size (number of serving the recipe yields).

Look for recipes that are relatively low in fat, especially saturated fat, low in sodium, have a generous serving size so you're satisfied, and don't send you beyond your meal's carb recommendations. Search especially for vegetable recipes, like salads or roasted vegetables with spices, so you can really enjoy the food group that should make up the majority of your diet.

Converting recipes

There's no rule that your collection of recipes that don't include nutrition information have to go into the trash. You can take advantage of the nutrition resources on the Internet to calculate the nutrition information yourself. Simply research the nutrition data for each ingredient — calories, total fat, saturated fat, total carbohydrate, fiber, protein, and sodium for a good start — and add it all up. Divide the totals by the number of servings you believe the dish should make, and check the result against what you've learned will qualify as a healthy and diabetes-friendly dish. If one of your old standards doesn't seem to make the cut (maybe the cup of lard couldn't pass muster), check Chapter 12 for some potential ingredient substitutions.

Considering Exchanges

Most dietitians and certified diabetes educators use the carbohydrate counting method for teaching nutrition to people with diabetes — counting carb choices. The Diabetic Exchange System was developed over 40 years ago as the best method for teaching healthy eating for diabetes at that time, and the Exchange System still holds some value for explaining healthy eating. The basics of the Exchange System is that all food we eat falls into one of, or a combination of, six categories — starches, fruits, milk, nonstarchy vegetables, meat and meat substitutes, or fats. Foods are placed into a group based on the nutrient makeup of the food item, and the portion size is already specified.

The Exchange System comes with a few benefits; exchanges guide heart-healthy eating by subdividing meats into lean, medium fat, and high fat meats, and the fat category into monounsaturated, polyunsaturated, and saturated subgroups; exchanges aid in weight management by placing food into the groups based on caloric content; exchanges encourage consuming a variety of foods instead of just focusing on familiar carbohydrates; and carbohydrate counting can be used in combination with the Exchange System.

The Exchange System works by promoting the equal exchange of foods within the same category. For instance, if your registered dietitian gives you three servings of the starch group at breakfast, you can choose either three slices of bread, two slices of bread and ½ cup cooked oatmeal, or 1½ cups cooked oatmeal with no bread at that meal. The choices for how you can mix and match foods from the same food group are endless, and some people find choosing from actual foods easier than strictly carb counting. In any case, looking over the exchange list shows you that healthy eating and effective diabetes self-management don't limit the variety of available food choices.

For a complete list of the exchanges, see Appendix A and B.

Part III
Meal Planning for Better Health

Top Five Fun Foods to Add to Your Grocery List

1. **Fresh vegetables and fruits:** These can be nonstarchy vegetables such as lettuce, spinach, kale, Swiss chard, soft-shell squash such as zucchini, asparagus, onions, and beets. Fruits can include mangoes, grapes, berries, apricots, and grapefruit.

2. **Go nuts!:** Nuts are a great source of protein, and they make a healthy snack if eaten in moderations. Go for the in-shell nuts so that you can get them unsalted.

3. **Lean meats, poultry, and fish:** Meat offers a way to get complete protein into your diet, but it also brings along some unhealthy fats. Rotate your favorite leans cut of mean (red meat, pork, and lamb) with skinless chicken or turkey and shellfish or fish. And don't forget that your favorite fish and shellfish are likely high in omega-3 fatty acids!

4. **Cluck and moo (eggs and dairy):** Eggs are an excellent source of protein, B12, and riboflavin, among others, but be sure to figure in the cholestoral. Two egg whites are equal to one egg, and you can always choose egg substitutes, too. And dairy offers protein along with fat and carbs. But there are low-carb yogurt options, and many low-fat milks, cheeses, sour cream, and cottage cheese.

5. **Pasta and rice and legumes . . . oh my!:** Some of your healthiest food choices are grains and legumes (beans). These foods are rich in nutrients, and some are high in both soluble and insoluble fiber. Pasta includes all noodles, including couscous. Although all pasta is high in carbohydrates, a small serving is fine. Just be sure to factor in whatever yummy sauce you want on top of it.

Measuring portion sizes is important; read about ways to measure at www.dummies.com/extras/diabetesmealplanningandnutrition.

In this part...

- Learn to plan ahead, before you take off to go grocery shopping. Make a list; spend your food dollars wisely; and avoid temptation.

- Humans have a natural emotional attachment to food. Many times, food becomes a means to dealing with sadness, loss, fear, or even happiness. Learn about the unhealthy physical and emotional attachments to different foods.

- Understand the triggers and cues that cause mindless eating, and how your eating behavior can be influenced by food descriptions and contain shape and size.

- Identify forces that work against you and your best intentions for healthier eating, and you can then create an environment that minimizes food-related temptation. And learn some tricks and tips to cut down on mindless eating.

Chapter 10

Exposing Barriers to Healthy Eating

*I*f *it was easy, everybody would do it.* That's an overused phrase for certain, but truly does apply to healthy eating. Healthy eating, apparently, is not easy, or everybody would be doing it. But healthy eating is essential for managing diabetes, so exploring the challenges and finding some simple solutions can have a huge impact on the quality of your life.

What makes healthy eating so difficult? Most people have access to healthy food choices, and healthy food can be just as filling and tasty as unhealthy food. Yet, a 2009 evaluation of the daily food logs of nearly 7,000 participants in the National Health and Nutrition Examination Survey found only 10 percent of adolescents and adults were meeting the recommended intake of fruits and vegetables — and French fries accounted for half of the vegetable consumption among adolescents. Interestingly, surveys which ask Americans directly about their fruit and vegetable consumption often find 60 percent claiming to eat five servings almost every day. Something's rotten in Denmark.

So, what accounts for this confusion? With two thirds of the population either overweight or obese, and type 2 diabetes rates skyrocketing, it's fair to say that healthy eating habits are not the norm. Is all the confusion about healthy eating, and the difficulty most people seem to have adopting healthier eating habits, all in the mind? In fact, in some significant ways it is.

This chapter explores how brain signals, culture, emotion, and the modern food environment all conspire to distort your concept of healthy eating, and to sabotage your sincere intentions to eat healthier. Fortunately, because thriving with diabetes means coming to grips with healthy eating, you can find some simple solutions that put you in the driver's seat on the road to better health.

Tracing Changes in the Food Environment

Just thinking of food can have physical effects on humans. But other images and impressions can have virtually the same effect and can keep you thinking about food even when you don't know you're thinking about food.

You may already be familiar with the story of Pavlov's dogs. Ivan Pavlov, a physiologist, was studying how dogs salivate when presented with food — a natural, *unconditioned* response in preparation for eating. But, when Pavlov began ringing a bell each time he brought food to the dogs, he noticed that their salivating could be stimulated by ringing the bell, even if no food was involved. The salivation in response to a bell was an unnatural, *conditioned* response — anticipation.

Your days and nights are now swamped with images and sounds designed to condition a certain response to a particular franchise or brand of food. Even if you've never tasted the food, chances are you have been conditioned to think about it in a certain way — to eat with your eyes. Of course, there's nothing new about advertising. What's new is the intensity of the sights and sounds, and the absolute saturation of media. It hasn't always been this way, but there's no changing it now. Commercial food, whether at restaurants or snack-type foods, may not be your only less healthy eating habit, but chances are it has a starring role.

The food industry spends as much as $10 billion dollars a year to influence consumers to a brand, and the effectiveness of advertising is a science itself. Don't underestimate the power of advertising — keep your eyes wide open, and your brain on duty.

Surviving scarcity

In this book about meal planning it would be nice to pinpoint its beginnings, but that's not really possible. Human populations began growing plants and domesticating animals with purpose before they were leaving written records. Whatever the date, these ancient attempts to better control the availability of food are the beginnings of meal planning. Some 7,500 years ago, the Sumerians were systematically planting, harvesting, and storing excess food. Agriculture, where the work of a few people can feed many, made large communities possible and helped to fill basic needs for sustenance and security.

But, in spite of this long, long history of attempts to control food supply, scarcity has always been common. And, severe scarcity in localized regions has decimated populations throughout recorded time. In the 20th century alone it's estimated that 70 million people died as a result of food shortages caused by political intention or incompetence, overpopulation, weather patterns, crop destruction by floods or insects, or shortages during war. The great Irish potato famine, caused by a plant disease, is well known in the United States for triggering a wave of immigration from Ireland, but this blight also resulted in more than one million deaths.

Food storage is as important as food production, and archeologists have found grain storage structures that predate agricultural production — ancients were storing foods they collected in the wild. Storing food protects it from spoilage and theft by other animals, protects humans from disease, and greatly increases the security of adequate food. Dry storage, root cellars, meat curing or dehydration, canning, and, of course, refrigeration have contributed mightily to fulfilling this basic human need.

Still, throughout most of history, humans have been forced to carefully plan for the production, acquisition, storage and preparation of food. Even in the relatively wealthy 20th century United States, family budgeting demanded careful planning for adequate food and sufficient nutrition. Selections were limited by transportation challenges, and the cost of some foods was significantly higher than now in relation to income during much of the 1900s. In 1920, the average American worked for nearly 3 hours to buy a 3-pound chicken, but today she earns the same chicken in less than 15 minutes. In very real ways, only the wealthy had access to excess calories.

In the 1920s, food expenses represented 25 percent of the average American family's disposal income, and only 14 percent of those food expenditures went for food away from home. By the early 1980s, the cost of food had declined to 12.5 percent of disposable income, but nearly 35 percent of food expenses went for food away from home. The cost of food in 2011 had declined further as a percentage of disposable income, to less than 10 percent, but away-from-home food now accounts for 42 percent of the food budget.

Numerous studies have shown that we consume more calories when we eat out rather than when we eat at home. One simple way to cut back on your calories is to enjoy more of your meals in your own dining room. And by eating at home, you save money, too!

The rise in the percentage of a family food budget spent away from home tells part of the story of the American diet. But quantity is one thing, quality is another. Entire books have been written about the economic and political forces that make foods packed with fat and added sugar more accessible, and often less costly, than healthier whole food. The important point, however, is that the trend in eating away from home means meal planning, even when a serious condition like diabetes puts long-term health at risk, is too often left to the influence of advertising, rather than the thoughtful consideration of a health-minded consumer.

Being overwhelmed by food

Supposedly, if you want to boil a frog for some unimaginable reason you should place the frog in cool water and then apply heat slowly. Frogs, it's said, don't notice the gradual rise in temperature and will remain calm in the pot until thoroughly cooked. If, however, you toss your frog into water that's already boiling, he is very aware of the temperature difference and will jump out immediately. The lesson in the frog tale is that you, like the frog, may not notice huge changes if they happen gradually. That's exactly what's happened to your *food environment,* and the impact is astounding.

You may realize, if you think about it, how you're physically surrounded by food constantly — bright-colored restaurants line the main streets, and every convenience store or gas stations hides the brake fluid behind rows of candy and snack chips. But, it's not unique signs or colorful packaging that subconsciously invites you to eat freely — it's advertising. Pavlov strikes again.

There are two important points to make it so you stay connected to this chapter's theme of what makes healthy eating difficult. With respect to the advertising for convenience food restaurants and snack foods, those two points are as follows:

✔ **Eating away from home is significantly less healthy than eating at home.** Study after study, some using data from the Continuing Survey of Food Intake by Individuals (CSFII), has shown that eating away from home, especially quick-service food, results in more calories, more fat, more saturated fat, more sodium, less fiber, less vitamins A and C, less calcium, less magnesium, and fewer fruits and vegetables. Eating snack foods, which are usually high in sugar and fat but lacking nutritional value, is obviously inconsistent with healthier eating.

✔ **Even if you are absolutely certain that advertising and atmosphere has no influence on you, it's almost certain that you're wrong.** Studies of eating behavior consistently show that humans are influenced by subconscious *cues* and *triggers* on where to eat, what to eat, and how much to eat. One study showed that matched groups of adults who were asked to evaluate the same TV program, but were shown different commercials, ate significantly more of the unhealthy snacks provided if their group was shown commercials for different unhealthy snacks. Participants in eating behavior experiments never believe they have been influenced by subconscious messages, and they're almost always wrong. Advertising has a powerful influence on your behavior.

When it comes to snack foods, the advertising for less healthy snacks almost always emphasizes something completely unrelated to the food — fun, happy faces, adventure, quenching extreme thirst, and friendship, for example. Advertisements for healthier snacks tend to focus on the health angle, a markedly less successful strategy.

So, what's the extent of your exposure to the advertising that subconsciously influences you to make unhealthier choices? Data for adults is difficult to find, but adolescents aged 13 to 17 are exposed to more than 6,000 food ads per year, equaling about 40 hours total. Their exposure to ads about nutrition, by contrast, is less than 30 minutes. That's an 80-fold advantage for the poorer choices. The story is, of course, the same for adults. When did you last see advertising for broccoli? The truth is that you are overwhelmed by food-related advertising, virtually none of which represents better choices for your health. You haven't noticed, but you're the frog, and the water has slowly gotten very hot.

Recognizing Our Emotional Attachment to Food

The phrase *emotional eating* has come to represent a psychological state where food becomes a means for coping with feelings of anger, sadness, loneliness, or even happiness. Eating in excess as a response to feelings can be emotionally and physically unhealthy, but responding emotionally to eating is something altogether different — it's truly part of your chemistry. Remember that cookie your mother gave you when you scraped your knee? Or that ice cream cone you got when you brought home good grades in second grade? Don't blame your mother. She got the same messages when she was a little girl.

When the physiological comfort and pleasure you feel from food is mixed with a sense of connection and emotional security associated with family or social interaction, powerful attachment to food results. Just as the development of agriculture allowed humans to form complex social relationships, food still keeps those relationships alive.

Identifying with our culture

Genealogy has become more and more popular, in part because the research tools for tracing your family roots through generations past are now at your fingertips. Sixteenth-century French author and gastronome Jean Anthelme Brillat-Savarin famously said, "Tell me what you eat, and I will tell you who you are."

The connection between culture and food is a subject of significant study. An Internet search turns up books, television series, academic studies, and a quarterly journal. Just as language, customs, music, and art arise with a cultural identity, so does food. And, as families, ethnicities, and cultures mix, new connections between food and cultural identity form.

Your cultural connection with food may be through certain holidays or celebrations, heirloom recipes, a favorite grandmother, your extended families, or your entire community. The important point is that your experience with food as something connecting you with others who are much like you is very deep, even representing, in some measure, who you are in a fundamental way. Food is love.

Your emotional connection with culture through food is neither good nor bad from the diabetes and health perspective. But, as you move toward making conscious decisions about how you are going to eat, remember that there are strong and fundamental forces that shape your relationship to food and can't simply be ignored. Culture is but one of those forces.

Making the social connection

Food is likely to be a centerpiece of your social connections too, and social connections are another aspect of emotional security — you belong somewhere. Whether it's drinking a cup of coffee or tea with friends, cooking hot dogs on a stick over a campfire, monitoring an important business transaction, or planning an elaborate affair like a wedding, food (or drink) is almost always prominent.

Sharing food, for most of history a valuable commodity, has always been a symbolic offer of peace or friendship; the preparation of food for guests or friends demonstrates caring and intimacy. In the most basic sense, sharing food is helping others survive.

Food as a gift is common in every society, and how many romantic relationships begin with a shared meal? Restaurants and drinking establishments strive to create a certain ambiance to match different social interactions, from peaceful and quiet to loud and celebratory — an atmosphere for every occasion and mood.

Food in society can convey messages that are less altruistic, too. Food can represent power, social status, separation, and exclusion.

All in all, food is woven intricately into society and into your social connections. Once again, the point is to simply understand that food has a larger role in your life than strictly sustenance and nutrition. When it comes to making conscious choices about your diet, it's important to look deeply into how food connects you to others.

Deferring To Our Inner "Caveman"

Your brain is amazing. The thinking part of your brain gets most of the credit, and who could really argue. Compared to the brains of other organisms, you take the grand prize for biggest brain to body size (an elephant's brain is bigger than yours, but an elephant is much bigger than you). And, what makes your brain so big for your size is your huge *cerebral cortex* — the thinking part. Your cerebral cortex is your brain's chief executive, responsible for self control, reasoning, abstract thought, and planning. It's the outer, folded layer often called gray matter, and because it is so superior to other animals you can speak and write, imagine, predict, deduce, decide, and calculate. Like any chief executive, your cerebral cortex not only gobbles up much of your resources, it's so wrapped up with high-level responsibilities it wouldn't know how to do the simplest things like breath, sleep, and swallow without assistance.

These basic, non-executive functions — involuntary, instinctive, and reflex — are handled behind the scenes with little fanfare by what you can think of as your working brain. Your working brain controls many of your behaviors, and responses to the world around you, in thousands of complex chemical ways. Making wise decisions about what you eat, to better manage diabetes and improve your overall health, is definitely a job for your marvelous thinking brain. But the messages your body gets from further down the organizational chart don't always agree with the big boss, and that can create a difficult conflict between eating decisions and eating urges.

Seeking the pleasure response

While your cerebral cortex is busy calculating away, something has to make sure you remember to drink, sleep, eat, form relationships, and reproduce. Your working brain is on the job, sending and receiving chemical messages here and there to keep essential behaviors humming along.

Take appetite, for example. Appetite isn't quite this simple, but in a simplified context the hormones *ghrelin* and *leptin* are fairly straightforward. Ghrelin is released by stomach cells to signal your working brain that you are hungry. As you eat, stored fat cells release the hormone leptin, signaling your brain you have had enough food — your hunger is satisfied. Because eating is a behavior that is absolutely essential to your survival, however, another part of your working brain wants to personally thank you for eating, and helps you create a fond memory so you remember that eating is good the next time you encounter food.

Your reward is a dose of the *neurotransmitter* dopamine, and dopamine is the ultimate feel-good chemical. Dopamine is so powerful that addictive drugs such as cocaine, heroin, and amphetamines, are addictive to some extent because they stimulate dopamine release. Dopamine keeps you coming back.

This *reward pathway*, which also can include other neurotransmitters like *serotonin* and *endorphins*, reinforces learning through reward, and is a factor in motivating the essential survival behaviors of all higher order animals. Your working brain rewards you for eating whenever you have food available. Your working brain does not understand that you always have food available, or that you really don't need special memories or rewards for eating whenever food is available. This particular responsibility assigned to your working brain is outdated in an advanced and affluent human society, but there's no off switch.

Without proper supervision, the wonderful, chemically induced feelings that are intended to reinforce essential survival behavior could make overconsumption difficult to control. Recent research employing powerful brain scans suggests that some foods activate the same areas of the brain as commonly abused drugs. And, just as decreasing sensitivity to dopamine keeps drug users increasing drug dosage for the same dopamine reward, recent research is finding that obese people may eat more food for similar reasons. Obese people, it seems, have fewer dopamine receptors than normal-weight people, and may not get the same reward.

The reinforcing role of the reward pathway also involves the creation of fond memories, as mentioned earlier. To the working brain it's important that when you encounter a hamburger you recall that previous hamburgers have been good. But this response isn't limited to encountering an actual hamburger — the reward pathway is stimulated by images of hamburgers or by thoughts of hamburgers, too. In this regard, you are Pavlov's dog, and advertising is the bell. Advertising images trigger a conditioned response to food through your outdated reward pathway.

Lastly, overeating for the sheer delight of dopamine and other pleasure stimulating neurotransmitters might not be much of a concern if broccoli triggered the same response as donuts; however, this part of your working brain is all about survival and scarcity, and, therefore, favors energy-dense food. Fat, with 9 calories per gram, is more than double the energy density of either carbohydrate or protein, and brain research shows that both fat and sugar activate the reward pathway. Some contend that a combination of fat, sugar, and salt is actually addictive. The bottom line is that a marvelous biological system, which is essential for survival when food is scarce, contributes to excessive eating when food is plentiful, and even stimulates addictive-like behavior when food and food images are inescapable.

Losing logic to impulse from stress

Your thinking brain has the power and the authority to override your more primitive survival instincts related to food. In fact, your ability to imagine and understand future consequences helps keep all sorts of impulsive behaviors in check every day. As long as your cerebral cortex is on duty, it has the final say. About the only time this chain of command gets short circuited is when you are threatened.

The primitive threat response is often called the *fight or flight* response, and the decision between fighting or fleeing has no time allowance for the sort of expert deliberative consideration your thinking brain is so good with. Instead, your working brain takes control in an emergency response to heighten senses, make energy resources available, and supercharge strength for fighting or fleeing by dumping adrenaline and other chemicals into your system. This intense response to threat puts your *sympathetic* nervous system in charge, and input from your thinking brain is irrelevant. The stress stimulated by a threat is all about reflex, impulse, and reaction — no thinking is required.

Fortunately, most of you are not subjected to real threats on a regular basis, and in a more controlled circumstance — a carnival ride or skydiving — you might even seek out the intense physical thrill of the threat response. In modern societies, however, researchers are beginning to identify potential consequences to health of chronic, low-level stress.

Low levels of constant stress from long work hours, too little physical activity, balancing relationships, financial worries, or health concerns like diabetes seems to have a distinctly negative impact on health. Chapter 4 mentioned a study where greater accumulations of the so-called stress hormone cortisol in hair, indicating stress over a period of months was more strongly associated with heart attack than other well known risk factors. Chronic stress may also inhibit your capacity to make wise decisions about food.

Some researchers believe that chronic stress levels keep the sympathetic nervous system turned on, literally reducing your willpower and making impulsive eating more likely. Stated simply, your difficulties sticking with a healthy eating plan, when you clearly understand the long-term advantages of healthier eating, may be in part because a threat-like response to low-level stress turns down the volume of your thinking brain.

Other stress-increasing situations are directly associated with eating behavior as well. Moderate sleep deprivation, certainly not uncommon, disrupts the appetite hormones by increasing levels of the hunger hormone ghrelin and reducing levels of the satiety hormone leptin. Ultimately, stress is not only unhealthy by itself, but may very well inhibit your capacity to makes logical decisions about your lifestyle.

The average adults needs seven to eight hours sleep every night — those who sleep consistently less don't perform as well on complex mental tests. Worse, studies show that adults who get less, or even much more, than seven hours sleep each night have a higher mortality rate, and a higher body mass index than adults who get seven to eight hours of sleep regularly.

Uncovering the mindless subconscious

Adults are not very gullible. It may take a hard lesson or two along the way, but eventually you can spot a load of manure a mile off. But, the truth is you are fooled every single day when it comes to food, and in some cases you're both the fooler and the fooled. And if you don't believe it, that's exactly what the research says you would think. Virtually everyone who's fooled in a food study swears they won't be.

Dr. Brian Wansink is a leading researcher into eating behavior, especially what he calls *mindless eating*. His carefully disguised experiments at the University of Illinois and Cornell University have demonstrated how your eating behavior can be significantly influenced by food descriptions, container size, whether your food waste is removed from your sight, and especially your surroundings. You can review Dr. Wansink's work on mindless eating at www.mindlesseating.org.

Controlled experiments on eating behavior demonstrate something you probably already know — it's a little unnatural to think about food. The truth is that this lack of awareness makes you a potential sucker for being tricked into overeating — but who's doing the tricking? A restaurant owner who's trying to maximize profit may be doing you a favor by tricking you into eating less. For instance, you will eat less, studies show, if you eat off of a smaller plate. That could explain why single price buffets often put out smaller plates, but the owners could increase their profits even more if they put the buffet out of sight. Mindless eating doesn't always work to your disadvantage, but more often than not it does.

Ultimately, you are more often your own worst enemy. Scan your kitchen or office, and note what kinds of foods are in plain sight, ready to be scooped up when you begin grazing. It's very likely that you don't apply the "out of sight, out of mind" strategy to foods that are best eaten in moderation. How often do you purchase the larger size snack because it seems like a better deal, even though the actual cost is greater? Is supersizing your convenience food meals irresistible as a financial investment to you? Do you always assume the salad is the healthier choice without ever bothering to actually find out?

Early in this chapter this question was left unanswered — is the difficulty most people seem to have adopting healthier eating habits all in the mind? You can see now that much of the difficulty is all in the mind — in the brain, to be precise. But, if you took the phrase *all in the mind* as hinting at some weakness in character, maybe you can see now how wrong that assumption would be.

Food is a fundamental need, and having an adequate supply of food is a biological mission for every human. Food is such a key to survival that it's woven into your emotional identity as a member of a family, a culture, or a society. In modern, affluent societies, however, you are surrounded by convenience foods. The formulations of these unhealthy, high-fat, high-sugar convenience foods are especially effective at triggering your brain's natural reward feedback loop, where the release of neurotransmitters like dopamine creates a biological urge to have more. Images and advertisements for these foods, which saturate your environment, stimulate the same urges as having the actual food. In a significant way, the interplay between human biology and the modern food environment is expressed in skyrocketing rates of obesity and type 2 diabetes, and this unhealthy cycle of stimulus and reward may be a frustrating part of your life, too. There are, however, solutions.

Beating the Odds — Eating Healthier Forever

It would be going too far to say that you are completely powerless to resist the subconscious influence of unhealthy food, and helpless to win the battle for control of your working brain against focused and well-financed advertisers. But, whereas awareness of what's responsible for your history of less-than-healthy eating habits improves your understanding, it's still true that if you keep doing what you've always done, you keep getting what you've always gotten. Something needs to change.

Obviously, eating healthier foods is the simple answer, but it probably hasn't been simple so far, and now you know how some of the influences on your eating behavior go much deeper than simply deciding to eat differently. With diabetes and your health so closely associated with the eating behaviors you are going to practice going forward, however, the stakes are greater than ever. Fortunately, you have one amazing asset on your side — your cerebral cortex, the most incredible thinking brain in the history of the world.

And the secret to eating healthy in this modern, affluent society, where unhealthy options exert so much influence, is to let your thinking brain do what it does best — plan. Planning is how individuals and organizations stay on track when surrounded by distractions and temptations — well thought-out, guiding decisions, made with a clear, long-term vision, can be more powerful than all distractions and temptations. Setting a new course for thriving with diabetes starts with minimizing the distractions and temptations in your life, and lets your thinking brain do the planning that keeps you on track.

Creating the right environment

Establishing an environment that minimizes the food-related temptations, which are reinforced by your working brain's chemical stew, could start by moving to the far reaches of Alaska or Wyoming, and declining TV, telephone, or internet service. That may make getting important regular medical care for your diabetes more challenging, however. A better alternative might be to simply modify your own food environment to whatever extent you can. Although it may sound overly simple, the benefits can be amazing.

The previous section explained how *cues and triggers* in the media, your community, and your immediate environment influence unhealthy eating habits, but this is only a problem because the huge majority of cues and triggers are associated with unhealthy choices. It's unlikely you see many influences toward healthier foods in media advertising, but you can build an environment in your home and office that turns mindless behavior in your favor. You can fool yourself to be healthier.

Start with an inventory of your home and anyplace else you hang out, like your office. What kinds of food have you stockpiled? Is there anything healthy, like fresh fruit, or some low-carbohydrate vegetables? Check to see if your less-healthy choices are the ones right out in plain view, begging you to grab a bite every time you glance up or walk by? Nobody says you can never snack, even on something that won't make anyone's list of healthy foods, but give yourself the chance to make better choices, or to forget you have cheese curls in the house. Make some decisions about what foods you must have now and then, like chocolate, and eliminate stuff that just happens to be lying around. Choose the best options for snacks, like dark chocolate instead of milk chocolate, and hide it away so you're not reminded constantly. Display healthier foods, like fresh fruit, in plain view so cues and triggers to eat work in your favor (and you remember to count the carbohydrates in foods like fruit).

And, when it comes to actually eating, try the following tricks:

- **Never eat snacks directly from the container.** Take an actual serving according to the label, and put the container completely away. This habit allows your thinking brain to ask you hard questions when you consider retrieving the container for another serving.

- **You eat less if you eat off of smaller plates.** If you're not in the market for new dishware, practice putting much less food on your plate, and leave the second helping across the room instead of in a serving bowl that's sitting right in front of you. A trip across the room can really discourage additional eating in a mindless way.

- **Incorporate a healthy, low-calorie appetizer.** Start with a salad of colorful vegetables (and low-calorie dressing), or bowl of low-sodium broth into your meals, and give the first course time to communicate with your brain before you gobble down the main course. It takes 20 minutes for your brain to get the all-full signal.

- **Chew your food thoroughly.** In fact, chew it beyond what it normally takes for you to swallow. Time is your friend in healthier eating habits.

✔ **Don't eat in front of the television.** Anything that takes your attention away from your food and your level of satisfaction and satiety opens the door for mindless overeating.

✔ **Change your habits.** If you always sit down at 10:00 P.M. with a bowl of ice cream, do something different to break the mindless pattern.

Your mind is both mysterious and amazing. Researchers in Pittsburg found, for instance, that subjects who were asked to imagine themselves in vivid detail eating a certain number of M&M candies resulted in that group actually eating fewer M&Ms after the thought experiment was over than subjects in groups asked to imagine they were doing other tasks. More interesting, subjects asked to simply think about M&M candies, without being asked to imagine eating them, did not show the same tendency to eat fewer M&Ms after the experiment. In a counterintuitive result, creating a vivid mental image of eating a food reduced the desire to actually eat the food.

Planning: Using your incredible brain

Your incredible thinking brain is a planner, and if you give it room to make your most important decisions, like how to improve your eating habits for diabetes, it will shine. If you call on your thinking brain to rescue you when you're stressed and surrounded by tempting, unhealthy food choices, it may ask you to call back later after it's had time to think about the issues for a while. When it comes to food, impulse often wins the spur-of-the-moment decisions. Impulse has a lot of support from that part of your brain, with its chemical reward system, that wants you to eat everything you see for survival in times of shortage.

The solution is actually simpler than you think, but it's something too many people in our society don't do anymore — decide what you're going to eat in advance. Making food-related decisions ahead of time, when you're not directly confronted with the cues and triggers that lead you down the wrong path, can disarm those influences that sabotage your best intentions, including your working brain. And, in some ways, facing the responsibility to manage your diabetes can be the final push that motivates you to begin thinking more about the foods you eat.

Planning ahead starts with a making a menu for your week's meals (or your month's meals, if planning is easy for you). Your diabetes meal plan provides a template for choosing food groups, especially your daily carbohydrate choices, but you fill in the actual foods and recipes. Chapter 17 gives you a sample menu, and Toby's website www.DiabetesEveryDay.com provides a new menu every week to subscribers. But, you can also plan a menu yourself after you accept that thinking about food is simply necessary, no matter how unnatural it seems at first. Chapter 13 gives you step-by-step instructions.

Your second assignment is to make a shopping list, and because you're making wise decisions in advance with the assistance of your marvelous thinking brain, load your list with wise choices for healthy eating. And, if you make your list carefully, you can float right by all of the temptations that impulse might have had you reaching for in the past. Chapter 12 takes you on a grocery tour, and explains how to make wiser choices and where you'll find them.

Your final assignment is to learn to plan ahead when you're eating out. Frankly, this couldn't be simpler now that restaurants post their menus and nutrition information online. By scanning the choices and making your decisions before you're bathed in ambiance and check out what was just delivered at the next table, impulse doesn't rule the day again. Eating out is challenging, but Chapter 15 guides you in making the better choices for your diabetes.

Eating healthy isn't easy, but you are perfectly equipped to take control of your diabetes by adopting better eating habits. Food will always be an important part of your life because humans are programmed to place great emphasis on survival and security, including emotional security. By giving your thinking brain the time and space to work for you, however, food loses its power over your behaviors. At the end of the day you can freely give healthier food its rightful place, because genuine survival and security is best assured by simply having your health.

Chapter 11

Setting Priorities and Staying on Track

. . . .

In This Chapter

▶ Accepting key personal and family commitments to health

▶ Learning simple eating habits that can improve blood glucose control

▶ Setting yourself up for success

▶ Getting help when you need it

▶ Patting yourself on the back

. . . .

*I*f you read almost any of the previous chapters you may have been surprised, or even shocked, to learn that you have so much responsibility for
your own health. It's your new management job — diabetes self-management.
Even though you never filled out an application and almost certainly weren't
prepared or fully qualified for the job, you were put in charge of your own
long-term health as soon as you were first diagnosed with diabetes. This
may be the most important job you will ever have, and the most challenging.
There's no paycheck, you can't resign, and you absolutely don't want to opt
in on the early retirement plan. There's much about your new job to dislike,
but you'll probably never have a better opportunity to positively impact the
quality of your life than by doing diabetes self-management well.

Some of you may have this eating-healthy-for-diabetes thing mastered already,
but for many, probably most, this represents significant lifestyle changes.
Lasting lifestyle changes are simply not easy to make, and anyone who has
tried to lose weight can back that statement up. New behaviors are necessary,
but before action comes attitude. And a new attitude can make all the difference.

In this chapter I show you the importance of acknowledging the challenges
of lifestyle change, how to stay committed to a healthier lifestyle, and some
expert tips for staying on track.

Committing to Your Future

The future can be hard to think about. After all, for most people the demands on time and attention today and tomorrow are enough to keep them completely occupied. If you have type 1 diabetes the daily contest to balance eating with your insulin injections probably puts the immediate dangers of very low and very high blood glucose in the front of your mind. But, for many with type 2 diabetes there aren't any daily reminders that diabetes needs more attention than taking a pill. A common response from patients to doctor or educator concerns about high A1Cs is, "But I feel fine."

The most serious threats to health for people with diabetes are in the future, something from the list of health effects we have innocently called complications. But, there is nothing innocent about diabetes complications. Some complications are life changing without being life threatening, like sexual dysfunction, but others are disabling or deadly, like kidney failure or heart attack. Two things all diabetes complications have in common, however, is they take time to develop — they are in the future — and they are much easier to prevent than to "fix" once they begin. Healthy eating for diabetes is about preventing complications later.

The process of changing your lifestyle today needs a commitment from you, a commitment to your future, whatever you want that to be. Experts suggest visualizing, and most of us do that already when we daydream or imagine what we would like our future to include. Maybe you look forward to grandchildren, or maybe your dream is playing professional basketball. Visualizing is simply serious imagining — really feeling the details of what that perfect future will be like. Visualizing is positive and optimistic, and your vision of your future should not include having your life derailed by serious diabetes complications.

Behavior change experts recommend making your visualizations more real by writing them down, and by collecting photos or objects that relate to your goals.

Making a personal commitment to managing diabetes well and eating healthy can keep diabetes squeezed down into the smallest possible part of your perfect future. Even if you don't quite have a grasp on exactly what you need to do (we're getting to that part), making this decision now is easy. It's all about attitude.

Making time for healthy eating

In the 1970s, as the potential for new technologies to improve worker productivity were becoming a reality, social scientists speculated that people in the

21st century would be challenged with how to spend an over abundance of leisure time. Things haven't exactly turned out that way. Ironically, the years since then have seen the appearance of convenience stores, fast food restaurants, ATMs, and all sorts of technologies and services marketed to save time (for some reason mobile dog grooming comes to mind).

Because time is limited to 24 hours each day you choose how you spend the time you have. It may seem like there aren't choices involved, but how you spend time represents how you prioritize time. Setting priorities always involves choices, and making a commitment to your future health may include reprioritizing how you spend some of your time.

Healthy eating involves time to plan, shop, prepare food, and keep yourself motivated. When you have committed to healthy eating the time spent on this commitment becomes, by definition, important. When an activity is accepted as an essential part of your schedule the stresses of feeling like time is wasted are removed, and you can give yourself permission to actually enjoy the time. Healthy eating can be special family time or an adventure. You don't have to be a chef to learn to love cooking.

Wondering where you'll find the time? Get out your pad and pen again (you will use more paper later, so bring extra). It's always revealing to write down where all of that time goes, and even more interesting to see what could be "adjusted" without missing anything. When you consider the importance of a healthy lifestyle to yourself and your family it will not be difficult finding a few minutes to improve your eating habits.

Accepting inconvenience

Inconvenience, like beauty, is in the eye of the beholder. The intent of this chapter's discussion about fully committing to diabetes self-management and healthy eating is to elevate the importance of this task among your many priorities. When tasks are seen as important, the effort required can be accepted as an investment, not an inconvenience. You may find, for instance, that when you accept the importance of preparing healthy meals at home, you begin to enjoy cooking.

The truth is that no matter how committed you become, there are aspects of diabetes self-management that are simply inconvenient. People with type 1 diabetes understand this all too well. There's really no case to make that sticking your finger for a blood glucose test eight or ten times a day should be enjoyable. Nor can lugging around syringes, insulin, a meter, and test strips; or dealing with low blood glucose in an important meeting; or getting an alarm from an insulin pump while waiting in line at the department of motor vehicles (the universal symbol for long lines).

People with type 2 diabetes don't usually share the same kind of frustration that comes with type 1, where it's impossible to "escape" for more than a few hours. Still, each person is different, and what comes easily to one person may be extraordinarily frustrating and inconvenient for another.

The bottom line is that dealing with a certain amount of genuine inconvenience is necessary if you're going to manage diabetes well and eat healthy. This book is filled with advice and tips that help make your diabetes meal planning easier, but accepting the unavoidable inconveniences with a smile is the only solution in some cases.

Learning new things — Old dog, new tricks

You may have noticed there is crucial but very simple information you need to know about food, such as which foods contain carbohydrate. Other necessary knowledge is somewhat more challenging — translating nutrition facts label information into a carb-counting format, for instance. Calculating insulin to carbohydrate ratios is another step beyond for those taking fast-acting insulin injections with meals, in part because being accurate is so important. But ultimately, this is not, as they say, rocket science.

Nevertheless, it's all too common to find otherwise extremely intelligent people who seemingly can't understand and apply the simplest facts about diabetes and nutrition. The issue isn't a shortage of brain power, but a refusal to think analytically about food. For some it's a rebellion against the unfairness of this demand, as if refusing to acknowledge diabetes can make it go away. For others, it's simply the view that eating should not require thinking.

Your new task as your own diabetes manager, that job you did not ask for, requires that you use your brain some. The thinking required is well within the range of most any adult who is willing to learn and, like any skill, gets easier as time passes. But no matter what your age, a commitment to your future health includes engaging your brain for healthy eating. In this case eating does not require thinking, but everything else until your plate is loaded does.

Some personalities are virtually the opposite, absorbing every detail about diabetes and healthy eating like a mad scientist. Knowing the information without applying it, however, accomplishes no more than not knowing in the first place.

Standing your ground

After you make a commitment to your future health, reprioritize your time, accept the inconveniences of managing diabetes, and engage your brain for learning new things, one unexpected stumbling block may remain. You may find a lack of support from family and/or friends. It may take the form of whining from the family about changes in food options, or of friends urging you to stop being a party pooper. In most cases there's no intentional effort to sabotage your commitment to healthy eating, and a serious discussion about your reasons may resolve the stress. If the conflict continues, something more confrontational may be required, including an option for family counseling or finding new friends.

A healthy diet for diabetes is a healthy diet for everyone. Targeted at heart health and weight management, the focus on carbohydrates is the only part of a healthy diabetes eating plan that's unique to people with diabetes. The changes you bring to your family's diet are most likely appropriate and beneficial to everyone.

Two generalizations should be put forward for your consideration. Albert Einstein is credited with saying, "All generalizations are false, including this one." But, accepting that disclaimer it is worth pointing to some common gender-associated pitfalls that can lead to lost focus and falling back to old habits.

First, most women truly do have a caretaker's heart, and the case of the whiny family can be overwhelming. It takes incredible resolve for anyone to both make a major lifestyle change and to carry along the extra weight of a family that's complaining about inadequate care. If these conflicts include the adult spouse or significant other (younger children can be forgiven) and remain unresolved after discussion, there's a relationship problem that goes beyond food.

Men, on the other hand, are more likely to revert to "macho," declaring by inaction that it takes more than diabetes to bend their iron will. The common scenario here is that a spouse, often without diabetes, initiates the changes in lifestyle, but the man with diabetes refuses to participate. This person hasn't made a commitment to change, so the behavior is not surprising to others. It can be an incredible frustration to the person trying to influence positive change, however.

Adopting Better Habits

So much of healthy behaviors, or not healthy behaviors, are simply the result of habits. The Merriam-Webster online dictionary defines *habit* as "an acquired mode of behavior that has become nearly or completely involuntary." Habits are learned, and old habits can be replaced by new ones. There are many habits that are helpful to improving blood glucose control, heart health, and weight management, but two are especially relevant to meal planning.

Eating at home more often

You only need to browse the nutrition information provided on the websites of your favorite restaurants to get an idea of how difficult it can be to eat healthy when eating out. Just scan the sodium content to keep your search simple, remembering that the population with diabetes falls into the "special" category with a daily sodium recommendation of 1,500 milligrams per day.

The U.S. Centers for Disease Control and Prevention, National Chronic Disease Prevention and Health Promotion's *Research to Practice Series #6*, entitled "Incorporating Away-From-Home Food into a Healthy Eating Plan," looked at available research on the question of eating away from home. Although the research is imperfect and tends to focus on quick-service food, there's little doubt that eating away from home results in higher calorie intake, higher fat intake, and lower nutrient intake.

A report from the Keystone Forum on Away-From-Home Foods, commissioned by the U.S. Food and Drug Administration and published in May 2006, cited research that showed the following:

- Eating out more frequently is associated with obesity, higher body fatness, and higher body mass index.

- Women who eat out more often (more than five times per week) consume about 290 more calories on average each day than women who eat out less often.

- Eating more fast-food meals is linked to eating more calories, more saturated fat, fewer fruits and vegetables, and less milk.

So, does this all mean you should never eat away from home? Of course not. One key to success in eating healthy for diabetes is to avoid feelings of being deprived, and eating away from home is often associated with important social connections. Skipping these social occasions would certainly lead to frustration. And, people with diabetes who travel for work or pleasure must eat away from home for all practical purposes. For these reasons Chapter 15 is dedicated to helping you learn to eat away from home wisely. But make no mistake about it, eating a healthy diet away from home is challenging and the more often one eats out the more important it becomes to plan carefully.

Eating more often at home not only makes it easier to know exactly what you are eating as it relates to diabetes management, it actually allows you to control what you are eating. Ask yourself if eating away from home as often as you do has simply become an ill-advised habit. If the answer is yes, it's time for a better habit.

Table 11-1 illustrates how one simple meal away from home compares to the daily recommendations in a 2,000-calories-per-day meal plan for diabetes management.

Table 11-1		The Nutrition Cost of Eating Out			
Food Item	**Calories**	**Carbohydrate (g)**	**Protein (g)**	**Fat (g)**	**Sodium (mg)**
Spaghetti and meatball dinner	920	98	50	36	1770
2 bread sticks	150	56	6	2	400
Side salad w/ dressing	290	23	5	20	1530
Diet soda	0	0	0	0	28
TOTAL	1360	177	61	58	3728
Daily Recommended	2000	250	100	67	1500

Timing is everything

To say that timing is everything may apply better to stock market trades or hitting a baseball than to eating with diabetes, but the timing of your meals and snacks and medication can be important in several ways.

The most direct timing relationship, and the most important, is the timing between injecting or bolusing with rapid- or short-acting insulin and eating carbohydrate food. These insulin varieties are formulated to take effect lowering blood glucose relatively quickly (5 minutes to one hour) and reach peak activity relatively soon (30 minutes to three hours). Unless taken specifically to lower high blood glucose levels, this insulin is intended to be followed by ingestion of a certain number of carbohydrate grams. A lapse in proper timing here can result in dangerously low blood glucose levels.

Timing is less critical, but still important for long acting insulin and for some oral diabetes medications where low blood glucose is a potential side effect.

Overall, eating on a regular schedule, following your dietitian's meal plan recommendations by spreading carbohydrates throughout the day, and not skipping meals can improve blood glucose control, especially after meals.

Meal skipping, especially skipping breakfast, can sabotage one other important mission for a statistical majority of people with type 2 diabetes weight loss. We have already discussed why weight management is so important and how even a modest loss of body weight can have profound benefits to blood sugar control. Although it may seem logical that skipping the calories from an entire meal would promote weight loss, that logic doesn't hold up. On the other hand, breakfast is not a magic meal where you eat anything you want and watch the weight fall off. Breakfast — breaking the overnight fast — should include carbohydrates for energy and protein for feeling full enough to pass on the donuts you find at the office or the bank — or the donut shop.

For many, skipping breakfast is not a misplaced weight loss strategy, but rather is an issue of time. Mornings can be frantic, and waiting two minutes for a bowl of oatmeal can simply seem difficult. But, a healthy breakfast is too important, and this problem of timing is too easy to resolve. Breakfast is a priority, and therefore gets its necessary time.

The National Weight Control Registry is a database of individuals who qualify by having lost at least 30 pounds and by keeping lost weight off for a minimum of one year. The group is a valuable source of information to define weight loss strategies that have proven successful. When it comes to eating breakfast, 78 percent of this group report eating breakfast every day, and 90 percent report eating breakfast at least five days per week. That is a strong hint that breakfast is a key part of reaching weight loss goals.

When traveling across several time zones, talk to your doctor about how to adjust your medication, including insulin. Going by local time at your destination can result in taking doses too close together or too far apart, depending upon which direction you travel.

Staying On Track

Your dedicated change in diabetes health behaviors sparked by a newly found commitment to your future health comes with one ironclad guarantee — detours. Other labels like setback, failure, falling off the wagon, relapse, collapse, defeat, or breakdown may be commonly used, but those labels don't apply if you stay committed. *Detour* is the word. Detours are diversions that not only find the way straight back to the intended route, but also make forward progress along the way. Staying on track includes the detours.

Declining deprivation — insisting on delicious

The word *deprivation* has been used most widely over recent years in the context of "enhanced interrogation techniques" and the debate about what constitutes torture. Deprivation is powerful at breaking down commitments. Feeling deprived is powerful, too.

If a new focus on healthy eating for diabetes management is going to take root and grow, then feeling deprived of food that satisfies your taste buds or an adequate amount of food can't be part of the plan. Even though you may be working to transition from too many calories and too much fat there is a distinct difference between feeling unfamiliar with a new habit and feeling deprived. Finding a reasonably acceptable balance is key.

Balancing starts with flavor. There's much empty space available between your mother's recipe for cheese and bacon broccoli casserole (with cracker topping) and a plain, steamed broccoli stalk, but this sort of drastic leap from one to the other is common. And, it's commonly not successful. For some people this feels like the right approach because they expect suffering to be key part of a better eating plan. Suffering and deprivation can motivate action, but the action is fueled by defiance and is simply not sustainable. Remember torture? Now picture a plain, steamed broccoli stalk for lunch.

So, how can you find delicious recipes that are still okay for diabetes? You look for them — they are everywhere. The U.S. market for diabetes is currently estimated at 26 million individuals, so you might expect to find recipe options targeted at a market that size, and you can. We suggest you begin with the *Diabetes Cookbook for Dummies* by Dr. Alan Rubin with Cait James (John Wiley and Sons). Ultimately, you can easily adapt virtually any recipe that's generally healthy to be "diabetes friendly."

Just don't settle for food that's less than delicious and satisfying. The challenges that naturally come with any effort to change habits are challenge enough. There's no rule that forbids enjoying yourself along the way.

Embracing imperfection

Want to know the surest and quickest way to become completely disenchanted with your diabetes management efforts? Simply expect perfection, and wait a day or two.

Starting any lifestyle change with unreasonable expectations is a certain path to disappointment. Unreasonable expectations could apply to both the anticipated results like an extreme weight loss or lofty goal to improve A1C, or your own capacity to carry out an overly ambitious plan. Going from a mostly sedentary lifestyle to running five miles every day, for example, is likely to be discouraging starting on day one.

But, even if you have kept your expectations reasonable, sometimes things just don't go the way they should. Religiously cutting 500 calories per day for a week to lose one pound, according to the standard formula, may not work precisely for you the first week. Covering 45 grams of carbohydrate with your mathematically perfect and proven five units of insulin won't keep your blood sugar levels perfect every time. There are simply too many variables for perfection.

The real risk with unmet expectations is that constant disappointment and frustration can lead you to stop trying. Wandering away from your meal plan one time shouldn't trigger weeks of unmanaged binge eating, but that's an all too common a response among dieters. Likewise, an unexplainable glitch now and then with your insulin/carbohydrate equation is no reason to stop pre-meal blood glucose testing in favor of guessing.

Embrace imperfection because imperfection is reality. Focus on the big picture, that being adopting healthier behaviors. Weight loss is about eating fewer calories on average and increasing physical activity slowly but surely. Glycemic control comes when you are more often in a normal blood glucose range than a higher than normal range. It's simple arithmetic that three steps forward and two steps back equals one step forward — and that's progress. If we reject expectations of perfection, accepting detours as reality, success is infinitely easier to find.

A survey of more than 2,000 members of the weight loss website `www.spark people.com` looked to identify keys to successful weight loss. Among the common characteristics of strong starters, who lost five times more weight than false starters, was listing their number one goal as "building a strong foundation of healthy habits." On the other hand, false starters tended to list a number, like lose four pounds in two weeks, as their main goal. Two thirds of false starters lost momentum in two weeks, 18 percent after just three days.

Ignoring quick fixes

A recent study by researchers at Oregon State University looked at available evidence for hundreds of weight loss supplements and concluded that no research evidence exists that any single product results in significant weight loss — and many have detrimental health benefits. The magic pill doesn't exist, yet Americans spend an estimated $2.4 billion each year on the promises of a shortcut. The language sounds legitimate — guaranteed, scientific break-through, money back if not satisfied. And most have personal testimonies, complete with before and after photos to prove the point. Don't believe it.

Dietary supplements are not approved by the U.S. Food and Drug Administration, nor are they tested for effectiveness or safety. Even invasive treatments like injections claiming to dissolve fat are not regulated in the way you might expect. And the FDA's case files support the Oregon State University study's statement that weight loss supplements can be dangerous.

By the way, the history of weight loss drugs that have been approved by the FDA is not a glowing success story. Drug after drug approved for weight loss has been pulled from use after side effects proved to be more dangerous than the extra weight. Fenfluramine with phentermine (Fen-phen), dexfenfluramine (Redux), and sibutrimine (Meridia) are a few examples. The search for safe and effective weight loss medication continues.

Claims for a diabetes cure are common also, often promoted with the omi-nous "what your doctor won't tell you" accusation or "the best kept secret" revelation. The story here is much the same; if it sounds too good to be true, it probably is. Ironically, reading the fine print of some diabetes-cure claims will reveal a program focused on a new healthy diet and plenty of physical activity, as if this approach was a secret.

The consensus is that diabetes can't be cured. Researchers focused on type 1 diabetes have done transplants of the insulin producing pancreatic islet cells with some limited success. Other type 1 research aims at stopping the renegade immune system attack on islet cells or developing an "artificial pancreas." For type 2 diabetes certain bariatric surgical procedures (gastric bypass) have proven effective at bringing blood glucose levels back into normal range even without medication. The success of these surgeries is generally not labeled as a cure, but rather a remission.

The artificial pancreas is actually a closed loop information exchange between a continuous blood glucose sensor and an insulin pump. Many people already use sensors and pumps, but the FDA has not yet approved a combination of the two that would be fully automated to keep blood glucose at a normal level without the participation of the patient.

In many cases the high blood glucose levels that define type 2 diabetes can be effectively kept in the normal range by practicing diabetes self-management. Learning about meal planning and nutrition gives you valuable tools for man-aging blood glucose with diet, and we've touched on other aspects of self-management, too. For an in depth and practical look at how to take control of your diabetes, Dr. Rubin's book *Diabetes for Dummies* (Wiley) has it all, including stories of his own patients who have put type 2 diabetes into remission.

The bottom line here is that promises of miracle weight loss formulas or a secret cure for your diabetes only serve to divert your attention away from what actually does work, where your attention and your commitment are necessary. Put your faith in what's tried and true, your effort into developing new healthier habits, and your money into a savings account.

Achieving Your Goals

This chapter has emphasized how your attitudes and willingness to participate in improving your own health are so important to adopting and staying with healthier habits. Your overall goal is to live a long an active life in spite of diabetes, but your doctor and dietitian may have defined individual goals for you. Weight loss is a common assignment because studies show that shedding even a little weight can greatly improve blood glucose control. An A1C less than 7 percent is recommended by the American Diabetes Association, and that organization sets ideal goals for blood pressure and cholesterol known all together as the diabetes ABCs.

Whatever your goals, healthy eating certainly plays a role in achieving them. And, a final few words of wisdom can keep you accountable, informed, and confident.

The American Diabetes Association recommends a hemoglobin A1C goal of less than 7 percent whereas the American Association of Clinical Endocrinologists recommends 6.5 percent. Although the latter goal is closer to the non-diabetic's 6 percent, the ADA feels that the frequency of low blood sugar to achieve that goal is too great a risk for the benefit a 6.5 percent provides.

Writing it all down

Recording what you eat, what time you ate it, what your blood glucose readings are at what time, when you take your medication, how much activity you got, if you are ill and even your mood can provide a wealth of important information to evaluate.

The more interesting thing is that even if you never evaluate anything about that information the simple act of writing it down has a significant impact on your success. Remember the National Weight Control Registry breakfast eaters earlier in this chapter? Tracking food intake was a consistent strategy among the members, all of whom have lost and kept off at least 30 pounds. Remember the strong starters and false starters from the Sparkpeople.com survey from a few pages ago, where the most successful strategy was not a number, but a goal to be healthier? Among the successful weight losers, the strong starters, 82 percent tracked their food intake daily.

Study after study shows this same connection between recordkeeping and success with lifestyle changes. Writing it down gets your brain involved and knowing you intend to write it down keeps you accountable to doing the right thing. Having the data is almost an extra bonus; the bigger motivation is simply the act of consciously writing down your diabetes-related activities.

If you're comfortable with technology there are websites or phone/tablet apps where you can record the relevant information in a database. If you're more a pen and paper person, use pen and paper. Just write it down. The time and effort is negligible, but the benefit is incredible.

Using blood glucose readings

Having the capacity to get an accurate reading of your own blood glucose level in a few seconds, at home, was a significant advance in diabetes care, and undoubtedly has literally saved lives among people with type 1 diabetes. But, the tremendous increase in cases of type 2 and the associated costs in medical care has some questioning whether the cost of testing supplies for type 2 diabetes should be reimbursed. (There's generally no debate about the critical role of blood glucose testing when low blood glucose is a risk as with anyone with type 1 diabetes, or with type 2 diabetes and taking insulin, or any of the oral medications that stimulate insulin secretion.)

The argument is that people don't use the information from blood glucose testing to make changes, so why test? Evidence tends to back up that statement, but evidence also shows that when people with diabetes receive instruction on how to recognize and respond to patterns, blood glucose control improves. It's probably fair to say that people who haven't been shown how to use the information aren't highly motivated to do the testing even once or twice a day.

Learning to use blood glucose test information gives you important insights into what effects your blood glucose levels negatively and allows you to make changes. Dr. Rubin's *Diabetes for Dummies* reviews how to test painlessly and how to time your testing to get useable information. The information gained from targeted testing is especially useful if your diabetes is not in good control. If you test after meals, for example, you can identify specific foods that spike your blood glucose and what spikes yours may not affect others the same way.

If your diabetes is not under good control your doctor can order a continuous glucose monitoring test. This test involves you wearing a small sensor for 3 days that reads blood glucose levels every few minutes, 24 hours a day. These particular sensors generally don't display the information for you to see like the ones some people with type 1 diabetes wear. Instead, your diabetes educator can download the data and display the ups and downs of your levels over the three-day period and compare the timeline with a record you keep of food, exercise, and medication.

Blood glucose levels can be influenced by your actions, but unless you collect the information and look for patterns you can't know what action to take. It's not possible to estimate your blood glucose level based on how you feel, so make a pledge to take advantage of this tool that is still, for the most part, available as a covered expense.

Asking for directions

Managing diabetes well is not always easy, but there is help available in all kinds of ways. From questions and concerns about blood glucose control or diabetes complications to just finding friends who understand what having diabetes is like, there are resources all around you. A diabetes educator is an excellent place to start.

The book that Certified Diabetes Educators (CDEs) use as a reference, *The Art and Science of Diabetes Self-Management Education*, is more than 800 pages long. So, it's a reasonable bet that a CDE is able to understand and help with your questions or concerns no matter what they might be. Certified diabetes educators include physicians, dietitians, pharmacists, and nurses, to name a few, all successfully passing a difficult exam to confirm their expertise. You may find a CDE associated with your physician's office, with a local hospital, in public health settings, or in private practice. A CDE who's also a registered dietitian can be especially helpful in helping with food-related issues.

Diabetes support groups are another excellent resource, especially for emotional support and connection. People with diabetes often feel like others, even close family or friends, don't really understand their worries and struggles, and support groups can really help. Support groups often are led by, or include, medical professionals like CDEs, and may offer both educational presentations and open discussions. Members can get advice from experts and learn from other members. The social connection shared with others is the most unique benefit to in-person support groups, and you may find that helping others adds extra motivation in your own life.

Depression is more common among people with diabetes. If you are or think you may be depressed, seek help from a mental health professional right away. Not only is depression itself miserable and potentially dangerous, but depression can limit your capacity to take care of your diabetes.

There are many excellent diabetes-focused magazines that typically offer insightful articles as well as practical resources like recipes and advice from professionals. *Diabetes Forecast* is published by the American Diabetes Association, *Diabetic Living* by the publishers of *Better Homes and Gardens*, and *Diabetes Self-Management* has a 30-year history providing information and support. There are many other credible periodicals you should sample to see if one or more work best for you.

Websites can be incredibly helpful, too. Major diabetes organizations and government health agencies, like the Centers for Disease Control and Prevention or the National Institutes of Health, provide statistics, research results and practical lifestyle advice. There are literally hundreds of credible websites, but a Google search for "diabetes help" brings millions of results so be discerning. For guidance and advice look for websites that include credentialed professionals — MDs, CDEs, registered dietitians — and look for product affiliations. Major pharmaceutical manufacturers all have diabetes-centered websites with credible advice and an understandable bias toward their own products. Dr. Rubin's book *Diabetes for Dummies* includes a listing of many web-based resources. Of course, Dr. Rubin's website www.DrRubin.com and Toby Smithson's website www.DiabetesEveryDay.com are excellent places to start, and both satisfy the credibility and unbiased "tests."

Social networking online is a different sort of resource, a place to connect "virtually" with others. There are a number of online communities where people with diabetes log in to discuss diabetes, diabetes management, complications, and frustrations. Social networks can provide camaraderie and a sounding board, but be cautious about taking medical advice from nonprofessionals. One study of diabetes communities on Facebook found one quarter of the posts to be promotional in nature, and often promoting one of those non-FDA approved products.

Lastly, books like this one offer information and insight into diabetes and diabetes treatments, and provide practical guidance and resources for the lifestyle issues so important to effectively managing diabetes. Dr. Rubin's books *Diabetes for Dummies, Type 1 Diabetes for Dummies, Diabetes Cookbook for Dummies*, and *Prediabetes for Dummies* are prefect examples.

There are all sorts of resources offering dependable help with diabetes-related concerns, and you should take advantage of them. However, be careful not to ignore or set aside advice and guidance from your most reliable resource, your medical team. Those who actually treat your diabetes have access to your individual medical history and the complete picture of your health status, and that gives them the best insight into what is right for you.

Rewarding small successes

Positive feedback is a powerful motivator, and there's no better place to get positive feedback than from you. After all, you know better than anyone else how many small challenges you face every day. Researchers at Cornell University found that you may make as many as 200 food-related decisions daily, each one an opportunity to choose what is best for controlling your diabetes.

Of course, the numbers, A1C, and other health markers are important in the long term, but you probably see those numbers only every few months. Plus, improvements aren't always instantaneous. Why not give yourself a pat on the back for the decisions you make wisely every day? That pat on the back motivates more wise decisions, and those small choices eventually add up to big improvements. You can be, and should be, your own best cheerleader.

Chapter 12

Shopping for the Best Food Choices

....

....

There is surely no doubt that most people want to preserve their health, and for some a diagnosis of type 2 diabetes offers a surge of motivation to change their ways. Maybe this describes you right now. Or, maybe you've already passed that point and still haven't figured out which of your ways you can change to really impact your diabetes for the better. It could be that you need to answer one very simple, but crucial question — paper or plastic?

OK, it's not fair to assume that you eat out too often, but the numbers hint that it's a good possibility. The average American household spends more than 40 percent of its food budget on food eaten away from home, and it's easy to understand why. Not only is eating away from home (or grabbing takeout food) convenient, but it's nice to get out of the house. And the food can be quite tasty. The food is also overwhelmingly less than healthy, to be kind. It's not impossible to eat away from home, and eat healthy — it's just very difficult. Chapter 15 can give you some tips on how to do diabetes meal planning when eating away from home. But, overall making the best choices for the foods you prepare and eat at home, and eating these foods at home more often, may just be the most important change you can make. This chapter helps you learn what foods to select and where you can find them.

Starting Healthy Meal Planning

Meal planning for diabetes starts by developing your menu and collecting the foods that make up your meals, and there is a wide range of possible destinations that offer everything you need. Figure 12-1 shows a typical floor plan for a supermarket, but you can find healthy choices at farmer's markets, local grocers, giant retailers, warehouse-like stores, web-based home delivery, and even at the local convenience store. But even though these establishments offer the best choices of foods for effective diabetes management, they're also chocked full of options that you're better off avoiding. Shopping for food is one more example of how preserving your health is all about the choices you make every day.

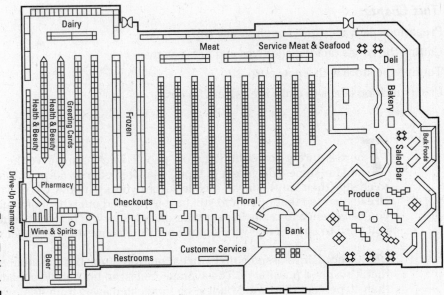

Figure 12-1:
Typical supermarket floor plan.

One of the great public health concerns is the lack of conveniently available, affordable, and healthy food in less-affluent and underserved neighborhoods, where rates of diabetes are often highest. Access to healthy food can be compromised by transportation difficulties, personal safety concerns, and crime rates that discourage retailers.

Heading For the Grocery Store

There are a few things you need to take along on your food shopping expeditions, but first things first — making time to go. Like it or not, managing your diabetes effectively can be inconvenient at times, and one category of inconveniences is making the effort to gather and prepare food at home. Once again, it's a matter of perspective and priority.

If you don't see the direct and intimate connection between what you eat every day and the potential impact of diabetes on your future health, then it's only natural that you'll find the other ways you can spend your time as more important than shopping. If, on the other hand, you're willing to accept that medical nutrition therapy — your diabetes meal plan — may help to add years of healthy living to your future, perhaps you'll be less willing to trust this key component of your diabetes treatment to today's special, free delivery, or food priced by the bucket.

If you accept the reality that food and your health are tied together, you clearly see the value in the time and effort you devote to planning your meals, and to gathering and preparing food yourself. Now, for a plan.

Making your list

You wouldn't dream of building a bookshelf, packing a suitcase, planting a tree, or jumping into just about anything else without some kind of forethought. If you have launched into a project or a trip with no plan, it's likely the outcome was less than ideal. By the same token, there's no doubt that you can visit a grocery and come home with a lot of food, but without a plan the outcome may be less than ideal. Your plan is your shopping list.

Plans are the nuts and bolts of a vision, and the vision that inspires your shopping list is your menu — the breakfasts, lunches, dinners, and snacks that will help keep your blood glucose levels steady, work to manage your weight, and protect your cardiovascular system. Having a specific menu is like knowing you want to build a bookshelf 4 feet tall, 4 feet wide, and 4 foot deep with three shelves. Making your shopping list is how you know you'll bring home 28 feet of 12-inch-wide boards, 16 screws, and 12 shelf holders.

Here is key advice for making and using your shopping list:

- Keep a running list so you can add replacement items as soon as you notice your supply is low.

- Organize your list according to the general plan of the grocery. Even if you're going to a store you're not familiar with, the foods will still be generally grouped in the same way, even if not in the same place.

- Make your list specific, and don't get anything that isn't on your list.

Ok, that last point may sound a little extreme, and it's OK, of course, to grab something you actually need. But, planning your meals and making a specific list has a purpose beyond saving you trips. Making a plan and then sticking to the plan is an effective way to resist impulse. You wouldn't be likely to grab a 2-foot-long board for your bookshelf project, when you only need 4-foot boards, just because you like the way the 2-foot board looks. But, coming face to face with half-priced premium ice cream you don't need can be a different story. Chapter 10 explains how food, or even images of food, can override your best intentions. Doing your thinking ahead of time by making a shopping list keeps food-related impulse buys from derailing your diabetes management success.

Stretching your dollars

There are people who are so incredibly proficient at managing discount coupons that their visits to the grocery are sometimes nearly free — can you say compulsive? It might be best to direct your compulsive tendencies more toward planning your meals than to collecting thousands of coupons, but store or brand coupons are one way to save money on groceries that you've probably done before.

Saving money on food is logical and very important to some. But, no matter which way you choose to save on groceries, it's very important not to get more focused on how much you're saving than on what you're buying. There is food that's clearly beneficial to your health, and there's food that's better avoided. Getting a great deal on food you should best avoid isn't such a great deal after all. Don't let a few dollars, or the thrill of victory from that great deal, steal your attention away from your health.

Here are some great ways to save on groceries:

- ✔ Look for coupons and sales on foods that work with your diabetes meal plan. Canned tuna or salmon are great examples of foods you can grab at a bargain.

- ✔ Register for every store's preferred customer plan, because some deals apply only to registered customers.

- ✔ Shop for fresh produce that's in season, because it's likely to be less expensive. You may also find better deals at farmer's markets or stores that specialize in produce.

- ✔ Check frozen and canned fruits and vegetables. As long as there's not added salt or sugar, frozen and canned food is as nutritious as fresh, sometimes even retaining more nutrients than fresh.

- ✔ Try generic foods, which are always less expensive than brand names. You may notice a difference in some specific products, but most of the time generic brands are virtually identical in nutrient content and taste.

✔ Buy foods in bulk. That doesn't mean a 50-pound sack of potatoes, but simply buying something like yogurt in a larger container saves significant money when compared to single-serving containers.

✔ Do your major shopping alone, if possible. It's important that you take time to read labels and ingredient listings and compare prices. It's easy to feel hurried if an uninterested companion or children are tagging along.

✔ Look on high and low shelves. The food at eye level is sometimes higher priced than foods stocked in less-convenient spots.

✔ Avoid buying prepared food that you can easily fix yourself.

✔ Consider growing a little of your own food. Not only is the food the best tasting and the freshest, but the satisfaction derived from seeing your seeds or plants turn into food at the table is enormous.

One way to save money at the grocery is to make sure you know what you already have on hand. Perfectly good food can get pushed to the back of the pantry or freezer, never again to see the light of day. Take a look in the way back of your freezer or cupboards every now and then, do an inventory, and make a point of using older items nearing their expiration date.

Avoiding temptation

Making your shopping list into an ironclad agreement with yourself is a surprisingly simple way to avoid impulse buying and assure that the foods you have at home are those that work to improve your health. But, in many groceries it's possible to eat enough food for an entire day one toothpick at a time — free samples.

Temptation is everywhere, and when it comes to food it's hard to connect what you choose to do today and tomorrow with the state of your health in five or ten years.

Unraveling Food Terminology

Food is always the subject of much debate in popular culture, but there are a few terms that can be confusing, especially when there's so much passion on either side of the discussion. For you to make the best decisions, it's important to sort through some of the terminology clutter so you fully understand what you're buying and why.

Picking prepackaged

Prepackaged food simply means food that is packaged before sale. If you think about it, that covers most everything in the grocery, whether it comes in cans, bags, boxes, bottles, jars, vacuum packed, or plastic wrap. So, how is it that prepackaged food has a bad reputation in some circles? Is prepackaged food getting a bad rap (pun intended)?

Well, the devil's in the details, as the saying goes. There are really two considerations when it comes to prepackaged food — the food itself, and anything else that may have been added to the food.

The story of the food itself is told to some extent by the nutrition facts label, where you find the amount of protein, fat, carbohydrate, and sodium for the specified serving size. Total fat is further divided into unsaturated fat, saturated fat, and trans fat. Total carbohydrates are divided into sugars, fiber, and sugar alcohols.

The ingredients list tells the rest of the story. Ingredients are listed in descending order, from the most to the least. The ingredients list allows you to see that a bag of frozen vegetables contains only vegetables, and that packaged mini blueberry muffins contain more sugar than any other ingredient, including flour. Because most recipes for homemade blueberry muffins call for two or three times more flour than sugar, the prepackaged muffins illustrate perfectly how some prepackaged foods include ingredients you're better off not having, like lots of added sugar.

The prepackaged muffins also include guar gum, sodium acid pyropophosphate, monocalcium phosphate, potassium sorbate, and sodium stearoyl lactylate — additives and preservatives. Food additives and preservatives are other ingredients or chemicals added to prepackaged foods to improve quality, shelf life, flavor, appearance, safety, or nutritional value. These other ingredients can be familiar to you, like salt or iron, or can seem like a chemistry lab experiment — disodium ethylenediaminetetraacetate or neohesperidin dihydrochalcone. There are, literally, thousands of additives or preservatives classified by the U.S. Food and Drug Administration (FDA) as *generally recognized as safe*. And, whereas the mini muffins wouldn't be recommended for your diabetes eating plan simply because of the added sugar, there are foods that could be considered healthy that still include the chemistry experiment near the bottom of the ingredients list. That leaves the choice up to you.

The bottom line on prepackaged foods is to make your judgments based upon blood glucose control and heart health first; then consider whether you want to make these additives and preservatives part of your diet, too.

Remember, some prepackaged foods, like most frozen vegetables, don't include any added ingredients.

Defining processed foods

The phrase *processed food* is another hot potato, generally viewed in an even more negative context than prepackaged food. But, processed foods are just foods that have been altered from their natural state and can include freezing, canning, cooking, dehydrating, or even pasteurizing milk for safety. You probably wouldn't consider the processing of a grape into a raisin as some horrible insult to a formerly healthy food. To judge whether a food has been processed for your benefit or to your detriment, you have to consider what processing does to the nutritional value of the food.

Whole grains, such as wheat and rice, provide good examples of how processing can reduce nutritional value. To make white flour, for example, both the germ and the bran of the original whole grain wheat are discarded. The same holds true for white rice. It wouldn't be accurate to say that white bread and white rice are unhealthy, but neither offers the health benefits of the natural whole grain versions.

The hydrogenation of liquid fats to create a solid *trans fat,* however, is processing with clear negative effects on health. Trans fats raise bad LDL cholesterol levels, and lower good HDL cholesterol levels, increasing the risk for heart disease. Consuming red meat processed into hot dogs and lunch meats appears to increase the risk for diabetes significantly beyond the risk of red meat alone, according to data from long-term observational health studies. Processed meat is mechanically manipulated, but also usually includes the addition of preservatives like sodium nitrite. These two examples illustrate processing that has a distinctly negative effect on your health.

Notice that hydrogenation and the addition of nitrites refer back to additives and preservatives, discussed previously as related to packaging. Much processing of food is to improve the quality, shelf life, flavor, appearance, safety, or nutritional value of the food products. Many cereals and breads are enriched with added vitamins, for instance, and the processing of milk by pasteurization reduces the risk for disease.

Once again, your focus should be on the nutritional benefits of food to blood glucose control and the risk for heart disease instead of on the popular idea that processed equals bad — in some cases that's true, but in some cases it's just the opposite. Knowing how the foods you choose can minimize the impact of diabetes on your long-term health and adopting those healthy eating habits is what's really important.

Analyzing organic foods

If prepackaged and processed foods are generally viewed in a negative light, then organic foods have the opposite reputation. But what does *organic* actually mean when referring to food? It turns out that laws and regulations are involved.

In general terms, organic foods are produced and processed with minimal input of chemicals, including fertilizers, pesticides, ripening agents, antibiotics, and growth hormones. And, producers must follow strict guidelines to claim the organic label. The objective of organic food production is not only to minimize the input of manufactured chemicals into food, but also to promote recycling of resources, facilitate ecological balance, and conserve biodiversity. It's not possible to say anything bad about organic food production, and organic foods are the fastest-growing segment of the food industry. Organic foods also cost more than conventionally produced foods.

So, how can eating organic foods improve blood glucose control, reduce your risk for heart disease, and improve your nutrition? Most evidence suggests that they can't. By most measures, producing food organically does not alter the nutrient content in any appreciable way. Studies have shown small differences in certain nutrients, but the differences can't be tied conclusively to their organic production or processing methods. Once again, what's most important is that you choose the best foods for your health.

 Studies have found that the consumption of organic foods is subject to the *healthy halo* effect, where people make unfounded health assumptions. One study found that university students inferred that organic cookies were lower in calories than conventional cookies, even when the nutrition labels showed the calorie content to be identical.

The questions about synthetic chemicals in your diet are unsettled. Conventionally produced foods probably expose you to more pesticide residues than organic foods, but the levels are very small and are considered safe by the regulatory agencies. Ultimately, if choosing organic foods is the right choice for you, there is no down side — that is, as long as you choose foods that promote good health.

Shopping Smart Aisle to Aisle

So, you've chosen a store, scoped out sales and coupons, made a detailed list of foods to buy from your week's menu plan, promised yourself you won't give in to impulse purchases (or food samples) — now what? First, grab your reading glasses, because the information on nutrition facts labels and ingredients lists is written in the same tiny font size as the expiration date. Next, ditch anyone who wants to tag along, but you know won't be patient while you shop or will insist on buying foods that don't help your diabetes. Finally, head for the grocery, and unless the weather is horrible, park far away from the door for a smidgen of exercise before you shop. Now you're ready to roll, literally.

 Grocery shopping can be an opportunity for some physical activity. If you've prioritized your time to allow for this extremely important activity, why not spend a few extra minutes taking a couple of laps around the store before you start shopping. All in all, you might get two days of improved insulin sensitivity (better blood glucose levels), and that's the best deal you see all day.

Picking produce

The produce section is the perfect place to start your shopping. OK, so you lose 30 minutes of freshness without refrigeration, and you have to be careful not to mash your fruit in the bottom of the cart. But, nothing beats starting your shopping by gathering what are arguably the healthiest foods in the store — fresh fruits, fresh vegetables, whole nuts, and probably some soy products hidden away someplace in produce. It's all about getting into a healthy mood.

Start with nonstarchy vegetables. These nutrient packed foods should make up half of your plate every meal, and this pattern is especially important with diabetes. Why? Because nonstarchy vegetables are very low in carbohydrates. So, with a variety of textures and colors you get a full stomach plus calcium, iron, magnesium, potassium, vitamin A, vitamin C, vitamin K, folate, fiber, antioxidants, and phytonutrients like beta-carotene, lycopene, lutein, anthocyanidins, and isoflavones — all with minimal impact on blood glucose. Nonstarchy vegetables include lettuce, spinach, kale, collards, broccoli, cauliflower, carrots, turnips, cabbage, tomatoes, cucumber, soft-shell squashes (think zucchini), peppers, asparagus, beets, Brussels sprouts, onions, green beans, eggplant, okra, and more. Nonstarchy vegetables are the foundation for healthy eating, and don't forget you can grow your own or get fabulous in-season vegetables at farmer's markets. Select nonstarchy vegetables that are colorful and crisp.

Starchy vegetables like potatoes, sweet potatoes, corn, peas, and hard shell squashes shouldn't be shunned. These foods are carbohydrate foods that you need to account for in your diabetes meal plan, but don't forget that carbohydrates should account for about half of your daily calories. Starchy vegetables offer many of the same nutrients as nonstarchy vegetables, and what would summer be without corn on the cob? Just be aware of serving sizes, and count the carbohydrates.

Fresh fruits are carbohydrate foods, too, but what a fine way to get your carbs and satisfy your sweet tooth. Today's food transportation efficiencies allow you to choose from an incredible variety of fruits from around the world, like papaya, mango, and kiwi, in addition to U.S.-grown oranges, apples, grapes, peaches, pears, grapefruit, cherries, blueberries, melons, apricots, and strawberries. Too numerous to mention all, eating a variety of fruits gives you a variety of vitamins, antioxidants, and powerful phytonutrients, as well as healthy fiber. Select fruits that are bright, free from blemish, and the appropriate firmness. Eat the skin of fruits with an edible skin, like apples, grapes, peaches, and pears, and remember to count the carbohydrate.

Often, the produce section of your store will include bulk nuts in their shell. Nuts are not carbohydrate foods, so they can make an excellent and healthy snack if eaten in moderation, and nuts offer a variety of healthy unsaturated fats. One benefit to buying nuts in the shell is you can generally get them without added salt.

You may also find soy foods in the produce section, such as tofu, tempeh, or soy processed into chicken-like or beef-like strips. Soy is a complete protein, and has been shown to help reduce bad LDL cholesterol and lower blood pressure. It's easy to add soy to your diet by trying these options with a vegetable stir fry.

Bread, cereal, crackers — grain in disguise

You may not think of bread, cereal, and crackers as grains, but of course the primary ingredient in these products is grain, or grain refined into flour. Like grains, bread, cereal, and crackers are carbohydrate foods — one slice of bread equals one carb choice, or 15 grams carbohydrate.

Whole grains that contain the bran, germ, and endosperm are the healthier choice, and that goes for bread, cereal, and crackers, too. Going for whole grain options does not change the carbohydrate content, but may slow the impact on blood glucose levels. More importantly, whole grains help lower cholesterol levels, work to reduce blood pressure, and provide nutrients lost in the refining process.

The bigger issue with the grains in bread, cereal, and crackers, however, is added ingredients — fat, salt, or sugar, in particular. Cereals are infamous for added sugar, but many healthy looking granola cereals can have 6 or more grams of fat in a half-cup serving. And, crackers would be the obvious place to watch for excess sodium from salt.

Fortunately, these items almost always have a nutrition facts label, and you have your reading glasses. Check the serving size and total carbohydrate content first; then look at the grams of sugar under total carbohydrate, and finally for sodium. It's common to see some sugar in all of these products, but when the sugar portion of total carbohydrate exceeds 30 percent it becomes a sweetened product.

There's definitely room to work bread, cereal, and crackers into your eating plan. It's worth noting that many of these products are fortified with vitamins — bread in the United States has been fortified with niacin since the late 1930s, and it's common to see vitamin C, vitamin D, folic acid, and several B vitamins including vitamin B_{12}, which is often missing in vegetarian diets.

Thinly sliced, whole-grain bread is great for sandwiches because you can get two slices for 20 grams, more or less, of carbohydrate. A sandwich needs two slices of bread, after all.

Choosing meats, poultry, and fish

Meat offers the highest quality, complete protein to your diet, but can also add unhealthy saturated fat that increases your risk for heart disease. Red meat, in particular, has also been associated with increased insulin resistance in large population studies. A healthy approach to meats is to rotate lean cuts of beef, pork, or lamb with skinless chicken or turkey, and fish or shellfish. Fish and shellfish are low in saturated fat and include healthy omega-3 fatty acids.

All meats are cut today with less fat than years ago, but you can reduce fat and saturated fat even more in your diet by choosing the leanest cuts. Table 12-1 lists the leanest cuts of red meats.

Table 12-1	Lean Cuts of Red Meats
Meat	*Cut*
Beef	Eye of round
	Top round
	Sirloin
	Flank steak
Pork	Tenderloin
	Top loin
	Rib chop
Lamb	Lamb shank

Choose USDA *select* cuts of meat, which are naturally lower in fat, and buy ground beef that's at least 90 percent lean when possible. You can further reduce saturated fat at home by trimming visible fat from meats and cooking without adding fat. Trimming visible fat can cut another 30 percent from your diet, and removing the skin from poultry (or buying skinless) reduces fat by as much as 50 percent.

Consider sandwich meats such as bologna or pastrami, bacon, sausages, and the like very carefully. This may be a difficult transition, but excess fat and sodium are not compatible with diabetes management. One slice of bologna can account for 25 percent of your daily sodium recommendations. There are reduced fat options for many items in this product line, but consider the nutrition facts labels and the ingredients list carefully, and you see that eating these foods in moderation makes sense for your health.

When buying fish or shellfish, freshness is important. Look for whole fish with bright eyes and shiny, moist skin, or filets that are translucent without brown spots. Fresh fish should not smell fishy.

For those who choose to eat meat, it can be an important source of protein and vitamin B_{12}. But manage red meat in your diet, eat fish twice each week, and consider going meatless once or twice a week to further reduce fat in your eating plan.

Ovo and lacto — eggs and dairy

Two additional sources of high-quality dietary protein are eggs and dairy, and both have seen their share of controversy.

For a time, eggs were outcasts due to their relatively high levels of cholesterol. But eggs have gained favor again as an excellent source of high quality protein, choline, riboflavin, folate, selenium, vitamin B_{12}, and vitamin D. As much as one egg per day falls within current dietary cholesterol guidelines if dietary cholesterol from other sources is minimized. Egg substitutes, made from egg whites, are cholesterol-free because the yolk is not included, but whereas the protein content is the same, some of the egg's natural nutrients have to be added. Egg substitutes, or using two egg whites as equal to one whole egg, can help moderate cholesterol intake and keep you enjoying eggs.

Dairy products such as milk, yogurt, sour cream, and cheese are a complex mixture of food options. And, dairy products contribute all three macronutrients to your diet — protein, fat, and carbohydrate — with some notable exceptions. One cup of whole milk, for instance, contains the three macronutrients in approximately the same proportion — 8 grams protein, 9 grams fat, and 12 grams carbohydrate. Cheese, however, does not retain significant amounts of carbohydrate.

The protein in dairy products is high-quality protein, easily absorbed by your body, and includes all of the essential amino acids that you can't manufacture. So, dairy products are a great way to start your day.

The fat in dairy products is mostly saturated fat, but all commercially available dairy products are available in reduced fat versions. Nonfat or low fat dairy is your best choice. One cup of 1 percent low-fat milk reduces the fat content from the 9 grams in whole milk to only 2.5 grams, and skim milk is fat free, although many people find skim milk a difficult adjustment.

The carbohydrate in dairy is primarily *lactose,* or milk sugar, and a large percentage of adults can't properly digest this carbohydrate — they are *lactose intolerant.* For those who can, the carbohydrates in dairy products need to be accounted for in your daily eating. The carbohydrate content of dairy products can vary significantly, from virtually zero in hard cheeses to more than 40 grams carbohydrate per cup for some yogurts with added fruit.

Dairy products can be a significant source of sodium, too, so get your reading glasses on and choose dairy products as follows:

- Select nonfat or reduced-fat options for all dairy products — milk, yogurt, cheese, cottage cheese, and sour cream.

- Select reduced sodium options where available.

- Check the carbohydrate content of yogurt — remember, you're not avoiding carbohydrates in your diet, but if you can start your day with 15 or 20 grams of carbohydrate from yogurt instead of 40 grams, you have more room in your breakfast meal plan for whole grain toast or fruit.

- If you're searching for a good source of calcium, choose dairy products that provide at least 30 percent of the *daily value,* like one cup of 1% milk.

Deli counter — no place for a novice

When you approach the deli counter with its long rows of meats, cheeses, and salads, in most cases you do so without your best friend — nutrition facts. That's not to say there aren't healthy choices available, but the trick is finding them. It simply isn't possible to tell by looking, because even though you see ingredients you know swimming around in those salads, you can bet there are ingredients you can't see. You need the nutrition information for these mixed dishes.

The information is available, but in most cases it's held in a secure location behind the deli counter. That makes planning for deli items even more challenging than eating out, because most restaurants publish nutrition information online for you to consider in advance — most groceries do not. The best strategy is to ask your deli counter how you can get copies of the nutrition information for products that you find appealing. They may hand you a book, or perhaps have preprinted tags or cards for the individual dishes. If you're comfortable evaluating the products on the spot, good for you. If you'd rather not do this while thinking under pressure, take the nutrition information home, and make your selections for the next trip. Remember, consider serving size and carbohydrates for blood glucose control, but watch for dishes that are high in fat, sodium, or added sugar.

Speaking of added sugar, the deli counter is often adjacent to the store's bakery goods department, where an assortment of cookies, cakes, and pastries may be softly calling your name. You may find some great, freshly baked bread selections in this area, and once again you should be able to get the nutrition information for those items from the bakery counter. As for the sweetened treats, walk swiftly. Sweet treats aren't forbidden — moderation, as you would imagine, is the strategy best adopted for diabetes management — but you are much better off preparing these kinds of items at home. First, you'll know exactly what goes into the recipe, and you can select from recipes that are lower in carbohydrate, fat, and sodium. Second, baked goods can often be modified by using non-nutritive sweeteners to replace sugar, and fruit purees to replace fat. Grocery baked sweets are best avoided.

Long-term storage — canned and frozen foods

Fresh foods are marvelous, but canned and frozen foods are, for the most part, equal in nutritional value. The nutrition profile of some foods, in fact, is improved in the canning process. Canned and frozen foods can be kept for a much longer time than fresh foods, meaning you can stock up when these foods are on sale.

Canning food dates back to the early 1800s, and the general idea is to kill microorganisms that can spoil food or cause illness by heating and sealing the food in an airtight enclosure to prevent contamination. Most foods are canned under pressure to achieve temperatures high enough to kill the spores of the organism that causes botulism. *Clostridium botulinum* is an organism that lives naturally in soil, but can grow in environments with no oxygen, like a sealed can, and produces a powerful toxin. Botulism intoxication from commercially canned foods is extremely rare, but always reject cans with dents in the seams or bulging ends. If you're considering home canning, be sure to read *Canning and Preserving For Dummies* (Wiley) to make sure you get a high quality and safe home canned product.

You can get just about any vegetable canned, but don't forget canned fruits, soups, and canned meats and fish, especially tuna and salmon. The key to selecting the healthiest canned goods is to read the labels and ingredients, a common theme in shopping for food (by now you're glad you got the advice on reading glasses). Many canned goods include added salt or sugar, so compare labels to get the least added sodium, always buy canned fruit packed in its own juice, and buy canned fish packed in water.

Frozen foods come in a wide variety of options, too, but plain frozen vegetables are particularly handy for healthy eating. Frozen vegetables are generally blanched with steam and frozen within hours of harvest. Because freezing temperatures inhibit microorganism growth, further processing or preservatives are not required.

Like most everything discussed in this chapter, the plainer the food, the more likely the food is to be healthier. Frozen vegetables also come in butter sauce, cheese sauce, and with other seasonings. Often, these varieties have — you guessed it — added fat, salt, and sugar. Once again, grab your reading glasses, and check the nutrition facts labels.

The same goes for carbohydrate containing vegetables and fruits — great options for convenient meals, as long as you count the carbohydrate and avoid added fat, salt, or sugar. Look for fruit with no sugar added — the nutrition facts label always shows sugar content because fruit has natural sugar, but if you see sugar in the ingredients, make a different selection.

Considering frozen entrées brings you back to the discussion earlier in this chapter about prepackaged and processed foods. Don't be surprised to find that the ingredients list reads like a chemistry lab stock room and the sodium content very high. Even low-calorie entrées with names that include lean or healthy can pack 600 to 800 milligrams of sodium into a frozen dinner. Frozen entrées demonstrate the importance of knowing the meaning of nutrition facts. Again, these aren't forbidden, and there are healthier choices, but don't put on the healthy halo — evaluate the information yourself.

Carb loading — pasta, rice, and legumes

Some of your healthiest food choices are grains and legumes (beans), main elements of the healthy Mediterranean diet and DASH eating plans described in Chapter 14. These foods are rich in nutrients, and some are high in both soluble and insoluble fiber. Grains and beans are also carbohydrate foods, so you manage them in 15-carbohydrate-gram serving sizes at your meals.

The story with grains and beans is much the same as with the other foods — keep track of what else is included, and go for the whole foods. Pasta is a great place to start.

Pasta includes all varieties of noodles too numerous to mention — and couscous. Pasta is often made from the endosperm of durum wheat, and even though it tends toward a yellowish color, typical pasta is not whole grain. However, whole-grain pastas, which also include the bran and germ, are available in many of the standard models and are always your better choice from a nutrition standpoint. All pasta is high in carbohydrate, and a 15-carbohydrate-gram carb choice is ⅓ cup cooked pasta. Diabetes and the giant plate of spaghetti, therefore, is not a good match for you. Some boxed pasta dishes, like macaroni and cheese or various couscous dishes, come along with a flavor packet, and you know the drill by now. Check the nutrition facts label on these products, as well as for whatever sauces you may intend to combine with your pasta — added fat, salt, and sugar can sabotage your healthy intentions.

One pasta manufacturer uses a patented process to make some of the carbohydrate indigestible, having no affect on blood glucose. The pasta must be cooked according to specific instructions, and your blood glucose response may vary. Test your blood glucose levels before and after, and you may find extra pasta can fit on your plate.

Rice is an extraordinarily popular staple starch worldwide, including in the United States, and it's another food high in carbohydrate — ⅓ cup of cooked rice equals 15 grams carbohydrate. Rice is also more popular in its white form, where only the endosperm portion of the grain is included. Choose whole-grain brown rice instead to improve your nutrient load and blood glucose response with a simple swap.

Rice may have a broader assortment of boxed dishes with the flavor packet than pasta, but the advice remains the same. Check the nutrition facts label for added fat, salt, and sugar, and search for healthier recipes that you can make at home.

Beans and lentils are super foods that contain carbohydrate, albeit with a slightly larger serving size for the 15 gram carb choice — ½ cup. Beans and lentils come unprocessed in bags, or many beans are canned for your convenience. Either way, beans and lentils are a nutritional bonanza, including cholesterol lowering soluble fiber. For vegetarians, beans are an important source of protein as well. Watch for added salt, even in plain canned beans, and check the nutrition facts on specialty beans, like bar-b-que beans, for added fat and sugar, too.

Whole grains and legumes such as lentils are a very important part of a healthy diet. Although having diabetes requires that you manage the carbohydrates with your meal plan, don't shy away from including these healthy options in your eating plan every day.

Oils and condiments

Oils are liquid fat at room temperature, so they're all more or less the same in calories and fat grams. Oils are about 120 calories and 14 grams of fat per tablespoon, period. Most vegetable oils are the healthier unsaturated oils and vary by their proportion of monounsaturated fat to polyunsaturated fat. Some *tropical oils,* such as palm oil and coconut oil, are considered saturated fats, but these are rarely offered in the grocery. Chefs have preferred oils for cooking based upon the particular smoke point or other characteristic, but in everyday life the vegetable oils commonly available are fine for managing diabetes. However, remember the healthy halo. Just because you're eating healthy fats doesn't make the 120 calories and 14 grams of fat disappear. That said, olive oil, the foundation of the Mediterranean diet, seems to have a very beneficial impact on the LDL cholesterol/HDL cholesterol ratio.

Condiments can include mayonnaise, ketchup, mustards, salad dressings, salsa, relish, or other sauces, and although the refrain may be getting old, check the nutrition facts labels. Mayonnaise and salad dressing can be high in fat, but low-fat or no-fat versions are usually available. Ketchup and bar-b-que sauces often include added sugar, high fructose corn syrup, honey, or other sweeteners, and salt. The same goes for mustard as well as soy sauce — even the reduced-sodium blends are extremely high in sodium. Generally speaking, these products are used sparingly, and for the most part won't cause your healthy eating plan to crash and burn. Still, manage fat, sodium, and sugar with care. Check the section "Adding in the add ons" in Chapter 13.

Chipping away at snack foods

Who doesn't love crunchy snacks? If you do, it's best to share your love only with the snacks that love you back, and that means studying the nutrition labels for fat, carbohydrate (both potatoes and corn are carbohydrate foods), sodium, and added sugar. About 12 to15 potato or corn chips make a 15 carbohydrate gram carb choice, and those few chips can come with 10 grams of fat or more, and 10 percent of your daily recommendation for sodium.

Better choices for snacking would include nuts, but even though carbohydrates aren't an issue, added salt can be, and the fat content of nuts keeps the recommended serving size modest.

Your best option for snacking may very well be popcorn. You can eat 3 cups of air-popped popcorn for the same carbohydrates you'll get in 12 tortilla chips, plus popcorn is a whole grain. The small amount of oil added for microwave cooking gives you a couple of grams of fat, and if you select non-salted popcorn you put the sodium amount in your own hands. Other snacks may work well in moderation, but moderation and snacking often aren't compatible concepts. Give popcorn a try.

Surprises in the "health foods" aisle

You don't really require any special health foods, but grocers often place some very useful foods in a location that suggests they're special. Here's what you might find in the health food aisle.

- ✔ Alternative milks, for those who are lactose intolerant, can help add a dairy-like touch to cereals and hot chocolate. Soy milk, nut milks, or coconut milk offer a milky texture with fewer calories, less fat, less carbohydrate, and are usually fortified with vitamin D and other nutrients.

- ✔ Gluten-free products are essential for those managing celiac disease, which is much more common among people with type 1 diabetes than among the general population.

- ✔ A variety of uncommon grains can add a little zip to your food life. Amaranth, barley, flax, millet, quinoa, rye, spelt, and other grains, seeds, and flours can fit well into your diet and add extra nutrients.

There's just no way around developing an understanding of and an appreciation for nutrition facts labels (you may have noticed). Managing carbohydrate, fat, and sodium in your diet are the keys to blood glucose control and heart health. If the discussion of nutrition facts labels in Chapter 9 didn't click, try reading *Nutrition For Dummies* (Wiley). Better yet, meet with a registered dietitian. Remember, the information is not difficult — it's a subconscious reluctance to think too much about food that keeps the light bulb from lighting up. Just don't give up.

Part IV
Ready, Set, Plan

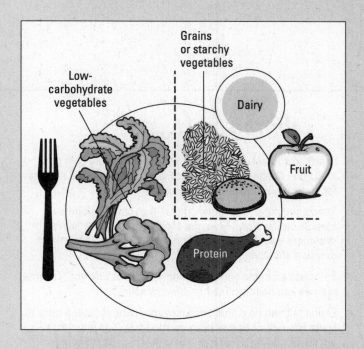

In this part...

- ✔ Learn how to eat . . . not with a knife and fork, but with healthy foods and healthy eating habits. For some this comes naturally; for many of us, however, it takes a little practice.

- ✔ Read about several popular "diets" that can be diabetes-friendly eating plans. From the Mediterranean diet to Weight Watchers, see what you need to know to make an informed decision about your food.

- ✔ Calculate amounts and modify ingredients to turn your favorite recipes into healthy diabetes-friendly dishes.

- ✔ Eating out can be a challenge, but you learn about the tools to make good choices that keep you on track. You learn that it's not about making sacrifices, but rather it's about finding a healthier eating plan you can stay with over the long run.

- ✔ Give up snacks? No way! You learn which foods are snackable, and which to avoid.

Chapter 13

Customizing Your Meals

In This Chapter

▶ Getting a personalized meal plan

▶ Modifying the USDA MyPlate for diabetes

▶ Assembling your meals

▶ Figuring out the unknown foods

Forrest Gump was a wonderful movie. The storyline followed a young boy, faced with significant mental challenges, through an extraordinary life, where random events propelled him from one achievement to the other. With no plan or purpose, each of Forrest's amazing successes was essentially a complete accident. Throughout his totally random, but world-changing adventures, he was anchored by his Mama's sage advice — *life is like a box of chocolates, you never know what you're gonna get.*

For everything Forrest Gump accidentally became — Elvis's dance instructor, star football player, military hero, international ping-pong champion, shrimping magnate, and father — he clearly was not managing diabetes. And, the giveaway isn't the box of chocolates reference. The giveaway is that when someone addresses diabetes with no plan or purpose, things don't just randomly work out for the best, as everything always did for Forrest Gump. Without a plan and purpose for taking control of your long-term health, diabetes doesn't all work out for the best.

Maybe you already learned that lesson the hard way, or maybe you wisely understand you shouldn't take your chances with fate. Either way, you're on the right track now. Managing diabetes can't be separated from managing what you eat, and it's probably fair to say that managing what you eat is the most important, and the most challenging, element to managing diabetes. But, managing what you eat every day puts you in charge of your own future health, a sobering responsibility to be sure, and also an incredible opportunity. Forrest Gump's Mama had another piece of advice for those who fail to take advantage of opportunity.

In this chapter you learn the nuts and bolts of meal planning for effective diabetes management. For most people, this doesn't come naturally — not the meal planning itself, but meal planning with a health-related purpose.

Laying the Foundation

It's really not possible to eat in a way that's best for your health if you don't even know what you should be doing. And, knowing what you should be doing means knowing exactly what you should be doing — having precise and personalized information that comes from a registered dietitian. Registered dietitians provide a service known as *medical nutrition therapy* when a metabolic disorder like diabetes is involved, and when diabetes is involved food really is medicine. The drugs you're prescribed for diabetes can only do so much, even if you have type 1 diabetes and take insulin injections to directly control blood glucose levels. Preserving your health over the long run means addressing your lifestyle choices, especially the food you eat.

So, step number one in laying a strong foundation for managing diabetes effectively with food is to see a registered dietitian, and you may need to request a referral from your doctor. There really is no shortcut to getting an effective eating plan — a meal plan tailored to your specific physical and medical needs is an integral part of your diabetes treatment, and you can't get that from a friend, or off of the Internet. And, if you want to impress a dietitian on your first visit, begin keeping a food journal before you go, recording everything you eat, the time of day, and your blood glucose level whenever you take one over several days or weeks.

Whereas a personalized meal plan may be the most valuable result of your visit, your dietitian can also explain why a meal plan is so important, and work with you so you can identify carbohydrates in your diet. Maybe most importantly, you can evaluate your food journal together, and make adjustments — maybe only minor ones — to your normal eating pattern. If you have also kept a record of your blood glucose levels — and you should — you're able to see how certain food choices can have a greater impact than others. Don't let one visit with a dietitian be the end. Most insurers cover multiple visits, and your department of public health likely has dietetic services as well.

Knowing your personal meal plan

Your personalized meal plan, which guides your daily choices for managing your diabetes with food, isn't a menu, telling you exactly what to eat. Instead, it's a framework, like a house under construction where the various rooms have been established, but leaving you a world of options for how you're going to finish the décor. In general terms, your personalized meal plan will be based on the following criteria:

✔ Your daily calorie requirements, which depend to some extent upon whether your health status would benefit by gaining weight, maintaining your current weight, or losing weight over time.

✔ Your recommended carbohydrate consumption, based upon your calorie budget, your diabetes-related health status, and your medications. Usually, your daily carbohydrate recommendation is expressed as a certain number of carbohydrate, or carb, *choices,* which is a food portion containing approximately 15 grams of carbohydrate.

✔ Your health status related to possible conditions, and medications for conditions, other than diabetes.

✔ Your personal food preferences are always a consideration in developing your personalized meal plan.

Your daily calorie needs are based upon your current body mass index (BMI calculates weight for height), your activity level, your age, gender, and a goal for reaching a weight that makes sense for you. It's no secret that most people with type 2 diabetes are overweight, and losing excess weight clearly promotes better blood glucose control. If you fall into that group, your meal plan helps you both manage blood glucose levels and lose weight at a healthy pace. Any effective diabetes management plan also addresses prevention of the most common diabetes complications and *comorbidities* — related health conditions caused by diabetes, or often occurring with diabetes. High blood pressure, high LDL cholesterol, low HDL cholesterol, and high blood triglycerides are all related, to some extent, to diet.

Your body mass index (BMI) is your mass (weight) in kilograms, divided by your height in meters squared. You can calculate your own BMI in English measures by dividing your weight in pounds by your height in inches squared, and multiplying that number by 703 to correct for using English measures. If, for instance, you weigh 190 pounds and are 5'7" tall (67 inches) the formula is $190 \div 67 \times 67 = 190 \div 4489 = .0423 \times 703 = 29.75$. A BMI higher than 25 is considered overweight, and higher than 30 is in the obese range.

Based upon your daily calorie needs, your meal plan divides those calories among the three macronutrients — protein, fat, and carbohydrate. You may expect to see the calories allotted as follows:

✔ Calories from protein likely account for 20 percent of your daily calorie total. Each gram of protein stores 4 calories of energy. Some diabetes eating plans suggest that a higher percentage of calories come from protein, and in some cases, especially where kidney function is compromised, protein may be restricted.

✔ Calories from fat likely account for about 30 percent of your daily calorie total. Each gram of fat stores 9 calories of energy, and your eating plan suggests that saturated fat make up only a modest percentage of your daily fat intake, with trans fat strictly limited.

✔ Calories from carbohydrate often account for a full 50 percent of your daily calorie total. Like protein, carbohydrate stores 4 calories of energy per gram, and it's carbohydrate that has the greatest effect by far on your blood glucose levels. For that reason, carbohydrates deserve a lot of attention, and are the main focus of your meal plan.

The key to understanding your meal plan, and to getting the benefits of following one, is learning the correct portion sizes for food. Even though your meal plan is set to provide a certain number of calories each day, you don't have to add up calories as you go along. Instead, with each meal you have set amounts of carbohydrate, protein, and fat, and the sum of the calories from those recommended amounts over the whole day should hit the correct calorie mark. Nobody, except maybe an accountant, likes keeping a running tally of their daily calories, so this approach is much more user friendly, and extremely effective as long as you eat the correct portions.

Portion sizes need to be specific. If someone told you the proper portion for an apple is the size of a ball, you wouldn't know whether they meant a golf ball, baseball, basketball, or a giant beach ball. And, the difference is obviously significant. With diabetes, knowing the correct portion sizes of carbohydrate containing foods is essential — a baseball-sized apple would be the proper size for one carb choice (15 grams of carbohydrate), but only 1 tablespoon of maple syrup would give you the same amount of carbohydrate. In general, both portions have the same effect on blood glucose.

It's not necessary to learn every portion size of every food. The best strategy is to learn the correct portion size of the foods you most commonly eat, and refer to a carb counting book or an exchange list for foods you haven't memorized. A comprehensive exchange list is included in Appendix A, and Appendix B provides that information for some ethnic favorites.

Be aware that you probably have a natural resistance to thinking too much about food — it just seems that eating shouldn't require any thinking. Unfortunately, you need to get beyond that barrier if you intend to take control of your health — thinking about food is required. And not just for carbohydrates. Even though carbohydrates have the most direct impact on blood glucose, dietary fat contributes to excess body weight by piling on calories, and saturated fats contribute to unhealthy cholesterol and triglyceride levels. Your personalized meal plan, however, accounts for all of these issues, and minimizes the amount of thinking and calculating you have to do.

Blood glucose control is very important and must be a clear focus of your meal plan. But, for most people with diabetes the greatest threat to well-being is heart disease. Because diabetes increases your risk, it's as important to concentrate on an eating plan that's heart healthy, too.

Making MyPlate into YourPlate

In 1992 the U.S. Department of Agriculture published its first Food Guide Pyramid. The idea was to demonstrate how foods represented as the wider base of the pyramid — whole grains — should be consumed in greater quantities than the foods associated with the tiny tip of the pyramid — fats, oils, and sweets. The USDA pyramid was revised in 2005 to an image that represented the various food groups in colorful vertical sections, rather than stacked in layers, complete with a stairway and a stickman. Other pyramids, including one developed by the World Health Organization, have followed the original Swedish version put out in 1972. All of the pyramids have been criticized by nutrition professionals for misrepresenting, or failing to clearly articulate, various aspects of a healthy diet. Ultimately, the pyramid concept may have resonated with ancient Egyptians, but was too abstract for the general public.

In 2011, the USDA replaced its pyramid with MyPlate, a visual representation of relative portion sizes for different food groups in a dinner place setting, including a dinner plate and a separate section for dairy. Figure 13-1 is the current official icon representing the general categories of food that make up a healthy diet, showing recommended portions of protein, grain, fruit, vegetables, and dairy. One key take-home message is that vegetables and fruits should make up one half of your plate, more or less.

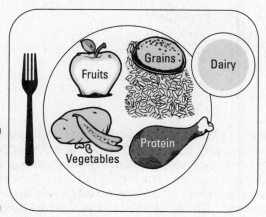

Figure 13-1:
The USDA
MyPlate
icon.

Unfortunately, the USDA MyPlate doesn't address the particulars of a diabetes eating plan, where identifying carbohydrate foods is the key to success. Although it's not completely obvious looking at the icon, the official MyPlate has carbohydrate foods spread through every single category, because beans are included in the protein group, and starchy vegetables like potatoes and corn are included in the vegetable group. Fruits, grains, and dairy, except for cheese, are always considered carbohydrates.

You could make the case that MyPlate encourages you to get your carbohydrates from a variety of different food groups, and that certainly fits in with a healthy diabetes eating plan. The importance of segregating carbohydrate foods, and increasing your consumption of low-carbohydrate vegetables, really justifies a special plate for people with diabetes.

Figure 13-2 is a variation of USDAs MyPlate adjusted for people with diabetes.

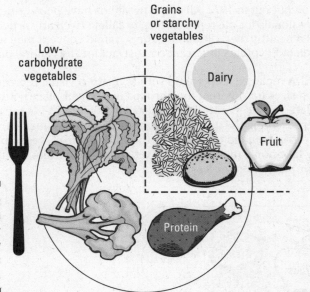

Grains
or starchy
vegetables

Low-
carbohydrate
vegetables

Dairy

Fruit

Protein

Figure 13-2: MyPlate is adjusted for a healthy diabetes eating plan.

This representation of your plate emphasizes two important healthy eating strategies. Eat lots of nonstarchy vegetables — cover half of your plate. Nonstarchy vegetables are low-calorie, low-carbohydrate, packed with vitamins and essential nutrients, and keep you feeling full. Also, limit your protein portion to about one-quarter of your plate, usually about three ounces (no fair cutting your 16-ounce T-bone into pieces and stacking them high).

Most importantly, this plate gathers the carbohydrate foods together — grains, fruit, starchy vegetables and beans, and dairy (except for cheese). From this group you select the appropriate number of carb choices your meal plan recommends for each meal.

Coming to grips with carb portions

Carbohydrates — sugars, starches, and fiber — liberate single molecules of glucose during digestion, which are promptly absorbed directly into the bloodstream. When blood glucose levels begin to rise, insulin is released from special cells in the pancreas to assist in getting glucose out of circulation, stored away inside of certain cells, bringing blood glucose levels back to normal. Carb loading is something athletes do before competition to make sure their body's storage capacity for glucose, your body's favorite and most efficient source of energy, is filled and ready for action. Diabetes, however, interferes with your body's ability to store glucose quickly and efficiently, so glucose that's loaded doesn't necessarily get stored.

The glitch in this systemic imbalance is an inadequate amount of insulin, a diminished response to insulin by those cells that should be storing glucose for later, or both. Glucose that can't be stored continues to circulate in the bloodstream, keeping blood glucose levels high. High blood glucose levels cause damage to cells over time, and lead to serious complications of diabetes like heart disease, vision loss, kidney damage, and more.

Carbohydrates are desirable and necessary in a healthy diet, however. The secret to eating healthy carbohydrates and keeping blood glucose levels in better balance is, in part, managing the amount, timing, and the quality of the carbohydrates you eat. That means knowing how much carbohydrate is in the food you're eating, spreading your carbohydrate consumption throughout the day, and choosing some of your carbohydrates from foods that don't get digested and absorbed as quickly. Carb *trickling*, rather than carb *loading*.

Timing your carbohydrate consumption means don't skip meals; eat meals around the same time each day; and eat an approximately equal proportion of your daily carbohydrate budget at each meal. Your meal plan may even set aside one or two carbohydrate choices for between-meal snacks. Giving your body a lighter load of glucose at any one time helps blood glucose levels come down more efficiently.

Carbohydrates that digest and absorb slowly are usually *whole* foods, like unrefined grains, beans, and whole fruit. These foods have a low *glycemic index value*, meaning their impact on blood glucose levels is slower, giving your body extra time to find vacant storage for the excess glucose. Managing diabetes is partly about getting blood glucose levels to come down after eating carbohydrate foods. Carbohydrates make the blood glucose levels of people with normal glucose metabolism go higher, too, but a normal response between insulin and cells storing excess glucose brings blood glucose levels down significantly in a couple of hours. Managing the amount, timing, and quality of carbohydrate intake works to get blood glucose levels decreasing more efficiently in people with diabetes.

Knowing the amount of carbohydrate you're eating is a more complicated issue because the portion of a food that contains a set amount of carbohydrate — look for 15 grams, which is called one *carb choice* — is different for different carbohydrate containing foods. You can get one carb choice, 15 grams of carbohydrate, all of the following ways:

- One tablespoon of sugar or concentrated syrup
- Two tablespoons of raisins or dried cherries
- One-quarter cup granola
- One-third cup cooked rice, barley, pasta, or plantain
- One-half cup beans, corn, cooked oatmeal, mashed potatoes, parsnips, or applesauce
- Three-quarter cup blackberries or canned grapefruit
- Two-thirds cup yogurt
- One cup canned pumpkin, papaya, honeydew, or acorn squash
- One-and-a-quarter cups strawberries or watermelon
- One-and-a-half cups of cooked nonstarchy vegetables
- Three cups raw, nonstarchy vegetables or popcorn

The difficulty many people with diabetes have with modifying their eating habits for better management is with the staple grains and starches — potatoes, rice, pasta, and corn. It's obvious from the list earlier in this chapter that there are plenty of healthy carbohydrate foods with a generous portion size for one carb choice — see Appendix A for the long list. But one-third cup of rice or pasta, one corn tortilla, or the pointed end of a giant baked potato can seem drastically insignificant if you're used to eating these grains and starches by the pile or by the pound.

That makes managing these foods all the more important. You likely have a meal plan recommendation of between 9 and 15 carb choices per day — three to five per meal. That definitely leaves room for your favorite staple foods if you manage portion sizes, and include other carbohydrate foods in your diet. You might consider alternative recipes, like mashed potatoes and cauliflower, or a pasta that's processed to make some of the carbohydrate indigestible. You might even splurge on rice as your only carbohydrate for a meal — choose whole-grain brown rice, keep the number of servings you eat consistent with your carbohydrate budget for that meal, and get your carbs from different foods groups most of the time.

Finally, how can sweets fit into a diabetes management plan? There are really two different considerations when it comes to sweets — empty calories and portion size. Empty calories are calories that don't bring along any compensating nutritional value. With diabetes and sweets, the concept can be extended to include both empty calories and carbohydrates — a cost to your weight and blood glucose without any redeeming benefit. A 20-ounce sugar-sweetened soft drink crosses off more than four of your daily carb choices; for example, 65 grams of carbohydrate for a negligible amount of phosphorous from phosphoric acid. Getting your sweet calories and carbs from foods with real nutritional value, like fruits, is a better choice. And, non-nutritive sweeteners can eliminate both the calories and carbohydrates from sweets when appropriate for a recipe. But, in the big picture it's not necessary to avoid sweets, or even sugar, like poison, as long as you fit them responsibly into your diabetes eating plan. Your author Toby Smithson, who has effectively managed her type 1 diabetes for decades, regularly has a serving of slow-churned chocolate ice cream before bedtime. Remember, eating healthy isn't torture.

Starting simple

It's unlikely that Michelangelo started with a paint-by-numbers set, but he didn't start with the ceiling of the Sistine Chapel, either. Diving into anything without starting simple is a recipe for discouragement, and diabetes meal planning is no different. It's not that you can't prepare a five-star Russian Salmon Coulibiac — it's that figuring out the appropriate serving size of a complex fish and rice loaf baked in a pastry shell leaves much room for error. If you're just starting to get serious about managing your diabetes better by getting serious about food, it's important that you see positive results. And the less room you leave for error, the better the result.

Starting simple, therefore, means focusing on foods that contain predominantly only one of the macronutrients — carbohydrate, protein, or fat. In practice, that's not always completely possible, but you can get close. And it is feasible to actually eat this way, but that's not really the intent of this section. The intent is allow you to concentrate on one food at a time so that you can get the hang of where your macronutrients come from and understand how you can construct meals that manage carbohydrates, keep your eating habits heart healthy, and keep your appetite satisfied. It's like practicing with a paint-by-numbers project before you tackle your chapel ceiling.

Picking a perfect protein

About 20 percent of your daily calories should come from protein, although your personalized meal plan could vary somewhat from that. Nevertheless, protein is an important macronutrient for building and repairing tissue, to create enzymes which accelerate important biochemical reactions, and for constructing important hormones like insulin. Proteins are assembled from amino acids, and there are 20 specific amino acids your body needs to build all the different proteins you need. The protein in your diet is broken down into its various amino acids during digestion, and your body recycles those amino acids to make your proteins from scratch. You can even make some amino acids by modifying other amino acids in some cases, but there are nine amino acids you must get intact from your diet — these nine are referred to as *essential* amino acids (refer to Table 6-1 in the previous chapter for the list).

When considering which foods supply all of the essential amino acids in a useable form, and in sufficient quantity, there really are perfect proteins — they are called *complete* proteins. And, there are scoring systems, one of which is called the *protein digestibility corrected amino acid score*. By this scoring system, which measures both the essential amino acids and your ability to easily absorb them, the perfect proteins are egg white, soy protein, and the casein and whey proteins in milk. It's only fair to point out that meats score well on this scale, too.

Proteins are all complex foods. Egg whites are a great source of protein, but whole eggs bring along just as much fat as protein and are also a source of dietary cholesterol. Soy and milk both contain carbohydrates, and whole milk is a significant source of saturated fat (soy contains healthier unsaturated fats). Likewise, meats always include some saturated fat. So, contrary to the title of this section, for keeping meal planning simple there is no perfection in protein. But, for almost perfect you can consider the following options:

✔ Egg substitutes are 99 percent egg white, so these products supply the high-quality protein without the saturated fat and cholesterol found in the egg yolk.

✔ Soy beans (edamame) contain about the same amount of carbohydrate as protein, but when processed into tofu the carbohydrate content is significantly reduced compared to the remaining high quality protein. Tofu does retain the fat content of the beans, but the fat in soy in primarily healthy unsaturated fat.

✔ Trimming the visible fat from lean cuts of beef and pork, or removing the skin from poultry, can reduce the fat content profoundly. Removing the skin from a chicken breast, for example, can cut the fat to only about one gram. Or, start with a lean cut of beef like flank steak, round, or tenderloin, and you'll know you're on track.

The take-home lesson is that you can choose your protein in this manner without having to account for carbohydrates, too, and with some comfort that the included fat is either healthy unsaturated fat, or a minimal amount of saturated fat from lean meats.

Isolating carbohydrates

Carbohydrates account for approximately one half of your daily calories, and carbohydrate foods are the foods that have a direct impact on your blood glucose levels. For that reason, carbohydrates are the main focus of your eating plan. You can track carbohydrates bundled into 15-gram portions called a *carb choice*, and with type 1 diabetes especially you always look to match insulin injections with the carbohydrate content of your foods.

Anyone with diabetes considers, at some point, the prospect of eliminating carbohydrates from his or her diet. At first glance the logic makes sense — carbohydrates equal higher blood glucose levels, and higher blood glucose levels are unhealthy. In reality, however, that strategy could be compared to deciding you can walk everywhere on your hands to save wear and tear on your feet. Just like humans are made to walk upright, you're made to run on carbohydrate fuel. Plus, eliminating carbohydrates from your diet isn't really going to leave much for you to eat. It's natural to have that passing thought, but be sure it passes so you can get down to the business of managing carbohydrates in your daily eating.

Carbohydrates in your food come in the forms of sugars, starches, and fiber, going from the simplest sugar molecules with six to ten connected carbon atoms to the most complex, and often indigestible, fiber with thousands of carbon atoms in a chain. The simple sugar glucose is a frequent participant in building carbohydrate, and glucose is liberated from these complex molecules in digestion and absorbed directly into your bloodstream. A certain level of dissolved glucose circulating in your blood is essential — too little, or too much, has consequences.

Isolating carbohydrates in your diet is similar to isolating protein — many excellent sources of carbohydrate also come along with protein and fat; but like the previous search for the perfect protein, perfection isn't necessary for this simple lesson in meal planning. Here are a few relatively pure carbohydrate foods, and your meal plan might recommend three to five carb choices you can choose from the following:

✔ Fruit is perhaps the purest carbohydrate, often without any protein or fat. Virtually every fruit has at least ten times more carbohydrate than protein, and if you discount a few outliers like avocado (which has so much fat and so little carbohydrate it's placed in the dietary fat group), fruit is mostly fat free. A carb choice for fruit varies depending upon the fruit itself, and whether or not it's dried. Two tablespoons of raisins or one and a quarter cups of watermelon are both one carb choice. Canned and frozen fruits are excellent as long as there is no added sugar, and whole fruit offers more nutritional value than fruit juice. Having fruit with every meal is a wise choice, and you'll always know to count the carbohydrate.

✔ Brown rice, the whole-grain version of rice, contains protein and fat, but in negligible amounts. The same is true for most whole grains — even quinoa, a grain noted for its protein content, contains five times as much carbohydrate. A carb choice for whole grains, including pasta, is one-third cup cooked, and you can also get your whole grains from bread, where one slice of a whole-grain bread is equal to one carb choice.

✔ Starchy vegetables (potatoes, corn, and peas, for example) contain significantly more carbohydrate than protein, and are nonfat foods unless fat is added. Peas have three times more carbohydrate than protein, and both corn and potatoes have an even higher ratio. One carb choice for a white potato is 3 ounces weight, and for peas and corn the correct volume is ½ cup.

These represent the simplest categories of healthy carbohydrate foods, and if you recognize other healthy carbohydrates foods that aren't included here (dairy products and beans) it's because they are not quite as simple. That doesn't mean they aren't extremely beneficial to your health and an essential element of your eating plan. I discuss dairy, beans, and other complicated foods in the next section.

Filling up on vegetables

Vegetables, specifically nonstarchy vegetables, are special to diabetes. Not only are they packed with vitamins, loaded with water to help keep you hydrated, and a source of dietary fiber, they are your best choice for the volume you need to feel full. Nonstarchy vegetables are your best choice because these foods are low in calories, low in carbohydrate, and nonfat — 1 whole cup of sliced cucumber, for example, has but 16 calories and 4 grams carbohydrate. A carb choice, 15 grams of carbohydrate, would be about 4 full cups.

The MyPlate representation adapted for diabetes suggests that one half of your plate should be nonstarchy vegetables. In general, a carb choice for these foods is considered to be 3 cups raw, or one and ½ cups cooked, but the foods do vary some. Nonstarchy vegetables include:

Artichoke	Carrots	Mung bean sprouts
Artichoke hearts	Cauliflower	Mushrooms
Asparagus	Celery	Okra
Baby corn	Chayote	Onions
Bamboo shoots	Cucumber	Oriental radish or daikon
Beans – green, Italian, wax	Eggplant	Peapods
Bean sprouts	Greens – collard, mustard, turnip	Peppers (all varieties)
Beets		Radishes
Bok choy	Green onions or scallions	Rutabaga
Broccoli	Kale	Salad greens (all types)
Brussels sprouts	Jicama	Sauerkraut
Cabbage – Chinese and green	Kohlrabi	Soybean sprouts
	Leeks	Spinach

Sugar snap peas

Soft-shell summer squash

Swiss chard

Tomato – raw, canned, sauce, or juice

Turnips

Vegetable juice cocktail

Water chestnuts

Zucchini

And more!

Nonstarchy vegetables can go into omelets, on sandwiches, make a colorful tossed salad, be used for dipping, become the featured ingredients in a stir fry, be eaten as a snack without worrying about raising your blood glucose, or served as a side dish to any meal. The only caution is to watch for added fat or salt, and that means keeping an eye on yourself, too. When all is said and done, nonstarchy vegetables can be your most powerful weapon for controlling blood glucose, losing weight, and improving heart health.

Mix and match meals for you

Figure 13-3 illustrates how you can choose foods from different categories to create a lunch that fits into your diabetes meal plan perfectly. The number of servings from each group will depend upon your daily calorie levels, but you can do this with your favorite foods for breakfast or for dinner, too.

This little exercise demonstrates perfectly how simple it can be to put healthy meals together when you think about the components separately. It's something like ordering at a restaurant — pick a protein and choose three carbohydrate side dishes — except the options you have to choose from are healthy foods in an appropriate portion.

You can easily adapt this list to your own tastes, too — think of all the fruits that could go under the carbohydrate section, or other nonstarchy vegetables that could work to create your favorite salad. And, you can start from scratch to build your own menu options for your breakfasts and dinners.

One of the major themes of this book on diabetes meal planning is the planning part — making decisions in advance. Planning ahead allows you to take advantage of the thinking part of your brain and minimize the influence of impulse. A logical and organized chart like the one illustrated in Figure 13-3 works both ways, however. The options are selected with care for how they fit into your meal plan, but the fact that there are many options allows you to make impulsive decisions regarding what sounds good at any particular time. It's the best of both worlds.

Lean Protein
(Choose 1-3 servings per meal)

- ☐ 1 ounce lean beef, pork or lamb
- ☐ 2 ounces tuna (packed in water)
- ☐ 1 ounce fish (broiled, baked or grilled)
- ☐ 1 ounce chicken or turkey (no skin)
- ☐ 1 egg
- ☐ 1 ounce low fat cheese
- ☐ ¼ cup cottage cheese

Low Carbohydrate Vegetables
(1-2 servings with meals)

- ☐ Baby carrots
- ☐ Celery sticks
- ☐ Bell pepper strips
- ☐ Cucumber slices
- ☐ Sliced tomato
- ☐ Dark leafy greens
- ☐ Cauliflower
- ☐ Broccoli
- ☐ Jicama
- ☐ Mushrooms
- ☐ Salad

Carbohydrates
(Choose 3 servings at each meal)

- ☐ 1 slice bread
- ☐ ½ bagel, pita, hamburger or hot dog bun or English muffin
- ☐ 1 tortilla
- ☐ 1 small dinner roll
- ☐ ¾ cup dry cereal
- ☐ ½ cup cooked cereal
- ☐ ½ cup peas or corn
- ☐ ⅓ cup cooked beans (also count as 1 ounce protein)
- ☐ ⅓ cup pasta
- ☐ 5 ounce sweet or white potato
- ☐ 1 cup plain or low fat yogurt
- ☐ 1 cup skim or 1% milk
- ☐ 1 medium apple, banana, orange, peach or pear
- ☐ ¼ cup dried raisins or cranberries
- ☐ 17 grapes
- ☐ 1 cup melon
- ☐ ½ cup 100% fruit juice
- ☐ ½ cup canned fruit packed in its own juice

Healthy Fats
(1-2 servings per meal)

- ☐ 1 teaspoon mayonnaise
- ☐ 1 teaspoon tub margarine
- ☐ 10 peanuts
- ☐ ⅛ avocado
- ☐ 1 T. salad dressing
- ☐ 2 T. fat reduced salad dressing

Figure 13-3:
Mix and match food choices to create a healthy lunch.

Moving Beyond Simple

Like any true artist, after you paint by the numbers for a short time, you're ready for something more challenging. With diabetes and food, that's a good thing. There are excellent food choices waiting in the wings to join those simple foods reviewed in the previous section, and now that you've had a little practice it's time for some introductions.

Knowing the sneaky foods

Don't misunderstand the word sneaky here — there's nothing malicious about these foods. In fact, these are some great choices for your diabetes meal plan because they are complex, offering more than one of the macro-nutrients in addition to a host of other nutritional benefits. In general, the most significant issue with these foods comes if you fail to recognize them as carbohydrates, and it's possible you don't think of these foods as carbohydrates. But you will, because you are becoming a carbohydrate expert.

Beans are the sneakiest of sneaky. Beans are included in the protein section of the USDA's MyPlate, and with good reason. Soy beans, called edamame, are the only vegetable source of complete protein, a food containing all nine essential amino acids in an easily digestible form. Chickpeas (garbanzo beans), and other beans score well on that scale, too. Beans, like kidney beans and black beans, will give you about 15 grams of high-quality protein per cup, and that protein comes with very little fat unless it's added. And, beans are an excellent source of fiber, including soluble fiber which helps lower LDL unhealthy cholesterol. Those beans are one healthy source for protein. But, that cup of beans also counts as two carb choices — about 40 grams of carbohydrate reduced by one half of the 10 to 12 grams of fiber, leaving between 30 and 35 grams total carbohydrate per cup. So, what's that mean for your diabetes eating plan? It means eat lots of beans — beans of all kinds are very healthy little packages of nutrition. Just remember to count the carbohydrates and to consider the beans as a significant part of your mealtime protein.

Dairy products bring to mind calcium, protein, and maybe even fat because you are probably familiar with the 2 percent, 1 percent, and nonfat skim milk options. Lately, Greek yogurt is gaining popularity thanks to its higher concentration of protein than regular yogurt. But don't forget the carbohydrates in dairy products, thanks to lactose, commonly called milk sugar. One cup of milk is considered one carb choice, even though it's actually 12 grams of carbohydrate, and yogurt can vary remarkably in its carbohydrate content depending upon added sugar or fruit. Plain Greek yogurt can supply almost 25 grams of protein per cup, but also contains as much as 8 grams of carbohydrate. What does that mean for your diabetes eating plan? Dairy products can fit very well into your meal plan — just remember to count the carbohydrates, and go for low- or no-fat choices.

There's one other sneaky thing about dairy products — cheese. The carbohydrates in milk feed the microorganisms that turn milk into cheese, and these bugs are hungry. As a result, cheese contains very little of the original carbohydrate, but retains its protein. Be warned, however, that cheese can be a significant source of saturated fat, so choose low-fat varieties whenever possible.

Sugar free or *no sugar added* are labels that can grab the attention of anybody with diabetes. There's something about those phases that can get mysteriously translated into *carbohydrate free*, but don't be misled. Although it's likely that a sugar-free food has less carbohydrate than its thoroughly sugared variety, all carbohydrates aren't from sugar. Baked items contain flour, for example, which includes the carbohydrate from the original grain. And *no sugar added* doesn't mean that the sugar naturally there, like the lactose in ice cream, was removed. Often it also means that sugar alcohols were added to sweeten the food, and sugar alcohols are included in total carbohydrate content separately from sugar. What's this mean for your diabetes eating plan? It means always read the label so you can always count the carbohydrates.

In fact, that's the best lesson for this section, because no matter what your preconceived notions about any food may be, the nutrition facts label always makes sure you get the real story before you eat.

Trying mixed dishes and casseroles

A recipe for Salmon Coulibiac includes flour, cornstarch, rice, sour cream, butter, eggs, salmon, mushrooms, shortening, milk, white wine, shallots, bell peppers, and dill. What's the carbohydrate content you must count for your meal? Time's up.

Of course, you can't answer that question without knowing how much of each ingredient goes into the dish, the nutrition facts for each ingredient, and the number of servings. Even then, you're talking about a project to compile all of the information you collect. This recipe made 8 servings, and each serving was 1130 calories, 62 grams of total fat (35 grams saturated fat), 28 grams protein, 1750 milligrams of sodium, and 117 grams of carbohydrate. This particular recipe for Salmon Coulibiac would not fit well into your eating plan, but that doesn't mean there aren't fabulous mixed dishes that will.

Mixed dishes and casseroles often contain combinations of all three macronutrients and can seem overwhelming. These dishes commonly include foods that you know are dense carbohydrates, like potatoes, rice, or pasta, and can include flour or sauces you're not so familiar with. Even foods you've been enjoying for your whole life, like pizza, can be a varying mix of ingredients that are hard to decipher. But, it's not as complicated as it seems if you take an organized view of mixed dishes.

Have an idea of how your daily protein, fat, and carbohydrate recommendations divide out for each meal. You can find this information on your meal plan. For a 1,700 calories per day meal plan, an approximate target for each meal would be 25 grams of protein, 19 grams of fat, and 70 grams of carbohydrate. It's also worth remembering that your daily recommendation for sodium is 1,500 milligrams, or about 500 milligrams for meal.

Compare these mealtime macronutrient recommendations with the per serving nutrition information for the dish in question. You can already see how the Salmon Coulibiac works well for your mealtime protein but is significantly higher for the other dietary concerns. There is, of course, room for adjustments, but that dish would require a profoundly smaller serving size. You can usually get the per serving nutrition information from the recipe, or from a restaurant website, and starting from scratch with an ingredients list is always an option. It's a much better option for dishes that have four ingredients than for dishes that have 12 ingredients, however. You can also adjust the serving size of a combined food if a smaller portion fits better into your meal plan. If the serving size that fits best seems too small, add a salad or nonstarchy vegetable side dish to your meal.

Evaluate recipes from a general health viewpoint, and consider modifying a recipe to improve its nutrition profile. You may want to avoid cured fatty meats, like bacon and sausage, as well as lard, shortening, or butter. If the dish fits well into your meal plan otherwise, substitute ingredients with less fat, like Canadian bacon or margarine.

If you don't have access to the nutrition information, consider carbohydrate-dense casseroles with rice, pasta, corn, or potatoes, as about 30 grams of carbohydrate per cup. You'll be surprisingly close, but it's always an excellent idea to check your blood glucose levels a couple of hours after eating.

Table 13-1 offers some estimating tricks that include protein and fat in addition to carbohydrate.

Table 13-1	Nutrition Estimates for Mixed Dishes			
Dish	**Portion size**	**Carbohydrate**	**Protein**	**Fat**
Tuna and pasta casserole	1 cup	30 grams	14 grams	10 grams
Lasagna/ spaghetti and meatballs	1 cup	30 grams	14 grams	10 grams
Tuna or chicken salad	1 cup	15 grams	28 grams	10 grams
Thin crust pizza with meat	¼ of a 12" pizza	30 grams	14 grams	15 grams
Broth soup with noodles	1 cup	15 grams	0 grams	0 grams

Don't forget that a good, pocket-sized reference book can be invaluable in getting relatively accurate nutrition information for all sorts of dishes. Appendix A is a fairly detailed list of exchanges.

Mixed dishes aren't as tricky as they seem if you've taken some time beforehand to understand what your meals should provide. After all, mixed dishes are just single foods joining together to give you a different flavor and texture — the single foods still have the same nutrition facts as before.

Remembering breakfast and lunch

With diabetes, it's important to spread your food, especially your daily carbohydrates, over time. Spreading your carbohydrates minimizes blood glucose spikes and gives your body an opportunity to bring levels down. The same holds true for both type 1 and type 2 diabetes. Spreading your meals out also is associated with successful weight loss. That means, don't skip meals.

It also means that breakfast and lunch give you two new opportunities each day to incorporate foods into your eating habits that benefit your health. So, are you? Or are you hitting the drive-through in the morning for your driving entertainment and picking up a sandwich and chips for lunch? The truth is that breakfast and lunch can sabotage your best efforts at managing diabetes if you don't treat those meals with the same consideration as dinner.

The week of menus offered in Chapter 17 has seven different, diabetes-friendly options for breakfasts and for lunches. Breakfast and lunch are the perfect times to work healthy dairy foods into your day, like low-fat milk or yogurt. And, what other time are you likely to enjoy the benefits of the soluble fiber in oatmeal? Canned fish, like tuna packed in water, and portable fruits are perfect to grab and go for lunch, and whole-wheat bread gives healthy grains a place to shine.

Breakfast and lunch do take some planning, but many people find they're perfectly happy to eat the same thing every day for these meals, or rotate a few favorites. If that's the case with you, the planning for these meals into the foreseeable future requires an incredibly small investment of your time. By the way, if you're thinking you can find a way to make takeout food work well for these meals, think again. Better yet, visit a few websites with your pen and pad handy, and read Chapter 15 for a look at typical restaurant food.

Adding in the add ons

A little more than two pounds of uranium-235 fueling electricity generation in a nuclear power plant has the potential to produce as much energy as 6.5 million pounds of coal. And, 1 tablespoon of soy sauce contains more sodium than 20 cups of shredded bok choy. The lesson is that it's possible to pack a lot into a small container. When you don't account for that small container, if that container happens to be a condiment going onto your healthy food, you may be symbolically pitching your healthy diabetes meal plan onto the considerable fire 6.5 million pounds of coal can make.

Not all condiments are a nutrition disaster, and in fairness to soy sauce the low sodium versions reduce the 900 milligrams of sodium per tablespoon down to less than 600 milligrams — that is an improvement. Condiments are concentrated little doses of flavor, so you might expect the sources of those flavors to be high, and it's not always sodium that deserves attention. Whatever the case, it's to your advantage to check the nutrition facts for condiments you enjoy and look for alternative varieties that might have lower amounts of the item that's out of bounds. Here are a few tidbits, good and not so good, about your favorite condiments:

- Soy sauce dates back to the second century, and it is made from healthy soy beans, and is fat free without any carbohydrate. But, as mentioned earlier, the sodium is incredibly concentrated in the dark liquid, and even the low-sodium versions deserve a second look before you douse your food. Remember, excess sodium is associated with high blood pressure, and high blood pressure increases your already increased risk for heart attack, stroke, and kidney failure.

- Mayonnaise is a mixture of egg yolks, oil, and vinegar or lemon juice, and is a popular addition to sandwiches and creamy salads. The combination of oil and egg yolk gives mayo a load of fat, both saturated and unsaturated. One tablespoon of full-strength mayonnaise is about 100 calories with 11 grams of total fat. Consider low-fat or fat-free mayo, or try avocado for a really creamy texture and half the calories and fat.

- The National Mustard Museum is located in Middleton, Wisconsin, and displays more than 5,000 different mustards from around the world. Mustard is made with the ground seeds of the mustard plant mixed with vinegar, water, and secret spices — well, salt isn't really a secret. Obviously, mustard is a very popular condiment with so many commercial varieties available, but it does tend to be high in sodium. There are low-sodium varieties of mustard, and if it's the kick you're looking for you might consider horseradish, which has only about a third the sodium as regular mustards.

✔ Ketchup was originally known as table sauce, and it's made with pureed tomatoes, vinegar, spices, and a sweetener. Ketchup has more calories, almost as much sodium, and more carbohydrate than mustard. And, even though the carb content is only 4 grams per tablespoon, that can add up when you're shaking that bottle. Freshly sliced tomatoes are a better option — you can have a whole cup of chopped tomatoes for the same carbohydrate investment.

✔ Sour cream and butter are traditional baked potato toppings, and in some ways it's fortunate that the appropriate diabetes-friendly serving size for a baked potato doesn't resemble a football. Sour cream and butter are both relatively high in fat. Sour cream is the less-fat choice, with 23 calories and 2 grams of fat per tablespoon. Butter, by contrast, has 100 calories and 11 grams of fat for that same tablespoon. But, plain, non-fat Greek yogurt can give you the creaminess you desire at 8 calories, no fat, and a scant 6 milligrams of sodium per tablespoon.

✔ Salsa has become quite popular in the United States as a dipping sauce, and without any commentary on what food you might be dipping your salsa with, salsa is a pretty healthy condiment. Most salsa in a jar has no fat, only 4 or 5 calories, and 100 milligrams of sodium per tablespoon. You can make your own salsa, or *pico de gallo* (uncooked salsa from fresh ingredients), and cut the sodium way down.

✔ Salad dressings deserve mention here, in part because there are so many varieties, and in part because they represent a clear and present threat to a healthy bowl of salad greens. A tablespoon of common salad dressings can have 85 calories, 9 grams of fat, and more than 100 milligrams of sodium. And, contrary to what you may be inclined to believe, it's not necessarily the creamy salad dressings that are highest in calories and fat, although the creamier dressing can include 3 grams of carbohydrate in that tablespoon. The potential issue with salad dressings is the tablespoon — who actually uses only one on their salad? The bigger your healthy salad, the more salad dressing you may be inclined to apply. Adding high-calorie, high-fat, and high-carbohydrate ingredients to your healthy salad, including excess salad dressing, is sometimes called *wearing the healthy halo*. It amounts to conferring high honors to a food you think is healthy, and to yourself for eating that food, when a real look at the add-ons tells a different story.

Gobbling Around the Globe

One of the more interesting food phenomena in the United States over the past decades has been the proliferation of restaurants offering foods of different ethnic and cultural persuasions in smaller cities and towns around the country. Large cities have always enjoyed genuine foods from around the world because large cities often have genuine populations of genuine ethnic people who want to enjoy the genuine ethnic foods they have known. Whether the franchised American restaurants that serve Mexican, Italian, and Asian cuisine actually approach authentic is a question best answered by people in those genuine ethnic groups. The fact is that Americans love their authentic ethnic foods, even if they aren't really authentic.

Ultimately, other countries are exactly like the United States — there is no singular way of eating. For instance, the American view of Mexican food is that the people in a country with literally thousands of miles of coastline on both major oceans mostly eat ground beef tacos and refried beans — they haven't discovered seafood? It's almost certainly the same with other ethnic franchise restaurants — the food offered represents only a caricature of the diversity one would find when traveling in that country. And in true American fashion, the foods you can choose have often been Westernized to provide excess calories and fat.

So, apologies in advance to the marvelously healthy ethnic foods that could be offered in American franchises, because this discussion may spend more time on what people with diabetes should be cautious about. Fortunately, there are authentic options in some areas, and, of course, there are healthy recipes for dishes with one or the other ethnic origin you can find if you look. And, to be completely fair to other countries, your first look will be at an iconic American cuisine.

Satisfying Southern and "soul"

It could be just a coincidence that a geographical area of the United States now labeled as the *diabetes belt,* where the rate of diabetes (mostly type 2) exceeds 12 percent of the population, is concentrated in the American South. Or, maybe not. Maybe a cooking tradition that can turn a serving of very-low-carbohydrate carrots into two carb choices, or no-fat turnip greens into a fat exchange is an ongoing demonstration of the destructive power of added sugar, fat, and salt. Adding sugar, fat, and salt to otherwise healthy food really sums up the tradition of Southern and soul food, and some credible professionals, including David Kessler, MD, a former chief of the U.S. Food and Drug Administration, suggest that this very combination of added ingredients has made modern fast food actually addictive. In that regard, Southern food and soul food has been way ahead of its time.

The important point is that many traditional Southern and soul foods aren't unhealthy from the start — it's the addition of less healthy flavoring ingredients that can overwhelm the nutritional value. Some common additions are as follows:

- Frying foods always adds fat, but frying foods in lard or shortening can add lots of unhealthy saturated fat.

- Adding sugar to cut fruit is a tradition that creates a tasty syrup, but adds loads of empty calories and carbohydrate to a food that is sufficiently sweet to start with.

- Cured meats have been associated with significantly increased risk for type 2 diabetes in long-term studies. Bacon and ham, for instance, should be eaten on a limited basis, but adding these fatty foods to vegetable dishes for flavoring also adds fat and sodium.

- Shortening or lard makes for flaky biscuits but can bring a load of saturated fat to these bread products.

- Butter is mostly saturated fat — seven grams of saturated fat per tablespoon. Adding butter to flaky biscuits, along with a dose of carbohydrates from jelly or honey, is a Southern tradition that could stand improvement.

- Batter adds fat and carbohydrates to food that is generally fried after dipping.

- Creamy vegetables means you've added fat and carbohydrate to otherwise healthy dishes.

- Gravy is made by adding carbohydrate, and sometimes fat, to the saturated fat cooked out of meat products.

Traditional Southern and soul food is represented in some U.S. fast food restaurants, most prominently by restaurant chains that specialize in fried chicken. There you can get coleslaw with 19 grams of carbohydrate and 10 grams of fat, all from the dressing, or a biscuit with more than 500 milligrams of sodium. Add a chicken breast for 11 grams of carbohydrate (breading), 21 grams of fat, and nearly 1,100 milligrams of sodium, and you have a traditional Southern lunch that exceeds your daily sodium recommendation and invests four of your daily carb choices in white flour and added sugar.

Making Southern and soul food healthier for diabetes is mostly about limiting what's added to healthy food. That means less frying in favor of grilling or baking, and there are great recipes around for oven-fried chicken, which is not really fried. The addition of fat from lard and butter and cured meats, like ham hocks, can be minimized by using unsaturated oils and soft margarines sparingly. A smoked turkey neck can add Southern-style flavor to greens without leaving fat behind. Breading and cracker toppings add carbohydrates without significant nutritional benefit. And, adding sugar to foods that are already sweet, or to vegetables like corn, only piles on empty calories and carbohydrates.

The extraordinary rates of type 2 diabetes in the American South and among African Americans is probably related to some extent to eating habits passed down with this traditional diet. And a diet pattern that's associated with developing diabetes is definitely not a template for effectively managing diabetes. But simple modifications can go for big improvements in health, and planning for healthier food, especially limiting stray carbohydrates and fats that find their way into Southern and soul foods, is step number one.

Loving Latino

In many ways, the conflict between diabetes and Mexican food is similar to the issues with traditional Southern and soul food — it's mostly about what's added. A standard Mexican dinner in an American restaurant, however, also offers the person with diabetes a steady stream of carbohydrates — tortilla chips as a warm up, tortillas on the side or as a wrap, a generous helping of beans, and so-called Mexican rice.

Even though added fat, like lard in refried beans, deep-fried poblano chili rellenos, or the generous use of cheese and sour cream, is something a person with diabetes should avoid, the carbohydrates may be the real challenge with Mexican food. The good news is that the carbohydrates aren't usually hidden away in sweetened sauces or gravies — they are right there in front of you. A look at the menu items of a popular Mexican franchise shows that the entrée items — tacos and burritos — come in at 15 to 20 grams of carbohydrate for single tacos, with larger burritos ranging from 40 to 100 grams.

A dine-in franchise offers fish tacos and rice that ring in at 158 grams of carbohydrate, more than ten carb choices, 121 grams of fat, and 3,500 milligrams of sodium. Making the assumption that fish is always the healthier choice would be the wrong assumption in this case because of add-ons.

Mexican cuisine also includes wonderful fresh food, like pico de gallo (salsa fresca) and grilled vegetables. Whole-grain tortillas in your grocery often have so much healthy fiber that the total carbohydrate for a large one can come down to less than 10 grams after subtracting half of the fiber grams. Burritos or tacos made with lean meats, low-sodium beans, fresh vegetables, salsa, and whole-grain tortillas can make an entire diabetes-friendly meal. Again, it's only a matter of planning what goes in. Some franchise Mexican restaurants focus on these kinds of healthy choices, and you can decide what you want to eat from the nutrition information on their websites.

It's worth mentioning the pre-meal tortilla chips, which are usually served with healthy salsa . . . anytime food is placed within your reach is an opportunity for what's called *mindless eating*. That's where your hand automatically travels back and forth from the tortilla chip basket to your mouth while your brain is preoccupied with deciding what to order. A few tortilla chips aren't going to ruin your meal plan, but if you don't stay conscious of this temptation, you can easily get well beyond a few chips.

Assessing Asian

At first glance, the American concept of Asian food would seem to be extremely healthy — stir-fry dishes are like a healthy salad that's simply been cooked. It's clearly possible to make or find very healthy Asian food.

The theme is much the same with Asian food as with other ethnic cuisines — it's what gets added that can make the most difference. With Asian foods it's often the sauces that add fat and sodium in amounts that are inconsistent with healthy eating. Soy sauce is extremely high in sodium, an issue discussed earlier in this chapter, but so is miso, teriyaki, oyster, and black bean sauces. Remember, excess dietary sodium increases your risk for high blood pressure. Some Asian sauces are high in fat as well, and some include added sugar.

While stir frying is an especially healthy was to cook, many Asian foods are deep fried, which adds fat, often to otherwise low-fat foods. Eggrolls would be an example most people know, but some meat dishes like General Tsao's chicken include deep-fried food.

The generosity shown by your favorite Chinese restaurant with the giant pail of rice which accompanies every order may lead you to suspect that carbohydrates could be a concern in enjoying Asian cuisine — you would be correct. A 1-carb-choice portion of white rice is ⅓ cup, and that paper bucket could easily offer you ten or more servings. Plus, Asian food generally highlights white rice, which is no longer a whole grain. A study published in the Archives of Internal Medicine in 2010 found that replacing white rice with brown rice was associated with a 16 percent reduction in developing type 2 diabetes. Exercising some discipline with rice when you're dining Asian can help keep your blood glucose in check.

Incorporating Italian

Once again, it's entirely likely that the American concept of Italian food is colored by the Americanization of Italian food. Nevertheless, when you eat Italian in America it's carbohydrates and fat you need to manage.

The carbohydrates often come from bread and pasta, and the bread may be already waiting for you before you're seated. The bread at an Italian restaurant is exactly like the tortilla chips at a Mexican establishment — an excellent opportunity to eat your way through two or three carb choices before you realize what you're doing. A glass or two of wine can add additional calories, and another carb choice to your running tally.

Pasta is a dense carbohydrate food, with one carb choice coming from a ⅓-cup portion. And, like the Asian takeout rice bucket, most Italian restaurants include pasta in an unmeasurable serving size that could be called a pile. A pile of pasta is not compatible with effective blood glucose control.

Finally, Italian restaurants often offer creamy sauces like Alfredo, made with butter and cheese, and extremely high in fat. Plus, Italian food is known for its assortment of cured meats — prosciutto, mortadella, pancetta, soppressata, and more. These meats are cured with salt, and are often high in saturated fat as well. These should be avoided, or eaten in extreme moderation.

Like any ethnic cuisine, Italian food also offers healthy selections for diabetes management. Fish dishes and vegetables cooked lightly in olive oil are wonderful; tomatoes play a featured role in many Italian dishes. If you're eating out, check the nutrition information before you go. And, if you're preparing Italian food at home, find recipes that are low fat, low sodium, and with a carbohydrate content that fits into your meal plan.

The same advice goes for all of your eating adventures. Every culture has its share of foods and flavors that will fit perfectly into your meal plan. It's up to you to find the ones that fit. Bon appétit.

Chapter 14

Modifying Popular Diet Plans

On a National Geographic documentary film you might hear a biologist quietly whisper something like, "these mountain gorillas live primarily on a diet of tender leaves and stems." In everyday language, however, the word *diet* is rarely used to simply describe a general eating pattern. Instead, *diet* more often refers to a temporary, unwanted, and unpleasant assignment that you must tolerate in order to lose weight — "I need to go on a diet." For this book, and for a more enjoyable life, the National Geographic use of the word is a better way to think.

In the descriptive context of *diet*, you already have one. Your diet is simply your general eating pattern as it might be described by a whispering biologist who has followed you around every day for years. Maybe you love your diet, but know it's hurting your health. Maybe you have a diet you hate, whether it's protecting your health or not. What you want and need is a diet you can love and also protects your health. It's the only certain way to make healthier eating your diet for the long haul. Mountain gorillas go for tender leaves and stems — you have a much wider range of options.

This chapter reviews some popular diet plans, including a few commercial ones you've seen advertised, to evaluate how they might fit with accepted diabetes management principles. The chapter also takes a look at the lure of fad diets and how you can modify some of your favorite recipes to make them diabetes friendly.

Basking in the Mediterranean

The so-called Mediterranean diet is a perfect example of a diet you can live with, not a diet you'll go on — the Mediterranean diet is a general pattern of eating. The primary benefit of this eating pattern was first identified in the Seven Countries Study, which started following middle-aged men in 1958 across four different regions of the world to systematically look at the effects of lifestyle on health. This study contributed to current understandings about the health risks of high blood pressure, smoking, cholesterol, and obesity, and about the health benefits of physical activity and dietary fiber. But, researchers noted something odd in the data. Deaths from heart attacks were much higher in the United States and Northern Europe than in Southern Europe, even when statistics were adjusted to account for age, weight, physical activity, smoking, cholesterol, and blood pressure. The diet and lifestyle in this Mediterranean region seemed to be protecting the population.

A diet for effective diabetes management controls blood glucose averages, helps you manage body weight, and reduces risk factors for heart disease like cholesterol and blood pressure.

The Mediterranean diet, as a contemporary eating plan with health distinct benefits, began gaining popularity in the mid-1990s, and the characteristic foods are modeled from the dietary patterns of Southern Italy, Greece, Crete, Morocco, and Spain in the 1960s. Literally hundreds of studies have examined the health effects of the food and/or the Mediterranean lifestyle, which includes physical activity and stress reduction. Two studies published in 2013 added credibility to the Mediterranean diet's benefits to heart health and diabetes.

- Researchers in Spain followed more than 7,000 individuals at high risk for cardiovascular disease over nearly five years after placing one group on a low-fat diet and two groups on different Mediterranean eating patterns. The Mediterranean diet groups experienced 30 percent fewer major cardiovascular events (heart attack, stroke, or death).

- A meta-analysis published in the January 2013 issue of the *American Journal of Clinical Nutrition* evaluated 20 different studies to determine the effectiveness of different dietary approaches for the management of type 2 diabetes. The analysis showed the Mediterranean diet improves average blood glucose levels (A1C), improves HDL (good) cholesterol, reduces blood triglycerides, and effectively promotes weight loss, all-important to reducing risks for diabetes-related complications.

A meta-analysis is essentially a study of the results of other studies. A meta-analysis evaluates whether the results from multiple independent studies looking at the same issue, more or less, gave statistically consistent results so that the data from those studies can be combined to strengthen a conclusion.

One interesting aspect of many studies involving the Mediterranean diet is that researchers often observe the eating pattern is easy to sustain over time. In the study from Spain, the group assigned to a low-fat diet dropped out of the study at a high rate and ultimately could not stick closely with their assigned diet. By contrast, participants assigned to the either of the two Mediterranean diet groups showed a high level of adherence to their assigned plan. Because no healthy eating plan is effective if it can't be followed, the desirability of this eating plan may be its most important feature. *Mediterranean Diet for Dummies* and *Mediterranean Diet Cookbook for Dummies* (John Wiley and Sons) can help you really explore the possibilities of this healthy diet and lifestyle.

Balancing grains, legumes, and fruit

Dietary fiber is a key component of the Mediterranean diet, and the fiber comes along with carbohydrates and other key nutrients from unrefined grains, legumes (beans and peas), fresh fruits, and vegetables. One benefit of dietary fiber is simply making you feel full sooner and for a longer period between meals. That's called *satiety*. A satisfied appetite often leads to fewer calories, and consuming fewer calories leads to weight loss. But the health benefits of these foods don't stop with satiety.

Legumes — beans, chickpeas, peas, and lentils — are a key source of low-fat protein in a Mediterranean diet and are a rich source of soluble fiber. Soluble fiber helps reduce cholesterol, especially LDL (bad) cholesterol, a key risk factor for heart disease. Whole grain consumption is associated with lower blood pressure, even in relatively small amounts. High blood pressure along with diabetes is a double whammy for your kidneys, as well as a risk factor for heart disease and stroke.

Fruits and vegetables in the Mediterranean diet also contribute to satiety and add an assortment of vitamins and nutrients to the mix. Fresh fruit is the dessert of choice, and the fruits and vegetables should be enjoyed without added sugar, fat, or salt (sodium). The dietary fiber from this fruit and vegetable part of the Mediterranean diet, as well as from legumes and grains, can benefit your health in another very important way — blood glucose control.

A typical Mediterranean diet gets about 50 percent of daily calories from carbohydrate, and the great majority of the carbs come from legumes, unrefined grains, and fruit. These sources tend to have a lower *glycemic index* than added sugars or refined grains because the liberation of glucose during digestion is slower. The *glycemic index* is discussed in more detail in Chapter 8, but the key issue is that the effect on blood glucose levels from low glycemic index foods is gradual. The Mediterranean diet has been shown as appropriate, even beneficial, to blood glucose control. And, while the glycemic index of the primary sources of carbohydrates surely is important, that fact alone doesn't seem to account for the total picture of this eating plan and diabetes. The meta-analysis, mentioned earlier in this section, found the Mediterranean diet reduced A1C more than any of the diets in the comparison, including, by the way, low glycemic index diets.

If you have diabetes, type 1 or type 2, you need to account for your consumption of carbohydrates, even those from low glycemic index foods. These foods do elevate blood glucose at a slower rate than high glycemic index foods, but it's still your supply and response to insulin that brings your blood glucose levels back to normal. At any rate, whether the Mediterranean diet seems like the best eating plan for you or not, it should be clear that getting the majority of your carbohydrates from legumes, unrefined grains, and fruit is a strategy you should try to adopt.

If your idea of beans and grains is bland and blander, you're in for a surprise. Mediterranean cuisine livens up the main ingredients with vinegars, capers, rosemary, mushrooms, citrus, mint, garlic, honey, fennel, peppers, cumin, paprika, onions, saffron, thyme, tomatoes, sage, bay leaf, oregano, nuts, dill, yogurt — to name just a few.

Swapping meat for fish and olive oil

The predominant sources of protein and fat in the typical Mediterranean diet are what sets this eating plan apart from other patterns, especially from the eating patterns typical in the United States (sometimes called the Western diet). On balance, the protein component is relatively low (15 to 20 percent of daily calories), and the fat component relatively high (35 percent of daily calories). But, the specific foods providing the bulk of these macronutrients are somewhat unique to the Mediterranean diet.

For starters, the consumption of dairy products is low, especially milk. Yogurt and cheese make up the dairy component of this eating plan, and these foods, even if eaten every day, are consumed in moderation. Likewise, poultry and eggs provide a portion of the diet's protein, but are eaten in moderation also. Poultry or eggs may be on the menu a few times each week.

The most distinctive trait of the Mediterranean diet, especially when contrasted with the Western diet, is the focus on red meat. More accurately, there is no focus on red meat in the Mediterranean diet — red meat is consumed very sparingly, and in small 2- to 4-ounce portions. Limiting meat consumption leads to a general reduction in unhealthier saturated fats, enhancing the cardiovascular benefits of a Mediterranean diet. But, red meat consumption, especially processed red meat products like hot dogs or salami, has recently gotten attention for its role in blood glucose imbalance, too.

Looking at more than 440,000 participants in the long-term Nurses' Health Study and similar groups, researchers at Harvard University's School of Public Health found a 2-ounce serving of processed red meat product per day increased the risk for developing type 2 diabetes by 50 percent. The ATTICA Study of men and women in Greece (carried out in the Greek province of Attica in Athens), all without cardiovascular disease or diabetes, showed that red meat consumption was associated with reduced insulin sensitivity and excess insulin secretion, typical of type 2 diabetes. Red meat consumption clearly has a negative effect on blood glucose balance. Any factor that accelerates the development of type 2 diabetes or promotes insulin resistance in healthy people is certain to make controlling blood glucose more difficult if you already have diabetes. Limiting red meat intake, therefore, likely accounts for some of the compatibility between the Mediterranean diet and improvements seen in A1C.

So, if cheese, poultry, eggs, and especially red meat are only a minor part of this eating plan, what are the remaining sources of protein and dietary fat? The answer is probably the key to what makes the Mediterranean diet easy to follow for the long term — fish and seafood, nuts, and olive oil.

Fish, seafood, and nuts not only supplement the dietary protein already provided by legumes, but also add healthy unsaturated fats, including omega-3 fatty acids, into the mix. Your Mediterranean diet might add a small serving of nuts every day and a serving of fish or seafood several times a week. Fresh fish, of course, was plentiful along the coast of the Mediterranean in the 1960s when the Seven Countries study first noted the mysteriously low cardiovascular risk associated with living there.

Fish and nuts aside, the final touch to the Mediterranean diet is olive oil. Olive oil contains mostly healthy mono-unsaturated fats (oleic acid), vitamin E, and natural phenols with healthy antioxidant properties. Clinical data suggests that olive oil has anti-inflammatory and anti-thrombotic (preventing blood clots) properties, and improves the flexibility of blood vessels. With respect to diabetes, a 2011 study actually looked at individual variations in the composition of a fat that is part of cell membranes, *phosphatidylcholine*, and found when oleic acid was a component of this complex molecule insulin resistance was lower. Among the 360 participants in Spain, none with diabetes, every 1 percent increase in the oleic acid composition of phosphatidylcholine represented a 20 percent reduction in insulin resistance (prediabetes). Olive oil, therefore, may offer clear benefits for both cardiovascular health, and blood glucose control.

As a food, olive oil replaces the saturated fats other societies consume as butter, and adds flavor to vegetable dishes in particular. Olive oil can be used for cooking or can be drizzled directly into salads, vegetable dishes, onto bread, or in marinades. Olive oil even appears to increase satiety. Extra virgin olive oil is generally recommended for direct consumption.

Finally, the Mediterranean diet's combination of fats seems to strike a beneficial balance between omega-3 fatty acids and the less famous omega-6 fatty acids. You need both omega-3 and omega-6 fatty acids, and both are healthy fats. But when omega-6 consumption is much higher than omega-3 consumption, the imbalance in fats can lead to inflammation and atherosclerosis. The typical Western diet may favor omega-6 fatty acids by 20 to 1 or more, but in a typical Mediterranean diet the balance is closer to a healthy 4 to 1.

Having wine with dinner

Encouraging a glass of red wine with dinner is the perfect way to cap off this discussion of the Mediterranean diet, because having wine in moderation is typical for the people of this region. Moderate consumption of alcohol, defined as no more than two drinks per day for men or one drink per day for women, has health benefits when compared to heavier drinkers or tea totalers. And red wine, in particular, contains antioxidants including the phenol *resveratrol*, which is somewhat famous for anti-aging properties. This is great news if you happen to be a yeast cell or a certain round worm, but human studies are inconclusive about resveratrol and aging. Nevertheless, a little wine with dinner is clearly consistent with good health.

Alcohol consumption is not advised for some health conditions that are common among people with type 2 diabetes, like high blood pressure or high triglyceride levels. Excessive consumption of alcohol is clearly not healthy over the long term, and in some people with diabetes excessive consumption at any time can trigger severe and dangerous low blood glucose levels. Some alcoholic beverages, including wine, contain carbohydrates, although the carb content in wines that are not excessively sweet (dessert wines) is usually less than 5 grams per 5-ounce serving.

Always consume your alcohol with food to avoid hypoglycemia, especially after the evening meal when you go to bed.

A Mediterranean diet has benefits to cardiovascular health, to weight management, and to blood glucose control, and is, by most accounts, easy to sustain over time. Maybe most important, it's an eating plan adopted from real life. What's not to like?

Dining With DASH

High blood pressure, *hypertension*, is too common among people with diabetes. By some estimates two of every three people with diabetes have high blood pressure, too, in some measure because the risk factors for type 2 diabetes — overweight, lack of physical activity, and age — are also risk factors for high blood pressure. Having both high blood pressure and diabetes multiplies the risk for some serious complications, like kidney failure, heart attack and stroke, and problems with the eye.

DASH is an acronym for "dietary approaches to stop hypertension." DASH is an eating plan developed experimentally by the National Institutes of Health when that agency conducted clinical trials on three distinct diet plans through five medical centers between 1993 and 1997. The study clearly demonstrated a capacity to lower blood pressure with diet.

Controlling high blood pressure with diet

Blood pressure is a measure of the force of blood pushing on the walls of your arteries as your heart pumps blood throughout your body. High blood pressure can be caused by a loss of flexibility in blood vessels and arteries, by deposits that decrease the size of arteries and decrease the smoothness of blood flow, by changes in blood volume or thickness, or by unknown factors. Blood pressure measurements are expressed in millimeters of mercury (a measure of pressure) when the heart pumps, *systolic* pressure, and the pressure when the heart is resting between beats, *diastolic* pressure. A normal blood pressure is considered to be lower than 120/80. If you have either number higher than a systolic/diastolic 140/90, you are considered hypertensive.

The National Institutes of Health study found that a particular eating plan, now known as DASH, lowered blood pressure by an average of 5.5 systolic and 3.0 diastolic compared to the typical U.S. diet eaten by a matched group. The DASH plan lowered blood pressure even more among the African American and other ethnic participants, who are at a statistically higher risk for hypertension. And, for participants with hypertension, systolic pressure dropped by an average of 11.4 and diastolic by an average of 5.5. The original DASH eating plan notably did not include a reduced sodium component.

Considering grains, fruit, and dairy

The DASH eating plan is typical of most healthy diet recommendations in its emphasis on more vegetables, fewer added sweets, and less saturated fat. The DASH plan is somewhat unique, however, in its strong emphasis on whole grains. A typical DASH eating plan also incorporates several servings of fruit and low-fat dairy into a daily menu, and taken together with the grains there are a lot of carbohydrate containing foods you need to balance for blood glucose management.

Table 14-1 shows the recommended number of servings from the various food groups as they're divided in the DASH plan. For a 2,000 calories per day diet, the plan could (emphasizing could) include up to 25 carb choices per day. A typical eating plan for diabetes management would be more likely to include closer to 15 carb choices each day (remember that a carb choice is 15 grams of carbohydrate). This kind of variation could be significant in managing blood glucose effectively, but it's easy enough to adjust the daily carbohydrates and still follow the DASH plan.

Table 14-1	DASH Plan Recommended Servings and Examples for a 2,000 Calories per Day Diet	
DASH Plan	**Number of Servings (Per Day Unless Noted) Examples**	**Food Group**
Grains	6-8 servings	Whole wheat bread or rolls, whole grain pasta, cereals, grits, brown rice, quinoa, popcorn, oatmeal, pretzels
Vegetables	4-5 servings	Broccoli, carrots, greens, squash, potatoes, sweet potatoes, tomatoes, peas, cucumbers, green beans
Fruit	4-5 servings	Fresh, frozen, dried, canned without syrup, or juices
Fat free or low-fat dairy products	2-3 servings	Milk, buttermilk, cheese, yogurt
Lean meats, poultry,	6 or fewer 1 ounce	Lean meats, trim fat, broil, roast fish, eggs servings or one egg or poach, remove skin from poultry, limit eggs to four per week
Nuts, seeds and legumes	4-5 servings per week	Almonds, walnuts, peanuts, sunflower seeds, peanut butter, beans, lentils
Fats and oils	2-3 servings	Margarine, oil, salad dressing
Sweets and sugars	less than 1 serving	Candy, syrup, jelly, sugar

Chapter 13 discusses how the USDA's representation of a healthy and balanced diet with MyPlate spreads carbohydrates into more than one group. The DASH eating plan does this, too, so it's important to know where carbohydrates are hiding.

All grains contain carbohydrate, so the DASH recommendation for 6 to 8 servings per day is pretty clear — always count grains as carbohydrates. But, did you notice some starchy vegetables hiding in the vegetable category? Potatoes, sweet potatoes, peas, lima beans, and hard-shell squashes are carbohydrate foods, and you would need to account for them as carb choices. You know that everything in the fruit category should be counted as carbs, but while cheese has no carbohydrate, both milk and yogurt in the dairy group should be accounted for in your daily carbohydrate consumption. The sweets group is, of course, all carbohydrate, and there's no need to look for carbs in the fat and oils or in the lean meats groups. But, the nuts and seeds group also includes the legumes beans and lentils, and these legumes are candidates for carbohydrate counting.

When following the DASH eating plan you simply need to remember your diabetes meal plan's carbohydrate recommendations and know that carbohydrate foods are not completely segregated with grains, fruits and sweets, but also can be found in with vegetables, dairy and nuts. If you, for instance, decide to go with the full 8 servings of grain in a day, then you won't throw in 5 servings of fruit, 2 glasses of milk, a bean burrito, a baked potato, a mocha latte, and a frozen yogurt.

Finding Potassium, Magnesium, and Calcium

The DASH eating plan has a focus on providing three substances that can help keep blood pressure levels lower — potassium, magnesium, and calcium. And, the plan focuses on getting these elements from food.

Tomato gardeners know that when their fertilizer says 18-18-21, it means 18 percent nitrogen, 18 percent phosphorus, and 21 percent potash. Potash is a potassium compound, and potassium (scientific symbol K) is essential for you and your tomatoes. Potassium is an *electrolyte* that plays a key role in important activities like helping your heart beat in rhythm, and many studies have shown that adequate levels of potassium help lower blood pressure. Fruits, vegetables, legumes, fish and dairy are all DASH sources of potassium, and the eating plan looks to provide 4,700 milligrams per day.

If you're familiar with milk of magnesia, you're familiar with magnesium. This common earth element has more important roles than bringing relief from constipation, however. Magnesium is involved in hundreds of biochemical processes in your body, including regulation of blood pressure and blood glucose. The DASH eating plan looks to increase your intake of magnesium by emphasizing whole grains, fruits and vegetables, nuts, seeds, and legumes. People with type 2 diabetes tend to have lower levels of magnesium. The DASH plan's goal for magnesium is 500 milligrams per day.

Calcium is known for its relationship to bone health. But calcium also plays a complex role in blood pressure. The first studies exploring the effects of dietary calcium on blood pressure were published in the early 1980s, and the benefit has become clearer since. The DASH plan aims to provide 1,250 milligrams per day from fat-free and low-fat dairy, green vegetables, fish, and beans.

Losing sodium is even better

The Centers for Disease Control and Prevention (CDC) estimate the average American diet includes 3,436 milligrams of sodium per day, compared to your body's requirement of less than 500 milligrams. Excess sodium consumption is related to hypertension, and the DASH plan limits sodium intake to 2,300 milligrams per day. The dietary recommendation for people with diabetes, however, is no more than 1,500 milligrams of sodium per day. Interestingly, a follow-up to the original DASH study looked at the effect on high blood pressure of a lower sodium DASH eating plan — 1,500 milligrams per day. The lower sodium plan reduced blood pressure more than the original plan.

Don't think that throwing your salt shaker out in the yard automatically solves the challenges with reducing sodium. If your sodium intake is average, it's likely that 70 percent comes from foods, not that shaker. The most likely culprits are canned foods, cured meats, and restaurant food, and reducing sodium is so important you should really learn to look for it in your diet.

 Go to your favorite restaurant's website, and check the sodium content of some of the dinners. You're likely to find one meal can give you two days' worth of sodium. Sodium in restaurant food is another reason that eating more often at home is good for your health.

The DASH eating plan can be consistent with effective diabetes management, but you need to locate the carbohydrate foods to balance DASH with your meal plan. Talk with your doctor before you jump in, especially if there are concerns about kidney function.

Preferring Plants

There is an impressive body of evidence demonstrating the effectiveness of a vegetarian diet in weight management, A1C improvement, increased insulin sensitivity, and cardiovascular health indicators. But, can you really get adequate nutrition from plants? According to the Academy of Nutrition and Dietetics, "appropriately planned vegetarian diets, including total vegetarian or vegan diets, are healthful, nutritionally adequate, and may provide health benefits in the prevention and treatment of certain diseases." Maybe this is worth a look.

The Vegetarian Society was founded in Manchester, England in 1847, and that event marks the beginning of what could be called the modern era of this approach to diet. Defining a vegetarian depends to some extent upon whom you ask. A *pollo-pescetarian* vegetarian, for instance, eats poultry and seafood. Most likely, only pollo-pescetarians can add the word vegetarian to that lineup with a straight face — a giant turkey leg with a shrimp cocktail appetizer may leave only limited space for the vegetarian part of their meals.

Many people around the world, however, fall under more accepted variations of vegetarianism, and it's reasonable to address the question of diabetes management as it applies to a couple of different views on plant-based eating. The truth is that most people could stand to lean more toward vegetarian to add more vegetables and to cut down on red meat. But, there's one surprising nutrient most Americans could use a little more of, and getting enough of this from plants while managing blood glucose levels takes a little thought.

In 2008 the *American Journal of Clinical Nutrition* published an assessment of average Americans' protein consumption based upon an ongoing survey called the *National Health and Nutrition Examination Survey* (NHANES). In the broad picture, a surprising number of Americans are not getting enough protein relative to the recommendation that protein should account for 20 percent, more or less, of total calories. One challenge of a plant-based diet is finding nutrients, including protein, to replace what's lost when giving up meat and other animal products.

Adopting the ovo-lacto view

Movie credits often run the disclaimer, "no animals were harmed during the making of this film." Ovo-lacto vegetarians take a similar view, and include eggs and dairy products into their primarily plant-based diet because no animals are harmed in the making of those foods. Adding eggs and dairy provides additional options for dietary protein, the best dietary source of calcium from dairy and better access to vitamin B_{12} (more on that next). But, it isn't that these nutrients aren't available from plant foods.

Eating protein is all about getting the *amino acids*. Protein is built from amino acids, and your body uses about 20 different amino acids to build everything it needs for good health. Of the 20, a specific 9 are called *essential amino acids* because your body cannot produce them from scratch — these must be in your diet. Protein is readily available from plants like beans, nuts and seeds, and grains, but whereas most animal sources of protein include all nine essential amino acids, single sources of plant protein are often missing a few. In practice, that simply means that vegetarians should eat a wide variety of protein foods. Adding eggs and dairy, however, does provide a couple of one-stop shops for essential amino acids, but soy protein is of equal quality. All in all, concerns about inadequate protein in a vegetarian diet are irrelevant as long as a variety of foods are included and adequate protein consumption is a focus.

Adequate calcium is only slightly more a concern in a vegetarian diet. Calcium is available in dark greens like collards or kale, green soy beans (edamame) and soy, and sesame seeds, to name a few, but calcium in plants may not be as available for absorption as calcium in dairy or fish. And, dairy is the richest source of calcium.

Consuming dairy products as part of a plant-based diet, therefore, adds some distinct benefit. In the big picture, eggs and dairy in the diets of ovo-lacto vegetarians may be valuable if only by adding more variety.

To be sure you get enough calcium in your diet, you need to have enough vitamin D, which promotes the uptake of calcium in your intestine. The best source of vitamin D is definitely sunlight, but there is a fear of overexposure to sunlight, which might lead to skin cancer or possibly malignant melanoma. And there are many places far from the equator where the sun comes in at such an angle in the winter that you get little or no vitamin D from sun exposure. You can get some vitamin D from food, especially from milk and fatty fish like salmon, but the easiest source is a little gel capsule, which is cheap and available in any drugstore.

If you are concerned that you are not getting enough vitamin D, ask your doctor to perform a blood test for your level.

Being vegan

The word *vegan* describes a person who eats only foods from plants, or in some cases avoids, using any animal products at all, like leather or silk. With respect to diet, you have already seen how plants can provide well-balanced nutrition. Plants are a primary source of carbohydrates in any diet, plant protein is sufficient when the diet is varied, and plant fats are, for the most part, healthy unsaturated fats. There's one nutrient that vegetarians, and especially vegans, cannot get in a plant-based diet, and that is vitamin B_{12}.

Eggs and dairy products do contain vitamin B_{12}, but there are no reliable sources of this essential vitamin from plants. Vitamin B_{12} has some very important responsibilities, including brain and nervous system function, and a deficiency of this vitamin can lead to severe neurological damage.

Vegans must either consume vitamin B_{12} fortified foods or take a vitamin supplement. Breakfast cereals are commonly fortified with vitamin B_{12} and provide a convenient source for vegans. Soy and nut milks are often fortified, as are meat substitutes, and vegans must look for this nutrient on nutrition labels. Products targeted to vegetarians and vegans are certain to list this essential fact on the nutrition label.

A vegetarian or vegan diet can be completely consistent with diabetes, especially when nonstarchy vegetables are liberally included. The heart benefits to this eating strategy are clear, and as long as you remember that carbohydrates are found in fruits, grains, legumes (beans), and starchy vegetables, you can manage your health and your diabetes quite nicely.

Counting Points — Weight Watchers

Weight Watchers is a successful weight loss program that is not, by its own admission, "designed for those with diabetes." However, successful weight loss can have profoundly positive effects on blood glucose control and on risk factors for diabetes complications like heart disease. Weight Watchers promotes a healthy lifestyle, including regular exercise, and offers programs that include regular, in-person meetings as well as an online program.

A basic Weight Watchers philosophy is that foods are not forbidden. Instead, foods are assigned a specific point value, and the participant budgets for a daily points target. The targets are designed to provide a daily calorie deficit, resulting in weight loss. Foods that are low calorie, low fat, and high fiber are assigned a lower point value than high-calorie, high-fat, low-fiber foods. The advantage to the participant is in being able to see the relative advantage to choosing healthier foods, even though less healthy options can be freely chosen as long as the higher points are counted.

Additionally, following the Weight Watchers program requires at least some focus on food portion sizes in order to arrive at the points value for any particular food. Diabetes management also requires an understanding of portion sizes.

So, on the positive side, Weight Watchers has the following benefits:

- ✔ Potentially helps some achieve weight loss
- ✔ Encourages healthier foods and physical activity
- ✔ Teaches that all foods can fit into a healthy diet
- ✔ Requires a focus on portion size and the nutritional quality of food to arrive at a point value

On the cautionary side, the points are completely unrelated to the carbohydrate content of food. In practice, that means that tracking Weight Watchers point values is no substitute for tracking carbohydrates in your meals and snacks. Carbohydrate foods are some of the healthiest foods around, and Weight Watchers often assigns a lower point value based upon the calorie, fiber, and fat content. In fact, a recent attempt to encourage healthier choices left some fruit as 0 point free foods. For effective diabetes management, eating healthy food is important, but so is managing the volume and timing of your carbohydrates, and you can't ignore the carbs in a fruit even if Weight Watchers says so.

Secondly, there is, of course, a financial cost to the Weight Watchers program. Expect an initial sign up fee, and a monthly fee for both the traditional and online programs. Weight Watchers doesn't require the purchase of its branded food products, but should you decide to go for Weight Watchers foods or its *Smart Ones* brand frozen entrees (found in a store near you) be aware that the cost of food is extra.

Lastly, weight loss is an appropriate goal for many people with diabetes — remember that more than 80 percent of people with type 2 diabetes are overweight or obese. Diabetes is a serious condition and is often joined by other related health problems. You should discuss any plan to modify your diet with your doctor, and with your registered dietitian. Severely limiting calories or restricting food choices without considering health conditions and your medications shouldn't be undertaken with consulting your medical team.

Food By Mail

Some weight loss programs claim to do all the work for you by delivering your meals already made. But, is doing all the work for weight loss the same as doing all the work for controlling blood glucose? Two of these popular commercial weight loss plans have a specific program targeted at diabetes management.

Nutrisystem

Nutrisystem was founded in 1972, and in 1999 began its current business model selling prepackaged foods directly to customers. The current Nutrisystem program offers weight loss programs tailored to men or women, each with a subcategory for seniors, vegetarians, or people with diabetes. The plans are calorie restricted for weight loss, and deliver meals and snacks for 28 days each month to the participant's door. Fresh produce, dairy, and some protein foods must be purchased separately. Nutrisystem offers transition and maintenance plans when you're ready to leave the program, or to maintain a target weight. A members' website offers educational information and tracking tools, and some membership levels include telephone counseling.

The Nutrisystem plan is built, according to its promotional information, on the *glycemic index*, and its diabetes plan, called Nutrisystem D, offers access to Certified Diabetes Educators at all membership levels. The women's diabetes plan is 1,250 calories per day, and 2,300 milligrams sodium. Many of the food choices are specifically for the diabetes plan, and the cost at the lowest level for 28 breakfasts, lunches, dinners, and snacks is advertised at $260.00 per month for men (slightly less for women) if you select the automatic shipping option. Remember, the participant must supply some food.

A 2009 study involving 69 obese participants, funded by Nutrisystem, concluded that the Nutrisystem D was significantly more effective for weight loss, A1C reduction, and other health indicators than a program described as "a diabetes support and education program." This group participated in a group session about diabetes management every four weeks, but its diet was not controlled.

The Nutrisystem D plan is almost certainly suitable for diabetes management, but some qualification may be necessary. One important note to the Nutrisystem-funded study of the Nutrisystem D plan is that participants consumed a certain number of Nutrisystem food servings as well as additional sources of dairy, fruit, and vegetables. It is fair to deduce that some of the daily carbohydrate choices that are part of the Nutrisystem D plan are purchased weekly at a grocery by the participant, prepared by the participant, and portioned by the participant. Including fresh foods is a good thing, but this element of the Nutrisystem D program suggests that you won't escape thinking about, and planning for, carbohydrates in your diet.

Jenny Craig

Jenny Craig is another commercial weight loss program that delivers food to their members and advertises a plan for diabetes. The Jenny Craig program began in 1983 in Australia and moved to the United States in 1985. The company is now owned by Nestle. This diet plan emphasizes an approach known as *volumetrics*, where a focus on less energy-dense foods (lower-calorie foods) allows for more volume. The Jenny Craig program includes a tailored physical activity plan and weekly one-on-one sessions with a Jenny Craig consultant. These individuals aren't necessarily nutrition professionals, however, and focus on motivation. Even though the program delivers meals, there are Jenny Craig centers where you can pick up your food and meet with your consultant. The Jenny Craig program can be expensive, with membership costs running from $7.00 to $10.00 per month plus the cost of Jenny Craig food. Like Nutrisystem, you shop for your own dairy, fruits, and protein.

The Jenny Craig diabetes program is called *Jenny Type 2*, and claims to help you maintain healthy blood glucose levels, manage blood pressure, and control cholesterol and triglyceride levels. The actual program, however, isn't separate from the standard weight loss regimen. That doesn't mean a Jenny Craig plan isn't compatible with managing your diabetes effectively. Weight loss always benefits people with type 2 diabetes, and the volumetrics philosophy emphasizes healthy nonstarchy vegetables almost by default. You're not going to escape managing your own carbohydrate intake, however.

Saying Farewell to Carbs

The Atkins Diet, surely the best-known low-carbohydrate weight loss plan, is based on a theory that excess weight is mostly related to excess carbohydrates. And this eating plan may be attractive to people with diabetes because the constant focus on carbohydrates in diabetes management plans could be interpreted to confirm the notion that carbs are inherently bad.

The Atkins plan, or other low carbohydrate diet, aims to switch your body into burning fat as an alternative to glucose, and as a weight loss strategy these diets are effective. The popularity of the Atkins plan skyrocketed in 2003, with nearly 10 percent of Americans gloating over the diet that required consumption of bacon and steak. Sales of carbohydrate foods like rice and pasta plummeted, and food manufacturers began marketing low-carb versions of their standard products. The death of Dr. Robert Atkins from a fall in 2003, followed by autopsy results suggesting heart disease and high blood pressure, marked the beginning of the end to this frenzy.

The long-term health controversies surrounding this approach to weight loss are still unresolved, and a few of the concerns relate to diabetes. Some doctors, for instance, worry that high protein consumption over a long term eventually takes a toll on kidney function, and bone loss is another common concern. In practice, the grand celebration over eating all the foods other diet plans look to minimize often gives way to craving the carbohydrates (and maybe other nutrients) you've been missing. This diet is usually not sustainable.

The meta-analysis, first mentioned in this chapter's section on the Mediterranean diet, included diets described as low carbohydrate and diets described as high protein. Whereas the extent of carbohydrate restriction didn't always fall to Atkins standards, that analysis found neither a low-carbohydrate nor high-protein diet reduced A1C as much as the Mediterranean plan.

Extremely low-carbohydrate diets may be fun and effective as a weight loss option for healthy individuals over a short term, but adding diabetes to the mix is cause for concern. Considering that other dietary approaches are proven to effectively manage diabetes and associated health concerns, low-carbohydrate diets need more research to justify an endorsement for people with diabetes.

Resisting Fads

The cabbage soup diet of the 1980s is alive and well, apparently outliving cabbage patch dolls of the same period. But, those who own the original dolls may find they still have value — those who tried the diet lost any value almost immediately. In fairness to the cabbage soup diet, it only claims on its website that you can lose 10 pounds in seven days. If you're 28 years old and want to drop a few pounds before your ten-year class reunion, it could be that feeling light-headed, weak, and unable to concentrate is worth a week of cabbage. If you have diabetes, however, the cabbage soup diet is maybe not such a great idea.

Americans are on a constant search for an easy way to lose weight, spending more than $2 billion dollars each year on ineffective weight loss supplements. Fad diets, although not nearly so expensive (cabbage is cheap), somehow seem irresistible to many. And, while you might be perfectly able to see through the claims of diet plans like the Hot Dog Diet or Dr. Siegal's Cookie Diet, the desperation that comes from unsuccessful efforts at weight loss can cloud judgment. The guilt about weight that sometimes goes with diabetes can increase that sense of desperation, too, but having diabetes makes fad diets potentially dangerous.

Promising the quick fix

Medical professionals generally consider weight loss of about 1 to 2 pounds per week fast enough unless close supervision is provided. Diet plans that guarantee rapid weight loss, perhaps by resetting or revving up your metabolism, are either fraudulent or dangerous.

The HCG diet, where HCG stands for *human chorionic gonadotropin*, is an excellent example. The plan focuses your attention on injections of this special hormone recovered from the urine of pregnant women, but the extreme weight loss is actually related to the diet's 500 calories per day food allowance. A diet that includes only 500 calories per day is not safe. The U.S. Food and Drug Administration issued warning letters to companies that market HCG as a natural weight loss supplement, but startling claims and persuasive testimonials are everywhere still.

The bottom line is that ultra-quick weight loss is unhealthy, is often only a loss of water (the weight is regained immediately), and the method is not sustainable. Just ask those who tried the Apple Cider Vinegar Diet.

Trumpeting miracle foods

Sorry, there are no miracle foods or secret combinations of foods that burn fat while you sleep. The constantly resurrecting Grapefruit Diet, or the Wu-Yi Tea Diet are examples — there are others, and there will always be new ones.

Losing weight and losing fat is about using more calories than you ingest, and any of these plans that actually leads to weight loss inevitably does so by coming in with low calories. Unfortunately, these plans also restrict foods that are healthy, and sometimes essential.

A few other keys to recognizing fad diets would include the following:

- It sounds too good to be true (your mother was right!).
- It's the food (or diet) they don't want you to know about (if it was healthy, they really would want you to know about it).
- Claims are based on a single unpublished study, or simple conclusions are drawn from a complex study.
- A diet special for only some people (the Blood Type Diet).
- It includes a miracle food only available from one place (at a low price today only, plus shipping and handling).

Having diabetes makes it especially important that you not waste time (or money) or risk your health by looking for shortcuts to better health. The sooner you decide to follow a proven path, the better your future looks.

Salvaging Your Heirloom Recipes

Finding an eating plan that facilitates weight management, blood glucose control, and is heart healthy doesn't mean everything about your old life goes on the trash heap. People have interesting relationships with food, and sometimes an emotional connection with the past is strong. It's entirely probable that your grandmother's pumpkin pie can fit somewhere in your eating plan now and then. But to know just where and how often that old favorite can fit, you really need to review the nutrition facts label. On Grandma's pumpkin pie, however, there is no nutrition facts label.

Calculating nutrition facts

Fortunately, in this age where information is literally at your fingertips, you too can be dietitian-for-a-day. Calculating the basic nutrition facts for that Thanksgiving favorite may include calories, carbohydrates, fat, protein, sodium, and serving size. To make the calculation you simply find a website that provides information for each individual ingredient, add the values to find the nutrition facts for the entire pie, and then divide each by the number of pieces the pie could yield. The grand tally is illustrated in Table 14-2, and you can probably predict that a healthy slice of Grandma's pumpkin pie will be a decidedly small one.

If you were to declare that this recipe makes 8 servings, each serving would be more than 300 calories, 41 grams carbohydrate, 13 grams saturated fat from lard, and 204 milligrams sodium. Of course, after a piece of that pie, Grandma would spend the rest of the afternoon hoeing the garden. If five hours of garden hoeing isn't on your agenda for the day, you could recalculate this recipe with a few choice ingredient substitutions.

Table 14-2	Nutrition Calculation for Grandma's Pumpkin Pie				
Ingredient	**Calories**	**Carbohydrate**	**Fat**	**Protein**	**Sodium**
1¼ cups all-purpose flour	569	119g	1g	16g	3mg
½ teaspoon salt	0	0	0	0	1,163mg
⅓ cup lard	610	0	68g	0	0
4 tbsp water	0	0	0	0	0
1 pound canned pumpkin	167	40g	1g	5g	25mg
¾ cup sugar	540	144g	0	0	0
1 tsp. cinnamon	6	2g	0	0	1mg
½ tsp. ground ginger	3	1g	0	0	0
½ tsp. ground nutmeg	6	1g	0	0	0
3 eggs	221	1g	15g	19g	210mg
⅔ cup evaporated milk	226	17g	13g	11g	179mg
½ cup whole milk	73	6g	4g	4g	49mg
Totals	2421	331g	102g	55g	1631mg
Per serving @ 8 slices	303	41g	13g	7g	204mg

Modifying ingredients

Many recipes can be modified to improve the nutrient picture, and every little bit adds up. Grandma's pumpkin pie, for example, could lose the salt (and 146 milligrams sodium) and could go into a premade pie shell to eliminate most of the saturated fat. Substitute 1% or skim milk for whole milk, egg substitute for the eggs, and half of the sugar with a no-calorie sweetener suitable for baking, and you may find Grandma's memory can come with a much better nutrition picture.

Healthier substitutions can be incorporated into your diet in many ways. Here are just a few other difference-makers for your consideration:

- ✔ Remove skin from poultry.

- ✔ Always look for reduced sodium soups, broths, soy sauce, and cheese.

- ✔ Select leaner cuts of meat — substitute pork tenderloin for pork chops, turkey bacon for bacon, or ground round or lean ground beef for higher fat mixes.

- ✔ Use whole-wheat pasta and flours.

- ✔ Substitute applesauce or other fruit puree for some of the fat in baking recipes.

It's not about making the biggest sacrifice; it's about finding a healthier eating plan you can stay with over the long run.

Chapter 15

What's On the Menu: Having a Plan for Eating Out

Once upon a time, in the land of Dontyouwish, the restaurants made magical food for people with diabetes. This magical food was delicious and inexpensive, but most magically, the food at the restaurants in Dontyouwish didn't have the same effect on blood sugar and heart health as the foods the people ate at home. The people with diabetes were relieved from thinking about food, and lived happily ever after.

Don't you wish. But, the truth, of course, is that foods you eat away from home, whether at a restaurant or a party, have exactly and precisely the same effect on your blood glucose and long-term heart health as the foods you eat at home. The only real difference is that you don't control what goes into the food you eat away from home. And to pretend that eating away from home doesn't make effective diabetes management more challenging would be to live in a fairy tale.

It would be unrealistic to suggest that you must never stray from your diabetes meal plan or that you should never, ever eat away from home. But, it is completely realistic to say that if you don't manage how far or how often you stray, your health will surely suffer. This chapter helps you find a balance between diabetes management and eating away from home by employing the same strategies that can keep you on track at home — planning ahead. And, if planning is your key to conquering impulsive eating at home — and it is — imagine how important planning can be when you're enveloped by the sights and sounds and aromas that encourage you to eat with abandon. There really is no such place as Dontyouwish.

Making Decisions First

Eating away from home almost certainly means eating less healthy foods overall. Studies show that people eating away from home are consistently confronted with higher-calorie foods, larger portion sizes, and an atmosphere that encourages overindulgence. Consequently, eating away from home results in a higher intake of calories, fat, saturated fat, and sodium as well as a lower intake of fiber, vitamins A and C, carotenes, calcium, and magnesium. With diabetes well-being so closely connected to food, eating away from home, while staying true to your medical nutrition therapy, is definitely a challenge.

Table 15-1 compares a full day's recommendations for carbohydrate, fat, and sodium for a 1,700-calories-per-day eating plan to a few single meals at popular restaurants. Remember, the first line is the recommendation for a whole day.

Table 15-1	Restaurant Meals Compared to Daily Recommendations			
Meal	*Calories*	*Carbohydrate*	*Fat*	*Sodium*
Daily for diabetes	1,700	212 grams	56 grams	1,500 milligrams
Honey chipotle chicken	1,700	200 grams	77 grams	4,110 milligrams
Hibachi chicken skewers	1,330	187 grams	41 grams	4,760 milligrams
Angus deluxe, large fries, large diet soda	1,260	124 grams	64 grams	2,025 milligrams
Tostada chicken salad	1,551	102 grams	94 grams	2,480 milligrams

Standing face to face with food, or with images of food like in a menu, is not the time to be making decisions about healthy eating. The thinking part of your brain is no match for biology in the spur of the moment — it needs time to consider all of the variables and reach a logical conclusion. Giving your thinking brain the time and information to do what it does best is one thing that makes meal planning so powerful.

So, making decisions first, before you're confronted with overwhelming choices, means actually making decisions. It doesn't mean considering in some general way whether you might go for the salad at dinner tonight. Your thinking brain needs information, and it's up to you to collect the facts.

Remembering your meal plan

If you don't have a personalized meal plan from a registered dietitian as part of your diabetes *medical nutrition therapy*, get one. Food is extremely important to controlling your diabetes, and a personalized meal plan tells you how many grams of carbohydrate to eat at each meal, what your daily calorie goal should be, how to best address blood pressure and cholesterol, how your diabetes medications work most effectively, and includes nutritional guidance for other medical conditions.

The most unique element of your diabetes meal plan is its focus on carbohydrates, because carbohydrates raise blood glucose levels directly. Because diabetes is all about unhealthy high blood glucose levels, it makes perfect sense that managing the foods that raise blood glucose levels is important. The amount and timing of carbohydrate foods you eat works hand in hand with the amount and timing of your medications, including insulin, to keep blood glucose levels as close to normal as possible. When you can keep your blood glucose levels as close to normal as possible, your risk for serious diabetes complications is reduced, so keeping your blood glucose under control makes perfect sense too. Your thinking brain is pleased when things make perfect sense.

Your meal plan helps this whole process by recommending a specific number of grams of carbohydrate with each meal and by giving general guidance on which carbohydrate foods give you the most nutrition-related bang for your buck. Generally, about 50 percent of your daily calories comes from carbohydrates — 1,000 calories from carbohydrates if your calorie recommendation is 2,000 calories per day. Because carbohydrates store 4 calories of energy per gram, 1,000 calories translate to 250 grams of carbohydrate per day. Carbohydrates, in diabetes-related nutrition, are discussed in 15-gram portions called a carbohydrate (or carb) choice. Your 2,000 calories per day eating plan, therefore, recommends about 16 carb choices per day — maybe 5 with each meal, and one 15 gram snack, depending upon your personalized plan. Your meal plan never recommends that you save all, or even most, of your 16 carbohydrate choices for the all-you-can-eat buffet. So, making decisions in advance about what you're going to eat for a meal away from home should include a strong preference for about four to six carb choices, whatever is consistent with your meal plan, for the entire meal — drinks, finger food, appetizers, soup, salad ingredients and dressing, entrée and sides, and dessert.

Food that's sitting around in plain view — bar snacks, appetizers, or bread — is difficult to ignore. Try taking a small serving, then have the food removed from your sight. Most people believe they are not influenced by such temptations, but studies show that having food in reach translates to eating more.

With the immediate focus on carbohydrates, don't forget your healthy eating recommendations for protein, fat, and sodium. A 2,000 calories per day eating plan would call for about 100 grams of protein per day, and about 67 grams of total fat, only about 15 grams of that from saturated fat. And, the daily recommendation for sodium is 1,500 milligrams per day. Going off the tracks for protein, fat, or sodium in one meal away from home may not have the same immediate impact that a surge in blood glucose levels from excess carbohydrates will have, but if excess protein, fat, and sodium become routine, the long-term negative impact on heart health is clear.

Checking ahead

You can't always tell what you're eating by looking. Some things you'll know, such as the carbohydrates in a giant baked potato, but other dishes are a mystery. For instance, from the dishes in Table 15-1 is there anything in the name *hibachi chicken skewers* that would tip you off that this entrée would be 12 carb choices, 72 percent of your daily carbohydrate budget, and more than three times your recommended daily sodium limitation? The only thing you can be sure about is that it isn't the chicken. It's probably not the skewers, either. So, either a hibachi is a terribly salty and starchy food, or there are added ingredients (soy sauce would be a prime suspect for the sodium) that aren't given away by the dish's name.

Fortunately, you don't have to find out that the hibachi chicken skewers were not a good choice for diabetes after you've already eaten them. There are great resources online and in print which give nutrition information for many specific restaurant menus. And most restaurant websites provide the information, too. As long as you know where you're going to eat, it's usually possible to pull the information for virtually every food item you find at any larger restaurant.

Sticking to a plan

Having a plan goes a long, long way in helping you resist impulse eating, but it's up to you to stick to your plan. There will be chef's specials you didn't know about in advance, finger foods in the bar or appetizers somebody wants to share, and one of your companions will rave about the hibachi chicken skewers she had last week — "you have to try it."

Sticking with your plan is a matter of your overall commitment to diabetes self-management, and having the confidence that you've made the right choices. But, here's an important point: The fact that you took a few minutes to actually think ahead about what you see as the best choices for you is most of the battle. Whether you made the perfect choices is almost beside the point — it's virtually certain that your advance choices were better than the ones impulsive eating would have led you to make.

Dining Out

It's easy to see how deciding on eating plan ahead of time is a great idea — you can ignore the temptations and be confident you've accounted for your health. But, what if your eating-out opportunity comes up suddenly or isn't at a restaurant with nutrition information available? There are visits with friends, parties, banquets, and unexpected schedule changes. How can you get the information you need when you don't have time or access to the menu in advance, and how can you make good decisions if you can't get the information?

Analyzing the menu

If an occasion to eat at a restaurant comes up without time for preplanning, you can still make the healthier choices. The biggest difference is that you're making your choices surrounded by distractions and engulfed in an atmosphere created to trigger your eating instincts. These are powerful influences, but you can make healthy choices if you concentrate on what you know about your diabetes meal plan — manage carbohydrates from all sources, look to reduce dietary fat, and reduce sodium.

You can access nutrition information from your table on mobile devices, either from websites or *apps*. Some apps even evaluate the menu items with a letter grade or rating system, but whereas these can be great for calories, fat, and sodium, the rating criteria generally doesn't take carbohydrate content into account (but the detailed information provides a number for you). Alternatively, you can request nutrition information from the restaurant — most are able to bring you the information at your table, or while you're waiting.

So, now you can spend 30 minutes ignoring your friends while you evaluate every single item on the menu, right? Of course you can't, and that's part of the challenge when you haven't been able to plan ahead. The menu descriptions can give some valuable clues about healthy and not-so-healthy choices, however, so you can narrow your options down to a few, check the details on those, make a choice, and join the conversation.

Here are some tips for analyzing menu items:

- Look for clues in the cooking method. Healthier cooking styles include baked, grilled, steamed, poached, and broiled. Not-so-healthy methods are deep fried, flash fried, escalloped, or creamed.

- Be careful with breaded or batter-dipped foods, crusts or double crusts, sweet and sour dishes, or syrups because of the added carbohydrates.

- Be cautious about sauces and glazes — most are high in calories and fat, and some are sweetened.

- Be aware of portion sizes for foods you know are carbohydrates — bread, pasta, rice, and potatoes are often served in liberal portions. One slice of bread, 3 ounces of baked potato, and ⅓ cup cooked rice or pasta are all 15 grams of carbohydrate.

- Don't assume that a meal-sized salad is healthy just because it's a salad — read the ingredients, and take the dressing on the side (or go for an alternative nonfat dressing like lemon or lime juice, or plain balsamic vinegar).

- Look at the appetizer menu. Often it's possible to get similar foods in smaller portions.

There's not much you can do differently when it comes to fast foods. Go for broiled or grilled rather than fried, avoid mayonnaise and special sauces when possible (you can scrape them off), watch the carbohydrates in bread, buns, French fries, and sweetened drinks, and go for thin-crust pizzas to minimize the carbohydrates from thick crusts.

Nonstarchy vegetables, like lettuce and tomato, can fill you up, and add almost no carbohydrates to your meal. Sandwich shops and pizza joints always offer a variety of nonstarchy vegetables.

One way to know whether you've made the best choices is to test your blood glucose levels two hours after you eat. Over time, patterns can inform your choices the next time you find yourself choosing from the same menu.

Asking the right people

Don't be shy — what's in your food has a direct affect on your health. If you're taking insulin to match your carbohydrate consumption, it's not just about your long-term health either — having accurate information helps you avoid dangerous low or high blood glucose levels after you eat. So, whether you're at a restaurant, a banquet, a party, or eating at a friend's home, ask questions — somebody has information you can use. There are basically two barriers to quizzing others about what's in your food.

First, you might be uncomfortable being assertive, or you could feel that asking about food is bad manners. You're more likely to feel reluctant about quizzing friends than about asking questions in a restaurant — most everyone is comfortable getting details when they're paying. But, if someone else is buying, or if the food is at a party or a friend's house, there can certainly be a reluctance to ask questions. You may feel you're insulting the person who prepared the dish — trying to determine if it's good enough for you to eat. Everyone will be more comfortable if you acknowledge that your concerns are health related, and not about whether you think the food is tasty. And, if you say you're trying to determine how much you should eat, as opposed to whether you can eat a certain dish or not, people will understand.

Second, you need to know what you're wanting to know. Again, because carbohydrates have a direct and immediate impact on blood glucose levels, carbohydrates are your main concern. That's not to say that calories, fat, and sodium aren't important, but it's difficult to focus on too many things unless you've been able to give your thinking brain the time to evaluate all the options. You want your overall lifestyle to manage calories, fat, and sodium, too, but an occasional adventure won't have the same effect that overloading on carbohydrates can have. Plus, you can control your calorie intake to some extent based simply on how much you eat.

Your search for carbohydrates is most effective if you can simply know the recipes for the foods you're planning to eat — so ask. Ultimately, it's the hidden carbohydrates you want to find. You know that potatoes, corn, peas, beans, rice, pasta, bread, and fruits contain carbohydrates. Sugars, honey, syrups, flour, corn meal, fruit juice, milk, yogurt, and other carbs can be unseen in sauces, gravy, stuffing, spreads, dips, or drinks. Bar-b-que sauces, for instance, are almost always high in carbohydrate. If you can't get a peek at the recipe, consider asking questions about the possible hidden carbs.

If food isn't already prepared, don't be shy about asking for modifications. Your options might be limited at parties or fast food restaurants, but full service restaurants are generally more than happy to modify a menu item. You should feel free to request a healthier cooking method, different sauces, added or omitted ingredients, or menu substitutions for the side dishes. Don't forget, restaurants want you back, and most of the changes are really no big deal.

Bringing your own

Bringing your own food may not be a very good option in some cases, but for a family get-together or meals with close friends it's a sure fire way to make sure you've got food that fits your meal plan perfectly. If you know what's on the menu, maybe you only bring foods where the one's available don't work well for diabetes, or perhaps a healthy salad to help dampen your appetite. Bringing your own food can work for office lunches, on trips, or anyplace else your choices are going to be limited.

Anytime you're going to a potluck or bring-a-dish affair, bring a dish that you know works well with your diabetes eating plan. It could be the only item that fits in your healthier diet.

Taking some home

Refer to Table 15-1 and notice that the nutrition information shows that all of the listed dishes give you your lion's share of daily calories, carbohydrates, and fat — although protein isn't provided in the table, it's the same story. In today's food environment, this is common. Even menu choices labeled as "lighter" or "lunch portions" are likely to give you more than one meal's share of calories, fat, protein, and carbohydrate when you divide up a daily total. One could make a strong case that the excess food Americans have become accustomed to getting at restaurants carries over into other meals and has contributed to the skyrocketing rates of obesity and type 2 diabetes. Nutrition professionals call this *portion distortion*. As you look over the menu nutrition information from any restaurant, when planning your meals in advance, this becomes obvious.

So, it's fair to say that with most any meal you eat from the menu at a restaurant, you can't eat the entire meal and at the same time stay somewhat committed to your meal plan. That means that unless you're splitting the meal with someone else, which is often a great idea, you'll have leftovers to take home.

Now, if you already know in advance that you shouldn't eat the entire meal, there's a secret to making sure that you don't. Because eating behavior is so subconscious, ask for a take-home container as soon as your food is served and stash the excess amount out of sight while you eat. You can be almost certain that you won't take your doggy bag out of its hiding place to add more food to your plate — you can't be certain that you won't nibble away until the entire meal is finished if you leave the food on the plate.

Taking food home isn't always practical — maybe you're traveling with no way to refrigerate or reheat the food later. But if you're just going to a movie after dinner, bring along an insulated bag and some ice packs. Cooling your leftovers to 40 degrees Fahrenheit keeps it safe until you make it home. Don't forget that if you separate your leftovers before you ever begin eating, you can send them home with somebody else without sending your germs along, too.

Toby once attended a potluck holiday gathering of her husband's family in Kentucky where the menu consisted of a ham, many desserts, and exactly nine creamy, cracker-topped casseroles, which were impossible to identify without digging beneath the crispy surface. Because she had asked about the menu ahead of time, she was able to bring her own food, which happened to be left-over from the previous evening's meal in a restaurant. At one event she pulled out every strategy described in this chapter and was able to keep her blood glucose on the mark without hurting any feelings.

Keeping it Honest

Don't be offended — maybe honest isn't the best choice of words, but keeping it accurate sounds too nitpicky. The point is, it's possible to pile on calories, fat, sodium, and carbohydrate a little at a time when you're in a social environment, and calories, fat, sodium, and carbohydrates count just the same whether you get them in many small packages or all at once from the hibachi chicken skewers. So, in a real sense it's important to be honest about being accurate, even if that's both offensive and nitpicky.

Drinks and bar snacks

Alcohol is not a carbohydrate, so alcohol doesn't raise blood glucose levels directly; however, alcohol stores more energy per gram than the 4 calories per gram in carbohydrates or protein, and almost as much as the 9 calories per gram stored in fat. So, at 7 calories per gram 1 ounce of 80 proof liquor adds about 60 calories to your day. Alcoholic beverages are rarely just alcohol, however, and a 12-ounce beer can come in at 150 calories, a glass of wine about the same, and mixed drinks or liqueurs can bring along two or three times as many calories. Beer, wine, and many mixed drinks and liqueurs also contain carbohydrate, and the grams can vary significantly by brand or according to the mixer.

Bar snacks aren't free foods, either. Twenty pretzel sticks is 120 calories and 26 grams of carbohydrate, and 1 ounce of beer nuts can bring along 185 calories, 15 grams of fat, and 6 grams of carbohydrate — an ounce of beer nuts is only about 25 or 30 nuts. Many snack mixes get their calories from carbohydrate and fat, complicating blood glucose control if you're eating mindlessly. A 1-ounce nibble of some snack mixes can add 15 to 25 grams of unexpected carbohydrate to your diabetes meal plan.

If you have a tequila sunrise with 1 ounce of the free snack mix before dinner, you're starting out with 325 calories and three carb choices (45 grams carbohydrate) already in your tank. That may be OK if you made the drink and snacks part of your advanced meal planning, but if you're not planning on a drink and bar snacks, be sure to make a specific plan not to have a drink and bar snacks. Leaving more than 300 calories and 45 grams of carbohydrate up to chance is no way to do meal planning unless you're equally prepared to deduct that amount from what you intended to have for dinner.

Just to be clear, you can have a drink and some bar snacks without cashing in the big calories and carbohydrates before your meal. Drinks are easy to research, and you can find one you like that's lower in calories and carbohydrates than the 200 calorie, 25 grams of carbohydrate tequila sunrise. A glass of wine will usually have less than 5 grams of carbohydrate, low-carb beers are popular still, and liquor with a sugar-free mixer contains no carbohydrates. Plus, you can ask the bartender to modify recipes just like you're prepared to ask a chef.

The snacks are a different story. Most nuts might load in extra calories but are very low in carbohydrate; however, the mixed snacks with crackers, pretzels, and sesame sticks are going to be carbohydrate rich. If you can't avoid them completely, put a small amount on a napkin or plate to eat slowly, and ask someone to remove the remainder from your field of vision.

Hors d'oeuvres, appetizers, bread, and dessert

These are the foods that seem to find you, even if you're trying to hide from them, especially hors d'oeuvres — with those little party bites it may seem there's a conspiracy at work to put you face-to-face with a tray of bacon-wrapped scallops. Once again, these are foods that seem to just appear, are powerfully tempting, can seem insignificant, but can add up quickly.

Technically, hors d'oeuvres are not necessarily associated with a meal, so they're often circulated at parties or events where an actual meal isn't included. In some ways this can be a good thing. If you keep reasonable track of what you've eaten from passing trays or long tables, you can potentially adjust your foods at a later meal to compensate. In theory there's nothing wrong with, and even some benefits to, eating more than three smaller meals in a day. But, the operable word is smaller. There can be a tendency in some circumstances to try and make a meal of hors d'oeuvres, and that can make keeping track of what you've eaten very difficult. These finger foods can disappear in one bite, and large events can have many different varieties floating around. Plus, hors d'oeuvres aren't necessarily healthy choices, and nutrition information may be hard to find. If you're at a party or an event, have an hors d'oeuvre or two, preferably something without carbohydrates, and then have a reasonable dinner later. Don't try and make a dinner from finger foods unless you're confident you have options that are healthy and let you keep reasonably accurate track of what you've eaten.

Appetizers and bread often appear before a meal and are intended to stimulate an appetite or to keep you busy while waiting for the food you ordered to be prepared. Most often the bread is standard, but appetizers are part of an order. Even if you don't order an appetizer, somebody will almost surely want you to share his or hers. Appetizers come in all kinds of forms, from downsized entrées, flatbreads, deep-fried anything, potato skins, or corn chips covered with meats and cheese to some reasonably healthy choices available at some establishments. Bread is usually served with butter, margarine, olive oil, or a special spread.

The story with appetizers and bread is the same — if you have planned ahead to include these foods in your advance meal plan, and chosen healthy options, then dig in. Unplanned food sitting in plain sight, however, makes healthy eating more difficult that it has to be. If possible, let the unplanned appetizers and bread be quickly passed and removed from the table.

Dessert is purely optional but can be one of the great pleasures of eating out. If you've planned in advance for dessert, good for you. Chances are, however, that restaurant desserts go for 500 calories or more and almost by definition include a sizable dose of carbohydrates. Sorbets, sherbets, or fresh fruit are your best options. For most other desserts, splitting them four ways may still leave you with 300 extra calories and 30 to 40 grams of carbohydrate.

Salad bar foolers

Since the appearance of salad bars in restaurants, people have often seen them as the healthy choice. Even though salad greens make a great foundation for a healthy meal, the range of ingredients available to add to your salad can leave you with an unexpected load of calories, fat, and carbohydrates. It's the small amounts you add that can lead you to consider those ingredients as irrelevant. Table 15-2 compares two salads built at the same salad bar.

Table 15-2	Comparing Salads from the Salad Bar		
Salad 1	*Calories*	*Salad 2*	*Calories*
Lettuce (2 cups)	110	Lettuce (2 cups)	110
Small tomato	20	Small tomato	20
Cucumber	5	Cucumber	5
Carrots	12	Carrots	12
Cauliflower	14	Avocado	188
Green peppers	6	Diced ham	115
Beets	20	Hard-boiled egg	72
Green onions	11	Bacon bits	50
Kidney beans	50	Sunflower seeds	100
Radishes	5	Olives	75
Snow peas	15	Croutons	135
Tuna	78	Shredded cheese	175
Light dressing	30	Salad dressing	140
Total	376	**Total**	1197

You can see that the higher fat items — avocado, ham, sunflower seeds, and salad dressing — can really pile on calories. Because you're adding these items with a spoon, it's difficult to keep up with what, and how much, you need to account for. Plus, you've probably noticed that some salad bars have expanded to include prepared creamy salads, like macaroni salad, and even dinner-type food like fried chicken. Oh yes, and it's the same price to go through ten times as it is for one.

The salad bar can still be a great place to make a complete and healthy meal, but it's necessary to know where you're likely to grab extra calories and carbohydrates in small packages. Otherwise, sticking to the salad bar for your health is wearing the healthy halo — feeling good about a healthy behavior that really isn't healthy after all. Here are a few items typically found at salad bars that add calories fast if you don't manage the amounts you add carefully:

- Bacon, pepperoni, or salami
- Black or green olives
- Bleu cheese and feta cheese

- ✔ Croutons, sunflower seeds, and nuts
- ✔ Anchovies and fish packed in oil
- ✔ Marinated salads, like oil-based coleslaw
- ✔ Raisins and other dried fruit
- ✔ Canned fruit (often in syrup)
- ✔ Salads made with mayonnaise
- ✔ Shredded cheese
- ✔ Creamy salad dressings

Carbohydrates are especially important, because losing track of your carbohydrate food is losing control of your blood glucose. Watch for carbohydrates in fresh or canned fruits, raisins and dried fruit, beans and peas, potatoes, croutons, crackers, rice, pasta, and any mixed or creamy salads that include these items — potato salads and three-bean salads are common.

The point is not to declare salad bars off limits or label them as a bad choice without reservation. The point is to demonstrate that it's not only possible to lose track of what you're eating from the salad bar, it's easy to lose track. If your dinner meal recommendations are in the 700-calorie and 90-grams-of-carbohydrate neighborhood, it's difficult to imagine you can sail past those numbers scooping ingredients with a tablespoon. But, when you add it up — refer to Table 15-2 — it's actually way too easy.

So, here's the secret. Start your salad with nonstarchy or low-calorie vegetables like lettuce, spinach, alfalfa sprouts, bean sprouts, broccoli, carrots, cauliflower, celery, cucumber, peppers, mushrooms, onions, radishes, tomatoes, and zucchini. Then, if you need to add carbohydrates to your meal, add them from beans, potatoes, corn or peas, whole-grain bread or crackers, and fresh or dried fruit. Find some healthy protein — tuna, egg, or soy — and a little healthy fat from nuts, olives, or a touch of a noncreamy salad dressing.

Just know what you're adding to your salad (the nonstarchy vegetable part) before you start adding — the calories mount up quickly. You have to know your stuff — 2 tablespoons of bleu cheese dressing is 150 calories and 16 grams of fat, for instance. The information is available in pocket reference books, at numerous websites or phone apps, or you can make your own cheat sheet on an index card. Contrary to popular belief, the salad bar is no place for amateurs.

You can save calories, fat, sodium, and sometimes carbohydrates by passing completely on the salad dressing and using vinegar, salsa, or freshly squeezed lemon or lime juice instead.

Wanting it all — buffets

If the salad bar is no place for amateurs, access to the dinner buffet should require a year of classes with a final exam. Buffets are tempting because of the variety of food and the price. In fact, it's easy to get swept up into a competition, where the more you eat the better the deal. This kind of fun may work well for active teens, but managing diabetes requires a little discipline, as you know.

The buffet is a challenging assignment not only because of the variety of foods available, but also because planning ahead isn't possible. There is only one inherently positive thing about the all-you-can-eat buffet. The owners are aware of mindless eating cues, and almost always provide small plates — people who eat from smaller plates tend to eat less. From the business owner's perspective, five trips through the buffet with a smaller plate saves her money compared to five trips with a larger plate. From your perspective, taking diabetes and weight management into account, the small plate is only a benefit for one trip through — without stacking.

So, how can you responsibly approach eating from a buffet? First, take your seat as far away from the buffet line as possible . . . out of sight, if feasible. Then, do a reconnaissance mission to look specifically for foods that seem healthiest. Finally, eat responsibly.

In evaluating the foods and making your eating plan, consider the following:

- ✔ If there's a salad bar, go for a salad of nonstarchy vegetables with vinegar or lemon/lime juice as a dressing. If you skipped the previous section of this chapter on salad bars, go back and see why you should avoid many of the add-ons provided for your salad.

- ✔ If there's a broth-based soup, have a little. A healthy salad and broth-based soup helps reduce your appetite without adding excess calories to your meal, but salad fixings and creamy soups only add calories, fat, and even carbohydrates. (Broth-based soups in restaurants are likely to be very high in sodium, so if you eat out often, this strategy may have a downside over the long term. Broth-based soups can include added carbohydrates, like noodles, as well.)

- ✔ Look for meat or fish that has been roasted, poached, or steamed, and is not floating in buttery-looking sauce. A plain fish filet or the carved roast beef may be your best choices — pick one.

- ✔ Go for vegetables with the same idea — no sauces, not fried, and be careful about casseroles and mixed dishes.

- ✔ Get your carbohydrates from whole-grain bread, fruit, or grain and potato dishes without added fat from cooking methods or sauces.

- ✔ Be cautious with desserts.

Don't be shy about asking questions of the servers, and even the chefs. Somebody has information you may need to decide on certain dishes, and it's perfectly reasonable that you should have it.

Eating away from home has become much more routine than in years past, and there's no denying the convenience of having someone else do the work. But there is a cost, and the cost to people with diabetes can be significant. Eating away from home makes it more challenging to identify healthy options that fit with your diabetes management plan, and more difficult to resist the emotional triggers and cues that lead to over consumption. Managing diabetes well requires understanding how food influences blood glucose levels and heart disease risk factors, and having enough information about the food you're eating to make decisions. Even if you've made the commitment to understand how food works to manage diabetes, the essential information about foods at restaurants is not always easy to come by and healthy choices not always easy to find even when you have the information.

The greatest challenge with eating away from home, however, may be the greater need for planning because the food can be so extreme. Eating away from home is seen as an opportunity to relax from all things stressful, like meal planning. Just when the need for planning is greatest, the temptation to avoid thinking about food is strongest. What will it hurt to splurge just this once? Eating out has become so routine for some people that the splurging may happen three, four, or five times a week, and that makes it a lifestyle. Plus, the food you encounter when eating out is likely to be way beyond the bounds of a normal meal and can have immediate consequences. The carbohydrate content of some entrées and most desserts could send blood glucose levels to dangerous heights, especially for someone with type 1 diabetes who underestimated his insulin requirements.

This connection between diabetes and food can be stressful, but that stress doesn't have to spoil your opportunities to eat away from home. The most effective way to separate the stress of thinking about food from the relaxation of eating away from home is to plan ahead. And, in most cases, it's possible to gather the information you need and to make a specific plan for exactly what you can eat when you're out. Having a plan in advance equips you to resist the powerful biological, psychological, and social influences that lead to over consumption. When your advanced plan is consistent with healthy eating for diabetes management, you can not only leave the stress of thinking about food behind while you're eating out, but also can forget feeling guilty about what you ate afterwards.

Chapter 16

Choosing Sensible Beverages and Snacks

"*W*ould you care for something to drink, or a snack?" Don't you wish you had a nickel for every time you've heard those words in your lifetime? Offering liquid refreshment and nourishment to guests is good manners, sound business practice, and in many cultures a formal offer of goodwill.

In today's ultra-commercial, convenience society, drinks and snacks have taken on a much bigger role. You've probably noticed that every commercially available drink or snack also comes with great friends, vitality, perfect weather, the woman or man of your fantasies, peak athletic performance, never-ending fun, a bonfire on the beach at sunset, and maybe even world peace. Your main choice, it appears, is which kind of wonderful life is right for you.

So you're not completely convinced by billions of advertising dollars that every drink or snack is the one missing piece that will make your life perfect. In that case, maybe it's a good time to leave fantasies at the door and take a closer look at how drinks and snacks best fit into your regular life. In this chapter you learn how to manage drinks and snacks without sabotaging your diabetes management plan. You also find some drinks and snacks that are surprisingly healthy.

Mixing with Alcohol

Not many things could better illustrate the concept of moderation than alcohol. Your first thoughts seeing alcohol and moderation used together in a sentence probably go to traffic safety, addiction issues, social embarrassment, or scores of other cautions related to alcohol as mood-altering substance. But, putting aside the confusing behavioral, social, and moral issues, what about alcohol as something you consume?

It turns out that moderate alcohol consumption can have beneficial health effects. You're probably not surprised that moderate alcohol consumption might be healthier than heavy alcohol consumption, but moderate consumption might also be healthier than no consumption. Studies have shown that people who consume moderate amounts of alcohol have improved cardiovascular risks, possibly from alcohol elevating levels of good HDL cholesterol. Alcohol may act as a blood thinner as well, and some studies have shown moderate consumption associated with lower blood pressure.

Moderate consumption can be defined as no more than one glass of wine or its equivalent per day for women, and no more than two glasses of wine or their equivalent per day for men. And, it is important to note that any beneficial health impacts not only disappear with heavier drinking, but actually turn full circle to distinctly negative effects on health. Alcohol consumption of more than three drinks per day is associated with high blood pressure.

Even moderate alcohol consumption may not be right for some people with diabetes. Diabetes-related problems with sensation called neuropathy can be made worse by even small amounts of alcohol. As a general rule, nondrinkers should not begin drinking for the potential health effects. Anyone with diabetes should honestly discuss their alcohol consumption patterns with their health care team.

Finding the calories and carbohydrates

Alcohol is not a carbohydrate, and by itself has virtually no impact in raising blood glucose levels. Alcohol, however, does have calories. In fact, alcohol stores 7 calories per gram — significantly more than the 4 calories stored by a gram of carbohydrate or protein, and only slightly less than the 9 calories stored by fat. So, the calories in alcohol can mount up, with a 1½ ounce jigger of 80-proof spirits like gin or whiskey packing about 100 calories.

Many alcoholic beverages, like wine and beer, do include carbohydrates, and mixed drinks bring along whatever carbohydrates and calories are in the mixer. Table 16-1 shows common alcohol containing beverages with the typical serving size, and the calories and carbohydrate grams per serving.

Table 16-1	Nutrition Information for Alcoholic Beverages		
Beverage	*Typical Serving*	*Calories*	*Carbohydrate*
80 proof spirits	1.5 ounces (jigger)	97	0 grams
Beer	12 ounces	120-150	10-12 grams
Light beer	12 ounces	60-100	2-8 grams
Stout beer	12 ounces	up to 300	up to 20 grams
Cabernet red wine	5 ounces	120	4 grams
Riesling white wine	5 ounces	120	6 grams
Sweet dessert wine	3.5 ounces	170	15 grams
Margarita	8 ounces	368	16 grams
Piña colada	4.5 ounces	245	32 grams
Coffee liqueur	3 ounces	275	44 grams
Irish cream	3 ounces	351	22 grams

You can see that a relaxing margarita every night before dinner would equal 25 percent of a 1,500-calories-per-day eating plan, making weight management very difficult. Sipping Kahlua on ice grabs not only 18 percent of your calories, but also 25 percent of your daily carb choices.

For weight management and blood glucose control it's important to evaluate both the calorie and carbohydrate content of alcoholic beverages. When you look carefully, you may be surprised to find that reducing the calories and carbs you're drinking every day results in more effective weight and blood glucose control. All calories and carbohydrates count.

Caution about hypoglycemia

In certain cases, alcohol consumption can contribute to dangerous, even life threatening, low blood sugar. Anyone who is taking insulin or other diabetes medication, or combination of medications, where low blood glucose is a possible side effect must be extremely careful with alcohol.

Falling blood glucose levels normally stimulate a release of stored glucose from liver cells, but alcohol interferes with this process. Recent research also suggests that alcohol stimulates insulin secretion by changing blood flow patterns in the pancreas. As a consequence, if alcohol is being consumed without food, blood glucose levels in people with diabetes can continue to fall at an uncommon rate. Since the symptoms of hypoglycemia and alcohol intoxication are similar, you (or those with you) may attribute the telltale signs of acute low blood glucose to the alcohol. In circumstances where alcohol consumption goes beyond moderate, hypoglycemia can be extremely serious.

To avoid the dangers of alcohol-induced hypoglycemia follow this advice:

- ✔ Always drink in moderation.
- ✔ Have your alcoholic beverage with your meal.
- ✔ Always test your blood glucose levels, even in the morning, and especially after excessive consumption.
- ✔ Make sure your companions are aware of the potential for low blood glucose, and always wear medical alert identification.

For information on treating hypoglycemia, see the last section in this chapter.

Coffee and Tea

Coffee and tea may be best known for delivering the stimulant caffeine, but evidence is mounting to support significant health benefits for both. On the caffeine point, coffee takes the prize, delivering about two to five times as much per cup. That's good news for sleepy heads, but most of the health benefits of coffee and tea seem unrelated to the caffeine. And, caffeine is not well tolerated by some people. Coffee, by the way, is more popular than tea in the United States by about 2.5 to 1 in gallons consumed annually, but worldwide, tea is in second place as a beverage, behind only water.

Both coffee and tea appear to reduce the risk of cardiovascular disease, and while the effect is often attributed to the antioxidants contained in both, the actual mechanisms are not clear. Recent research shows a decreased risk for stroke for both coffee and tea drinkers. Coffee drinking has a fairly clear association with reduced risk for dementia and Parkinson's disease. And, studies involving hundreds of thousands of subjects show heavy coffee consumption may reduce the risk for diabetes by more than 30 percent. A review of weight loss supplements found that only green tea provided a genuine benefit to weight management.

All in all, the health data on coffee and tea looks solid, and both can be recommended as being consistent with effective diabetes management. Like alcohol, however, the pitfalls can be in added ingredients. Sugar and creamers can add calories, fat, and carbohydrates, and specialty coffee or tea drinks can take a significant bite from your daily calorie and carbohydrate budget. A large white chocolate mocha frappuccino weighs in at 440 calories, 16 grams total fat, with 69 grams carbohydrate if made with whole milk — a green tea latte is 390 calories, 7 grams fat, and 57 grams carbohydrate.

Soft Drinks and Flavored Waters

Soft drinks are sometimes called soda, pop, soda pop, Coke, or something else, in large part depending upon where you happen to live. And, soft drinks have been around for a long, long time. Soft drinks are, of course, carbonated.

Flavored waters, on the other hand, are a recent comer to the commercial drink market. They come ready-to-drink in bottles or cans, and some varieties are carbonated like soft drinks. The difference between carbonated flavored water and a soft drink may be only a question of the manufacturer's target market. Flavored water also comes as a dry powdered mix that can be added to water. Many flavored waters advertise certain formulas of vitamins and nutrients, or are labeled with descriptive words hinting at a particular effect — relax, flex, think. View these claims as advertising's subtle attempt to convince you there are no other options for finding these nutrients, and always check the nutrition facts label for calories and carbohydrate.

As you might suspect, the primary issue with soft drinks and flavored waters related to diabetes would be whether the drinks are sweetened with sugar. A 12-ounce, sugar-sweetened soft drink has 140 calories and 39 grams of carbohydrate. Soft drinks are commonly packaged in 20-ounce bottles, too, listed as one serving on the nutrition labels with 240 calories and 65 grams carbohydrate. Supersized fountain drinks, 32 ounces or more, can pack 300 calories and 80 grams carbohydrate.

Of course, most soft drinks and flavored waters come in no calorie varieties, meaning they are either not sweetened, or are sweetened with non-nutritive sweeteners. For diabetes and weight management, no-calorie or reduced-calorie beverages are a better choice because they allow you to get your calories and carbohydrates from foods that also provide nutritional benefits.

A final thought on soft drinks relates to excessive consumption. The acid in soft drinks can contribute to dental cavities by eating away at the enamel coating of teeth. There is also some evidence that the phosphoric acid content in some soft drinks can contribute to bone loss. Soft drinks, even no-calorie varieties, should be consumed in moderation.

You may think if you consume drinks that are sweetened with sugar substitutes containing no calories that you have reduced your energy intake by a large number of calories. For example, 12 ounces of Coca-Cola has 140 calories, but Diet Coke has none. In fact, studies have shown that you tend to replace those calories to the extent of 25 percent or more with other foods.

Sports and Energy Drinks

The advertising behind sports drinks is slightly different than for soft drinks. Sports drinks actually do provide benefits in carbohydrate replacement and in electrolyte replacement. But the need to quickly replace carbohydrates and electrolytes comes as a result of intense exercise. If you're not a marathoner, or participating in some other high intensity exercise for an hour or longer, chances are that you don't need a sports drink.

Sports drinks contain varying amounts of carbohydrate from sugar, and the electrolytes potassium and sodium. If you're eating a balanced diet, you're already getting enough carbohydrates and potassium — and sodium, almost certainly more than you need. Sports drinks have a high glycemic index value, to rapidly raise blood glucose and make that energy available. Again, this is essentially the opposite of what you want from your carbohydrates.

Sports drinks may have some use among athletes with type 1 diabetes in combating hypoglycemia during and after intense workouts, but that's a specific use that is uncommon to the great majority of people with diabetes. Unless you can realistically see yourself in head-to-head competition with the athletes starring in sports drink commercials, sports drinks aren't really for you.

Today's advertising for energy drinks definitely targets youth, and annual sales in the United States exceeded $10 billion in 2012. Adults with diabetes may be tempted to try these products because their energy levels can be chronically low as a consequence of diabetes. So, energy drinks deserve a closer look.

The secret to the energy in energy drinks is caffeine — lots of caffeine. Many energy drinks also contain carbohydrate in the form of sugar, although most offer sugar-free versions, too. The list of special ingredients can feature a range of B vitamins, ginseng, taurine, guarana, and glucuronolactone. A review of research on energy drinks published in the New York Times in January, 2013, found that there isn't much research to review. The consensus among experts, however, is that energy drinks have no effect other than the effect of caffeine and sugar. The additional, often featured, ingredients are lacking sound evidence for any benefit whatsoever.

Energy drinks vary in caffeine concentration, from an amount about equal to brewed coffee at 10 milligrams caffeine per fluid ounce to as much as ten times that concentration according to *Consumer Reports'* testing of one brand. The dose of caffeine depends both on the concentration and the size of the drink.

Ultimately the question becomes one of purpose and cost. It's fair to say that people with diabetes don't need additional carbohydrate, and many of these drinks also include unwanted sodium. Some research suggests that caffeine has a negative effect on blood glucose and insulin balance in people with type 2 diabetes that is not well controlled. And, whereas caffeine does raise blood pressure, the effect seems to be temporary. Nevertheless, consuming caffeine when you already have high blood pressure should be discussed with your physician, and caffeine in the amounts contained in many energy drinks is unnecessary. Lastly, the cost of energy drinks, at $2.50 to $3.50 per container, is an expensive way to get caffeine, which inevitably also comes with ingredients you don't need.

Nuts and Seeds

Nuts and seeds may sound like professional advice for attracting squirrels to your yard, and there's no doubt those fuzzy rodents would appreciate the consideration, but maybe squirrels know more about healthy eating that you give them credit for.

Healthy snacking is an important part of any healthy eating plan, and in some ways especially important for managing body weight and blood glucose when you have diabetes. But, when people think of snacks, they often think of the high-calorie, high-carbohydrate, and high-fat kind like chips, cookies, or candy bars on racks in your local convenience market. Healthy snacks can help reduce between-meal hunger, give a boost of energy, and even reduce mealtime calorie intake, all without piling on extra calories, unhealthy fats, or excess carbohydrates. Portion control is always important and so are added ingredients like salt, but all in all nuts and seeds fit the bill for diabetes snacking pretty well.

In the practical sense, nuts and seeds contain enough protein, fiber, and fat to help you feel full. You can easily guess that managing hunger can go a long way toward reducing impulsive eating. Nuts and seeds are relatively low in carbohydrate, too, so they work well for most people with diabetes by not raising blood glucose levels. In fact, if you've been advised to have a snack during the day or in the evening to avoid periods of low blood glucose, nuts or seeds would not be your best choice. Later in this chapter you find a list of healthy snacks that do offer enough carbohydrate to stabilize lower blood glucose levels between meals.

The real story with nuts and seeds is fat — healthy mono and poly unsaturated fats, to be specific. One ounce of nuts contains 13 to 22 grams of these heart-healthy fats. Walnuts, Brazil nuts, pumpkin seeds, and sunflower seeds contain more polyunsaturated fats. Almonds, cashews, pecans, hazelnuts, macadamia nuts, peanuts, and sesame seeds contain more monounsaturated fats. Although the fat in nuts is predominantly these healthy fats, any fat is calorie dense. A 1-ounce serving of nuts packs 150 to 200 calories. Packaged nuts and seeds often include added salt or sugar, neither of which are helpful for the main purpose of snacking, so check the nutrition label on packaged foods.

Several studies have looked at nuts and seeds as a desirable element of diabetes management. Research from the University of Toronto in 2011 found nuts to be a favorable replacement for carbohydrate snacks when a group with type 2 diabetes showed improvements in A1C and bad LDL cholesterol after three months. A study involving 13,000 subjects by Louisiana State University found consumers of tree nuts (the study excluded peanuts, which are a legume) had smaller waist measurements, lower weight, lower blood pressure, lower fasting blood glucose, higher levels of HDL ("good") cholesterol, and lower levels of proteins linked to inflammation and heart disease. In fairness, regular nut eating was also linked with higher consumption of whole grains and fruits, and lower consumption of alcohol and sugar. Still, the association between nuts, seeds, lower weight, and better cardiovascular health is strong.

Chocolate and Candy

Do any food products have a greater connection to emotions than chocolate and candy? There's a candy associated with virtually every holiday, especially the Valentine's Day celebration of romance. And most people — at least those of us raised in the United States — hold an affection for candy that goes back to childhood. But mentioning chocolate and candy in a discussion about weight management and diabetes has a hint of the proverbial good news/bad news conclusion. Well, not so fast. There's still some room for love.

Defining candy is not so simple. One definition specifies two categories of candy based upon the how sugar molecules are organized in the final product. *Crystalline* candies are easy to bite or cut into, like fudge or creams. *Amorphous* candies concentrate the sugar more, but into a more disorganized structure resulting in a chewy, hard, or brittle texture. Peppermints or toffee fit the amorphous category. All classic candies contain high concentrations of sugar, but candies also contain other ingredients like cocoa, fat, and milk powder to make milk chocolate.

As with all foods related to diabetes and/or weight management, looking at the nutrition information best shows whether chocolate or candies are good choices. With chocolate or candy, the important information will be calories, carbohydrate, fat, and sodium.

So, the bad news first. Most candy bars are high in calories, high in carbohydrate, high in fat (especially unhealthy saturated fat), and added sodium. A Milky Way bar comes in at 240 calories, 37 grams carbohydrate, 7 grams saturated fat (35 percent of the daily recommended intake of saturated fat), and 75 milligrams sodium. Candy bars are not an especially good choice for weight management or blood glucose control. The same goes for most homemade candies.

Hard candies like peppermints, cinnamon, and butterscotch have a more favorable profile, in part because the serving size is much smaller. One piece would typically contain about 5 grams carbohydrate and 20 calories. Hard candies are purely sugar, so don't usually contain the added fat from nuts, milk products, or added oils. These products are fine for refreshing your breath, dampening your appetite, or shedding nervous energy, but hard candy adds calories and carbohydrates without nutritional benefits.

Sugar-free candies do paint a different picture in some respects, but maybe not exactly what you would expect. If you look at the nutrition facts labels for most sugar-free candies you'll notice the carbohydrate grams per serving is virtually identical to the regular recipe. So, what benefit could there be? Chapter 6 discusses certain deductions you can make from total carbohydrate when fiber or sugar alcohol exceeds 5 grams — the deduction is one half the grams of whichever subcategory exceeds 5 grams subtracted from total carbohydrate. Well, most sugar-free candy is made with sugar alcohol, often exceeding 5 grams.

Table 16-2 compares the nutrition information for a popular brand's regular and sugar-free miniature peanut butter cups.

Table 16-2   Nutrition Information for Regular and Sugar-free Miniature Peanut Butter Cups (Serving Size = 5 Pieces)

	Regular	*Sugar-free*
Calories	220	180
Total fat	13 grams	13 grams
Saturated fat	5 grams	6 grams
Total Carbohydrate	26 grams	27 grams
Sugar	23 grams	0 grams
Sugar alcohol	0 grams	20 grams
Dietary fiber	1 gram	6 grams
Adjustment to carbs	no adjustment	-13 grams
Adjusted total carbohydrate	26 grams	14 grams

You can see there is a reduction in calories and in adjusted total carbohydrates, after deducting 10 grams for one-half the sugar alcohol and 3 grams for one-half the fiber. But, while the adjusted total carbohydrate is half of the regular recipe, the fat content is higher, and both recipes register more than 100 milligrams sodium per the 5-pieces serving size. Sugar-free hard candies usually eliminate the fat (check the nutrition label), but the story with carbohydrate is the same. In both cases, moderation is best for diabetes and weight management.

Finally, what about the chocolate teaser earlier in this section — a cruel joke or a strange twist? Well, it's true that chocolate includes calories, carbohydrate, and fat, but cacao also contains chemical compounds that have been associated with a range of health benefits. The specific health benefits identified in studies, often when comparing chocolate eaters to non-eaters, include the following:

- There's a reduced of risk of stroke in women who ate more than 45 grams (about 1½ ounce) of chocolate per week.

- In an Italian study, chocolate eaters show improved insulin sensitivity.

- Improved muscle cell function by production of new mitochondria, the cell structure where glucose is converted to ATP, in profoundly ill subjects with major muscle cell damage. The subjects were fed cocoa fortified with additional epicatechin (an antioxidant flavonol occurring naturally in cacao).

- Chocolate acts to lower blood pressure and increase good HDL cholesterol.

- Studies have shown that chocolate improves blood flow.

Is there a catch? Well, the beneficial cardiovascular effects are associated with plant phenols (cocoa phenols), and the darker the chocolate, the higher the levels of these antioxidants. Most experts, therefore, recommend eating chocolate that's at least 70 percent cacao, and, of course, consuming this dark chocolate in moderation — perhaps one ounce per day.

Low-Carb Healthy Snacks

So far you've gotten relatively good news about nuts, seeds, chocolate, and candy — eat in moderation, watch the fat, and know your carbohydrates. You may now be asking if there are low-calorie and low-carb snacks. And, what about snacks that are more in the carbohydrate family — grains, fruit, starchy vegetables, or dairy?

There are options here, too, and in some cases carbohydrate snacks are a specific part of your meal plan. In other cases, where insulin or pills that can cause low blood glucose are part of your treatment plan, these snacks may come in handy when blood glucose needs a slight boost between meals or before bedtime. For the most part, these snacks aren't suitable for treating serious low blood glucose levels, where a quick response is preferred.

Low-carb snacks

Snacks without significant carbohydrate can help calm the appetite between meals, yet have no affect on blood glucose levels. A few recommendations for low-carbohydrate snacks are as follows:

> One ounce, low-fat string cheese
>
> A sugar-free popsicle
>
> One or two ounces of jerky
>
> One cup raw, nonstarchy vegetables
>
> Water with a sugar-free drink mix added, or tea made by boiling cinnamon sticks
>
> One tablespoon of peanut butter
>
> Raw vegetables with salsa

Raw vegetables always offer the best deal on volume when trading for carbohydrates, calories, or fat. Cucumbers are particularly refreshing, but bell peppers, zucchini, green beans, carrots, or other choices may suit your tastes even better.

15-gram snacks

Snacks that offer 15 grams of carbohydrate — one carb choice — elevate blood glucose levels 30 to 45 milligrams per deciliter if necessary to head off mild hypoglycemia. For those wearing an insulin pump, carbohydrate snacks when blood glucose levels are normal can be offset with a bolus dose of insulin (a carbohydrate snack may not be worth an injection when low-carb snacks are just as satisfying).

A few lower calorie, 15-carbohydrate-gram snacks are as follows:

> One cup berries or cubed melon
>
> Six ounces no-sugar added ice cream, or sugar-free, no-fat yogurt
>
> Three graham cracker halves
>
> Three-quarter cup unsweetened cereal
>
> One-half cup canned fruit (packed in juice)
>
> Ten potato or tortilla chips (the baked kind)
>
> A low-fat granola bar

Twelve small pretzels

One-half grapefruit or mango

One-half cup sugar-free pudding

Be sure to monitor the affect of snacks on your blood glucose levels — not everyone responds the same way to the same food.

30-gram snacks

In general, 30-carbohydrate-gram snacks will be worked into your meal plan in a balance with fewer carb choices at meals. Having one of these two-carb-choice snacks should require an insulin bolus for those with type 1 diabetes, because these snacks may raise blood glucose by 60 mg/dl or more. These snacks are not intended for treating hypoglycemia.

With type 2 diabetes these snacks can be matched to your medication to help spread carbohydrate consumption more evenly throughout the day. A few 30-carbohydrate-gram snacks would be the following:

One cup unsweetened cereal with one-half cup low-fat milk

One-half cup regular pudding

One-half bagel with low-fat cream cheese

Sixteen animal crackers

One-quarter cup dried fruit

One-half cup beans on a 6" tortilla

Alternative Sweeteners

The term *alternative sweetener* refers to sweeteners that are alternative to sucrose, which is typical table sugar and primarily produced from sugarcane and beets. Sucrose in different forms is the sugar most people know — table sugar, brown sugar, confectioner's sugar, and so on. But there are many alternatives to sucrose, some confined primarily to commercial food production uses, that can generally be divided into alternatives with equal calories to sucrose or alternatives that are no-calorie (often called non-nutritive). Other common terms attached to some products are *artificial sweetener* and *sugar substitute*.

Alternative sweeteners are often shrouded in controversy, and this isn't the place to sort those issues out. Alternative sweeteners that are in common use are presumed safe and without acute health effects when used in moderation.

The U.S. Food and Drug Administration terminology is GRAS, meaning Generally Recognized as Safe, and that agency has banned or refused to approve many sweeteners. The rumors and conspiracies surrounding sweeteners that are generally recognized as safe will have to wait for a different book.

No-calorie or zero-calorie sweeteners are manufactured compounds or natural extracts that taste many times sweeter than sucrose, so can be added to foods or drinks in extremely small amounts for equal sweetness. The big three in the United States are saccharin (in the pink packets), aspartame (in the blue packets), and more recently sucralose (in the yellow packets). These sweeteners are everywhere, from diet soft drinks to no-sugar-added ice cream, to the table at restaurants and coffee shops, and into your home-baked desserts. No-calorie sweeteners allow people with diabetes to enjoy sweetened food without calories and without carbohydrates from sugar (calories and carbohydrates can come from other sources, like flour in baked goods). Two newer products representing sweetener extracted from natural plants are stevia and mogroside (produced primarily from monk fruit). These substances have calories but are 200 times sweeter than sucrose, so the caloric amount is negligible.

Sugar alcohols — mannitol, sorbitol, xylitol, and others — have about half the calories of sugars but are listed under total carbohydrate on nutrition labels. In an earlier review of peanut butter cups you saw how sugar alcohols enable you to reduce the total carbohydrate content of foods when carb counting by subtracting one half of the sugar alcohol grams. Reducing the calories and carbohydrates of sweetened foods makes these easier to work into your meal plan. Some people experience bloating or diarrhea in response to sugar alcohols.

Some alternative sweeteners provide no caloric or carbohydrate advantage to your eating plan. High-fructose corn syrup, honey, molasses, fruit juices, and agave nectar are popular alternatives. High-fructose corn syrup is a common commercial sweetener used in soft drinks and many other food products as a replacement for sucrose. Honey, syrups, and nectars are promoted as being healthier and less processed than sucrose. For all intents and purposes, these sweeteners all have calories and carbohydrates that should be accounted for equally, and should represent a small part of your healthy diet.

Treating Hypoglycemia

Episodes of low blood glucose — hypoglycemia — are not uncommon for anyone taking insulin and can be a side effect of other pills or injectable medications used to treat type 2 diabetes. Left untreated, hypoglycemia can be life threatening. Hypoglycemia is defined by blood glucose levels below 70 mg/dl.

The symptoms of hypoglycemia vary by individual, as does the blood glucose level when symptoms appear. Common symptoms include nervousness, sleepiness, sweating, weakness, confusion, irritability, difficulty sleeping, and unconsciousness. Hypoglycemia can quickly become a medical emergency and in severe cases needs immediate medical assistance. People with diabetes who frequently experience episodes of severe hypoglycemia should carry a glucagon injection kit, which can rapidly stimulate a release of glucose from liver cells. Milder hypoglycemia can be treated with carbohydrate food.

Hypoglycemia and alcohol intoxication are an extremely dangerous combination. Alcohol consumption can trigger hypoglycemia, but the symptoms of low blood glucose and alcohol intoxication are similar, making the medical concern difficult to recognize. Glucagon, ordinarily an effective remedy for hypoglycemia, is less effective when the liver is preoccupied processing alcohol. If an intoxicated person is experiencing severe hypoglycemia, call 911.

Treating hypoglycemia with food should follow the *rule of 15*. That is, eat 15 grams of a fast-acting carbohydrate food, wait 15 minutes, test your blood glucose level, and repeat if necessary. Fast-acting carbohydrates include

- Glucose powders, tablets, and gels made especially for treating hypoglycemia
- Fruit juice
- Regular soft drinks (not diet)
- Honey or table sugar
- Hard candy

Choose candy that can be easily chewed, and don't depend upon candy that includes chocolate or other sources of fat. If hypoglycemia occurs at mealtime, treat the low blood sugar before eating. Don't depend upon being able to easily find a suitable carbohydrate food. Always carry a food with you that can counteract falling blood glucose levels.

Part V

Putting It All Together: Seven Delicious Days Managing Your Diabetes

Breakfast	Lunch	Dinner
Cheese Danish 1½ ☺	Tuna Niçoise 1½ ☺	Flatbread pizza ☺ ☺
6 ounces of low-fat, fruited yogurt ☺ ☺	10 whole grain crackers ☺ ☺	Tossed green salad, 2 table-spoons regular balsamic vinaigrette
½ cup raspberries ½ ☺	12 almonds	1 cup berries with whipped topping ☺
1 cup canned fruit cocktail ☺ ☺	Coffee or tea, sugar-free drink, or water	Sugar-free drink or flavored water with non-nutritive sweetener

You can find more valuable information about managing your diet at www.dummies.com/extras/diabetesmealplanningandnutrition.

In this part...

- Take a running start on what you need to plan three meals a day. You get recipes plus all the nutritional info you need to take charge of your food and your health.

- Learn that making small changes in your meals and snacks can keep you healthy and feeling good. It's not about giving up your favorite dishes; it's about making tweaks.

- With 22 new recipes to try, you have a week's worth of breakfasts, lunches, and dinners at your fingertips.

Chapter 17

Reviewing a Seven-Day Menu

The most common comment registered dietitians hear from people with diabetes has got to be, *"just tell me what to eat."* And, if this was a line in a Broadway play, the note in the margin would cue the actor to speak this line with extreme exasperation. But, planning healthy meals for diabetes isn't that miserable an experience. If you're exasperated trying to get started with healthier eating habits, it could be something else that's holding you back. Maybe you see this as the first step into a life of restriction and deprivation — no more tasty food, and never again feeling the satisfaction that comes with a good meal.

That would be a misconception, however. To prove the point, this chapter provides you with a whole week's menu — three meals a day for seven days. The intent is not to tell you what to eat — you'll get pretty tired going through the same food every day, week after week. The idea is to provide a wide range of options that demonstrate how you can plan your meals, and to show how diabetes-friendly meals can be marvelous.

The menu is presented each day in two different tables, as both a 1,300 calories per day eating plan, and a 1,700 calories per day plan. For many people, these calorie levels represent a common weight loss number for women and men, respectively, but see your registered dietitian for your personalized plan to get the right calories and carbs for you.

Because a critical skill in managing diabetes is to manage carbohydrate intake, each carb choice (15 grams of carbohydrate) is marked with a ☺, sometimes preceded by a number, ½ or 1½, for example, before the ☺ to be more precise on carbohydrate content. The 1,300 calories per day menu includes 9 carbohydrate choices throughout the day, equally distributed across the three meals. The 1,700 calories per day menu includes 12 carb choices.

Your personal meal plan may include a carbohydrate snack at some point, so a list of various snack choices is provided at the end of the chapter. Whenever a dish is highlighted, you can find the recipe in Chapter 18.

Day 1

The menu for this day includes pizza, a dish that can send blood glucose levels soaring from the dough and sweetened tomato sauces. Flatbread or whole grain tortillas can make a great crust, and you can feel free to add nonstarchy vegetables to the recipe included in Chapter 18. If you can't go vegetarian on pizza, try a little Canadian bacon instead of fatty meats like pepperoni. Be conservative with the cured meats, however, because the sodium content is high.

The Tuna Niçoise for lunch includes lots of nonstarchy vegetables, a foundation for healthy eating. But this salad also incorporates potatoes, another food that people with diabetes often think must be avoided, and egg as a protein source in addition to the tuna.

Whole grains for Day 1, shown in Tables 17-1 and 17-2, include the whole-grain waffle of the cheese Danish and whole-grain crackers for lunch.

Table 17-1   Day 1 — 1,300 Calories with 9 Carbohydrate Choices

Breakfast	Lunch	Dinner
Cheese Danish ½ ☺	Tuna Niçoise 1½ ☺	Flatbread pizza ☺ ☺
6 ounces plain Greek yogurt ½ ☺	5 whole grain crackers ☺	Tossed green salad balsamic vinaigrette
1 sliced peach ☺	½ cup berries with 1 tablespoon regular whipped topping ½ ☺	
6 almonds	½ cup canned fruit cocktail ☺	Coffee or tea, sugar-free drink, or water with non-nutritive sweetener

Table 17-2 Day 1 — 1,700 Calories with 12 Carbohydrate Choices

Breakfast	Lunch	Dinner
Cheese Danish 1½ ☺	Tuna Niçoise 1½ ☺	Flatbread pizza ☺ ☺
6 ounces of low-fat, fruited yogurt ☺ ☺	10 whole grain crackers ☺ ☺	Tossed green salad, 2 table-spoons regular balsamic vinaigrette
½ cup raspberries ½ ☺	12 almonds	1 cup berries with whipped topping ☺
1 cup canned fruit cocktail ☺ ☺	Coffee or tea, sugar-free drink, or water	Sugar-free drink or water with non-nutritive sweetener

Take every opportunity to limit fat in your diet because a gram of fat packs more than twice the calories of a gram of either carbohydrate or protein. The cheese Danish uses low-fat cottage cheese, and the tuna for the Tuna Niçoise should be packed in water instead of oil, both to reduce fat.

Whole-grain tortillas make an excellent thin crust for pizza. Remember that you can subtract one half of the fiber from total carbohydrate if the fiber amount is equal to or exceeds 5 grams per serving. Some large tortillas can be only about 10 grams of total carbohydrate after subtracting half of the fiber grams, and using sliced tomatoes on your pizza instead of tomato sauce can cut sodium, and often carbohydrate, significantly.

Day 2

The menu for your second day includes grits, a dish that those of you from the southern United States know and love. Grits are a whole grain, meaning grits includes the germ, bran, and endosperm of corn. Grits are great for any meal, as is the Italian side of the corn meal family, polenta.

Lunch highlights a low-calorie condiment you may never have tried — ajvar. Ajvar is a condiment made from roasted red peppers and eggplant, with garlic and olive oil, sometimes called vegetarian caviar. Ajvar ranges from mild to hot, so pick your favorite.

Today's dinner, shown in Tables 17-3 and 17-4, is a wonderful pork dish, selecting the lower-fat tenderloin cut of pork, and flavoring the dish with apples and a little cider. The dinner side dishes include sweet potato, a healthy starchy vegetable rich in vitamin A.

Table 17-3   Day 2 — 1,300 Calories with 9 Carbohydrate Choices

Breakfast	Lunch	Dinner
6 ounces plain Greek yogurt with 10 chopped peanuts and cinnamon ½ ☺	2 ounces sliced turkey on 1 slice of rye bread, 1 tablespoon ajvar ☺	Spiced pork tenderloin with gala apples ½ ☺
1 cup cooked grits ☺ ☺	1 ounce baked chips 1½ ☺	1 medium sweet potato 1½ ☺
½ cup papaya ½ ☺	Clementine orange sections ½ ☺	2"-square cornbread, 1 teaspoon margarine ☺
Coffee or tea with a non-nutritive sweetener	Bell pepper and celery sticks	Sautéed spinach and garlic with salsa
Sugar-free drink or water, sugar-free drink, or water		

Table 17-4   Day 2 — 1,700 Calories with 12 Carbohydrate Choices

Breakfast	Lunch	Dinner
6 ounces plain Greek yogurt with 20 chopped peanuts and cinnamon ½ ☺	4 ounces sliced turkey on two slices rye bread ☺ ☺	Spiced pork tenderloin with gala apples ½ ☺
1 cup cooked grits ☺ ☺	1 tablespoon ajvar	Large sweet potato 2½ ☺ ☺
1 ounce baked chips 1½ ☺	1½ cup papaya 1½ ☺	Clementine orange sections ½ ☺
2"-square cornbread, 2 teaspoons margarine ☺	Coffee or tea with a non-nutritive sweetener	Bell pepper and celery sticks
Sautéed spinach and garlic with salsa		Sugar-free drink or water

Fresh fruit eaten whole, like the papaya and orange sections in this day's menu, bring you all of the nutrients and fiber that occurs naturally in fruit, in addition to the sweet carbohydrate content.

Day 3

Your menu today (see Tables 17-5 and 17-6) has a couple of unique main dishes — shrimp for lunch, and a zesty chicken dish for dinner. Both shrimp and skinless chicken breasts are lean meats, helping to reduce saturated fats in your daily eating. Lunch also includes cake and cherries for dessert, and even a rice dish included at dinner. Rice is another food that some people with diabetes think needs to be avoided — rice is a high-carbohydrate food, but it's always about portion size.

A dinner side dish — steamed green beans with roasted red peppers — includes, not surprisingly, roasted red peppers. Try roasting your own by literally burning the whole pepper over an open flame (outside on the grill may be safest) until the skin is charred. Then, place the pepper in a sealed dish for a few minutes to steam, peel off the blackened skin, clean the seeds, and slice your roasted red peppers for a gourmet's delight.

Table 17-5   Day 3 — 1,300 Calories with 9 Carbohydrate Choices

Breakfast	*Lunch*	*Dinner*
1 whole grain tortilla with 1 tablespoon peanut butter ☺ ☺	Shrimp salad rolls ☺ ☺	Chicken with lemon
1 small banana ☺	Sliced cucumber with lime juice	¾ cup rice pilaf with currants ☺ ☺
½ ounce slice angel food cake ½ ☺	Steamed green beans with roasted red peppers	1 whole grain roll ☺
Coffee or tea with non-nutritive sweetener	6 fresh cherries ½ ☺	10 peanuts
1 teaspoon margarine	Sugar-free drink or water	Sugar-free drink or water

Table 17-6   Day 3 — 1,700 Calories with 12 Carbohydrate Choices

Breakfast	*Lunch*	*Dinner*
1 whole grain tortilla with 2 tablespoons peanut butter ☺ ☺	Shrimp salad rolls ☺ ☺	Chicken with lemon
1 small banana ☺	Sliced cucumber with lime juice	1 cup rice pilaf with currants 2½ ☺ ☺
1 cup low-fat milk ☺	1-ounce slice angel food cake ☺	Steamed green beans with roasted red peppers
Coffee or tea with non-nutritive sweetener	12 fresh cherries ☺	1 whole grain roll ☺
20 peanuts	2 teaspoons margarine	Sugar-free drink or water
Sugar-free drink or water		

It's important to learn how to judge carbohydrate content for fruit based upon size, especially if you're calculating insulin doses. A small banana is about 4 ounces, and going for a large banana instead could easily double the carbohydrate content, raising blood glucose levels by 50 to 70 mg/dl more than expected.

You probably loved having peanut butter for breakfast as a kid — why not now? Peanut butter has enough protein and healthy fat to help keep you feeling satisfied until lunch, and if you want to mash today's banana and spread it on your tortilla along with the peanut butter, who's going to stop you?

Day 4

Breakfast on Day 4, as shown in Tables 17-7 and 17-8, features oatmeal, a traditional breakfast favorite, but more importantly an excellent source of soluble fiber. This healthy whole-grain cereal has earned a government sanction to make specific claims for reducing the risk for heart disease by lowering bad LDL cholesterol levels. Breakfast also welcomes Canadian bacon, which is significantly lower in calories, fat, saturated fat, and sodium than American bacon. Calories, fat, and sodium are three things most people with diabetes should reduce whenever possible.

Day 4 also contrasts a hamburger for lunch with a meatless stir fry for dinner, using a meat substitute product made from soy. The stir fry includes lots of healthy, nonstarchy vegetables, and whole grain brown rice as well. Adding edamame increases the protein without increasing the carbohydrate significantly.

Table 17-7   Day 4 — 1,300 Calories with 9 Carbohydrate Choices

Breakfast	Lunch	Dinner
½ cup cooked oatmeal ☺	3-ounce lean hamburger and ½ hamburger bun ☺	Quick soy stir fry with ¼ cup edamame ☺
Baked apple with 4 walnut halves ☺	Lettuce, tomato, and 1 tablespoon low-fat mayonnaise	⅓ cup brown rice ☺
1 slice Canadian bacon	1 cup baked French fries ☺	Baked vegetable egg roll, 1½ ☺
1 cup low-fat milk ☺	¾ cup fresh pineapple ☺	Sugar-free drink or water
Coffee or tea with non-nutritive sweetener	Sugar-free drink or water	

Table 17-8   Day 4 — 1,700 Calories with 12 Carbohydrate Choices

Breakfast	Lunch	Dinner
1 cup cooked oatmeal ☺ ☺	4 ounce lean hamburger and hamburger bun ☺ ☺	Quick soy stir fry ☺ with ½ cup edamame ½ ☺
Baked apple with 8 walnut halves ☺	Lettuce, tomato, and 2 tablespoons low-fat mayonnaise	⅓ cup brown rice ☺
2 slices Canadian bacon	1 cup baked French fries ☺	Baked vegetable egg roll ½ ☺
1 cup low-fat milk ☺	¾ cup pineapple ☺	Sugar-free drink or water
Coffee or tea with non-nutritive sweetener	Sugar-free drink or water	

All meat includes saturated fat, but you can reduce calories and fat substantially by selecting lean cuts, like Canadian bacon or lean ground beef. And, because ground meat can mix bacterial contamination throughout the product, never eat ground meats rare — always cook to a safe internal temperature of 160 degrees Fahrenheit.

Soy is a high-quality, complete protein, containing all of the essential amino acids your body can't manufacture itself. Soy delivers its protein without saturated fat. Food producers are constantly introducing high-quality soy products that replicate meat in dishes, such as the stir fry on today's dinner menu, and green soy beans called *edamame* add a nutty taste to salads or other recipes. Four ounces of soy has twice the protein of a large egg, or an 8-ounce glass of milk.

Day 5

Day 5 in Tables 17-9 and 17-10 features a couple of fast food favorites, made at home for a healthier touch. Your Egg Muffin and Panko Chicken Tenders may have neighbors driving up to your kitchen window to place a takeout order if the word gets out. Be sure you have the proper license from the Department of Health before you start selling food, but you can enjoy these yourself whenever you want with both recipes provided in Chapter 18.

Lunch features a healthy version of the iconic twice-baked potato, to keep the restaurant food theme intact for the entire day. As mentioned earlier, potatoes are a high-carbohydrate, high-glycemic index value food that many people with diabetes think they must give up — no way! As long as you account for the carbohydrates, you can reap the nutritional benefits of potatoes in your diabetes eating plan.

Table 17-9   Day 5 — 1,300 Calories with 9 Carbohydrate Choices

Breakfast	Lunch	Dinner
1 egg muffin ☺	Meal-in-a-potato ☺ ☺ ☺	Panko chicken tenders
1 cup cubed melon ☺	Spinach salad with 2 tablespoons low-fat dressing	Roasted Brussels sprouts
1 cup low-fat milk ☺	Sugar-free drink or water	½ cup Lindsey's quinoa salad 1½ ☺
Coffee or tea with non-nutritive sweetener		½ cup cubed cantaloupe ½ ☺
		Sugar-free drink or water

Table 17-10   Day 5 — 1,700 Calories with 12 Carbohydrate Choices

Breakfast	Lunch	Dinner
1 egg muffin ☺	Meal-in-a-potato ☺ ☺ ☺	Panko chicken tenders ☺
½ English muffin with 2 teaspoons margarine	Spinach salad with 4 tablespoons low-fat dressing	Roasted Brussels sprouts
1 cup cubed melon ☺	½ cup sugar-free chocolate pudding	¾ cup Lindsey's quinoa salad 2½ ☺ ☺
1 cup low-fat milk ☺	Sugar-free drink or water	½ cup cubed cantaloupe ½ ☺
Coffee or tea with non-nutritive sweetener		Sugar-free drink or water

Melons are a great source of vitamin C, and vitamin A, potassium, and lycopene, depending on the variety. The nutritional value of melons increases as they ripen, so select fully ripe melons whenever possible. And, watermelon is 92 percent water, so eating this favorite summertime fruit can help keep you hydrated.

Quinoa is a whole grain native to South America that's gaining popularity for its taste and high protein content.

Day 6

One theme for today's menu is transportation efficiency — not for you — for food. Day 6 includes two fruits that travel far to reach your table, but thanks to the incredibly efficient worldwide food transportation network, these fruits are available at your grocery down the street (see Tables 17-11 and 17-12). Mangos are a tropical fruit native to South Asia, and India leads the world in production, although mangoes are grown in tropical regions around the world. Kiwi, or kiwifruit, is synonymous with New Zealand, which is also home to the flightless kiwi bird from which the fruit eventually got its marketing name. (Here's a little-known fact: Italy actually leads the world in kiwi production, with New Zealand second, and Chili third.) The variations in growing seasons for these fruits, plus transportation efficiencies, keep a supply of these nutritious, and interesting, foods ready for you all year around.

Table 17-11   Day 6 — 1,300 Calories with 9 Carbohydrate Choices

Breakfast	Lunch	Dinner
2 pancakes ☺ ☺	Chipotle beef tacos ☺ ☺	Teriyaki salmon with ginger and orange juice ½ ☺
Topping of 6 ounces plain, low-fat Greek yogurt with ¼ cup cubes mango ☺	Tossed salad with jicama and 1 tablespoon salad dressing	Spaghetti squash ☺
4 chopped pecan halves and sugar substitute	½ cup fancy fruit salad ☺	Roasted asparagus
Coffee or tea with non-nutritive sweetener	Sugar-free drink or water	1 whole grain roll ☺ with 1 teaspoon margarine
		1 sliced kiwi ☺
		Sugar-free drink or water

Table 17-12 Day 6 — 1,700 Calories with 12 Carbohydrate Choices

Breakfast	Lunch	Dinner
2 pancakes ☺ ☺	Chipotle beef tacos ☺ ☺	Teriyaki salmon with ginger and orange juice ½ ☺
Topping of 6 ounces plain, low-fat Greek yogurt with ¾ cup cubes mango ☺ ☺	Tossed salad with jicama and 1 table-spoon salad dressing	Spaghetti squash ☺
8 chopped pecan halves and sugar substitute	1 cup fancy fruit salad ☺ ☺	Roasted asparagus
Coffee or tea with non-nutritive sweetener	Sugar-free drink or water	1 whole grain roll ☺ with 1 teaspoon margarine
		2 sliced kiwi ☺ ☺
		Sugar-free drink or water

Spaghetti squash is a hard-shell, winter squash that resembles pasta when the meat is separated from the shell after cooking. Pasta is another food that some people with diabetes think is off limits, and although that isn't true, pasta is high in carbohydrate, so keep serving sizes modest. Spaghetti squash, on the other hand, is low calorie, low carbohydrate, and tasty in its own right, as you see at dinner tonight.

Adding small serving of unsalted nuts to your meals increases satiety (feeling full), and gives you a dose of healthy, unsaturated fats.

Day 7

You can end your week in style with French toast for breakfast, your own made-from-scratch polenta at lunch, and a marvelous vegetarian lasagna for dinner (see Tables 17-13 and 17-4). Oh yes, how about banana pudding for dessert? That would be with real bananas, vanilla wafers, and whipped topping, by the way.

This is the first appearance of beans on this sample week-long menu, but that doesn't mean that these healthy legumes shouldn't appear often in your real life meals. Beans are a carbohydrate food, so you need to count every ½ cup serving as a carb choice (15 grams of carbohydrate). But, there's room for beans in your diabetes eating plan because beans help reduce cholesterol, and lower blood pressure. You can, in fact, have some beans at every meal.

Table 17-13   Day 7 — 1,300 Calories with 9 Carbohydrate Choices

Breakfast	Lunch	Dinner
2 slices of whole-wheat French toast with red berry sauce ☺ ☺ ☺	Baked polenta with turkey sausage ragu ☺ ☺	Mushroom lasagna with zucchini noodles ☺
6 sliced almonds	Steamed broccoli with 1 teaspoon margarine	Green leafy salad with ¾ ounce of soy nuts and 1 tablespoon balsamic vinaigrette ☺
Coffee or tea with non-nutritive sweetener	½ cup red beans ☺	Banana pudding 1½ ☺
	Sugar-free drink or water	Sugar-free drink or water

Table 17-14   Day 7 — 1,700 Calories with 12 Carbohydrate Choices

Breakfast	Lunch	Dinner
2 slices of whole-wheat French toast with red berry sauce ☺ ☺ ☺	Baked polenta with turkey sausage ragu ☺ ☺	Mushroom lasagna with zucchini noodles ☺
6 sliced almonds	Steamed broccoli with 1 teaspoon margarine	Green leafy salad with ¾ ounce of soy nuts and 1 tablespoon balsamic vinaigrette ☺
1 cup low-fat milk ☺	½ cup red beans ☺	1 slice garlic bread ☺
Coffee or tea with non-nutritive sweetener	17 frozen grapes ☺	Banana pudding 1½ ☺
	Sugar-free drink or water	Sugar-free drink or water

The red berry sauce for the French toast is made with frozen fruit. Most frozen fruits and vegetables aren't packaged with additives or preservatives unless they're part of a prepared dish of some sort, like a fruit pie. Plain frozen fruit is about as close to freshly picked as you can get, and for all practical purposes the nutrition profile is the same as fresh.

The Baked Polenta with Turkey Sausage Ragu uses ground turkey because it's always lower in fat than ground beef — true or false? The answer is false — ground turkey is not, by default, lower in fat than ground beef. So, look for leaner mixes of ground turkey just as you look for leaner mixes of ground beef.

Snacks

It's likely that your personalized meal plan includes a carbohydrate snack or two, and it's important to choose snacks that don't impact your blood glucose dramatically yet fill you up. Nothing on this list of snacks is appropriate for treating low blood glucose, where you do want to raise blood sugar quickly.

Each of these snacks provides 15 grams of carbohydrate, but one carb choice, small amounts of nuts or any nonstarchy vegetable can provide a snack with virtually no impact on blood glucose levels provided the calories, and fat in the case of nuts, fit into your meal plan.

The following snacks provide one carbohydrate choice, 15 grams of carbohydrate, to your daily eating plan:

- ✔ One-half cup sugar-free pudding
- ✔ Three graham cracker halves with 1½ tsp. peanut butter
- ✔ Raisin bread with 1 tsp. margarine
- ✔ One small granola bar
- ✔ One-half cup no-added-sugar ice cream
- ✔ Three ginger snaps
- ✔ Five vanilla wafers

The menu provided in this chapter takes 50 percent of the calories from car-bohydrate. Most of those carbohydrates are noted as carbohydrate choices (15 grams of carbohydrate) or even one-half a carb choice. But 7 or 8 percent of your carbohydrates come in small doses from nonstarchy vegetables and other minor sources, so the number of carbohydrate choices provided won't quite reach one-half of the calorie levels specified.

Having diabetes doesn't mean you avoid carbohydrates — it's hard to say that too often. Having diabetes means you choose your carbohydrates wisely, and you spread them throughout the day. Carbohydrate foods like fruit, whole grains, starchy vegetables, beans and legumes, and low-fat milk or yogurt, are nutritious and delicious. Getting your carbohydrates from sugar and refined grains, which often come with little redeeming nutri-tional value, is not a successful strategy for managing diabetes effectively. Ultimately, it's you who makes the choices about how you're going to eat, and what effect your eating has on your long-term health.

Chapter 18

Starting Your Recipe Collection

In This Chapter

▶ Sampling healthy foods to find your favorite eating plan

▶ Preparing healthy recipes you're sure to love

Food is like music in many ways. Food can soothe your emotions, bring a smile to your face, and keep you vibrating with anticipation. But like music, one person's masterpiece may be another's nightmare.

Many people approach diabetes and diet like they would a bus trip with a middle school marching band — with dread. But, while a road trip with a huge bass drum and novice clarinetists really would be dreadful, there is a diabetes eating plan that will resonate with you waiting to be discovered. And when you find it, your diabetes eating plan can soothe your emotions, bring a smile to your face, and keep you vibrating with anticipation.

Where should you start looking? Look first at recipes that others in your situation have found satisfying. Throughout this book you've seen that there isn't one single option for managing diabetes effectively with diet. But just as different musical genres can follow a similar pattern, there's a pattern connecting the many food choices that can fit into a diet that's healthy for you. The most pleasing patterns emphasize vegetables, lean protein and low fat dairy products, whole grains, and healthy fats. Ultimately, managing your carbohydrate consumption and timing within an eating plan that pleases you is like having a great drummer who can help you stay on a steady beat.

The recipes in this chapter, with nutrition information provided, start your search for an eating plan that's right for you; each recipe is folded into the sample week's menu in Chapter 17. With all you've learned about healthy eating and meal planning you can find thousands more recipes that fit the bill. It may take a little time and effort, but the payoff is pure harmony.

Enticing Entrées

Entrée is a French word meaning *entrance,* and in that country the term applies to a dish served before the main course. Somewhere along the way, the word entrée in the United States and much of the English speaking world has taken on reference to the main course itself. This must puzzle the French, but whatever you want to call your main dishes, the following recipes steal the show.

Spiced pork tenderloin with gala apples

This dish demonstrates some of the secrets to fabulous food that's healthy too. A lean cut of pork, an interesting combination of spices, onion and garlic, and sweet apples go together in perfect harmony. This dish is begging for sweet potatoes, cornbread, and sautéed spinach.

Panko chicken tenders

These tenders might tempt you to drive up to your kitchen window and have someone hand them out in a bag, but maybe it's better if you just sit quietly and enjoy. Be sure and make enough for the grandkids.

Chipotle beef tacos

These lunch or dinner favorites will grab your attention. Your two-taco serving adds some refreshing lime juice to help extinguish the chilies in adobo sauce.

Chicken with lemon

Juicy chicken breasts make this a simple, but elegant, dish that you'll be proud to share with anyone. Add a whole grain, vegetables, and a fruit dessert to find perfection.

Teriyaki salmon with ginger and orange juice

This healthy fish with a tangy touch will put your search for omega 3 fatty acids in a different light.

Spiced Pork Tenderloin with Gala Apples

Chef Lindsey Singleton, DiabetesEveryDay.com

Prep time: 10 minutes • **Cook time:** 15 minutes • **Yield:** 4 servings

Ingredients	*Directions*
¼ teaspoon coriander seeds	**1** Mix first five ingredients together in small bowl.
¼ teaspoon black pepper	
¼ teaspoon cumin	**2** Rub tenderloin with olive oil, coating evenly.
⅛ teaspoon nutmeg	**3** Rub spice mixture over pork, evenly coating all sides.
¼ teaspoon salt	
½ teaspoon olive oil	**4** Heat a large skillet over medium-high heat; place tenderloin into skillet, cooking about 3 to 4 minutes on each side.
1 pound pork tenderloin	
2 tablespoons light margarine	**5** Remove from heat, wrap with aluminum foil, and place in 375°F oven until internal temperature reaches at least 145°F.
2 cups thinly sliced gala apples (leave skin on)	
¼ yellow onion, diced	**6** Meanwhile, in same skillet, add light margarine, swirl to coat.
1 garlic clove, minced	
¼ teaspoon salt	**7** Add onion, garlic, and salt. Sauté about 2 minutes, add apples, and continue until apples are soft.
½ cup apple cider	
½ teaspoon fresh thyme	**8** Add apple cider and let mixture reduce for 2 minutes.
	9 Add thyme, stir, and remove from heat.
	10 Slice pork into 8 medallions, drizzle with apple mixture, and enjoy.

Per serving: Calories 207 (From fat 59); Fat 7g (Saturated Fat 2g); Cholesterol 60mg; Sodium 386mg; Carbohydrate 15g (Dietary Fiber 3g); Protein 22g.

Panko Chicken Tenders

Chef Lindsey Singleton, DiabetesEveryDay.com

Prep time: 10 minutes • **Cook time:** 15 minutes • **Yield:** 4 servings

Ingredients	*Directions*
1¼ **pound boneless chicken breast, cut into 3 inch pieces**	*1* Preheat oven to 400°F.
¼ **cup whole wheat flour**	*2* Mix together panko bread crumbs, parmesan cheese, garlic salt, pepper, and parsley.
⅓ **cup egg substitutes 1 tablespoon buttermilk, low fat**	*3* Set up breading station with 3 medium size, flat bottom dishes.
¾ **cup panko bread crumbs**	
2 tablespoon grated parmesan cheese	*4* Place flour in first dish, egg substitute and buttermilk (give it a quick mix . . . in second, and panko bread crumb mixture in the third.
¼ **teaspoon garlic salt**	
¼ **teaspoon. black pepper**	*5* Dredge chicken pieces in flour, dip in egg substitute/buttermilk, and then coat with bread crumb mixture.
1 teaspoon chopped parsley	
Non-stick vegetable spray	
	6 Spray baking sheet lightly with nonstick vegetable spray.
	7 Place chicken pieces on baking sheet, and spray top side with vegetable spray. (You might need to do this in batches.)
	8 Bake for 15–17 minutes

Per serving: Calories 335 (From fat 78); Fat 6g (Saturated fat 2g); Cholesterol 123mg; Sodium 224mg; Carbohydrate 17g (Dietary fiber 1g); Protein 49g.

Chipotle Beef Tacos

Chef Lindsey Singleton, DiabetesEveryDay.com

Prep time: 10 minutes • **Cook time:** 10 minutes • **Yield:** 4, two taco servings

Ingredients	Directions
12 ounces beef round steak	**1** Place steak between two pieces of plastic wrap, pound to ¼-in thickness using meat mallet.
1½ tsp finely grated lime rind	
1 tablespoon fresh lime juice	**2** Remove plastic wrap and cut beef into thin strips.
2 teaspoon minced fresh oregano	
1 teaspoon brown sugar	**3** Combine beef, lime rind, lime juice, oregano, brown sugar, chopped chipotle chiles, garlic, and salt; let rest for a few minutes.
2 teaspoon chopped chipotle chiles in adobo sauce	
2 teaspoon minced garlic	**4** Heat olive oil in a large nonstick skillet over medium-high heat, add shallots, and sauté for about 30 seconds.
¼ teaspoon salt	
1 cup thinly sliced shallots	**5** Add beef mixture and sauté for about 4 minutes, or until beef is no longer pink.
2 teaspoon light olive oil	
8 low-carb, high-fiber tortillas	**6** Warm tortillas in 350°F oven wrapped in aluminum foil.
¼ cup reduced fat sour cream	
2 teaspoon chopped cilantro	**7** Spoon ⅛ of mixture into each tortilla, top with sour cream and cilantro.

Per serving: Calories 385 (From fat 135); Fat 15g (Saturated fat 4g); Cholesterol 63mg; Sodium 764mg; Carbohydrate 35g (Dietary fiber 16g); Protein 27g.

Chicken with Lemon

Chef Lindsey Singleton, DiabetesEveryDay.com

Prep time: 5 minutes • **Cook time:** 20 minutes • **Yield:** 4 servings

Ingredients	*Directions*
1 pound boneless chicken breasts cut into 4 oz. portions	*1* Pre-heat oven to 375°F.
1 tablespoon light olive oil	*2* Lightly salt and pepper both sides of chicken.
Salt and black pepper, to taste	
1 teaspoon garlic, minced	*3* In a medium ovenproof skillet, heat oil until hot and sear breasts for about 4 minutes, or until golden brown. Flip, and sear other side for another 2 minutes.
¼ cup dry white wine	
¼ cup lemon juice	
2 teaspoon lemon zest	*4* Move pan to oven to finish cooking, bake about 10 minutes (use a baking dish if you don't have an ovenproof skillet). When chicken is fully cooked, remove from pan and keep warm by covering with aluminum foil.
2 tablespoon light margarine	
1 tablespoon fresh parsley, chopped fine	
	5 Place pan back on stove, add garlic. Sauté about 1 minute. Add white wine (deglaze), and reduce by half (scraping bottom of pan to free any residue).
	6 Add lemon juice and zest. Sauté about 2 minutes, and then add cold margarine and stir until melted.
	7 Pour mixture over chicken breast, top with fresh parsley, and garnish with lemon slices.

Per serving: Calories 184 (From fat 79); Fat 9g (Saturated fat 2g); Cholesterol 63mg; Sodium 245 mg; Carbohydrate 2 g; Protein 23 g.

Teriyaki Salmon with Ginger and Orange Juice

Chef Lindsey Singleton, DiabetesEveryDay.com

Prep time: 1 hour • **Cook time:** 20 minutes • **Yield:** 4 servings

Ingredients	*Directions*
1 clove garlic, minced	**1** Mix garlic, ginger, soy sauce, orange juice, olive oil, black pepper, and sesame seeds in gallon-size ziplock bag.
½ teaspoon ginger, minced	
2 tablespoons reduced sodium soy sauce	
	2 Add salmon to bag, seal air tight, and place in refrigerator for 1 hour to marinate.
½ cup orange juice	
1 tablespoon olive oil	
⅛ teaspoon black pepper	**3** Preheat oven to 375°F.
1 tablespoon sesame seeds	**4** Place salmon in a single layer into a shallow dish.
12 ounces salmon	
2 teaspoons brown sugar, packed	**5** Cover with marinade and bake for 10 minutes.
	6 Remove from oven and sprinkle salmon with brown sugar.
	7 Place back in oven and continue baking for remaining 10 minutes, or until salmon is easily flaked with a fork.

Per serving: Calories 212 (From fat 97); Fat 11 g (Saturated fat 1g); Cholesterol 53mg; Sodium 334mg; Carbohydrate 7g (Dietary fiber 0g); Protein 21g.

Great Grains

Whole grains are an important part of your healthy diet. All grains are carbohydrate foods, and need to be planned for in your meals. But, the nutritional benefits whole grains provide are significant, and the recipes in this section offer a snapshot look at a few of the many ways great grains can become a regular part of your diabetes meal planning.

Flatbread pizza

Pizza can wreak havoc on blood glucose levels, and you never know what you're going to get when you eat pizza out. Here's a recipe for a tasty pizza using a whole grain flatbread with low carbohydrate vegetable toppings. Sliced tomato replaces sauce, which can often be the blood glucose culprit.

Rice pilaf with currants

Rice shouldn't be banned from your table, but with only ⅓ cup ringing up 15 grams carbohydrate this recipe gives high returns on that investment.

Shrimp salad rolls

You can get whole grains in a fabulous sandwich, by the way. This recipe turns a hot dog bun into a seafood delight.

Baked polenta with turkey sausage ragu

Polenta is whole grain corn cooked to a marvelous mush. This recipe has you making polenta from scratch, and topping with a rich, red wine meat sauce.

Lindsey's quinoa salad

Quinoa is a whole grain native to South America that contains significant protein too. This recipe adds sweetness from cucumber, dried apricots, and champagne vinegar to the great grain salad.

Flatbread Pizza

Toby Smithson, RDN, CDE, DiabetesEveryDay.com

Prep time: 5 minutes • **Cook time:** 10 minutes • **Yield:** 4 servings

Ingredients	*Directions*
4 thin-crust, whole-grain flatbread (spicy Italian; check the deli section of your store)	*1* Preheat oven to 450°F.
½ cup part-skim mozzarella	*2* Prepare vegetables and herbs.
⅔ cup finely shredded Italian-style cheese	*3* Place thin crust flatbread on a baking pan lined with aluminum foil and sprayed lightly with nonstick spray.
4 fresh sliced tomatoes	
2 cups sliced mushrooms	*4* Place thinly sliced tomato on top of flatbread, add vegetable ingredients, and cover with cheese. Sprinkle finely chopped basil on the top of the cheese.
2 cups chopped bell pepper	
4 tablespoons finely chopped fresh basil	*5* Bake in oven until the cheese is completely melted.
	6 Remove from oven and serve while hot.

Per serving: Calories 300 (from fat 104); Fat 12g (Saturated fat 5g); Cholesterol 22mg; Sodium 557mg; Carbohydrate 33g (fiber 4g); Protein 15g.

Rice Pilaf With Currants

Chef Lindsey Singleton, DiabetesEveryDay.com

Prep time: 5 minutes • **Cook time:** 45 minutes • **Yield:** 8 servings

Ingredients	Directions
1⅓ cups long-grain brown rice, uncooked	1 Heat medium size skillet over medium heat, add margarine, and swirl to coat pan.
2⅔ cups water	
1 tablespoon plus 1 teaspoon light margarine	2 Add onions and sauté about 2 minutes.
½ cup yellow onion, minced	3 Add pine nuts and toast about 30 seconds.
2 tablespoon pine nuts	4 Add rice, stir to coat rice with margarine, and sauté about 1 minute.
½ cup mushrooms, minced	
½ cup currants	5 Add water, currants, and mushrooms. Bring to boil.
2 tablespoons parsley	6 Reduce heat, stir, cover, and simmer for about 50–60 minutes, adding water if necessary.
	7 Uncover rice, fluff with fork, and add parsley.
	8 Season lightly with salt and pepper.

Per serving: Calories 168 (Form fat 30); Fat 0g (Saturated fat 1g); Cholesterol 0g; Sodium 22mg; Carbohydrates 32g (Dietary fiber 3g); Protein 4g.

Shrimp Salad Rolls

Chef Lindsey Singleton, DiabetesEveryDay.com

Prep time: 5 minutes • **Cook time:** 15 minutes • **Yield:** 4 servings

Ingredients	*Directions*
1 tablespoon light margarine	**1** Preheat broiler.
1 pound fresh, uncooked large shrimp, peeled and deveined	**2** Heat margarine in large non-stick skillet over medium-high heat, and swirl to coat. Add shrimp to pan, sauté 4 minutes or until no longer pink.
¼ cup mayonnaise	
1 tablespoon fresh lemon juice	**3** Cool shrimp in refrigerator for 10 minutes. When cool, coarsely chop shrimp.
1 teaspoon lemon zest	
1 teaspoonchopped parsley	**4** Combine shrimp, mayonnaise, lemon juice, lemon zest, parsley, basil, black pepper, and salt in large bowl.
1 teaspoon chopped basil	
½ teaspoon freshly ground black pepper	**5** Open hot dog buns and place on baking sheet. Broil 1 minute, or until golden brown.
⅛ teaspoon salt	
4 whole-grain hot dog buns	**6** Fill each bun with 2 lettuce leaves, and top with ½ cup shrimp mixture.
8 Boston lettuce leaves	

Per serving: Calories 255 (From fat 72); Fat 8g (Saturated fat 1g); Cholesterol 166mg; Sodium 535mg; Carbohydrate 25g (Dietary fiber 3g); Protein 27g.

Baked Polenta with Turkey Sausage Ragu

Chef Lindsey Singleton, DiabetesEveryDay.com

Prep time: 10 minutes • **Cook time:** 1 hour • **Yield:** 4 servings

Ingredients	Directions
4 cups water	**1** Add water and ½ teaspoon salt to large saucepan, bring to a boil.
1 clove garlic, minced	
½ teaspoon salt	
1 14-ounce can crushed tomatoes	**2** Reduce heat to simmer, and very slowly stream in polenta, stirring constantly.
1 cup polenta (or coarse-ground yellow cornmeal)	**3** Continue to cook until polenta is thickened and begins to pull away from the sides of the pot, this will take about 25–30 minutes.
1 cup low-sodium chicken stock	
1 tablespoon olive oil	**4** Moisten a large flat surface (such as a baking sheet), pour polenta onto surface. Let cool.
½ cup red wine	
12 ounces lean ground turkey	**5** Meanwhile, to prepare turkey sausage ragu: Heat a large skillet over medium-high heat, add oil, and swirl to coat.
½ teaspoon dried oregano	
½ teaspoon black pepper	**6** Add ground turkey, cooking for 6 minutes or until turkey is lightly browned.
1 teaspoon parsley, chopped	
¼ teaspoon salt	**7** Add remaining ¼ teaspoon salt, pepper, onion, and garlic. Sauté for 3 minutes.
1 teaspoon basil, chopped	
½ large yellow onion, minced	**8** Add tomatoes, chicken stock, red wine, and oregano. Simmer about 20 minutes over low heat, stirring occasionally. Remove from heat, and add parsley.
	9 Chop polenta into 12 rectangles, and place on serving dish.
	10 Cover with ragu sauce and garnish with freshly chopped basil.

Per serving: Calories 364 (From fat 91); Fat 10 g (Saturated fat 2 g); Cholesterol 58 mg; Sodium 651 mg; Carbohydrate 46g (Dietary fiber 6 g); Protein 24 g.

Lindsey's Quinoa Salad

Chef Lindsey Singleton, DiabetesEveryDay.com

Prep time: 10 minutes • **Cook time:** 30 minutes • **Yield:** 4 servings

Ingredients	Directions
1 cup quinoa	*1* Rinse the quinoa with water, and drain.
1 cup water	
Pinch of salt	*2* Combine rinsed quinoa with water and salt, bring to boil, lower heat, cover, and simmer until grain is cooked (about 15 minutes).
¼ cup red bell pepper, small dice	
½ cup cucumber, small dice	*3* Cool grain before combining with other ingredients.
2 tablespoons chopped dried apricots	*4* Mix cooled quinoa, bell pepper, cucumber, apricots, and green onion.
2 tablespoons green onion, chopped	
Dressing	*5* Whisk together dressing ingredients and pour over salad mixture, and toss to coat salad with dressing.
2 tablespoons olive oil	
1 tablespoon champagne vinegar	
½ tablespoon lemon juice	
2 tablespoons no-calorie, non-nutritive sweetener	
¼ teaspoon salt	
⅛ teaspoon black pepper	

Per serving: Calories 233 (From fat 83); Fat 9g (Saturated fat 1g); Cholesterol 0g; Sodium 172mg; Carbohydrate 31g (Dietary fiber 4g); Protein 6g.

Running it Through the Garden

Adding more vegetables to your diet, even going vegetarian now and then, is a key to healthy eating. Vegetables help fill you up, they are packed with healthy nutrients, give you important fiber, add a boost of color to your plate, and most are very low in carbohydrate.

One of these recipes isn't vegetarian, but they all feature vegetables as the main ingredient. And remember, when it comes to nonstarchy veggies you can usually add more to your meal without increasing your blood glucose level or your weight.

Tuna Niçoise

Here's a meal in a salad with room to add a piece of whole grain bread or two. Tuna and potatoes are the featured event, but fresh steamed green beans steal the show.

Meal in a potato

Speaking of potatoes, how about using one as a container for bright vegetables and low fat cheese? A sprinkle of Italian seasoning tops off this dinner or lunch favorite.

Mushroom lasagna with zucchini noodles

Pasta is another food that can send blood glucose sailing, but not if your lasagna noodles are strips of zucchini. This vegetarian dish has everything a great lasagna should except the carb load.

Quick soy stir fry

This dish is a great meatless Monday option. The beef or chicken soy strips honestly bring the flavor and texture of meat to this dish that actually has none.

Tuna Niçoise

Toby Smithson, RDN, CDE, DiabetesEveryDay.com

Prep time: 5 minutes • **Cook time:** 10 minutes • **Yield:** 4 servings

Ingredients	Directions
1 16-ounce white potato or 16 ounces red skin potatoes	**1** Quarter potatoes, boil for 10–15 minutes until fork tender, cool, and cut into thin slices (⅛-inch).
¼ pound fresh green beans, trimmed	**2** Steam green beans in a microwaveable dish in steamer basket or blanch until tender. Drain well, and cool.
2 tablespoon water	
4 cups Romaine lettuce, shredded	**3** Arrange lettuce leaves on a large platter. Top with potato slices and green beans.
1 6½-ounce can tuna in water, drained and flaked	
2 tomatoes, cut into wedges	**4** Add tuna, tomato, and egg wedges. Drizzle with dressing mixture of vinegar and oil.
2 hard-cooked eggs, cooled and cut into wedges	
6 tablespoons balsamic vinegar	
3 tablespoons olive oil	
Freshly ground pepper	

Note: Canned potatoes or green beans as a substitute will almost certainly add significant sodium to each serving.

Per serving: Calories 311 (From fat 126); Fat 14g (Saturated fat 3g); Cholesterol 108mg; Sodium 181mg; Carbohydrate 29g (Dietary fiber 4g); Protein 16g.

Meal in a Potato

Toby Smithson, RDN, CDE, DiabetesEveryDay.com

Prep time: 5 minutes • **Cook time:** 15 minutes • **Yield:** 4 servings

Ingredients	*Directions*
4 medium baking potatoes	*1* Scrub potatoes, and pierce several times with a fork.
2 tablespoons margarine	
2 cups frozen California-blend vegetables	*2* Wrap each potato in a microwave-safe paper towel; arrange potatoes 1 inch apart in microwave oven. Microwave on HIGH 8 to 14 minutes, or until done. Let cool to touch.
1 cup shredded low fat cheddar cheese	
1 cup shredded mozzarella cheese	*3* Slice away skin from top of each potato; carefully scoop out pulp, leaving shells intact. Mash pulp in medium bowl.
2 teaspoons Italian seasoning	
	4 Microwave frozen vegetables in a small microwave safe bowl for 3–4 minutes, drain, and set aside.
	5 Place 2 tablespoons margarine in with potato mixture, add the cooked vegetables, cheddar cheese, and Italian seasoning, mixing well. Fill potato shells with mixture and sprinkle with mozzarella.
	6 Place stuffed potatoes on microwave safe plate. Microwave at HIGH 2 minutes, or until thoroughly heated.

Per serving: Calories 366 (From fat 126); Fat 14g (Saturated fat 6g); Cholesterol 28mg; Sodium 440mg; Carbohydrate 42g (Dietary fiber 6g); Protein 18g.

Mushroom Lasagna with Zucchini Noodles

Chef Lindsey Singleton, DiabetesEveryDay.com

Prep time: 20 minutes • **Cook time:** 90 minutes • **Yield:** 8 servings

Ingredients	*Directions*
1 tablespoon olive oil	**1** In a large saucepan, heat olive oil over medium high heat. Swirl to coat.
1 pound sliced mushrooms (cremini or portabella)	
½ yellow onion, chopped	**2** Add mushrooms, onions, and garlic, and sauté for 5 minutes.
3 cloves garlic, minced	
1 28-ounce can crushed tomatoes	**3** Add tomatoes, ¼ teaspoon salt, pepper, and basil. Simmer for 30 minutes.
¼ teaspoon salt	
1 teaspoon black pepper	**4** Preheat oven to 350°F
2 tablespoons fresh chopped basil	**5** Lightly salt zucchini strips with remaining salt (to remove excess water). After 10 minutes, blot water off with a paper towel.
3 medium zucchini, sliced lengthwise ⅛-inch thick	
¼ teaspoon salt	**6** In medium bowl, mix ricotta cheese, Parmesan cheese, and egg.
15 ounces low-fat ricotta cheese	
¼ cup reduced-sodium Parmesan cheese	**7** In large casserole dish, line bottom with thin layer of mushroom/tomato sauce, then add a layer of zucchini, top with the ricotta mixture, and a thin layer of mozzarella cheese.
1 large egg	
8 ounces part-skim mozzarella cheese	**8** Repeat this process until all of the ingredients are used. Be sure to end with layer of sauce and mozzarella cheese on top.
	9 Cover with aluminum foil, and bake for 45 minutes. Uncover and bake for 10 more minutes. Let stand 10 minutes before serving.

Per serving: Calories 235 (From fat 111); Fat 12g (Saturated fat 6g); Cholesterol 63mg; Sodium 655mg; Carbohydrate 17g (Dietary fiber 4g); Protein 20g.

Quick Soy Stir Fry

Toby Smithson, RDN, CDE, DiabetesEveryDay.com

Prep time: 5 minutes • **Cook time:** 15 minutes • **Yield:** 4 servings

Ingredients	Directions
Nonstick vegetable cooking spray	**1** Pre-heat large skillet over medium heat. Spray with vegetable cooking spray.
8-ounce package beef or chicken soy strips	**2** Saute ginger and garlic for 1 minute; add soy strips and stir fry until cooked through. Remove from pan, and set aside.
16-ounce bag frozen vegetables	
½ tablespoon freshly grated ginger	**3** Add package of frozen vegetables with about ¼ cup water and cover with a lid to let vegetables steam cook.
½ tablespoon minced garlic	**4** When vegetables are almost cooked, add the soy strips back into the pan and stir fry for about 5 more minutes.

Vary It: Add additional nonstarchy vegetables, if desired.

Per serving: Calories 119 (From fat 19); Fat 2g (Saturated fat 0g); Cholesterol 0g; Sodium 232mg; Carbohydrate 14g (Dietary fiber 4g); Protein 14g.

Starters and Sidekicks

Starting your day off in an interesting and healthy way is important for controlling blood glucose well. A good fast breaker (breakfast) allows you to spread carbohydrates throughout your day and can help with between meal grazing.

Creative side dishes can keep your food interesting and keep you interested in adding healthier pieces to your eating plan. Plain vegetables tossed into the microwave aren't going to win any prizes, but it takes only a few seconds to create a sure bet.

Egg muffin

Look at what 10 minutes can get you for breakfast. And, you're getting whole grain with the muffin, low fat dairy with a little cheese for a shot of calcium, plus protein, and a dose of vitamin B_{12} with the egg. Oh yes, no frightening clowns.

Cheese Danish

Try this unique way to combine a waffle, cottage cheese, nuts, cinnamon, and your choice of berries. Once again, whole grain, low-fat dairy, some protein from cottage cheese and almonds, and this recipe adds a carb choice of sweet berries.

Spaghetti squash

Spaghetti squash is actually a fun food if you haven't tried it. The meat of this hard shell squash comes loose in long, spaghetti-like strings. This recipe turns the spaghetti into a genuine Italian feast.

Roasted Brussels sprouts

These tiny cabbage heads, miniatures of its giant cousin, are wonderful when roasted. This recipe is simple, easy, and will leave you wondering why you haven't always loved Brussels sprouts.

Egg Muffin

Toby Smithson, RDN, CDE, DiabetesEveryDay.com

Prep time: 5 minutes • **Cook time:** 5 minutes • **Yield:** 4 servings

Ingredients	Directions
2 English muffins, 100% whole wheat, toasted	*1* Spray skillet with vegetable cooking spray and fry each egg sunny side up.
2 ounces cheddar cheese, low fat	*2* Top egg with ½ ounce cheese, and cover pan until cheese melts.
4 eggs	*3* Place each egg on an English muffin half.

Per serving: Calories 163 (From fat 58); Fat 6g (Saturated fat 2g); Cholesterol 189mg; Sodium 278mg; Carbohydrate 14g (Dietary fiber 2g); Protein 13g.

Cheese Danish

Toby Smithson, RDN, CDE, DiabetesEveryDay.com

Prep time: 5 minutes • **Cook time:** 5 minutes • **Yield:** 4 servings

Ingredients	Directions
4 frozen whole-grain waffles	*1* Toast waffles according to package directions.
1 cup low-fat cottage cheese	*2* While waffles are still warm layer each with ¼ cup cottage cheese, ¼ tablespoon cinnamon, 1 tablespoon almonds, and ¼ cup berries.
¼ cup sliced almonds	
1 tablespoon cinnamon	
1 cup berries	

Per serving: Calories 190 (From fat 59); Fat 7g (Saturated fat 1g); Cholesterol 1mg; Sodium 440mg; Carbohydrate 24g (Dietary fiber 4g); Protein 11g.

Spaghetti Squash

Chef Lindsey Singleton, DiabetesEveryDay.com

Prep time: 10 minutes • **Cook time:** 1 hour • **Yield:** 4 servings

Ingredients	*Directions*
1 small spaghetti squash (about 3.5 - 4lbs)	**1** Preheat oven to 375°F.
1 tablespoon light margarine	**2** Pierce squash with sharp knife 3 to 4 times to allow steam to escape. Bake about 1 hour or until squash can easily be pierced with sharp paring knife. Let cool 10 minutes.
¼ cup minced onion	
2 cloves minced garlic	
½ cup cherry tomatoes, halved	
1 teaspoon chopped fresh basil	**3** While squash cools, heat margarine in large non-stick skillet over medium-high heat, and swirl to coat. Add onions and cook about 2 minutes. Then add garlic and tomatoes. Sauté until tomatoes begin to soften.
¼ teaspoon salt	
⅛ teaspoon black pepper	
¼ cup grated parmesan cheese	**4** Cut squash in half lengthwise and use a spoon to remove all seeds. Use a fork to scrape out squash into long spaghetti like strands and then add basil, salt, pepper, and squash to pan.
Basil leaves for garnish	
	5 Remove from heat and toss with Parmesan cheese. Garnish with freshly torn basil leaves.

Per serving: Calories 131 (From fat 41); Fat 5g (Saturated fat 2g); Cholesterol 1mg; Sodium 293mg; Carbohydrate 22g (Dietary fiber 5g); Protein 4g.

Roasted Brussels Sprouts

Toby Smithson, RDN, CDE, DiabetesEveryDay.com

Prep time: 10 minutes • **Cook time:** 40 minutes • **Yield:** 4 servings

Ingredients	Directions
3 tablespoons olive oil	*1* Preheat oven to 350°F.
1 pound Brussels sprouts, halved	*2* Place Brussels sprouts in a medium-size bowl.
1 tablespoon balsamic vinegar	*3* Mix oil and vinegar, drizzle on sprouts, and toss.
1 teaspoon sesame seeds	*4* Spread sprouts on baking sheet, sprinkle with sesame seeds, and bake 40 minutes or until tender and browning.

Per serving: Calories 143 (From fat 99); Fat 11g (Saturated fat 21g); Cholesterol 0g; Sodium 28mg; Carbohydrate 10g (Dietary fiber 3g); Protein 3g.

Fun with Fruit

Fruit is an essential part of your diabetes meal plan. It's carbohydrate, fiber, and a satisfier of sweet cravings. And fruit comes in an incredible assortment, almost always available at your local grocery thanks to global shipping efficiency.

This chapter finishes with fruit done four ways. From the simplest push of the microwave button to a healthier version of a favorite pudding, it's not a bad idea to make fruit a part of every meal.

Baked apples

It hardly gets any easier than core, sprinkle, push button, and eat fruit. This express baked apple is great for breakfast or a snack. And, as a bonus this comfort food will leave your home smelling wonderful.

Fancy fruit salad

You can call this dish a salad, but you'll find it's very closely related to dessert. It's just that if you call it a dessert everyone else will want some, too.

Whole-wheat French toast with red berry sauce

Here's a Sunday morning breakfast you can enjoy right before your walk. This is another dish that bears a startling resemblance to dessert, but there's no denying there's whole grain and healthy fruit there.

Banana pudding

Banana, vanilla wafers, and whipped topping give this dish all of the bonafide credentials. Just be prepared to listen to everyone telling you that you can't eat food like this.

Baked Apples

Toby Smithson, RDN, CDE, DiabetesEveryDay.com

Prep time: 5 minutes • **Cook time:** 2 minutes • **Yield:** 4 servings

Ingredients	Directions
4 medium apples	1 Core a medium apple, slice in halves, and place in a microwave safe bowl.
4 teaspoons cinnamon	
4 teaspoons sugar substitute that can be heated	2 Sprinkle apple halves with cinnamon and sugar substitute; cook in microwave for approximately two minutes.

Per serving: Calories 84 (from fat 3); Fat 0 g (Saturated fat 0g); Cholesterol 0g; Sodium 2mg; Carbohydrate 23g (Dietary fiber 5g); Protein 1g.

Fancy Fruit Salad

Toby Smithson, RDN, CDE, DiabetesEveryDay.com

Prep time: 15 minutes • **Yield:** 9 one-cup servings

Ingredients	Directions
1, 20-ounce can pineapple chunks packed in water	1 Drain pineapple chunks, and wash fresh fruit.
3 apples	2 Core and cube apples.
2 kiwi	3 Peel and slice kiwi.
1 cup grapes, stems removed	
2¼ cups strawberries	4 Top and quarter strawberries.
1 8-ounce tub lite whipped topping	5 Place fruit in a large bowl and mix with whipped topping.

Per serving: Calories 133 (From fat 29); Fat 3g (Saturated fat 3g); Cholesterol 0g; Sodium 28mg; Carbohydrate 28g (Dietary fiber 3g); Protein 1g.

Whole-wheat French Toast with Red Berry Sauce

Toby Smithson, RDN, CDE, DiabetesEveryDay.com

Prep time: 10 minutes • **Cook time:** 5 minutes • **Yield:** 4 servings

Ingredients	*Directions*
4 slices whole-wheat bread	*1* Microwave frozen berries until hot and soft (3 to 5 minutes); set aside.
1 egg	
⅓ cup skim milk	*2* Cut each slice of bread in half diagonally.
1 teaspoon vanilla	
1 teaspoon cinnamon	*3* In a medium bowl whisk together egg, milk, vanilla, and cinnamon.
Nonstick cooking spray	
4 ounces frozen strawberries	*4* Dip bread slices into egg mixture until well coated.
4 ounces frozen raspberries	
	5 Spray skillet or griddle with nonstick cooking spray, and grill toast on medium heat until golden brown on both sides.
	6 Top toast with warm berry mixture.

Per serving: *Calories 121 (From fat 20); Fat 2g; Cholesterol 139mg; Sodium 139mg; Carbohydrate 19g (Dietary fiber 4g); Protein 6g.*

Banana Pudding

Chef Lindsey Singleton, DiabetesEveryDay.com

Prep time: 5 minutes • **Cook time:** 5 minutes • **Yield:** 4 servings

Ingredients	*Directions*
⅓ cup Splenda™	**1** In medium saucepan, mix together egg yolks, flour, and salt.
2 egg yolks	
1¼ tablespoon flour	**2** Slowly add milk, and vigorously whisk to combine, ridding any lumps.
⅛ teaspoon salt	
1 cup 2% milk	**3** Heat mixture over medium high heat, whisking constantly, for about 5 minutes, or until mixture thickens to custard-like consistency. (Adjust heat as necessary to prevent eggs from cooking; do not let mixture boil!)
1 teaspoon vanilla extract	
1 large banana	
8 tablespoons cool whip	**4** When the desired consistency is reached, turn off heat and allow custard to cool; stir in vanilla extract and Splenda.
8 reduced fat vanilla wafer cookies	
	5 Meanwhile, cut banana into 12 slices.
	6 Layer three banana slices in the bottom of a small glass bowl or cup. Drizzle with one fourth of custard mixture.
	7 Top with 2 tablespoons of cool whip and two vanilla wafer cookies.

Per serving: Calories 155 (From fat 48); Fat 5g (Saturated fat 3g); Cholesterol 98mg; Sodium 127mg; Carbohydrate 22g (Dietary fiber 1g); Protein 4g.

Part VI
The Part of Tens

Enjoy an additional Diabetes Meal Planning and Nutrition Part of Tens chapter online at
www.dummies.com/extras/diabetesmealplanningandnutrition.

In this part...

- You probably know that some foods are better for you than others. In this part, you learn about ten diabetes "power foods," including oats, beans, and yes . . . even dark chocolate.

- On a budget? Most of us are. Check out ten diabetes-friendly food that cost under a buck! Do you like peanut butter? Read on!

- Learn how swapping out one of your favorite foods for another can keep you on track and lower your calorie intake.

- Little changes make big results. Discover little changes that are simple and easy and can become new habits that eventually happen without thinking.

Chapter 19

Ten Diabetes "Power Foods"

In This Chapter

▶ Sweeping out cholesterol with soluble fiber

▶ Fishing for omega-3 fatty acids

▶ Keeping kale in the crisper

▶ Enjoying dark chocolate

▶ Settling the stink about soy

*E*verybody understands that some foods are better than others. If you made your list of best foods, however, chances are that subjective measures — taste, texture, and your emotional attachment to particular foods — would be your main focus. That's how most people think of food.

Most people also understand some foods are more nutritious than others, and nutritional value isn't so subjective. For the most part, what's healthy for one is healthy for all. Some foods, though, are just big-time healthy, and with diabetes so closely connected to food and nutrition, these are the foods you want to incorporate into your daily eating habits.

None of the ten diabetes power foods mentioned in this chapter are a miracle cure you can order by phone late in the night for $19.99 plus shipping and handling. There aren't any such shortcuts to good health with diabetes — taking your medication, monitoring blood glucose levels, counting carbohydrates, and getting some physical activity need to remain on your to-do list. But, these ten foods can provide amazing benefits to your health, and are an infinitely better way to invest $19.99 in your future; no shipping and handling charges apply. The only requirement — you have to add them to your diet.

Oats

Oats are a whole grain, so they are a great start toward healthy right off the bat. Oats are most noted for bringing a specific soluble fiber called *beta-glucans* to the rescue. Beta-glucans, technically in a class of carbohydrates called gums, are especially effective at lowering bad LDL cholesterol levels (remember the low density lipoproteins from Chapter 6) and reducing the risk for the buildup of plaque in arteries known as atherosclerosis. The effectiveness of the soluble fiber in oats in impacting cholesterol levels has earned authorization from the U.S. Food and Drug Administration to make a heart-healthy claim on the packaging.

Studies have also shown that oats help moderate after-meal blood glucose response and improve insulin sensitivity. Oats also contribute to satiety — fullness — helping to reduce appetite. Oatmeal, of course, has long been a breakfast standard, and it's hard to argue with a strategy that starts your day with this power food. But a bowl of hot oatmeal in the morning isn't the only place you can get the soluble fiber from oats. Oatmeal makes great filler for meat dishes like meatloaf, and you can add oats or oat bran, which concentrates the beta-glucans even more, to yogurt or smoothies.

Remember, oatmeal is a grain, grains are carbohydrates, and carbohydrates need to be counted for blood glucose control. One-quarter cup of dry oatmeal equals one carb choice — 15 grams carbohydrate. Also, be conscious of what's known as the *healthy halo* effect. Adding healthy oat bran to a not so healthy food does not turn the not so healthy food into a healthy one.

Beans

Every child learns that beans, beans (are) good for the heart, and that beans, the musical fruit, have certain side effects related to the fermentation of the oligosaccharides raffinose and stachinose by bacteria that live in the large intestine. All true.

Beans are good for your heart by providing both soluble and insoluble fiber, as well as folate, magnesium, and potassium. That makes beans a cholesterol-reducing, blood-pressure-lowering, and gas-producing powerhouse. But, beans also improve blood glucose control, having a low glycemic index due to the fiber and protein content.

Speaking of protein, beans are an invaluable source for vegetarians and the best dollar value on protein for anyone. One-half cup of beans has as much protein as an ounce of meat. Ultimately, these complex legumes are starchy vegetables, so don't forget that your ½-cup serving is a 15 gram carbohydrate portion after you deduct half of the fiber from total carbohydrate.

Remember that managing diabetes is not only about controlling blood glucose levels as effectively as possible, but also about reducing your risk for heart disease, which is significantly elevated simply by having diabetes. Remember also that eliminating carbohydrates is no way to go about controlling blood glucose levels — the energy and nutrients you get from healthy carbohydrate foods are too valuable to surrender, and you can manage blood glucose levels with carbohydrates in your diet.

Beans come in a wide variety and fit into every cuisine. Beans can be added to soups and stews, mixed into salads, wrapped in a tortilla, or mashed into a burger. As long as you avoid added salt or sugar and account for the carbohydrates and the potential for embarrassment, it's hard to top beans as an all-around healthy food.

Salmon

Salmon is a fatty fish that's readily available fresh, frozen, or canned. It's an excellent source of complete protein, one of the best sources of dietary vitamin D, an excellent source of niacin (vitamin B$_3$), and a good source of selenium, vitamin B$_6$, and omega-3 fatty acids. Wild salmon does offer some nutritional benefits over farmed salmon, like less saturated fat, but salmon is a power food either way.

Omega-3 fatty acids may be specifically important in reducing the chronic state of inflammation that's associated with insulin resistance. Research from the University of California at San Diego Medical School identified how omega-3 fatty acids can activate a receptor associated with immune responses, and commonly associated with fat tissue, to reduce inflammation and insulin resistance in obese mice.

Salmon is great grilled, broiled, on salads, or packed into patties. The bones in canned salmon add to its calcium content, and salmon can be an essential source of vitamin B$_{12}$ for vegetarians who eat fish.

Nuts

Nuts come in an amazing variety of tastes — walnuts, almonds, pecans, cashews, Brazil nuts, hazelnuts, macadamia nuts, and even peanuts (which are actually legumes). Nuts are a good source of B vitamins, vitamin E, fiber, iron, protein, magnesium, and zinc, and are a great source of mono and poly unsaturated fats. Nuts are also very low in carbohydrate, making them a great snack food for people with diabetes who aren't snacking to raise blood glucose levels. A small serving of nuts can satisfy your appetite for hours.

Peanuts, almonds, and walnuts are all associated in studies with improved insulin sensitivity, and improvements in A1C among people with diabetes. Nuts have been shown to improve cholesterol levels as well, and without weight gain; walnuts even provide valuable omega-3 fatty acids.

Watch for added salt or sugar in packaged nuts, but otherwise nuts make great snacks, a tasty addition to salads or yogurt, an interesting crusting for fish, and, of course, the marvelous nut butters. Try an ounce of your favorite nut, or a tablespoon of nut butter, the next time you're tempted to reach for a snack.

Oranges

Oranges are a citrus fruit, cousin to grapefruits and lemons, and oranges are a great source of another cholesterol-reducing soluble fiber, called *pectin,* as well as folate and potassium. Oranges also contain the antioxidant *hesperidin,* which can help prevent damage to cells And face it, sometimes it's great to have something really sweet, and it's hard to top an orange when it comes to sweet (certainly cousins grapefruit and lemon aren't close).

A medium-sized orange is one 15-gram carbohydrate choice, making an orange or one half cup orange juice an effective treatment for moderate hypoglycemia. If you want the full bang for your nutrition buck, however, go for the orange instead of the juice. You get more fiber and a better dose of antioxidants.

Kale

Kale is a fabulous representative of a star group of nonstarchy vegetables, belonging to the same species of plants as cabbage, broccoli, cauliflower, collards, kohlrabi, and Brussels sprouts. From a nutrition standpoint, kale is rich in vitamin A, vitamin B_6, vitamin C, vitamin K, folate, calcium, magnesium, fiber, and powerful flavonoids and antioxidants. Kale also contains substances known as bile acid sequestrants, which reduces cholesterol levels and limits the absorption of dietary fat. Kale contains oxalates, which can interfere with calcium absorption, and can be an issue for people prone to kidney stones.

Kale may be the superstar, but leafy greens are an important part of a healthy diet. Even iceberg lettuce, nearly absent in nutritional value, can help fill you up, and Popeye's affinity for spinach was on target. Kale is great steamed, added to salad, or even sprayed lightly with oil and baked until a crispy chip.

Dark Chocolate

Need any more be said? Yes, probably so, but you'll still like the result. British researchers looked at the chocolate eating habits of more than 100,000 people from seven previous studies and divided them into groups ranging from never to more than once a day. The analysis produced consistent results, that those who ate the most chocolate had a 37 percent reduced risk of heart disease, a reduced risk of stroke, and a reduced risk of diabetes when compared to subjects who ate the least chocolate.

For the most part this analysis adds to evidence that chocolate, especially dark (more than 60 percent cocoa) chocolate, has benefits related to cardio-metabolic health. These benefits are likely related to polyphenols present in cocoa and the beneficial effects on blood pressure, insulin resistance, and blood lipids of these compounds.

So, can chocolate fit into your diabetes management practices? Of course! In an effective diabetes management lifestyle, mindfulness and moderation are keys to good health. But, don't forget that mindfulness and moderation should be keys for everyone else too — this isn't punishment, it's being responsible. A square or two of dark chocolate is a great addition to your day, but half a box of chocolate covered coconut cookies is not great. Managing diabetes effectively is a balance. Learning to savor fabulous foods like chocolate in appropriate portions helps an effective diabetes lifestyle fit more easily into your regular life.

Soy

The soy bean is a remarkable little fellow. It's relatively close to one-third each of protein, fat, and carbohydrate. Also, it's the only source of plant protein that is *complete,* which means providing all of the amino acids humans can't make internally, and soy protein is highly digestible. Too, the fat content of soybeans is 88 percent healthy mono or poly unsaturated fatty acids, and the soybean even includes omega-3 fatty acids. And whole soy beans, as opposed to soy processed into tofu, have 16 grams carbohydrate per cup, but also 8 grams of fiber. The combination of protein, fat, and fiber gives soy beans a very low glycemic index value, meaning its impact on blood glucose levels is very gradual.

Soy has been shown to reduce total cholesterol, reduce bad LDL cholesterol, lower blood pressure, and improve *endothelial function,* a measure of the flexibility of arteries.

Soy also contains *isoflavones,* sometimes called phytoestrogens, and certain isoflavones mimic estrogen. Because some breast cancers are fueled by estrogen, information about the safety of soy, with respect to breast cancer, has been swirling around for years, and the issue is not completely clear. Part of the confusion relates to soy supplements, which concentrate isoflavones to much higher levels than you would get from soy foods. Information over the years has gone back and forth about whether soy increases or decreases the risk, and about soy in the diet of cancer patients and survivors.

In Asian populations, soy seems to be protective against breast cancer, but it's not possible to isolate soy from other potential foods or lifestyle factors. But, studies in the United States have shown there is no association between soy consumptions and the risk for breast cancer, and studies of breast cancer survivors have shown that soy reduces the rate of recurrence, especially among cancers that are not *estrogen receptor positive.* The American Cancer Society's guidelines conclude that current research finds no harmful effects to breast cancer survivors from eating soy.

As with most things, Mother Nature knows best. Responsible advice on soy says get your isoflavones from soy foods and not from supplements. You can increase your soy consumption by adding edamame (green soy beans) to your stir fry dishes or to salad. Tofu and tempeh make great meat substitutes and are now marketed as substitute chicken or beef strips to use in stir fry or stroganoff, or to enliven your cooking imagination. Tempeh contains the whole soy bean, and its fiber; tofu does not.

Dairy

Many adults are lactose intolerant, so it may surprise you to find dairy on a list of beneficial foods for diabetes. But, many lactose intolerant adults can enjoy cheese, and one diabetes benefit to dairy products is a compound called trans-palmitoleic acid, which is found in the milk fat. Researchers examining data from the long-term Cardiovascular Health Study being conducted by the National Heart, Lung, and Blood Institute found that participants with higher levels of this naturally occurring trans fat had healthier levels of blood cholesterol, inflammatory markers, insulin levels, and insulin sensitivity, after adjustment for other risk factors. During follow-up, individuals with higher circulating levels of trans-palmitoleic acid had a much lower risk of developing diabetes, with about a 60 percent lower risk than participants with the lowest level. If you caught that this substance is a trans fat, which is considered profoundly unhealthy when manufactured by adding hydrogen to unsaturated fats, you can note that it's just one more example of how nature knows best. Still, go for lower fat options of milk, yogurt, cheese, and other dairy products.

Barley

Surprise — bet you didn't expect to find this pearly little grain in the list of diabetes power foods, but surprises are fun. Remember the cholesterol-lowering soluble fiber called beta-glucans found in oats? The soluble fiber in barley includes beta-glucans too, so it won't surprise you to find that barley has been shown as effective in lowering total cholesterol and LDL cholesterol in human studies.

OK, but a carbohydrate can't improve diabetes can it? Don't tell barley. A study of people with type 2 diabetes who consumed a healthy diet that included 18 grams of soluble fiber each day from barley showed a reduction in A1C of 30 percent, from an average of 8.4 percent down to 5.9 percent.

That's an incredible result, and you can get barley by adding it to soups, stews, salads, or vegetable dishes. Remember, ⅓ cup cooked is a 15-gram carbohydrate choice.

Chapter 20

Ten Diabetes-Friendly Foods Costing Less Than $1.00

In This Chapter

▶ Picking legumes for heart health

▶ Loving potatoes in spite of the carbohydrates

▶ Searching for colorful phytonutrients

▶ Getting protein from eggs, yogurt, and a children's favorite

Much about managing diabetes can be costly, but food doesn't need to be one of them. A diet that's right for diabetes is a diet that's right for virtually anyone, and there are enough foods that fit the bill for blood glucose control and heart health that your budget can remain flexible, and your choices are still many. The short version of diabetes nutrition is to eat lean protein, mostly unsaturated fats, whole grains, fruits, low-fat dairy, beans and starchy vegetables, nuts in moderation, sweets in moderation, lots of non-starchy vegetables, and all the while keeping sodium low.

Black Beans

Beans are incredibly nutritious, and one of the most versatile foods you can find. And, at $0.12 per ¼-cup serving for dry black beans it's hard to beat the price. Beans are a carbohydrate containing food, so you need to count the carbohydrates in your eating plan — ½-cup cooked beans is one carb choice, or 15 grams total carbohydrate, but beans also are rich in fiber, both soluble and insoluble, and work to reduce cholesterol levels. Beans are an important source of protein as well, and one-quarter-cup dry black beans packs only 70 calories.

Apples

An apple a day may not keep the doctor away, but apples can play a prominent role in healthy eating for diabetes. Apples, as a fruit, are a carbohydrate food, and a medium apple, about the size of a baseball, counts as one carb choice. Apples also contain both soluble and insoluble fiber, and help to control cholesterol levels, and an apple gives you only about 80 calories.

There is an incredible assortment of apple varieties, and they are grown in temperate climates all over the world. Whatever your tastes, there's an apple for you, and you should easily find crisp apples ready to take home for less than $0.50 each. Try the recipe for *Spiced Pork Tenderloin with Gala Apples* in Chapter 18 if you want a taste of apples at their finest.

Yogurt

Yogurt is fermented milk and includes both carbohydrate and protein as macronutrients. For diabetes management, non-fat yogurt is the better choice. Yogurt can be eaten plain, served with fruit, or substituted in dishes for sour cream or mayonnaise. It's an excellent source of protein and calcium, and the fermentation process may improve your absorption of calcium and B vitamins in yogurt as compared to milk. Greek yogurt, which is strained, contains more protein than other commercially available yogurt. You can purchase plain yogurt in larger containers (not single servings) for about $0.60 per 6-ounce serving.

Potato

The potato sometimes gets a bum rap in the diabetes realm because of its high carbohydrate content and its high glycemic index. About 3 ounces of white potato is 15 grams of carbohydrate. But, this starchy root vegetable is a bargain staple food, and brings its own nutritional contributions to the table too. Potatoes are high in vitamin C, contain more potassium than any other fruit or vegetable, and are a good source of vitamin B_6, which helps your body make its own amino acids.

Whole potatoes are always on sale, and a 12-ounce baking potato should go for something like $0.20 — remember, a 12-ounce potato is four carb choices. By weight, potatoes are the least-expensive vegetable.

Banana

You won't find many bananas produced in the United States, but bananas don't have any problem finding their way here — Americans eat more than 20 pounds per person per year. Bananas will cost you less than $0.40 apiece, and they are a rich source of fiber, vitamins C and B_6, and especially potassium, which is effective in controlling blood pressure. Bananas are a carbohydrate food, and about half of a medium banana will make one 15-carbohydrate-gram carb choice.

Carrots

What's up doc? Carrots are a colorful and healthy, nonstarchy vegetable, and like many nonstarchy vegetables, their color gives away some of the nutritional benefits — carotenes, and especially beta carotene, the precursor to vitamin A. Their high levels of beta carotene are what give carrots such an unblemished reputation for eye health. Carrots also contain other active compounds, antioxidants, and other carotenoids. At a cost of $0.05 per ounce, $0.30 for a 6-ounce carrot, these roots are a nutritional bargain for certain. Carrots are great raw, and add beautiful color to salads, make a great scoop for healthy dips, or can be boiled or roasted as a side dish for any entrée.

Lentils

Lentils are a legume, and therefore contain carbohydrate — a ½-cup serving of cooked lentils is 15 grams carbohydrate, one carb choice. About 30 percent of the calories from lentils, however, is from protein, making lentils one of the highest protein-containing foods among plants. Lentils also offer soluble and insoluble fiber, folate, magnesium, vitamins B_1 and B_3, and healthy minerals like iron. Notably, lentils have a very low glycemic index value, which means their impact on blood glucose levels is slow and steady, giving insulin time to act. This makes lentils an excellent carbohydrate for diabetes. Dry lentils cost less than $0.10 per ounce, about a nickel per serving, and have an advantage over dry beans because they don't need presoaking before cooking.

Eggs

Eggs are a marvelous source of dietary protein. In fact, the amount and balance of amino acids in eggs sets the standard for how the protein in other foods is measured — eggs are a complete source of high-quality protein, containing all of the essential amino acids. But, that's not all eggs have to offer. You also get vitamin A, vitamin D, vitamin B_{12}, the antioxidant lutein, and choline, a nutrient essential for regulating your nervous system and cardiovascular system.

Eggs have spent time out of favor due to a relatively high content of dietary cholesterol, but recent research has shown that moderate consumption of eggs does not negatively impact blood cholesterol levels. At about $0.15 per egg, you get quite a deal for the highest quality protein available.

Beets

Beets are an interesting addition to a list of diabetes-friendly foods because sugar beets are the source of about 30 percent of the world's sugar, which is the disaccharide sucrose. Sugar beets provided a source of sugar that was easier to acquire in days before high-speed transportation than the sugar from cane, which grows only in tropical zones. But, while commercial sugar beets contain as much as 20 percent sucrose, *table beets* (also known as beet-root, garden beet, or red beet) aren't nearly as sweet. A 3-ounce table beet contains only 8 grams of carbohydrate, and is about 35 calories, even though table beets and sugar beets are the same species. For about $0.50 per 4-ounce serving, beets are an amazing find.

Peanut Butter

At a cost of about $0.20 per ounce, your favorite childhood food can still be your favorite adult food. Peanut butter has been shown to improve blood glucose control, prevent blood glucose spikes, and lower cholesterol levels in people with type 2 diabetes. The effect on blood glucose may be related to arginine, which causes the body to release more insulin. Peanut butter is best known for its protein and healthy fat, but peanut butter also brings fiber, folate, potassium, vitamin E, thiamine, and magnesium to your table. Although not considered a carbohydrate, peanut butter does contain about 7 grams per 2-tablespoon serving.

Peanut butter contains a relatively balanced mixture of healthy poly and mono unsaturated fats, which help lower bad LDL cholesterol and blood triglycerides, and help raise good HDL cholesterol. Peanut butter also helps increase satiety (fullness), and has been incorporated into successful weight loss strategies for this reason. Peanut butter makes an excellent snack for people with diabetes, because a small amount is filling, and there is virtually no effect on blood glucose. Peanut butter — still the one.

Chapter 21

Ten Healthy Food Swaps for Losing Weight

An elevated body mass index (BMI), where body weight to height falls into the *overweight, obese,* or even higher category on that scale, is very common among people with type 2 diabetes, and it isn't just a coincidence. Excess weight is a distinct risk factor for developing type 2 diabetes, and excess weight makes blood glucose more difficult to control after diabetes is diagnosed. Excess weight is also an independent risk factor for high blood pressure and heart disease, so the combination of excess weight and diabetes, which is also an independent risk factor for heart disease, is serious business. Excess weight results from an accumulation of excess calories stored as body fat.

The connection between weight and type 2 diabetes is insulin resistance, where cells that normally respond to insulin, by allowing glucose molecules to leave the blood and enter those cells, become unresponsive to this powerful hormone. When cells won't take glucose in, the simple sugar continues to circulate in the bloodstream at levels higher than normal. And over time, higher than normal blood glucose levels cause enough damage to arteries, blood vessels, capillaries, and even nerves, that essential body functions are upset. Heart attack, stroke, kidney failure, blindness, uncontrollable infections of the feet, numbness and nerve pain, sexual dysfunction, digestive problems, and more are innocently called *complications of diabetes,* and these conditions certainly do complicate things.

The trigger for insulin resistance seems to be related much more to an accumulation of fat around internal organs than to excess subcutaneous — under the skin — fat. Called *visceral fat,* this internal fat releases chemical signals that interfere with the communication between normal cells and insulin.

Losing weight, and losing visceral fat in particular, can improve insulin sensitivity, making blood glucose levels easier to control, and reducing the risk for complications of diabetes over the long term.

Fortunately, losing only a modest amount of weight — as little as 7 to 10 percent of your current weight — can have a profound effect on insulin resistance. That's in part because visceral fat appears to be the first fat to disappear as the pounds come off. Modest weight loss can have a huge effect on the course of diabetes.

A list of ten food swaps should not be considered a weight loss program in any sense. But, this simple list represents an important concept — little changes make big results. And importantly, little changes that are simple and easy can become new habits that eventually happen without thinking.

One note — this list leans toward swaps that reduce fat in your diet, but you shouldn't take that to mean that excess carbohydrates, protein, or alcohol, which are other sources of calories, are less important. All calories add up, but cutting fat becomes a natural target for the following reasons:

- People tend to get many of their excess calories from fat.

- Fat packs more than twice the calories per gram as either carbohydrate or protein, so cutting a gram of fat gets double the result.

- A diet high in saturated fat increases the risk for heart disease, and managing diabetes effectively has to target both blood glucose control and heart disease risk.

Lighten Up Your Mayo

Mayonnaise is a popular condiment in the United States, finding its way into sandwiches, sauces, and especially into salads and salad dressings. Mayonnaise is made by combining egg yolk, oil, a little vinegar or lemon juice, and sometimes other ingredients such as mustard, salt, or sugar. Mayo has been commercially available for so long that it's easy to forget it's a culinary sauce you could whip up in your kitchen. Commercial producers don't always follow the strict traditional recipe, often using whole eggs instead of just the yolk.

At home you might use mayonnaise on sandwiches or in salads like potato salad, coleslaw, or pasta salads. Mayonnaise is typically 80 percent fat, and a tablespoon of regular mayo will be about 10 grams of fat and 90 calories — because fat has 9 calories per gram, you can see that regular mayonnaise is essentially all fat.

But other formulations of mayonnaise are available, and swapping your regular mayonnaise for a lower-fat version can save significant calories.

Light mayonnaise reduces calories per tablespoon to 35 or so, and total fat to between 3 and 4 grams per serving. *Low-fat* or *reduced-fat* varieties usually cut calories and fat to 15 and about 1 gram, respectively. Going from 90 calories per tablespoon to 15 is a significant reduction, and when it comes to losing weight over the long term, these are the kinds of changes that really add up.

Try Bacon of Canadian Descent

The U.S. Department of Agriculture defines *bacon* as "the cured belly of a swine carcass." You might think such a description of a food would discourage all but the most adventurous eaters, but Americans go for American bacon to the tune of close to a billion pounds per year. Even the most uninformed would probably concede a product that is mostly saturated fat and cured with salt won't make anyone's annual list of healthy foods.

But bacon is a term that describes meats that vary surprising around the world, both by cut and processing. And, other cuts and varieties of bacon are significantly more in line with healthy eating than good ole American bacon. Canadian bacon, for example, is lower in calories, fat, saturated fat, and sodium than American bacon, and is generally available in your grocery.

Swapping one ounce of American bacon for Canadian bacon saves 100 calories, 9 grams of total fat, 3 grams of saturated fat, and 285 milligrams sodium. That is an incredible difference in nutritional composition for an incredibly simple change, and Canadian bacon also makes a wise swap for other meats like pepperoni. Swapping your bacon is an excellent example of how you don't have to completely abandon your dietary preferences to get big benefits.

Baked Potato, Meet Greek Yogurt

Standard toppings for baked potatoes are butter, margarine, or sour cream, but you can save calories and fat by trying nonfat Greek yogurt on your potato instead. And, Greek yogurt has the same thick and creamy consistency of sour cream. Two tablespoons (1 ounce) of nonfat Greek yogurt has only 24 calories and no fat, compared to 50 calories and 5 grams of fat for sour cream, 140 calories and 16 grams of fat for margarine, and 200 calories with 23 grams of fat for butter.

Greek yogurt, because it's thicker and creamier than regular yogurt, can replace sour cream or margarine just about anywhere, and you'll get some high-quality protein and calcium that you won't get from margarine as a bonus.

Freshen Your Salads with Lime

Everybody knows that a fresh green salad is a healthy choice, and for diabetes management nonstarchy vegetables like those commonly included in green salads are especially desirable because of their low carbohydrate content. So, after you've prepared your healthy tossed green salad, how are you going to top the lettuce, spinach, cucumber, tomato, carrots, and peppers? Maybe with three or four tablespoons of honey mustard salad dressing for 220 calories and 16 grams of fat, or blue cheese for 240 calories, or thousand island for 260, or French dressing for 280 calories and 26 grams of fat?

Or, maybe think about swapping any kind of salad dressing for fresh lime juice, with no fat, and calories you can count on one hand. Fresh lime juice will give you a burst of flavor, and complements the garden vegetables of your salad without compromising your healthy intentions. Salad dressing is one of those condiments you can tend to ignore because it's added in what seems to be such small amounts. But, the calories from fat mount quickly, and you can do a lot of damage with a tablespoon.

By the way, at restaurants have your salad without dressing, and ask the waitress or waiter for a few fresh lime slices. If they can't come up with limes in the kitchen, the bartender will know exactly where to find them.

Moooooove to Lower-Fat Dairy Products

Whole milk contains almost 4 percent fat, and 1 cup of whole milk has 156 calories, 9 grams of total fat, and 34 milligrams of cholesterol. Low-fat, 1 percent milk has 54 fewer calories, 7 grams less fat, 22 milligrams less cholesterol, the same amount of calcium, and more vitamin A per cup. Nonfat, or *skim* milk, has only 86 calories per cup.

If you don't drink much milk, think about the products made from milk that find their way into your diet — cheese, cottage cheese, sour cream, cream cheese, ice cream, and yogurt. And, don't forget recipes that call for a cup of milk, or shredded cheese. Every opportunity you take to use reduced fat or nonfat dairy products in place of the full fat versions takes calories out of your daily diet. Taking calories out of your diet without completely eliminating an entire group of foods is an opportunity you shouldn't miss. Even if you don't think you can make the leap straight to nonfat, there are perfectly delicious reduced fat options, and every little bit makes a difference.

Chipping and Dipping

Snack chips and dips are everywhere, from the office break room to Super Bowl parties to the free sample displays at your grocery. But chips are fried, and relatively high in fat. A one-ounce serving of potato chips, corn chips, or cheese snacks — 10 to 15 chips — will pack about 150 calories and 10 grams of fat. Add dip — nacho, queso, onion, ranch, or bean — and you add 50 to 70 more calories per two-tablespoon serving.

Substituting baked chips, however, cuts the calories and fat significantly. You save 20 to 30 calories per ounce, and 3 to 5 grams of fat by switching to the baked variety. And, if you adopt salsa as your dipping favorite, you lose 80 percent of the calories, and all of the fat from the dip, too. Make your own salsa by dicing fresh tomatoes, onions, cilantro, and peppers, and you can impress your friends with your kitchen skills, and your nutrition knowledge.

Spice it Up

Fat adds flavor to food, and one reason you like higher-fat foods is for the flavor. But, you can add incredible flavor with no calories and no fat by adding spices. And, you can add spices to anything, especially where your first thought might be to add butter and salt.

Popcorn is the perfect example. Instead of adding butter, and salt for that matter, try spices instead. Sprinkle your popcorn with Italian spices, or add a southwest flavor using chili powder, ground cumin, paprika, and garlic powder. For a sweet treat , combine a non-nutritive sweetener with cinnamon, ground nutmeg, and allspice, and sprinkle the mixture liberally over your popcorn.

Cinnamon is a great addition to hot cereal too, instead of butter or margarine. And, season your vegetables with herbs and spices instead of adding margarine. For every tablespoon of margarine you eliminate, you save 70 calories and 8 grams of fat.

A Healthier Chocolate Fix

Chocolate is a food processed from the fermented seeds of cacao trees, coming to Western societies from the Mayan and Aztec cultures. But while the ancient Mesoamericans brewed bitter drinks of chocolate, the addition of sugar and milk to make the chocolate you know today has also added significant calories, carbohydrates, and fat.

Chocolate is a dietary must have, however, and fortunately it brings some clear health benefits along with its addictive stimulation of your brain's serotonin levels. But even for dark chocolate, which has the greatest health benefits, an appropriate portion might be only ½ ounce, which for 60 percent cacao chocolate would be 76 calories, 5 grams total fat, 3 grams saturated fat, and 9 grams carbohydrate. A 2-ounce milk chocolate bar brings along 280 calories, 17 grams of fat, 11 grams of saturated fat, and 35 grams of carbohydrate.

When you need your next chocolate fix, try nonfat, sugar-free chocolate pudding instead. If you use nonfat milk to mix your pudding, you can enjoy a ½-cup serving for 80 calories, 0 grams of fat, and one carb choice — 15 grams of carbohydrate. You save 200 calories, 17 grams of fat, and 20 grams of carbohydrate. If you're feeling especially frisky, stir a tablespoon of peanut butter into your pudding, and you still save 100 calories, 10 grams of fat, and 15 grams of carbohydrate compared to the milk chocolate bar.

Roasted Garlic Spread

Garlic roasted in the oven for 30 minutes, or zapped in a terra cotta roaster for only about two minutes in the microwave, loses much of its strong, pungent bite, and takes on a mild, buttery sweetness. And, roasted garlic can be smashed into a rich paste, and used on anything where you would otherwise get your buttery sweetness from butter or margarine — bread, potatoes, vegetables, pasta, or wherever.

One tablespoon of roasted garlic is only 12 calories, with no fat, saturated fat, or sodium. Compared to a tablespoon of margarine, roasted garlic saves you 58 calories, 8 grams of total fat, and 100 milligrams of sodium. And, eating garlic does have some beneficial effects on heart health, specifically lowering blood pressure and helping to prevent atherosclerosis.

Keeping Your Fish in Water

Canned tuna is a great source of high quality protein, and healthy omega-3 fatty acids. But, you can get your tuna packed in water, or you can get your tuna packed in oil. You guessed it — having tuna packed in water will save you 69 calories, 6 grams of fat, and 14 milligrams of sodium compared to the same 3-ounce serving of tuna packed in oil.

So, what about taste? Well, you may hear expert sounding talk about the richness of oil-packed tuna compared to tasteless water-packed tuna, but ultimately it's about the fish itself. In a blind taste test conducted on 13 different tuna brands by a popular food lovers website, water-packed tunas captured first and third place among the expert judges.

Part VII
The Appendixes

Visit www.dummies.com/extras/diabetesmealplanningandnutrition to find more important info.

In this part...

✔ Use the carbohydrate exchange list as a reference to help you learn carbohydrate counting.

✔ Get nutritional information about many of your favorite ethnic foods, from Asian to Mexican and a few in between.

✔ Understand how to convert measures and food portion sizes so that you can control the amount of carbs you eat.

✔ Learn the difference between dry and cooked carbohydrate foods, such as beans and pasta.

Appendix A

Diabetes Exchange Lists

· ·

Diabetes exchanges were the best way for patients to learn about healthy eating for diabetes before carbohydrate counting became the standard. It's true that carb counting offers more accuracy and flexibility for managing the foods that directly affect blood glucose levels, especially in matching insulin doses to carbohydrate consumption, and in many circles diabetes exchanges have gone by the wayside as a teaching tool.

But these exchange lists still have some life. Some people with diabetes find exchange lists easier to deal with than carbohydrate counting, and exchange lists don't address only carbohydrates, but other food groups as well. In that regard, exchange lists can illustrate healthy eating concepts beyond carbohydrate management better than carb counting. And exchanges encourage people with diabetes to select their carbohydrate choices from a variety of carbohydrate containing foods, rather than just one group.

A meal plan incorporating exchanges may suggest, for example, that your breakfasts include one starch, one fruit, and one dairy exchange rather than simply three carb choices. While your carbohydrate intake would be the same either way, exchanges would discourage you from choosing three pieces of toast as your three breakfast carb choices.

The exchange concept means you can exchange any food within an exchange list for any other food in that same list. As your breakfast fruit you are free to select 17 grapes, 2 tablespoons of dried cherries, or any other portion given for another fruit or fruit juice.

Exchanges are also helpful in following a weight management plan, which addresses more than simply carbohydrates. If your registered dietitian has recommended a 1,500 calorie per day eating plan, you can find your best choices and the appropriate portions for protein and fat in your daily diet from the *meat and meat substitutes* list, and from the *fats* list. There is also a list of *free foods*, which are very low-calorie and low-carbohydrate choices you can eat as often as three times each day as a snack, or add to your meals.

Throughout the exchange lists, foods marked with an asterisk (*) indicate choices that may be high in sodium. People with diabetes should restrict sodium intake to 1,500 milligrams per day.

Carbohydrate Exchanges

Exchange lists are an effective way to make sure you get the correct portions of any particular food, especially the carbohydrate foods in Tables A-1, A-2, and A-3. Exchange lists may also help you add a variety of carbohydrate foods to your diet, simply by listing many available foods that are all equal to 15 grams of carbohydrate in the portions specified.

Starches

One exchange of a starchy food contains about 15 grams of carbohydrate, up to 3 grams of protein, up to 1 gram of fat, and 80 calories. Beans, peas, and lentils are an exception with respect to protein, where each portion also includes 7 grams, and is considered a very lean meat substitute exchange. Starches in the amounts listed in Table A-1 equal one carbohydrate exchange. Choose whole-grain and low-fat starches when possible.

Table A-1	Starches	
Type	*Food*	*Portion Size*
Bread		
	Bagel large (4 ounces)	¼ bagel (1 ounce)
	Bread	1 slice (1 ounce)
	Bread (reduced calorie)	2 slices (1½ ounces)
	Hamburger or hot dog bun	½ bun (1 ounce)
	English muffin	½ muffin
	Pita	½ pita
	Tortilla (6" corn or flour)	1 tortilla
	Pancake (4" by ¼" thick)	1 pancake
	Barley, cooked	⅓ cup
	Bulgur wheat, cooked	½ cup
	Bran, oats, shredded wheat, frosted cereals	½ cup
	Cereal, puffed, unfrosted	1½ cups
Cereals and grains		
	Cereal, unsweetened, ready to eat	¾ cups
	Couscous	⅓ cup

Type	Food	Portion Size
	Granola, low-fat or regular	¼ cup (+ 1 fat exchange)
	Grits, cooked	½ cup
	Pasta, cooked	⅓ cup
	Quinoa, cooked	⅓ cup
	Rice, cooked, brown or white	⅓ cup
	Tabbouleh, prepared	½ cup
	Wheat germ, dry	3 tablespoons
Starchy vegetables		
	Corn	½ cup
	Corn on the cob, large	½ cob (5 ounces)
	Mixed vegetables, with peas, corn or pasta	1 cup
	Parsnips	½ cup
	Potato, baked with skin	3 ounces
	Potato, mashed	½ cup
	Pumpkin, canned	1 cup
	Spaghetti or pasta sauce	½ cup
	Squash, acorn or butternut	1 cup
	Succotash	½ cup
	Yam or sweet potato, plain	½ cup
Crackers and snacks		
	Animal crackers	8
	Graham crackers (2½" squares)	3
	Matzoh	¾ ounce
	Melba toast (2" × 4")	4
	Oyster crackers*	20
	Popcorn, low fat microwave* or no fat air popped	3 cups
	Pretzels*	¾ ounce
	Rice cakes (4 inches across)	2
	Saltine crackers*	6
	Snack chips, baked*	15-20 piece (¾ oz.)

(continued)

Table A-1 *(continued)*

Type	Food	Portion Size
Beans, peas, lentils (count as 1 carbohydrate and 1 ounce lean meat)		
	Baked beans	⅓ cup
	Black, garbanzo, kidney lima, navy, pinto, white (cooked)	½ cup
	Lentils, cooked	½ cup
	Black eyed, split, green peas (cooked)	½ cup
	Refried beans, canned, fat free	½ cup

Fruits

One fruit exchange equals 15 grams of carbohydrate and 60 calories. Watch the serving sizes for dried fruit, and choose whole fruits over juices most of the time. Table A-2 shows you a wide variety of fruits you can eat, as well as the appropriate portion size equal to 15 grams of carbohydrate.

Table A-2   Fruits

Type	Food	Portion Size
Fresh		
	Apple, small 2" across	1 (4 ounces)
	Apricots	4 (5½ ounces)
	Banana, extra small	1 (4 ounces)
	Blackberries, blueberries	¾ cup
	Cantaloupe, honey dew, papaya, cubed	1 cup (11 ounces)
	Cherries	12 (3 ounces)
	Dates	3
	Grapefruit, large	½ (11 ounces)
	Grapes, small	17 (3 ounces)
	Kiwi	1 (3½ ounces)
	Mango, cubed	½ cup
	Nectarine, small	1 (5 ounces)

Type	Food	Portion Size
	Orange, small	1 (6½ ounces)
	Peach, medium	1 (6 ounces)
	Pear, large	½ (4 ounces)
	Pineapple, cubed	¾ cup
	Plums, small	2 (5 ounces)
	Raspberries	1 cup
	Strawberries	1¼ cup
	Watermelon, cubed	1¼ cups (13½ ounces)
Dried fruit		
	Apples	4 rings
	Apricots	8 halves
	Blueberries, cherries, cranberries, mixed fruit	2 tablespoons
	Figs	1½
	Prunes	3
	Raisins	2 tablespoons
Canned fruit, unsweetened		
	Applesauce, apricots, cherries, peaches, pears, pineapple, plums	½ cup
	Grapefruit, mandarin oranges	¾ cup
Fruit juice		
	Unsweetened apple, grapefruit, orange, pineapple	½ cup
	Fruit juice blends of 100% juice, grape, prune	⅓ cup

Milk

One milk exchange equals 12 grams of carbohydrate, and 8 grams of protein. Note that 2% or whole-milk products also count as one or two fat exchanges, so choose low-fat milk products more often. Table A-3 reflects different milk products.

Table A-3		Milk
Type	**Food**	**Portion Size**
Fat-free and low-fat milk and yogurt products		
	Buttermilk *	1 cup (8 ounces)
	Chocolate milk	1 cup (counts as 1 milk + 1 starch)
	Evaporated milk	½ cup
	Milk, skim or 1%	1 cup
	Yogurt, plain or flavored with a non-nutritive sweetener	⅔ cup (6 ounces)
	Yogurt, low fat with fruit	⅔ cup (6 ounces) (counts as 1 milk + 1 fruit)
Reduced-fat milk and yogurt products		
	Milk, 2%	1 cup (counts as 1 milk + 1 fat)
	Soy milk, light	1 cup (counts as 1 milk + 1 fat)
Whole milk and yogurt products		
	Buttermilk	1 cup
	Chocolate milk	1 cup
	Evaporated milk	½ cup
	Milk, whole	1 cup (counts as 1 milk + 2 fats)
	Soymilk	1 cup
	Yogurt, plain	1 cup
Other		
	Eggnog, whole milk	1 cup (counts as 1 milk + 2 fats)
	Rice drink, fat free, plain	1 cup fat free milk
	Rice drink, low fat	1 cup milk + 1 fat

Meat and Meat Substitutes

A meat and meat substitute exchange is carbohydrate free (negligible carbohydrate) and contains seven grams of protein. The different exchange lists are based upon the fat and calories in a portion that gives you seven grams of protein. Beans, peas, and lentils are an exception with respect to carbohydrate, where each portion also includes 15 grams and is considered a starch exchange, too (see Table A-1).

Lean and very lean meat, and meat substitutes

Very lean and lean meat and meat substitutes contain 0 carbohydrates, 7 grams protein, 1 gram or less fat, and 35 calories. Lean meat or meat substitutes contain 0 carbohydrate (except for beans, peas, and lentils), 7 grams of protein, 3 grams of fat, and 55 calories. Table A-4 list the portion size containing 7 grams of protein for your best choices when you have diabetes.

Table A-4 Lean and Very Lean Meat, and Meat Substitutes	
Food	*Portion size*
Beef, select or choice, trimmed of fat: ground round, roast, round sirloin, tenderloin	1 ounce
Beef jerky*	½ ounce
Fish, fresh or frozen: catfish, cod, flounder, haddock, halibut, orange roughy, salmon, tilapia, trout, tuna	1 ounce
Herring, smoked*	1 ounce
Hot dog, 3 grams or less of fat per ounce (Note: May also contain carbohydrate)*	1
Lamb: roast, chop, leg	1 ounce
Lunch meat, 3 grams or less of fat per ounce: chipped beef, deli thin-sliced meats, turkey ham, turkey kielbasa, turkey pastrami*	1 ounce
Oysters, medium, fresh or frozen	6
Pork, lean: Canadian bacon,* chop, ham, tenderloin	1 ounce
Poultry without skin: chicken, Cornish hen, duck, goose, turkey	1 ounce
Sardines, canned*	2 medium
Shellfish: clams, crab, imitation shellfish, lobster, scallops, shrimp	1 ounce
Tuna, canned in water or oil, drained*	1 ounce
Veal: loin chop, roast	1 ounce
Cheese, 3 grams or less of fat per ounce*	1 ounce
Cottage cheese, fat-free, low-fat or regular*	¼ cup
Egg substitute, plain	¼ cup
Egg whites	2

(continued)

Table A-4 *(continued)*

Food	Portion size
Baked beans	⅓ cup
Black, garbanzo, kidney lima, navy, pinto, white (cooked)	½ cup
Lentils, cooked	½ cup
Black eyed, split, green peas (cooked)	½ cup
Refried beans, canned, fat free	½ cup

Medium-fat meat and meat substitutes

Medium-fat meat or meat substitutes contain 0 carbohydrates, 7 grams of protein, 5 grams of fat, and 75 calories. Table A-5 lists the portion sizes for meat and meat substitutes containing 7 grams of protein, and a notable amount of fat.

Table A-5   Medium-Fat Meat and Meat Substitutes

Food	Portion Size
Beef: corned beef, ground beef, meatloaf, prime rib, short ribs, tongue*	1 ounce
Cheese, 4 to 7 grams of fat per ounce: feta, mozzarella, pasteurized processed cheese spread, reduced-fat cheeses, string*	1 ounce
Eggs (limit to 3 a week)	1
Fish, fried	1 ounce
Lamb: ground, rib roast	1 ounce
Pork: cutlet, shoulder roast	1 ounce
Poultry: chicken with skin, dove, fried chicken, ground turkey, pheasant, wild duck or goose	1 ounce
Ricotta cheese*	¼ cup (2 ounces)

High-fat meat and meat substitutes

High-fat meat and meat substitutes contain 0 carbohydrates, 7 grams protein, 8 grams of fat, and 100 calories. These foods are high in saturated fat and calories. Table A-6 lists foods containing 7 grams of protein and this significant amount of fat. Your diet is healthier if you make these choices only rarely.

Table A-6   High Fat Meats and Meat Substitutes

Food	Portion Size
Bacon, pork*	2 slices (1 ounce each before cooking)
Bacon, turkey*	3 slices (½ ounce each prior to cooking)
Cheese, regular: American, bleu, Brie, cheddar, hard goat, Monterey Jack, queso, Swiss*	1 ounce
Hot dog, regular: beef, chicken, pork, turkey or combination*	1 (counts as 1 fat and 1 meat exchange)
Lunch meat, 8 or more grams of fat per ounce: bologna, pastrami, hard salami*	1 ounce
Pork: ground, sausage, spareribs	1 ounce
Sausage, 8 or more grams of fat per ounce: bratwurst, chorizo, Italian, knockwurst, Polish, smoked, summer sausage*	1 ounce

Fats

One fat exchange equals 5 grams of fat and 45 calories. Table A-7 lists fats and a portion size according to whether they are predominantly monounsaturated, polyunsaturated, or saturated fat. The unsaturated fats are your best choice for heart health.

Table A-7   Monounsaturated, Polyunsaturated, and Saturated Fats

Type	Food	Portion Size
Monounsaturated fats		
	Almonds*	6
	Avocado	2 tablespoons (1 ounce)
	Brazil nuts*	2
	Cashews*	6
	Filberts (Hazelnuts)*	5
	Macadamia nuts	3

(continued)

Table A-7 (continued)

Type	Food	Portion Size
	Nut butters, trans-free: almond butter, cashew butter, peanut butter (smooth or crunchy)	1½ teaspoons
	Oil: canola, olive, peanut	1 teaspoon
	Olives, black*	8 large
	Olives, green with pimento*	10 large
	Peanuts	10*
	Pecans*	4 halves
	Pistachios*	16
Polyunsaturated fats		
	Margarine, low-fat spread, 30 to 50 percent vegetable oil, trans fat-free	1 tablespoon
	Margarine, trans-free: squeeze, stick, tub	1 teaspoon
	Mayonnaise, reduced-fat	1 tablespoon
	Mayonnaise, regular	1 teaspoon
	Mayonnaise-style salad dressing, reduced-fat*	1 tablespoon
	Mayonnaise-style salad dressing, regular	2 teaspoons
	Oil: corn, cottonseed, flaxseed, grape seed, safflower, soybean, sunflower	1 teaspoon
	Pine nuts	1 tablespoon
	Salad dressing, reduced-fat	2 tablespoons
	Salad dressing, regular*	1 tablespoon
	Seeds: flaxseed, pumpkin, sesame, sunflower*	1 tablespoon
	Walnuts	4 halves
Saturated fats		
	Bacon, cooked, regular or turkey*	1 slice
	Butter, reduced-fat	1 tablespoon

Type	Food	Portion Size
	Butter, stick	1 teaspoon
	Butter, whipped	2 teaspoons
	Coconut, shredded	2 tablespoons
	Cream: half-and-half, whipped	2 tablespoons
	Cream, heavy	1 tablespoon
	Cream, light	1½ tablespoons
	Cream cheese, reduced-fat	1½ tablespoons
	Cream cheese, regular	1 tablespoon
	Oil: coconut, palm, palm kernel	1 teaspoon
	Shortening or lard	1 teaspoon
	Sour cream, reduced-fat	3 tablespoons
	Sour cream, regular	2 tablespoons

Free Foods

The specified portion sizes for free foods are less than 20 calories, and five or less grams carbohydrate. If you spread these throughout the day, up to three servings is often recommended for appetite control without affecting blood glucose levels. Remember that one exchange of a nonstarchy vegetable falls into this category, too. Table A-8 lists common free foods and a portion size fitting the free food definition. A portion size listed as *Unlimited* would refer to the calorie and carbohydrate content of normal use. For instance, drinking a couple of glasses of "cooking wine" would be outside of its normal use.

Table A-8	Free Foods	
Food	Type	Portion Size
Beverages		
	Bouillon*, club soda, coffee (unsweetened or with sugar), flavored water (carbohydrate free),tea (unsweetened or with sugar substitute),tonic water (sugar free), water (plain, carbonated, mineral)	Unlimited
Condiments		
	Horseradish	Unlimited
	Lemon juice	Unlimited

(continued)

Table A-8 *(continued)*

Type	Food	Portion Size
	Mustard*	Unlimited
	Vinegar	Unlimited
Seasonings		
	Vegetable cooking spray	Unlimited
	Cooking wine	Unlimited
	Extracts (vanilla, peppermint, etc.)	Unlimited
	Garlic	Unlimited
	Herbs	Unlimited
	Hot sauce*	Unlimited
	Pimento	Unlimited
	Spices without salt as an ingredient	Unlimited
	Worcestershire sauce*	Unlimited
Other		
	Gelatin, sugar free or unflavored	Unlimited
	Sugar-free gum	Unlimited
	Salad greens	Unlimited
Condiments with a limit		
	Barbeque sauce*	2 teaspoons
	Cream cheese, fat free	1 tablespoon
	Creamer, liquid nondairy	1 tablespoon
	Creamer, powdered nondairy	2 teaspoons
	Pickle, dill*	1½ medium
	Gherkin pickles	¾ ounce
	Honey mustard*	1 tablespoon
	Jam or jelly, light or no sugar added	2 teaspoons
	Ketchup	1 tablespoon
	Margarine spread, fat free	1 tablespoon
	Margarine spread, reduced fat	1 teaspoon

Type	Food	Portion Size
	Mayonnaise, fat free	1 tablespoon
	Mayonnaise, reduced fat	1 teaspoon
	Mayonnaise-style salad dressing, fat free	1 tablespoon
	Mayonnaise-style salad dressing, reduced fat	1 teaspoon
	Miso*	1½ teaspoons
	Parmesan cheese, freshly grated *	1 tablespoon
	Pickle relish	1 tablespoon
	Salad dressing, fat free Italian*	2 tablespoons
	Salad dressing, fat free or low fat*	1 tablespoon
	Salsa	¼ cup
	Sour cream, fat free or reduced fat	1 tablespoon
	Soy sauce, regular or Light*	1 tablespoon
	Sweet and sour sauce	2 teaspoons
	Sweet chili sauce	2 teaspoons
	Syrup, sugar free	2 tablespoons
	Taco sauce	1 tablespoon
Other		
	Cocoa powder, unsweetened	1 tablespoon
	Hard candy, regular or sugar free	1 piece
	Whipped topping, light or fat free	2 tablespoons
	Whipped topping, Regular	1 tablespoon

Sweets and Desserts

Sweets and desserts are often very high in carbohydrates, fats, and calories, and with diabetes should be eaten in moderation. This limited list of exchanges is provided for demonstration purposes, illustrating a few better choices for sweets and desserts, contrasted to a few choices that are going to be frustrating because of the portion size. Table A-9 gives the portion size containing 15 grams of carbohydrate for common sweets and desserts. Note than some of these foods also include more than 5 grams of fat for the serving size listed.

Table A-9	Sweets and Desserts — Portions for 15-Grams Carbohydrate
Food	*Portion Size*
Hot chocolate, sugar free or light	1 packet
Gingersnap cookies	3 cookies
Frozen yogurt	½ cup
Ice cream (fat free)	⅓ cup
Vanilla wafer	5 cookies (+ 1 fat exchange)
Cake, unfrosted	1 ounce (+ 1 fat exchange)
Soft drink, regular	5 ounces
Glazed donut	½ donut (+ 1 fat exchange)
Chocolate kisses	5 pieces (+ 1 fat exchange)
Pumpkin pie	½₁₂ pie (+ 1 fat exchange)
Lemonade	¼ cup
Large muffin	¼ muffin (+ 1½ fat exchanges)
Banana nut bread	½ ounce

Appendix B
Ethnic Carbohydrate Foods

. . . .

*F*abulous ethnic foods and exotic fruits are becoming more and more available to everyone, especially in urban areas. And, just as with any food, having some nutrition information, especially on carbohydrate containing foods, is essential. This list may also be helpful to people of Asian, Eastern European, or Mexican descent, but will undoubtedly fall short of being comprehensive. Start with Asian foods in Table B-1.

Table B-1	Asian Carbohydrate Foods —15-grams Carbohydrate Portion
Food	*Portion Size*
Gingko seeds, canned	½ cup
Lotus root, 2½ in. diameter	10 slices
Mung beans, cooked	⅓ cup
Red beans, cooked	⅓ cup
Rice congee or soup	½ cup
Rice noodles, cooked	½ cup
Taro, cooked	⅓ cup
Chinese spinach, cooked	½ cup
Bamboo shoots, canned	½ cup
Bittermelon, raw	1½ cups
Chayote, raw	1 cup
Chinese celery, raw	1 cup
Chinese eggplant, cooked	1 cup
Chinese mushroom, dried	2 medium
Hairy cucumber, raw	1 cup
Leeks, cooked	½ cup
Peapods, cooked	½ cup
Sprouts	½ cup

(continued)

Table B-1 *(continued)*

Food	Portion Size
Straw mushrooms	½ cup
Turnip, raw or cooked	1 cup
Water chestnuts, canned	½ cup
Water chestnuts, raw	4
Winter melon, cooked	1 cup
Avial	½ cup
Idli, plain	3" round
Naan	¼ of 8" × 2"
Pita	½
Phulka/chapatti (6")	1
Dosa, plain	1
Mumra (puffed rice)	1½ cups
Roti (6")	½
Sambar	½ cup
Toor dahl	½ cup
Rasam	1 cup
Mung, dahl (soup)	½ cup
Dholka (chickpea cake)	1" square
Dhansak (lentil curry w/meat)	½ cup
Paratha (flatbread w/oil)	1 (6 in.)
Poha	1 cup
Matki usal	½ cup
Lassi, regular	1 cup
Paneer, 1%	1 ounce
Masala tea with 1% milk	1 cup
Lychee	½ cup
Jujube	⅓ cup
Loquat	¾ cup
Lyokan	1 medium
Kyoho grapes	1 cup
Mutsu apple	½ medium
Korean pear (Asian pear)	1 medium
Korean melon	1 medium

Food	Portion Size
Persimmon	½ medium
Pitaya (dragon fruit)	1 medium
Mango	½ medium
Durian	¼ cup
Rambutan	2 medium
Jackfruit	½ cup
Mangosteen	½ cup
Santol	1½ medium
Carambola (starfruit)	1½ cups
Bael	½ cup
Bignay	2 cups
Gamboge	½ cup
Java plum	¾ cup
Sapota (chiku)	1 medium
Seetaphal	1 medium
Guava	1½ medium
Guava juice	½ cup
Jambu	6

Mexican food has become increasingly popular in the United States over the past several years. Using cilantro and citrus such as lime and lemon to flavor a dish can help cut down on carbs, calories, and sodium. Table B-2 shows some of the more popular Mexican dishes.

Table B-2	Mexican Carbohydrate Foods — 15-Grams Carbohydrate Portion
Food	**Portion size**
Bolillo	¼ (4½-5 in. long)
Tortilla, corn	1, 7½ in. across
Tortilla, flour	⅓ ,9 in. across
Pan dulce	¼, 4½ in. across
Frijoles cocidos	⅓ cup cooked
Mango	½ cup
Papaya	1 cup cubed
Nopales, raw	½ cup

Table B-3 shows the correct portion containing 15 grams of carbohydrate for some popular Eastern European foods. Bagels, in particular, have become popular in the United States over the past several years, coming in a wide variety of flavors and tastes. Some bagels are huge, however, and like any bread are relatively carbohydrate dense. This table helps you manage carbohydrates while enjoying these favorites.

Table B-3	Eastern European Carbohydrate Foods — 15-Gram Carbohydrate Portion
Food	**Portion Size**
Bagel or bialy	½ (1 ounce)
Challah	1 slice (1 ounce)
Pumpernickel bread	1 slice (1 ounce)
Rye bread	1 slice (1 ounce)
Matzoh	¾ ounce
Bulgur, cooked	½ cup
Farfel (dry)	½ cup
Kasha (cooked)	½ cup
Kasha (raw)	2 tablespoons
Matzoh meal	2½ tablespoons
Potato starch	2 tablespoons
Matzoh balls	3 balls-1½ ounce
Potato pancake	½ pancake
Borscht (no sugar)	½ cup
Sorrel (schav)	½ cup

Appendix C

Conversions

● ●

Diabetes management, and cooking for that matter, involves some mathematics, but if you're like most people you'd just as soon skip the math whenever possible. Appendix C may help a little by providing some simple conversions for various diabetes-related issues.

Blood Glucose and Blood Lipid (fat) Measures

Blood glucose, total cholesterol, HDL cholesterol, LDL cholesterol, and blood triglycerides are important health indicators for people with diabetes. Blood glucose levels can be taken in real time with home glucose meters for real time diabetes management decisions, and blood lipids are often taken on a yearly or semi-annual basis to evaluate risks for cardiovascular disease. In most countries, the United States included, all of these values are expressed as milligrams (of the substance) per deciliter (of blood), abbreviated as mg/dl — a weight (or mass) to volume concentration. Many other countries, including Canada and the United Kingdom, have adopted the International System of Units expressing these measures in millimoles per liter (abbreviated mmol/l). Because mmol/l concentrations depend upon the molecular weight of the compound rather than the measured-on-a-scale weight, the conversion factors from mg/dl to mmol/liter are different depending upon the molecular weight of the compound. The following conversion factors apply to the health indicators of concern.

Blood glucose	mg/dl × .0555 = mmol/l
Cholesterol (total, HDL, or LDL)	mg/dl × .0259 = mmol/l
Triglycerides	mg/dl × .0113 = mmol/l

Hemoglobin A1C (A1C) to Average Blood Glucose

A1C is a test measuring *glycated* or *glycosylated* blood hemoglobin — hemoglobin molecules with attached glucose molecules. Higher blood glucose levels over time result in a higher percentage of hemoglobin that has been glycated, and A1C is interpreted to represent average blood glucose levels over a period of one to three months. Blood glucose levels nearer the time of sampling have a greater influence on A1C than blood glucose levels two months or three months prior. A1C is an important measure for people with diabetes, and higher A1C values have been correlated with an increased risk for complications. A1C in the United States is commonly expressed as a percentage, and target values have been set at 7 percent by the American Diabetes Association and 6.5 percent by the American Association of Clinical Endocrinologists. A1C correlates with average blood glucose (bg) levels in mg/dl and mmol/l is shown in Table C-1.

Table C-1	A1C Values Equated to Average Blood Glucose (bg) in Milligrams/Deciliter (mg/dl) and Millimoles Per Liter (mmol/l)				
A1C	*bg mg/dl*	*bg mmol/l*	*A1C*	*bg mg/dl*	*bg mmol/l*
5.0%	97	5.4	5.5%	110	6.1
6.0%	126	7.0	6.5%	140	7.8
7.0%	154	8.6	7.5%	168	9.3
8.0%	183	10.2	8.5%	197	10.9
9.0%	212	11.8	9.5%	226	12.5
10.0%	240	13.4	10.5%	255	14.1
11.0%	269	14.9	11.5%	284	15.8
12.0%	298	16.5	12.5%	308	17.0
13.0%	326	18.1	13.5%	340	18.9

Not all sources agree precisely because there are statistical variations.

International Units (IUs)

It's common to see vitamin doses from supplements expressed as International Units (IUs). The IU value of a compound is based upon biological activity or effect, and there is no standard conversion factor to convert from metric or U.S. measures to IUs. For example, vitamin A can be formed from different precursors, which differ in biological activity. So, 100 IUs of vitamin A is equivalent to 30 micrograms of the more available retinol, or 60 micrograms of the less-available beta carotene.

Dry verses Cooked Measures for 15 grams of Carbohydrate

The correct portion size for grains, legumes, and some starchy vegetables is often given as the cooked volume, but the cooked volume and dry volume are often very different. Table C-2 gives the dry volume equal to the cooked portion for 15 grams of carbohydrate for common grains and starches.

Table C-2	Dry Measure Equivalents to Make One Carb Choice (15 Grams Carbohydrate) of Common Foods Cooked	
Food	*Dry*	*Cooked*
Oatmeal	3 tablespoons makes	½ cup
Cream of Wheat	2 tablespoons makes	½ cup
Grits	3 tablespoons makes	½ cup
Rice	2 tablespoons makes	⅓ cup
Dried beans	¼ cup makes	½ cup
Dried peas	¼ cup makes	½ cup
Lentils	3 tablespoons makes	½ cup
Linguini, spaghetti, vermicelli	0.7 ounces makes	⅓ cup
Macaroni, Penne, or Rotini	0.6 ounces makes	⅓ cup
Egg noodles	0.6 ounces makes	⅓ cup

These pasta measures are somewhat impractical. One cup of small, whole-grain pasta shells weighs 2½ ounces dry, meaning it will prepare about 1⅓ cups, or four carb choices (60 grams carbohydrate total).

Non-nutritive Sweeteners

These sweeteners are *Generally Recognized As Safe (GRAS)* by the U.S. Food and Drug Administration. These compounds can substitute for natural carbohydrate-containing sweeteners, like sucrose (table sugar), and may be useful for reducing calories and carbohydrates for people with diabetes. Table C-3 lists non-nutritive sweeteners by common brands, their relative sweetness compared to table sugar, and whether they are suitable for cooking.

Table C-3	Generally Recognized as Safe Non-nutritive Sweeteners		
Sweetener	*Notable Brands*	*x Times Sweeter than Sugar*	*For Cooking*
Aspartame	Equal, NutraSweet	200 ×	no
Saccharin	Sweet n Low	300 ×	yes
Sucralose	Splenda	600 ×	yes
Acesulfame potassium	Sunette	200 ×	yes
Neotame	NA — commercial use	7,000 – 13,000 ×	yes
Rebiana (Stevia)	Truvia, Pure Via	250 ×	yes
Mogrosiades (Monk fruit)	Nectresse	300 ×	yes

Index

• *N* •

About the Authors

Toby Smithson is the founder of `DiabetesEveryDay.com`, a website offering practical, consistent, and credible lifestyle support to people with diabetes. She is a registered dietitian nutritionist (RDN), a certified diabetes educator (CDE), a national spokesperson for the Academy of Nutrition and Dietetics, and her professional experiences extend from public health and research to patient counseling and media work. Toby was diagnosed with type 1 diabetes in 1968, and her passion for diabetes self-management is reinforced daily by her own good health.

Alan L. Rubin, M.D., is the author of several successful diabetes books, including *Diabetes For Dummies, Diabetes Cookbook For Dummies, Type 1 Diabetes For Dummies,* and *Prediabetes For Dummies.* Dr. Rubin regularly speaks to professional audiences around the world, hosts the interactive website `drrubin.com`, and often appears on radio and television talking about the cause, prevention, and treatment of disease.

Dedication

From Toby: Without a question, this book is dedicated to my number one cheerleader, supporter, confidant, business partner, and best friend — my husband Tony. I'm thankful for my good health and lucky to have Tony on my team. He is the person who had the insight to turn my successful management of diabetes into platforms that can help fellow people with diabetes.

From Alan: I dedicate the book to my granddaughters, Eliana and Rachel Ross. I am certain that the joy they have brought to my life makes every day a pleasure to live.

Author's Acknowledgments

From Toby: Writing my first book about something near and dear to my daily life was an incredible opportunity, and I owe Acquisitions Editor Michael Lewis a huge thanks for his confidence. Project Editor Susan Hobbs was patient and encouraging over many months, and I have valued her guidance very much. Lela Fausze tirelessly gathered and organized reams of research, helping me keep the facts current. And, we can all heap praises on Chef Lindsey Singleton for developing some incredible diabetes-friendly recipes for this book. A special thanks to Dr. Alan Rubin who shared his insights and experience with me, and his expertise with our readers. Last, but not least, I am especially indebted to my husband Tony who patiently helped organize the book, evaluate research, edit, rewrite, guide, critique, question, and encourage me.

Publisher's Acknowledgments

Acquisitions Editor: Mike Lewis

Project Editor: Susan Hobbs

Copy Editor: Susan Hobbs

Technical Editor: Dr. Pamela Coates

Art Coordinator: Alicia B. South

Project Coordinator: Sheree Montgomery

Cover Image: ©Keith Ovregaard/Cole Group/ jupiterimages

Two Fabulous Deals for You!!

If you read this book carefully you learned about the best deal you'll ever get – for every two days you manage your diabetes, you could add an extra day to your life

Now,
here's another great deal that will help you claim that big prize

50% off of your membership at DiabetesEveryDay.com

for expert and practical diabetes guidance and support 24-7-365

www.DiabetesEveryDay.com

- A new 7-day dinner menu and shopping list every week
- Featured recipes on video each week
- Videos, podcasts, and articles on exercise, motivation, lifestyle, and medical issues
- Hundreds of diabetes-friendly recipes
- A weekly email newsletter to keep you engaged with your health
- No advertising

Join author, spokesperson, registered dietitian nutritionist, and certified diabetes educator Toby Smithson on the road to good health in spite of diabetes

For details on both incredible offers visit

www.DiabetesEveryDay.com/dummiesdeal